STAGE COSTUME DESIGN

A costume sketch by Tanya Moiseiwitsch for Paul Scofield as Coriolanus in Shakespeare's play of the same name, as produced by the Stratford Shakespearean Festival, Stratford, Ont., 1961. Courtesy of Tanya Moiseiwitsch.

STAGE COSTUME DESIGN

Theory, Technique, and Style

by DOUGLAS A. RUSSELL
Stanford University

PRENTICE-HALL, INC., *Englewood Cliffs, New Jersey*

PRENTICE-HALL INTERNATIONAL, INC., *London*
PRENTICE-HALL OF AUSTRALIA, PTY. LTD., *Sydney*
PRENTICE-HALL OF CANADA, LTD., *Toronto*
PRENTICE-HALL OF INDIA PRIVATE LIMITED, *New Delhi*
PRENTICE-HALL OF JAPAN, INC., *Tokyo*

To Marilyn, Malcolm, and Andrea

Foreword

The fact that Doug Russell got me my first job as an actor in the theatre twenty years ago has absolutely nothing to do with the great and thoroughly justified praise I intend to lavish on his book.

This book answers a tremendous need in the professional theatre, for it gives a complete definition of the role of costume designer, covering every aspect of training, professional relationships, research, studies in fabric, patterns, budgets, shop personnel—in short, it provides a statement of what any professional director expects in his artistic and practical relation to the stage designer. This comprehensiveness is the book's glory and principal value. In his own right, Doug Russell is one of the brilliant American interpreters of clothes for the stage. He has incorporated here the high standards of work which he requires of himself. His language is direct, concentrated, and extremely clear for any member of the professional theatre. It will be a joy to read. He puts into engaging prose many aspects of the designer and his work which have hitherto, to my knowledge, remained unsaid.

The art of design for the stage requires of the artist a tremendous sensitivity to the life of the play. The costume designer must be sensitive to styles of literature, to the art of acting, to the coordination of visual effects with the stage designer and the lighting designer; the costume designer must have a tremendous sympathy and understanding for the actor who is creating a role. He must be a leader and an inspirational force among his shop crew. He must have a deep personal responsiveness to the art, music, and architecture of all historical periods. He must have a passionate belief in the power of individual and composed color. And most important, he must have a vivid sense of "the theatrical."

This book unfolds as a series of revelations to the young designer. Of great importance are his detailed observations about relations with the director, preliminary discussions of the play, the ever-important budget, scheduling, and charts. He provides invaluable information on how to prepare the most readable costume sketches, what medium to work in, and how to reveal significant details without losing the overall production tone. His discussions of color control and color relationships are unmatched.

The pages are bursting with information which must be part of the working kit of any professional. At the same time the writing and illustrations are sure to prove tremendously fascinating to the imagination of the beginner.

With an inspirational vividness, this book plants in the mind of the reader many imaginative questions that will lead him to go on in the profession, to test and explore techniques in order to develop and shape his own style. With absolute conviction I say that this book is a must for any student who intends to make costume design, stage design, or directing his profession.

In the theatre we rarely come upon a book which sets forth standards which will command the respect of the profession. This is such a book and it is my hope that the principles presented in this volume will awaken new standards and an enlightened approach to costume design throughout the profession in our country.

William Ball,
American Conservatory Theatre

Preface

This book is an introduction to the study of costume design. Its aim is to arouse interest in the subject on a variety of levels—critical, aesthetic, practical, and historical—and to give a well-rounded view without attempting to dwell on any one area in great detail. For instance, it does not attempt to examine the history of dress except briefly in Part III, since that has been well covered by many other volumes. The book is intended primarily for courses that introduce the student to the problems of sketching, principles of design, and practices of costume construction and style in period plays. It should also be of general interest to actors, directors, and teachers in general theatre.

Part I includes an analysis of what is meant by costume design and the nature of the field as it exists today. A discussion of sketching and presentation of costume plates follows. Design principles and the use of color are briefly discussed, and the complex area of patterns and fabric follows. Part I closes with two chapters on costume construction and the organization of the wardrobe and wardrobe personnel. Part II is devoted to the problems of style in costume design and begins with a chapter introducing the problems of style in relation to the history of art. Succeeding chapters treat each major period of art and drama in Western history and generally discuss its art and culture, the theatre, the drama, and at least one representative play, including the problems of costume design for production. Part III is devoted to a capsule review of the periods of dress in Western history with a representative male and female costumed figure, a list of costume terms used, and a representative list of useful books for each period. Part I and Part II are independent of one another and can be used separately in a course or combined and used with other related sources.

In the discussion of plays in Part II, a method of play analysis has been used that should lead the designer to consider the structure of the play as well as its story line as the basis for the costume designs. The plays were selected as famous and frequently anthologized representative dramas from the periods in which they were written, and each was chosen to reinforce the discussion of visual style in a particular chapter. Each is intended as a clear and direct example of a particular period style or a particular aspect of that style. The aim is to provide the student designer with a foundation scheme for planning the style for his costume designs from script to production.

The Bibliography, though not exhaustive, attempts to indicate useful books for each chapter. Additional reading suggested under each chapter heading will give greater dimension to the particular subject under discussion.

This book is based on many years of experience as a costume designer and teacher of costume history and design. Ideas have come from students, teachers, other designers, historians, the costume examination of the United Scenic Artists of America, other colleagues in the field, and from many books.

A book such as this could not be written without the aid of students and colleagues directly or indirectly involved during the period of writing and the collecting of illustrative material. I am indebted to my teachers, Virginia Opsvig, Hubert Heffner, and Frank Bevan, for the will to do this book and to Lewis Spitz of the Stanford University History Department for getting me to sit down and begin the actual writing of what had long been in mind. I also want to thank the staffs of the Stanford University Library, Department of Art, and Department of Drama for assistance along the way. I also wish to acknowledge specialized help from Robin Coon, Ruth Henderson, and Barbara Cleveland, patient checking of the manuscript by my typist, Carolyn D. Hill, and the kind help of all the people who are credited with providing sketches, photographs, and other illustrative material. Thanks are particularly due to Norman Philbrick, both for the very kind use of illustrative materials from his extensive theatre library, and for his careful, patient reading of the manuscript for content, balance, and style. His service has been invaluable. Finally, I wish to thank my wife, Marilyn, for her helpful advice and editorial assistance.

D.A.R.

Contents

I. Theory and Technique

II.   Theory and Style

Visual Presentation of *Six Characters in Search of an Author* Today; *The Blacks;* Visual Presentation of *The Blacks* Today.

The Meaning of Style; The Various Style Labels in Relation to Life; How the Various Style Labels Affect the Costume Designer; The Problem of Costume Design in Our Present Culture; A Production of *Prometheus Bound;* Contemporary Plays.

III. *Outline History of Western Costume*

I

THEORY
AND TECHNIQUE

1

Introduction

The Visual Environment of a Production

The art of the theatre is often understood to consist of two parts: the literary and the visual or, more specifically, the writing of the play and its presentation before an audience. The playwright tells his story and creates his characters in words, while the theatre artists must re-create the play on the stage in concrete visual terms. They must make the ideas, characters, story, and dialogue visible and audible by translating the playwright's words into acting, music, dancing, costumes, scenery, and lighting. The theatre artists must create a visual and aural equivalent on stage for what occurs in the script. If the interpreters are fine artists, and if they have understood the text and have been intelligent in their interpretation, the same thought and spirit should govern the re-created vision that governed the original. Words, however, are only symbols for ideas, and it is possible to interpret symbols in a number of different ways. Theatre artists who are expert in dance, pantomime, speech, stage design, costume design, and lighting may each gain very different ideas about stage presentation from an author's stage directions and dialogue. If the approach of any one of these artists is placed on the stage, an audience will probably feel that what it sees is a true interpretation of the script; but if the views of the various artists are combined in a single production, the result will be complete confusion, like an orchestra without a conductor. The recreation of a script's imagery in visual and aural terms must, therefore, be unified in all its elements, and the effect of a performance on an audience must be one. The conductor of this orchestration of dance, acting, music, costume, scenery, properties, and lighting is the director, and it is through his eyes that the audience should see a production of a play.

3

The most important element in this re-created vision is action: not just the physical action of pantomime and speech but the spirit of "man in action," that vital flow of dramatic movement that brings a play to life on the stage through the medium of rhythmic speech and gesture. As Sheldon Cheney says in *Stage Decoration* (1928):

> . . . the art of the theatre has to emphasize the presentation of a play by actors on a stage, through a flow of action, with that fusion of all the contributive stage arts which makes the drama live for its audience at its highest possible emotional intensity. Within this larger definition there should be special emphasis on action as the essential theatric core of the arts; . . . action in the sense of movement (as in early ritual drama and in . . . highly developed dance drama), or in the sense of the unfolding of a story or drama by actors using speech largely for expressiveness.

Scenery and costume, as the re-creation of the text, must always serve the play's dramatic action, developing and enriching it, but never dominating it or distracting from its flow and movement. Scenery and costume should be the visual expression of the play's dynamic spirit—an environment for the action. It was Robert Edmond Jones, the famous American scene designer, who used the word "environment" to describe the function of scenery and costumes (Figure 1–1). Although theatre ideas have changed greatly since Jones wrote *The Dramatic Imagination* (1941), the term "environment" is still useful if one thinks of it not as used in psychology and sociology, but rather as an envelope for the mood and ideas of the playwright—a visualization in color, line, and texture of the actors' actions and emotions. Seen in this way, environment can be as broken and inconsistent as the action in the script, and absurdist dramas and dramas of multileveled reality will not remain outside the definition.

The Function of Environment

The most obvious use of environment is to place or illuminate the dramatic action. In setting the place and time of the play *realistically,* costumes and sets should try to re-create fully the places and times of the action, although not in as much detail as if actual properties and costumes were used. Costumes and setting may also be used to suggest the locality and period, as in a production on the Elizabethan stage. With a few simple scenic forms, a few properties, costumes of strong silhouette and not too much detail, the audience is made to feel the presence of a much larger and fuller action than is shown. The environment also may be used to *express* an idea through the presentation of

Figure 1–1   A costume sketch by Robert Edmond Jones for the 1945 production of *Lute Song*. From *The Theatre of Robert Edmond Jones* by Ralph Pendleton, Wesleyan University Press, Middletown, Conn., 1958, p. 137. Sketch courtesy of The Museum of Modern Art, New York.

distorted or abstract forms in which some inner vision of the playwright is projected with little or no reliance on forms in nature. Finally, there may be no specific environment except the space formed by stairs, platforms, and plain wall surfaces. These are very broad statements about the visual environment of a play and will be examined historically and conceptually in the second part of this book when we begin to discuss the great periods of the drama and the visual styles they engendered.

Aside from placing the action, a second function of the visual environment is to reinforce the action by reflecting the characters' personalities. A number of little touches about a room, a property or two, or an individual costume may tell the audience more about a character than does the dialogue. The visual environment may reinforce the action through the use of symbols, for example, in a Shakespearean historical play, red costumes and banners showing the Lion of England for the British forces and blue costumes and banners showing the gold Fleur de Lis for the French forces. The visual environment frequently sets the weather, time of day, or year. The geographical location of the action may be indicated by the texture and weight of clothing, the use of hats and outer wraps, or the inclusion of lamps and fireplaces in the setting, while the social and economic state of the characters may be shown by the quality and style of clothes, furniture, walls, and properties. Or more broadly still, the visual environment may reinforce the dramatic action through the creation of mood and atmosphere. Costumes and settings can become emotionally charged through the subtle and careful use of color, line, and texture and can suggest loneliness, sadness, joy, fear, or laughter and thereby put the audience in the appropriate mood for the action of the play. In the last act of *Cyrano de Bergerac*, for example, the soft fall of leaves, the quiet movement of the darkly gowned and crisply hooded nuns, the light slowly fading through the trees together help the audience sense how the aging poet's life is finally drawing to a close. Such scenes attune the audience to the emotional mood of the action.

A third function of environment is to make a play visually attractive through an appealing use of line, texture, and color. The environment may be beautiful, ugly, harmonious, disruptive, or shocking, but it should not be flat, monotonous, dull, or boring. In addition to its functions in placing the action and reinforcing the play symbolically and atmospherically, the environment must be pleasing as an abstract work of art created in time, one that achieves its effect during the two to three hours of action onstage. No matter how drab the setting, nor how many levels of visual effect are used, an artistic design or plan behind the entire visual presentation must capture and hold the attention of the audience.

Elements of the Visual Scene

The four elements that comprise the visual scene or environment of a production in the modern theatre are scenery or stage space, properties or stage furniture and incidental objects, costumes and makeup, and lighting or illumination. Scenery gives the physical placement, background, and shape to the action, and sometimes the relation of the action to the audience viewing it. The properties have a strong dramatic value in that they are the objects that the actors handle, talk about, and on which they lie and sit; they frequently place the action without the aid of scenery, and they are part of the color and composition of the total scene. Costumes are the moving scenery of a production, and when worn by the actors, who are the center of all dramatic action, they are the strongest element of the visual scene; they project personality and individual emotion and obtain the strongest audience focus. Costumes usually are the most pronounced accents of color, line, and texture on stage. Lighting is the strongest element in unifying and composing the various visual effects through the manipulation of color, highlights, shadows, and focus. It is lighting that can most fully intensify the dramatic values in the total stage scene.

Three functions of the environment of a play's action are, as we stated earlier, to locate or place the play, to express its spirit or mood, and to make the play visually interesting. Regarding this last category, more should be said about the concept of the well-composed visual scene. In teaching design for the theatre, for many years great stress was placed on the fourfold concept of *unity, variety, balance,* and *harmony.* The *unity* of a well-composed scene meant that all of the parts—mass, line, color, texture in costumes, properties, scenery, and lighting—should appear to belong together. Achieving unity in a design depended on (1) selection of only those elements that could properly be related to one another to gain the specific environment required; (2) arrangement of the chosen elements into a plan that emphasized those features or motifs most clearly expressing the environment; and (3) maintenance of a single style throughout the entire design. A unified scene was said to be a scene with a sharp focus on central details. *Variety* was thought of as a subcategory; a unified scene always avoided monotony by means of successful contrasts. The design should be alive and interesting, but still subordinate to the dominant motif or mood of the production. *Balance* was also thought of as being integral to the unified or well-composed scene. Each costume, each piece of scenery, each property, and the stage as a whole was designed to weigh certain elements of mass, color, line, or texture against other elements so that a certain equilibrium was established. Finally, the well-composed scene was said to have a *harmony* in which all of the different elements combined together to make an attractive whole, the result achieved through skilled application of the principles of unity, variety, and balance to the work of scene composition.

In recent years, however, many plays have deliberately distorted or violated these principles and often seemed to give the designer license to place anything on the stage without regard for principles of composition. But no matter how confused, distorted, or disunified a work may seem, a plan underlies its construction, even if the audience has difficulty discovering it. The plan must be found and expressed by the designer; for once he has the unifying thread running through the work, he will be able to use a variety that may seem to verge on violent and excessive contrast, a balance that may seem to be all imbalance, and a harmony that may appear to be shockingly inharmonious; but the final impression, though not creating "an attractive whole," will have a unity of opposites, contrasts, and confusions—a logic underlying what at first may have seemed incomprehensible or meaningless. In Jean Gênet's *The Blacks,* the audience sees the action of the play as if in a set of reflecting mirrors, each distorting the image previously reflected. Each image may for a moment be mistaken for reality; but upon examination it always proves to be an illusion. Truth, or the beginning of the set of reflections, can never be found. The characters assume roles, but when the disguises are removed, the true persons are never discovered; each appearance is only a new disguise. But two or three unifying threads weave through the play: the concept of life as a series of reflecting mirrors or disguises; the idea of what would happen in Western imagery if white became black and black, white; the contrast between a black, African civilization and a white, Western one. A play such as *The Blacks* demands as much care in arrangement of artistic elements as does a more conventional and outwardly logical play. By concentrating on two or three unifying images, the designer can create unity—the unity of the absurd and irrational.

Requirements of the Visual Scene

In addition to the aesthetic problems of unity, variety, balance, and harmony, a number of physical requirements should be a part of the well-conceived visual scene or environment. The visual scene should be clear—it should be designed to be seen and understood at a distance. Most of the audience may be anywhere from twenty to seventy-five feet away from the action, so all parts of the scene must be simplified and exaggerated. Indeed, the motto "Simplify and exaggerate" is used in most classes in costume and set design; it is the basic concept behind turning source material into stageworthy costumes or scenery. One is always leaving out details from the painting or print used as a source while strengthening and exaggerating the lines and motifs for the finished stage costume. Simplicity does not mean bareness or meagerness. It means the use of essentials, those elements that contribute to the main idea of the costume's design. In this way, the design becomes uncomplicated in the best sense and can easily be grasped by the spectator.

Another important physical requirement in the visual scene is that sets, costumes, and properties must be designed to be used efficiently and effectively by the actors. They must be safe enough and strong enough to weather the problems that arise in dress rehearsals, in the course of the play's action, and throughout the run of the production. Scenery, costumes, and properties must be practical. They must be clearly and easily translatable from sketch to final form, must fit within the budget limits of the production, must be capable of being constructed within the required time limitation, must satisfy the demands of costume changes or scene shifts, must be practical for the size of the stage, and must be able to be packed and shipped easily if the production is to travel. In short, the designs for sets, costumes, and properties must be the work of an efficient craftsman's mind as well as of an artist's imagination.

Finally, the visual scene must be part of the organic whole that is the entire production. The designers of sets, of costumes, and of properties must not try to occupy first place in the audience's attention. They must not be swept away by the picturesque nature or decorative aspect of their work; they must not lose sight of the living, human element that is the actor, the dancer, or the singer. The visual scene must never be thought of alone, but only in conjunction with the directorial lines of the dramatic action. In the organic design of any theatrical presentation, the visual scene is the servant rather than the master of "man in action."

Costume as Part of the Visual Scene

Now that we have looked in a general way at the total visual scene or environment and discussed briefly how it functions in relation to the dramatic action of a play, we can introduce a specific discussion of costume design as one of the key elements in the formation of the total visual scene. The concept of costumes as moving scenery has already been mentioned. What does costume include and what does it do for the actor?

Costumes include all the body garments worn by the actor, all the accessories he carries as part of his character, all the items related to his hairdressing, and everything associated with his face and body makeup, including masks if they substitute for facial makeup. A costume tells us many things about the character played by the actor and about the nature of the play in which he appears. The list of things costumes can tell about characters and the whole play is lengthy.

Costumes can provide understanding or identification of the period in which the play occurs. If a play is placed in a period other than that envisioned by the playwright, the costumes become more important than usual in bringing out new themes and ideas that have been sought by the director in consultation with his designer.

Costumes can establish the locale of a production, that is, whether it is set in the city, the country, a particular nation, or north, south, east, or west of a particular continent or country.

Costumes can point up the time of day and thereby clarify the nature of the occasion taking place, such as an informal morning at home, a dinner party, a midnight rendezvous.

Costumes can establish the social class and economic stature of the characters by distinguishing between rich and poor, aristocrats and peasants, those on the way up and those on the way down.

Costumes frequently establish occupation, especially when a type of uniform is used to indicate that a character is a maid, a postman, a policeman, a milkman, or a soldier.

Costumes can establish the age of the characters, since certain garments are appropriate only to the aged, others only to the young. Costumes can indicate that characters are trying to appear older or younger than they are.

Costumes help to clarify character relationships; they can tie together members of a family, group, faction, or party through identifying elements of ornament, line, and color. Sympathetic and antagonistic relationships can be shown through similarities and contrasts in costume elements. Changes in costume can indicate alteration in the relationships among characters or in the psychological outlook of a character.

Costumes can point out the importance of the various characters through emphasis and subordination, for instance, the use of strong colors against weaker ones or the placement of a solid black costume in the midst of color.

The items above give us information about the characters and the play. But, more important, as a visual art, costume design can express intangible ideas that can strengthen the visual mood, style, and theme of the play. Costume design functions on two levels: the aesthetic or formal level, as pure art; and the associative or symbolic level, where it suggests by stimulating an audience's visual experience and sense of association.

On the aesthetic or formal level, the costume designer organizes and composes his media to appeal to the eye of the audience. He exploits the sensuous values of material and textural surfaces and their ability to reflect light. He develops the formal relationships among colors, lines, and shapes. He works with fabric, ornament, color, and line to develop a costume or a group of costumes that create an interesting visual picture—a combination of line, texture and color that will attract, and hold the attention of the audience. Even if the desire is to shock the audience's visual sensibilities, the artist always works for just the right aesthetic balance to obtain the audience reaction he and his director desire.

But one cannot design on the aesthetic level alone. There is also the associative or symbolic level. Any visual experience will play in some manner on the audience's associations—a given set of shapes, colors, textures, and lines will evoke certain symbolic meanings. Jean Gênet probes this fascinating area in *The Blacks* when he tries to suggest through varying images the shock to Western sensitivity that takes place when one poses such reversals as virginity as black, devils as white, evil as white, and purity as black. The visual connotations or associations in the symbolic meaning of white and black or any other color have been ingrained in Western culture for so many centuries that a designer will be in grave trouble if he deliberately defies them; and, if he does, he must expect to disturb the audience. In any visual experience there are, of course, two levels of association; the primary level sets certain shapes, colors, and textures as having more or less the same meaning for everyone in Western culture; and the secondary pertains to the background and experience of each member of the audience. The designer cannot design for individual association, but, unless he wishes his work to be a cliché, he would be advised not to follow every cue leading him to the stock associative responses of our culture; for example, red for the fallen woman, white for purity, the gray flannel suit for the businessman. The designer should learn to balance primary associative values with secondary ones from his own imaginative experience. This associative or symbolic level is a very difficult one for the teacher and the student of costume design, since it is easier to talk about formal and aesthetic values than about the personal, shifting nature of associative values. As society changes, these also change. But it is through associations and their symbolic use that the most exciting and the most deeply felt audience reactions are achieved. In a production of Ibsen's *Ghosts*, a designer, through a dusty, darkened palette and controlled use of braid and lace, can awaken in his middle-aged audience childhood memories of Victorian clothes and interiors.

Figure 1–2   A scene from *The Wild Duck* by Henrik Ibsen, as produced by the Stanford Players, Stanford Universty, 1957. Directed by Robert Loper, sets by William Allison, costumes by Irene Griffin. Photo courtesy of The Stanford Collection, Stanford University Libraries.

Figure 1–3   The final scene from Shakespeare's *The Tempest* as produced at the Memorial Theatre, Stratford-upon-Avon, England, in 1951. Reproduced by permission of the Governors of the Royal Shakespeare Theatre, Stratford-upon-Avon, England. Photo by Angus McBean.

On the intangible and expressive level then, costumes can establish the overall mood of a play or the atmosphere of a scene. They can express a play's style; much more will be said of this in chapters to follow. But even at this point, it can be readily seen that the costumes for an Ibsen drama such as *The Wild Duck* demand a closer fidelity to real-life garments than do the costumes for *The Tempest* (Figures 1–2 and 1–3). It can certainly be said that the costumes should always reflect the level of reality embodied in the script.

Finally, we can also say that the structure of a play should be subtly revealed through costume, so that the rise to climax and the fall from it to denouement are paralleled in dress. If the same costumes are worn throughout, they must sustain interest over a long period of time and be as effective in a certain combination at the climax of a play as they were in a different combination at its beginning.

Costumes can and do bear a great weight of fact and suggested meaning to an audience. It takes an accomplished and experienced costume designer to meet fully the demands of a complex production.

The Meaning of Costume for the Designer, the Actor, and the Director

Now that we have discussed the meanings and suggested effects resulting from well-designed costumes, let us consider the meaning of costume design for the various artists most closely involved with it. Do the scene and costume designers, the director, and the actor think of costume in the same way? Is each aware of all the meanings we mentioned when he thinks about the designs for a play or for a character? The answer is obviously no. Each artist thinks of costume subjectively, as a means of artistic expression, rather than as an artistic effect on the audience.

The designer, whether he is in charge of the whole visual scene or of the costumes alone, wishes to see a certain emotion or mood made manifest in fabric of a certain shape and color on an actor moving in and out of light on a stage. Sometimes his aim is to astonish and excite an audience by exaggeration and distortion of the actor's body; at other times, his aim is to beautify and enhance the human form. He may wish to hide an actor in a visual character creation that is so unlike himself that the individual will seem transformed, or he may wish to find the actor's best points, the qualities of personality, form, and movement distinctively his, and to design all the actor's costumes, no matter what the character, subordinate to that personal image. There are times when the designer is not interested in actors at all but only in the creation of rich, sensuous effects in movement on a stage; while at other times he is interested only in textural and draped effects as they are actuated by light. All costume designers recognize in themselves these urges to expression. Because of their own personalities and experience, they find certain spurs to expression stronger than others, and many work in only one or two of these directions. In fact, if a designer is flexible enough to work in all directions, he may become too facile and eclectic; while a designer who concentrates on expressing himself in one or two modes may develop greater depth and artistry.

For the actor, the costume is at the same time a mask for his everyday character and personality and a release into the world of the play and the character he is portraying. If he is an actor who subordinates the character he plays to his own strong personality, then he will want his costume always to express both the personality of the character and his own stage personality. If he is an actor who subordinates his own personality to the role, then each costume for each role he plays will be very different, a mask to conceal himself and project his idea of the character. But an actor will always want a costume (even if uncomfortable and unfamiliar at fittings and first dress rehearsal) to become a part of him and his role. Ideally, the actor and the designer can share a vision of a character and his relation to the play and work cooperatively toward a common goal. However, friction may arise if the designer has some mood vision of the particular costume in his visual scheme and the actor can see only that the costume seems uncomfortable and wrong for his interpretation of the character. The actor feels unable to express himself in such a costume, unable to release himself fully into his role, while the designer feels that to fulfill the actor's idea he will have to sacrifice his overall visual view of the play. At this point, the more objective view of the director must effect a compromise.

In what way does costume act as a form of expression for the director? Ideally, it combines both the actor's and the designer's ideas in a broader, more objective view of the visual scene. If the director is a *régisseur*, all the visual ideas emanate from his overall view of the production, and the designer refines and embodies these ideas in the finished costumes. However, there have been many instances in the history of the theatre when an actor became the manager of production and supervised design of all the costumes to suit his taste as a star; conversely, there have been other cases, like that of the early twentieth-century design theorist, Gordon Craig, when all phases of the production were in the hands of the designer, and actors were but visual puppets in the hands of a great master. The ideal director should have as much knowledge of the visual arts of the theatre as he does of the art of acting, but he should remain on a plane above both, working with actor and designer to release them artistically and to translate their ideas into concrete form. The most successful productions are those in which actors, director, and designer collaborate—when only a directorial outline of a role or a visual idea is given to actors and designer, when each brings to the director ideas that they mutually explore, and when the final effect can truly be said to be the creation of all the artists involved in the production.

The Meaning of Costume as Personal Expression

Unless the actor and designer communicate, there is danger that the actor will think of costume only as a means of expressing his character, while the designer will see it only as one part of his visual expression of the play. Although the director must keep the balance, all three need to understand the function of clothing in society, the way in which costume expresses a person's idea of himself. Only then can the actor, the director, and the costume designer translate clothing into theatrical costume.

Since man first painted himself and wore primitive adornments, clothing has been one of his best means of self-expression. Clothing is also one of the clearest ways in which he can show his relationship to his society. The two most obvious poles of expression in a society are *conformity* and *rebellion,* and clothes speak more clearly about them than any other social custom. If a person wishes to seem securely a part of his culture, for each social occasion he will choose only the dress prescribed by the leaders of society. Conformity gives security and relieves a person from thinking about why he chooses certain clothes for certain occasions. If a person wishes to establish his own personality, his independence from the social ideals of his culture, he will choose dress that is opposed to that enjoined by his culture. Sometimes rebellious dress remains on the fringes of a culture; at other times it modifies the styles of a culture or overthrows them in favor of a modified form of the original fashion. Today's T-shirts, tight trousers, uncontrolled hair, and bare feet are symbols of rebellion against the business suit and the afternoon dress. Such dress speaks loudly for a simpler, more natural way of life, and it attempts to brand the business suit and the afternoon dress as the uniforms of social robots trapped in a machine-made society.

We have talked about a deliberate rebellion against society in one's choice of clothing; but there is also the person who wishes to be comfortable at any cost, even if he appears unconventional. Or there is the person who may look ridiculous because he is preoccupied with his work and completely unconscious of his dress. Or there is the person who is genuinely careless in dress, who does not look well groomed by society's standards because of slovenly personal habits. A variation on these two is the man who is indifferent to clothing and its meaning in society. Still another type is the person who is so self-effacing that he dresses in a way that seems to erase him from memory; clothes to him are a means of hiding. Then there is the person who moves in the face of conformity to become a style innovator. And so it goes into ever more subtle breaks with or interpretations of the accepted fashions of the day. It is a fascinating study, this picture of man's relationship to his society as expressed by clothing.

There are other basic dress instincts in man, and one of the most important for the theatre is the instinct to *dress up,* to don rich fancy dress garments for special occasions. We have gowns for the opera ball, uniforms for lodge groups, special costumes for weddings, inaugurations, and funerals. We are excited and satisfied by observing the rich ecclesiastical robes in church ceremonies, the brilliant uniforms of a coronation, or the rich costumes of opera, ballet, and the theatre.

Another basic instinct, perhaps the most basic following the use of clothing as protection against the elements, is dress used to enhance a certain *sexual ideal* of manhood or womanhood. The history of feminine dress in particular can be read as an ever-changing game of revealing and concealing certain portions of the body. There are periods when the arm is bare, others when it is completely concealed; periods when the decolletage is so low that it creates the imminent danger of an accidental overexposure; others when not even the neck is left uncovered. In some periods, bare arms and decolletage for evening wear alternate with complete covering for day wear, as in the late nineteenth century; at other times, the legs are revealed above the knee; and in some eras, it is shocking to uncover the ankle. The changing image and sexual ideal of manhood is more related to silhouette or figure outline than to revealing or concealing parts of the body. One can contrast those periods that use the decorated codpiece with other periods when all trace of the sex organs is hidden. The male image shifts from padded shoulders or balloon sleeves to tight-fitting torso coverings, from loose garments to tight ones, from grotesque exaggerations of key parts of the body to a stress on the natural.

Personal expression through dress may appear in the way an individual uses clothes to clarify his relation to others in a particular *social situation*. Choice of a business suit, riding habit, tuxedo, sport shirt, slacks, or swimsuit are ways in which a man places himself clearly in a particular social situation. A woman sets her social level and the social occasion by how she selects her wardrobe and how it corresponds to the other dresses at a particular function.

Closely related to social expression is society's use of uniforms and vestments to express a person's authority, position, and expected duties. Such clothing may also appeal to our sense of fancy dress, but in its basic form it gives station and identity. We know what to demand and expect of a woman dressed as a nurse, of a man dressed as a policeman, of a youth garbed as a choirboy.

The director, actor, and designer must understand dress as an expression of human personality, identity, and position before stage costumes can be created that are both aesthetically and psychologically appropriate to a play and its characters.

The Structure of Costume as Personal Expression

We have discussed how costume is more than mere body covering; the way it is made and the shape it takes are the psychological and aesthetic results of the individual's interaction with his society. The designer, the director, and the actor must have some idea of how and why costume structure has changed through the centuries, even if the designer alone has full knowledge of the intricacies of costume history.

From the beginning of man's history, when skins or leaves were used as a protection against the elements and for adornment, man had a choice about how he would dress. If the skins or leaves were wrapped tightly around the body, they were used primarily for protection; if they were hung or draped from the body, the intention was more adornment, prestige, and display. For example, if a full animal skin is wrapped tightly about the human form it merely warms the figure, but if the head is placed on the human head, the skin of the forelegs hangs over the arms, and the hind legs and tail fall behind, then a grand image of control over the animal world is created as well as a suggested fusion of the power of man and beast. From this difference come two widely used costume structures that are still the basis for much costume design: the wraparound effect and the hanging or draped effect. These two structural forms, of course, took on new significance when the art of weaving developed in the Neolithic or New Stone Age, for many more variations are possible in wrapping or draping woven fabric. It is also in the Neolithic period that man invented the third basic structural form in dress, cutting fabric to fit the form of the body and sewing, pinning, or belting it into place. If one contemplates these three primitive structural forms, one realizes that all costume since has merely been a refinement of the wrapped, draped, or cut-to-fit methods.

In pre-Greek times, most garments were either of the wraparound or hung variety, although Near Eastern dress showed a tendency toward the cut-to-fit. Then, if one follows through from Greek to late medieval times, one sees the gradual change from the fully draped line of the fifth century B.C. to the more fitted costume of the fifteenth century. The most rigid and distorted human silhouette in the history of Western dress was achieved in the sixteenth century, and since that time there have been recurring cycles that have moved from a soft, indistinct, draped silhouette to a rigid, fitted, and even distorted costume line. Since the Renaissance there has been a much greater reaching back to the past for costume effects than in previous centuries. Looking at the history of costume, then, to its beginnings in the wraparound, the hung, and the crudely fitted garments of primitive times, one can see the four general structural types that have continued in the later history of dress: *the draped costume, the semifitted costume, the fitted costume,* and *the artificial or distorted costume.*

The draped costume stresses a maximum amount of free movement of the human body under the draped fabric and a minimum amount of sewing and pinning. Draped dress is dependent on the supple grace and movement of the wearer, and is usually stressed in periods such as the Greek, where there is openness, belief in natural movement, and admiration of the human body (Figure 1–4a).

The semifitted costume applies to most T-shaped tunics and gowns, kimonos and pajamas, and loose shirts and trouser combinations of all

Figure 1–4a   Example of a costume structure based on draping. Statue of L'Arringatore, first century B.C. Archaeological Museum, Florence. Photo courtesy of Alinari, Florence.

kinds. It is basic to the Romanesque and early medieval period, most oriental dress, costumes for *commedia* clowns, and much peasant dress. It is often a transition from a draped to a fitted costume period or structural relaxation from a heavily artificial and distorted costume period (Figure 1–4b).

The *fitted costume* strives to clothe the figure in a smooth-fitting outer skin of interesting texture that both limits body movement and reflects its strain in the pull and stretch of the fabric surface. This least frequent of all costume structures is often coupled with elements of the artificial or the semifitted structural approach. Again, an ideal form is demanded beneath the tight-fitting skin of fabric. The fitted costume is difficult to cut and fit correctly. In our own day, the fitted costume appears in tight-fitting trousers and knitted blouses, and it was boldly used in the fourteenth-century tight-fitting tunic or cotehardie (Figure 1–4c).

Finally, there is the *artificial or distorted structural costume*. Fabric is forced to fit an arbitrary shape created by padding and boning the human figure, and the silhouette produced is unlike the form of the human body. The costume of the late sixteenth century is the most obvious example of the artificial approach, but it can also be seen in the bustles of the late nineteenth century and the grotesque wigs of the late seventeenth century (Figure 1–4d).

In general, one can say that any of the four structural types are related to man's view of the human body and nature in a particular society. If the society is not too rigid, the body accepted, and nature admired, then fabrics will be used for their sensuous value. Costume structure will usually be of the semifitted or draped variety. If unrest, repression,

Figure 1–4b Example of a costume structure of the semifitted variety. A gentleman's spring costume for 1823. From Max von Boehn's *Menschen und Moden im 19 Jahrhundert,* Bruckman, Munich, 1905.

and inhibition prevail and the normal human form is not admired, costume structure will cover and distort or actually change the human figure.

Stage costume falls into the artificial structural category more often than civil dress because it must exaggerate for effect and must be built on a solid foundation; folds, puffed effects, and draped lines must stay in place through the performance. But the theatre artists involved in stage costume must understand the various psychological and social reasons for the structural methods used throughout costume history before they move to the artificial methods of the theatre workshop.

Figure 1–4c Example of a costume structure that is form fitted. A cotehardie from the middle of the fourteenth century. Drawing by Herbert Norris from *Costume and Fashion* by Herbert Norris, E. P. Dutton, New York, 1927, Vol. II, p. 220.

Figure 1–4d Example of a costume structure that is completely artificial. A portrait of Queen Elizabeth from an engraving of 1589 by William Rogers in the British Museum. Photo courtesy of the Trustees of the British Museum, London.

Historic Use of Costume in the Theatre

We have now seen how costume functions as part of the visual scene, as a means of expression for the director, actor, and designer, as a statement about an individual and his relation to society, and as a structure in fabric that reveals much about man's view of himself. Let us now turn our attention to what costume tells us about society's view of the theatre.

We have already noted how a costume designer can treat the formal and sensuous values of his work as abstractions to be presented in a purely visual manner. We have also talked of the symbolic or associative values of costume; a designer can suggest all manner of moods, ideas,

Figure 1–5a   Statue of Melpomene, Muse of Tragedy, from the Vatican Museum, Rome. Photo courtesy of Alinari, Florence.

and feelings by playing on the audience's primary and secondary associations. In the history of stage costume, the pendulum swings from costumes that are symbolic to those that are close to civil dress, from costumes that suggest cultural and religious ideals to costumes that express personality and social position.

In Greek plays, heroes and gods represented idealized mankind, while comic figures and humanized birds and animals represented the unregenerate aspects of human nature. The masks, enlarged costumes, and symbolic ornaments used were more than extensions or enlargements of civil dress; all had been handed down from archaic times (Figure 1–5a).

Roman stage costume borrowed from the Greek, although there was more stress on realistic or melodramatic touches in masks, wigs, and garments, as there was in Roman plays and art. Medieval stage costume was a marvelous mixture of the real and the symbolic—at one moment saying something obvious about the psychological and socio- logical position of a character and the next commenting symbolically on his religious significance. The dualism apparent in all the visual aspects of medieval theatre, and, of course, in medieval art, is nowhere more obvious than in the costumes of the mystery, miracle, and morality plays.

In the Renaissance theatre, costume came much closer to the civil dress, overlaid with accessories and ornamentation that still acted sym- bolically to lift a character or a scene above an ordinary psychological or sociological situation (Figure 1–5b). In the Elizabethan theatre, the audience was willing to accept an actor as a king of France, a Roman leader, or a Moorish general if he wore a few symbolic or exotic ac-

Figure 1–5b A pageant costume from the original drawing by Leonardo da Vinci at Windsor Castle. Reproduced by the gracious permission of H.M. Queen Elizabeth II.

cessories on his rich contemporary dress (Figure 1–5c). In the eighteenth century, costume was still rich and decorative, with symbols of position, nationality, and historic period added to fancy dress (Figure 1–5d).

At the end of the eighteenth century and the beginning of the nineteenth, a new, scientific view of history developed, and for the first time in the history of the theatre, historical accuracy appeared in stage dress (Figure 1–5e). But historical accuracy limited the designer, director, and actor. With the new stagecraft of the late nineteenth and early twentieth centuries, stage costume once again became aesthetic and picturesque as well as unified, simplified, and controlled.

Figure 1–5c   An original drawing for a theatrical costume by Henri Gissey. Courtesy of the Victoria and Albert Museum, London.

Figure 1–5d Mrs. Baddely as Joan la Pucelle in Shakespeare's *Henry VI, Part 2*. From Bell's Edition of Shakespeare's Plays, 1776.

Costume Design as a Profession

The new stagecraft brought the designer to one of the strongest positions he had ever held in the history of the theatre. In the past, the actor, director, or person in charge of stage wardrobe was responsible for costume. Rarely did the set and costume designer control all the visual aspects of a production. In the Renaissance, the great painters designed *intermezzi;* in the seventeenth century, Inigo Jones designed masques; and in the Baroque period, Jean Berain designed *divertissements*. But only in the last fifty years has a person trained in the visual arts and the theatre had control of the visual presentation of a production.

Figure 1–5e   An original sketch by James Robinson Planché of Leopold of Austria for a production of Shakespeare's *King John*, 1823. Courtesy of the Stark Collection, University of Texas Library, Austin.

Today there are various opportunities for work in the field of stage costume. In Europe, Latin America, Canada, and the United States, the field of professional costume design includes films, fashions, legitimate theatre, opera, extravaganza, and dance, and is usually controlled by labor union practice. In Europe and Latin America, there is a much less rigid pattern than in the United States, but the person who makes a living as a professional is usually a member of an organization if not a union that sets standards, wages, and hours and usually provides some form of benefits. Sometimes the costume designer merely pays a fee to join the organization, sometimes he is invited to join or is elected to membership, and sometimes an examination must be passed before he becomes a member.

Probably the most lucrative area for the costume designer today is in films. In large-scale film epics, a costume designer assisted by an army of specialists may design a thousand costumes or more and control the costume effects on movie sets that cover acres. Costume design on this scale becomes an industry, and there are many people involved in research, sketching, choosing fabric, cutting, fitting, sewing, and accessory making. The work is carefully controlled by a union that oversees the settings, costume design, and art direction, and the fees paid to the designer as well as funds available for costuming a production are handsome.

Fashion design is only indirectly related to costume for the theatre, but it is one of the most publicized aspects of our present culture. In the great urban centers, fashion designers who have been apprenticed to great fashion houses or designers develop a line of clothes each season to fit all social occasions. These styles are meant to attract the attention of society's fashion leaders through a combination of shocking, eye-catching, or strikingly different ideas. It is a multimillion dollar business, and if a particular line attracts widespread attention and filters down to the mass buying public in adapted form, the design house sponsoring the line may have tremendous control over the fashion industry and the visual aspects of our culture. Only when a play requires high fashion does fashion design come close to costume design, and even then the high-style garments must be designed to be viewed at a distance rather than in the close proximity of a drawing room. Few designers have achieved a reputation in both the fields of stage costume design and high fashion.

The major area that captures attention in costume design is the legitimate theatre and opera, and although this is a rather limited profession, in many ways it offers more challenge to the talented costume designer than other fields. In Europe and Latin America, costume designers belong to loosely organized groups that only occasionally approximate our design unions, but in the United States, all major work is controlled by the United Scenic Artists of America, Local 829 of the Painters and Decorators Union of the American Federation of Labor. Two other unions, Locals 850 and 816 in Chicago and Los Angeles, respectively, work closely with the parent organization in New York. The United Scenic Artists is divided into several divisions: there are the full scenic designers who design sets, costumes, and lighting, and there are costume associates, lighting associates, mural artists, and display associates who work only in those areas. Membership in the union is limited, and a thorough examination must be passed for admittance. Entrance fees and dues are fairly high, but the union does excellent work in gaining benefits and fees for the designer and in seeing that employers do not default on payments. In the professional theatre, many costume designers who belong to the union work as resident designers for a theatre company or a television network; others work as assistants to major designers and as off-Broadway costume designers, while a top few are employed designing the individual plays that make up the New York theatre and opera season and national touring companies. Many of these designers do work in other fields or have incomes from other sources; however, with the increasing number of resident professional companies, there is more opportunity for the costume designer in legitimate drama today than in the past.

Another design area is extravaganza. Although the challenge may be more limited, the richly decorative aspect of extravaganza appeals to many designers. Ice shows, circuses, night clubs, and dance revues demand costumes that emphasize purely decorative effects. Such costumes use strong color, brilliant ornamentation, and such light-reflecting surfaces as sequins, beads, and metallic fabrics. Extravaganza is a well-paid professional area which demands of the designer a minimum of subtlety and a maximum of surface effect.

In the related area of dance, there are a number of established ballet companies and a smaller number of dance troupes that need a costume designer; and although the opportunities are limited, the challenge to the designer interested in ballet and dance problems is exciting. The costume problems of the dancer are complex and very different from those of the actor or the entertainer, and the costume designer who can solve them brilliantly is always in demand.

Connected to the design field is the costume-servicing profession. This includes the great costume houses, the costume workshops for large theatres, and all the persons who work at wardrobe maintenance in theatres around the world. Most of the costume-servicing profession is also unionized, and its union is usually affiliated with the seamstresses of the garment industry. In the large costume houses and the costume shops for large theatres, the personnel include cutters, fitters, designers and makers of accessories, milliners, makers of footwear, dyers, and finishers, as well as the people employed to maintain the wardrobe, handle its movement in and out of the shops, and its rental after its original use in production. The same operation on a larger scale occurs in the film industry. This field, usually known as wardrobe, appeals to those people who do not wish to design, but who are fascinated by costumes of all kinds and usually have a craft or skill that can be used to excellent advantage in building or maintaining a wardrobe.

There are a number of opportunities in education for those interested in costume design. In the large universities and professional schools with a school of fine arts, the theatre department often gives training in costume design, and has a designer-teacher to supervise the work and teach the courses, a small core of professional wardrobe personnel, and well-equipped shops. Each season the department usually presents a number of productions that make use of student talent, and it often helps place the graduating student in a beginning professional position. In departments of drama that are part of a liberal arts college or a small university, stress is on teacher training and there is less orientation toward the profession. Positions open after graduation are usually in other university and college drama departments. In small colleges and high schools with no emphasis on theatre, there is usually a production course that includes material on costume for the stage, or there may be a strong extracurricular drama society that gives training and experience in the arts of production.

Finally, there are the community theatres and many amateur groups around the country where much practice and training in costume for the stage is available, usually without cost but also without pay. Sometimes a large community theatre with city support will hire the services of a full-time person in costume; at other times a person may be hired to design and supervise a particular production. Although the quality of design work varies greatly in community theatre as it does in schools and universities, at its best it may reach a near-professional character. Opportunities here are usually for the person with some training who has not followed costume design as a career. Housewives and business-men who may have done costume work in college are often called upon to give their time and talent to community theatre productions.

2

Planning and Presentation of the Costume Sketch

Reading the Script

The first order of business for the costume designer, as for the other artists collaborating on a production, is reading the script. For an opera or a musical, the designer may listen to the music before reading the libretto; for a ballet, he may see part of the choreography before reading the story outline. The script may be a full play or it may be an outline of music and movement in a dance presentation, an ice show scene, or a circus sequence. If there is no dialogue or story line, the designer must look for other clues to lead him to his costume scheme. Perhaps music or a historical theme will indicate the mood. If the script leaves matters open, the designer must bring his sense of the occasion and the theatrical effect required to the visual solution of the problem. When the designer creates a visual sequence in a musical or dance presentation, he is limited only by a choreographer's or director's ideas and by the patterns of motion and gesture that have been developed for the sequence. But most often there is something to read besides an outline of music and movement, and it is usually from this first reading that the designer develops many of his deepest visual reactions to the play.

During the first reading of the script there should be no thought of costume changes, problems of period, or methods of construction. The designer should absorb as much as possible of the author's story, mood, characterization, imagery, and pictorial intent before he challenges himself as designer. He may wish to make notations about the play's progression or rhythmic development, the underlying pattern, the prevailing atmosphere, the nature of the verbal imagery and how it suggests visual effects, and especially the level of reality in the script. This last is a delicate problem, since the designer's response to the level of reality may be quite different from that of the various members of the audience. As we shall see in Part II, the visual style in a production depends on an understanding of the plot, character, thought, language, rhythm, and spectacle in the script. Only after he has analyzed the entire play should the costume designer continue with a closer appraisal of its costume demands.

During the second reading of the script the designer will read specifically for costume data. First, there are the factual questions: Where and under what circumstances will the play be performed? How much time has the designer for design and execution? How large is the theatre? What is the distance from the stage to the first row of seats? How many people will the house hold? What backstage facilities are available? What is the nature of the audience? How long will the play run? At what time of year will the production take place? If the play is to tour, perhaps many of these questions cannot be answered. It may only be after conferences with the producer and director that the designer will know the date and the theatre for the opening.

Second, the costume designer will want to know if any casting has taken place or if the production is being built around a particular star. Ideally, all casting should be completed before the designer begins work, but it seldom is; often he must do his preliminary planning without knowing full casting. If some actors have been cast, the designer should meet them, learn their methods and personalities, and try to envision them in their parts during his second reading. If he knows none of the actors cast, he may do his reading with certain people or types in mind, but this is frequently dangerous until after a first conference with the director.

Third, the designer should mark anything in the script that pertains to costume. He should make notes on the geographical location, the historical period, and the time of day and year for the play and for each scene. He should list any indication of a costume item or accessory and any description or image in the dialogue. Any action that would affect the construction or wear of a costume should be written down, and all possible changes of a full costume or parts of a costume should be clearly charted. Also, he should estimate the time needed and time available for such changes (Figure 2–1).

Finally, before he attends conferences, the designer should make a rough estimate of the number of costume changes he finds, the number of costumes he thinks will be needed, and the costs he sees involved, assuming that he has some idea where the costumes will be constructed and where and under what circumstances the buying will be done.

And 'scape detecting, I will pay the theft.

Ham. They are coming to the play; I must be idle:

Get you a place.

Danish march. A flourish. Enter KING, QUEEN, POLONIUS, OPHELIA, ROSENCRANTZ, GUILDENSTERN, *and others.*

King. How fares our cousin Hamlet?

Ham. Excellent, i' faith; of the chameleon's dish: I eat the air, promise-crammed: you cannot feed capons so. 100

King. I have nothing with this answer, Hamlet; these words are not mine.

Ham. No, nor mine now. [*To Polonius*] My lord, you played once i' the university, you say?

Pol. That did I, my lord; and was accounted a good actor.

Ham. What did you enact?

Pol. I did enact Julius Cæsar: I was killed i' the Capitol; Brutus killed me.

Ham. It was a brute part of him to kill so capital a calf there. Be the players ready?

Ros. Ay, my lord; they stay upon your patience.

Queen. Come hither, my dear Hamlet, sit by me.

Ham. No, good mother, here's metal more attractive.

Pol. [*To the King*] O, ho! do you mark that?

Ham. Lady, shall I lie in your lap?

　　　　　[*Lying down at Ophelia's feet.*

Oph. No, my lord. 120

Ham. I mean, my head upon your lap?

Oph. Ay, my lord.

Ham. Do you think I meant country matters?

Oph. I think nothing, my lord.

Ham. That's a fair thought to lie between maids' legs.

Oph. What is, my lord?

Ham. Nothing.

Oph. You are merry, my lord.

Ham. Who, I?

Oph. Ay, my lord.

Ham. O God, your only jig-maker. What should a man do but be merry? for, look you, how cheerfully my mother looks, and my father died within these two hours.

Oph. Nay, 'tis twice two months, my lord.

Ham. So long? Nay then, let the devil wear black, for I'll have a suit of sables. O heavens! die two months ago, and not forgotten yet! Then there's hope a great man's memory may outlive his life half a year: but, by 'r lady, he must build churches, then; or else shall he suffer not thinking on, with the

hobby-horse, whose epitaph is 'For, O, for O, the hobby-horse is forgot.'

Hautboys play. The dumb-show enters.

Enter a King and a Queen very lovingly; the Queen embracing him, and he her. She kneels, and makes show of protestation unto him. He takes her up, and declines his head upon her neck: lays him down upon a bank of flowers: she, seeing him asleep, leaves him. Anon comes in a fellow, takes off his crown, kisses it, and pours poison in the King's ears, and exit. The Queen returns; finds the King dead, and makes passionate action. The Poisoner, with some two or three Mutes, comes in again, seeming to lament with her. The dead body is carried away. The Poisoner wooes the Queen with gifts: she seems loath and unwilling awhile, but in the end accepts his love. [*Exeunt.*

Oph. What means this, my lord?

Ham. Marry, this is miching mallecho; it means mischief.

Oph. Belike this show imports the argument of the play. 150

Enter Prologue.

Ham. We shall know by this fellow: the players cannot keep counsel; they'll tell all.

Oph. Will he tell us what this show meant?

Ham. Ay, or any show that you'll show him: be not you ashamed to show, he'll not shame to tell you what it means.

Oph. You are naught, you are naught: I'll make the play.

Pro. For us, and for our tragedy,
　　Here stooping to your clemency, 160
　　We beg your hearing patiently. [*Exit.*

Ham. Is this a prologue, or the posy of a ring?

Oph. 'Tis brief, my lord.

Ham. As woman's love.

Enter two Players, King and Queen.

P. King. Full thirty times hath Phœbus' cart gone round

Neptune's salt wash and Tellus' orbed ground,

And thirty dozen moons with borrow'd sheen

About the world have times twelve thirties been,

Since love our hearts and Hymen did our hands

Unite commutual in most sacred bands. 170

P. Queen. So many journeys may the sun and moon

Figure 2–1　Costume notations in a playscript. A page from Shakespeare's *Hamlet* as printed in the Globe Edition edited by William Clark and William Wright, 1864.

Conferences

Obviously, much of the preliminary planning during the second reading of the script may be drastically revised or nullified by subsequent conferences with the producer, the director, the set designer, the lighting designer, and sometimes the playwright, but it is still wise to come to the first conference with a full understanding of the play and its costume problems and with an estimate of cost and numbers. At the first conference, the director should set forth as clearly as he can his interpretation of the play. The costume designer must listen carefully to determine whether the director is visually oriented or not. If he is, there may be a fruitful collaboration on the designs for the production; if not, he will prefer to wait to see the sketches and will then accept or reject them. There must also be a preliminary understanding among the other visual artists about the general direction in which each will work, although there is seldom immediate agreement about all the visual matters discussed, and seldom does one meeting serve to elucidate everyone's ideas of the production's aims. Sometimes the costume designer makes almost no contribution to the discussion, or he may have an approach that in no way agrees with that of the author or the director. Sometimes the playwright and the director cannot develop a common interpretation of the script. Sometimes the director finds that the principal actors desired by the producer or the playwright do not envision the characters as he does. Many times misunderstandings or breakdowns in communication at the conferences can ruin the unity of effect in the final product. And there are times when disagreements or failures to reach mutual understanding result in the cancellation of contracts or even of the production. The importance of communication at the start cannot be stressed too strongly. Many a disaster is due to a failure of a group of theatre artists to reach a candid interchange of views before the production opens. Prominent and experienced theatre artists must not ignore what they know to be basic differences of opinion merely for appearance's sake, or as the work progresses, each person will set out to achieve his own end at the expense of the artistic production.

True, it is difficult for the various workers to reach an understanding: each is a specialist in his field; every production is in many respects unprecedented; and there are often as many opinions, theories, experiences, and schools of thought as there are theatre artists. But misunderstanding and vagueness must be eliminated as completely as is humanly possible from the proceedings. For example, in later conferences with the director, the costume designer must have certain key visual sources, rather than merely verbal descriptions with him. He must do thumbnail sketches or small figure layouts for the director to see, and he must urge the director to articulate his reactions to each item. The costume designer must learn to watch the director's face to see if he is really reading the sketch as a costume or is merely viewing it as an illustration, and the designer must never leave a conference feeling that he has not made clear contact with the director.

At the first conference, the costume designer will want to know the budget he has to work with, the amount of time available for design and construction, the final acting version of the script, and the director's changes, special interpretations, or specific requests.

At later meetings, the costume designer should have ready all the sketches, color plates, costume charts, accessory lists, and fabric swatches to make his visual concept as clear as possible to the director. Unless the costume designer is specific, the director may discover at dress rehearsal that many elements do not operate as he had envisioned. This may still occur, but one should try to avoid it. Last minute changes are costly and sometimes impossible.

After all sketches and plans have been approved, the designers and technicians move on to building the production while the director turns full time to rehearsals, and although there may be further conferences at regular or irregular intervals, the work of the designers and the director and actors progresses more or less independently until the first technical and dress rehearsals.

Research

We have said that the costume designer, like the other artists in a production, must make a thorough study of plot, character, dialogue, thought, rhythm, and spectacle, so that he has a secure grasp of the whole play as well as an understanding of the individual characters. But the costume designer can seldom go directly from the script to his imagination to produce the finished designs. Even in a play that seems to have few ties to reality or period, background research is still necessary, if only to learn more about the playwright and his ideas. If he is designing a period play, the designer should have a solid background in the social history of the period. He should be thoroughly familiar with the garments worn in the age: the characteristic silhouette, the typical textures and materials, the favorite colors and ornamental motifs, and the key accessories.

What are the usual sources from which the costume designer works? Obviously, this depends on the play and its interpretation; there are productions in which the costume ideas have come from books on marine life, texts on biology, treatises on zoology, or manuals on flower arrangement. Most frequently, however, a script presents some aspect of historic or present-day society that demands careful study. The resource material for such plays is usually located in the following places.

Books on the history of dress, especially those of the past few years, are fully documented with excellent original visual sources. If the books use modern drawings and sketches rather than original sources such as paintings and sculptures, there is a danger that one will miss the facts and quality of a past era. (See the recommended sources in Part III, p. 455.)

Magazines of the period (for the past two centuries) give the true flavor of the times, although with certain limitations. If one concentrates on fashion drawings, the costumes will follow the fashion ideal rather than what was actually worn; if one concentrates on illustrations, one comes close to the truth, but the information will be filtered through the illustrator's view; if one is able to use magazine photographs for periods after 1850 or 1860, one will get at the truth of the period but not at how people saw themselves.

Prints, paintings, engravings, etchings, and sketches of past periods are often difficult to locate, since the most frequently reproduced artistic products of the past may not provide insight into costume styles and accessory details. Often, much detective work must go into unearthing primary source material that is not to be found in volumes on fashion history.

Books on the plastic arts are another source: works on sculpture may be useful, and so may works on architecture if one is pursuing a certain artistic idea behind the costume and architecture of a period. Because it is three dimensional, sculpture is more helpful than painting in giving a sense of the form inside a costume.

The minor arts of jewelry, mosaics, pottery, textiles, and glassware provide information about accessories and details of costume. They also provide a more general kind of information: the color, line, and texture favored by a society. Sometimes the inspiration for a whole production may evolve from a small bit of tableware, a piece of furniture, or an item of jewelry.

Original garments from past periods can be found in museums or private collections. These usually date back only to the eighteenth century, but there are some from the Middle Ages. Original garments are particularly useful for learning the methods of cutting and fitting period costumes.

Finally, source material may be obtained from anything that strikes a response. No area should be closed; the designer should keep his eye open for possible inspiration and information from everything in the world around him.

Most of the material listed above will be found in the visual arts sections of libraries under the 700s in the Dewey decimal system, although books on the history of dress are frequently placed with social customs under the 390s. Books on theatre costume are often found under 809. Many libraries have picture files that are useful if certain paintings or a phase of an artist's work cannot be found in art books, and some libraries have slide files that cover the history of the visual arts far more fully than do volumes on the subject. A fine arts library is an ideal place for research.

Much material will be found only in museums, especially original garments, paintings, sculpture, and minor arts. If excellent museums are within easy reach during the design period, they should certainly be visited; if not, material can be sent in slide or print form. Certain large museums, like the Metropolitan Museum of Art in New York City, have a separate costume library and museum in addition to their larger collections, and here people trained in costume history can help the designer find the needed sources.

Most designers also develop their own files of pictures from magazines, newspapers, and journals, and some keep detailed files of costume fabrics that can be used in texture layouts.

Another source the designer uses is his background reading. Social histories give the broadest view of a society, while biographies provide detailed portraits of people and the age in which they lived. Memoirs, reminiscenses, and diaries are helpful in giving a direct, spontaneous, informal view of a period. For example, no book offers subtler insight into Restoration England than the diary of Samuel Pepys.

But what about the use of source material in developing a costume approach? The artist has collected much valuable information from his research, and he is tempted to use all of it. It takes great discipline and self-criticism to pare away material as one works to the core of a particular approach. Repeatedly, one sees productions in which all the costume designer's research is still on the stage on opening night; one sees an illustration of a period, a pageant of dress from past times, an unrolling of historical facts that are fascinating in themselves but stand in the way of the audience's concentration on the mood of the play. The most creative costume designer neither lifts costumes from books and source material nor copies the dress of past times; he is not obsessed with historical accuracy, but he attempts to get at the essence of the period as seen through the eyes of the dramatist and his director and to make this ordered artistry operate in terms of the theatre. Theatrical appropriateness to the character and play are far more important than historical accuracy and an abundance of historical detail.

Schedules, Lists, and Charts

We noted earlier that the designer should mark the script with notations about any matters pertaining to costume; he should start recording this material in chart form while he is doing his research. To make a chart, he divides a large sheet of paper or cardboard into squares. Down the left side, in each square, he writes the name of each character in the production along with the name of the actor playing the role. Then, across the top of the chart, each act or scene is listed, with one square allotted to each actor. In each square, the designer indicates the costume item worn by the actor in that scene, including all accessories, and sometimes he attaches color samples for the costume. The color range and overall color scheme can thus be seen at a glance, and the list of costume items can be used as a guide in dressing the actors and in keeping the costumes organized in the designer's, director's, and actor's minds (Figure 2–2).

	ACT I								ACT II					
	Lonely Landscape	Sarastro Palace	A Grove	Palm Grove	Court or Temple	Garden	Hallway	Inside Pyramid	Garden	Wild Mountain Spot	Small Garden	Rugged Cliffs	Temple of Sun	Comments
Sarastro			✓ 1ST COST	✓		✓ 2ND COST		✓					✓ 3RD COST	
Tamino	✓		✓		✓		✓	✓		✓			✓	
Papageno	✓	✓	✓		✓		✓	✓		✓				
Queen of Night	✓					✓					✓			
Pamina		✓ 1ST COST	✓			✓ 2ND COST	✓	✓	✓	✓			✓ 3RD COST	
Monostatos		✓	✓			✓					✓			
Papagena						✓ disguised as old lady	✓ disguised				✓			Throws off disguise on stage
1st Lady	✓				✓							✓		
2nd Lady	✓				✓							✓		
3rd Lady	✓				✓							✓		
1st Boy Genie			✓				✓		✓	✓				
2nd Boy Genie			✓				✓		✓	✓				
3rd Boy Genie			✓				✓		✓	✓				
1st Priest					✓			✓		✓		✓		
2nd Priest				✓	✓		✓	✓		✓		✓		
3rd Priest					✓			✓		✓		✓		
Speaker			✓	✓	✓		✓	✓				✓		
Slave		✓												
1st Man In Armor										✓				
2nd Man In Armor										✓				
Female Chorus Slaves			✓	✓				✓				✓		
Male Chorus Slaves		✓	✓	✓				✓				✓		
Chorus Guards			✓	✓				✓				✓		
Chorus Priests			✓	✓				✓				✓		
Chorus Priestesses			✓	✓				✓				✓		

Figure 2–2   Example of a costume chart for Mozart's *The Magic Flute*. From the notebooks of the author.

THE MAGIC FLUTE

COSTUME LIST

Principals - Male

    Sarastro - age 50 - High Priest of Isis
- (1)   1. fantastic headdress, corselet, overskirt, tonnelet, tights, boots, mantle, jewelry.
- (2)   2. headdress, gown, robe, tights, boots, staff, jewelry.
- (3)   3. turban-headdress, cuirass, gown, sash, underskirt, mantle, tight boots, jewelry, staff.

    Tamino - age 25 - An Egyptian Prince
- (4)   1. plumed helmet, corselet with labels, arm guards, tights, boots, mantle.

Principals - Female

    The Queen of the Night - age 40 - Mother of Pamina
- (14)   1. fantastic headdress, corsage, overskirt, underskirt, mantle, staff, petticoats, corset, stockings, slippers, jewelry.

Chorus - Male

    1st Male Guard
- (26)   1. headdress, robe, tonnelet with belt, tights, boots.

    2nd Male Guard
- (27)   1. headdress, robe, tonnelet with belt, tights, boots.

    3rd Male Guard
- (28)   1. headdress, robe, tonnelet with belt, tights, boots.

Chorus - Female

    1st Priestess
- (55)   1. headdress, corsage, skirt, mantle, jewelry, petticoats, corset, stockings, slippers.

TOTALS

Total Number of Costumes	75
Total Women's Costumes	37
Total Men's Costumes	38
Principal Men's Costumes	13
Principal Women's Costumes	12
Chorus Men's Costumes	25
Chorus Women's Costumes	25

Figure 2–3   Excerpts from a costume list for Mozart's *The Magic Flute.* From the notebooks of the author.

Similar in scope, and usually used to present a breakdown of costs to the producer, is the costume list. The characters in the production are listed in categories, the men divided from the women and the principals from the supporting cast and from the chorus or extras. After each character's name is written every item of clothing worn or accessory carried for each costume change. There are two sets of numbers to the left of the costume changes: the first set runs consecutively from the first to the last full costume in each category and tells the designer and the producer exactly how many full costumes he has in each grouping and in the play as a whole. The second runs consecutively for each character and gives only his total number of costumes. After each character's name, there is usually his age and a brief identification. At the end of the list are totaled the number of costumes in the production; the number of women's costumes; the number of men's costumes; the number for principal men and principal women; and, finally, the numbers each for chorus or supers, men and chorus or supers, women and chorus or supers (Figure 2–3). The costume list is invaluable when the designer talks with a producer about costs or negotiates with a costume house that may build the wardrobe. It is also helpful when he fills in the Costume Designer's Contract for the United Scenic Artists, which sets a certain fee for the costume designs of featured or principal players, another fee for the costume designs of supporting players, and a lesser fee for repeats of a costume design, for instance, for a chorus or an army.

Another chart, used later in the production preparation period to help the actor keep the parts of his costumes in order, is the character or actor costume chart, which gives at the top the dresser, the dressing room, and the title of the play. The body of the chart lists the character, the actor playing the role, and a notation of footwear, garments, headgear, and accessories (Figure 2–4). A chart like this should eventually be in each actor's dressing room, but earlier in the design period it is useful to pin it to the back of the sketch.

One final chart the designer should have for his private use is really a work calendar. Here the periods for each phase of the work can be penciled, and the designer can see how to budget his time and perhaps minimize the emotional crises that frequently accompany the pressure of production. The calendar should be divided generally into six periods: (1) reading the play; (2) conferences; (3) research; (4) design; (5) the date the show must go into the shop, and the time needed to build the show; and (6) the rehearsals and previews leading up to opening night. The calendar always gives the designer a guideline and an added confidence in planning (Figure 2–5).

Other charts related to construction and handling will be explained in a later chapter, but the overall costume chart, the costume list, and the individual actor's costume chart are aids that are best prepared when one is in the final stages of preliminary sketching and layout.

				Outer	Wigs &	

Dresser _____

COSTUME CHART

Dressing Room _____   Play _____

Character	Actor	Footwear	Basic Garments	Outer Garments	Wigs & Headdresses	Accessories

Figure 2–4   Example of a character-actor costume chart. From the notebooks of the author.

Figure 2–5 Example of a costume calendar for design and construction periods. From the notebooks of the author.

Preliminary Sketching and Layout

Once the research period has ended and the designer has clarified the costume requirements on his overall costume chart, preliminary sketching begins. Obviously, each designer will have his method of working, but almost everyone, his research fully in mind, goes through a period of doodling with pen and ink, pencil, or paint in an attempt to bring into focus his ideas for the production. Sometimes his research material is at his drawing board with him, sometimes sketches and inspirational notations from a research notebook are before him as he develops his early sketches. The designer may use swatches of fabric at this point if he thinks of texture and draped line before he thinks of form. The preliminary sketching period is one of the most exciting periods of the entire design process, because now the designer attempts to take hold of the vague concepts that have been intriguing him since he first read the play. At this point, the designer must not force a design to appear. He must let his ideas and research join at the subconscious level before surfacing on the pages of a notebook or sketch pad. Sometimes the idea for a costume will come quickly and remain intact even after later criticism, while another costume may elude the designer for days, and he will cover pages of a sketch pad or notebook as he tries to crystallize his sense of exactly what is required for the role. These pages of doodlings and half-ideas are often meaningless to anyone but the designer; for him they are a trail leading, often with many false starts, to the final costume form (Figure 2–6).

In plays where an abstract idea has been conceived as the key to all the costumes, the designer may work for every possible variation he can drain from his original idea before he is ready to piece together the individual costumes for character. In a production of *The Tempest*, if the designer wishes to use the basic costume forms of the English masque in conjunction with the visual imagery of the sea, he will first do research into the masque designs of Inigo Jones and then into books on sea life; the doodling period may then be devoted to pages and pages of masque forms combining, contrasting, and recombining the shapes of seaweed, crustaceans, and fish fins until masque design principles become a part of his inner consciousness. Only then can he move to the more concrete level of preliminary sketches for the characters.

When the preliminary sketching begins to approach its final form, the designer should again consult with his director so that each assures himself he is developing his ideas in the same direction. At a consultation like this, one or two costumes will usually create a problem. If there seems to be no immediate solution, the designer can either keep working at his preliminary designs or bypass those costumes and do a layout for the remainder of the play, hoping that by further clarifying the overall concept for the production he and the director will be led to a solution of the problems.

The layout is usually a string of small figures in pen and ink, sketch

Figure 2–6   Idea sketches from a designer's notebook. From the notebooks of the author.

Figure 2–7   Example of a costume layout for Molière's *Les Fourberies de Scapin* as produced by the Stanford Repertory Theatre, 1965. From the notebooks of the author.

pencil, colored pencil, or pigment that shows the director at a glance what the entire costume concept will look like. Sometimes, especially if the layout designs are in pen and ink with no indication of color, swatches of fabric will be pinned above each sketch. If the layout is in full color, then samples of the textures to be used are included at the side. The figures themselves may be strung out horizontally on several sheets of drawing paper or mat board; they may be on small individual pieces of sketch paper or mat board; or they may all be grouped on a large board or sketch sheet so that all changes for one character are clustered together and characters are grouped according to visual relationships in the play. Whatever the layout method, the small sketches should be simple and clear so that one will not waste time explaining one's intentions to the director (Figure 2–7). The layout is only an aid to the director and designer, not a finished statement to show actors, producers, backers, and interested friends.

The Costume Sketch

One should be careful to make the final sketches clear and large enough so there is no confusion about detail. Some designers' sketches are so vague that much marginal information is necessary for the cutters and seamstresses. Other designers make their sketches so detailed that the mood they wish to convey is lost. Obviously, some middle ground is pref-

Figure 2–8   Costume diagrams to aid in sketching. After sketching ideas in *The Art of Costume Design* by Marilyn Sotto. Courtesy of The Walter Foster Art Service, Inc., Tustin, Calif.

erable: the designer should retain the feeling he had about the costume when he conceived it, yet also show that the costume is wearable clothing. This is a difficult balance to achieve, and many designers do not try; they use whatever sketching style suits their personality. One time-consuming solution used by the famous American designer Lee Simonson was to do a set of beautifully vague and imaginative color sketches for the designer, producer, and actor, and another set of sketches—three or four simple, small, face-front figures on a board surrounded by detailed construction information—for those who were to make the costumes.

The average size of a costume figure in a finished sketch should be from ten to fourteen inches high; the figure should be either full-front or in three-quarter view with a minimum of foreshortening. The arms should be open, and the pose should tell as much about the costume as possible (Figure 2–8). Many designers like to suggest a figure in movement, because onstage the costume will almost never be still. Each sketch should carry four items of information: (1) the name of the production; (2) the name of the character; (3) in which act and scene he wears the costume; and (4) the designer's signature. Although there is no hard and fast rule about the placement of this information, the production name most often goes in the upper left-hand corner, the character's name with act and scene number in the lower right, and the signature or initials of the designer at the foot of the character (Figure 2–9).

Surfaces for the Costume Sketch

It is always difficult to decide on what surface to present the finished costume sketch. Mat board will not bend, can be easily stood against a wall, and will wear far better during shop use than watercolor or sketch paper. But mat board will seldom suit the watercolorist, who uses the surface and texture of the paper for the effectiveness of the sketch, and many mat board sketches together make a heavy portfolio. Some designers choose a surface and texture to suit each play; there are no limits to presentational possibilities. The designer may always use the same medium, surface, and technique as a sort of personal signature, or he may try to suit the presentational approach to the atmosphere of the play and its costumes.

Here are some of the surfaces that can be used:

Watercolor paper is used most frequently, because watercolor is still the most frequently used medium for costume sketching. Watercolor paper comes in many weights and textures, from very stiff and rough to quite light and smooth. Most designers prefer the medium to heavier weight, which holds up better, wrinkles less easily, and takes a heavier use of water and pigment. The costume designer who is to have his original watercolor sketches used in the shop needs a sketch that will not

Queen and The Rebels

Act II sc 3

Figure 2–9   Example of the labeling and placement of the costume sketch. From the notebooks of the author.

deteriorate easily, and unless he is going to fasten it to a solid mat board surface, he will want a fairly sturdy surface background. (Suggested watercolor papers: Andrews-Nelson-Whitehead; Bainbridge Sons; Grumbacher; Strathmore; Winsor & Newton.)

Mat board is another favorite background surface, since it is sturdy and does not easily bend or deteriorate. It is not as ideal for watercolor as watercolor paper, but for gouache, pen and ink with wash, colored

Figure 2–10   A costume sketch for Macduff for a production of Shakespeare's *Macbeth*, showing the use of black mat board as a background, as produced by the Yale Drama School, 1961. From the collection of the author.

pencil, acrylics, or colored inks it is satisfactory if the appropriate surface texture is chosen. Mat board usually comes in sheets 80 inches by 120 inches, which can be divided into eight sketch surfaces 10 inches by 15 inches. Surfaces vary from rough to smooth, and if gouache or any kind of opaque color is used, great variety of effect can be achieved by choosing colored or tinted boards that will suggest the background mood of the play. Black is a favorite, since it allows the designer to paint in only what the audience will see under stage lighting; the shadows are provided by the board surface. Black board is especially fine for presenting costumes if a play requires much shadow onstage and lighting from specific rather than general sources (Figure 2–10). Rough-surfaced mat board lends itself well to dry-dragging or dry-brushing with opaque color for a soft, fresco-like surface. (Suggested mat boards: Andrews-Nelson-Whitehead; Bainbridge Sons; Grumbacher; National American.)

Drawing paper, which comes in various weights and qualities, is useful for the artist who prefers to work dry, with pen and ink or colored pencils. The choice of a surface depends on how it reacts to the artist's pen or pencil stroke. If colored surfaces are required, the designer may use colored construction paper, which takes soft colored pencils effectively. (Suggested drawing paper: Andrews-Nelson-Whitehead; Bainbridge Sons; Strathmore; Winsor & Newton.)

Velour paper is usually chosen for pastel renderings, but the sketches must be protected with plastic spray or they will smear and disappear. Black velour paper gives a beautiful velvety background of great depth, and pastels or thick dry-brushed opaque colors can be effective in bring-

Figure 2–11   A costume sketch for the Baroness in Anouilh's *The Cavern*, showing the use of black velour paper as a background, as produced by the Stanford Repertory Theatre, 1967. From the collection of the author.

ing out what the audience will see of the costume under stage lighting (Figure 2–11). One can choose colored velour paper to suggest the mood of the play. (Suggested velour paper: Andrews-Nelson-Whitehead; Grumbacher; Strathmore; Winsor & Newton.)

Other surfaces can certainly be used. Some designers use a paste-up technique; that is, they paste various cut-out colored surfaces onto a roughly indicated human form placed against a fabric background, metallic paper, a patterned wallpaper background, or a thin rice paper surface. Even when a designer uses pen and ink, he may choose surfaces ranging from thin rice paper to heavy metallic paper, and some artists will also attempt to paint on these backgrounds. Certainly nothing should be ruled out if it projects the designer's feeling about a production and how he would like to work during the sketching process. But if the same design is to be used by shop personnel, the design must be readable and capable of having construction information attached to it.

Rendering the Costume Sketch

The sketch surface the designer chooses depends on the medium he chooses for the final costume rendering. The media usually include pencils, inks, transparent color, opaque color, casein, acrylics, or cut-out or paste-up materials.

PENCILS   Drawing, as opposed to painting, is usually the first step for any designer: he clarifies his ideas in the preliminary design stages and then he sets down the forms and outlines of the final sketch before he moves to the painting process. Very few designers rely exclusively on the drawing process, but all will use it at one time or another. Drawing is usually divided into three modes: (1) delineation or line drawing; (2) form drawing; and (3) color-value drawing. Line drawing is rare even in preliminary sketching stages, since some indication of dark or light is usually given, even if unconsciously. Often a designer mixes all three modes without being aware of it. All steps in the drawing process can be done either with pen and ink, with pencil or, as in the Orient, with a brush. At the time he begins his finished renderings, if the designer feels most at ease with a pencil he may draw his figure with great detail, bringing in all elements of form and light, and then tint the results with color. Or he may wish to use pencil for the entire sketch, even to adding his color with colored pencils. (Suggested drawing pencils: No. 1 or 2 American Crayon; Eagle; Eberhard Faber; Grumbacher; Winsor & Newton.)

Colored pencils usually come in hard and soft varieties; the hard are useful for various pencil lines, for example, crosshatching, clustered diagonal strokes, thinner and thicker lines, to bring out form through the various colors chosen. The hard colored pencil is excellent for linear ef-

Figure 2–12   A costume sketch for Alice in Bolt's *A Man for All Seasons,* show-ing the use of soft colored pencils on gray mat board, as produced by the Renaissance Festival, Victoria, B.C., 1965. From the collection of the author.

fects in color application, but one cannot merge color strokes into a smooth, colored form. Soft colored pencils are like pastels, but without their softness and their tendency to blur and smear. With soft colored pencils one can approach the softness of conté crayon as used by the eighteenth-century French artist Jean-Antoine Watteau. Blended color is possible, and on the correct surface a nonlinear result can be achieved. Colored pencils, both hard and soft, work best on tinted or colored sur-faces, where highlights can be placed with a white pencil (Figure 2–12). (Suggested colored pencils: Eberhard Faber; Eagle Prismacolor—highly recommended.)

INKS   In costume sketching, inks are used mostly for setting the line and form before adding color washes, although colored inks can be used

Figure 2–13   A costume sketch for M Perrichon in Labiche's *The Voyage of M Perrichon,* showing the use of a pen-and-ink drawing filled in with gray value washes of ink or watercolor. From the collection of the author.

in place of watercolors. For costume sketches without color, black indelible ink sets a clear, flat outline with any width of line from very thin to quite heavy, in preparation for a value wash in grays that is usually done with washable black ink. Fabric swatches must be attached to costume sketches without color (Figure 2–13). (Suggested drawing inks: Arthur Brown; Carters; Higgins.)

Another possibility is a flat ink outline with shadowed or receding areas inked in with indelible ink. This gives a stronger effect than the line and flat tone washes (Figure 2–14).

If one varies the thickness of the sketch lines when drawing with indelible ink, as did the fifteenth-century Italian artist Antonio Pollaiuolo, one can get form without shadowing or working in value washes. Color swatches will provide the color.

One can also develop a sense of three-dimensional form through crosshatching and clustered horizontal, vertical, or diagonal stroking (Figure 2–15).

Finally, we have the method of most Japanese art and also much poster art: the flat indelible ink outline with flat color washes added. The washes can be either watercolor or colored ink washes and, for the best effect, the result should be absolutely flat and transparent. If opaque color is used with strong, flat ink outlines, the result will be very like poster art (Figure 2–16).

Although the brilliant transparent results of colored inks are exciting, there is not much possibility for variation. They must be used as a trans-

Figure 2–14 A costume sketch for Bernardo in Shakespeare's *Hamlet* set in 1820, showing the use of indelible ink crosshatching and shadow used under watercolor washes to give depth to the sketch, as produced by the Stanford Players, 1963. From the collection of the author.

parent wash, although varying amounts of the surface beneath may be allowed to show. Occasionally, inks used with a dry-brush technique can be effective. (Suggested colored inks: Arthur Brown; Grumbacher; Higgins; Winsor & Newton.)

WATERCOLORS   The most common way to use watercolors in the preparation of a costume sketch is to execute a pencil drawing and then quickly brush in watercolor to suggest texture and color (Figure 2–17). If the drawing is complete in pencil form, the designer may color in the areas with a minimum of brushwork; if the drawing is vague, the folds, highlights, shadows, and accessory details can be suggested by the brush-

Figure 2–15   A costume sketch for Fouquier-Tinville in Büchner's *Danton's Death,* showing the use of indelible ink crosshatching to suggest German Expressionist woodcuts. From the collection of the author.

Figure 2–16   A costume sketch for the Doctor in Hindemith's *Hin und Zurück,* showing an indelible ink sketch filled in with flat opaque color, as produced by the Stanford Opera Theatre, 1962. From the collection of the author.

stroke. Watercolors are most effective when the paper beneath the costume is allowed to show through. If the surface of the paper or board used is rough, a dry-brushing or dragging technique can be effective, and with heavy pigment one can draw rather than paint with the brush. Always remember that watercolor sketches must retain their transparency and must give a feeling of spontaneity and rapid execution to be effective; the artist must paint in color and shadow, leaving highlight to the white surface beneath the sketch (Figure 2–18). Probably the simplest use of watercolors is as flat color washes that fill in areas of ink or pencil drawing with an indicated color, with no attempt at brushstrokes, feathering,

Figure 2–17   An original sketch by Leslie Hurry for Richard III in Shakespeare's history play, showing a rich and complex watercolor technique. From The Norman Philbrick Library. Courtesy of Leslie Hurry.

bleeding color, or more complicated techniques. (Suggested watercolors, tube: Grumbacher, Craftint; Weber; Winsor & Newton; cake: Arthur Brown; Grumbacher; Weber; Winsor & Newton.)

OPAQUE COLOR   In many ways, gouache colors or opaque watercolors are easiest for a beginning designer with little experience of the transparent media. Opaque color gives an excellent flat surface and a true sense of color, since one is not confused by surface effects in transparent color. With opaque color, highlights can be painted into the sketch, and one can make excellent use of colored and tinted backgrounds.

The most common use of opaque color and the simplest is to draw in the full, strong figure outline with indelible ink, and then fill in the areas of the costume in flat color. The result is like poster art (Figure 2–19). One can allow small amounts of the paper to show through the gouache application to give variety and a fuller sense of the sketch process. One may also use a dryer brush, and especially if a rough surface is used, one can achieve a pleasing rough plaster or fresco-like effect. Still another variation is to draw rather than paint with the brush. This works best on a dark or black surface, and with a full range of values from white to the black of the board, one can create vivid figures. Shadowing and highlighting in opaque color can become quite an art; and, on a dark or black surface, one can develop a figure as if seen in theatrical spotlighting, achieving a three-dimensional effect with a minimum of effort (Figure 2–20). One can also outline one side of the figure in white and the other in black to indicate a light source. An interesting surface on

Figure 2–18   An original sketch by Alix Stone for Katharina in Shakespeare's *Taming of the Shrew,* showing a watercolor technique combined with sepia ink drawings. From The Norman Philbrick Library. Courtesy of Alix Stone.

which to work with gouache is velour paper; here great thick pigment strokes give a rich, soft, textural sketch (see Figure 2–11).

In general, opaque color is easier to use than transparent watercolor, because it can be used in a drier way, it allows for more control, does not puddle and grow muddy the way beginners' watercolor sketches do, and gives a better idea of possibilities in fabric colors than does watercolor. (Suggested opaque or gouache colors: Grumbacher; Shiva; Winsor & Newton.)

CASEIN, OIL, ACRYLICS   Although used by commercial and professional artists, oil and casein are usually not used by the costume designer because they take a long time to dry. The need to work rapidly forces the

Figure 2–19   A costume sketch for Valentine in Shakespeare's *Two Gentlemen of Verona*, showing a pebbled mat board background containing a sketch in opaque color done with a dry brush, as produced by the Stanford Players, 1964. From the collection of the author.

Figure 2–20   A costume sketch for King Duncan in Shakespeare's *Macbeth,*
showing the placement of fabric swatches on the sketch, as produced by the
Yale Drama School, 1961. From the collection of the author.

costume designer to use a medium that can be managed easily and speed-
ily. Within the last few years, however, new plastic acrylics have entered
the market, and these offer the designer another choice because of the
wide range of effects they can achieve and the speed with which they can
be used. With water as a thinner, the designer can move all the way from
the impasto and glaze of oil to the transparency of watercolor; impasto
can be used without a drying time; and colors will not fade, crack, or
age. When dry, they are water resistant, and various transparent layers
may be overlaid in any sequence without erasing or obliterating the layer
below. Many designers have abandoned the older media for the possibilities that can be achieved with acrylics (Figure 2–21). (Suggested

casein and oil colors: Grumbacher; Talens; suggested acrylic and polymer colors: Grumbacher; Polyart; Polyform; Shiva; Talens.)

CUT-OUTS AND PASTE-UPS   Some designers use collage, a cut-out and paste-up method, instead of a sketch. They choose an interesting background, such as fabric, metal, wallpaper, construction paper, or velour paper, and construct the figure on it by pasting fabrics or colored or patterned papers to the background in appropriate shapes. Ralph Koltai used this method in his designs for the Shakespeare Memorial Theatre's production of *The Merchant of Venice* (Figure 2–22). The artist may draw or paint on top of the paste-up to clarify the design, but frequently the cut-out and paste-up method is used alone.

Figure 2–21   A costume sketch for Lady Macbeth in Shakespeare's *Macbeth*, as designed for a class project by Jean Schultz Davidson, showing the use of acrylic paints. Courtesy of Jean Schultz Davidson.

Figure 2–22   Costume sketches for the Prince of Aragon and the Duke of Morocco by Ralph Koltai for Shakespeare's *The Merchant of Venice,* showing the use of cut-out paper and paint against a metallic paper background. From The Norman Philbrick Library. Courtesy of Ralph Koltai.

Backgrounds, Framing, and Preservation of the Costume Sketch

Many designers will not be content to present a simple figure on a blank sheet of paper. They will wish to help the viewer see better how the designer envisions the particular costume and the play as a whole. We have already mentioned that an interesting surface can help enhance a particular rendering technique, and that colored or tinted surfaces can contribute to setting the mood of the play. Many designers use brush or colored pencil to lay in a colored area behind the costume figure to give it further importance on the sketch surface. Some use a pen-and-ink stroke

Figure 2–23   A costume sketch for Pantalone-Géronte in Molière's *Les Four-beries de Scapin*, showing the use of pen-and-ink crosshatching to set off the sketch from its background, as produced by the Stanford Repertory Theatre, 1965. From the collection of the author.

to build up a background or frame for the figure, or they may cover the surface behind the figure with an interesting texture and color pattern laid in with brush, pen, or pencil (Figure 2–23). Whatever he chooses to do here, the designer must be certain that the background does enhance the sketch and does not distract from or blur its artistic effect or make the construction notes surrounding it difficult to read.

If a designer intends his sketches to be used in the shop, that is, to be handed about instead of hung on a wall, he will want to preserve them by covering them with polyethylene or plastic. If he has used pastels or soft pencils, he should spray the sketch thoroughly with a plastic preservative before covering it. If the sketches are to hang on the walls of the costume room or be shown in public exhibition, the designer may wish to consider matting—adding a 2- to 3-inch border of mat board in an appropriate color and texture to set off the effect of the original rendering. Framing in mat board also gives a border on which to clip any typed information that might be needed if the sketch is exhibited. If the designer wishes, he can cover the matted sketch with plastic to protect the rendering.

Construction Notes

One of the dilemmas facing the designer is whether to treat his rendering as a sketch plan for the costume shop staff with full construction notes surrounding the sketch, or as an artistic idea that only suggests the finished product and is intended to sell the costume and the artistic approach to the actor, director, producer, and public. It has already been mentioned that the leading American designer Lee Simonson made two sets of sketches, one an artistic evocation of the mood of the play, the other a set of figures and plans for construction. Most designers try to strike a balance, and many still prefer construction drawing on a separate sheet or on the back of the sketch.

If the construction notes and drawings are on a separate sheet, they are usually attached to the left-hand side of the sketch and fold over it when it is carried or fold behind it when it is shown (Figure 2–24). A separate sheet gives more space for notations than does the space around the costume figure, but one cannot draw arrows or lines from the sketch to the notation or detail drawing. The same is true if the costume information is on the back of the sketch. If it surrounds the figure, it is certainly easier to relate the sketch to the detail drawing or construction notes.

Costume construction notes generally explain something that cannot be seen clearly in the sketch. They do not need to show the patterns for basic garments; the experienced people in the costume shop should know the patterns. In fact, conferences with an expert cutter will often teach the designer a better way to make a garment or costume detail. But anything in a costume sketch that is not self-explanatory to trained people should be blown up in a small construction sketch with accompanying notes. A hat shape or hairdo; a form of collar; the way something is to be draped, laced, or belted; small ornaments such as bracelets, buckles, brooches, and pins; patterns on fabric or elsewhere; and armor, complicated headdresses, swords, canes, or snuffboxes should be shown if they present any problems in construction, purchase, or rental. It is obviously best not to clutter a sketch with this information, so if a great many construction notes must be set down, the designer should use a separate sheet rather than crowd his costume rendering with drawings and notes. Most designers tend to limit their clarifying notes and drawings to two or three major items if the information surrounds the sketch (see Figure 1–1).

Finally, although more will be said of this in Chapter 5, the costume sketch in the upper left-hand corner should contain sample swatches of the fabrics to be used in building the costumes. Sometimes swatches from the designer's collection will be placed on the sketch for the director to see or for the designer to refer to when buying, but the swatches should be replaced by the fabrics to be used when the renderings reach the shop (Figures 2–10, 2–12, and 2–20). Some suggested books on rendering methods and materials are *The Craftsman's Handbook* (New York: Dover, 1954); Rutherford J. Gettens and George L. Stout, *Painting Materials: A Short Encyclopedia,* (New York: Van Nostrand Reinhold, 1966), a paperback; Ralph Mayer, *The Artist's Handbook of Materials and Techniques* (New York, Viking, 1957); also see the Bibliography at the end of the book.

Figure 2–24   A costume sketch for the First Priestess in Mozart's *The Magic Flute,* showing construction notes appended to the sketch. From the collection of the author.

3

Principles of
Characterization and Design

The Fundamentals of Design

Although preparing the costume sketch is in many ways the most reward-ing part of the design process, it is only a means to an artistic end. The costume-sketch is the plan for the finished costume, which will involve an interplay of line, form, texture, and color. The beginning designer often thinks of the sketch merely as a picture or an illustration of a cos-tume to be built, rather than as a design formed consciously or intuitively from a knowledge of certain common design principles.

In this book we shall view costume design not merely as a set of tech-niques for dressing plays, but as an art form. In developing an approach to costume design, now is the time to say something about art and about the principles of artistic theory. The study of aesthetics has usually pro-duced a great many questions such as: What is art? How do we perceive it? Is there such a thing as beauty? For our purposes, such philosophical questions are far less important than a pragmatic look at how artistic principles work in various artistic media. Problems of truth and beauty, theories of how man relates to art, definitions of what is art and what is not do not really concern the practicing designer as much as understand-ing and working with limited concepts such as line, proportion, mass, shape, and balance.

Philosophers of art have divided art into three categories or fields of value: sensuous, formal, and associative. The responses aroused by each of these values is distinct, and even a beginning student of design should have no difficulty in distinguishing one from the other. *Sensuous* values are those that arise from a perception of and response to colors, textures, and tones of light and shade, independent of the formal organization, the story, or the meaning of the work. For example, fabric surfaces of a costume may have visual or tactile appeal without creating in us an involvement in the period of the costume or the nature of the character wearing it. *Formal* values are less obvious, more complex, and more difficult to understand than the sensuous. Here we respond to the intellectual relationships that can be perceived in the work. In costume, one is particularly aware of the parts of the individual costume, how they relate to each other, and how each costume in the production relates to the total design concept. In this chapter we shall consider formal values as we look into the nature of line, the problems of repetition and balance, the nature of proportion, and the concept of unity. Finally, as mentioned in Chapter 1, there is an important category of symbolic or *associative* values, in which art objects gain meaning by reminding the viewer of things, ideas, or events outside the work itself. Such values are usually tied to memory, to past experiences, to a general cultural inheritance, and can be divided into two levels: primary and secondary. Primary associations are those that have universality and appeal to all people, while secondary associations are personal and are not necessarily understood by others.

If the costume designer were to design only for circus, dance, and extravaganza, it would be possible at this point to move directly from an introduction of the three types of aesthetic value to a discussion of the formal values or the principles of design, but most designers are involved with costume designs for specific characters with specific functions in a play. Therefore, before discussing the problems of formal design, it is important for us to establish how the designer develops a costume for a character in his visual imagination.

Principles of Characterization

The designer usually begins to develop a costume by covering pages and pages of a notebook with idea sketches that attempt to solve the problems of characterization. As he does preliminary sketching, he puts aside for the moment the results of his research and concentrates on the size, shape, posture, and silhouette of each character. He tries to visualize the habits, gestures, physical actions of the characters, the things they handle, the physical actions demanded by the director and the script, and to relate them to the characters' ages and social stations in the play. Often, the designer may sketch an actor (or a human form) without clothes or in a leotard and then gradually add the minimum clothing necessary to create the characterization (Figure 3–1). If any roles have been cast, the designer may wish to see the actors in leotards performing basic movements and gestures required in the play. At this stage of the idea-sketching process, the designer should think of each piece of clothing not as moving scenery or period decoration, but as something that will further underline an aspect of character. For each piece of clothing added to the sketch, the designer should ask himself: How will it move? How will it work? How will it help the actor on the stage underline some aspect of his characterization? A piece of clothing may have an intellectual reason for appearing on a character, but one must always remember that the audience will see the costume before knowing the reason that the character is wearing it. One must avoid clothing that is false to the visual image the character should project. A production of *The Cherry Orchard* comes to mind in which Madame Ranevsky appeared in an ugly wrapper that was alien to her visual personality. The director chose to have her wear it because it was a gift from her lover in Paris, and reflected the lover's taste, not her own. If the wrapper gave a subtle insight into her personality, it did so through intellectual, not visual means. For the audience, it did not relate to the mood of the scene, the dramatic needs of the action, or the character of Madame Ranevsky.

The production that has all parts cast by the preliminary design period invariably presents an easier and more rewarding experience for the designer, since he can get to know the actors personally and learn how they wear costume and makeup on the stage. If older actors are playing

Figure 3–1   Padding under a leotard used to emphasize pose and character. Drawings by the author.

younger parts, or if the actors are of established reputation and feel they must always appear handsome onstage, the designer may have to make an extra effort to hide less desirable points and stress the best points of their physical appearances. In this regard, much attention must be placed on the hairdo or wig and the makeup, and although specialists other than the costume designer may be in charge here, the designer must supervise and be responsible for the final results. In designing for well-known actors, the designer must attend more than usual to the comfort, fit, and perfection of costume lines. This means that the preliminary idea sketching must explore every possibility for creating just the right effect, and the designer may require several conferences and even working periods with the leading performers before the right level of subtle character delineation is achieved.

One cannot stress too fully the need to build the costume characterization from the inside out, no matter who the actor performing the role. It is in the basic structure underneath the costume that the secret of success is to be found. A little padding at the shoulders, at the bustline, or at the hips, a little cinching in at the waist, the upper arm, or the hips, a little boning of the torso and the back, and one can often achieve exactly the right combination of period line and personal characterization. Each item of underclothing worn in a period should be analyzed for its function, not its looks or its charm, and nothing should be worn or discarded until its necessity for the final physical characterization is established. As we said in Chapter 1, most theatrical costume is of the artificial structural type rather than the fitted, semifitted, or draped variety; and it is the structural foundation that makes possible the variety of subtle changes in silhouette, movement, and gesture that cannot be achieved when clothing is worn directly over the human form.

Accessories must also be considered when making preliminary sketches of costume silhouette and line, and all adornments and ornamentation should be a reflection of the basic character line inherent in the costume. By character line, it should be clear by now that we mean the importance of a character in a play, the posture and stance of a personality, the height of a figure, and the other ways in which we take in a character at first glance. The only times the basic character line is relatively unimportant is when a character in a play is less a personality onstage than a moving decoration for the stage scene. Once a character has been developed, and if the character is not to sustain major physical changes (such as aging, injury, or illness), the designer is well advised to have as few costume changes as is consistent with the play's action. A dazzling display of costume changes may be rewarding for the audience and challenging for the designer, but many changes will weaken the physical characterization established at the beginning of the play.

There are a number of basic costume lines that designers, through many years of experience, have found helpful in stressing the actor's best

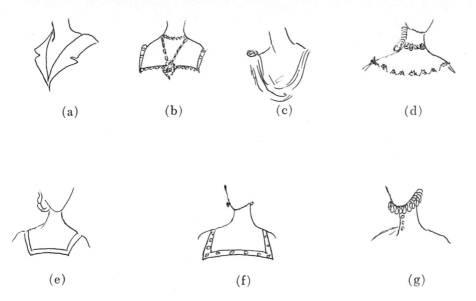

(a)   (b)   (c)   (d)

(e)   (f)   (g)

Figure 3–2   Line problems in necklines. Drawings by the author.

physical attributes, although the use of these will vary with the general physical ideal in vogue at the time.

First, beginning at the top of the figure, an actor will profit by having his face show clearly. Hats should not cover the forehead and shade the eyes, wigs should not hang across the sides of the face, collars should not hide the jawline and chin. Second, the neck should be lengthened so that the head does not appear to sit directly on the shoulders, although overly long necks can also present problems. In Figure 3–2 a number of variations in neckline are shown, each accomplishing something quite different. The V neckline (a) will draw the eye down from the neckline and will stress the area from the neck to the center of the bust. The square neckline (b) will widen the shoulders and the figure below the neck and the area above the bust. The U-shaped neckline (c) will give a gentle line to the area below the neck and draw little attention to the area above the bust. A boat or crescent neckline (d) will give the same soft line but with more stress on the width of the shoulders and will not draw attention to the bust. A keystone neckline (e) is used infrequently even in period dress, since it is not particularly flattering; it tends to widen the shoulders and narrow the bust. The trapezoidal neckline (f), usually associated with the sixteenth-century Tudor style, tends to draw attention from the shoulders and give great breadth to the bust. A high neckline (g) of any kind appears to enclose and suppress the area below the chin.

Third, although we have seen how the bust can be greatly influenced by the neckline, it should usually be shaped by careful padding or boning on a foundation garment or in the foundation of the bodice or gown. It can be remade to suit any period ideal or characterization. The waist is always seen in connection with the bust, and it can be pulled in by a foundation garment, or the area between hip bone and rib cage can be stretched out by boning. For some periods and for some personalities, the waist must be balanced with the bustline to give a boyish or straight line to the torso; at other times, it must be especially small in contrast with an exceedingly large bust. The same is true of the hips; they will need to be enlarged or contracted depending on the proportions desired in a particular period or character silhouette. They can be large in contrast to a small waist or slimmed so that bust, waist, and hips are all more or less equalized. These proportion changes also apply to men; chest, waist, and hips can be built up or contracted for a particular character or period line. For example, the male silhouette of 1830 had a padded chest, cinched-in waist, and padded hips comparable to the feminine ideal of the period.

One must decide whether it is best to expose or cover the arms. If they are exposed, they must not be overbalanced by the remainder of the costume; if they are partly covered, three-quarter-length sleeves may make them look too long or the sleeves too short. If the sleeve is full length, one must decide whether the line is to be broken at several points by decoration, puffs, or an over- and an undersleeve, be all of one piece, or be sharply divided at the elbow into an upper and lower sleeve. If great puffs are used on the upper arm, will the lower arm and hands seem too small? Can the arm be enlarged without looking grotesque against the rest of the costume? The same is true of legs: they can be left uncovered to the hips, covered to below or above the knee, or covered all the way to the floor, including or excluding the feet. In each case, the covered and uncovered areas must be balanced against one another to gain the right balance and proportion and the particular character silhouette desired.

Elements of Design

The next step in developing a design consciousness involves a more formal, abstract, and less subjective approach to theatrical costume. A study of the elements and principles of design will develop the eye of the designer, so that he sees with his mind as well as his feelings. Twentieth-century art has taught us to see abstractly. We have learned to see lines, colors, shapes, and textures in themselves, unrelated to a story, scene, or particular subject matter. We have learned to look at one or two things at a time, and as we look up and down and across an arrangement of color, line, and texture, we find that subtle differences create in us emotional responses often as great as those we feel when we see great religious or historical paintings.

Line, shape, measure, mass, position, color, and texture are the elements of design. They make up what are usually referred to as the form of a work of art—the "design form," which implies that a composition has been created using these elements of design. A costume designer must learn what these terms mean and make them part of the way he sees.

LINE   We might say that line is a record of the movement of the eye when it examines an object. In primitive drawings and in children's sketches, we can see the visual shorthand that may allow a single line to stand for a full, complex shape. Even the simplest lines have mood, meaning, and emotional associations, and thus we feel a strong difference in the effect of vertical and horizontal lines, of curved and serpentine lines. Line in costume is manifested primarily in the silhouette of garments, but it may also be seen in seams, darts, and ornamentation. It may be complex, with zigzags, scallops, and intricate patterns of brocade and embroidery. The line used in one costume must relate to the overall pattern of line used in the other costumes in a production and to the line pattern used in the visual setting for the production.

SHAPE   One role of line is to define an object as a shape. Line can define and limit the size of a particular area, but it also does more; as soon as an outline for an area has been established, the line that surrounds the shape will appear to have movement, rhythm, and emotional connotations. In costume, shape refers to the area of a shirt, doublet, cloak, or coat, or to the area of a particular ornament or pattern decoration.

MEASURE   One of the most important characteristics of a trained eye is the ability to measure without the aid of tapes or yardsticks. One must be able to judge sizes and the distances between shapes and lines. For the costume designer, measure is one of the most vital elements in the creation of quality designs. It involves the size of buttons, the distance between buttons or ornaments, the width of a collar, the length of a skirt, and a host of other sizes and distances that must be correct in any design.

MASS   The effects of line, shape, and measure are combined so that an area of a certain size is seen to have bulk and depth; in other words, mass is three-dimensional shape. In costume, this involves the mass of a particular garment that an actor wears or the mass of an entire costume in relation to other costumes and the entire spatial arrangement of the stage. We can see the importance of mass as a design element when we view a stage full of costumes at a distance that allows us to take in all the costumes at once.

POSITION   Position indicates not just the distance between shapes, but the placement of a shape in relation to another shape and in relation to the area around it. If a shape is not symmetrical, then the strongest or most important side of the shape can lead the eye in a particular direction. Thus, the position of an asymmetrical brooch or decorative ornament can be extremely important in a costume. For example, a rectangular shoulder brooch for a medieval mantle can be placed horizontally on the shoulder to give more width to the figure, or it can be placed vertically to stress the vertical line of the mantle.

Color   Color is obviously one of the most important design elements, because it captures associative and emotional responses from an audience. We shall discuss color more fully in Chapter 4, where it will become evident that color can be used to create effects in all three areas of aesthetic value: the sensuous, the associative, and the formal. Rich, thick, intense colors can elicit a sensuous response from a viewer, and color can be used to organize and direct the eye's response to a stage full of costumes.

Texture   Costume design is different from other arts because it uses fabric as its major medium. Texture refers to the tactile response the surfaces and folds of the fabric arouse in the viewer. Texture is usually thought to be a sensuous value, but it can also be viewed associatively and, to some extent, as a formal series of arranged relationships. In costume design, one of the major factors in the choice of textures is the effect of a surface under light. Textures with a thick, fuzzy surface such as velour or heavy woolen will absorb light; shiny, smooth surfaces such as satin or metallic armor will reflect light. It is the interplay of texture and light that creates the complex subtleties of tactile response in an audience. The distance between the viewer and the stage often requires that texture be stimulated or artificially enhanced through painting, scraping, polishing, brushing, or other processes. A detailed discussion of texture will be found in Chapter 5 and at the end of Chapter 7.

Principles of Design

Having looked briefly at the elements used in producing a composition with a "design form," let us now look at the terms that describe the principles of organization used to create the artistic product. By these principles of organization a designer seeks to manipulate his ideas and his visual material in such a way as to bring unity, interest, and meaning to his design. Although in the work of the experienced costume designer many of the principles are used unconsciously or instinctively, it will be helpful to the beginning designer if we discuss them here.

Unity   Probably the key word in any discussion of design principles is unity, or the linking of the separate parts of a composition in such a way as to create a whole that is greater than the sum of its parts. In costume design, unity involves organizing the parts of a single costume and the total costumed stage picture into an overall plan. If disunity, not unity, seems to be required in many modern productions, one merely has to reverse one's thinking; the planning is the same. One has to calculate just as carefully the correct balance of clash and opposition, the right proportion of disparate elements, so that the final design approach has the "unity of disunity" correct for the production.

HARMONY   Unity is achieved through the use of harmony and contrast. Harmony is the pleasing grouping of lines, textures, and colors with certain similar characteristics. When similar effects are repeated and sequences of effects are created, an artistic organization and control can be achieved that we feel to be harmonious. However, if there is too much repetition, or too obvious a sequence, the result may be monotonous. For example, too many closely related colors, or two few variations of line in a set of costumes may produce results that are dull and unexciting because they lack variation and contrast.

CONTRAST   Diversity in the grouping of the design elements creates contrast and gives interest and life to a design scheme that may lack variety because it has a strong harmony. Without contrast, form cannot be revealed: in war, for example, men and weapons are concealed from the enemy—camouflaged—by the use of color harmony. In the theatre, sharp contrast is obviously preferred to the color harmony that can occur accidentally when a green costume sinks into a green chair. What is needed in a production is the right balance between harmony and contrast.

VARIATION   When repetition produces monotony, regularly introduced variation will add interest to the composition. A variation in the shape of every third ornament on a doublet sleeve or the space between every third appearance of a particular motif in a pattern is more interesting than identical forms or identical distances between forms in a sequence. To create variation in a sequence, a motif can be alternated so that it shifts its position in relation to its central axis without changing the direction of the pattern: it can be placed in opposition so that every other repetition of the motif opposes the preceding one; or it can be inverted so that the direction of the pattern keeps reversing as the sequence of motifs moves in a particular direction. As can be seen in border or overall fabric patterns (Figures 3–3 and 3–4), the different means of variation can be used in many combinations.

BALANCE   When one creates a sense of stability by the careful distribution of the forces or weights within a composition, the result is said to be balanced. A costume will appear balanced when one has distributed color, line, and texture in such a way that those elements that attract the most attention are spread evenly over the figure. In a stage scene, one group of costumes must not attract all the attention; it may have to be weighted against another group. The visual tension between individual costumes and groups of costumes gives a production a feeling of balance. There are tensions of balance between upstage costumes and downstage costumes, between costume groups right stage and left stage, and in a

Figure 3–3   Variation in patterns. (a) Repetition of elements. (b) Variation of shape. (c) Variation of measure. (d) Variation of position. (e) Variation of color. (f) Variation of texture. Drawings by the author.

single costume between head and toe and arm and arm.

The stage has an element that a painting does not have: movement, or the change of the composition in space and time. It is the harmonious maintenance of different balances as the eye of the audience is led through changes in color, shape, size, and texture that gives the theatre its particular fascination. Even the balance of the individual costume is ever-changing as an actor sits, raises his arms, runs, or falls.

There are two kinds of balance: symmetrical and asymmetrical. In

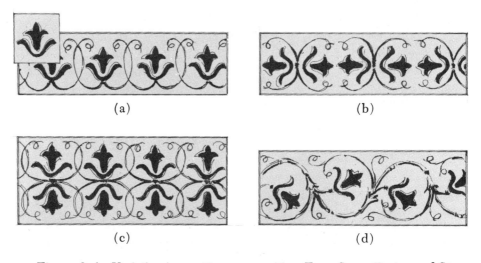

Figure 3–4   Variation in a pattern composition. From *Scene Design and Stage Lighting* by W. Oren Parker and Harvey K. Smith, Holt, Rinehart and Winston, New York, 1963, Chapter III, Figure 2.

the individual costume, the more common form is symmetrical balance, where both sides of the costume are alike. But asymmetrical balance is not to be neglected, for there are many costumes in which a drapery may pass across the figure and trail at one side, or ornamentation and accessories may follow diagonal lines across a figure rather than balance horizontally or vertically. Sometimes an entire sleeve or a leg covering may be a different cut or color from the one opposite (Figure 3–5).

PROPORTION   The relationship of one element of a design to another is proportion. If a young designer has an innate sense of scale and proportion, he will be on his way to good costume design. Although much can be learned by training, and the eye can be sharpened by continual analysis, a great part of one's sense of proportion is intuitive.

In the theatre, the human form is the measure of all decisions of proportion. Even in a large theatre presenting an operatic production, the designer cannot overlook the human form of actor or singer when he develops his scale of proportions in costume and setting. To exaggerate or overscale costumes and accessories may achieve a heightened size or grandeur for the human form, but it also may weigh the actor down, hide his movements, and inhibit his expression. To underscale a production may be to present an audience with a blur of textures, lines, and details that never make their point because they are too small and weak.

Proportion is especially important in the individual costume. The

Figure 3–5   Symmetrical (left) and asymmetrical (right) balance in costume. Drawings by the author.

designer must give attention to the amount and distribution of color, the length of a bodice in comparison to a skirt, and the width of shoulders in relation to hips, waist, and bust. Through the manipulation of proportions, one can improve an actor's appearance. For example, by emphasizing vertical lines, a plump actor can be made to appear more slender, while horizontal lines will increase his width. In short, what we consider to be beautiful, graceful costumes usually come from right proportion, awkwardness and ugliness from disproportion (Figure 3–6). In modern drama, much use is made of disproportion for the sake of shock, surprise, violence, or ugliness.

EMPHASIS   As does a painting or a piece of sculpture, a costume design needs a focus or center of interest, a point to which the eye is first directed (Figure 3–7). Emphasis may be created by a patch of color, converging lines, a change in texture, or ornament and accessories. Through emphasis, a good costume designer can direct attention to an actor's good points and minimize or disguise his poor ones. In the full-stage picture of grouped costumes, some should obviously be more important than others; the eye should be led to the principal rather than the subordinate characters.

RHYTHM   A sequence of visual impressions that has been ordered into a recurring pattern with certain accents and emphases creates a sense

Figure 3–6   Proportion (left) and disproportion (right) in costume. Drawings by the author.

Figure 3–7 Emphasis in costume design: emphasis below waist (left) and emphasis at neck (right). Drawings by the author.

of rhythm. Rhythm is one of the most deeply felt, innate responses that man has, since its pulsing quality is related to the two fundamental life processes of the heartbeat and breathing, as well as to the rhythms of the sexual act and the progression and decline of human life. As John Dewey said in *Art as Experience* (1934): "So far as nature is to us more than a flux lacking order in its mutable changes, so far as it is more than a whirlpool of confusion, it is marked by rhythms." An audience in a theatre responds instinctively to the rhythm of music in a production, to the rise and fall of the plot, and to the recurring patterns and accented groups of visual stimuli projected by sets and costumes. It reacts both emotionally and physically, usually at a subconscious level.

In costume design, a unifying rhythm is achieved by the way lines, shapes, textures, and colors of a costume direct the eye from the major points of interest to the subordinate parts and from one grouping of costumes to another throughout the play. The rhythm of the costume designs should support the play's action, visual atmosphere, and emotional climate.

Problems in Line

The designer must remember that the two-dimensional lines in his costume sketch will be translated into the three-dimensional costume of a moving actor onstage. He should know exactly how each linear effect in

Figure 3–8   Short-line (left), medium-line (center), and long-line (right) costumes. Drawings by the author.

the sketch will appear in the finished garment, and he should be consistent in his use of line for all the costumes in the production.

Some designers stress line, some stress color or texture, and some combine the three; after a designer has worked for many years, he becomes aware of his preferences and learns his strengths and weaknesses. Ideas for designs may come from the line treatment of fashion illustrations, from the work of other designers, and from the art of the past, but the designer always attempts to see the two-dimensional linear effects as they will appear in three-dimensional garments.

In the outer lines of a costume, the designer can work for a harmony of long lines, short lines, or medium lines. While he will usually try to avoid the clash of too sharp a contrast of line, there are many modern plays in which a disproportionate effect is needed. Most period fashions are a harmony of lines that do not contain too sharp a contrast. For example, a modern suit is a harmony of medium straight lines; a Roman soldier's costume is composed primarily of short lines; ecclesiastical vestments usually involve an interplay of long lines (Figure 3–8). Mid-nineteenth-century women's costumes, which call for tiers of fabric and small pattern pieces, are a play of short lines.

The outer lines of a costume may show a play of curved lines, such as one finds in eighteenth-century dress or in the costume lines of the Romantic period. The curved line of the upper puffed sleeve is contrasted with the curved lines of the skirt and underskirt, and in the eighteenth-century costume, the harmony of curves is further accentuated by the draped curves of decoration on the outer skirt or by the draping of the outer skirt itself in a series of curves over the panier. Often, such harmonies of curves have contrasting accents of angles at the bodice front, in the trim, or even at the neckline, so that the lines of the costume do not become too monotonous. A costume based more on a harmony of angles than on curves is the early sixteenth-century Tudor gown. Here angularity is apparent in the neckline, waist, overskirt, and gabled headdress. Minor accents of curves are sometimes added by a necklace or in the shape of the sleeves (Figure 3–9).

A harmony of direction is achieved when the major lines of a costume are horizontal, vertical, or diagonal; if the lines go equally in all three directions, complete confusion and fragmentation of effect result.

Let us consider the possibility of a harmony of curves and angles. If we take a dress that has almost all of its exterior lines as curves, and add a series of scalloped flounces also in curves, we have a harmony of curves. If we then add a zigzag bottom flounce, we destroy the total effect by destroying the expectation set up by the three curved flounces. Unless we can include a series of repeats for the zigzag line as a subordinate accent, the one strong zigzag must be left out. The strength of the curves and the zigzags cannot be equal or they cancel each other.

Or, let us take the example of a strong circular pattern down one side of a costume and a triangular pattern down the opposite side. Each side has a strong harmony through repetition, but the two sides are opposed in their decorative patterns; the result is an opposition between the two sides of the costume.

Figure 3–9 Angular-line (left) and curved-line (right) harmony. Drawings by the author.

Compositional Problems in Shape and Measure

Problems of shape and measure have to be solved during every step of the design process. The designer must train his eye to judge proportion and shape in the objects about him and the clothes he sees in the street. Just how large and what shape should a belt, sleeves, neckbands, and wristbands be? Only when a designer achieves a fine eye for shape and measure can he tell immediately that a belt is too large or the wrong shape, or that the shape of a bodice and its length are disproportionate to a particular female form.

The most common decorative harmonies with a definite shape and measure are the circle, the band, and stripes. There are any number of variations derived from them. When the designer repeats a shape three or more times, the size of the shape and the space between the repeats become a problem to be solved in relation to the rest of the costume. He must not overdo the repetitions; he should work to achieve the correct placement, shape, size, and space between shapes so that a focus or accent is created instead of a monotonous repetition of decorations.

Compositional Problems of Sequence and Repetition

The designer who works with simple geometric shapes is doing something basic to the most primitive societies: abstracting pattern from nature, and ordering and controlling it. In Neolithic wall paintings and decorative pottery, one is aware how much importance man has placed on the abstraction and ordering of objects taken from the apparent disorder of nature.

When one repeats a shape more than twice, a sequence results. If the decoration on a costume is subtly done, a sequence permits the eye to move from point to point rather than to remain focused on a single motif. The problem with a sequence is that it must not be too obvious, and the eye must follow from point to point easily (Figure 3–10a); it must not confuse the eye by too large a jump from one point to the next, nor must some larger and differently shaped motif interrupt in the middle of the sequence to destroy its effect (Figure 3–10b). When two sequences in a costume are about equal in interest and strength, they fight for dominance and cancel each other. The costume can never achieve a unity or a single focus until one sequence is subordinated to the other (Figure 3–10c). When the designer sees a conflict in a sequence, he must learn the simplest method of correcting the focus so that his original idea for the costume need not be discarded. One area of the body that often causes trouble is the waistline. Frequently, a sequence of motif that runs

Figure 4–4a   Example of the use of neutralized color and its mood effect in painting: *The Angelus* by Jean-François Millet, The Louvre, Paris, 1857–1859. Photo courtesy of the Directeur des Musées de France.

Figure 4–4b   Example of the use of intense color and its mood effect in painting: *The Houses of Chatou* by Maurice Vlaminck, Chicago Art Institute, Chicago, ca. 1904. Photo courtesy of The Art Institute of Chicago.

Figure 4–5a   Example of the linearist approach in Renaissance painting: *The Doni Madonna* (Holy Family) by Michelangelo, Uffizi, Florence, ca. 1506. Courtesy of the Uffizi Gallery, Florence.

Figure 4–5b   Example of the colorist approach in Renaissance painting: *The Rape of Europa* by Titian, Isabella Stewart Gardner Museum, Boston, ca. 1559. Photo courtesy of the Isabella Stewart Gardner Museum.

Figure 4–7 Example of a painting used as a source for a rich sixteenth-century color scheme: *The Feast at Cana* by Paolo Veronese, The Louvre, Paris. Photo courtesy of the Directeur des Musées de France.

Figure 4–8 Example of color imagery based on marine life: a scene from a production of *The Tempest* by Shakespeare as produced by the Oregon Shakespeare Festival, Ashland, Ore., 1960. Photo by the author.

Figure 4–9   Example of a famous El Greco painting as a source of color imagery for a production of *Hamlet: The Burial of Count Orgaz* by El Greco, Church of San Tomé, Toledo. Courtesy of D. P. Domínguez-Párocco.

Figure 4–10   Example of the first layout of costumes for a production: a color layout of small figures for a production of *Twelfth Night* as produced by the Actor's Workshop, San Francisco, 1962. From the collection of the author.

In a sequence the eye must follow a line easily from beginning to end.

This is a blocked sequence.

With too large a jump, there is no sequence.

This does read as a sequence.

(a)

No sequence

Sequence

(b)

Here, floral ornaments fight the bands at the bottom — one sequence cancels out the other.

Unless the floral element is repeated, it fights with buttons.

Here, the buttons and flowers complement one another and carry the eye from neck and shoulders to hemline.

(c)

Figure 3–10   Problems in sequence and repetition. Drawings by the author.

up the figure from floor to neck can be blocked by a belt that is too wide or has a sequence of horizontal direction that is too strong. One has to pay particular attention to the width and decoration of a belt. When a sequence of decoration is involved, any transition from one area to another can cause difficulty and must be handled with great care.

A sequence is more interesting if it is a sequence of alternation rather than mere repetition. In Western art, some of the great basic sequences of alternation are those used by the Greeks and Romans as architectural ornament. The egg and dart, bead and reel, and leaf and dart moldings are excellent examples of rhythmic alternations of shape. The accent comes at regular intervals, and one can sense oneself reacting rhythmically when one looks at the sequences or when one develops them as an artist. An even more interesting use of sequence, but one often difficult to work into a design without creating too obvious an effect, is a sequence of progression. Here the designer works to increase or decrease the size of the shape or the interval between the shapes so that a sense of growth or decay, a sense of enlargement or contraction is added to the sense of movement in the sequence (Figure 3–11a). For example, buttons can become larger and farther apart as they march up the torso to a climax in a large collar or ruff; or they may enlarge and grow farther apart as they

Figure 3–11   Sequences of progression. Drawings by the author.

come down from the neck to a very portly stomach (Figure 3–11b). Most progressions run downward; it is always easier to come down the figure than to go up it because of our sense of the pull of gravity. Another important use of the sequence is in enlarging the size and space between motif shapes as they go down a skirt front or edge a divided overskirt, since the expanding lines of the costume are complemented by the expanding progression of the decoration (Figure 3–11c).

Sometimes, especially in certain comic costumes or in classically simple costumes, the entire design scheme is based on a calculated play of curved versus straight lines, bands of decoration in exactly the right proportions, and sequences of motifs that expand and contract to fit the expanding and contracting lines of the costume. It is a rational rather than an emotional kind of design, and the results can give the audience a sense of controlled humor.

Let us use as an example a comic costume designed for Sir Andrew Aguecheek in a production of *Twelfth Night*. To make the figure look taller and thinner and to make the lines of the body contract and expand in an exaggeration of the typical Elizabethan figure, the braiding on the doublet might deliberately get smaller toward the waist, the bands on the leg might outline the thighs like separate parts, and the bows at the shoulders and knees might make the whole figure look like a tightly packaged gift. All would give a calculated play of linear effects using

Figure 3–12   Harmony, sequence, and balance in a costume design for Sir Andrew Aguecheek in *Twelfth Night* as produced by the Actor's Workshop, San Francisco, 1962. From the collection of the author.

repetition, alternation, and progression to exaggerate the human figure (Figure 3–12).

Characterization and Design When Costumes Are Rented or Taken from Wardrobe

Ideally, costumes are designed for each production and "built from scratch" in a well-equipped shop, but a word or two should be said about the more common necessity of renting costumes or choosing them from the costume wardrobe.

First of all, a few costume houses will build costumes to a designer's specifications at a price that is well below that which they would charge to a commercial management; this may prove helpful when a designer does not have the trained personnel to build frock coats and other tailored garments. Costume houses will send out design layouts that include sketches for an entire production, but do not assume when you rent a production that all the costumes will mirror the lines in the sketches. The layout is primarily a promotional device to increase rentals, although when a costume house owns the costumes from a professional New York production, one may receive all the costumes designed for the original presentation. Usually, when renting, one receives a coordinated group of costumes related to the sketches in a costume layout but chosen to fit the measurements of one's actors.

For the best results, the designer or costume coordinator should go to the rental house and pick out the costumes with the company personnel. Only in an emergency should costumes be rented sight unseen on the basis of a description, a thumbnail sketch, and a few measurements. In preparing to visit a costume house, the designer or coordinator should do a complete layout as described in Chapter 2. To each small sketch he may attach colored fabrics in the appropriate textures to remind himself of his preferred costume scheme. Then his plans will not be frustrated if he cannot find exactly the color scheme he wishes for each costume. The designer should have a clear idea of the unified result he wants to achieve in the production, and he must keep it in mind throughout the trying process of choosing rental items. There will always be some costumes or parts of costumes that will not satisfy him and will call for a compromise in the design plan.

Measurements usually needed by the rental house are bust or chest, waist, hips, shirt size, collar size, hat size, shoe size, inseam, overarm, and possibly the shoulder measurement. Costume rental houses that will usually give competent service will be found in the section on "Sources of Theatrical Supplies" at the back of the book.

When the designer receives costumes from a rental house, he will be allowed certain changes in the garments as long as they do not basically alter the costume. New buttons and trim may be applied if the original ones are replaced before the costumes are returned, and garments may be altered to fit more smoothly.

When a designer works with costumes from his wardrobe or from local thrift stores, army surplus stores, or secondhand stores, he will use much the same procedure that he would in choosing from a rental house, except that now any amount of change and alteration is possible. Often, disparate items from a wardrobe may be brought together by trim, buttons, or the way waistcoats, ties, or costume accessories are used. Color will help to give a unified feeling to a production in spite of great varieties in cut, line, and texture. Items also can be dyed or a felt pen or textile paint can be used to strengthen patterns or outlines of trim. One method of establishing a unity of atmosphere among a "grab bag" of wardrobe items is to texture the costumes with spray paint, dye, or dry-brushing. In this way the designer can still control the effect of the costume even though he must use ready-made items from the wardrobe.

4

Color

Color Theory

An audience will generally react more readily to color than to line or texture. Thus, the strength of color as a part of design demands that the designer have full control of its use. The costume designer, like the scene designer, must know color theory before he begins to work with color. Knowledge of color theory does not inhibit imagination; it gives the designer control over his color effects in fabric. Color theory is something that is learned, becomes a part of one's approach, and is forgotten as a series of rules, although it is retained as a critical way of seeing.

A color has three properties that can be varied: hue, value, and intensity.

Hue When the radiant energy from the sun passes through a triangular prism of glass, the light beam is broken up into various wavelengths and a series of colors are seen by the eye like those one sees when one looks at a rainbow. Hue is the name given to the various colors that are formed from the refraction of sunlight. Objects, or, in our case, fabrics, do not actually contain color; they have the capacity to absorb some wavelengths and reflect others so that only certain wavelengths reach the viewer's eye. It is the viewer's psychological and physical response to these wavelengths that make him call an object or fabric a certain color. There is, of course, great variation in the human response to color: one man's red is another man's purple.

Many systems attempt to codify the basic colors of the spectrum in relation to each other and to black and white. But for our purposes, it is necessary only to know the standard color wheel used in grade school art classes, art schools, and courses taught in introductory color theory.

The full color wheel is made up of twelve colors or hues: three primaries, six basic colors that include these primaries, and six intermediate hues. The three primaries are yellow, red, and blue. From the three primaries all the other colors of the wheel can be achieved by mixing. The secondary colors, orange, violet, and green, can be obtained by mixing equal amounts of two primaries. The intermediate colors, yellow-green, blue-green, blue-violet, red-violet, red-orange, and yellow-orange, can be obtained by mixing a primary color and a secondary color. Colors that are next to each other on the color wheel are said to be *analogous* colors, those directly opposite one another are *complementaries.* The center of the wheel is neutral or gray and, theoretically, if one mixes equal parts of two complementaries, one will achieve a neutral gray. An axis or line running up through this center neutral point of the color wheel will, in four even steps of gray, reach white above the color wheel and black below. By drawing lines from each of the colors on the wheel to the central axis that contains black and white, two cones are created, one above and one below the color wheel. Thus, one can see what happens to a color when it is mixed with black and white: it is both grayed and lightened or darkened at the same time. One can also understand that when two colors are mixed, they produce a color that is somewhat closer to the center of the wheel than any single color on the outside of the wheel; thus, all mixtures are less intense in color than a pure color (Figure 4–1).

VALUE   The lightness or darkness of a hue or color is its value. Lightness or darkness is determined by the amount of black and white mixed with a basic hue. A color of high lightness is known as a *tint*, one of low lightness or darkness is known as a *shade*. The color wheel, when viewed as the circular base that divides the two cones—one leading up-

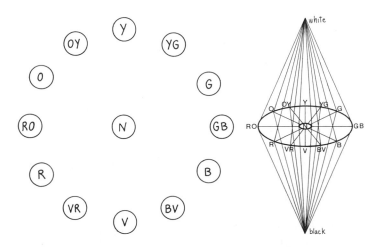

Figure 4–1   The color wheel (left) and the color solid (right). Drawings by the author.

ward to white, the other leading downward to black—is not quite perpendicular to the axis through the two cones. It is tipped at a slight angle, and yellow is therefore lighter than blue, violet is darker than orange, blue is darker than green. One can arrange the twelve colors of the wheel on a scale that travels up the axis of the wheel from black to white. Since the untutored eye can see only so many different levels of gray, the scale of grays or neutral values up the axis of the wheel from black to white is usually limited to seven steps: low dark, dark, high dark, medium, low light, light, high light. It is important to realize that all the hues on the wheel, if grayed, do not correspond to medium gray or medium neutral. In other words, in the diagram of the wheel with the neutral axis through the center, the wheel is tipped so that yellow corresponds to high light, yellow-orange and yellow-green to light, green and orange to low light, blue-green and red-orange to medium, blue and red to high dark, blue-violet and red-violet to dark, and violet to low dark (Figure 4–2).

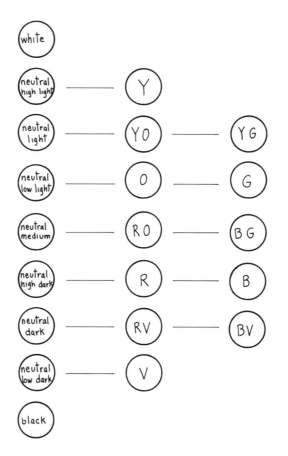

Figure 4–2 Value scale and value relationship of the twelve principle hues. Drawing by the author.

INTENSITY The saturation or intensity of a color is determined by its purity as a hue. If a color is pure and has full brilliance, it is said to have full intensity. It loses intensity if it is mixed with another hue or grayed with black or white. Usually, three steps are shown in moving a hue from full intensity to its value of neutrality or gray on the axis of the color wheel. These three steps are three-fourths intensity, one-half intensity, and one-quarter intensity; or, if they are read as steps toward neutralization and away from full intensity, they are labeled one-quarter neutralization, one-half neutralization, and three-quarters neutralization. If we crossed the full wheel from, let us say, orange to its complementary hue of blue, we would have seven full steps—three on each side of the axis of neutralization.

When one changes the value of a hue toward a tint or a shade by adding white or black, and thereby raises or lowers the value of a color, one also changes and lowers its intensity. In other words, one can change the intensity of a hue without changing its value, but one cannot alter the value without lowering the intensity. One can see from the diagrams that accompany this explanation that in going from a hue on one side of the wheel to its complement on the other side, the line from one to the other is not direct unless, as in the case of red-orange and blue-green, the complements meet at the same neutral value on the axis of the wheel (Figure 4–3).

Color theory both helps to explain color relationships and to describe in comprehensible terms the nature and appearance of a particular hue under particular conditions. If someone asks you to produce a red-orange color that is at one-fourth intensity and at a low light value, you can reproduce this tint without a great deal of difficulty. In short, color theory is not just an accurate way to describe color, but a tool artists and scientists use to reproduce color precisely.

Color Mixing

In practice, colors seldom do exactly what they are supposed to do according to color theory. Particularly in pigment mixing, color theory cannot take into account the effect of chemical reactions among ingredients, the purity of the pigments, or the variations in the textures on which the pigments are used.

There are two basic methods of color mixing: additive and subtractive. Both have to do with the way color is created by light. When a ray of light strikes any object, it is broken up into wavelengths that are reflected, absorbed, or transmitted. If the object on which the light falls is transparent, then the resultant pattern of absorption and transmission is known as a subtractive color mixture. For example, when a small amount of white light falls on a red fabric, a small amount of white light is re-

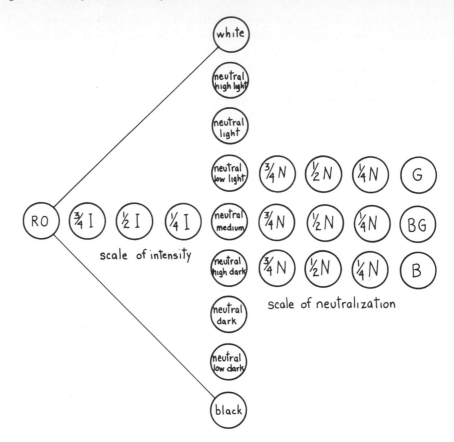

Figure 4–3 Intensity-value steps for red-orange and scale of neutralization for green, blue-green, and blue. Drawing by the author.

flected (the exact amount depends on the angle at which the light strikes the surface), and this reflected light is dominated by the red wavelengths. Thus, red is transmitted to the eye of the viewer, and the remainder of the white light is subtracted. Theoretically, if one placed a green filter in the path of the red light, nothing would be transmitted because the red would be absorbed by its complementary hue of green.

When two different beams of light, each with a different composition of wavelengths, fall on a surface and are reflected to the eye, what the eye sees is a single hue or color. For instance, if a green and a red beam were reflected to the eye from the same surface, the viewer would theoretically see yellow. In other words, one color is added to another color to form a third color; this is called additive mixing.

ADDITIVE MIXING   Additive mixing is usually considered to be mainly the province of the lighting designer, who mixes colored light instead of pigments, but additive mixing can be extremely effective for the costume and the set designer, too. When a surface is spattered with dots of varying hues, the eye will mix the dots. At a distance, the dots will appear as a single hue, but with more intensity than a single hue achieved by colors mixed before painting. This was discovered by the nineteenth-century French pointillist painters, particularly the scientifically oriented Seurat. Additive mixing can enhance the appearance of a costume onstage by giving more depth to fabric, more three dimensionality to form, and stronger contrasts between highlight and shadow.

SUBTRACTIVE MIXING   Subtractive mixing is the mixing of color, usually pigment of one kind or another, before the rays of light are reflected to the eye. Here the designer is mixing hues directly, as he does when he attempts to achieve subtle tints and shades in his sketches. As any art student knows, when colors are mixed on a palette or in paint tins, the colors added subtract from the intensity and from the color of the original hue. When red paint is poured into yellow and the result is orange, all other wavelengths are subtracted except the orange one. The impressionists and the pointillists discovered that subtractive mixing grayed and neutralized the brilliance of primaries and secondaries. That is why they shifted to additive color mixing. By applying primary colors in dots or strokes, and allowing the eye to do the mixing, they retained a much greater intensity of color. In painting his sketches or in preparing paint or dye for costumes, the costume designer sometimes uses the pointillist technique, but he far more frequently employs the subtractive method and develops his palette from a large array of commercial pigments.

Color and Light

When a color in a fabric or in paint is seen onstage under light, the color is modified or changed by the light that strikes it. The costume designer not only has to consider the color and texture of his costumes in relation to their background, but he must know how the color of his costumes will be modified by colored light. The appearance of color under stage light is a particular problem if there is unusual lighting in a scene, such as that produced by a fire, moonlight, or some supernatural source. The basic principle here is similar to that in subtractive mixing: a red light makes a red fabric look redder, grays or neutralizes a green fabric, and makes a yellow fabric look orange or at least have an orange quality.

One way to visualize color modification is to view the costume color scheme through a sample of the gelatin or color medium to be used in the production. Well-equipped theatre plants may have a viewing room or a miniature theatre stage where the costume designer can check various fabrics under a duplication of the lights to be used onstage. The costume designer can get some idea of his color effects under stage light by using two spotlights in a darkened room, one with cool and one with warm gels. The real challenge is to have colored light that is equally effective both for sets and costumes. It need hardly be noted that color planning for a stage production demands the closest cooperation among the light designer, the scene designer, and the costume designer. Some useful reference books on color theory are Ralph M. Evans, *An Introduction to Color* (New York: Wiley, 1948); A. H. Munsell, *A Color Notation* (Munsell Color Company, 1941); Maitland Graves, *The Art of Color and Design* (York, Pa.: The Maple Press, 1941).

Color Consciousness for the Designer

One approach to color is not superior to another, nor are the color schemes of one age to be preferred to those of another. The art of each age has its own color formulas and restrictions, and so does the costume of an age. In taking any color usage for stage costume, the designer, whether he uses strong primaries or neutralized secondaries, must work for the control and unity that is right for a particular play. Bright colors may please the color sense of the average viewer, but they should be used only if they support the mood of the play to be produced. A musical comedy done in bright hues is often a visual success, not because of subtlety or color control, but because the bright colors have the same appeal as those on banners, flags, or heraldic emblems. Red, white, and blue for a musical can be designed just as effectively as grayed hues for *Pelléas and Mélisande,* even though the grayed hues may look more controlled because of the subtlety of color used.

One essential for the designer in developing a keen sense of color is the ability to separate color from the line, form, and texture that contain it. The designer must train himself to see color as an isolated phenomenon of a certain hue, intensity, and value. This is often difficult to do with clothing, because one tends to see color as part of a garment rather than as an area of blue or green or red of a certain shape. We are all too conditioned to see intellectually rather than visually, to register the facts and associations about an object rather than to see it without preconceptions. Modern abstract art has attempted to teach people to see in a new way. For example, the early twentieth-century French fauvists, revolting from the muddied and neutralized colors of nineteenth-century academic art, painted only with primary colors (Figure 4–4a). They revived the viewer's pleasure in vivid color for its own sake (Figure 4–4b). But many beginning designers, as well as most audiences, connect color with associations or facts. They do not see color visually. Thus, the designer always tries to balance the visual and intellectual ways of seeing, attempting to plan his color in terms of hue, value, and intensity, while still fitting it to people's associations and preconceptions. To stress the latter without full control of the former is to produce color clichés.

As a designer develops, he may find, as did the great artists of the past, that he is either a linearist or a colorist. Either he will instinctively stress line and form over color, or vice versa. We know, for example, that Michelangelo stressed line and form, while Titian stressed color. Delacroix stressed color, while Ingres concentrated on line (Figures 4–5a and 4–5b). The instinctual preference for line or color can be found in most costume designers, and a designer must become aware of his bias. He may then perfect his work or broaden his feeling for color or line, depending on which receives the weaker emphasis in his work. A well-trained designer will take pleasure in working with both line and color, but one will probably always interest him more than the other. This has been true of artists through the ages, and it is certainly true of costume and set designers in the theatre today.

In developing a color sense, a costume designer, unlike the easel artist, must develop a sense of color in movement. While the set designer sees his color move or shift with changes of lighting on the stage, the costume designer observes his entire color palette moving and shifting with each new grouping, each new picturization, each small cross or large gesture. This is difficult for the designer to remember when he sketches, since he is then working like any other draftsman or painter. Before bringing color to a static costume on paper, the designer should experiment with colored cut-out swatches on a miniature stage, or with colored fabrics draped or hung over the actors in rehearsal, until he has a clear picture of his color palette in movement, developing and shifting with the progress of the production. Eventually, a designer may be able to see color movement in his imagination; but in the beginning, anything that will assist in making the designer aware of the problem is helpful.

Developing a Color Palette

In developing a color palette for a production, there are two avenues of approach. One, the technical approach, is based on color theory. The other is an emotional approach based on some strong image, mood, or association that struck the designer when he first read the play. One of the favorite schemes for the beginning designer is the use of monochromatic color in a costume. By working with a gray-blue dress with rich blue trim and a pastel blue accent, a designer assures himself of a costume that will be pleasing and harmonious without difficult color balances to be solved. Sometimes a whole scene will be designed monochromatically, with a possible accent of another hue. A designer will often find that a fascinating game can be played with the variations on a single hue through shifts in intensity and value, or with the limited palettes that can be devised through the use of neutrals and a single color. In *Macbeth*, the color palette can be all grays and blacks with an accent of red, and one can bring color movement to the production by increasing the amount of red in the costumes as the play progresses. Or one can do a play completely in black and white, the black creating the silhouette or form and the white creating the accent, or vice versa. A production of Schiller's *Don Carlos* that wished to stress the El Greco-like silhouette in Spain in the late sixteenth century might use all black costumes with white accents in ruffs and cuffs, against changing lighting on a back wall seen through simple arches. It would be limited in concept but effective (Figure 4–6).

Many designers with a developed color sense like to use a palette that plays with intensity and value variations in analogous colors. For example, a pleasing scheme of warmth and gaiety can be achieved by taking orange as the key color and working out a series of variations in red-orange and yellow-orange. For the band of exiled courtiers led by the banished Duke in *As You Like It,* one might develop a scheme that ranges from red-orange darkened to brown, orange-browns, and dark yellow-orange to the pure intense hues of each color, and on into accents of lighter red-orange, orange, and yellow-orange. Carefully done, it would be limited but still give a feeling of variety.

One may also expand this scheme into the cool or warm palettes so often used by designers. Here one group in the production is dressed only in warm colors, the other in cool. One frequently sees productions of *Romeo and Juliet* in which the Capulets wear warm hues—reds, oranges, warm browns, and golds—while the Montagues wear blues, greens, and blue-violets. *Antony and Cleopatra* is frequently designed

Figure 4–6   The use of black and white costumes silhouetted against a colored background: a scene from a production of *Don Carlos* by Schiller as produced at the Yale University Studio Theatre, 1961. Costumes by the author. Photo by the author.

with the forces of Egypt in the warm hues associated with that climate, while the forces of Rome wear much gray, white, and purple, the cool colors that seem appropriate to coldly intellectual Rome.

Finally, there are the schemes that can be developed using contrasting colors. The most obvious is found in complementary hues: orange and blue, yellow and violet, green and red. But such color contrasts are difficult to create without harshness and unpleasantness, unless there is a careful play of intensity and value in the way the colors are used together and a careful proportioning of the amounts of the complementaries used. To use equal amounts of full saturation complementaries is to arrive at a scheme that would be acceptable only in band or football uniforms. However, in a production of *Twelfth Night*, Orsino's costume for the scene in which he listens to music and dreams of Olivia was designed in purple with accents of yellow and neutrals of black and white. There were lavenders and grayed purples with touches of pale yellow among the lords, all leading to the bright yellow costume of Feste. It worked as a use of the violet–yellow complementary contrast, even though it did not seem appropriate to the particular scene. A variation of the complementary scheme is the split complement, in which, instead of using the hue directly across the color wheel, the two hues that lie on either side of the complementary hue are selected. Instead of using yellow and violet, the split complement would use yellow with red-violet and blue-violet. The split complement gives a slightly greater range of color play and is effective when used with many variations in intensity and value. The expanded contrasting-complement scheme could have been used in the *Twelfth Night* production to give further variety to the courtier costumes surrounding Orsino.

Another use of contrasting colors is the triad. Colors that are equidistant from each other on the color wheel are used together, for example, yellow–orange, red–violet, and blue–green. The triad gives a variety of color effect when there is wide play of intensity and value variations, but proportion is again important. One hue should probably be dominant, and the others remain secondary or act as accents. Such a scheme might be useful in a play that had a triangular grouping of characters or an interplay of three forces. For *Antony and Cleopatra,* one might work out the Egyptian forces in the orange–yellow area, Rome in the red–violet area with neutrals, and the forces of Pompey in the blue–green area. Sometimes an obvious contrast such as red–blue is useful, even necessary, to differentiate between opposing forces. There are scenes in Shakespeare's history plays, where French forces are pitted against English, in which the French could be costumed in variations of blue with accents of white, black, gray, and metallic gold, and the English in variations of red with accents of black, white, gray, and gold. Such an obvious scheme is sometimes necessary for identification and clarity.

All of the above schemes are based on some limitation on the value-intensity scale or the color wheel itself, and are arrived at technically or intellectually rather than emotionally. The usual impetus for a designer's color scheme is his emotional response to the play, although he may later translate the color images into a technical scheme. For example, in Shakespeare's tragedies, such as *Lear, Macbeth,* and *Hamlet,* one thinks of color of low value and intensity, of costumes seen in darkness or by flickering torch or sconce. There are almost no full daylight scenes in these plays. But the designer's color palette must be developed from more specific visual images in the play, from the period chosen in which to present the play, and from ideas or characterization about key personages. What the designer and the director arrive at first is a color image, even if only for one character or one scene that is for them important. Once a color image is set, the designer is free to work out a scheme that may use any or all of the technical schemes already mentioned to support and expand his color image. If the color image that strikes both director and designer in *Macbeth* is blood, then the color scheme might work out similarly to the technical scheme we mentioned, but it might also lead to more variety in low-keyed neutral colors than would be the case with grays, blacks, and whites used with red. In *Hamlet,* Hamlet's costume is black, since there is reference in the play to an inky coat of black. Black becomes a color image of strong emotional association and has great influence on what one does with the color of the other costumes in the play. Must the court be rich and gaudy, dark and austere, limited or varied in color? The answer lies in the director's and the designer's image of Hamlet as he stands against the court. There is no easy, step-by-step process for working out a color palette from emotionally felt color associations. In the beginning it is instinctive, and only after the key image for a play has been set can the designer's keen eye and knowledge of color theory be brought into play to develop a full color scheme for a whole production.

Color Associations

The first images that leap to mind as the designer reads the script must be sifted, rearranged, or revised many times during the preparation of a color scheme for a production, but the original color associations are usually valid and useful. Yet everyone has color associations that are clichés. We recognize the red and green of Christmas, the red for stop and the green for go, the red, white, and blue of Uncle Sam immediately. These colors must be developed carefully in relation to other colors if they are to achieve an artistic effect. Color clichés are useful for pop art effects, where the banality of our culture is exaggerated and satirized, and they are useful in expressionist productions, where the red, white, and blue of Uncle Sam or the American flag is made to dominate the audience and overwhelm it with this symbol of patriotism.

As we said in Chapter 1, a designer must be careful to distinguish between primary and secondary color associations. The primary color associations, such as the red, white, and blue of the American flag, the white of virginity, the red and green of Christmas, will mean the same to everyone in our Western culture, but secondary color associations are personal. They come from events in a person's past in which a color has been associated with an event or emotion. The designer who uses personal color images is in danger of having his audience miss his color idea. He must use the associations carefully; he must lead the audience into them in the same way he was led into the experience that set up the association for him in the first place. A designer may have a vivid remembrance of clothing of a certain color that he grew to hate as a child, and that color in any garment of a similar kind may still stir up a strong emotional reaction in him; but to use the association effectively on the stage, the designer would have to lead the audience along the same emotional path he had traversed as a child, or the color association would fail.

Besides personal color associations, there are those connected with theatrical productions seen in the past. If a designer has seen a particularly exciting color scheme in a production of a play he is later asked to design, it is often difficult for him to break with the remembered scheme when he begins his own color layout. There is no harm in using a scheme one has seen work well in a previous production, but one must make it one's own. One must not just borrow a color scheme and repeat it secondhand.

Source of Color Images

Color images for a production must come from the feeling for the time and place of a play. If, after reading a script for the first time, one analyzes the nature of the color images or associations that have been aroused, one can usually trace them to a response to the play's setting, or the particular period demanded for the production. Think how the Scottish setting, the barbaric period, and the number of night scenes set up specific color images in *Macbeth*, or how the ancient English setting and the storm scene set up color associations for *King Lear*. Color associations arise from social levels in a play as well as age levels. We usually associate neutralized, earth colors with the lower classes and brilliant, rich colors with the aristocracy, just as we associate bright colors with young people and grayed and muted tonalities with age.

Most costume designers have a thorough knowledge of period fashions; the color usage of a period will come to mind by the very choice of a period for a play. Since each period has its color schemes, the designer will often unconsciously be influenced in the colors he uses by his knowledge of period clothes. Yet too close a reliance on period color usage may inhibit the color statement for the modern audience. Colors in period clothes should follow accurate period usage only when such a scheme helps the play to work for a modern audience. The designs must not exhibit a period color scheme that has no relation to audience taste. The designer is not demonstrating his historical knowledge of period color; he is attempting to make a particular play and a particular set of characters come vividly to life for his audience. A costume historian may object that certain hues were not available in fabric dyes at the time that the play is set, but this should not inhibit the designer. He is designing for today, and the actors must play before an audience that generally does not know period color schemes. Accurate period color schemes are useless if the audience loses contact with the visual scene.

One of the great sources for color schemes that truly reflect a period is painting, since it is an artistic expression of period color rather than a reflection of the fashion colors of the time. Many times a single painting, by being from the same period and by having the same mood as the play, will give the designer an entire color scheme for a production. While a color scheme based only on the fashion colors of a period may be charming but unrelated to the play, a color scheme based on a painting from the period may give a visual equivalent to the play's verbal style. A good example of this may be seen in the paintings of Paolo Veronese, an Italian contemporary of Shakespeare's. Veronese's canvases, which depict a Renaissance idea of the richness and sumptuousness of classical times, are analogous in many ways to Shakespeare's *Antony and Cleopatra*. A color scheme for this play from *The Feast at Cana* or *The Feast in the House of Levi* may not follow the fashion colors of the period, but it works easily and effectively without great alteration. Also, because Veronese is a great colorist, a modern audience can appreciate his effects, whereas they might not follow the color vagaries of late sixteenth-century fashion (Figure 4–7).

Still other sources of color are the minor arts of a period: the tableware, lamps, furniture, tapestries, mosaics, jewelry. An interesting Victorian lamp may inspire a color scheme that is more valid than a scheme borrowed from the fashion plates of *Godey's Lady's Book,* or a set of Baroque tableware may be the key to a color layout for a play by Molière. Fine artifacts may be closer to the spirit of a period than its fashion because fashion is often personal, set by influential people who are not artists, while fine artifacts are the work of craftsmen-artists who have a deeper insight into the culture of the period.

Architecture can also be a source of color imagery, if color as well as form are important in a particular structure. For example, a richly decorated Romanesque church interior might suggest a color palette for a medieval production.

Certainly a designer should never overlook nature as a source of color imagery. In many productions, intricate and beautiful color schemes have come from marine life, flower gardens, rocks, insects, animals, and other natural sources. If the natural source is appropriate to the play, such a scheme has a freshness that cannot be found in mechanical use of color theory or borrowing from painting and the minor arts. For example, *The Tempest,* which stresses sea and marine imagery, can be beautifully costumed in a color scheme taken from the hues of undersea life, while *Twelfth Night,* which centers around a formal garden, can effectively take a color scheme from a flower garden (Figure 4–8).

There are many other possible sources for color images, and any of them, when matching the mood of the play, may provide a brilliant scheme The designer must always be alert to all sources of color images.

Color Layouts

Once he has his color images in mind, the designer must try his scheme to see if it will encompass all the individual costume requirements in the production. By taking colored cardboard (like that found in the Color-aid swatch book in art stores), cut-out colored papers, or colored fabric swatches, or by building a color collage in paint, the designer can develop color groupings for the various sets of characters. The designer should work with his layout technique until he feels comfortable with his scheme. The scheme should be flexible enough to adjust if extra characters are added, if further courtiers and guards are needed by the director, or if a cast change calls for a different colored costume for a lead. In working with a layout, a designer should always leave enough room in any direction for fairly full groupings of characters, or he may create a scheme that backs him into a corner. For example, a children's play or a comedy that tried to rely completely on full-intensity primaries and secondaries would run into difficulty if there were many characters. Either colors would have to be repeated after all the primary and secondary colors had been used, or neutrals would have to be introduced with primaries and secondaries acting as accents. One should always allow for a fairly wide range of variation in value and intensity, even if the color scheme is limited to only two or three hues plus neutrals.

As we mentioned earlier, many designers prefer to do their color collages or color layouts in fabric. They keep extensive files of color swatches in carefully marked intensity and value steps for each hue. The swatches are arranged until a color scheme is developed that follows a particular color image and yet also shows the amount of each color to be used in the production.

While developing a color layout, a designer must remember that no matter how carefully a scheme is planned, it is the integration of the scheme with the other design factors—the costumes, the textures of the fabrics, the movement of the actors—that is the test of the scheme's workability.

Color Planning in a Play

There are a number of ways to proceed with color planning and the allocation of color groupings when developing a color layout. First, one must determine the script requirements. A change of scene or the passage of time may require a change of color. Perhaps a key character must wear a certain color, and groupings around him will have to take this into account. A cardinal in full red robes for *The Duchess of Malfi* or *Henry VIII* is an insistent color block onstage, and all surrounding costumes must coordinate with his robes. Perhaps class divisions must be indicated in color: aristocrats must be distinguished from the bourgeoisie and from the servants. In *Der Rosenkavalier*, it is important to set off the aristocratic Marschallin household from the upper-bourgeois Faninal home, and to distinguish both of these from the lower-class atmosphere of the third-act inn scene. Colors are important in making these distinctions. We have already mentioned the color schemes of opposing armies, such as red for England and blue for France. Even though the script may not demand such color division, confusion results if the two forces are not differentiated.

Should the designer stress the mood and atmosphere of the total production, or should he design in terms of character? Often a color scheme that is appropriate for the play is not appropriate for a particular character. For example, in a production of Gluck's opera *Iphigenia in Tauris*, I chose to use a color scheme based on the colors of Wedgwood ware. The soft blues, the light seaweed green, the earth red in the vases were appropriate for the cool, sophisticated, neoclassical mood we wanted for the production. None of the Wedgwood colors seemed right for the hero, Orestes. For his costume, I moved beyond my color sources and chose the standard gold and white of the typical late eighteenth-century operatic hero. Thus, there is no one answer to the problems of mood and atmosphere versus character. It all depends on the production, the direction, and the designer's ability to integrate character designs into the overall mood of the production.

A second method of color planning is the "big scene" approach. The designer works out the colors for the most important scene, and then works backwards and forwards to take in the smaller scenes and the characters that do not appear in the important scene. The climactic scene in *Hamlet* is the mousetrap scene. If one can achieve the appropriate color image for the key characters in this scene, with a color range for the surrounding courtiers, small changes for the earlier and later scenes will often solve the color scheme for the entire production. In a production of the play presented at the Oregon Shakespeare Festival in 1961, the color scheme for the mousetrap scene was based on the famous El Greco painting, *The Burial of Count Orgaz.* By taking the young child in black who acts as the "presenter" in the painting as Hamlet, the nobles behind the body of the Count as courtiers, the church fathers in their gold and red robes as Claudius and Gertrude in their court robes, and color accents from the heavens as the color accents for Polonius, Ophelia, Rosencrantz, and Guildenstern, the color layout for the scene was established. In earlier scenes, Claudius and Gertrude wore tight, quilted black costumes with a few jewels; in the mousetrap scene, they added to their costumes the court robes; in later scenes they wore dressing gowns. Changes were kept to a minimum, and it was possible to keep El Greco's color scheme intact throughout the play (Figure 4–9).

In another method of color planning, the designer follows the changing emotional climate of the play, or the emotional progress of the leading character. By having costumes that project a character's psychological development in color, one develops a scheme around which colors for the supporting characters can be grouped. In *The Heiress,* there is the progress from a cherry red dress in the first scene to the heavy, dark, almost colorless dress of the last scene. In *Richard II,* Richard's costume changes from the flamboyant colors of the early scenes to the simpler, more reserved colors in the deposition scene to the coarse-textured black of the death scene, while Bolingbroke's costume changes from somber hues in the early scenes to full royal colors at the end of the play. The colors of the other characters can be developed around the changes for Richard and Bolingbroke.

The most difficult kind of color planning is the contrast and coordination of three or four equally important characters. It is difficult to get the right color balance in *Agamemnon* for Agamemnon, Clytemnestra, Cassandra, and Aegisthus so that color will set character and position, yet so that all four will relate to one another according to the emotional demands of the play. In opera, a similar problem occurs with four singers in a quartet: each of the four should be equally important and yet each should reflect his character's relationship to the other three. In Verdi's *Otello,* it is difficult to obtain the right color scheme for the Otello–Desdemona–Iago–Emilia quartet and still keep their characters, personal relationships, and social stations in the correct balance. Once such problems have been solved, however, the colors for the costumes in the remainder of the production will usually fall into place.

The methods for approaching the problem of color planning can be as complicated or as simple as the play being designed. There is no single best way to plan the color scheme within a production. Each designer must work out his own approach for each production, and as his experience increases, he will find a half-dozen methods that he uses most frequently and that serve his design needs best (Figure 4–10).

Color Relationships Between Costume and Scenery

Thus far we have talked about the planning and development of color schemes without reference to the background against which the costumes will appear. Yet it is important for the costume designer to coordinate his color scheme with that of the set designer.

The most obvious approach to color coordination between sets and costumes, and the one most frequently used on open stages, in Shakespearean unit sets, and in formal staging, is to keep the backgrounds primarily neutral in tone and allow the costumes to provide the color accent. On the Greek stage, the background was architectural, and color accents came primarily from costumes and secondarily from decorated panels. In the medieval theatre, the interior of the church, the town square, or the front of the cathedral provided a neutral background; the color was provided by the costumes and the decoration of the little booths

Figure 4–11 Example of the importance in lighting on costume when the background is neutral and very simple: a production of *Salomé* by Strauss based on designs by Wieland Wagner, San Francisco Opera, 1968. Courtesy of the San Francisco Opera. Photo by Carolyn Mason Jones.

or mansions that were used as settings. On the Elizabethan stage, the facade against which the plays were presented was neutral. The color was provided by the costumes, banners, and hangings. Only with the arrival of the proscenium stage did a complex color coordination have to take place between sets and costumes. The new stagecraft of the late nineteenth and early twentieth centuries returned to the neutral background for many productions. Sketches by Adolphe Appia and Gordon Craig indicate a neutral architectural arrangement of space against which the costumes would provide the color. This is still a workable and effective method today for Shakespearean and classical productions and has been used for many years for the Wagnerian operas at Bayreuth, Germany. It leaves the costume designer free to choose his color palette; color coordination with the set designer is thus not as important as coordination of line and form (Figure 4–11).

If the background is not to be neutral, then there should be contrast between sets and costumes, not so much that unity is destroyed, but enough so that costumes do not blend into sets. If the settings are done primarily in cool colors, then the costumes might be in warn hues. If the background is relatively dark, then the costumes might be lighter in value, or the reverse effect might be used. If a setting is grayed, then more brilliant or intense colors in costume might be used against it; but if the set is bright, the reverse, the use of grayed colors in the costumes, is not particularly effective. Obvious but often effective in achieving a high style and mannered color coordination is the subtle interaction of color from sets to costumes; a color accent in each costume is reflected in value and intensity variations in the setting. This can often turn comic, however, if upholstery, draperies, and wallpaper are too obviously color-keyed to costume. Probably the most effective color interaction between sets and costumes is a mood-evoking palette in the setting that is insistent but not obvious, in which individual colors stand out less than all-over tonality of mood. If costumes are of the same general range but stronger and more intense, they both accent the scheme and blend into it as a part of the atmospheric whole.

It is important that costume color and scenery color complement one another, that each is made stronger by the addition of the other, that the entrance of a costume strengthens rather than disrupts the color scheme of the setting. A red dress on a figure seated in a red chair of the same hue or a blue costume lost against a blue wall must be avoided at all costs.

The lighting designer's scheme must work for both sets and costumes, and the gel plan used must not kill but enhance colors in both sets and costumes. Many thrust or open-stage theatres have now given up colored gels altogether in favor of white light that sculptures the form of the actor in costume and brings out the true color of the fabric. Usually, the gel colors are adjusted to the costume colors instead of fabric colors being selected to fit a certain gel scheme. But the lighting designer and the costume designer should certainly confer well in advance of costume construction about colors to be used. If the costume designer knows what each of the major gel colors will do to fabric colors on the stage, he can avoid the problems that may arise when a scene must be lit by firelight or moonlight.

The watchword is coordination between the lighting designer, the costume designer, and the set designer. Each must try to visualize in advance what will happen in each scene onstage, and each must strive to create the unified visual scene conceived by the director.

Unity Through Color

In closing this chapter on color, we must stress again how important it is to set up a color limitation for a production that will give a unity of effect. To say that a production is colorful is not to say that it is well designed. Unless a scene is supposed to look like a riot, the color layout should be carefully composed to give the correct accent and focus to the right characters and to the desired part of the individual costume. A riot of color onstage is just that; color fights color, character relationships are blurred, major and minor character contrasts are lost, and confusion reigns. Everyone has at one time or another seen a production in which a jumble of color prevented the principals from being seen among the chorus, a lead character had so many colors in his costume that an overall view of his costumed form was impossible, or the audience was unable to tell to which group or social class a character belonged.

Color cannot be divorced from the texture and the shape of the garment of which it is a part, nor can it be divorced from the movement of acting and the blocking of a scene. The designer is always working with color in movement, and he must never design as if color, as in a painting, will stay in repose.

5

Fabric

Fabric for the Stage

The designer must know a great deal about fabrics, the basic element of stage costume design. He must be sensitive to draping quality and to surface texture—to how the fabric drapes on an actor's moving body and how the surface of the fabric appears under stage lights. The costume designer always considers these two aspects of fabric when he makes his choices for stage costumes.

Fabrics can be divided into two groups according to their draping qualities: limp fabrics, which hang in soft folds; and stiff fabrics, which hang in angular folds. For example, chiffon is a soft fabric with light, fluid draping lines, while organdy, which has the same weight and transparency as chiffon, is quite stiff. Of course, there are many variations within these two fabrics groups, but in most productions the costumes will fall into one group or the other.

Fabrics can also be divided according to their surfaces into dull and shiny. Dull fabrics have no reflective quality and absorb light; this group comprises woolens and cottons. Shiny fabrics have a smooth surface such as one finds in satin and chintz; this group comprises silk, rayon, nylon, and other synthetics.

Surface texture is the quality that first attracts the beginning designer and untutored layman. Many period plays are done in velvets, satins, and brocades, not because the surfaces or the draped lines of these textures are appropriate for character or visual mood but because the effect is rich and sensuous. In many ways, these are particularly difficult fabrics to use. Brocades are frequently effective at close view but ineffective at a distance, while velvets must be used with restraint or the various surfaces chosen will war with each other onstage.

The Basic Fabric Fibers

Before one can use fabrics effectively onstage, one must have an understanding of the nature and composition of fabrics. When a beginning
designer first shops for fabrics, he may look at the surface and feel the
weight without knowing much about the content; but gradually he will
develop a knowledge of fabric composition and how fabrics are woven,
treated, and finished.

One of the first phrases that the young designer or costumer will
learn is "fiber content." A fiber is the basic unit of the fabric, a filament of
the raw material from which cloth—cotton, wool, silk, nylon—is made. To
see what a fiber looks like, unravel a thread, called a *yarn*, from a piece of
fabric. The tiny hairs you see when the yarn is untwisted are the fibers.
Cloth can be constructed from fibers or yarns in a number of different
ways:

Weaving. Two sets of yarns are interlaced at right angles, the warp
threads running lengthwise and the woof or weft threads (sometimes
called the filling) running crosswise. The woof or weft threads are carried over and under the warp threads. The outer finished edges of the
fabric are known as the *selvage.*

Knitting. Rows of loops formed by the yarn are drawn through another series of loops of a single yarn by needles, the loops supporting one
another like chains. An elastic, porous fabric results.

Crocheting. A looped fabric is made from a single yarn with a hook
that creates a chain of loops.

Braiding. Yarns are interlaced one over another at an angle of less than
ninety degrees to form a flat, tubular fabric. Braiding can be done over a
core of another yarn.

Knotting. An openwork fabric is made by knotting threads or yarns
together into a pattern. In tatting, which is a variation, a knotted lace is
formed by a shuttle filled with yarn passing through loops of yarn to
form knots.

Felting. Fibers are pressed together by heat, steam, and pressure to
create a matted fabric.

Laminating. Fibers are pressed together into a sheet of fabric and
held together by adhesives. Frequently, several layers are held together
by adhesives.

Fabrics are known as textile fabrics when they are made from fibers
by one of these methods. (Leather is therefore not a textile fabric.) Textile
fibers used to create textile fabrics fall into two major categories: the
natural fibers from vegetable and animal sources, and the man-made,
synthetic fibers that have become so important in recent years. Cotton,
wool, silk, and linen are the most-used natural fibers for clothing. Ramie,
jute, and hemp are sometimes used for certain coarse, rough-textured
fabrics.

First, let us look at the vegetable fibers.

COTTON   Cotton comes from the cotton plant, which is a small bush whose blossoms become cotton bolls or pods that produce cotton fibers. Unless treated, it has no pronounced luster of its own, yet its strength, compared to that of other fibers, is considerable, increasing when wet, decreasing when dry. It is not nearly as elastic as silk or wool; it conducts heat better than silk or wool, although not as well as linen. Cotton fades and loses strength under prolonged exposure to the sun, but it can take heat up to 300 degrees Fahrenheit without injury. When it does burn, it smells like burning paper. It takes dyes less well than wool or silk, but still presents no great problems when dyed and can be bleached fairly easily without injury to the fibers. It can be made up into a tremendous variety of fabrics with greatly varied surface effects, but because of its lack of elasticity and weight per square inch of fabric, it does not drape particularly well. As a fabric, it ranges in price from most reasonable to very expensive.

LINEN   Linen is a vegetable fiber taken from inside the stalk of the flax plant. It has been one of the most basic fibers since early Egyptian times. The fibers are longer and wider than those of cotton, and their strength and natural luster are greater. Linen is even less elastic than cotton; it feels hard and smooth and wrinkles very easily. Accordingly, it irons into creases and folds beautifully. It conducts heat away from the body more readily than cotton, and is often used in hot climates. It has a poor affinity for all dyes, and is usually seen bleached or in its natural buff color. Linen will take about the same amount of heat without burning as cotton, and when it burns it smells like burning rope. When made up into fabric, it has an uneven thread, a shiny, hard surface, and costs more than cotton.

RAMIE, JUTE, AND HEMP   Ramie, jute, and hemp are used more often for rope and heavy matting than for fabric. Ramie is sometimes used in place of flax, and it has many of the same characteristics as linen when made up into fabric. It is more often seen in upholstery, mats, draperies, and rugs than in clothing. Jute comes from a tall, flax-like plant, and when made up into fabric it resembles linen, although it is much weaker, coarser, and does not take well to dye, bleach, or sunlight. It is usually seen in bags, sacks, rugs, and coat interlinings. Hemp comes from a tall, fibrous plant that produces a fiber stronger than linen, jute, or cotton. It is less elastic and coarser than linen, and is usually seen woven into heavy webbings or gauzes. The most common fabric that comes from these three fibers is burlap, which is usually woven from jute.

Some seldom-used fibers are sometimes mixed with the standard ones. Paper can be used in conjunction with cotton threads in very cheap fabrics. It is not washable, and the paper fibers disintegrate in water, leaving only the cotton. Kapok is a fluffy fiber used for stuffing, but it is not adaptable to spinning into cloth. Asbestos is a mineral that is mixed with cotton yarn and woven into fireproof cloth. Metal threads that make up lamé fabrics usually consist of a thin ribbon of metal wound over a core of cotton yarn. Lamés are popular for rich, light-reflecting fabrics used in theatrical costumes and evening wear.

Now let us examine the natural animal fibers.

SILK   Silk originated in China, reached the Mediterranean basin after the birth of Christ, and for centuries was the most costly and prized fabric of princes and kings because of its scarcity. It is the product of the silkworm, of which there are two varieties: the wild and the cultivated. The fibers of the wild silkworm are brown and have a coarse hard texture. The wild silkworm feeds on the scrub oak, and the resultant fabric is known as wild silk. The cultivated silkworm requires much care. It feeds on the mulberry leaf and its fibers are yellow to gray. During the two months that it lives it goes through four stages: the egg, the worm, the cocoon, and the moth. The fine, gummy filaments that exude from under the worm's mouth and from which it spins its cocoon are eventually made into silk. Three thousand cocoons will make one yard of silk. There are two ways of removing the filaments from the cocoon: by spinning and by reeling. In reeling the filament, the longest threads are retained and a minimum of twisting takes place. In spinning, the shorter threads are used and much twisting takes place. Reeled silk is stronger and more lustrous than the spun variety. When made up into fabric, silk can be woven into the lightest of all the natural fiber fabrics, although raw silk fabrics can also be woven to be relatively heavy, depending on the amount and weight of the fiber used. Light weaves are sometimes weighted with metallic salts, but the fibers are thereby weakened and the resultant fabric cannot be called pure silk. The basic characteristics of silk are lightness of weight, great elasticity, and a high, subtle luster. It is smooth, soft, pliable, dyes beautifully, holds heat, making it excellent for warmth, absorbs moisture without appearing damp, and if it burns it has no animal odor. Because for centuries it was so scarce and costly, silk has a certain value in the history of our culture, and people will usually choose it over less costly rayons or cottons with comparable surface effects.

WOOL   Wool comes from the fleece of sheep and goats and has been one of the most staple fibers since man first began to weave. There are three categories of woolens: new wool, which has never been processed before; reprocessed wool, which often comes from felting cuttings from the garment manufacturer's cutting room; and reused wool, which is made from discarded woolen garments that have been remade into fibrous form. Wool is also mixed with cottons, rayons, nylons, and many other man-made fibers. Today the term wool often includes such exotic fibers as camel's hair, alpaca, llama, and vicuna. Wool comes in a great many yarn variations, in two-, three-, and four-ply layers of thickness, some heavily twisted, some combed and fluffed. When it is made into fabric, one gets great surface variety, from a hard, tightly woven fabric to a soft, pliable, loosely woven pile surface. Wool is quite strong, very elastic, and takes dyes well if it has been treated so that it will not shrink. Water or moisture makes wool give off a damp animal odor; the same is true if the fabric is burned. Wool wears very well and is excellent for warmth.

Finally, let us consider a few of the man-made fibers.

RAYON Rayon was the first of the man-made fibers; the name applies to all textile fibers derived from cellulose. Cellulose comes from wood pulp and cotton linters (the short hairs covering the cotton seed) treated with a variety of chemicals. Until 1924, rayon was called artificial silk, but in that year the National Dry Goods Association invented the name rayon to apply to all synthetic fibers, since the luster of the fabrics was like the reflecting rays of the sun. When it was first produced, the fibers were exceedingly lustrous, and one could clearly see the harsher effect of a rayon surface compared with that of silk, but today rayons are woven in almost every subtlety of surface texture formerly reserved for silks. Rayon is not as elastic as silk, nor can it be woven into as light a fabric as china silk; it also burns more rapidly than silk. Acetate rayon is made from certain chemical compounds of cellulose that cause it to melt rather than burn. Both forms of rayon dye relatively well, although acetate rayon requires a special dye treatment, and both usually sell at prices far less than silk.

NYLON A man-made textile fiber with a chemical base, nylon was created by the du Pont Company in 1928. Nylon is derived from coal, air, and water by a complicated process, and although it seems similar to rayon in many ways, it is the strongest fiber yet made into fabric. It does not dye well, but it dries very quickly, irons easily, holds a crease well, and holds bodily warmth very well. In fact, its major problem when warm is that it does not breathe, but holds in perspiration and heat. It is often mixed with rayon, cotton, and wool to obtain many textile variations. Like acetate rayon, it will melt rather than burn. Recently, orlons, dacrons, and other fabrics have been created with slightly different properties but the same basic fiber structure.

The Basic Weaves

Now that we have listed and briefly discussed the basic textile fibers, let us discuss the weaving and processing of the fibers into finished fabrics. Weaving developed as man experimented with weaving grass mats and baskets; when man learned how to twist short fibers together into yarn and to work the yarn into a fabric, the art of weaving was born. The first hand looms were crude and simple, while today's machine looms are very complicated, but the process is basically the same. The warp threads are the threads running lengthwise in a piece of fabric. The filling or weft or woof threads are carried between the warp threads in an in-and-out pattern known as *picking*. Each time the filling is carried across the cloth, one pick is made. Each filling is pushed against the previous filling, and this is called *battening*. When the warp threads are released from the warp beam, the finished cloth is said to be *let off* and *taken up*. The outer edges, or *selvages,* are finished off with more closely spaced warp threads than the rest of the fabric.

The ways in which the warp thread and the filling yarns are interlaced change the appearance of the fabric and produce many intricate designs. Weaves are named according to the system or design followed in interlacing warp and filling yarns. The basic weaves are plain, twill, satin, pile, jacquard, dobby, leno, and the ornamental weaves.

PLAIN WEAVE   Plain weave is the simplest weave. The yarn filling is passed over one warp yarn and under the next, alternating in this manner across the cloth. The second time across, the filling passes over the warp yarns it previously went under and under the warps it went over on the row above. Alternation takes place throughout the remainder of the fabric piece (Figure 5–1). Cottons are the textiles most often woven in the plain weave, and they are usually simple in effect, inexpensive, and long wearing.

Variations on the plain weave can produce many more interesting surfaces. By using fillings much heavier than warp threads, a *ribbed weave* can be produced, while a *patterned rib* can be produced by alternating a fine and a coarse warp thread at regular intervals. A *basket weave* results when two or more filling threads are passed alternately over two or more warp threads; Oxford cloth and monk's cloth are good examples (Figure 5–2). If uneven threads are used at irregular intervals, a roughened, bumpy texture is produced, as in shantung; if the number of warp and filling threads is varied, a tight or loose weave is produced. A tight weave, such as cotton broadcloth, is called a high-count cloth; a loose weave, such as cheesecloth, is called a low-count cloth. One can get variations in the surface by changing the amount of twist in the yarn, as in crepe, or by mixing different fibers, or by dyeing the fibers different colors before weaving. Finally, the yarns may be printed with a design before

Figure 5–1   Examples of plain weaves. Photo by Keeble and Shuchat.

Figure 5–2 Example of basket-weave variation on a plain weave (monk's cloth). Photo by Keeble and Shuchat.

weaving, the cloth may be dyed after it has been woven, or a pattern may be stamped on the cloth after it has been woven.

TWILL WEAVE   Twill weave is the most durable of all weaves. The filling yarns are interlaced with the warp yarns so that diagonal ridges are formed across the fabric. These diagonals, called *wales,* may run from upper right to lower left, from upper left to lower right, or both ways in the same cloth. There are uneven twill weaves, even twill weaves, and a variation called herringbone in which the diagonal reverses direction at regular intervals. The diagonals may also be formed so that diamond patterns appear. Different effects are made possible by varying the yarn sizes and qualities, mixing fibers, varying yarn colors, and adding special finishing processes. Twill weaves usually give a close texture that is heavier and stronger than plain weaves; this is why twill is the most common weave in men's clothing. Twills do not show dirt readily, but when dirty they are difficult to clean. Twills are usually found in woolens and cottons rather than in silks, rayons, nylons, and linens.

SATIN WEAVE   When one touches the surface of a satin, the hand slips more easily lengthwise than crosswise because more warp threads than filling threads are exposed on the right side. In satin weaves there is a semblance of a diagonal pattern, and the satin weave is sometimes considered rearranged twill; but the interlacings of the warp and filling are placed far apart to avoid the forming of wales. In satin the warp may not interlace with the filling for from four to twelve yarns. Varying lengths of warp are thus left exposed on the surface, and if a warp or "float" (an exposed warp thread) skips twelve fillings before it interlaces, it is called a twelve-float warp satin. Obviously, a long-float satin is not a strong fabric, although it is lustrous. A short-float satin is much stronger. Creped yarns can be used in the filling to produce a satin crepe; twists in the warp and filling threads can be varied; and filling threads can vary in color or in yarn fiber. Satin is used primarily in coat linings, vests, and in lustrous gowns for formal wear.

PILE WEAVE   Fabrics such as velours, velvets, and plush, with a soft, downy texture that absorbs a great amount of light, are examples of the pile weave. The pile weave uses the plain or twill weave as a ground. A third or extra yarn is woven or tied between each warp and filling thread, projecting up from it as a cut end or loop. The third threads can be cut off at any length to give a high or low pile. The pile effect can be achieved in a number of ways, but only in the terry weave method is the pile uncut and formed from loops rather than cut ends. Silk, rayon, and nylon are at their richest and most luxurious when pile construction is used. Silk pile appears rich and deep in color when one looks directly into the pile or up the nap. (The nap is the direction in which the third or pile thread lies when woven into the ground of the fabric.) If the pile is pressed down or one looks directly down the nap, the color is lighter and the fabric has a silvery sheen. Piles must be brushed and steamed, not ironed, and many cannot be washed, but must be dry cleaned. A pile weave is used in silks, rayons, cottons, and wools; in wools it is the basis for most rug and upholstery surfaces.

JACQUARD WEAVE   Complex patterns are not possible in the weaves that have been discussed. After the invention of the jacquard loom in 1801, elaborate designs could be woven into fabric. In the jacquard weave, cards are punched with a pattern of holes (similar to the holes on the rolls of player pianos), and needles going through the holes bring the warp threads to the surface to create the pattern. It is a complex process, and large amounts of yardage in a pattern must be run off to keep the price of the finished fabric within a reasonable range. The jacquard weave uses elements of the satin, plain, and twill weaves in the ground of the fabric, so one might say that a combination of weaves is used to bring out a pattern. In cotton, jacquard weaves are usually called damasks or tapestries; in linen, they are called damasks; in silk and wool, they are called damasks, tapestries, or brocades.

DOBBY WEAVE   The dobby loom does small, uncomplicated designs in a simple way by using a chain of narrow wooden strips instead of the cards of the jacquard loom. The strips or pegs pick out the design as the filling threads are worked through the warp threads. Small geometrical patterns are the result, as are found in toweling, shirts, and tablecloths.

LENO WEAVE   Lace-like or open effects like those in curtains are made by a loom with a leno or tying attachment and are called leno weave. Adjacent yarns are twisted around each other, usually in pairs, the filling threads passing through the twisted warps. Sometimes the leno weave is combined with the plain or basket weave to produce a lacy mesh called lace cloth, or a fabric of plain weave may have strips of leno weave. Considering their open construction, cloths of leno weave are durable; the twist not only adds strength but prevents the filling from slipping. The leno weave is usually found in cotton and rayon or a mixture of the two; occasionally it is found in silk.

ORNAMENTAL WOVEN WEAVES   Patterns similar to embroidery can be woven into fabric when it is made, but the result differs from the dobby or jacquard weaves because the embroidered effects can be pulled out by hand without injury to the rest of the cloth. In the *swivel weave* an extra shuttle on the loom for each figure in the cloth works the embroidery threads into the fabric with the raw end left loose on the back side. In the *lappet weave* the embroidery threads are carried from one figure to another across the back of the fabric by a needle attachment. The swivel weave is done with extra filling yarns, the lappet with extra warp yarns.

KNITTED CLOTH   Knitted cloth is not a woven fabric, since knitting uses one continuous thread rather than two. Knitted cloth is constructed of rows of loops, each row caught into the previous row and depending for its support on the row below and the row above. The yarns are more loosely twisted than they are for weaving, and the result is a very elastic, porous fabric. Cottons, wools, rayons, and silks are all knitted, but linen seldom is. There are many variations in the knit stitches that can be used to achieve interesting surface effects, and the size of the yarns and the size of the stitch can be widely varied.

Dyeing and Printing

Although the problems involved in dyeing fabrics for the stage must wait until Chapter 7, something should be said at this point about dyeing and printing fabrics for the textile market. (What is said here is compressed and necessarily brief. A fuller statement may be found in a du Pont booklet, *Modern Dyestuffs and Their Properties*.) Although the costume designer may not have to worry as much as the average consumer does about colorfastness in washing and under long exposure to sunlight, he should be sure that all colored fabrics he buys are resistant to perspiration and at least reasonably fast to washing and dry cleaning.

Until 1856, all dyestuffs were natural; that is, they were obtained from insects, minerals, plants, shellfish, and woods. In 1856, aniline dyes were derived from coal tar. But the great developments in chemical dyestuffs came after World War I. Dyestuffs may be classified according to their dyeing properties or according to how they take on various fibers. The principal synthetic dyestuffs are

1. basic colors
2. acid dyes
3. sulfur dyes
4. direct dyes
5. developed colors
6. mordant and chrome dyes
7. naphthol or azoic dyes
8. vat dyes
9. acetate dyes
10. pigment dyes

Basic colors are chemically alkaline, and *acid dyes* are chiefly acid. Both will dye animal fibers directly with no prior chemical treatment, but vegetable fibers must be treated with a mordant or chemical that has an affinity for both dyestuff and fabric. For a basic dye the mordant is acid; for an acid dye the mordant is alkaline salt. *Sulfur dyes* are used almost exclusively on vegetable fibers and appear most frequently in the dyeing of automobile upholstery. *Direct dyes,* such as acid dyes, are salts of colored acids. They are usually applied directly, are used mostly in the dyeing of cottons, and are usually not as brilliant as basic dyes. *Developed colors* are dyestuffs applied directly to fabrics and then treated with chemical developers that change, deepen, and set the color. Silk does best with these dyes; other fabrics tend to lose color in laundering. *Mordant and chrome dyes* are colored compounds that become insoluble when metallic salts are added, combine well with the fiber of wool or silk, and are colorfast. *Naphthol* or *azoic dyes* are used almost exclusively on cotton. The cotton is impregnated with a beta-naphthol that has been dissolved in caustic soda and then immersed in a basic dye. The name *vat dyes* originated in the making of the old indigo dyes, which had to steep for days. Modern indigo is still the most famous of the so-called vat dyes. The dyes usually come in powder form and are mixed with water, sulfonated oil, and caustic soda, with sodium hydrosulfate added when the dye is heated. It is difficult to match colors with these dyes, because the color changes sharply when dry. *Acetate dyes* are certain insoluble compounds of azoic or vat dyes kept in a gelatinous suspension and used almost exclusively on rayon and nylon fibers. *Pigment dyes* are usually printed or stamped into cloth using dry color pigments mixed with a synthetic resin solution.

Dyeing can be done in the original raw state of the fiber, after the fiber has been carded and combed, in the yarn, or in the final fabric. Printing of colored patterns into a fabric is usually done by large stencil rollers, although colored patterns are occasionally stenciled or even hand blocked on expensive fabrics. Hand-painted designs, silk-screen printing, and the new process of photoprinting a design onto fabric are also seen on the market. Today, most designs are set into the fabric so that they will remain after washing and extended usage, but some printed patterns obviously retain their original look much longer than others. Without a microscope it is difficult to tell which printed patterns have been set into the fabric most deeply, although one can tell something by unraveling some of the yarns in the pattern.

Fabric Finishes

The stiffness of organdy, the smooth, silky feeling of batiste, the colored print on cretonne, the watered or moiré effect on silk are all the result of finishing treatments to which fabrics are subjected after they are made. Finishes are mechanical (the older processes) or chemical (the newer ones), depending on whether they are done by machine or by dipping.

Permanent and nonpermanent finishes Finishes that will stand wear, washing, and sunlight are called *permanent*. They include bleaching, glazing, printing, dyeing, napping, water-marking, beetling, and preshrinking. Surfaces that rub off when a fabric is brushed or washed, such as sizing, certain kinds of glazing, weighting, some forms of creping, embossing, and some forms of moiréing, are called *nonpermanent*. Today, more and more of the finishes that used to be nonpermanent are treated to withstand wear, washing, and sunlight.

Pretreatments Before regular or functional finishes can be applied, fabrics are usually given pretreatments. The most common is *bleaching*, in which the natural color of the fiber is bleached to a pure white. *Scouring* and *carbonizing* are preliminary processes that remove oil and dirt from the natural fiber before dyes are applied. *Degumming* removes the natural gums from silk yarns by boiling before dyeing, while *immunizing* is a process whereby cottons can be made to take the same dyes as rayons, thus giving a much greater variety of color. *Mercerizing* is another such process in which cottons are given greater strength, a greater affinity to dyes, and a greater luster.

Regular finishes Regular finishes include both treatments that enhance a fabric for the eye and those that add weight, body, warmth, or appeal to the sense of touch. Those that enhance the look of the fabric are as follows;

Perching is an examination of cloth to catch defects in the weave.
Burling removes knots or irregularities from the weave.
Crabbing tightens up and sets the weave (for wool fabrics only).
Brushing removes all loose fibers by revolving fabric through cylinders covered with bristles so that a smooth surface results.
Singeing burns off all loose fibers to give a clean, clear surface.
Shearing removes raised fibers or fuzz or cuts a pile to a certain length.
Beetling subjects fabric to a pounding by steel or wooden hammers to flatten fibers and make them glossy and is a common finish for linen napkins and tablecloths.
Decating is a process in which steam is forced through a fabric in tension to add luster and set nap.
Tentering makes all fabrics on the bolt the same width.
Calendering is the final process, after all chemical and mechanical finishes have been applied, which smoothes and presses the finished fabric.
Moiréing, related to calendering, is a process in which the roller in the calender process is engraved with lines to give a watered pattern to the finished fabric.

Embossing imprints a design from the calender rollers to the fabric as it is pressed.

Creping uses steam or caustic acid to pucker or shrink fabric in a pattern in the calendering process (such creping should not be confused with the permanent creping process done at the weaving stage).

Glazing uses starch or a form of glue to polish a fabric with rollers to give the hard, shiny finish of glazed tarlatan or chintz.

The following finishes appeal primarily to one's sense of touch:

Fulling shrinks wool to close its weave and give the fabric further weight, compactness, and softness.

Gigging and *napping* raise the fuzz from the fiber with brush rollers to cover the weave (for woolens, cotton flannels, and duvetyns).

Steaming conditions the fiber and makes the fabric more compact.

Shrinkage control or *sanforizing* preshrinks fabrics so that they will not shrink after washing.

Weighting adds weight and substance to a fabric by adding a chemican component to silks or a steamed flocking to wool.

FUNCTIONAL FINISHES   Functional finishes are applied to fabrics to make them better suited for particular purposes. Most of them resulted from experimentation during World War II. They are as follows:

Absorbent finishes result when a fabric is treated with an ammonium compound to make it hold moisture (towels, washcloths).

Crease-resistant finishes result from experiments with various resins (cotton, linen, and rayon meant for clothing).

Flameproofing makes a fabric fire-resistant by dipping it in a solution of boric acid and borax (draperies and curtains and even much fabric for clothing).

Germ-resistant finishes, mildew-resistant finishes, and *moth-repellent finishes* aid in the storage of fabrics and clothes.

Permanent starchless finishes make stiff, firm fabrics that do not require starching after washing (collars, cuffs).

Waterproofing or *water-repelling finishes* are used for rainwear or bathing suits.

It can be readily seen that in the present fabric market as much is achieved through finishes as through the weaving of the various textile fibers, and new finishing processes are appearing every day.

A Basic List of Standard Fabrics

Before discussing the problems that arise when shopping for material, it may be helpful to list the standard fabric names that one will meet.

CRINOLINE   Crinoline usually comes in 36-inch widths in black and white only. Even the permanent-finish crinoline loses some of its stiffness after laundering, but it is still useful in making petticoats, bustles, panniers, puffings under sleeves, collars, cuffs, and interfacings for certain tailored garments.

PELLON   Pellon (a brand name) also comes in 36-inch widths or wider in black and white; it is a pressed pulp and can thus be used in any direction. Today, Pellon is often used instead of crinoline, since it is easier to handle and does not lose its stiffness until after many cleanings.

BUCKRAM   Buckram also comes in 36-inch widths in black and white and is much stiffer than crinoline or Pellon. It is used as a foundation for hats, headdresses, stiff collars, and other costume pieces needing major stiffening. Since it is usually of two thicknesses of crinoline bonded together with sizing, it can be dampened and shaped, then allowed to dry. It can then be painted and covered. The edges of buckram will wear and shape better, especially when used for hat brims, if they are wired.

MUSLIN   Muslin comes in 36-, 72-, 90-, and 108-inch widths, either in a bleached or unbleached state. The unbleached is the standard fabric for lining stage costumes, and when the starch or size has been washed out of it, unbleached muslin dyes well or may be used onstage as a white fabric to reduce light reflection. It is one of the staples of any costume shop and is very inexpensive, especially when bought in bulk.

CANVAS   Canvas usually comes in 27-, 36-, or 45-inch widths and is useful for heavier linings in its natural state. It also comes in a variety of colors and gives a heavy, very crisp costume line; a garment made of it will take the heaviest wear. Colored canvas is frequently used in outdoor productions in which a unified but nonrealistic effect is desired, because the fabric is durable in all weather.

PERCALE   Percale usually comes in 36-inch widths in a wide range of colors and patterns. It is used wherever a muslin would be appropriate but the designer does not wish to take the time to have the muslin dyed or printed. Percale launders well and is only slightly more expensive than muslin.

DENIM   Denim usually comes in 36-inch widths in many colors and some patterns, including a great variety of stripes. It is a twill-weave cotton that is heavier than percale and muslin, and it has a rougher texture. It is durable, launders well, and is excellent for lower-class, period costumes, peasant dress, and crisp, flat, stylized effects. Its colors are never deep and rich, but always slightly grayed.

SATEEN OR COTTON SATIN   Now being replaced in the market by polished cotton, sateen usually comes in 36-inch widths and is either soft or stiff depending on its finishing process. It has more luster than other cottons and is useful for shirts, blouses, and some inexpensive period dresses.

VOILE   Voile comes in 36-inch widths in many colors, and is easily dyed. It is fluid, semitransparent, and relatively inexpensive. It is useful for lightweight summer dresses.

MARQUISETTE   Marquisette usually comes in 45- and 50-inch widths in pastel colors, and it may be made up in rayon, nylon, or cotton. It is transparent and can be found in a medium stiff to a very soft texture. It is useful for soft blouses, kerchiefs, and scarves.

ORGANDY   Organdy usually comes in 36-inch widths in many colors. It is a stiff, semitransparent cotton, very useful for bouffant, ruffled costumes. It is also useful for the starched veils of the late Gothic and Renaissance periods.

TARLATAN   Tarlatan usually comes in 52-inch widths in many colors. It is a stiff, transparent cotton, but because it is starched it will not launder without losing its finish. Its primary use is in ballet skirts, but it also makes good lightweight petticoats under full-skirted dance costumes.

COTTON CREPE   Cotton crepe comes in 36-inch widths in light colors or floral designs, and its finish makes it look like crepe. It is good for lightweight draped costumes and summer dresses.

TERRYCLOTH   Terrycloth comes in 36-inch widths in white, colors, and patterns. It can be used as a substitute for heavier woolen fabrics if carefully dyed and textured, and when used in large amounts it will drape very well, even though it is a cotton. It is much less expensive than woolens.

COTTON FLANNEL   Cotton flannel comes in 36-inch widths in a fair variety of colors that are light rather than dark, and it will dye well. It is very inexpensive and is often used by amateur and community groups to replace lightweight woolens. It does not drape well, but it has a soft, dull surface with a nap that resembles wool.

SUEDE CLOTH OR COTTON DUVETYN   Suede cloth usually comes in 36-inch widths in many colors and is similar to flannel except that it has a nap only on one side and is heavier. It is relatively inexpensive and is sometimes used as a substitute for wool, especially for winter garments, servants' outfits, breeches, capes, and coats.

MONK'S CLOTH   Monk's cloth usually comes in 50-inch widths in a limited number of colors. It is used primarily as a drapery fabric and comes in a fine or coarse basket weave. In its natural tan color it can be easily dyed, although it does shrink, and it is excellent for inexpensive, heavy draped garments.

BURLAP   Burlap comes in 36- to 54-inch widths in a limited number of colors. It has a very coarse texture, is rather stiff, and works well for homespun effects, peasant costumes, and beggars' outfits. It is rough and scratchy, so it usually must be lined or worn over a protective under-garment.

Taffeta Taffeta usually comes in 40- to 45-inch widths in many colors and patterns and several degrees of stiffness. Silk taffeta is seldom seen anymore; most varieties on sale are of rayon. It has a smooth surface, a fairly high sheen, wears quite well, drapes crisply, and is used a great deal for men's seventeenth- and eighteenth-century vests and breeches as well as for nineteenth-century women's gowns.

Crepe Crepe comes in 40- to 45-inch widths in colors and some patterns. In addition to silk crepes, there are many synthetic crepes: rayon, nylon, dacron, and others. Costs vary from moderate to expensive. Crepe has a softer draping quality than taffeta, less sheen, and is excellent for lingerie and flowing costumes with softly draped folds.

Satin Satin comes in 40- to 45-inch widths in many colors and some patterns. It also comes in rayon, nylon, silk, and other synthetic fibers. It is far more lustrous than taffeta and must be checked carefully under stage lights to ensure that it is not too reflective. It comes in light to quite heavy weights; if lightweight, it must be heavily lined if it is to wear well.

Brocade Brocade comes in 36- to 50-inch widths in many colors and patterns. Brocades for costumes may be either dress, drapery, or upholstery fabrics. The patterns woven into the fabric can be one color or a combination of colors. The background and pattern have different textures that reverse on the wrong side. In choosing brocades for period plays, one must try to suit the pattern to the period so that the effect is not too modern. Although inexpensive brocades can be found, some of the most expensive fabric sold is brocade.

Chiffon Chiffon comes in 40- to 45-inch widths in a variety of colors and is more practical when made from rayon or nylon than from silk. It is a transparent, filmy fabric that is excellent for soft, floating, draped costumes. It is difficult to handle, since it creeps and puckers during costume construction. It is excellent for veils, clinging transparent dresses, scarves, fairy costumes, and impressionistic effects.

Net Net comes in 45- to 72-inch widths in a great variety of colors in cotton, rayon, or nylon. All nets are quite stiff but soften a bit after washing. The nylon net is inexpensive and the most practical. It is excellent for ballet skirts, ruffled gowns, stiff veils, Elizabethan ruffs, and other such effects.

Lace Lace usually comes in 36-inch widths or in trimming widths, in a limited variety of colors. Dress lace is used for complete dresses, especially the elaborate gowns of the early twentieth century, while lace trimming can be purchased in narrow widths for edges and borders of costumes. Lace usually does not ravel, so it need not be finished.

CORDUROY   Corduroy comes in 36-inch widths or sometimes wider, in a variety of colors and patterns. It is usually woven of cotton in pile ridges that form wales. A wide-wale corduroy is more lustrous and will be more expensive than a narrow-wale. Since the wale is not seen at a distance, it makes an excellent period velvet, and it is more serviceable than regular velour or velveteen.

VELVETEEN   Velveteen comes in 36-inch widths in a great variety of colors. It looks more elegant than corduroy, and in productions in which the audience is close to the stage it should be used instead of corduroy even though it is usually more expensive.

VELOUR   Velour usually comes in 50-inch widths in a limited variety of colors. With a much heavier pile than corduroy or velveteen, it is used chiefly for draperies, but it is sometimes used for bulky costumes and heavy outer garments.

VELVET   Velvet usually comes in 36- to 45-inch widths in a variety of colors. It has a pile similar to velveteen but is made of silk, rayon, nylon, or some other synthetic that gives it much more sheen. It is softer and drapes better than velveteen and is about the same price.

METALLIC FABRICS   Metallic fabrics usually come in 36-inch widths in silver, gold, and copper, sometimes mixed with another color. Theatrical fabric stores generally have wider selections than yardage stores and often have cheap varieties that look well but will not wear long. The fabric can be either stiff or fluid; the fluid type is more costly. Cottons and synthetics with metallic threads or designs are often as effective for less money. Metallics are widely used for musicals, circuses, nightclub costumes, and ice shows.

WOOL   Wool comes in 54- to 60-inch widths in a wide variety of colors, and is the best single fabric for heavy draped lines. Considering the width, the prices, though high, are not prohibitive, and there are no substitutes that will give the same soft, absorptive, rich draped effect, especially for medieval and classical costumes.

FELT   Felt usually comes in 72-inch widths in a wide variety of bright colors. A pressed rather than a woven fabric, it can be cut in any direction. It comes in wool, cotton, and rayon. The cotton and rayon are the cheapest; the wool is excellent for flat, stiff, bulky costumes and trimmings, and for hats; it will also steam and shape into headdresses.

PLASTIC   Plastic comes in 36- to 60-inch widths in various weights and colors that approximate the look of leather. It is usually used for upholstery, but can be used as a substitute for leather or as a special effect in which a shiny, synthetic, fairly stiff result is desired.

LEATHER   Leather can be obtained from old leather clothing if the expense of new leather is beyond the budget, or it can be bought by the skin and cut in any direction that will allow maximum use of the skin. It is available in many colors and its price is by the square inch, but it is often worth the cost to have the look of genuine leather in jackets or boots.

JERSEY   Jersey usually comes in 36-inch widths in many colors, and it drapes better than any other fabric because it is a knit rather than a weave. It comes in cotton, wool, rayon, and nylon, in weights from very light to heavy. It is moderately expensive.

TRIMMING BRAIDS   Trimming braids can be purchased by the yard in bolts of varying amounts and widths, both cloth and metallic, and can be found in upholstery, theatrical, and yardage supply stores. The cost depends on the quality and the width. Braids are essential for giving the proper period finish to the borders and edges of costumes.

JEWELS, SEQUINS, AND SPANGLES   These are not fabrics but can be listed here as items used in the trim and finish of costumes. They can be found in junk stores and secondhand shops or by the gross or dozen in theatrical supply houses, as well as in limited supply in yardage stores.

This is a partial list of the standard materials. The designer will learn many more fabric names when he shops for fabrics. The important thing is not the name of the fabric but its cost, its wearability, and its effectiveness onstage.

Buying Fabrics

The designer wants to spend the least amount of time possible buying fabrics for a production, yet he must not rush or he may have to make costly changes later on. Every minute must count, and every decision must be the right one.

First, the designer must have a good idea of fabric prices before he goes shopping, so that he can estimate the cost to his producer or director and can plan the price range for each costume he designs. Even though he may not know what specific fabric he intends to use, he should have a general group of fabrics in mind. He must be able to estimate the added expenses of trimming, lining, and finishing so that he will not figure the cost of the costume only by its main fabric.

The designer must also know yardage, since he cannot estimate cost without knowing how much fabric he will need. He must know in what widths fabrics come: How many yards of 54-inch wool will he need for a costume? How many more yards of 36-inch cotton would he need for the same costume? It is a good idea for him to prepare a chart of the general garments used in stage costume and the amounts of fabric they require in the various fabric widths. This will save him time in purchasing and prevent mistakes. If he does not buy enough fabric, he may find that it is not always possible to get more of the same; if he buys too much, he may not be able to find a use for leftover material. If there is time, he should note the estimated yardage and trim needed in the corner of the costume sketch before he shops.

The designer will usually find it difficult to tell from a bolt how a fabric will look onstage, but he must nonetheless be able to imagine the effect of a fabric in movement before he ever sees it at a distance under stage lights. He should never rely on the look of the fabric on the bolt. He should unroll a fair amount, drape it in various ways over other fabrics, his arm, or let it fall to the floor to check its elasticity and folds before he judges its effectiveness at a distance. Even if store clerks are aghast at these peculiar procedures, the designer should not be intimidated into buying any fabric until he has checked its textural and draping qualities thoroughly. To be rushed into buying a fabric without being convinced of its effectiveness for a particular costume is usually to invite a mistake. Unless the designer is certain that he has made the right choice of fabric, he should not buy the fabric; it is just that simple. Even if he is rushed for time and does not wish to look further, he will be making an unwise decision if he buys a fabric that is acceptable but not exactly what he had in mind. He must be absolutely clear about what the fabric is supposed to do: Is it to be lined and tailored? Is it to be soft and flowing? Is it to be heavy but soft? By asking himself the right questions as he looks over a group of fabrics, the designer may be able to pinpoint what it is he wants and which fabric will accomplish what he wants.

There will, of course, be times when the designer will despair of finding the right fabric in the right color. In such cases he should always buy the right fabric in white and dye it rather than buy another fabric merely because it is the right color. If one has to buy a fabric that is not exactly right, one can often treat it in the shop. For example, a fabric may have to be washed a number of times, its stiffness or fiber tightness broken down by heavy brushing, or its pattern brought up by outlining. In such cases the designer may wish to buy a very small amount of the fabric and test out his treatments on it before buying the fabric for the entire costume.

Like casting, buying for a production is one of the key moments of decision in the whole design process, and mistakes made at this time will cost in time, money, and nerves later in the building and rehearsal period. Through experience a designer must develop a sharp eye, the ability to envision fabric on a bolt made up into finished costumes, and the ability to make purchases that decisively solve his fabric problems for each costume in the production.

Fabric Images

To help set up the textural or fabric image for a play, the designer should create a fabric layout for a production before shopping. A fabric layout can be readily made if a designer keeps small swatches of fabric in white or in color in as many weaves and finishes as he can find. He can file the swatches in small boxes or drawers under weave and fabric names and then select and arrange them until the right balance of textures for a production is achieved. A fabric layout or collage may help in discussions with the director, who will be able to see and touch the fabrics and react to texture even though he may not be able to estimate the fitting and draping effect of the fabric in large masses. It may also help the designer and the director to clarify the feeling they wish to achieve in the fabric usage for the production. Is the production to have the light, soft, fluid, draped, transparent effect that one might wish for an impressionistic piece such as *Pelléas and Mélisande?* Or is it to have the heavy, dull-surfaced, deeply sculptured folds that one might use in *Macbeth?* Should the fabric reflect light and have the crisp, lustrous, hard, rich quality of taffeta and satin that one associates with many eighteenth-century paintings and with plays such as *The School for Scandal?* Or should the fabrics have the deep, thick, rich, subtle, absorptive qualities of heavy velvet and velour that one associates with Jacobean tragedy? By showing the director a fabric collage and by asking him careful questions, the designer can often get a much clearer idea of the director's feeling for texture and for fabrics under light than he can get from discussions alone. Sometimes reproductions of paintings or sculpture with particularly strong emphasis on texture are also helpful as a departure point for discussion. A comparison of the crinkled folds of a Dürer woodcut to the hard, sculptural folds of a statue such as *The Charioteer of Delphi* can help clarify a a vague discussion of fabric surface and fabric line (Figures 5–3a and 5–3b).

Fabrics in Movement

We have already mentioned how important it is for the designer to know before he buys fabric the effect he wishes from his costumes in movement. If some of the basic fabrics are on hand in a costume shop or in the designer's studio, the designer can gain a clearer idea of how his costumes will move onstage by draping the fabrics over himself or someone else in a manner that may approximate a particular gown, sleeve, or mantle. If the actor who will play the role is available, the designer can work with him and a large piece of fabric to refine his cos-

Figure 5–3a   Example of crinkled fabric folds: Woodcut of *The Three Bishops* by Albrecht Dürer. Photo courtesy of the Stanford University Department of Art.

tume line and determine the amount of fabric and the weight and texture that he feels will be needed.

If he has a key costume whose lines in movement are important to the play, the designer may refrain from buying the fabric until the production is well into rehearsal and he can understand the directorial demands to be made on the costume and see the blocking of the movement. Using a rehearsal skirt, gown, or cape, or even an uncut piece of draped fabric of approximately the right size, and working with the director and the actor, the designer may be able to determine the fabric requirements for a costume. Stairs, ramps, and platforms, the width and depth of steps, the width given for the passage of a flowing garment, surfaces and corners will affect the way a costume makes its point. No one should think of designing great flowing robes for Lady Macbeth's sleepwalking scene if the stair she descends to enter the scene is so narrow that it inhibits the effectiveness of her costume; no one should design a costume for Romeo until he knows the nature of the ladder and how the actor is going to use it in the scene in which Romeo leaves Juliet's bedroom.

It will save time and money if all the problems of the costume and its movement over the set can be solved before the final costume fabric is purchased. If this cannot be done, and the costume has to be built before the set and movement problems have been solved, the director, actor, set designer, and costume designer should go over sketches, models, fabric swatches, and the script in an attempt to foresee any problems.

Figure 5–3b   Example of hard, sculptural folds: *The Charioteer of Delphi,* bronze, ca. 470 B.C. Photo courtesy of Hirmer Fotoarchiv, Munich.

Fabrics Under Light

When he chooses his fabric, the designer must visualize what is going to happen to it under stage light. At this point he is not thinking of what happens to the colors of his costumes under the colored gels of the lights, but of the reflectivity and the absorptive qualities of the surface texture, and the highlights and shadows that will come from the costume folds.

The first consideration is certainly the reflective quality of a fabric. A lustrous, high-sheen satin under a full barrage of light can be blinding; the light bounces off the fabric so sharply that the fabric seems to leap off the stage. However, in a dimly lit production, fabric surface that is too absorptive may make a costume all but disappear at a moment when it should have at least a subtle strength. A designer must balance his reflective surfaces so that they are neither all exactly alike nor too sharply contrasted. There should be a range that is varied and interesting without being so great that it causes certain costumes to jump out of the general grouping. Violent contrast should be used only when a violent effect is desired.

The second consideration is the effect of lights on folds. Should there be form-fitting costumes without folds, in which highlights come from the raised areas of the body? Or should there be semifitted garments with some folds, or draped costumes with many folds, where the highlights are on the edges of the folds or drapes? Thick fabrics give deep folds with strong highlights and shadows; thin fabrics give many small highlights and shadows. In a production that stresses folds, the lights should usually be arranged at angles that will give the maximum sculptured effect to the ridges and valleys of the folds to make the strongest contrasts between highlights and shadows. The lighting designer and the costume designer should confer as carefully about the angle and placement of lighting as about gel colors, and if possible the costume designer should check his fabrics for folds, highlights, and shadows under an approximation of the stage lights before he begins final construction of the costumes. Some of the most exciting costume effects in the theatre come from the subtle interaction of light on fabric in movement, and such effects should not be merely accidental but carefully planned in advance.

6

Patterns

Introduction

After selecting and purchasing the fabrics for a production, our next concern is drafting the patterns, or adapting existing patterns to suit the requirements of the costume designs. It would be simple if the designer could buy patterns in stores the way one buys clothes. Unfortunately, except for a few standard, traditional garments or masquerade costumes, patterns for theatrical costumes are not manufactured. The designer and his shop personnel must expand patterns from diagrams in books or must draft patterns to suit the design lines. A well-equipped costume shop, whether educational, amateur, or professional, will have a file of patterns that will make even the most exotic and complicated costume possible. But a costume designer should know how to draft a basic pattern from an actor's measurements and how to adapt specialized patterns from these basics. There are times when a designer may have untrained personnel, no access to store patterns, and limited time at his disposal, yet have to translate his sketches into complete sets of simple patterns quickly so that construction can commence. At such times all the designer needs, aside from his basic knowledge of measurements and pattern layouts, are a T-square, triangle, ruler, tape measure, pencil, eraser, and the paper from which the patterns are to be cut. Often it is a good idea to draft on heavy wrapping paper and then transfer the finished pattern to muslin. A muslin pattern is easier to lay out on fabric, will last longer, and can be stored more easily than a paper one. Patterns of any kind must, of course, be fitted to the individual, even though both he and the pattern are a size 38. No one in the theatre depends on store sizes to fit perfectly; the costume designer must design and fit costumes to the actors the way

Measurement Chart

Play

Name of player

Role

<u>Height</u>--stocking feet

<u>Weight</u>

<u>Head</u>--around--circumference at widest point

Head--forehead to nape of neck

Head--ear to ear--over top of head

<u>Hat size</u>

Neck--loose to top center of collarbone

<u>Chest or bust</u>

<u>Waist</u>

Across the shoulders--front   --back

One shoulder--across the top

Armseye to armseye--narrowest measurement above chest and
      below shoulders in front

Shoulder to waist--front   --back

Shoulder to floor--front   --back

Armpit to waist

Arm length outside--to elbow   --to wrist--elbow bent

Armlength inside--to elbow   --to wrist--arm straight

Wrist--tight

Wrist--loose--so that the hand can slip through the tape

Armseye--loose--so that the tape does not bind under the arm

Arm above the elbow--widest measurement above elbow and
      below shoulder

Waist to floor--front   --back

Waist to thigh--front   --back

Waist to above knee--front   --back

Waist to below knee--front   --back

Inseam <u>to floor</u>--from crotch to the floor

Crotch--waist through crotch to waist

Hips

Thigh

Calf

Ankle

<u>Stocking foot size</u>--for tights

Shoe size

Figure 6-1   A measurement chart.

the tailor or the seamstress fits garments. A pattern to be included in a permanent file may be drafted to fit the standard measurements of a store size and altered to fit an individual, or it may be designed from the first to fit a particular person's measurements. If several costumes in different sizes will be made from one pattern, it saves time to draft one pattern in a medium size and then alter it for the different measurements. If only one costume is to be made from a pattern, it is easiest to use the actual measurements.

Measurements

A permanent workshop where many plays are costumed must have mimeographed measurement blanks with a space for the name of the play, the actor's name, and the role played in the production. Include every measurement the costume shop will ever use on this blank, even though all the measurements may not be needed on any one production. Such a measurement blank places an actor's measurements on file, and if the acting company is a permanent one, then only minor adjustments need be made on the measurement card for each new production. The cards are filed alphabetically in a cabinet or file box, or sometimes in a binder or folder for each production. Sometimes the designer fastens the actor's measurements to the back of the sketch. Figure 6–1 shows a typical measurement blank with explanatory comments. The underlined items are those especially necessary to know when renting.

The garment industry has standard measurement charts which are simpler than those used in the costume shop because they give measurements for the standard sizes of manufactured clothing. These charts are good for drafting basic patterns to fit a standard size rather than a particular individual. The measurements follow average figure proportions. A pattern can usually be altered by several inches in each direction, so that standard patterns in small, medium, and large would be adaptable to all the shapes and sizes in a cast. Commercial patterns, which are primarily for women, usually give only the bust, waist, hip, and back (base of neck) to waist measurements. Recently, the whole system of sizing for patterns was revised, so that a woman may now buy patterns by bust measurements alone in any of the six categories into which women's patterns fall: young junior teen, junior petite, junior, misses, women's, and women's half-sizes. The "new sizing" equates all the other measurements to the bust measure once the correct choice within the six categories has been made. The categories are based on age and build, and the "new sizing" attempts to provide patterns that correspond more closely to the standard ready-to-wear sizes of the store.

See Figure 6–2 for a typical set of proportions useful in pattern drafting for a man and a woman of average build, the man with a 38-inch chest and the woman with a 36-inch bust.

	Average Sizes (inches)	
Measurement	Male	Female
Chest or bust	38	36
Waist	31	26
Neck	15	13
Shoulder	5	4½
Width of back	15	13½
Width of chest	16	14
Hip	40	40
Back from neck to waist	17	16
Front from neck to waist	16	15
Underarm to waist	9	8½
Armseye	17	15
Sleeve from shoulder to elbow	14	13
Sleeve from elbow to wrist	11	10
Underarm to wrist	20	19
Wrist	8	6½
Front from waist to knee	26	25
Front from waist to hip	8½	7¼
Front from waist to ankle	41	40
Inseam	32	31

Figure 6–2   Measurements: male and female average sizes.

Standard Commercial Patterns

Although a designer will always prefer to have patterns drafted to his requirements by a trained cutter, time and effort can be saved by having in the workshop basic commercial patterns that can be quickly adjusted to a desired costume line. All patterns from past productions should be on file, so that when a particularly useful pattern has been developed, it can readily be produced and adapted to the requirements of the moment.

If possible, the commercial patterns should be on file in the three sizes that correspond to small, medium, and large: 32, 36, and 38 for women and 36–38, 39–40, 42–44 for men. The suggested patterns are as follows:

Men

A standard pajama pattern with a V neck and cossack neck and a side opening.

A cassock: Butterick or McCall's.

A surplice and choir cotta: Butterick or McCall's.

A devil, with a clown and a bullfighter variation: McCall's. With an animal costume: Butterick.

Colonial or George Washington, an eighteenth-century costume with an Uncle Sam and full-dress tails variation: Butterick.

Women

A standard pattern for a kimono nightgown, fitted bodice with tight long sleeves, and a high or low neckline.

A witch, with an angel variation: McCall's or Butterick.

Colonial, with Puritan, Spanish, Dutch, or Mexican variations: Butterick.

Centennial, variations of the gowns dating from 1840 to 1870: Simplicity, Butterick, or McCall's.

Bustle dresses, variations of the costume worn by women from 1870 to 1890: McCall's.

Gay Nineties, with shepherdess and early bathing costume variations: Butterick.

The fancy dress costumes suggested above are modern versions of period garments, evolved from a superficial study of period pictures and definitely affected by present-day fashions. They almost always call for less material than one should use to give a feeling of the period, but they give the basic structure of the period costume and can save time in the drafting process if the designer and the cutter use them as a guide rather than as finished patterns.

Expansion of Patterns Drawn to Scale

There are many sources where the designer can find reproductions of period patterns in a reduced scale. Many designers and cutters prefer to expand period patterns to full size because they achieve a more authentic line than they would if they drafted without a guide. A small-scale pattern may be expanded in many ways. It may be enlarged by using an opaque projector and tracing the outline; it may be enlarged with the mechanical enlargers used in mechanical drawing; or it may be enlarged by extending a series of lines outward from a single point until the original can be drawn full size. This last method, which is simple and requires no equipment, is as follows: If the scale for a particular set of small printed patterns is $\frac{1}{16}$ inch to 1 inch, from any given point (A) extend a line 16 times the original length in all directions until enough points (B, C, D, E, F, G, H) have been established to retain the original cut (Figure 6–3).

Readily Available Sources for Costume Patterns

In recent years many books have been published that present a wide variety of period patterns, some exactly as they were used originally, some simplified for the costume shop, and some originals that have been adapted to today's sizes. No matter how exciting a pattern may look on paper, no matter how accurate it may seem to be, it cannot be recommended for theatrical use until it has been cut, sewn, and fitted for an actor. Many period patterns will not fit today's male and female figures, even with the appropriate underpinnings. In the past century, because of changes in diet and health habits, men and women have become taller and broader. Therefore, even though the reproductions of some patterns may appeal more than others, and some may look more professional than others, each pattern must be tested before it is approved and filed in the workshop or in the designer's file.

First let us mention a few books with easy-to-read, simplified patterns for costumes that are not authentic. These patterns are intended to suggest period line and are meant for the amateur costume workshop. *Costume Design and Making* by Mary Fernald and Eileen Shenton gives patterns for English costume from Saxon times to the end of the nineteenth century. The patterns are easy to understand but overly simplified. *Dress the Show* by Daty Healy presents similar diagrams but concentrates on tunics, vests, trousers, jackets, skirts, and bodices. Fitted coats and complex gowns are not included. *Stage Costume Handbook* by Berneice Prisk gives clear diagrams and directions for basic bodice, sleeve, skirt, and trouser patterns, and for some basic costume shapes from Egyptian times to the late nineteenth century. Miss Prisk's latest book with Jack Byers, *The Theatre Student: Costuming*, also has simple, clear patterns. *Dressing the Part* by Fairfax Proudfit Walkup has tiny pattern diagrams with the line drawings that illustrate the book, but they give little more than the general shape of the pattern piece.

Few books present original patterns edited and adapted for stage use and adjusted to present-day sizes. *Period Patterns* by Doris Edson, with

Figure 6–3   One method of expanding a pattern diagram.

commentary by Lucy Barton, is intended as a supplement to Miss Barton's book, *Historic Costume for the Stage,* which is a text on the history of dress. Although *Period Patterns* presents only a sampling of patterns from each period, and these are taken from items available in this country, each is clearly presented and has been thoroughly tested on models before inclusion in the book. The *Costume and Fashion* series by Herbert Norris, which includes Vol. I: *The Earlier Ages;* Vol. II: *From Senlac to Bosworth;* Vol. III: *The Tudors,* Books 1 and 2; and Vol. VI: *The Nineteenth Century* by Norris and Oswald Curtis, is a monumental series intended for the costume designer. Although the many costume diagrams are not actually patterns, they give an accurate picture of original pattern shapes, and costume patterns can be easily drawn from them. Mary G.

Houston's series, *Technical History of Costume,* including *Ancient Egyptian, Mesopotamian, and Persian Costume; Ancient Greek, Roman, and Byzantine Costume;* and *Medieval Costume in France and England,* does much the same thing. Diagrams show the cut of a particular garment, and from these it is not too difficult to devise a full-size pattern. *A History of Costume* by Carl Köhler, a standard work for almost fifty years, is now available in paperback and includes many pattern diagrams. Unfortunately, the measurements are in the metric system. Mary Evans' *How to Make Historic American Costumes* has a set of simple, clear patterns for male and female American dress from the early seventeenth through the nineteenth centuries. *Masterpieces of Eighteenth and Nineteenth Century Women's Costumes* by Aline Bernstein, the American costume designer of the 1920s, has detailed patterns of some beautiful examples of feminine fashion. Blanche Payne's *History of Costume* has an appendix of costume patterns. *Medieval Theatre Costume* by Iris Brooke has helpful Gothic patterns.

A number of recent books contain patterns taken from old tailors' manuals, patterns derived from period garments, and patterns reproduced from those in private collections and museums. *The Cut of Men's Clothes 1600–1900* by Norah Waugh is a good example. Its companion is *The Cut of Women's Clothes 1600–1930.* Both contain many illustrations and contemporary quotations explaining the patterns, and almost every major style from 1600 to the present is included. Another is *Patterns of Fashion* by Janet Arnold, in two volumes. The first volume gives patterns from 1660 to 1860, the second, patterns from 1860 to 1940. The patterns are large and readable, without too many complex markings and complicated information. A third excellent new volume is *The Evolution of Fashion: Pattern and Cut from 1066–1930* by Margaret Hamilton Hill and Peter A. Bucknell. It has large, easy-to-read patterns of an excellent size. A standard work is still *Costume Patterns and Designs* by Max Tilke, which includes patterns for national costume around the world as well as the usual survey of patterns for the history of Western dress.

Patterns may also be found in a number of nineteenth- and twentieth-century periodicals with sections on women's fashions, such as *The Delineator, Godey's Lady's Book, Good Housekeeping, Harper's Bazaar, Illustrated London News, Journal des Dames et des Demoiselles, Ladies' Home Journal, Ladies Tailor, McCall's, Peterson's Magazine, The Studio,* and *Vogue.* Certain museum costume collections, such as those at the Metropolitan Museum in New York City, the Brooklyn Museum, and the County Museum of Los Angeles, have extensive pattern files.

Once patterns are copied, traced, or drafted, they should be carefully labeled and filed, in a manila folder, in a filing cabinet. In this way the designer or costume shop supervisor gradually will build up an extensive file of period patterns that are accessible at short notice. It is best to use heavy wrapping paper or muslin for the patterns, because the tissue-thin paper on which commercial patterns are printed soon deteriorates.

The Layout of Basic Pattern Shapes

When time is of the essence, or when books with diagramed period patterns are not available, the designer may have to draft a basic costume shape from measurements alone. Simple items such as a basic bodice shape, a basic sleeve, or a basic pair of trousers can be drafted quickly, and any lack of precision can be remedied in fitting. Often, when chorus members are added to a production or supers must be readied to fill up the stage, the designer must produce a finished costume directly from an actor's measurements without the luxury of a cutter and still achieve the look of a carefully prepared pattern. Here is a simplified procedure for drafting basic patterns from a set of measurements.

Figure 6–4a   Basic bodice or waist front—male.

BASIC BODICE OR WAIST FRONT—MALE (Figure 6–4a)

1. Lay out the neck-to-waist front measurement vertically in the center of a large sheet of paper, AB.
2. At the bottom of this line at A, lay out one-fourth the waist measurement to either the right or the left, AC.
3. Assuming that we have laid out one-fourth the waist measurement to the right of this center line, measure approximately 3¼ inches to the right of the neck- to waistline, AB, and lay out the shoulder-to-waist measurement, DE.
4. Draw in the curve of the neckline, BD, with right angles at neck and shoulder.

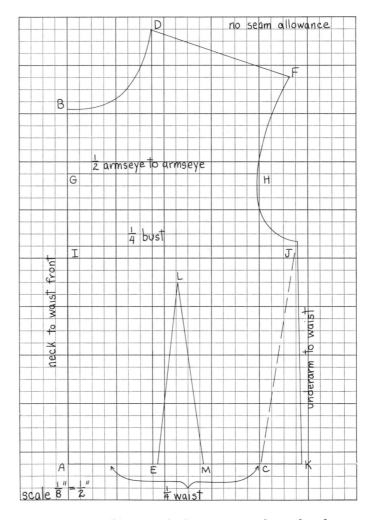

Figure 6–4b   Basic bodice or waist front—female.

5. Making sure that there is a right angle where the shoulder line meets the neckline, D, lay out the measurement of one shoulder, DF.
6. Lay out one-half the armseye-to-armseye measurement front, GH, approximately 3 inches below the base of the neckline.
7. Lay out one-fourth the bustline or chest measurement, IJ, approximately 3 inches below the armseye-to-armseye measurement.
8. Lay out the underarm-to-waist measurement, JC, so that it connects the end of the bustline measurement with the end of the waistline measurement.
9. Draw in the armseye so that its curve, FHJ, creates a right angle with the shoulder line at F and the underarm-to-waist measurement

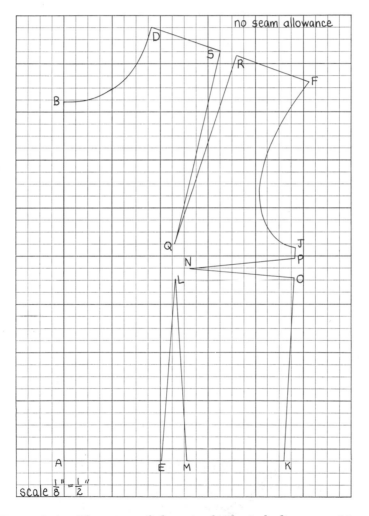

Figure 6–4c Placement of darts in the basic bodice or waist.

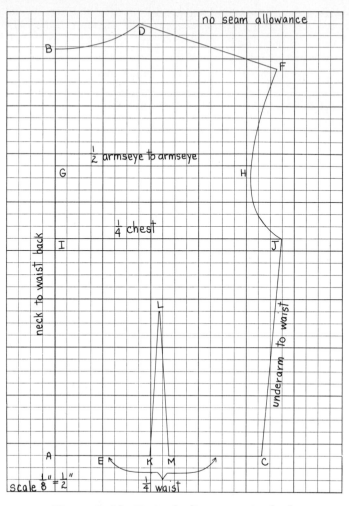

Figure 6–4d   Basic   bodice or waist—back.

at J, so that it makes a deep curve between the armseye-to-armseye measurement and the bust- or chestline.

BASIC BODICE OR WAIST FRONT—FEMALE (Figure 6–4b)

1. For women, add approximately 1½ to 2 inches to the waistline, AC, and redraw the underarm-to-waist line, as JK; take this 1½ inches out of the center of the side waist front in a triangular slice, ELM, to create a dart rising to a point 2 inches below the bustline.

PLACEMENT OF DARTS (Figure 6–4c)

1. The 1½ to 2 inches taken out at the waist, ELM, may be transferred either to the side under the armseye, PNO, or to the shoulder seam, SQR, either completely or partially, thus giving a fitted bust with

darts at waist or darts at waist and side, darts at side and shoulder, darts at shoulder and waist, or darts at all three places.

BASIC BODICE OR WAIST—BACK (Figure 6–4d)
1. This is laid out in the same manner as the front, except that no bustline darts are necessary, although small darts at the center of each side, KLM, may be needed in fitting.
2. It requires a more gradual curve to the armseye, FHJ, and a neck-line, BD, that is not as deeply cut in back as it is the front, since the neck-to-waist measurement, BA, is longer in the back.

ONE-PIECE SLEEVE (Figure 6–5)
1. In the center of a large piece of paper, lay out a vertical line the length of the overarm measurement, AB.

Figure 6–5 Diagram for a one-piece sleeve.

2. At B, lay out a horizontal line, CD, equal to the wrist measurement.
3. Lay out the underarm measurement, BL, on the vertical line up from the wrist, and lay out a horizontal line, ELF, at L. EL is 6½ inches, LF is 7 inches.
4. At M, 2 inches above this horizontal line, lay out a second horizontal line, GMH. GM is 4 inches, MH is 4½ inches.
5. At N, 1½ inches above this, lay out a third horizontal line, INJ. IN is 3 inches, NJ is 3½ inches.
6. Connect the ends of these lines, EGIAJHF, with a gradual curve, making adjustments until the length of the curve approximates the armseye measurement.
7. Connect the ends of the armseye curve, EF, with the ends of the wrist measurement, CD.

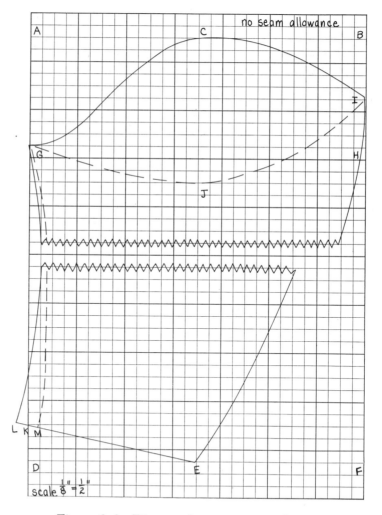

Figure 6–6   Diagram for a two-piece sleeve.

8. Take a 1-inch dart at the elbow, OPQ, halfway down the right underarm-to-wrist measurement, FD.

9. Extend FD 1 inch to K and redraw the wrist line along a new line, CK.

10. If more curve is desired in the sleeve, curve the two underarm-to-wrist lines, EC and FD, to the left 1 to 1½ inches and again connect their lower ends with the wrist measurement.

TWO-PIECE SLEEVE (Figure 6–6)

1. At the top of a large sheet of paper, lay out a horizontal line, ACB, one-half the armseye measurement, with the point C at the center.

2. Drop three vertical lines from points A, C, and B the length of the overarm measurement to create AD, CE, and BF.

3. Calculate the difference between the underarm and the overarm measurements. From horizontal line ACB, measure this difference from point A to G and B to H, creating a new horizontal line, GH.

4. At B, measure down one-half the distance between the overarm and underarm measurements and mark a point I.

5. Connect I in a gentle curve with point C. Connect C with a gentle dipping curve to G.

6. Mark a point J on the central vertical line, CE, 1½ inches below the second horizontal line, GH.

7. Connect the points G, J, and I with a gently curving dashed line.

8. Connect I with E in a gentle curve.

9. On line AD, measure up 1½ inches and mark a point K.

10. From E through this point K and ending at L, lay out a line that is one-half the wrist measurement plus 1 inch.

11. Connect K to L with a gentle curve.

12. Along line EL, mark off one-half the wrist measurement at M.

13. Connect G to M in a gentle dashed curve.

BASIC PAIR OF TROUSERS (Figure 6–7)

1. In the upper third of a large piece of paper, lay out a horizontal line, ADB, one-half the hip measurement.

2. At A, raise a perpendicular vertical line of 9 inches, AC.

3. At D, raise a perpendicular vertical line of 8½ inches, DE.

4. At B, raise a perpendicular line of 7½ inches, BF.

5. Lay out a horizontal line, GH, 7½ inches below the hip line, ADB.

6. At G, extend a horizontal line 5 inches to the left, creating IG.

7. At H, extend a horizontal line 3 inches to the right, creating HJ.

8. Connect points CEF.

9. On this new line, measure in 2 inches from C and establish a point K.

10. Connect this point K with A and I in a gentle curve.

11. Connect F, B, and J with a deep curve.

12. With the crotch line, IC and FJ, now established, the inseam or the waist-to-knee measurements may be laid out below IJ and the de-

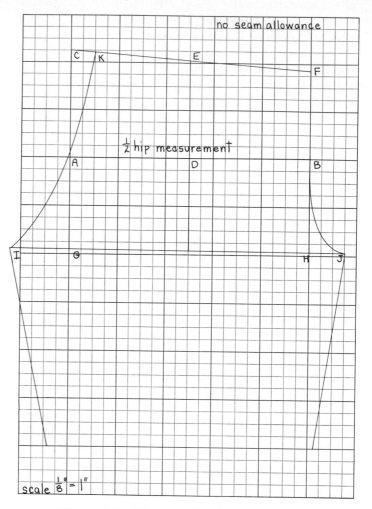

Figure 6–7 Diagram of a basic trouser top.

sired width of the trouser at the bottom or at the knee (in knee breeches) established. A dart may be taken at the side seam of the trousers at the waist, at E.

BASIC GORED SKIRT (Figure 6–8)
1. In the upper third of a large piece of paper, lay out a horizontal line, AFB, one-half the hip measurement.
2. Mark point C 6½ inches directly above point A and point D 7½ inches directly above point B and connect, CD.
3. At the middle of AB at established point F, draw a vertical line through it intersecting CD at G.
4. Mark point H 1 inch directly above point F.

5. Connect AH and BH with gentle curves.
6. Mark point I 1 inch directly above point G, and connect CI and ID with gentle curves.
7. Through point H, lay out a straight line, HJ, to make a right angle with CI at J and with AH at H.
8. Through point H, lay out a straight line to make a right angle with HB at H and with ID at K.
9. On KD, take two small darts, NOP and QRS, so that CJ and KD add up to one-half the waist measurement.
10. A single dart, TUV, on CJ may be necessary to keep the side seam at JHK centered on the side of the skirt.
11. CE may be laid in as the front waist-to-ankle or waist-to-floor

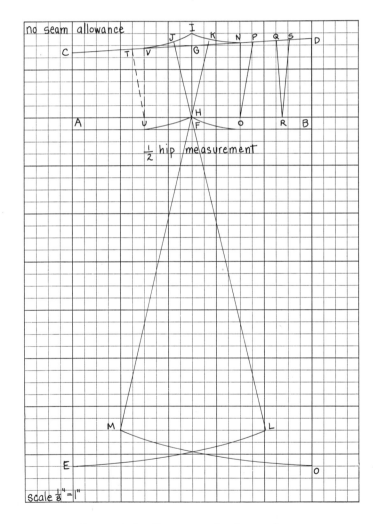

Figure 6–8   Diagram of a basic skirt.

measurement, while DO is the back waist-to-ankle or waist-to-floor measurement.

12. EL should follow a gentle curve to meet the extension of JH at L in a right angle.

13. OM should follow a gentle curve to meet the extension of KH at M in a right angle.

14. OM and EL may be shortened in length to gain a narrowed, pencil-line skirt.

15. OM and EL may also be lengthened to form a fuller gored skirt, as long as JL and KM continue to make right angles with CJ and KD.

These layouts are not accurate patterns; they are ways to make basic garment shapes from measurements and a few numbers that establish general proportions. The refinement must take place in the fittings. If accuracy is desired from the beginning, the designer should obtain his patterns from the appropriate source books and adapt them to the actors' measurements before cutting. Only when he is under pressure, when there is no time to refine a pattern, or when a costume is simple in line should the designer use a basic layout.

Pattern Adaptation

Changing a pattern size is simple if the designer remembers not to make his changes all in one place or all on one edge of the pattern. Only in lengthening or shortening skirts, trousers, or sleeves should one edge, the bottom edge, be used for the adjustment. If 2 inches must be taken from the bustline of a bodice pattern, then ½ inch should be taken from each half of the front and the back pieces of the pattern. Often it is best to split the pattern pieces down the middle and overlap them to reduce size or spread them apart to increase size. If one does not wish to cut the pattern, then trace halfway around it, move the pattern the necessary amount to add the extra width, and trace around the other half. The proper relationship between the two halves of the pattern must, of course, be kept.

To develop patterns for period garments for which one does not have pattern sources, or for fanciful garments for which there are no patterns, the designer needs a good set of basic patterns. He can draw and reshape them until he achieves a pattern suited to his sketch. If a commercial pattern is copied on heavy brown paper, it can be cut, spread apart, compressed, new seams added, and worked over until the right line is achieved. Much experimentation may have to take place before the right line is obtained. The pattern may have to be transferred to muslin and pinned together on the actor or dress form a number of times before the fabric can be cut for the final costume.

Pattern Pieces

Figures 6–9 through 6–15 illustrate the variety of pattern shapes that have resulted from experimentation with basic costume lines through the centuries. The diagrams are drawn $\frac{1}{16}$ inch to 1 inch, and no seam allowance is shown.

Figure 6–9 shows the basic male waist pattern for such fitted garments as the cotehardie, certain doublets, and certain male foundation garments for a size 38. With it are two waistcoat variations and a sixteenth-century doublet layout.

Figure 6–10 shows further variations on the basic waist pattern for

Figure 6–9 Diagrams of men's doublets and vests.

men for a seventeenth-century cassock with pleated skirt, an eighteenth-century coat, an Empire coat, and a late nineteenth-century evening coat.

Figure 6–11 shows the layout of the basic woman's waist, with measurements for a size 16. Variations include the bodice of a Spanish gown of the late sixteenth century, the bodice of a mideighteenth-century court gown, an Empire bodice, a bodice used with the hoop skirts of 1863, and a bodice of the last decade of the nineteenth century.

Figures 6–12a and 6–12b show a basic trouser pattern, with measurements for a size 38 man's suit and including cutting lines for eighteenth-century knee breeches. Other diagrams are for trunks, Elizabethan trunk hose, and tight-fitting trousers of the early nineteenth century.

The sleeve patterns in Figures 6–13a and 6–13b show the basic lay-

Figure 6–10. Diagrams of men's jackets and coats.

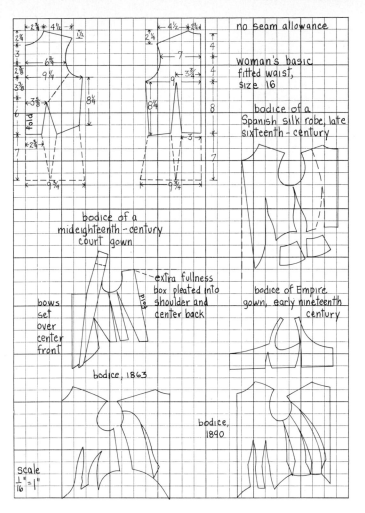

Figure 6–11 Diagrams of women's bodices.

out of a woman's one-piece fitted sleeve and a two-piece sleeve, both
with measurements for a size 16. Other diagrams show how to expand
the sleeve for added width and fullness at the top, with variations that
include a bell-shaped Gothic sleeve, a Renaissance bagpipe sleeve, an
eighteenth-century cap sleeve, a Renaissance open-hanging sleeve, a
slashed hanging sleeve, and a tiny Empire cap sleeve.

In Figure 6–14, a basic woman's skirt, size 16, is shown with measurements and dashed lines to indicate the method for making the skirt more
circular. With this diagram are layouts for an Empire skirt and a skirt of
the 1890s.

Figure 6–15 shows variations on the basic half-circular cloak pattern
by the addition of shoulder capes, sleeves, collars, and facings.

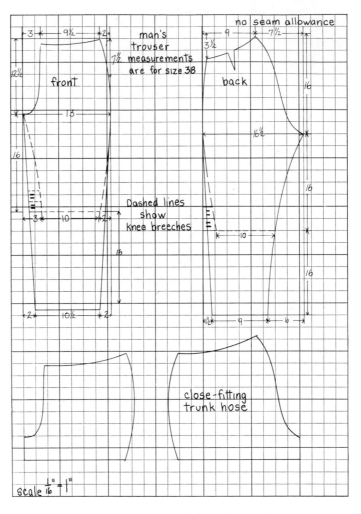

Figure 6–12a　Diagrams of breeches and trousers.

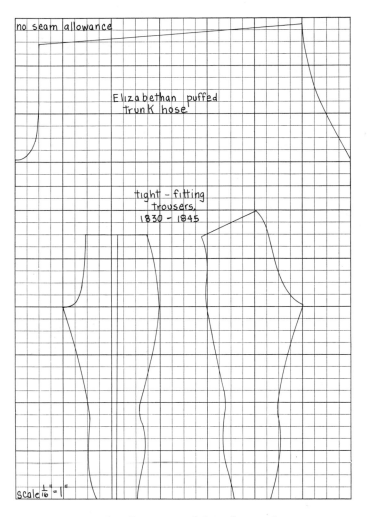

no seam allowance

Elizabethan puffed
trunk hose

tight - fitting
trousers,
1830 - 1845

scale $\frac{1}{16}$" = 1"

Figure 6–12b   Diagrams of breeches and trousers.

Figure 6–13a   Diagrams of sleeves.

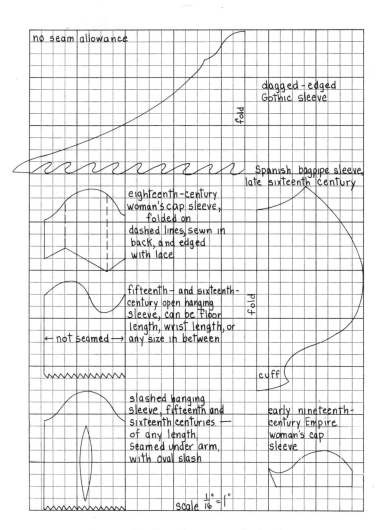

no seam allowance

dagged-edged
Gothic sleeve

fold

Spanish bagpipe sleeve,
late sixteenth century

eighteenth-century
woman's cap sleeve,
folded on
dashed lines, sewn in
back, and edged
with lace

fifteenth- and sixteenth-
century open hanging
sleeve, can be floor
length, wrist length, or
← not seamed → any size in between

fold

cuff

slashed hanging
sleeve, fifteenth and
sixteenth centuries —
of any length,
seamed under arm,
with oval slash

early nineteenth-
century Empire
woman's cap
sleeve

scale $\frac{1}{16}" = 1"$

Figure 6–13b   Diagrams of sleeves.

Figure 6–14   Diagrams of skirts.

Figure 6–15 Diagrams of capes and cloaks.

7

Construction and Ornamentation

Costume Construction

When the designs for a production have been completed and the patterns for the costumes devised, the actual construction of the garment begins. During this period the designer's time is occupied by countless details; and even when he is fortunate enough to have an excellent shop foreman and trained cutters, seamstresses, and personnel for dyeing, ornamentation, painting, and finishing, he must always be everywhere at once. No matter how carefully the sketches and working drawings have been prepared, no matter how carefully the patterns have been worked out, unless the designer spends time with each cutter and seamstress, he will find at dress parade that his ideas have not been fully executed. Robert Edmond Jones used to write little poems and inspiring notes to his construction staff to give them his feeling about the costumes, in hopes that the workers would capture some of his imaginative vision in the finished products. There is no one way a designer can work with his staff, but he must try to encourage and inspire them to do more than turn out a machine-like product. Each costume must be given that extra thought, that extra personal touch that keeps the original vision of the designer alive through long and grueling hours of work. Especially at the fittings, from the first one in muslin to the final one before dress parade, the designer must make known to the actor and the fitter his hopes and desires for the costume. Even though a busy professional designer is not always in the shop during costume construction, he must spend as much time as is necessary on the fittings to ensure that the final result fulfills his design image for the play.

Workshop and Storage Facilities

Although the university or repertory theatre designer seldom sets up costume workshop facilities, he will be asked to express his desires about workshop and storage space and costume equipment when a new theatre is being designed. Therefore, in this section we shall discuss the space and equipment requirements for the ideal costume department.

The proper facilities for the construction and storage of costumes are of great importance if a theatre is to produce plays in a professional manner. Nothing is more important in a continuing operation, whether repertory or run of the show, than the storage space to house costumes on hand and store new ones. It is best if the storage room and the workshop can be close to each other. Only if the storage is easily accessible from the workshop is the transfer of costumes from storage to workshop easily manageable. If the rooms must be on different floors, there should be a large elevator for rolling racks. The ideal is to have adjoining workshop and storage space areas, both easily accessible to the dressing rooms and the stage.

The Costume Storage Area

The room used for storage must be dry, because dampness can cause considerable damage to stored clothes. Its size must be determined by the extent of its use, but it should always be larger than what is at first apparently needed. After a theatre has presented several seasons of shows, wardrobe costumes will need a much larger area than would have been anticipated. A good average size is 1200 to 1600 square feet. The space should be divided between hanging space and shelves or drawers. Shelves are cheaper to build than drawers, and labeled boxes can be used on the shelves in the sizes needed, while drawers once built cannot be expanded. Costumes should be hung to avoid folds and wrinkles. The hanging space can either be open space equipped with pipes, or built-in wardrobes. The latter is preferable if the storage space is not completely dust free. If open racks are used, it is best to cover them with dust covers. The hanging space needs to be only the width of a coat hanger plus clearance for large padded sleeves or unusual bulk. A six-foot height will accommodate the length of most costumes, except gowns with long trains and large mantles. Long garments can usually be pinned up to clear the floor. A very good arrangement is two low-ceilinged rooms, one for hanging space, the other for shelves. High shelves that require one to climb a ladder to reach a box should not be used.

It is difficult to state exactly what the height between the shelves for storage boxes should be, but there should be several inches clearance above the storage box. Shelves should generally be three feet deep, with two feet between shelves. The storage box should be about 27 inches by 15 inches by 15 inches so that it can be conveniently handled by one person even when the box is fully packed. The box should be constructed of durable cardboard with detachable overlapping covers. Edges and corners that become worn with handling can be reinforced with gummed cloth tape. At least 1 inch of space should be left between boxes. All boxes and all racks of costumes should be clearly labeled so that items can be easily located on demand.

The Costume Workshop

The workshop size should be determined by the number of people most likely to be working in the room at the same time, the amount of work to be done, and the size of the largest productions costumed. The number of productions done during a season is another determining factor. The room should be well lighted. If one has a choice of lighting, it is best to request incandescent light instead of fluorescent light, because fabrics look different under fluorescent light than they do under stage light (Figures 7–1 and 7–2).

The following list of equipment includes everything commonly used in the construction of stage costumes. Some items are essential, others are merely a convenience. The essential items are as follows:

CUTTING TABLE   A 40-inch width allows for convenient cutting of 36-inch material with a margin on which to lay shears and other tools. Although a wider table is helpful for 54-inch fabrics, it is difficult to reach across its width. A table can be as long as the room will conveniently allow, up to ten feet, but it is preferable to have several tables about eight feet long if the room will accommodate them. If the room is large enough, it is possible to have three tables six to eight feet long and in heights for short, medium, and tall people. Since the cutter usually stands while he cuts, it is important to have the table the correct height to ease back strain. A height of 32 to 34 inches is best for short people, 36 inches is best as a general height, and 38 to 40 inches is best for tall people. The surface of the table should be smooth, so that fabric threads will not catch on it. One of the most practical surfaces is cork, because fabrics can be pinned directly to it and slippery fabrics will not skid on it.

SEWING MACHINE Three sewing machines are usually a minimum for a small shop. At least two of these should be the standard home cabinet models, which are simple to operate and easy to repair. If possible, at least one machine should do zigzag work for buttonholes, edging, and binding, and one should be a heavy-duty machine that can sew very heavy fabrics and leather without difficulty.

DRESSMAKER'S SHEARS Shears usually come 8, 10, or 12 inches long, should be well sharpened, and should be used only for cutting fabric. Other shears or scissors should be on hand for cutting paper, plastic, and gelatin.

YARDSTICKS AND TAPE MEASURES The yardstick is 36 inches long and the tape measure is 60 inches long, and both should be of the reversible type that can be read from either end.

WIRE-CUTTING PLIERS A small pair of pliers is needed to cut hat wire.

RAZOR BLADES OR SEAM RIPPERS Blades inserted in handles are easier to use than naked blades, and they will not get lost or cut fingers as easily.

Figure 7–1 An example of a costume workshop. The arrangement of the equipment and facilities in the costume room at the Department of Drama, University of Texas. Photo courtesy of Paul Reinhardt, University of Texas.

Figure 7–2   Another view of the costume workshop at the University of Texas, showing the arrangement of storage cabinets and cutting tables. Photo courtesy of Paul Reinhardt, University of Texas.

HAMMERS, SCREWDRIVERS, AND PLIERS   Hand tools are important when working with armor, leather rivets, jewelry, and costume properties.

ELECTRIC IRON   The shop should have two or three steam irons and one dry iron.

IRONING BOARD   In an area removed from other kinds of activity, the shop should have two or three ironing boards and a small sleeve board. The floor beneath the ironing boards should have carpeting on it or be covered to protect the costumes from dust and dirt.

COSTUME RACK   Costume racks may be built into one of the walls of the shop, but it is better if there is an open area for the placement of several movable racks on casters, so that costumes can be moved directly from the workshop to the dressing rooms. Shelves can be placed across the bottom and the top of the racks for footwear and headdresses.

STEP LADDERS   Small or medium ladders may be necessary to reach items on high shelves or in top cupboards.

CLOTHES, HAT, AND SHOE BRUSHES   Brushes are necessary for the maintenance of costumes.

LARGE BINS OR WASTEBASKETS   Receptacles are needed to hold the daily accumulation of trash.

LARGE SCRAP BOXES   All the scraps from the production in progress should be placed in a scrap box marked with the name of the production. When the production is over, small scraps should be thrown away and the larger ones placed in the fabric drawers or bins.

FABRIC BINS   The workshop should have fabric drawers or bins marked according to color or fiber, into which all large scraps should be placed for possible future use.

BULLETIN BOARDS   The workshop should have ample fiberboard-covered wall areas for the display of the costume plates.

FULL-LENGTH MIRROR   A mirror is essential so that actors may see themselves during fittings.

ELECTRIC WASHING MACHINE   A top-loading machine with an enamel inner tub is essential for dyeing and laundering.

ELECTRIC DRYER   An electric dryer saves time after washing and dyeing.

STRAIGHT PINS   Pins should be rustproof, bought in quantity in boxes, and in a medium size that is not so large they will not penetrate fabric easily and not so small they will be lost during cutting and sewing.

NEEDLES   The long-eyed needles in packages including sizes 5 to 10 are convenient for ordinary sewing. Carpet, darning, upholstery, and heavy embroidery needles are necessary for heavy work. Needles are best bought from a wholesale supply house in bulk quantity so that staff members need not be continually running to the local variety or department store.

SAFETY PINS   Safety pins should be on hand in assorted sizes and should be purchased in bulk.

TAILOR'S CHALK   Chalk comes in white and in colors and is used for marking around patterns and for alterations.

THREAD   In medium- and large-sized threatres only black and white thread is usually used, since thread color cannot be seen from a distance. In intimate productions, colored thread is necessary. Only a few sizes are necessary: mercerized #40 and #50 for machine and ordinary sewing, heavy button and carpet thread for buttons and leather, and mending thread for hose.

BIAS TAPE   Single-fold tape in black and white is usually all that is necessary unless the inside of a costume will be seen; then colored bias to match the costume must be used. Bias tape is useful for finishing openings, necklines, and various edges as well as for trimming.

COTTON TWILL TAPE   Cotton twill tape is usually purchased only in black and white unless it is to be used on the outside of a costume as trim. It should be stocked in ¼-, ½-, and ¾-inch widths and can also be used for ties and drawstrings and for trimming and binding off straight edges.

SNAPS   Snaps should be kept on hand in black and silver in sizes #000, #00, #1, and #2.

HOOKS AND EYES   Hooks and eyes should be kept on hand in black and silver in sizes #2, #3, #5, and #12. Metal pants hooks for heavy costumes are also frequently necessary.

LEAD WEIGHTS   Weights are necessary in small and medium sizes, usually cloth covered, for weighting corners and edges of costumes to keep them from clinging or fluttering.

FABRIC GLUE AND ALL-PURPOSE GLUE   Two forms of glue should be on hand: a fabric glue that is so flexible that even jewelry and patterns can be glued to fabric without peeling or cracking off under heavy use, and an all-purpose glue for gluing solid objects firmly together. 3M spray trim adhesive is useful for quickly gluing fabric or trim to other fabric surfaces.

THUMBTACKS OR PUSH PINS   These are used for putting up sketches, pinning wigs to headblocks, and putting patterns and swatches on walls.

HAT WIRE   Hat wire is sold in millinery stores in black and white and is used in finishing the edges of buckram when forming crowns and brims for hats.

HOOP WIRE   Flat, flexible, spring steel is needed for making hoop skirts and petticoats.

FEATHER BONING AND METAL BONING   Boning is needed in various sizes for building corsets and period bodices.

UNBLEACHED MUSLIN   Muslin should be in a medium weight, 120 count, and any width, although the 108-inch width is the most practical. The basic line and fit of a costume come from the way the muslin is cut and fitted. Unless the inside of a costume will be visible, muslin is used to line all stage costumes.

BUCKRAM   Buckram should be kept on hand in black and white in 36-inch widths for making hats and headdresses.

CRINOLINE OR PELLON   Crinoline and Pellon come in varying weights and are used for stiffening costumes.

ELASTIC   The ¼-inch-width elastic in black and white is the most useful. Other widths can be purchased when required.

TRANSPARENT TAPE AND MASKING TAPE   Tapes have many applications, from putting swatches on sketches, to piecing patterns, to covering cutting tables with brown wrapping paper.

ROLLS OF BROWN WRAPPING PAPER Wrapping paper is used for cutting patterns and for covering cutting tables.

BUTTONS Although boxes of buttons in various sizes and colors should be accumulated over a period of time, have on hand a range of button forms from small to large for making fabric-covered "self" buttons for costumes.

DRESS SHIELDS Shields should be washable in sizes 2, 3, and 4, and should be removed and laundered after each use of a costume in production.

COAT HANGERS Special shaped and padded coat hangers may be needed for special costumes; wooden hangers are needed for heavy garments; wire is adequate for most costumes.

PAPER TOWELS Paper towels are essential when painting, dyeing, and washing.

CLEANING FLUID The nonflammable type of cleaning fluid is the safest. One should experiment to find a cleaner that is an all-purpose remover of grease and dirt.

STARCH Starch is needed for stiffening shirts, collars, and petticoats.

SOAP AND DETERGENT Large boxes of soap and detergent should be kept on hand.

HEAVY METAL HAIRPINS AND BOBBY PINS Hairpins and bobby pins should be kept on hand in large quantities.

WHOLESALE DYES For a costume workshop that is in continuous operation, have a chemical company furnish a complete line of industrial dyes in bulk for the dye room.

SALT AND VINEGAR Salt and vinegar are needed for setting the dye solution in certain dye mixtures.

Less essential but valuable equipment items for a costume workshop include the following.

DRESS FORMS Moldable dress forms in several sizes are useful because the size and shape can be changed for the individual actor. Male forms can be made by wrapping a well-built actor in a T-shirt with six or seven layers of gummed paper tape, then cutting him out of the finished form, putting it together, setting it on a wooden template or base with a strong dowel up through the center to the neck, and placing it on a wooden stand. The plaster torsos covered in cloth that are used to display suits in men's clothing stores are also useful.

WIG BLOCKS Wig blocks should preferably be of soft wood, in a range of average head sizes from 21 to 24 inches. They are useful in making and dressing wigs, winding turbans, shaping hats, and making other headdresses.

PINKING SHEARS OR A PINKING MACHINE Pinking, a quick method of finishing seams, is a slow process when done with hand shears, even when they have been recently sharpened. A hand-operated machine that can be attached to the table requires less servicing than shears.

GROMMETING EQUIPMENT This kit for setting eyelets is very useful for making laced openings in boots, jackets, and vests. Eyelets and grommets come in various sizes and colors and are very useful in making certain period costumes.

CURLING IRONS, COMBS, AND HAIRBRUSHES These are all needed in the dressing of wigs and hair.

DYEING EQUIPMENT For large amounts of fabric, there are large steam vats that can be purchased at a fairly high cost. For normal dyeing, in which the fabric must be boiled in the dye solution, the equipment includes a gas or electric two-burner stove or hotplate, a sink with running water, granite or enamel buckets or dishpans, gloves, and smooth wooden sticks for handling the fabrics in the dye bath. A washing machine is needed for all dyeing in which boiling is unnecessary.

DEEP LAUNDRY TUBS Tubs are usually part of the dye-room equipment.

SPRAYING EQUIPMENT For fine spraying, a small air compressor with a number of interchangeable nozzles or air brushes that give a variety of textures is valuable.

A HEMMING PLATFORM It is useful to have a low, 18-inch platform on casters that can be locked for nonmoveability on which actors can stand when having hems set.

A further list of supplies for special uses might include the following.

SPLIT OR BIFURCATED RIVETS Rivets, available in nickel, copper, or brass, are used for nailhead trim or to hold leather or leatherette together.

GLASS JEWELS Glass jewels can be bought by the dozen in costume supply houses or hobby shops in all shapes and colors and are useful for building ornaments and stage jewelry.

SPANGLES AND SEQUINS Spangles and sequins are often useful.

BEADS Beads can be bought in quantity and variety so that they are in supply when needed.

TURPENTINE, DENATURED ALCOHOL, WHITE SHELLAC, AND SOLVENT These are needed for painting costumes and accessories.

Textile paints, dry color, spray paints   Various paints are also needed for painting costumes and accessories.

Armor and mask-making supplies   These include clay, materials for papier mâché, Celastic, plaster of paris, glue, fixative spray, muslin, paint, and trims.

Silver, gold, copper, and bronze powders and bronzing liquid   These are needed to achieve a metallic effect.

An active workshop needs all these items and more; otherwise time is lost in purchasing or in making substitutions. The best workshop is always fully equipped. Each new production can contribute some equipment, supplies, and costume accessories, so that over the years an active shop will be able to undertake any play without purchasing massive amounts of supplies and equipment for a single production.

Organization of the Shop Personnel

A minimum staff for the costume shop should include the costume designer, his assistant designer, the shop supervisor or foreman, the costume crew head, and the cutters, seamstresses, dyers, milliners, footwear and wig makers, and those involved with specialized items and accessories. Often the shop personnel must double up in their responsibilities. It is only in the best professional situations that one has separate personnel for each specialized area of costume construction. The major duties for which each member of the shop personnel is responsible may be summarized as follows:

Costume designer   The designer is responsible for all the artistic aspects of the costume designs.

Assistant designer   If a production is done under a union contract, the assistant designer is usually a beginning professional designer who is already a member of the union and is establishing himself in his profession through work with an older and more experienced designer. In schools and universities, the assistant designer is usually an intermediate design student working either with the professor of design, if he is the designer of the production, or with a more advanced design student. His responsibilities, aside from helping the designer in any way he can, usually include preparing working drawings from the designer's sketches, procuring various colored fabric swatches from which the designer can make final fabric choices, and finding and purchasing all fabrics not supervised directly by the designer. He assists the designer in buying the many small items for trim and ornamentation. He also acts as a liaison between the designer and the shop, supervising all fittings and checking on all construction that cannot be directly overseen by the designer. If

Actor:_____ Character:_____ Act:___Scene:___ Construction by:_____	fabric bought	costume cut	first fitting	second fitting	final fitting	costume complete
Actor:_____ Character:_____ Act:___Scene:___ Construction by:_____						
Actor:_____ Character:_____ Act:___Scene:___ Construction by:_____						
Actor:_____ Character:_____ Act:___Scene:___ Construction by:_____						
Actor:_____ Character:_____ Act:___Scene:___ Construction by:_____						
Actor:_____ Character:_____ Act:___Scene:___ Construction by:_____						

Figure 7–3   A costume construction chart.

164

the designer makes good use of the assistant designer's services, the position is an admirable one from which to learn all aspects of costume design. It is also a very demanding job in the amount of time and energy that must be expended.

SHOP SUPERVISOR In the profession, the shop supervisor may be either the person in charge of all construction for a costume house or the person in charge of the entire wardrobe operation in a repertory theatre organization. He must know all aspects of costume construction and be able to read and interpret a designer's sketches. The shop supervisor must also be able to work with actors and designers and supervise the shop personnel. In schools, universities, and amateur theatres, the shop supervisor is the keystone of the entire costume operation. In a school or university, he must grade students on their crew work, teach inexperienced people their craft, keep accounts of all expenditures and have accurate books to show on each production, and oversee all aspects of the construction process. In an amateur operation, the shop supervisor may be a volunteer or a paid position, but his assistants will usually be volunteer. The supervisor must command the loyalty of the volunteer staff, do much of the work himself, keep the wardrobe and shop in order, plan for the running of the production, and he may even have to serve the staff morning coffee or afternoon tea.

CREW HEAD In the profession, the crew head, who is an employee of the costume house or the repertory theatre staff, is in charge of the hours the shop personnel spend on the job. He must know the intricacies of union contracts and make sure that the shop personnel are paid for as much work as is needed while he keeps overtime costs to a minimum. In school, university, and amateur theatrical organizations, he may also carry out many of the costume designer's plans, although he does not have full supervision of seamstresses and cutters. In schools, universities, and in large amateur organizations, the crew head is responsible for all the crew work done by the shop staff. He must make a costume chart based on the one made by the designer (Figure 2–3), and a costume list that will show all the costume items in the production with the estimated and final cost of each costume (Figure 2–4). The crew head usually has a chart that shows the order of costume construction and indicates the stage of development of each costume from fabric purchased through the final fitting (Figure 7–3). Unless a time clock is installed in the shop, he records on the crew time sheet the time crew members spend on shop duties, and their absences and tardinesses. Personnel changes are noted fully on this chart (Figure 7–4). A costume measurement chart is also useful, and the crew head is expected to take the measurements from the actors' file cards and prepare a large chart that will give a quick rundown on the measurements for each role to be costumed (Figure 7–5). The crew head is usually in charge of keeping the workshop clean and in order during costume construction.

CREW MEMBERS   In the profession, the crew members usually include a head cutter, assistant cutters, and seamstresses, the head cutter having a position of authority second only to the shop foreman's and the designer's. The cutters are responsible for all patterns and cutting of garments and for much of the fitting. Seamstresses are hired to do only the sewing and finishing and are usually divided into those who do machine work and those who do handwork. Then there is always a person or two who does dyeing, others who do nothing but painting and texturing, and still one or two more who do armor, accessories, jewelry, and footwear.

In schools, universities, and amateur groups, there is seldom such careful division of work, although in a large production it is certainly better to have some people assigned only to armor, footwear, wigs, headdresses, and accessories. However, seldom is there a division of work between the cutter and the seamstress. Usually the person assigned to a costume does cutting, sewing, and fitting under the supervision of the

CREW TIME SHEET

Play: Hamlet	Aug. 8	Aug. 9	Aug. 10	Aug. 11	Aug. 12	Aug. 13	Aug. 14	Aug. 15
Crew Member: **Sam Penn** Assignment: jewelry	in 4:15 out 6:15	*in* 2:15 out 4:15	in 4:15 out 6:15					
Crew Member: **Bert Mall** Assignment: footwear	in 4:15 out 6:30							
Crew Member: **Sally Small** Assignment: hats & headdresses								
Crew Member: **Bella Gann** Assignment: under garments								
Crew Member: **Robert Pace** Assignment: armor								
Crew Member: **Cynthia Cole** Assignment: wigs								
Crew Member: **Bertha Gale** Assignment: accessories								

Figure 7–4   A crew time sheet.

COSTUME MEASUREMENT
CHART

Actor's Name	Hd	Nk	Sh	Ch	Wst	Hip	Arm	WtF	NtW	UAtW	Ins	WtK	Ft
Sam Barclay	22	16	16	39	31	40	$24\frac{1}{2}$	45	19	10	32	$16\frac{1}{2}$	$11\frac{1}{2}$
Julius Kurtz													
Brigid Neils													
Patsy Samson													

Figure 7–5   A costume measurement chart.

foreman and the designer, with hand sewing and trim left to less experienced hands. All crew members or shop personnel must keep their belongings away from the work area; they must not smoke or eat on the job, but only in designated places away from the work in progress; they must return all tools to the proper places in the shop; they must report to personnel in charge when supplies are low; they must use only the designated shears for cutting things other than fabric; they must turn off electrical appliances after use; and they must leave the shop in good order at the close of each day's operation.

Cutting and Fitting the Costumes

With a fully equipped workshop available for the execution of his costume designs, the designer is next faced with the supervision of the costume construction process. Supervision may mean anything from full-time presence in the shop during the weeks before the dress parade to super-vision of only the first and final fittings of each costume; but whichever he does, the designer must know the basic problems involved in the cutting and fitting of costumes.

The costume patterns cut from actors' measurements must be exact; they should have a full inch or more seam allowance; they should be cut on the straight grain of the fabric; patterned or figured fabric must be cut so that the figure in the fabric is not unduly distorted at the seams; pieces of fabric with nap must all run in the same direction; sleeves, trousers, and skirts must all be cut 2 to 3 inches longer than necessary to allow for last-minute changes, alterations, or recasting.

The first fitting of a costume can be done one of two ways, but whichever approach is used, the designer should supervise and comment on the cut and fit of the costume. The costume can be cut out of muslin and then pinned together and fitted on the actor as a muslin, or the fabric of the costume can be cut and pinned to the muslin, which acts as the costume lining, and the two can be pinned together and tried on the actor inside out. If the designer prefers to use muslin alone, he must take into account the thickness of the fabric to be used. If the muslin and the fabric together are pinned on the actor inside out, then the designer must be certain that the actor is symmetrical, that is, that both sides of his body measure roughly the same; otherwise, when right side out, the left side of the costume will be on the right side of the actor and vice versa.

THE FIRST FITTING   At this fitting, the actor should wear the under-garments he will wear under the finished costume. This includes all pad-ding, corsets, girdles, brassieres, and petticoats.

First let us deal with the problems in fitting bodices, jackets, and doublets.

If the actor is symmetrical and it is decided to fit the costume inside out rather than in muslin, the pieces of the garment should all be pinned together with the seams on the outside. The garment should be slipped onto the body, the front or back opening centered so that it is absolutely straight, and then the garment should be pinned closed.

The neck and armholes should be trimmed so that the garment fits smoothly, and the side seams should be adjusted, working from the top down so that the same amount is taken in or let out on each side of the garment and the pinning is symmetrical from underarm to waist.

Next the shoulder seams should be adjusted by repinning from the outside of the shoulders to the neck. Darts should be repinned, keeping them equidistant from the center back, the center front, and the sides of the garment. Darts can be taken under the arms, halfway between the sides and the center of the back or front, on the center back seam, or in the front in the center of the two shoulder seams. Allow for the thickness of the finished seams when pinning seams and darts.

The neckline should next be sketched in with tailor's chalk from center front to center back on one side only, and, with the appropriate seam allowance, the neck should be cut out, the second half of the neck matching the first. This must be done while the garment is still on the actor, because the fit of the neckline affects the fit of the entire garment. Enough material should always be left in the neckline so that it can be finished off without problems.

One armseye should be trimmed to give the actor freedom to move his arm easily, again allowing adequate allowance for seams; the other armseye should be cut out to match the first. The first fitting for the jacket, bodice, or doublet is then complete, but the garment should not be removed until the other parts of the costume have been fitted and the waistline and the placket opening have been clearly marked.

Next let us look at the problem of fitting sleeves.

Choose the arm most used by the actor and place the sleeve on it inside out. Pin the sleeve to the bodice or the doublet at the underarm and the shoulder seams, making sure that the actor can stretch easily. If a dart is to be taken at the outside of the elbow, it should be set into place, and the sleeve seam or seams (if it is a two-piece sleeve) should be adjusted to the correct fit. Have the actor move his arm in all the gestures he uses in his role in order to check the fit.

A tightly fitted sleeve may require a placket opening at the wrist. The placket opening should be long enough for the actor's hand to fit through before the sleeve is removed. The approximate length of the sleeve should also be marked, allowing for the reaching and bending that an actor may do in performance.

Now let us look at the problem of fitting a skirt.

A gathered or a pleated skirt will usually not need a first fitting, since it can be set onto a waistband or bodice that has been built to a certain waist measurement without trying it on the actress.

As with a bodice or doublet, a fitted skirt can be either fitted for the first time in muslin or pinned and fitted wrong side out. The placket opening should be pinned together first, whether it is at the side of the skirt or in the back, and the skirt should be carefully centered front to back so that the side seams are symmetrical.

The side seams should be taken in or let out the same amount on each side of the skirt, and the length of the placket should be marked carefully on both sides of the opening. The seam into which the placket is to be placed can then be opened to that point, and the skirt can be removed. The length should be marked not at this fitting but at the second fitting.

Finally, let us look at the problem of fitting trousers.

Again the fitting can be done in muslin or wrong side out by turning the garment inside out. The trousers should be adjusted so that the crotch is in the appropriate position for the actor's comfort when moving. In fact, unless the crotch fit is exactly right from the beginning, all other fitting adjustments will be off.

The center front, the center back, the side seams, and the inseam should be taken in or let out, working evenly from waistline to hips so that the trousers will stay in place while the adjustments are made on the lower part of the leg. The length should be tentatively marked when the actor is standing straight. Knee breeches should be marked several inches below the knee with the knee bent to ensure adequate length. Trunks should be marked at the back of the leg, with the actor bent to a ninety-degree angle.

Both sides of the placket opening should be marked with tailor's chalk, and the trousers should be removed, testing to see that this can be done easily with the placket opened as marked.

Before completing any first fitting, the designer should remind his crew to check all special items that go with the costume, such as collars, belts, cuffs, peplums, shoes, hats, and gloves, so that all such accessory items will be available to be tried with the costume at the second fitting.

After the first fitting, the designer should see that his shop personnel mark all new seam lines in tailor's chalk and that all pins are made perpendicular to the stitching line so that a sewing machine needle can sew over the pins. Check darts again to see that they are equidistant to the center, symmetrical, and correctly placed. If only one sleeve was fitted, the other one should be pinned and set in to match. When all seams have been marked as repinned, the garment should be stitched. Be certain that plackets are left open. Press seams open on the wrong side, stretching the seam as it is pressed. Each seam should be pressed before crossing it with another seam. Curved seams will have to be notched if an outside curve, clipped if an inside curve.

Neckline trimming should be checked, and the neck finished with bias tape, a bias facing of the same material, or a collar, as indicated in the costume sketch. On a curved edge, the second inside sewing should be done by hand. The armseyes should also be checked to see that they have been trimmed symmetrically before the sleeves are set in.

The sleeves should be finished off at the bottom if the length is correct; if there is still doubt, bias tape may be stitched to the bottom and the sleeve then turned up and hemmed after the next fitting. A sleeve gathered into a cuff or band can now have the cuff set on, cutting it three times larger than the wrist measure and twice as wide as the finished cuff, with a ½-inch seam allowance. The placket edges of the sleeve can be finished with a narrow hem or bias facing, and the sleeve can then be set to the cuff with right sides together, gathers or pleats being adjusted in the process. The cuff should usually extend ½ inch beyond the placket edges for ease in fastening. The cuff should now be folded in half, turned right side out, pinned, and sewn by hand to the inside edge of the cuff, with the edge turned under about ¼ inch. The sleeves should then be pinned carefully into the armseye, starting at the underarm seam, making certain that the right sleeve goes into the right armseye. If the sleeve is to be larger than the armseye or a full sleeve, pin it flat for 3 inches on both sides of the underarm seam and then distribute the fullness with gathers or pleats over the top of the sleeve. For a pleated sleeve, start with a box pleat at the shoulder seam, with additional pleats going down in either direction from the shoulder. Be sure that sleeves are symmetrically pinned into place before stitching the sleeves to the armseyes with a $\frac{1}{2}$-inch seam allowance. If the costume is to see a great deal of action, double seam it.

In attaching a skirt to a bodice, pin it to the waistline marked at the first fitting, setting center back and center front first and then distributing the fullness, if any, according to the design. If a zipper is to extend to the skirt from the bodice, there should be no fullness at the waistline for 1 inch on either side of the closing line. When the skirt has been accurately pinned into place on the wrong side, it should be checked from the right side, then stitched, and the seam pressed up or down, whichever works best with the particular fabric.

If a zipper must be set in a garment, the lines of the opening marked at the first fitting should be checked; and the side of the costume which would be the underside of the zipper (left side on women, right side on men) should be folded back and pressed so that the fold is $\frac{1}{4}$ inch beyond the original closing line. On the top side of the closing, fold the fabric on the line and press. Pin the zipper into place with the top side overlapping the bottom fabric by $\frac{1}{4}$ inch, which is adequate covering to hide the zipper in period garments. The zipper should then be basted, but not finally stitched until after the second fitting.

If hooks or snaps are used on skirts and trousers, waistbands and plackets should be finished with a narrow hem or bias tape; if a zipper is preferred, it should be set in before the waistband is added. Cut a waistband to double its finished width and at least 3 inches longer than the finished waist. Put on the band in the same way as collar and cuffs, distributing fullness according to the costume sketch, allowing less fullness across the front than across the back.

Other parts of the costume, such as ruffles, collars, belts, stoles, and drapes, should be finished and ready to pin into place during the second fitting. Footwear and headgear should be fully prepared, except for final adjustments, so that they also will be ready for the second fitting.

THE SECOND FITTING   The actor must wear the underpinning he will wear under the final costume. By the second fitting he should know all the action that takes place when he wears the costume.

This time the actor tries the costume on right side out, and runs through the actions he will perform onstage. All seams and openings should be checked for strength and appearance. All fastenings should be checked for security, and zippers should be examined for defects or improper installation.

Belts and waistbands should be marked for fasteners, and hems, including the bottom edge of skirts, trousers, sleeves, jackets, gowns, and mantles, should be marked with a careful line of pins. For skirts and gowns, a yardstick should be used to ensure that all parts of the hem are the same distance from the floor. Pins marking the lengths of skirts, mantles, gowns, and robes should be about 2 inches apart.

Finally, all pieces of the costume should be carefully checked to be sure that no accessory has been overlooked, and all items to be sewn to the costume should be pinned into place.

After the second fitting, the costume can be finished completely, taking into account the corrections that have been made. Zippers can now be stitched firmly in place and checked to see that nothing can get caught in them. All hems can be taken by hand and the garment trimmed so that the amount taken up is the same all around, unless the garment has a train. The easiest place to pin a hem is on an ironing board or table, with the skirt laid out flat and wrong side out. The edge should be trimmed and folded under ¼ inch before the hemline is pressed into place. If the edge of the hem on a circular skirt is much wider than the area of the skirt to which it is being sewn, then evenly distributed tucks must be taken along the edge of the hem to keep it flat. On heavy fabrics, it is better not to fold under the extra ¼ inch but to use tape or seam binding to avoid the extra thickness.

The trim can now be added to the costume by hand or machine, although trim at the bottom of a skirt should be put on before the hem is turned up. All fasteners, buttons, and ties should be finished, dress shields should be tacked in place, and the costume should be given a final steam pressing; or, if necessary, it should be sent out to be pressed professionally.

THE FINAL FITTING   The final fitting is a last check on the fit of a costume and is usually made a day or two before the dress parade.

The actor should now run through the sequence of his costume changes in order, checking each costume with the designer and the costume shop supervisor, so that every item he needs is ready with the costume, and so that he feels able to execute every action required of him during the performance.

The actor should check the itemized list that accompanies his costume in his dressing room so that there is no question in his mind about what is worn when and with which costume props and accessories.

Lining and Finishing

The costume is usually lined in muslin, the lining stitched together with the outside fabric. If the inside of the costume will never be seen, this may be enough; a separate lining such as that in a suit jacket or overcoat is unnecessary. The seams need only to be bound off with tape. Another plan followed by some rental houses is to lay the right sides of the lining and the outside together and then stitch them together section by section.

The pieces are turned right side out and pressed flat, and, after fitting, the sections are seamed together to make the finished garment. By this method the raw edges are finished and one can easily alter the size by ripping seams and restitching. The disadvantage of this process is that the seams are likely to be bulkier, and the lining may pull askew unless one is careful.

When finishing a costume, all the seams should be securely stitched and the threads tied, if they are not backstitched, to guard against ripping. Except in skirt hems, cuff facings, and collar facings, machine stitching should be employed, unless there is too much bulk to pass through the machine. In this case, hand stitching with very heavy thread should be used. It is wise to stitch all places of extra stress, such as armseyes and crotches, with a double stitch for strength and security. The object of the inside stitching should be security and comfort, not appearance. If an armseye scratches, it must be bound off; if material ravels, then the edges must be pinked, overcast, or bound off. If hooks and eyes are used as fastenings, they must be sewn carefully and securely, not forgetting the shanks, and sufficient overlap must be left in the garment so that there will be no gap between the hooks. Hook-and-eye tape may occasionally be used, but it is difficult to sew by machine and the hooks are usually too widely spaced for stage costumes. To get the best fit with hooks and eyes, alternate them so that the hook is first on one side, then on the other side of the opening. The hooks must be placed very close together. Snaps are very risky except on garments and accessories that are given no strain at all. They may open if used on cuffs, waistbands, and bodices. Zippers are the most expensive fasteners, but they can be put on with minimal hand sewing and give a neat appearance and a secure feeling to a costume, although one must be certain that they do not show. There are two schools of thought on zippers. The careful actor will find that they make for ease and rapidity in costume changes, but the impetuous actor may jam them, and the crisis that results is more than the use of the zipper is worth. Trouser flaps should use pants fasteners above the fly zipper as is done in men's ready-made trousers. All zipper openings profit by having a hook and eye or a pants fastener at the top. A new closing device is Velcro, which consists of two strips of tape with textures that mesh together when one is pressed against the other. Such tape holds firmly and is useful for fast changes. It does, however, make a ripping sound when the tapes are separated.

Trousers, breeches, and sometimes tights should be equipped with suspender buttons, since tight-fitting nineteenth-century trousers and cotton tights will wrinkle unless held up from the shoulder. Even knee breeches look better if they are worn with suspenders. An actor who becomes accustomed to the feel of suspenders will be more secure and comfortable wearing them. If garments lack suspender buttons, the actor may use the old stage trick of twisting six pennies along the top of trousers or tights and then buttoning suspenders over them. Clip suspenders are dangerous; they have a tendency to come unclipped. Care should also be taken in fastening separate doublets to trunks and skirts to bodices so that they will not separate when the actor or actress raises his or her arms.

Trim and Ornamentation

In choosing suitable trim and ornamentation to carry out the artistic spirit of the original design, the designer must always choose items that will show up at a distance and suggest the trim of a particular period without being too complicated. Braid is excellent if it is used to outline and accentuate the period lines of the garment and is not used to over-decorate and obscure the costume lines. Fine braiding is wasted on the audience, as are most embroidery effects. If braiding is done by machine, it should be done with a long stitch; but it is usually best to stitch it on by hand. When sewing braid on by hand would take too long and pro-

Figure 7–6   Painted ornamentation made from fabric glue and silicone caulking. Detail from costumes for Racine's *Andromache* as designed by Regina Cate for the Stanford Repertory Theatre, 1968. Photo by the author.

Figure 7–7   Ornamentation created with a hot glue gun by Ann von Kanel for a costume designed by the author for Richard III and produced at the Old Globe Theatre, San Diego, 1972. Photo courtesy of the San Diego Union.

duce tension in the fabric surface, braid can be glued on with flexible fabric glue. Sometimes the glue itself or silicone caulking used in sealing shower stalls can be used as a kind of braid if it is painted after the raised line of the glue application has dried (Figure 7–6). An even more effective use of the same technique can be made with an electric hot-glue gun (made by Sears and by USM Chemical Company). As one writes or draws patterns with it, one presses pellets of glue into the gun. Before the glue has completely dried, gold and silver leaf can be pressed onto the design, and when the excess is brushed away, the metallic pattern is quite permanent. This technique gives great flexibility and speed, and very complex raised patterns can be applied (Figure 7–7).

When still wet, flexible fabric glue can have flocking or metallic glitter dusted over its surface so that a complicated pattern of decoration can be achieved without braid. Flocking is a finely ground fabric fiber that is often commercially sprayed on metal surfaces to give a finish that has fabric texture.

Appliqué takes time, but it is both effective and durable. A decorative pattern shape is cut out in fabric, usually in felt since the edges do not ravel, and then sewn or glued into place on the costume. To give added definition, the pattern can be outlined in braid. If the result is too flat, the pattern can be given depth by dry-brushing in paint on the highlights and shadows suggested by its shape. Some of the most effective ornamentation of stage costume uses this combination of appliqué, braid, and painted accents (Figure 7–8).

When jeweled pins and clasps are used as accents and points of focus, items should be chosen that are large and relatively simple, with strong lines that will carry at a distance. Buttons must be larger and slightly farther apart than in everyday dress. For accenting necks and cuffs, use lace that is coarse by everyday standards but fine when viewed at a distance.

Dyeing and Painting

The use of dye and paint creates in the finished costume onstage a richer and more theatrical effect than can be gained by the use of fabric and braided trim alone. At close range, dyed and painted effects may look crude and inartistic, but under stage lights, and at a distance, the result may be very effective. When fabrics are available in a limited range of colors, only dyeing will give the subtlety and variety required by the original sketch. Often elaborate patterns are not available in modern fabrics, and only through painting can desired effects be achieved.

Dyeing and painting involve a considerable amount of time and expense, but the subtlety of the result will often repay the designer for the extra effort. Dyeing and painting are usually used to change or deepen the color of a costume, to age a costume, to create embroidery or appliqué designs, or to strengthen the lines of a costume and its decoration. There are no fixed rules by which any of these processes can be executed, and a certain amount of experimentation in mixing and applying is advisable before a craftsman in the shop or the designer himself begins a full-scale project.

DYEING   Any of the commercial dyes on the market can be used for most fabrics. The package will usually give directions and indicate the type of fabric on which the dye can be used safely. If dye is used frequently, it is cheaper to buy dyes by the pound, no less than a pound of each color. All-purpose or unified aniline dye will adhere to most fabrics, and only a few basic colors are necessary. Bright red, yellow, blue, brown, and black can be combined to make almost any color. The formula for mixing is enough water to cover the fabric and one teaspoon of powdered dye to each pound of dry fabric. A half cup of salt or vinegar for each teaspoon of dye can be used as a setting agent to prevent the dye from rubbing off. If one has nonunified aniline dyes, either an aniline meant for cotton fibers or one meant only for animal fibers, then each must be used only on the appropriate fiber. For nonunified aniline dyes, the cotton or basic dyes are set with salt; the silk–wool or acid dyes are set with vinegar.

In preparing a dye solution, bring to a boil enough water to cover the fabric completely. Dissolve the dye thoroughly and add the setting agent. Luke-warm water should be used for wool, warm water for synthetics, hot water for cotton. The dye must be completely dissolved before the fabric is added, and it is always wise to test the solution on a small fabric sample. The fabric should be rinsed in cold water before being added to the dye bath, and all folds should be shaken out so that the fabric does not form creases and tight wrinkles. If the water does not have to be brought to a boil, the best place for dyeing is in a washing machine, which will stir the dye solution automatically. The automatic top-loading washing machine is best for dyeing larger quantities of fabric, because the fabric can be inspected more easily during the dyeing process than when boiled in a pot or tub. If dyeing must be done on top of a burner or stove, then crockery, glass, copper, porcelain, or enameled

Figure 7–8   Braid and pearls glued to a costume and highlighted with paint. Detail from costumes designed for Shakespeare's *All's Well That Ends Well* by Jean Schultz Davidson for a production by the Stanford Repertory Theatre, 1966. Photo by the author.

receptacles should be used, because tin and other metals may corrode in the dye solution. All receptacles should be large enough so that the fabric can be stirred easily without knotting. While it is boiling, keep the fabric moving by stirring the solution with wooden paddles. Check the fabric from time to time by squeezing the dye out of one corner to ascertain the color. If additional dye must be added, the fabric should be removed from the dye bath, the dye added with the setting agent, the solution stirred until all powder has been completely dissolved, and the fabric added once again to the dye bath. When the fabric has reached the correct color, it should be lifted from the bath with the wooden paddles and rinsed in cold water until the water runs clear. In a washer, this usually means the full automatic cycle of rinses. The fabric should then be dried in a dryer or hung without folds. Finally, it should be pressed flat so that it is ready for cutting.

There are a few tips to remember about dyeing fabrics for the stage. First, if some small wrinkles are left in a dyed fabric, the fabric will look heavier and have more depth of color than if pressed completely flat. Second, if two colors of dye are to be mixed to achieve a certain hue, then a deeper, richer effect can sometimes be achieved if the fabric is dipped first in one dye bath and then the other rather than in a dye bath of mixed dyes. Finally, richer effects under light can frequently be achieved by dyeing fabric unevenly so that the shadows in the folds of the fabric show darker than the highlights. Sometimes the shadows can be brushed in with a slightly darker solution of the dye when the fabric is still wet. Dye may be sprayed onto a fabric after it has been dip-dyed to deepen and enrich the surface effect under stage lights. Either a hand spray or a small electric spray gun may be used.

Cotton fabrics dye readily, and almost any color can be achieved easily. Woolens can be dyed as long as cool water and the correct type of dye is used. Closely woven fabrics will not absorb dye as easily as those that are more loosely woven, and hard fibers are less absorbent than soft fibers. Synthetics are especially unpredictable, some absorbing easily, others shedding dye almost completely. Never begin fabric dyeing until samples have been thoroughly tested in the dye solution. All fabrics containing a starch or size should be thoroughly washed with soap and water before they are dyed, and all fabric must be rinsed in clear water before being placed in a dye solution. Many fabrics may shrink a bit in the dyeing process, and allowance must be made for shrinkage in the amount of fabric purchased. Obviously, it is better to dye fabric before cutting it, although it is possible to cut out the various pieces with enough seam allowance for shrinkage and then dye the individual pieces. Loosely woven fabrics shrink the most and usually become tighter and stiffer in the process. Cotton flannel and muslin will usually shrink about 1 inch to the yard, terrycloth as much as 2 to 3 inches, monk's cloth about 4 inches. Synthetics will shrink very little; wool will shrink only slightly in cool water but as much as 3 inches a yard in hot water.

CREATING PATTERNS WITH DYE   There are three ways to apply patterns to fabric with dye.

The first is an old process called *tie-dyeing*, which has just recently acquired a new lease on life because of the current fad for psychedelic swirls, blobs, and bursts of blending color in the fashions seen in the boutiques of the Sunset Strip and Madison Avenue. The first step in tie-dyeing is to tie the fabric into any of the five basic shapes known as rosettes, bunches, gathers, pleats, and marblings. String or dental floss can be used, but elastic bands are better since they are not permeated by the dye and can be easily clipped to free the fabric after dyeing.

After the fabric has been tied, it is immersed in a simmering dye solution for a time that varies with the fabric. Cotton soaks up the dye slowly, while silk takes it very quickly. The fabric is then rinsed in cold water. The process may be repeated up to five times with different colors or weaker or stronger dye solutions. Shadings of color can be achieved by painting or spraying on chlorine bleach when the fabric is wet. Other variations can be created by dropping dye into the bunched or twisted folds of the ties or knots with a medicine dropper or a squeeze bottle, while larger effects can be developed by squirting dye onto the damp fabric with a poultry baster.

Tie-dyeing is time consuming, but its rich, sensuous, seemingly spontaneous results cannot be achieved in any other manner.

A second method of producing patterns with dye is the *wax-resistant* or *batik* method. A pattern is drawn on the material with tailor's chalk or a soft marking pencil and the material is stretch on a frame. Melted paraffin or a mixture of paraffin and beeswax is painted on with a small brush, outlining the pattern which has been drawn on the material. If the material is transparent, then the pattern can be drawn on paper and the paper placed underneath the material. Within the edges of the waxed lines, dye can be painted without fear of its running. Many colors can be applied one next to another if there is wax to hold the dye within the edges of the pattern. After the patterns have been worked in, they can be covered in wax and the whole piece dyed to get the desired background color. The wax is removed by ironing the cloth between blotting paper, and if the cloth is still stiff, a little gasoline or naphtha will take out the remaining wax. While this method is most often used on silk, it can also be done on cotton with good results.

A third way to apply patterns to fabric is with a *stencil* through which dye is sprayed onto the fabric. The stencil must be thumbtacked to the fabric against a smooth upright surface, and one must make sure to cover all surfaces adjoining the stencil with paper. Usually the dye sprayed on should be warm rather than hot or cold, and if the patterns can be ironed while damp this will help to set the color.

PAINTING WITH DYE   In recent years many of the costume shops in the United States, Canada, and England have developed the technique of texturing and aging costumes to a fine art. In the shops at the Memorial Theatre in Stratford, England, at Stratford, Ontario, at the Guthrie Theatre in Minneapolis, and at certain costume houses in New York and London, painterly richness and sculptural form under light has been added to stage costumes by the artistic highlighting and shadowing of costumes with paint or dye. Although there are many variations, the dye solution most frequently used is a mixture of dry dye pigment and shellac thinned with alcohol. The exact proportions are best found by experimentation. The best method of application is with a small, easily controlled aerosol-can hand spray, or a small motorized air compressor with interchangeable air brushes of varying sizes that can produce anything from a ¼-inch line of sprayed dye to mass coverage of large areas. With the artistic and controlled use of an air brush technique, exciting effects of depth, richness, age, and an overall tonality can be added to costumes that normally might appear too new, flat, or direct in their effect. The air brush technique has great possibilities as a way to unify large and complicated productions.

TEXTURING AND PATTERNING WITH PAINT   Fabrics with smooth textures, such as muslins, percale, rayons, and most synthetic fabrics, will be easier to use as a base for painted effects than napped fabrics, such as wools, flannel, corduroy, and velour. Even with napped fabrics, textured effects that bring out shadows and highlights can be very effective. If hand-painted designs are to be used, fabrics may be laid out flat on paper that will absorb any paint that may seep through, or the fabrics may be fastened to a frame that will stretch them flat while painting.

There are a number of paint mixtures that may be used: textile paints, designers' colors, emulsion and acrylic paints, and French enamel varnish are all possibilities. A new textile paint called Versatex is the latest product for painting on fabric. It comes in a variety of colors, is quite permanent, and stiffens the fabric very little. Other possibilities are metallic powders mixed with bronzing liquid or thin glue, and dry scene pigment or tempera mixed with shellac thinned with a little alcohol. These media are usually best used on a fabric that is already rather stiff, since they will stiffen it further. Silk-screen ink thinned with water and Inko dye used commercially in creating flat patterns on fabric can also be used, and they will not stiffen the fabric to any appreciable extent. Spraying can be done with the above paints if textile colors are thinned with turpentine, emulsions and acrylics with water, and French enamel varnish with denatured alcohol.

There are three ways paint can be used: (1) freehand application, which will not have the stiff formality of a stencil, (2) with a stencil, or (3) freehand texturing, which ages or brings out highlights and shadows. In the Memorial Theatre, Stratford, England, the costume shops seldom use a stencil even when applying complex patterns. It is felt that a more imaginative, artistic effect is achieved if an artist–craftsman decorates an entire costume freehand than if he uses the more mechanical stencil

Figure 7–9 Costumes from the Stanford Repertory Theatre Wardrobe that have been sprayed and spattered to give depth and age. Photo by the author.

method. Another freehand method is that of accentuating or outlining a pattern that already exists in the woven fabric. This can be done with paint or with a crayon or thick pencil. If a stencil is used, one section of the design is drawn on stencil paper, and the parts that are to be colored are cut out with a stencil knife or razor. Enough bridges must be left between the various parts of the design so that the stencil will hold together during long and rough use, and the effectiveness of the stencil design should be tested on paper before application to the fabric. In applying the design to the fabric, a stencil brush is usually used with textile paint in a stippling rather than a brushing motion. The stencil should be wiped after each pattern application so that no excess paint rubs off where it is not desired. The third painting method, which is usually referred to as texturing or dry-brushing, is very much used today to give age and textural variety. It has become synonymous with the "Brechtian technique" of production. Coarse woolens and burlaps are dry-brushed in textile paint to bring out the wear lines of the garment, accentuate highlights and shadows, and give an overall patina of age (Figure 7–9). This brings the scene painter's art to the costume shop. When a costume craftsman really understands and has mastered the effects of painting costumes, he is a most valuable asset to the costume shop and to the theatre. In many modern productions, more than fifty percent of the visual effect of the costumes onstage comes in the final painting and texturing process.

8

Accessory Construction and Production Organization

The Construction of Special Costume Parts and Accessories

During costume construction, the designer will have to supervise work besides sewing and fitting. We have already discussed painting and texturing of finished costumes as an art closer to scene painting than sewing. There are also other items, such as hoops, masks, armor, headdresses, wigs, jewelry, and footwear, that demand knowledge and craft techniques often not related to the art of the seamstress or the tailor. In fact, in many of these areas the most creative work of the designer and his associates may take place. It is interesting to note how many costume designers, such as Desmond Heeley at Stratford, England, and Brian Jackson, at Stratford, Ontario, began their careers in the property department, involved in the construction of ornamental furnishings, tableware, and jeweled accessories. A designer who has mastered the art of ornamental design—jewelry, costume accessories, furniture, interior set ornament, and sculpture in miniature—has an excellent foundation for moving on to the larger areas of scene design and costume design. Often in the history of the fine arts, men (such as Cellini or Ghiberti) have begun as goldsmiths and developed into brilliant sculptors.

Mask and Armor Construction

Certainly the most challenging and exciting decorative accessories with which the designer must deal are masks, armor, and certain ornaments developed in deep relief. All require some form of molding to create the right surfaces and decorative shapes. In the past, molding meant making a clay mold and covering it with papier mâché. The clay mold was covered with six or seven layers of paper torn into strips and dipped in glue or paste. After the entire object was dry, the final layer was sanded and painted (Figure 8–1). Although papier mâché is inexpensive to make, it takes time, and the mask is at the mercy of wear and rodents, who love to eat the glued paper. In recent years, a fabric with the brand name Celastic has been devised. It can be dipped in a special solvent, shaped, and dried in a short time, and it is very strong when finished.

The materials required for making articles of Celastic are modeling clay, metal foil, cheesecloth, a parting agent or separator, the Celastic fabric, solvent, and paint for finishing the object. To begin, a model of

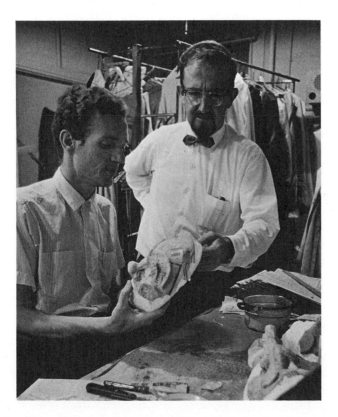

Figure 8–1   Herman George and the author making masks. Photo courtesy of News and Publications, Stanford University.

the object to be molded is made in clay. The entire object need not be created in clay if it is built over a form and the outside surface to be reproduced in Celastic is fully detailed. When building headdresses or helmets, a wooden head block is an ideal base on which to shape the clay. Because Celastic has a tendency to shrink while drying, particular care must be taken that the finished object will fit the head of the actor. Just as one allows for shrinkage in dyeing fabric, one should also allow for shrinkage in working with Celastic. If a small object is being created, then the entire mold is usually formed in clay; a layer of cheesecloth may be pressed into the wet clay so that the mold does not crack and break as it dries.

Many objects can be created directly from the clay mold by applying metal foil to the clay and then covering it directly with the Celastic, but for certain masks and articles in relief in which detail and smoothness of surface is important, a concave mold in plaster is necessary. This is made by covering a clay model with plaster of paris. Since the plaster hardens almost instantaneously, it must be handled very quickly. The plaster is mixed with cold water until it has the consistency of thin cream, and it is poured over the model. Any bubbles that form as it is applied should be punctured. After the model has been covered with a thin layer of plaster, a second, thicker layer can be added, until a fine mold of about an inch in thickness is achieved. The mold must be thoroughly dry before it is removed from the clay, and it should be thoroughly washed inside. If any bubbles remain on the inside, they should be filled in with plaster of paris and allowed to dry before the mold is prepared for application of the Celastic.

If the clay model is to be used directly as a base for the Celastic, it should be carefully covered with metal foil pressed down into all crevices and cracks until the surface is as smooth and as like the surface of the clay model underneath as possible. If a plaster of paris or other nonabsorbent mold is used, the foil can be eliminated and the entire surface covered with the parting agent or separator.

The Celastic fabric is prepared by tearing Celastic into strips 1 to 4 inches wide. The narrow strips should be used for areas of intricate detail. The Celastic solvent should be placed in a shallow pan. Moderate amounts should be used at a time, as it evaporates rapidly. Celastic comes in thin, medium, and heavy weights. It is best to use the heavy weight for armor and helmets, and the thin and medium weights for subtle effects. The Celastic strips are dipped in the solvent and then applied to the mold until the entire surface is covered. The strips should be overlapped. Be certain that the strips remain wet on all the edges in the area on which you are working. Sometimes certain edges or strips will have to be redampened with solvent as the work proceeds. When the entire area has been covered, special shaping can be done. If a helmet with a crest is difficult to build completely in clay or to cast in plaster of paris before the Celastic is applied, the crest can be cut of three-ply veneer board, set in place, and covered with the Celastic. Ears, noses, and other features for full masks can be formed by building up or by molding subtly with the dampened Celastic while attaching the features to the rest of the mask. Usually the Celastic should be allowed to dry on the mold for at least twenty-four hours. Even after it has been removed from the mold it will continue to dry and to shrink.

When a Celastic article is removed from the mold, it should be fully loosened around the edges and lifted carefully from the foil or the plaster of paris. If there are undercut edges, as in the neck part of a headdress, which is smaller than the large part of the head, cut the article with a knife from the edge up to its largest circumference, then pull it off, being careful not to break the edges. The edges can be seamed together with strips of Celastic dipped in solvent. Be certain that both surfaces of the Celastic are damp when this is done.

When the Celastic article is free of the mold, its edges should be trimmed and the item checked on the actor for fit. When this has been done, the edges can be bound off with bias cuts of the Celastic about ¾ inch to 1 inch wide. Both the binding piece and the edge must be damp, and the binding must be done very smoothly so that there are no folds or bumps.

At this point in making a mask, holes for ventilation and vision must be cut or designed into the Celastic. If the eyes of the mask will not be those of the actor, then wire screening may be set into the cheeks of the mask through which the actor can see. The screening is not seen by the audience because the paint on the outside blends into the rest of the mask area. Certainly the openings through which the actor is to see must be carefully checked so that his vision is not hindered, and all openings for ventilation should be placed so that there is a crosscurrent of air through the mask. Any ventilation holes large enough to be seen from the audience should be masked with screen or net before the mask is painted.

After the mask or piece of armor is smoothed with sandpaper, its edges bound, and all ornamental parts checked for clarity of projection, the article should be painted. If it is to be a metallic surface that is to appear aged, a ground coat of flat or semigloss black should be laid on the mask or armor before the metallic paint, which will act under lights as a highlight. This method is particularly helpful in adding to the three-dimensionality of the object. The dry metallic pigment is usually best mixed with shellac, and it can then be rubbed into the object or dry-brushed over the surface. A realistic aged metallic surface can be achieved with the use of graphite instead of aluminum paint to highlight the raised areas of the armor. In armor with intricate patterns of linear ornamentation that cannot be maintained in the final Celastic surface, sections of heavy lace can be used. These are glued into the appropriate places, the entire surface of the armor, including the lace, is painted black, and then

Figure 8–2   A Spanish sixteenth-century helmet made for the Stanford Repertory Theatre Wardrobe by Robin Coon from Celastic, braid, and heavy lace. Photo by Keeble and Shuchat.

the highlights are brought out in gold, graphite, or silver (Figure 8–2). The effect is rich and complex and cannot be easily achieved in any other manner. Another decorative possibility is the use of white or clear silicone caulking squeezed from the tube into the raised pattern desired or glue from a hot-glue gun. This allows the designer to draw his own design on the surface of the mask or helmet. Masks are often painted with oil paints so that an effect close to that of stage makeup is achieved, although a long drying period is necessary. If the final effect need not be realistic, then the mask can be given an even more durable surface finish with shellac.

A recent addition to the moldable plastics for masks, jewelry, and helmets is a thermoplastic rubber sheeting known as Polysar XB 407. Its results are somewhat like those achieved with Celastic, but the process of molding is quite different. Although semirigid at room temperature, Polysar XB 407 can be softened at temperatures around 170 degrees Fahrenheit (that is, in hot water or in an oven) and can then be easily molded by hand. It can even be molded directly onto the skin to give an exact fit to close-fitting body armor. When it cools, the plastic becomes rigid again. It will retain its shape through heavy use.

Polysar XB 407 sheets, which can be ordered in light, medium, and heavy weight, can be cut to the needed size and shape with scissors. Cutting is easier if the material is warmed to about 150 degrees Fahrenheit. Then either a heat lamp, an oven, or hot water can be used to soften the material for application. The higher the temperature, the quicker the material will soften. In an oven, the material must be placed on silicone-treated release paper to prevent it from sticking to oven trays. The material is self-adhering when dry-heated in this manner. If hot water is used for softening, the material must be left in the sink or basin until fully softened, and if self-adhesion is required, excess water must be blotted off and both surfaces painted with acetone before bonding will take place. Once the sheet has been softened, it can be molded easily over any shape desired, even a complex one. If the material begins to harden, it can be reheated. Hardening occurs after about ten minutes at room tem-

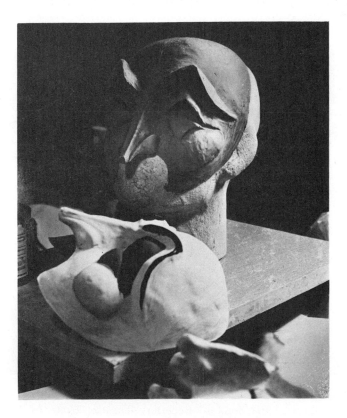

Figure 8–3   An example of Polysar XB 407 used for molding masks and helmets. Photo courtesy of the Polymer Corporation Limited, Sarnia, Canada.

perature, and immersion in cold water will speed hardening. When the material is completely hard, it can be removed from the mold and painted with quick-drying spray paints or thin layers of paint brushed on top of a base coat of quick-drying paint. The material should not be exposed to high temperatures while in storage nor exposed for long periods to strong lights. In some ways this new product is far easier to use than the more standard Celastic, since there is no solvent to bother with and there is less shrinkage in the construction process (Figure 8–3).

There is a process that is stronger than either Celastic or Polysar XB 407 in which fiberglass is used. There are both advantages and disadvantages to fiberglass for molding masks and armor, but fiberglass masks are heavier, stronger, and usually smoother than masks made from the other two plastics. Fiberglass comes in semitransparent sheets that are stiff until painted with fiberglass resin, which melts the fiberglass into every crevice and cranny of the plaster mold so that absolutely no detail is lost in molding (Figure 8–4). The fiberglass process excludes the use of clay as a positive mold over which masks and helmets can be formed. It demands a negative mold of plaster of paris before casting of the final forms can be undertaken. Fiberglass is in many ways more difficult to use

Figure 8–4   Fiberglass before use, and the inside of a plaster mold. Items used in the workshops of the Stanford Repertory Theatre. Photo by Keeble and Shuchat.

Figure 8–5 A group of finished masks and helmets of fiberglass from the wardrobe of the Stanford Repertory Theatre. Photo by Keeble and Shuchat.

than Celastic and Polysar XB 407, but the final results when sanded, painted, and finished are handsome, durable, and exact reproductions of an original mold or article (Figure 8–5).

Decorative Jewelry and Raised Ornaments

Decorative jewelry and other types of raised ornaments, including buckles, clasps, orders, crowns, and brooches, can be manufactured in papier mâché, Celastic, Polysar XB 407, or fiberglass into which are set glass beads, bits of metal, or pieces of glazed ceramic. Another method is to cut out the shape of the clasp, buckle, or brooch in wood and build up the decorative shape by gluing on bits of cording that has a strong twist in it. The end product is painted black and highlighted in silver, bronze, gold, or copper—only the raised areas of the cording pick up the metallic highlight—and a rich, three-dimensional metallic surface is achieved. Such pieces may also be set with glass jewels and beads, and by linking groups of these shapes together, one can devise decorative link belts and royal orders. In designing such decorative accessories, historical accuracy is far less important than the overall clarity and richness of the design, and its depth and ability to pick up and reflect light. Simplicity and the right amount of exaggeration are the key to good stage jewelry and ornament (Figure 8–6).

Celastic, papier mâché, or plastic wood can be used as a base on which to build small bits of glass, beads, earrings, and other decorative materials into a rich-looking order, pendant, or brooch. Finger rings can be created out of Celastic or a bit of soft wire built up with tiny cord and

Figure 8–6   Work in progress on the ornamentation for the coronation robe in Shakespeare's *Henry VIII* as produced at the Stratford Festival, 1966. Photo courtesy of the Stratford Shakespearean Festival, Stratford, Ont.

a large jewel. The result at close hand will be gaudy and cheap, but the effect onstage will be rich.

Another useful substance is foam rubber, which can be carved or cut with a sharp knife or scissors into bold decorative shapes for lightweight jewelry and accessories. Foam rubber takes dye, paint, or metallics, is very durable, and quite inexpensive.

A collection of junk jewelry should be kept in a workshop, separated according to size and use. Then, when the time comes to prepare the jewelry for a production, there is no need to rush about to locate the required items. The most satisfactory stage jewelry is that manufactured for the production rather than that purchased from costume supply houses. An excellent source of supply for odd bits of jewelry are the local stores of the Salvation Army and Goodwill Industries.

Chains for necklaces or large period pendants and orders can sometimes be bought at the hardware store, although they may be too heavy. Bamboo chain sold in garden shops and import stores is very light and, when textured with the appropriate metallic surface, is an excellent substitute for metal chain. Specialty shops, import stores, and theatrical supply houses often carry light aluminum or plastic chain that has been made to look heavier by adding a gold or silver surface. Aluminum or plastic chain can be useful onstage if the surface is properly textured. Small chains for necklaces usually must be purchased from shops specializing in costume jewelry.

An actor's personal jewelry should not be worn onstage unless it is absolutely right for the character and the period and style of the production. It is usually better to create from the junk jewelry on hand the desired items for each character. Additional dangles can easily be added to earrings with heavy thread, extra jewels can be appended to bracelets and necklaces, and bracelets can be fabricated to fit a number of wrist sizes if jewels are sewn to a metallic thread elastic rather than to a rigid bracelet. One thing that must always be checked is the light reflectivity of jewelry. Large rhinestones or fake diamonds may reflect too much light and blink at the audience in a distracting way. Their surfaces can be soaped, or they can be gone over with a thin dry-brushing of water-based paint. Flat metallic surfaces without decoration can present problems in light reflection; if they cannot be dry-brushed, they may be covered with a thin layer of black net, which will diffuse the light hitting the surface. Soaping, dry-brushing, or black net may also be necessary with shoe and vest buckles.

Footwear

Footwear is one of the most expensive accessory items on the professional stage. Usually some firm other than the house making the costumes is responsible for it. If the footwear is important to the look and feel of a production and the producer's budget allows a footwear firm to be contracted to provide shoes and boots that match the original designs, then this is the best arrangement for the designer. However, often the designer must include the footwear in the total costume construction budget.

The style of shoe that an actor wears makes a great difference in his stature and movement. In many period plays, the style of the actor is determined by his movement in the correct footwear. The height of the heels is particularly important in men's and women's shoes; the proper movement of hoop skirts, mantles, soft drapes, and other such items often depends on the correct footwear. Excessively high heels should never be worn onstage unless the style of the period demands them; this means that only in twentieth-century plays are high heels appropriate. For all other periods, medium and low-heeled shoes or slippers should be worn. If an actress has a floor-length dress it is often possible to find a plain low or medium-heeled shoe in lines that approximate those of the period and to allow these to be worn without great alteration. If the shoes are to be seen, they may be covered with the appropriate period brocade, recolored to match the costume, or decorated with bows, buckles, ties, or jewelry. For men's heels, one can buy either some of the more exotic present-day men's styles that have heels and resemble seventeenth-century shoes, or large-sized women's shoes. The shoes can be color-keyed to the costume, have tongues added, and bows, rosettes, and buckles set on to add the right period touch. Having a regular pair of men's shoes raised by having the shoemaker add height to the heel is usually not too successful.

House slippers are useful and inexpensive items of footwear for the costume designer. They are available in soft and hard soles, with or without heels, in leather or in cloth, in black and brown and often in colors. More varieties are usually available for women than for men, but if the men have small feet they may be fitted with large-sized women's slippers. Slippers can often be recut and reshaped on top, covered by gluing fabric over the basic lines, or dyed and trimmed to match the costume. The old-fashioned elastic-sided leather slippers for men are especially good. They are strong and durable and can be covered and cut down to make period shoes that can be worn for more than one production.

Various types of dance shoes are extremely useful when no heel or a very low one is desired, and many modern summer shoes or sandals are excellent for Roman, Greek, or Egyptian footwear with little alteration. Sometimes sandals may have to be manufactured from pieces of hard-sole leather and soft leather thongs, but if no one on the staff has experience in making sandals, it is probably better to have the sandals made by a sandalmaker. If soft shoes or slippers must be made, it is always better to build them over a pair of soft house slippers than to take the time to make them completely. Once the actor has been fitted with the slipper, it can be covered without another fitting. The covering can be cut and fitted over the slipper wrong side out, so that the seams can be easily stitched in the right places before the covering is sewn or glued to the slipper right side out. It is often easier to glue the covering to the slipper with flexible glue than to sew it around the edge of the sole, but if it is sewed, the stitches should be kept above the sole line so that they will not wear out quickly. A covering that has a center back and a center front seam is undoubtedly the easiest and quickest to make.

Boots may be made by making the boot top and then sewing or preferably gluing it to sturdy slippers with a hard sole or to low boots, unless a soft-soled boot is desired. Real leather, imitation leather, felt, or suede cloth can be used for the desired effect. If the part of the boot covering the slipper or low boot is carefully cut and sewn and the fabric is pulled tightly over the slipper or boot when it is glued, a realistic and wearable result can be achieved. If the boot is of a material that is too limp, it may have to be lined to give it more stiffness. Boots that are supposed to fit the leg must have a hidden zipper opening, preferably on the inside of the leg. If boots are to be laced, then either the center front or the outside of the leg is usually used. One should not rule out the use of real boots today, when it is easier than at any time in the past half-century to find in the stores boots of all shapes and styles for men and women. A costume shop should have boots in stock, especially

Figure 8–7   Leather over a slipper and leather over a short boot as a means of boot construction. From the Stanford Repertory Theatre Wardrobe. Photo by Keeble and Shuchat.

if they are high enough and simple enough to be adapted to a number of different styles and uses. Sometimes a good buy can be arranged for many boots, or they can be purchased through a discount house or outlet store. Sometimes a shoemaker can be coaxed into using a medium grade of leather to make boots for a production at a price that is not prohibitive. Boots are an invaluable addition to a costume collection (Figure 8–7).

Hoop Skirts

The farthingale or hoop skirt must usually be made for a production in a number of sizes. It is usually made of flat, flexible hoop wire purchased at a theatrical supply house, heavy wire from a hardware store, or the ½-inch spring steel used in clock springs. Although this light hoop is not really like the heavier farthingale of the sixteenth century, it is a practical stage device to be used for any bell-shaped skirt. The flat, flexible wire or the spring steel is by far the most serviceable and easiest for the actress to handle, because it collapses when she goes through doorways or sits and will fall back into place again no matter how much it is pushed out of shape. If the hoop must be oval or elliptical, the less flexible hardware wire will retain the shape more readily than the flexible hoop tied into an elliptical line.

An average nineteenth-century hoop is usually made by a series of four to six hoops of wire, depending on the length of the skirt, placed 4 to 8 inches apart and topped by a muslin waistband. The largest hoop is at the bottom, and each succeeding hoop should be enough smaller to make a smooth line from the bottom edge of the skirt to the hipline. The hoops are fastened together with cotton tape 1 to 1½ inches wide, running vertically from the waistband to the bottom hoop. To make an average-sized hoop that measures 109 inches at the bottom, the six lengths of wire should be 111, 100, 89, 78, 67, and 56 inches, and they should be overlapped and riveted or overlapped with clips that can be cramped with pliers until the hoops cannot spring open. The muslin waistband should fit the actress comfortably. Ties are preferable to hooks for fastening the waistband. Nine floor-length tapes can be fastened to the waistband, and then, with the waistband on a dress form, the bottom hoop can be pinned in at the ankle position and the other hoops pinned in

Figure 8–8   Hoop skirt or crinoline construction.

at equal intervals until the hip hoop is reached. If the skirt is not to stand out over the hips, the top hoop should not be pinned in. The hoops must be level before they are sewn firmly into place. If the hoop wire is covered with cloth tubing or tape, it will make the finished hoop easier to handle and more comfortable to wear (Figure 8–8).

The hoop can be worn easily under a petticoat and dress, with the effect but not the weight of many petticoats, and it can be stored by coiling and hanging on a hook. A ruffled petticoat is desirable over the hoop to smooth out the ridges and weigh down the hoop for easier handling. Wearing hoop skirts requires much rehearsal, and an actress should have her hoop and petticoat several weeks before the first dress rehearsal, because hoops not only take up extra space but affect all stage business.

Chain Mail

Chain mail is often required in medieval plays, and although it can be rented easily, it can also be simulated in a number of ways. If the production is not a realistic one, then a number of heavy-yarn open-weave fabrics can be used to suggest mail. If the weave is very open, a black jersey lining may be necessary, but the important things are that the outside surface is rough and the weave pattern is symmetrical. The open-weave fabric should be dyed a very dark gray or even black, and the entire surface can then be dry-brushed in silver. The resultant metallic surface can be pounded to give an even more metallic finish to the crossovers in the strands of yarn. Sometimes a cable-knit sweater and long stockings can be dyed and silvered in this way if the torso is fully covered by a surcote or tabard.

One can often buy from theatrical supply houses a knit metallic fabric that can be used for chain mail if its high reflectivity is removed by dry-brushing the brilliant metallic surface with black or gray. The problem with metallic knits is that the metallic surface is flat compared to the broken surface of actual mail.

The best way to make chain mail if you have the time and the help is to knit suits of mail out of heavy cord with the largest size knitting needles that are available. It is difficult to devise a pattern for arms, legs, and hood that all the knitters can follow, but once this has been done the pattern can be saved and new suits of mail added to the wardrobe whenever time permits. Use black cord for knitting or dye the finished suits black (although dyed suits tend to shrink). The suits can be silvered by dry-brushing and the knots pounded down to give a more metallic surface. Knitted mail will defy detection even at close quarters (Figure 8–9).

In Roman and early medieval times, the torso was covered with

Figure 8–9 Chain mail knitted from heavy string. From a production of Shakespeare's *Richard II* as produced at the Oregon Shakespeare Festival, 1960. Courtesy of the Oregon Shakespeare Festival, Ashland, Ore. Photo by Dwaine Smith, Classic Studio, Medford, Ore.

overlapping metal disks sewn to a base tunic. Here the base can be leather or imitation leather painted or decorated before the patterns in disks are set on or before the whole surface is covered with disks, scales, rings, or metal studs. The metallic pieces can be real metal or they can be manufactured from plastic.

Wigs

Wigs are an important part of the costume designer's concern, even though a wig department, hairdresser, or "wig man" may have the responsibility for obtaining, dressing, and caring for the wigs. The designer must make the final decisions, about the hairdressing styles and hair colors that complete a costume design. No designer should allow the wigs and hairdressing to be worked out between the actor or actress and the hairdresser.

If wigs must be of real hair and there is not a full range in stock, the wigs must be rented or purchased from a house that supplies wigs for the stage. It is always difficult to make a decision between renting and buying, but in any permanent theatrical organization it is important to build up a large stock of real hair wigs in excellent condition. If someone in the organization is appointed full time to supervise wigs, and has training or can be trained in professional wig making, over a period of time a permanent collection can be added to the wardrobe. It would be impossible to give anything but a brief description of professional wig-making methods here. The wig maker works on a reinforced, carefully fitted net cap with small amounts of hair that he attaches to the cap with a stocking darner. It is a slow and laborious process, but if the person has been trained by professionals, the result is a wig that can match the designer's sketch exactly.

Many different materials can be used for wigs that are supposed to be nonrealistic. Wigs for seventeenth- and eighteenth-century productions, for clowns, for animals, for fantastic characters, and for highly stylized effects can be made by unskilled labor with relatively inexpensive materials and equipment.

The best material for stylized wigs of the seventeenth and eighteenth centuries is probably a synthetic hair known as *rayon horsehair*. Rayon horsehair is manufactured for store mannequin wigs and comes by the pound in black and white, which can be dyed other colors. Sometimes it can be purchased in a wide range of natural colors. It takes about half a pound for a male eighteenth-century wig, while a full-bottomed seventeenth-century wig will use up to two pounds. *Dynel* is another soft synthetic wig material that gives a realistic effect at a distance and comes in a great range of natural colors, but it is expensive. For children's plays or stylized effects, *felt* can be cut in wavy or straight strips and sewn to a cap, *cellophane fringe* can be purchased at a theatrical supply house and used to give a wet, glistening effect, *metallic ribbon* can be looped into curls for nonrealistic sculptural effects, sheets of *plastic* can be cut into strips and tacked into curls, and *frayed rope* can be used for animal hair, horses' manes, and fringes of hair on clowns' skull caps.

The one piece of equipment that must be on hand before any work can begin on a wig is a *head block* (Figure 8–10). The blocks made of soft wood or styrofoam are probably best because they take push pins easily, even though they do not wear as well as those of hard wood. The wig department of a costume shop should always have at least a half-dozen such blocks in sizes ranging from 21 to 25 inches. A *revolving stand* is another useful item of equipment, because it allows the wig block to be easily revolved while one is working on the wig. *Heavy-duty mercerized thread,* an *ordinary needle,* a *long needle,* and a *curved upholstery needle* are also required, as well as *cotton net* for the basic wig cap. Cotton net is better than fabrics such as buckram, which can be shaped to the head but does not provide ventilation and is too hot for the actor to wear comfortably.

To begin construction, pin a piece of elastic around the head of the actor for whom the wig is being made so that it rests just above the hairline and the ears. If the actor has long hair, it must be pinned smoothly in place, because it will be under the wig. It is usually best to part the hair from front to back and wrap it smoothly about the head with a nylon stocking cap to keep it in place. Then take a piece of net a little longer than the head measurement and wide enough to cover the head and put it around the head, pinning it at the center back where the elastic is fastened. Pin the net to the elastic all the way around the head and fold the surplus net smoothly over the top of the head, pinning it in place. Cut off the excess net to keep the cap from being bulky, and trim off the extra net ¼ inch below the hairline. A new hairline can be drawn in, but care must be taken not to stretch the net. When the cap is removed from the actor's head, it should be handled by the elastic at its edge, not by the net.

The cap should then be placed on a wig block of the correct size and the seam sewn up the back and on the top. Edges should be sewn down flat, and when the cap is removed from the block, the net should be catch-stitched to the elastic on the inside. The elastic should be able to stretch and still not shift position inside the cap. The wig material with which the cap is to be covered should be measured out to double the wig length, and the hair should be placed on a piece of paper and

Figure 8–10   Wig blocks. From the Stanford Repertory Theatre Wardrobe. Photo by Keeble and Shuchat.

sewn across the center with a long stitch on the machine. The paper is then pulled away and the line of stitching can be used as the part, or the hair can be folded along the line and pinned in place. The hair must be securely pinned to the cap on the wig block, and the cap must not shift and change shape as the hair is pinned to it. The hair should now be sewn to the cap in sections so that it follows the direction of growth of the real hair, and the hair must be applied thinly enough so that it covers the cap but does not enlarge the normal head size. Rayon horsehair is best pinned in place while wet and sewn after it is dry. It shapes easily when wet, and curls can be set that will remain in place when dry. For eighteenth-century wigs, it may be wise to put a thin layer of cotton on the cap before adding hair, as this will cut down the amount of hair needed and will not allow a dark head of hair to show through from beneath. Cotton can also be used to build up a wig before the outer layer of hair is added. When all curls and styling have been set and sewn into place, the wig should be given a final fitting on the actor before being sprayed with a stiff hair spray and placed on a wig stand for transport to the actor's dressing room. Wigs must be carefully maintained during performance; loose waves and curls must be reset and sprayed with hair lacquer.

A method that can be used in place of sewing is gluing the hair into place with a flexible glue. The cap must be of a stiffer and firmer net or sometimes even of shaped buckram, and the wig may be warmer to wear, but a more satisfactory hairline can often be achieved by gluing groups of individual hairs into place.

Headdresses and Millinery

Hats and headdresses should also be made on a head or wig block if they are to fit properly. Allowance must be made if a wig is to be worn under the headdress. In fact, an old wig from stock that has the same thickness as the one to be worn onstage can be used on the block when the size of the headdress is being decided.

One of the most usable items for hats is the one-piece felt hat with a deep crown. Sometimes old hats that have been given to the wardrobe can be used, but more frequently felt hat shells sold in a millinery supply house can be purchased in the desired colors and brim sizes and reshaped by steaming on a hat block and possibly stiffening with lacquer or shellac. Shaping a hat on a block is time consuming but not difficult if an electrically heated hat block is part of the costume room equipment. This heated block will make the felt soft and pliable when dampened. Adequate steam must be available to make the felt really soft and pliable. The hat must be pulled and stretched slowly so that it does not break or tear in shaping, and the full shaping must take place while the felt is damp. Even some period helmets may be shaped out of felt in this way, shellacked inside and out, and then painted to obtain a metallic surface. Shellacking inside and out also protects the hat or helmet from perspiration and makes it more durable. If a very heavy felt is used, hats without too high a crown can be steamed and shaped directly from a flat piece of the fabric, but only a trained milliner will know all the subtleties and tricks that will achieve intricate and professional results.

For other styles of hats and headdresses, buckram, crinoline, or Pellon may be used as a foundation, depending on the degree of stiffness desired. Buckram is the most common foundation used in millinery because it can be cut and used stiff if the edges are overlapped at darts and seams, or it can be moistened and shaped over a head block and then allowed to dry. A great variety of hat crowns can be shaped in this way over a block and then painted or covered with fabric. Buckram softens when painted with dye, tempera, or oils, and it shrinks a little, but it can be stiffened again with shellac or glue. Its raw edges will scratch and fray and should be bound with bias tape, and it can only be sewn successfully by hand or machine before it has been painted or stiffened with glue. When a buckram foundation is covered with fabric, millinery wire sold at any milliner's supply house should be sewn around the brim. If the hat is tall, it should be sewn around the top of the crown before the cloth covering is added. If the brim is wide, a series of concentric circles of hat wire may have to be run around the brim to give the desired stiffness. In covering the buckram frame with fabric, care must be taken to remove all wrinkles and pulls so that the final result is absolutely smooth. The fabric should be kept tightly pulled over the foundation at every step of the sewing process.

Other materials may be used as headdress foundations, including wire frames of various kinds and even lampshade frames, but most headdresses can be built with a combination of wire, felt, buckram and glue, or plastic materials such as Celastic or Polysar XB 407.

Specialized Surface Textures

For certain fantastic, nonrealistic productions, modern synthetics can be used to excellent effect when surfaces are burned and melted, and then painted with acrylics or plastic-based paints. For example, in a production of *Prometheus Bound*, described in Chapter 19, in which all characters were intended to look prehuman, the chorus and the character of Io were dressed in overlapping petals made of muslin covered with melted nylon chiffon. Other costumes were made of burned styrofoam balls glued to a muslin background, foam rubber was burned to create rock-like shapes and set with pieces of chipped resin, sisal hemp was burned and added to surfaces of melted nylon, and overlapping scales were pressed out of plastic sheets with a child's Vacu-Form play set. All finished costumes were heavily painted or spattered with plastic paints. The finished textural effects and the costume shapes were unique and unlike the usual concept of what constitutes a stage costume (Figures 8–11a and 8–11b).

Through experiments with new synthetic materials, many of which will at first seem unrelated to the construction of stage costumes, a variety of new and interesting effects can be achieved. The designer must experiment with all forms of plastics for theatrical textural effects, and he must be ever alert to new possibilities of craftsmanship in costumes and costume accessories.

Figure 8–11a Textural effects achieved with spattered canvas for a production of *Hamlet*, 1963. From the Stanford Repertory Theatre Wardrobe. Photo by Keeble and Shuchat.

Figure 8–11b Textural effects achieved with melted nylon highlighted in white, for a production of *Prometheus Bound*, Stanford Repertory Theatre, 1966. Photo by Keeble and Shuchat.

Sources of Theatrical Fabrics and Supplies

As most designers and costumers know, finding sources for the wide variety of fabrics and supplies needed in production sometimes presents a problem. One can always start with the classified telephone directory of the nearest large city, but it is helpful to have a basic list of sources for the purchase of theatrical supplies and fabrics that cannot be purchased in the local department store or dry goods house. A basic list, to which firms can be added as sources are discovered, will be found on p. 551.

The Organization of a Costume Crew

Now that the specialized items and accessories that complete the costume designs have been briefly dealt with, something should be said about the wardrobe personnel who will take over from the costume shop and handle costume problems during dress rehearsal and production. Only too often there is chaos and confusion backstage in the dressing rooms at dress rehearsal and dress parade. With a little planning and organization, many of the headaches and problems of dress rehearsals can be avoided. If final fittings of all parts of an actor's costume have been completed during the week before dress rehearsal, and the actor is aware of all his costume problems, a smoother dress rehearsal period will result and all major costume problems will have been solved before the opening of the production.

The wardrobe personnel are in a different union from those who work in the shop. They are separated from the construction process, and usually do not see the costumes until the dress parade. Once the costumes leave the shop, the wardrobe personnel are in charge. During the run of the production, they see to mending, ironing, cleaning, and general maintenance. In the nonprofessional, educational, and semiprofessional theatre there is seldom a clear-cut division; it is often advantageous if the person who has headed the costume crew also heads the running crew for the production. In this way there is a follow-through from the beginning of the construction process until the closing of the production; one person organizes the time and hours in the shop, and the costumes and personnel backstage during the run of the production. This is, of course, a long and time-consuming job, and it may well be impossible for one person to devote his time to it, especially if the run of the production is extended.

In a theatrical organization that is part of a school, college, or university, the crew, crew head, and the designer and his assistant usually come from a costume or a production class, and the work for crew members, heads, and assistants must be based on individual experience and the experience to be gained from the current production. The professor or teacher in charge of the costume division of the theatre department must plan so that all those assigned to crew or head positions have adequate experience to carry out their duties smoothly and at the same time handle a job that is part of a larger learning process. One of the faults with much crew work in universities and colleges is that it is often easier to use the same people in the same positions production after production. This may make for a smoothly running show, but it does not provide the changing experiences so desirable in a learning situation.

In a theatrical organization on the amateur level in which the crew heads and crew members are volunteers, the designer or the costume supervisor, who oversees the running of the production, may have to spend a good amount of time stressing the importance of each crew member to the success of the final production. Some effort should be expended to develop in volunteer crew members a sense of responsibility to fellow theatre workers and to the theatre in general, even though the volunteer may have joined the organization as a leisure-time activity.

The organization of the backstage costume operation should be based on the following general plan:

MASTER OR MISTRESS OF WARDROBE OR THE CREW HEAD   The wardrobe master is in charge of the entire wardrobe personnel for a production. All other dressers work under the wardrobe master's supervision. In many small productions, especially those that tour, one person may be able to handle maintenance, but usually the leading actors will require a dresser if there are any costume changes during the production.

In schools, universities, and amateur groups, the title "crew head" is usually used instead of wardrobe master, and the people working under this supervisor are usually labeled "crew members" rather than dressers, but the duties of the crew head and wardrobe master are similar. Before dress rehearsals begin, the crew head must have a list of the costumes and accessories worn by each actor in the production (Figures 2–3 and 2–4) and the name, address, and telephone number of everyone on the running crew; he must know who is assigned to each of the actors in the company for each change; he must have a time sheet on which each crew member can check in and out before and after each call. The crew head must meet with his staff, stress the conduct to be followed backstage, give information regarding the clothes and footwear to be worn, and work out the placement of each member of the crew during the course of the play.

During the dress rehearsal period the crew head, with the stage manager, should post the dressing room assignments for the actors. Information should include the names of the dresser or dressers who will help each actor, a list of any items the actor may have provided for his characterization, any makeup instructions that may affect the dressing process, and a statement about the location of quick changes that cannot take place in the dressing room. The crew head must also arrange with the stage manager for space for quick changes. During the dress rehearsal period the crew head is responsible for all work done by the crew members, both during the production and in maintenance between rehearsals, although for major changes or alterations the costumes must go back to the shop. The crew head should make sure that neither crew members nor actors make costume alterations nor change the appearance of a costume without the designer's permission.

During the performances the crew head is responsible for seeing that the routine established during dress rehearsals is maintained and that precision in changes and dressing does not slacken. He must also see to laundry and cleaning during the run and check to see that costumes are pressed and repaired as needed. If a production tours, then the crew head or wardrobe master must be dependable and resourceful, since the visual freshness of the production is primarily his responsibility.

After a production has closed, the costumes are returned to the costume workshop or a central location from which they can be disposed into a storage wardrobe, sent to the cleaners, or returned to the costume house in which they were constructed. In schools, universities, and amateur groups, the costume "strike" usually takes place directly after the final curtain on closing night, and before this period the crew head should determine and then list the disposition of all parts of every costume. Rented costumes must be packed and returned, borrowed costumes must be cleaned or laundered and returned, and all items that were worn next to the body should be cleaned or laundered before they are stored. No soiled or used garments should be placed into a costume storage area. The "striking" of costumes after the closing of a production should be done in a minimum amount of time, with the costume running crew carefully organized so that no time is wasted and each crew member knows exactly what to do. The costume crew head should make a final check to see that everything has been accomplished; then his duties for that production are terminated. Professionally, this means that the contract stipulations of the wardrobe master have been completed and that he is now free to take another wardrobe position.

DRESSERS OR CREW MEMBERS In general, the dressers or members of the running crew are expected to remain on duty in or near their assigned dressing rooms throughout a dress rehearsal or a performance unless they have been assigned jobs elsewhere by the wardrobe master or crew head. They are also responsible for checking to see that all the costumes and accessories are in the dressing rooms assigned to them between rehearsal and performances and for having a full costume list for each actor posted in his dressing room. Dressers or crew members are usually expected not to eat, drink, or smoke while on duty, in order to avoid accidents with the costumes, and not to have friends visit them backstage while they are working. Crew members are expected to arrive when called and leave only when they are released; substitutions should be accepted only when a crew member has an excused illness.

In assembling the costumes for the dress rehearsal period, the crew members are expected to hang up and label each costume in each dressing room until a complete group of costumes for each character has been checked off and every item has been marked off on the costume list provided by the crew head. Costumes should be grouped together by character and hung carefully so that they all face the same way. No one hanger should be overburdened, skirts should be hung on skirt hangers or by clothespins, trousers on pants hangers or by clothespins, and all costumes should be easily seen and easily removable for wearing. Shoes and boots should be pinned together in pairs and placed under the costumes or on dressing room shoe racks. Headdresses should be placed on shelves above the dressing table or above the costume rack. Small accessories such as jewelry should be placed in small cloth bags pinned to the costumes or in small boxes in the drawers of the dressing tables. Assuming that each part of a costume has a label tape sewn inside before it is brought from the shop, a paper label should be pinned to each costume in the dressing room so that dresser and actor will have a complete picture of all costume parts and accessories as they are lined up in order on the costume rack. All nonwashable items should be equipped with dress shields, and protective dust catchers should be pinned and basted on all floor-length costumes and those with trains. The crew member should fold in half a strip of muslin or inexpensive cloth 12 to 18 inches wide and long enough to go around the hem, press the crease, insert the hem so that it fits inside the fold touching the crease, and baste along its top edge through the skirt, catching the inside of the strip. The dust catcher protects both the inside and outside bottom edge of skirts and mantles while the actor is rehearsing. The dust catchers can be removed before the last dress rehearsal. Finally, in preparation for the dress rehearsal period, the crew members should equip each dressing room with a tool or supply box, which should include shears, razor blade or seam ripper, straight pins, safety pins, black and white thread, needles, hooks and eyes, a clothes brush, and dry cleaning fluid. All should then be ready for the period of dress rehearsals, but each crew member should have his dressing room checked out with the crew head before the first dress rehearsal.

During dress rehearsals the crew members must see that costumes are in place in the dressing rooms before each performance. If the company is performing in repertory, it is usually impossible to keep the costumes for all the productions in the dressing rooms at the same time. In that case movable racks must be rolled into the dressing rooms before each performance with the costumes for the production carefully arranged in order of use during the performance. The racks for the other productions should be stored in some central area or near the dressing rooms unless maintenance work is necessary. The crew member should see that actors are in full makeup before dressing in costume in order to minimize makeup stains, and the costume labels should be neatly placed so that they can be replaced on the costumes after the performance. The actor should be encouraged to hang up his own clothes in an area removed from the costumes. When he is dressed, he should check with the crew member the line of the costume, the security of fastenings, the angle of wear for accessories and headgear. The actor should be encouraged to check himself in a full-length mirror before every entrance. All changes during the performance must be carefully planned in advance with the actor, and if there is not enough time to return to the dressing room, arrangements must be made with the stage manager for space close to the actor's stage exit. The crew member must be responsible for having the space equipped with all emergency repair items and all the costume parts to be worn by the actor after the change, and he must be responsible for getting all items back to the dressing room after the performance. The crew member must also be responsible for any costume item used as a stage property even if the property man accepts responsibility for picking up and returning the item before and after its use onstage. He must also see to it that no actor deposits any of his costume or costume accessories anywhere backstage during a performance and that no actor makes changes, alterations, or additions to his costume without the designer's consent. Any additions or changes in the costume list for an actor should be made as they take place, and after each rehearsal the crew member should check his list to see that each item is in the dressing room and in its proper place. The crew member should help the actor undress at the end of each dress rehearsal, but should not act as a valet. He should question the actor regarding any repairs that must be made before the next dress rehearsal. The crew member should also see as much of the production as possible when he is not performing specific duties so that he has a clear idea of how the production and the actors should look from the front of the house, but no crew member should be in the audience during the final dress rehearsal, previews, or performance. Dust catchers should be removed, a final check on the accuracy of the costume list and the order of the costumes in the dressing room should be made, and a final conference should take place with the head of the crew before the final dress rehearsal or first preview.

During the run of a production the routine established during the dress rehearsal period should be followed, and careful maintenance should take place each day after one performance and before the next. Cleaning and pressing should take place whenever required to maintain the costumes through the run in a condition approximating that on opening night.

When a production closes, the costume crew is responsible for carrying out the "strike" as smoothly and as efficiently as possible under the supervision of the crew head. Dress shields should be removed, pins should be taken out of costumes, zippers should be closed, trim that cannot be cleaned or laundered should be removed, shoes and boots should be pinned or laced together in pairs, and all pockets should be completely emptied. Laundry and cleaning lists should be made in duplicate, and items such as hats, wigs, and headdresses that are not going to the cleaners should have all makeup removed and be labeled for storage. Laundry should be sorted and labeled by color and be placed in bags ready to be sent out, while rental items should be checked, packed, and labeled for return to the company from which they were rented. Dressing rooms should be emptied of all items except what permanently belongs there, and any personal items left by actors should be turned over to the stage manager. The crew is finished with its work only when the crew head has checked on each crew member's work and has released him from further responsibility on the production.

Release from responsibility can bring a sigh of relief to crew head and crew member alike, but also a sense of loss—of friendships, of commitment and contribution to an artistic enterprise, and of routine—and if the run has been an extended one, the leave-taking may be sad and poignant.

II

THEORY
AND STYLE

9

The Problem of Style
in Costume Design

What Is Style?

The word "style" is often an obstacle in discussing a design plan for a
theatrical production. Theatre people aver that a production should have
a unified style, and they will frequently talk about finding the right style
for a presentation without knowing exactly what is meant by the term
or how an overall style should be achieved. The term is treacherous, as
are terms such as "form" and "content." But if we accept costume design
as an art form that can be approached in the same way as we approach
painting, architecture, sculpture, and the minor arts, then we must make
some attempt to define what is meant by "style."

First, we must distinguish between the style of the individual artist
and the style of the period in which he lives. The artistic style of a
period is a reflection of the social and political history of the times, and
the changes that occur in society are eventually reflected in the patterns
and shifting artistic trends of the period. Artists contribute to these
overall patterns, some directly, some indirectly, and some by working in
an opposing direction; no one work by an artist fully reveals the style
of the period in which it was created. A period style is not an absolute,
and it is almost never fully operative in a poem, play, painting, or theatrical production. Each work generates its own style, and we must analyze an entire lifetime of work to assess an artist's overall style. The
compilation of all the creativity of an entire era is what finally gives us
an overall sense of a period style.

An analogy given by James S. Ackerman, in an essay entitled "A Theory of Style," gives an excellent picture of the development of style:

> We might visualize a style as a great canvas on which generations of artists have painted. The earliest ones sketch a composition, later ones keep some of it, rub some out and add some of their own, the next do the same and so on. At any moment in the process there is a complete picture, but no indication of what it will look like after the succeeding artist has done his share. At the close of the process, when some artists have started on another picture, this one is abandoned. But the final image, although composed of contributions from every artist, cannot be said to represent the aims of the earlier ones, nor to represent a solution to the problem posed by the first of them.

Reality and Style in Costume Design

If Ackerman's picture of the formation of period style is true for the literary and the visual arts, it is also true for a more limited art such as costume design. But what is the relation of period style to visual reality? As with painting and sculpture, the finished work of the costume designer does not reproduce period reality. What is presented, even when a designer or an artist insists that he is merely recording and presenting facts, is a personal interpretation of a period's visual reality. The public is freed from actuality by the artist's approach—his scheme for a painting or a set of costumes, the things he chooses to stress or ignore, and the form his visual statement takes. In costume design, the designer's style, influenced by the culture in which he lives, makes it impossible to set on the stage the visual phenomena of another era. Art filters life, and the artist or designer always places his technique of representation between actuality and the public. The designer should put aside the idea that he can recreate the past in his costume designs. No matter how honestly he tries, he is doomed to failure. He cannot escape his own time and place; he cannot escape himself. No matter how objective and self-critical he may be about his work and no matter how much time he spends studying every possible visual source from the past, what he finally presents to the public is a personal interpretation, colored by training, personality, and the culture in which he lives.

Particularly in the nineteenth century, many theatrical designers believed that absolute fidelity to the past was possible. In every case their failure was complete. Examine, for example, the case of the actor-manager Charles Kean. In his overly serious way, he was determined to make his Shakespearean revivals complete, annotated tableaux of the eras suggested in the plays. His program notes boasted that it was more worthwhile to see a Kean production of Shakespeare than to spend time doing research in the British Museum. Pages of program notes and production footnotes explained in detail how each costume, each property, and each bit of scenery was based on careful research and documented fact, and how the whole production was intended to give the public a visual experience of a past era. The more astute critics of the day often teased him about his methods, and they would announce that they had heard Kean was about to contract with the zoo for two alligators to appear in *Antony and Cleopatra,* or that he had sent an archeological crew to find the sea coast of Bohemia for a production of *A Winter's Tale* (Figure 9–1). The fact that Kean was one of the first to have photographs taken of his production merely added humorous proof that his production method was misguided. The photos are deadly serious but the results are amusing, since even Kean could not remove the Victorian corsets

Figure 9–1 Charles Kean as Leontes and Ellen Terry as Mamilius in Shakespeare's *A Winter's Tale,* The Princess Theatre, London, 1856. An example of archeological accuracy in nineteenth-century theatrical design. Photo from Clement Scott's *The Drama of Yesterday and Today,* Vol. I, Macmillan, London, 1899, p. 282.

from under authentic Greek costumes, persuade Victorian actresses to use other than Victorian makeup and hair styles, and get nineteenth-century actors to look, even in a general way, like people from the first century. But Kean never learned, and he thought the critics and the public equally ungrateful. Only a membership in the Royal Society of Antiquarians soothed him and made him feel that at least in archeological circles his theatrical efforts had been appreciated.

Other theatrical producers followed the same method, although usually admitting that reality had to take second place to theatricality when box office receipts were at stake. From David Belasco to Cecil B. de Mille, the same mistaken idea was put forward: that one could actually create the reality of the past for an audience. What was achieved was always a transparent falseness of feeling and effect, a second-hand production that was neither artistic nor unified and that had no overall sense of style.

Thus one is always brought back to the necessity for a unified style or, to put it another way, a unified technique for presenting one's interpretation of real life, past and present. The word "technique" is important because all art is limited, controlled, and defined by the technical experience of the artist. Nature offers the artist only the materials for style, and these materials are modified by the craft, the medium in which he creates. The costume designer of today is strongly influenced in the way he works by modern fabrics, certain methods of machine sewing, and certain forms of pattern layout, which always result in period costumes having a modern look, that is, a relationship to modern styles. The designer cannot escape his time and place; he cannot send himself back in time so that he can design with the fabrics, patterns, and sewing techniques of the period he wishes to place on the stage. As a designer, I have often heard a production design being ignorantly praised as "authentic," and seen publicity and advertising people use the same term. Even though twentieth-century design has tried to kill the chimera of historical accuracy in design, there are still many people who confuse art and archeology, who allow the nineteenth-century belief in the scientific approach to interfere with their intuitive response to an artistic experience.

Stylization in Art and Costume Design

If costumes cannot be authentic, what can they be? This is obviously a complicated question to answer, but it can be said at this point that they can be as close to reality or as far from it as the director, the designer, and the playwright wish, as long as they do not attempt the impossible: the recreation of a period on the stage. Many a brilliant, unified artistic production has costumes that give the audience the illusion of period reality, but careful analysis and examination will show that the costumes are actually limited in line, texture, and color, are seen from the artist-designer's point of view, and create a world of the play and of the production before they create a world of the past. Any well-designed "realistic" production will create the world of the play before it creates place and time in some past era, just as a "realistic" painter such as Velasquez creates a world of pigment and light before he creates the brilliant illusion of Spanish court life in the seventeenth century. It is a matter of the artistic choices an artist makes. One artist will stress an illusion of reality rather than the line, texture, and color of his medium for its own sake, while another artist will manipulate these abstract values of the medium with little or no regard for reality. As for the gallery- or theatre-going public, one can never be certain at which point they will be more attracted by an artist's abstract manipulation of artistic values than by his interpretation of reality. It depends on the visual values stressed in the general culture, the amount of knowledge the viewer has about visual processes, and the educational and intellectual level of the audience to which the painting, sculpture, or theatrical production is being presented. A designer will think he has designed what he calls a "stylized" production—that is, sets and costumes that stress line, texture, and color more than visual reality—only to find the audience accepting the entire scheme as authentic period reality. Today, many theatrical presentations are almost completely abstracted from visual reality without the audience feeling that this interferes with their appreciation of the characters' psychological reality, while a half-century ago the audience would have been distracted by such designs (Figures 9–2a and 9–2b).

The problem of reality in art and the visual aspects of theatre is a very complicated and relative matter. One must know about the visual values of a culture and of an audience within that culture before one can estimate how an audience will respond to a particular visual approach.

Form and Content in the Visual Arts

Any discussion of the level of reality in theatrical presentation or in a work of art must certainly take into account the way in which each age has viewed reality, and especially how much stress, and what kind, has been placed on the content of a work of art versus the form that it takes. At this point let us discuss briefly the arguments that have been formulated by art critics and commentators down through the centuries about the importance of form and content in art, and then let us see how these broad concepts can be narrowed to specific ways of seeing. A

Figure 9–2a   A scene from *The Return of Peter Grimm* by David Belasco, as produced by the Stanford Players, 1949. An example of a completely realistic production. Photo courtesy of the Stanford Collection, Stanford University Libraries.

student of visual design for the theatre will have a better picture of how his art is tied to the history of the visual arts if he understands the progress of the artistic pendulum that swings from abstraction to reality and back again.

There has always been a tendency for man to turn from emotional stress to the analytical and the abstract in the visual arts, from the wish for submission to the reality of an impenetrable, natural world to the desire to organize and control nature. In fact, the great contrast between

Figure 9–2b   A scene from the short comic opera, *There and Back (Hin und Zurück)* by Hindemith, as produced by the Stanford Opera Theatre, 1962. An example of stylized costumes. Photo by the author.

Paleolithic and Neolithic art is based on the swing from one of these poles to the other. In the famous cave paintings in northern Spain and southern France, which provide some of our best records of Paleolithic art, there is a striking naturalism, an attempt to counterfeit the animal portrayed in a ceremonial, mysterious, magical way—to identify with the animal in order to capture and kill it. In the cave paintings, art is a form of sympathetic magic with which man identifies and becomes a part of the mystery of the natural world (Figure 9–3a).

With the rise of Neolithic culture, art assumed a different form. During this period, man began to control nature, organize life, and exert his will against the forces of the universe. His art reduced nature to simple, often abstract patterns. The artist stressed structure and layout, certain accidental effects in the artistic process became regularized, and a geometric clarity or formal repeat of patterns replaced the irregularities of nature. Art became a matter of planning; it celebrated man's new power over nature (Figure 9–3b).

Later, when a culture has developed a high level of humanistic values, a balance may develop between the values to be found in nature and the values of pattern, organization, and structure developed by man. When fear has been subdued, when optimism about man versus nature is at its height, we observe a period that balances the formal and the

Figure 9–3a   A polychrome bison from the Caves of Altamira in northern Spain, ca. 80,000–8,000 B.C. An example of naturalism found in Paleolithic art. Photo courtesy of the Spanish National Tourist Office.

Figure 9–3b Stylized figures on painted fabric from a tomb at Chanchan, Peru, 1200–1400 A.D. An example of the abstract geometric qualities in Neolithic art. Photo courtesy of the Staatliches Museum für Völkerkunde, Munich.

natural, the analytical and the sensational. These periods are called "golden ages" in the history of art and culture. From Greek times to the present, we can observe cycles of development that swing from a formal geometric style to a balance between the analytical and the sensational style. We find this in Greece as we proceed from archaic to classical to Hellenistic art. We find it in medieval times as we move from Romanesque to high Gothic to late Gothic; we find it in the Renaissance as we move from early to high Renaissance and then on to Baroque. Whether this cycle is or will always be operative is certainly open to question, since one cannot force neat patterns on the history of art any more than one can on human history; but art is usually in the process of swinging from one pole to the other or is balancing the two competitive outlooks. We can see this in modern art, where the sensational effects of expressionism are matched by the analytical and formal effects of hard-edged abstraction. With our strong nineteenth-century inheritance, we are inclined to talk of the opposition between romanticists and classicists, but analysis of a classicist will show an artist who places structure first; analysis of a romantic will show an artist who places sensation and the mystery of nature first.

In all men there is a tendency toward either the sensational or the analytical; the history of art as well as human history has seen a continuous attempt to reconcile such polar opposites. In great men as in great artists, the right balance is sometimes achieved; but this balance is based on a precarious foundation, and it seldom can be continued beyond the life of a single man or artist, or beyond a limited time in the history of a culture. Today, in our increasingly complex civilization, there are much stronger attempts to achieve this balance than ever before. When the attempts fail and either reason or emotion becomes disconnected from man and nature, chaos results.

Major Polar Opposites in the Visual Arts

The dividing line between the analytical and the sensational view of life and nature is never simple and clear, any more than is the political line that divides liberal and conservative, but critics often try to explain a particular period in art by using this method of comparison. One widely known attempt to do this is Heinrich Wölfflin's *Principles of Art History* (a comparison of Renaissance with the Baroque), which sets up five opposing forms of representation. These opposites are used to explain and organize the art of other periods, literary as well as visual. They are useful to the student of theatrical design who is attempting to create visual equivalents for a playwright's mode of seeing and organizing his material.

The first polar opposition is the distinction between the painterly approach and the linear approach. A linear style emphasizes clarity of

Figure 9–4a   *The Allegory of Spring* by Botticelli. Uffizi Gallery, Florence, ca. 1485. An example of a painting based primarily on a linear compositional method. Photo courtesy of Alinari, Florence.

contour, sharp edges, clear-cut boundaries, and the decorative isolation of ornamental details, while a painterly style blurs the limits and boundaries, merges objects and forms, and gives an illusory and shifting appearance to objects and forms. For example, if Botticelli is linear, then Rembrandt is painterly; if Bramante's architecture is linear, then that of Borromini is painterly; if classical Greek statuary is linear, then Hellenistic Greek statuary is painterly—or, to be more specific, if Michelangelo's *David* is linear, then Rodin's *Balzac* is painterly. If you apply this concept of polarity to the visual theatre, then the plays of Racine require a linear visual style in sets and costumes while the plays of Maeterlinck require a painterly approach (Figures 9–4a and 9–4b).

The second polar opposition is the distinction between depth in plane and depth in recession. With depth in plane, space is organized as a series of receding planes, one behind the other, until a horizon is

Figure 9–4b　*Self-portrait* by Rembrandt. The Frick Collection, New York, ca. 1656. An example of a painterly approach in brushwork and compositional method. Photo courtesy of The Frick Collection.

Figure 9–5a "Joseph Panel" from *The Gates of Paradise* by Ghiberti, Baptistry of the Cathedral of Florence, ca. 1430–1450 (bronze). An example of action in a series of shallow, receding, horizontal planes. Photo courtesy of Alinari, Florence.

reached or a vanishing point is located. In painting, this leads to one- or two-point perspective backgrounds; in sculpture, to the several planes located one behind the other, as in Ghiberti's second set of bronze doors for the Baptistry in Florence; in architecture, to the several planes of relief placed one on another in the interior and exterior of early Renaissance palaces. In a recessional use of space the plane is broken, and visual space goes back in depth on diagonal and sharply foreshortened lines. Here, real depth replaces the several planes that stand one behind the other and hold close to the surface. Recessional depth is seen in paintings by Tintoretto and Rubens, in Baroque buildings that have a strong forward and backward movement and lead the eye up stairs and through arches to create an illusion of great depth, or in Baroque sculpture that has great movement and leads the eye backward and forward along imaginary lines of progression and recession. In the theatre, depth in plane and depth in recession can be seen by comparing *Romeo and Juliet,* with its suggestion of horizontal movement on a series of shallow planes against a flat, planar background, with *Hamlet,* in which the Prince moves directly from a forward soliloquy back into the depth of a full court scene in a recessional manner, while the space and background around him create a labyrinthine illusion of great depth. In

Figure 9–5b   *The Cathedra Petri* by Bernini, behind the altar in St. Peter's, Rome, 1657–1666 (marble, gilt, bronze, and stucco). An example of recessional depth. Photo courtesy of Alinari, Florence.

Romeo and Juliet one thinks of a shallow series of horizontal planes, while in *Hamlet* we see Hamlet move backward and forward on lines of great recessional depth (Figures 9–5a and 9–5b).

The third polar concept is a closed versus an open composition. In a closed composition things are rigidly framed and enclosed, and boundaries are the absolute limits of the composition. In an open composition there is no limit but a flow, a merging with the space outside the design. In a closed composition vertical and horizontal balance usually predominates, while in an open composition such stability is lacking, and a balance is achieved only by imagining a continuation into space. One suggests a stable, unchanging world, the other a world in flux that flows toward infinity. Leonardo's *Last Supper* is certainly closed, while El Greco's *View of Toledo* is very open. A building such as the Tempietto by Bramante is closed, while a church such as Borromini's San Carlo alla Quatro Fontana is open. Donatello's *David* is closed, while Bernini's *David* is open—it leads one beyond the statue to the imagined figure of Goliath. In the theatre one can compare the rigidly framed proscenium picture to the production scheme that breaks through the frame, moves out toward the audience, or even down into it. It is the difference between the rigidly classical comedies of the Renaissance, carefully framed and limited, and the operatic Baroque productions, in which the ballet came down the steps onto the very floor of the stage house.

In the fourth polarity, one can make the distinction between multiplicity of incident and a compressed unity. In the first, individual details retain their identity even though they fit harmoniously together into

Figure 9–6a   *St. George* by Donatello in the Bargello Gallery, Florence, 1415–1416. An example of multiplicity of individual details. Photo courtesy of Alinari, Florence.

the design, while in the second, the details disappear in the overall effect and one cannot distinguish the individual elements. This contrast is particularly clear when we compare any early Renaissance painting with a Baroque painting. In Botticelli, all parts are separate yet fit together harmoniously; in Rubens, one cannot separate the clouds from the whipped up details of drapery. In Donatello's *St. George,* all is clearly seen as separate interlocking parts; in Bernini's *David,* it is only the overall impression of action that is seen. Most classical plays demand costumes and sets in which each part is seen for its own effect, while in romantic drama the details are intertwined to create a rich and complicated overall effect (Figures 9–6a and 9–6b).

Wölfflin's fifth and last polarity is a distinction similar to that be-

Figure 9–6b   *David* by Bernini in the Borghese Gallery, Rome, 1623 (bronze). An example of a compressed, complex unity in overall effect. Photo courtesy of Alinari, Florence.

Figure 9–7a   *The City* by Léger, Philadelphia Museum of Art, A. E. Gallatin Collection, 1919. An example of absolute clarity in a painting. Photo courtesy of the Philadelphia Museum of Art.

tween painterly and linear, but it stresses light rather than composition. In this contrast between absolute clarity and relative clarity, the light and color of a painting, statue, or building may be used to clarify and illuminate, or it can be used to blur and distort until strong images are reduced to flickering subjective symbols or objects that stir the sense of mystery and the imagination. In the theatre such contrasts are made evident in what the lighting designer does in a production, or how the set and costume designers use surfaces and textures that reflect the light (Figures 9–7a and 9–7b).

Other Polar Opposites in the Visual Arts

In *Four Stages of Renaissance Style*, Wylie Sypher develops other polar opposites based on concepts and ideas to be found in the critical works of a number of twentieth-century art historians. One very basic and quite simple contrast is that between rest and motion. Gothic architecture

Figure 9–7b   *Hide and Seek (Cache-cache)* by Pavel Tchelitchew, The Museum of Modern Art, New York, Mrs. Simon Guggenheim Fund, 1940–1942. Oil on canvas. An example of relative clarity in painting. Photo courtesy of The Museum of Modern Art.

creates a feeling of restless motion, while Houdouin Mansard's additions to Versailles are heavy and static. Poussin's paintings are static, while those of Rubens are in full motion. In the theatre, we can compare the slow and static rhythm of Racine with the swift motion in most Shakespearean drama (Figures 9–8a and 9–8b).

A distinction can be made between artists who are either in or out of phase with their culture and reality. The "in phase" artist frequently presents a design that follows an easy circular pattern in a unified composition, while the "out of phase" artist presents a design that is confused, violent, and broken. Raphael's *School of Athens* is cyclical and calmly rhythmic, while El Greco's *View of Toledo* is broken and distorted. This is a major contrast between most high Renaissance art and most mannerist art, between much nineteenth-century and midtwentieth-century art. In the theatre, the violent rhythms and sharp shifts of mood in *Measure for Measure* can be contrasted with the relaxed and unified cyclical rhythms of Greek tragedy.

The polarity between representational (natural) and nonrepresentational (abstract) art is a major consideration in all theatrical approaches.

Figure 9–8a *The Triumphal Entry of Henry IV into Paris,* oil sketch by Rubens, The Metropolitan Museum of Art, ca. 1621. An example of motion in painting. Photo courtesy of The Metropolitan Museum of Art, New York, Rogers Fund, 1942.

Figure 9–8b *The Holy Family on the Steps* by Nicolas Poussin, National Gallery of Art, Washington, D.C., Samuel H. Kress Collection, ca. 1656. An example of immobility in painting. Photo courtesy of the National Gallery of Art.

Abstract art usually occurs when man senses that the natural world is hostile or beyond his power to comprehend and control, while natural art results when man reads into nature his own sense of assurance and power. Abstract art is transcendental, crystalline, often geometric, and sometimes distorted, while natural art shows man submitting to or identifying with a nature and a natural world he finds pleasing. The high Renaissance uses and loves nature, the mannerist period distorts and rearranges it to suit inner subjective patterns. In the theatre there is a continuing battle between the realism of the nineteenth century and the abstraction of the absurdists and the *avante garde* (Figures 9–9a and 9–9b).

Another distinction one can make is between the visual and the tactile approaches to art: art that stresses only optical effects and art that stresses the surface of things, the feel of forms. Paintings that stress textural surface as much as the optical scene are tactile; some statues, such as those by Rodin, are far more tactile than those by classical Greek sculptors. Some modern buildings project no sense of surface, while others, like many Baroque structures, place great stress on tactile surfaces. We find that some playwrights stress tactile images; for example, Shakespeare's images are more tactile than Racine's. In stage design we

Figure 9–9a   *Good Morning Monsieur Courbet (Bonjour M Courbet),* Musée Fabre, Montpellier, France, 1854. An example of representational painting. Courtesy of the Musée Fabre, Montpellier. Photo by Claude O' Sughrue.

Figure 9–9b *Girl Before a Mirror* by Picasso, The Museum of Modern Art, New York, Gift of Mrs. Simon Guggenheim, 1932. Example of the nonrepresentational in art. Photo courtesy of The Museum of Modern Art.

often contrast the painted set on a flat surface with the rich, textural effects of solid-built scenery. In costume design tactile contrasts are achieved through fabric effects; one can easily distinguish designs that primarily stress texture from those that stress line and color (Figures 9–10a and 9–10b).

Ortega y Gassett made the distinction between near seeing and far seeing, which is based on the contrast between early Renaissance landscapes, such as those by Sassetta and Gozzoli, and landscapes such as those by El Greco and Cezanne. In far seeing, a wide horizon is covered, embracing a whole field of distant objects with sharp clarity, whereas in near seeing, the eyes focus onto a single close-in area in which all edges of surrounding areas become blurred and indefinite. In El Greco's *View of Toledo*, for example, the space about the fringes of the composition seems to curve away from the central focus. Over the past few

Figure 9–10a   *Suprematism* by Kasimir Malevitch, Stedelijk Museum, Amsterdam, ca. 1915. Example of the intellectual-visual in modern art. Photo courtesy of the Stedelijk Museum, Amsterdam.

hundred years there has been a gradual retraction from the clearly seen object to the close-in subject and finally to the interior focus on the subjective or abstract. In plays we can see the same contrast between those that view everything from a clear but removed point of view and those that concentrate so much on one personality or one subjective idea that the surrounding characters and atmosphere are distorted or out of focus. In costume design this is the distinction between costumes that are designed to give a clear picture, in which all characters are treated equally and no subjective touches are added, and costumes that are designed to assault the senses through the distortions and exaggerations concentrated on the central character. It is possible to envision *Hamlet* this way, and one would tend certainly to design Brecht's *Man Is Man* in this fashion.

Similar to the contrast between multiple and unified vision is the discrimination between intensified seeing and relaxed seeing. It is the difference between the tense, wire-like vision of Botticelli and the sweeping, relaxed, saturated vision of Rubens. It is the difference between a statue by Rodin and one by Maillol. It is the intensified vision of Racine in *Phèdre* versus the exuberant story telling to be found in *Antony and Cleopatra* (Figures 9–11a and 9–11b).

Then there is contrast between dark vision, as in the art of Rembrandt and the play *Macbeth*, and light, uniform illumination as in Botticelli or in a play such as *Two Gentlemen of Verona*. The contrast of lightness and darkness is a major element in costume design and one of the first considerations in planning designs for a production (Figures 9–12a and 9–12b).

When one sees the balance between horizontal and vertical energies in high Renaissance composition and the oblique and spiraling imbalances of mannerist art, one realizes that this contrast is also apparent in both art and theatre. In two realistic interiors, one by Degas and one by Winslow Homer, one can see the difference in effect between the tipped-up floor and oblique table angle in the Degas and the balanced and stable symmetries of the Homer. In the theatre, the raked stage, which was a device for projecting a geometric and stable recession into space, has been used in recent years to tip the action toward the spectator

Figure 9–10b *Cow with the Subtle Nose* by Dubuffet, The Museum of Modern Art, New York, 1952. Example of the emotional-tactile in modern painting. Photo courtesy of The Museum of Modern Art.

Figure 9–11a   *Burghers of Calais* by Rodin (bronze), Rodin Museum, Philadelphia, 1884–1895. An example of intensified vision in art. Photo courtesy of the Philadelphia Museum of Art.

and project a heightened and rather unstable equilibrium. In a costume one can replace the balanced symmetries of horizontal and vertical line with diagonal and spiraling lines that give an unsettled feeling to the viewer (Figures 9–13a and 9–13b).

Analogies Between Visual and Literary Style

How does one determine style in theatrical art—specifically in costume design? How does one transform the literary style of the script into the visual style of the stage production? It has always been tempting to form

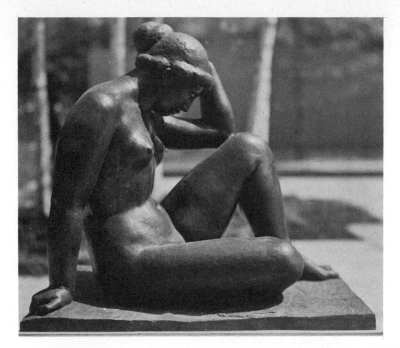

Figure 9–11b *La Méditerranée* by Maillol (bronze), The Museum of Modern Art, New York, 1901. An example of a relaxed vision in art. Photo courtesy of The Museum of Modern Art.

Figure 9–12a *The Birth of Venus* by Botticelli, Uffizi Gallery, Florence, ca. 1485. An example of a uniform lightness of tonality in painting. Photo courtesy of Alinari, Florence.

Figure 9–12b   *The Education of the Virgin* by Georges de la Tour. The Frick Collection, New York, ca. 1645. An example of a dark tonality in painting for dramatic effect. Photo courtesy of The Frick Collection.

Figure 9–13a   *The Country School* by Winslow Homer, City Art Museum of St. Louis, 1871. An example of a balanced equilibrium in composition. Photo courtesy of the City Art Museum of St. Louis.

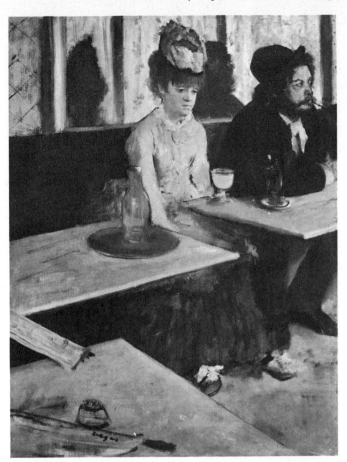

Figure 9–13b *The Absinthe Drinkers* by Degas, The Louvre, Paris, 1876. An example of unbalanced equilibrium in composition. Courtesy of the Directeur des Musées de France and S.P.A.D.E.M. 1969 by French Reproduction Rights, Inc.

parallels between art and literature, but because they are so different one often feels that the parallels must be false. However, if a stage designer or a costume designer hopes to be true to a script, he, above all other artists, must believe that analogies can be developed between the literary and visual arts, or he will always feel that he is imposing his visual artistry on a play. Many critics have noted that compositions in different media resemble each other in technique. A style will usually express itself in similar ways in many media. If, for example, we find that the organizational scheme for a Renaissance play appears to be similar to the organizational pattern in a Renaissance painting, building, or sculpture, it should be useful for the designer to study the way both are organized in order to create a visual scheme for the play. There is no problem in designing a direct and simple play in a direct and simple manner, nor in taking a play with sharp, staccato dialogue rhythms and short scenes and designing sets and costumes made up of short lines, small changing forms, and sharp dashes of color. But more complicated plays demand a more varied and complex development of the visual scheme. Every artist—whether literary, plastic, or visual—thus begins with a concept or a scheme, and the subject matter is then molded by it.

The old idea of approaching the design of a play on the basis of content, story line, and period setting is not enough. One must also design a play from the point of view of the director's and the author's plan or scheme for projecting the story onto the stage. Old arguments about whether one should always play Shakespeare in Elizabethan dress disappear, and the discussion moves to how one can relate the use of line,

Figure 9–14   James Mason as Oedipus and Eleanor Stuart as Jocasta in *Oedipus Rex,* produced at the Stratford Shakespearean Festival, Stratford, Ont., in 1954. An example of line, texture, and color related to the structure and organization of a drama. Photo courtesy of the Stratford Shakespearean Festival, Stratford, Ont.

texture, and color to the way the playwright has organized and presented his plot, characters, dialogue, theme, rhythm and spectacle. When one designs a production of *Oedipus Rex,* it is the tone and structure of the drama that should affect the designs far more than the story (Figure 9–14).

With this approach in mind, a costume designer would no longer design costume only for storytelling and character values; he would analyze the structure of the plot to see how various scenes were developed, how many lines of action were intertwined, whether transitions were abrupt or smooth, whether contrasts among scenes were sharp or subtle. He would look to see if one character dominated, two antagonists rose above the other characters, or whether a group or a series of paired individuals were the key to the play. He would analyze dialogue to see whether it was spare or rich, full of imagery or sharply telegraphic, tightened into sharp give-and-take character exchanges or expanded into long, full individual speeches. The theme and the rhythmic progression of the play would also be explored for qualities that could be translated into visual terms. Finally, the designer, with the help of the visual information given by the author, would prepare a design scheme for costumes that took into full consideration the choice of line, texture, and color.

As already established, when the director and the designer discuss the costumes for a play, both the story and the structure must be evaluated in making visual decisions. However, the story line frequently takes precedence, and the subtler visual needs suggested by the play's structure are frequently overlooked. For instance, while complicated, fashionable costumes for Molière may indicate the designer's knowledge of Louis XIV costuming, it is the spare, simple, clean-cut plotting and direct characterizations in Molière's plays that are important (Figure 9–15). In a production of *Le Bourgeois Gentilhomme,* the designer frequently attempts to show M Jourdain's lack of taste through extravagant and tasteless decor and costumes rather than relying on the strong unity and simplicity in the play's structure. Also, when a producer or director chooses, for the sake of novelty, to set a play in a period other than the one for which it was written, the superficial change will usually distort the script; but if the structure of the play is kept in mind and an instinct for the line, texture, and color required by the play's composition is retained, then the new period can be interestingly and successfully fitted into the drama. Certain plays are so tied to specific dress styles and cultural morés that to change the period is extremely difficult, if not impossible; but for those plays that have a human or philosophic universality, one can often achieve new and exciting visual effects by a shift of period or a move to abstraction—if the designs are closely related to the structure of the play. By attempting to attune one's "fundamental brainwork," as Dante Gabriel Rosetti used to say, to that of the playwright, the theatre artist should be able to achieve, through his plan-

Figure 9–15   A scene from Molière's *Tartuffe,* as produced by the Stanford Repertory Theatre in 1965. An example of strong unity and simplicity in costume and setting based on the structure of the drama. Photo by the author.

ning and layout, effects analogous to those achieved by the playwright.

Such a statement may seem overly simplified because it does not consider how a director is going to interpret a playwright's work to his designer and actors. The excitement and interest for theatre artists occurs during these discussions in which it may be determined that the audience is to see a "new" play in place of the one read in an anthology. It is then for the audience and critics to discuss whether the "new" play is better than the old one, a distortion of the playwright's intent, or a fascinating but not necessarily helpful new look at an old script. But even in the wildest deviation from what the play seems to be on the printed page, the designer cannot stop analyzing the basic compositional method of the script, even though he must, of course, see the scheme through the eyes of his director.

Although we are always looking for new ways to present old plays or exciting theatrical devices for producing new plays, no designer can afford to be superficial or arbitrary in his visual concept for a play. The more he studies how playwrights gain absolutely different effects from the same subject, how the same story is changed by playwrights in different cultures, how even the poorest play with the least planning is still strongly imbued with the world outlook or artistic style of the times, the more he himself develops as a designer. Only when a designer has a healthy respect and a secure feeling for the relationships between the visual arts of an age and the playwrights of that era is he really ready to work with a director in presenting an old play in a new light.

The plan for the remainder of this book will be guided by the fact that since theatrical design must transform a literary work into a visual work, a designer—specifically a costume designer—must understand the relationship between the literary and artistic developments in the period that shaped the play. This relationship should influence the visual concept and presentation of that play. Since one can find parallels between the literary works and the artistic works of a period, a costume designer should make a careful study of a play's plot, character, dialogue, theme, rhythm, and spectacle. He should devise his costume scheme so that the use of line, texture, and color will support the play's structure. He cannot use a rigid methodology. His plan of attack has to be personal, it has to come from his sensibility, and the result cannot be called right or wrong. Theatre costume design is far more than just a vehicle for developing a talent or merely an opportunity to design period clothes— it is all encompassing both artistically and intellectually, and one must approach the job well fortified with a background in cultural and social history and dramatic structure.

10

Classical Plays

Ritualistic Beginnings of Theatre

Much has been written about the origins of the theatre, and much speculation has taken place about where and at what time aspects of nature worship and religious ritual entered the realm of drama and theatre. Certainly theatre grew out of ritual forms in which early man, fearful of the changes in nature and the unpredictability of life, offered sacrifices to influence the powers of the unknown and the forces behind nature. The more these ritual sacrifices were performed, the more they became complex ceremonies displaying many theatrical effects, including body movement, vocal chanting, recitations, and special items of dress, accessories, and hand properties. Those persons who were especially effective in performing the rituals became the priests who planned the presentation of the rites and led in their performance. With the ability of man to disguise himself as an animal or as a god and perform before others, the seeds of theatrical presentation had been sown; and with the acting out of a hunting scene, the death of an animal, or the cure of a tribesman, the priest assumed many of the characteristics of the actor (Figure 10–1).

Gradually, stories grew up around the rituals that attempted either to explain them or to veil them in awe and mystery. As such tales grew in complication and character, the origin of the stories was often lost and the material itself became supernatural and mysterious, while the characters became either gods or people closely connected with gods. Links were established from one legend to another through the re-appearance of the same character, part of the story carrying over into another, or a series of stories being grouped together. The mythology that resulted was both fascinating as story telling and deeply symbolic —it intended to illuminate many of the unanswerable questions about man in his universe. Because primitive man made little distinction between religion and life, work, and play, there was a close relationship between the myths' rhythmic, sequential, and verbal development and the way the tribe or social group lived. Hence, the rituals or rites performed in the presentation of such myths embodied the customs, beliefs, and life rhythms of the society.

There is an innate histrionic sensibility in every human being—an instinct to imitate—that makes man enjoy imitating others and seeing

Figure 10–1   A wall painting of a medicine man wearing the antlers and skin of a deer, ca. 25,000–15,000 B.C. From a cave in the southern Pyrenees, France. Reproduced from *Theater Pictorial* by George Altman, Ralph Freud, William Melnitz, and Kenneth Macgowan, University of California Press, Berkeley, 1953. Photo courtesy of William Melnitz.

Figure 10–2   A mask of the Southern Dan style from northeast Liberia. From the Ralph Altman Collection. Photo courtesy of the Stanford University Art Department Slide Files.

such mimicries performed by others. The use of imaginative masks, mystical properties, and exciting ornamental costumes are all combined in primitive theatre to project this histrionic instinct. (Figure 10–2). It is the love of mimicry and imitation that sustains the theatrical instinct in society even when interest in myth and ritual begins to pale. It is one of the most basic of human instincts, and with those members of society who become actors it is merely a much deeper, stronger drive. Couple this with the story-telling instinct, which is another basic human impulse, and the result is two of the strongest psychological reasons why theatre and drama, from primitive times to the present, have remained such powerful forces, even in ages when both theatre and drama were heavily frowned upon, if not prohibited, by society.

Greek Art and Drama

Although there is some indication that a static form of drama existed in Egyptian ritual ceremonies during the period of the Empire, it was in Greece that the first great drama of the Western world developed. In the festivals honoring the Greek god Dionysus, the god of wine and fertility, drama was born and gradually matured to the written form we now find in the great plays of the fifth century B.C.

Although the Dionysian festivals were dedicated to a god of irrationality, Greek drama and philosophy clearly reflected the Greek belief in balance—that a failure to do honor to any part of nature may lead to destruction. One of the great precepts of Greek art and culture is that man must achieve a balance and harmony among all the conflicting forces of nature. It is this drive for balance and moderation which gives Greek Golden Age culture its unique character.

The fifth century B.C. is one of the great periods in the development

Figure 10–3a Poseidon (Zeus?), ca. 460–450 B.C. (bronze). National Museum, Athens. One of the finest transitional or severe classical statues from fifth-century Greece. Photo courtesy of Hirmer Fotoarchiv, Munich.

Figure 10–3b   Roman copy of *The Diadoumenos* by Polyclitus, 430 B.C. The Metropolitan Museum of Art, New York. One of the finest examples of high classical Greek sculpture in the fifth century B.C. Photo courtesy of The Metropolitan Museum of Art, Fletcher Fund, 1925.

of naturalism, and the Greek impulse to be true to nature is almost as strong as the desire for proportion and balance. It is this balance which distinguishes Greek art from the later styles derived from it, and it is also closely tied to the political and social balance between aristocratic organization and democratic individualism. When individualism and particularism began to triumph, at the close of the fifth century, classical perfection in art began to falter and disappear (Figure 10–3a).

One cannot separate the two forces or opposing stylistic trends in Greek art and theatre; naturalism and formalism are one. With the exception of Greek classical art, one cannot find the human form presented with such complete relaxation combined with complete control, simplicity achieved through complexity, freedom and lightness combined with poise and serenity (Figure 10–3b).

Classical Greek Tragedy

Tragedy is a primary creation of fifth-century Athenian society, and only in theatre are the inner conflicts of the social order seen so directly. Whereas the external presentation of the dramatic festivals to the masses was democratic, the tragiheroic content was strictly aristocratic. The plays treat questions of current politics in connection with a mythical background, and the religious basis of the story uses tragedy as an excellent mediator between religion and state policy, between religion and art, between the irrational and the rational in the Greek spirit. The rational factor, called *Apollonian*—Apollo was the god of reason—is almost as fundamental to tragedy as the irrational or *Dionysian* element of religious ecstasy; and as tragedy developed, it was the rational element that became paramount. Those elements in the story which had been dark, confused, mystical, and ecstatic were brought into the light of experience, meaning, and logical thought. Drama, more than any of the other classical arts, shows the major part played by rationalism and naturalism and clearly demonstrates that the two principles are not incompatible (Figure 10–4).

Figure 10–4   The tragic actor studying his mask. Wall painting, Naples, first century A.D. National Museum, Naples. Photo courtesy of Alinari, Florence.

Figure 10–5   Drawing of a reconstruction of a fifth-century Greek theatre. From a drawing in the Stanford University Art Department Slide Files.

Figure 10–6   Tragic masks from Medinet el Fayyûm, Egypt, early Roman period (first century A.D.). Photo courtesy of The Metropolitan Museum of Art, New York, Carnarvon Collection, Gift of Edward S. Harkness, 1926.

Greek Theatre

The theatre for tragedy began as a hillside grouping of spectators seated above a flat terrace, usually located near a temple dedicated to Dionysus, on which was placed a central altar and a chorus. In the case of the famous Theatre of Dionysus located on the slopes of the Acropolis in Athens, many changes took place from the sixth century B.C. to Hellenistic and Roman times; but basically the theatre was made up of a three-quarter circle of seats, first wood, later stone; a flat, circular orchestra or dancing place around the central altar or *thymele;* and a scene house or *skene* opposite the circle of seats, which was first used as a changing room for actors and later as a background for the play's action—certain props were utilized to suggest a temple, palace, or some other dwelling. Later this scene house or skene building was elaborated into a second story with side wings, machinery was added for mysterious appearances and other special effects, and the possibility of acting on a level above and away from the chorus developed. It is also supposed that scenic effects became much more complex (Figure 10–5).

The chorus was the backbone of the Greek tragedies and, in unison or in groups, delivered opinions, expressed sympathy, deepened the mood, and, most important, reacted to the events and characters as the author would wish his audience to respond. The chorus also added color and movement and a sense of spectacle to the proceedings; through the chanting and movement, with the help of accompanying music, it kept the rhythmical development of the drama organized, changing the pace, allowing for the deepening of audience reaction, and establishing mood pauses in the development of the tragedy.

Besides the chorus, there were three actors in each tragic trilogy, with "extras" brought in if they were needed. The three actors played numerous roles, male and female, and used lightweight masks of linen, cork, or wood and costumes based on the full draped folds of the Greek chiton and himation of civil dress (Figure 10–6). These costumes were often decorated with large symbols and ornaments to increase theatrical effect. The high-topped boot or *cothurnus* was the standard footwear. As a whole, the costume allowed for great flexibility and freedom of movement, and only at a later date did enlarged masks, raised shoes, padded shoulders, and violently exaggerated masks develop (Figure 10–7).

Oedipus the King

STRUCTURE   The story of *Oedipus* may be complex, but the plot is simple, the events are inevitable, there are no subplots, the time on stage is actual time, and all action takes place in one location. Sophocles, the author, keeps the distilled ritual rhythms inherent in the myth and merges them with the rational organization of his dramatic form so that the tragic rhythm, common to both, becomes as one and gives a deeper vision of life than is possible with either alone. On one level, the situation at Thebes as the play opens is analogous to the withering of winter in the ancient ritual of the seasons, followed by death and the hope for renewal. On a rational level, the play can be understood as an exciting murder mystery, with Oedipus as a prosecutor who eventually convicts himself in a marvelous theatrical resolution. As with Greek architecture and sculpture, the concentration on the simplest and most rationally perfect form leads to a heightened sense of the natural world around us and the mysterious world beyond.

Figure 10–7   Ivory statue of a tragic actor; probably Roman, but similar to the dress worn by tragic actors in Hellenistic times, with high headdress, distorted and exaggerated mask features, thick-soled shoes, and a heavy robe. Photo courtesy of The Archives Photographiques, Paris.

CHARACTERIZATION   In matters of characterization, the playwright pays little attention to age and appearance; we know only that the leading characters are mature, while the other characters are labeled simply as old, blind, or children. The same is true of levels in society; we need only know that Creon, Jocasta, and Oedipus are rulers, that the other characters are a Priest, a Herdsman, a Messenger, and a Seer. It is clear that the playwright is interested only in the psychological and ethical content of his characters, not in their looks and social positions, and even here he is interested only in those psychological and ethical attributes necessary to the story. It is well to remember that all the speaking roles would originally have been played by three actors: one playing Oedipus, another probably playing Creon and the Messenger from Corinth, and the third probably playing the Priest, Tiresias, Jocasta, the Herdsman, and the Second Messenger. The first actor would have required the most sustained power, but the third actor would have needed great range and the most help from masks and costume. Numerous extras were required, and they could also double in roles.

THEME   There are a number of themes in the play. One lies in the final lines of the drama: "Count no mortal happy till he has passed the final limit of his life secure from pain." Man's vision is limited, and a sharp contrast is drawn between man seeking his own destiny and the relentless fate or "will of the gods." Oedipus accepts his fate, yet sees himself as responsible for Laius' death and his own downfall. It is implied that man must submit to his fate, that to attempt to avoid it is to become more deeply entangled in a web of evil and wrongdoing. Behind this lies the one strong note of irrationality within the play: that the gods represent an unknown force in the life of man over which none can triumph.

A minor theme is that of Oedipus as a symbol of the dismembered god-king, and on this plane an audience in classical times would have viewed the play as a ritual atonement—a pre-Christian passion play celebrating the mystery of human destiny. Still another motif is the contrast of sight versus blindness. The strongest statement of this is the comparison of the blind Tiresias' inner sight with Oedipus' physical sight: the blind see truth while the one with sight lies in darkness.

DIALOGUE   The language makes great use of images based on these key themes; it creates a "life" that lies below the surface of the play. It is in the dialogue of the play that we find action continuously moving between passion and reason. It is this complex histrionic usage which creates the power of the play. The simplicity, directness, and beauty of the speech can all be appreciated rationally, but the mystery, the suggestion of primitive roots, the stream of feeling and subjective imagery can only come through emotion.

RHYTHM   The rhythm or music of the play is tied to the carefully alternating structure of the script, which swings from forward movement to backward-looking exposition broken by choral interludes that serve to deepen the mood and atmosphere. The play's choral passages would have been performed to musical accompaniment, and the dancing of the chorus would have been a direct reaffirmation in visual terms of the pattern and movement of the playwright's structural method.

SPECTACLE   The visual spectacle originally involved in a tragedy such as *Oedipus* was really quite limited. The play calls only for the stage house to represent the palace, no machinery or changes are called for, and an altar, in addition to the one at the center of the orchestra, is required. Costumes need only suggest the station of the character and the nobility of his personality, and the masks would indicate the age and personality of each character, with a change of masks required when Oedipus enters blind. Most of the visual effects in the drama would come not from scenery and costumes but from the patterns of movement of the actors and the chorus (Figure 10–8).

Visual Presentation of Oedipus *Today*

In making a decision about a visual approach to *Oedipus* today, one quickly has to answer a major question: should the emphasis be placed on the rational or on the irrational elements in the play? Throughout this discussion of the nature of Greek classical tragedy and Greek classical art, it has been noted that the balance between the formal and the natural, the rational and the irrational, the direct and the mysterious created a precarious equilibrium in fifth-century drama. Today, with our fragmented view of life, it would probably be impossible to present a live and vital production of *Oedipus* that managed to achieve this balance in all aspects of production. Usually a director decides to take an approach to *Oedipus* that will bring out a wide spectrum of the play's meaning and moods without trying to encompass them all. Should one choose the formality, the classic restraint, the structural pattern of the play, the Apollonian elements? Or should one choose the primitive, ritualistic, violent Dionysian qualities of the script? Fifty years ago, when the Gilbert Murray translations of the Greek classics were in vogue, productions frequently stressed the sonorous and rather removed beauties of the script, while today, especially since the great Olivier production of *Oedipus* in 1946, the stress has more often been on the modern aspects of the play—the violence, primitivism, ritual, and unseen forces working behind the play's structure. Given this basic choice, even though a near balance may still be a goal, the director usually has to choose between symmetry and balance and the more mysterious and evocative, with possibilities of asymmetry and imbalance for dramatic effect.

Figure 10–8 A scene from Max Reinhardt's production of *Oedipus Rex*, starring Sir John Martin-Harvey as the King, as produced at Covent Garden, London, 1912. From the Enthoven Collection of the Victoria and Albert Museum, London. Photo by Malcolm Keep.

Should the palace be placed squarely and absolutely symmetrically before the audience or, as in the Olivier production, should there be an off-center placement that disrupts and unbalances this basic formality? The first choice presses on the director patterns of formal movement, balanced arrangement of chorus, and a great symmetry in the overall action of the play; the second gives room for ambiguity and imbalance, for gaining disturbing and far more varied effects, for achieving mystery and sharper contrasts in placement and movement. These latter elements are the ones that the sixteenth-century mannerists pitted against the balanced beauties of the high Renaissance, that the early twentieth century, with its interests in African masks and primitive art forms, placed against the *beaux arts* tradition of the nineteenth century. This may appear to be too clear cut and obvious a choice, but a director of *Oedipus* will finally make this choice regarding every aspect of the production to a greater or lesser extent.

In planning costumes for *Oedipus*, the choice must be made as to whether the characters should look like fifth-century statues brought to life or whether it is desirable to stress the archaic, mysterious aspects of the play in order to make the production less remote, less connected

Figure 10–9a   A scene from the Tyrone Guthrie production of *Oedipus Rex* as produced at the Stratford Shakespearean Festival, Stratford, Ont., in 1955. Production designed by Tanya Moiseiwitsch. Courtesy of the Stratford Shakespearean Festival, Stratford, Ont. Photo by the Piper Studio, Ltd.

with book illustrations, and more related to current artistic and visual values (Figure 10–9a).

The decision the designer and director reach regarding masks will set the tone for everything else done with movement and costume. The use of masks, whether exaggerated or subtle, will move the production away from psychological realism, no matter what the director's approach. Masks immediately establish the illusion that the actor and the character are not one; they create the illusion of the play as ritual, ceremony, a working out of forces behind and beyond reality. Masks obviously work best in a theatre that is not too small, since the removal of the actor's personality from the audience seems to require that the audience be at a distance from the action of the play. In a small theatre, seating about 300 people, it might be best to use makeup that would remove the character to a plane above the personality of the actor, but in the average or large theatre, holding 700 to 1200 persons, masks may become an important and integral part of the ritualistic mood in a Greek tragedy.

In creating masks one must establish the right sense of balance between the outer form of the mask and the expression of personality through the mask. Fifth-century busts, statue heads, and statuettes are excellent sources as well as inspirations. The famous statue of Zeus from Cape Artemision (Figure 10–3a) is an excellent work from which to gain a sense of the strength, severity, and careful form that weighs as heavily with the viewer as the personality projected. This monumental head sums up the great balance between form and content, ritual and mystery, and naturalistic statement that provide the key to the great Greek tragedies by Sophocles—especially *Oedipus*. For this tragedy, to create masks that are too naturalistic is to neglect the sense of structure at work in the play; but to concentrate too much attention on the formal, archaic aspects of the mask is to lose the sense of individuality that is so important to the play. A compromise that is a balance between the formal and the naturalistic, carrying the best qualities of both, is the ideal. One of the problems with the famed Guthrie production of the play at Stratford, Ontario, in 1955 was that the masks tended to stress the theatrical aspects of archaism and formality at the expense of character. It is better to use fifth-century sculpture as source material rather than the theatrical masks in the sculptural interpretations of theatrical performance from Hellenistic or Roman times; these later sources indicate a self-conscious piling up of theatrical effect that is not compatible with *Oedipus*.

In designing the masks, one should be careful to keep them as lightweight as possible, fabricating them out of leather, light plastic, or fiberglass; and usually, for modern performance, it is wise to cut the mask entirely away around the mouth and chin for a three-quarter rather than a fully masked face. Visibility must be as full as possible, even if areas around the eyes must be made of open screening painted to look opaque; and the mask must fit the head to allow air to circulate within the mask for proper ventilation.

Next in order of importance to the costume designer of *Oedipus* is the question of the weight and line in the costumes. With the use of masks, the costumes must be fuller and scaled larger than in Greek civil dress, and the folds and draped lines must be of a scale that matches the masked face of the actor, not the actor without the mask. This often means shoulder padding to give the appropriate support to the draped lines of the garments, and possibly gloves to keep the hands from looking like tiny naked appendages appearing from the folds of a huge Greek chiton. Although garments for certain characters may have to show bare arms or legs, these should be kept to a minimum, and wherever possible the body should be treated as a completely covered and whole design. Great importance should be given to the correct weight and softness of the fabric so that the folds of the garments will have the size and monumentality that will suit the formal aspects of the play's structure and yet have the ease and pliability to make movement and characterization perfectly natural. Woolens are the obvious choice, but they must be exactly right if they are to capture a balance between formality and flexibility. One should guard, in particular, against relying for inspiration only on the subtle, soft beauties of late fifth-century sculptural draping. Although the draping may conjure up a picture of Greece, it does not take into account that *Oedipus* is a Greek tragedy. Costumes executed in nylon or rayon jersey will be beautiful but too feminine. It is also wise to forget actual Greek practice in the cut and drape of the chiton and to build the folds and draped lines into the costume when it is constructed. This will free the actor from any need to pose like Greek statuary, strengthen the form of the total figure when masked, and ensure that the costume retains its original designed form from one performance to another.

In matters of texture, there is a choice between a rougher texture that may take light with more interest and give a slightly more primitive feel to the production, or a flat and smoother texture that will reflect more light and give a more civilized atmosphere to the play. Something that is a balance between the two effects, perhaps wool with a maximum of drapability and a minimum of texture, is probably most desirable as long as the choice does not result in a dull textural surface that has no character. Textural variety among the costumes may be very desirable, but it must not confuse the overall visual plan for the production.

Color is often thought to be unimportant in costumes for Greek tragedy. Because the statuary that has remained from Greek times lacks color, we tend to see the plays in some neutral tone, with color appearing only in the ornamentation. We know, however, that Greek statuary was originally brilliantly colored, and we know that theatrical and civil dress used strong colors even during the fifth century. However, in tragedy the tendency is usually toward somber or neutral hues; and although more concentration on the strength of form and line in costume can come from less color, rich color can be very effective in small areas of ornamentation, borders of garments, and accessories. Color in the costumes is more effective if it is kept to a single hue for each costume and if color is subordinated to a limited scale of value. Despite the bright color used on Greek statuary, sharp contrasts of strong color from costume to costume are probably a mistake if one thinks about the way the script is written and the characters are developed.

In ornament one must decide whether to concentrate on simple flat patterns for the garments, which usually can be best derived from Greek vase painting, or whether to stress the three-dimensional ornamental effect of large accessories, including brooches, belts, bracelets, tiaras, and pins (Figure 10–9b). The strong three-dimensionality of the masks tends to suggest three-dimensional ornament, especially if the lighting is to give strong three-dimensional form to each actor. The flat, decorative effects of Greek vase painting do not seem compatible with the structural nature of *Oedipus*. Three-dimensional accessories of lightweight plastic can be painted to give a sense of weight and substance, and, with appropriate highlighting and shadowing, when properly lit these ornamental accessories can give great strength and focus to those areas of the costume on which they are used.

The costumes for *Oedipus* should create a world larger, older, and more severe than the world of fifth-century Greek statuary. They should be both ritualistic and mysterious—natural in the use of simple, severe masks, formal yet natural in the draped folds of the chiton. Color should be simple, subordinated and complemented by the lighting. Ornament should be strong, severe, simple, and used to focus attention on one or two key areas of the human figure (Figures 10–10a and 10–10b).

Figure 10–9b   Ray Reinhardt as Creon and Carol May Jenkins as Jocasta in the American Conservatory Theatre production of *Oedipus Rex,* directed by William Ball, designed by Robert Fletcher, 1970. Courtesy of the American Conservatory Theatre, San Francisco. Photo by Ganslen Studios.

Figure 10–10a   Design by Tanya Moiseiwitsch for Tiresias in the Tyrone Guthrie production of *Oedipus Rex* as produced at the Stratford Shakespearean Festival, Stratford, Ont., in 1955. Courtesy of the designer. Photo from the Tenth Season Souvenir Collection of Costume Designs, Stratford, Ont., 1962.

Roman Art and Drama

Although tradition reports that Rome was founded in the eighth century B.C., the culture was for a number of centuries, overshadowed by the Hellenistic influences of the Eastern Mediterranean. But Roman art did have a character of its own, just as did Roman drama. One way to contrast the two civilizations is to compare their respective sculpture. The Romans tended to use sculpture as portraiture in private homes or

Figure 10–10b   Donald Davis as Tiresias in the Tyrone Guthrie production of *Oedipus Rex,* 1955. Courtesy of the Stratford Shakespearean Festival, Stratford, Ont. Photo by Piper Studio, Ltd.

palaces, while the Greeks designed sculpture primarily for public monuments. Thus, Roman sculpture is far more naturalistic and less idealized than Greek; and in the Roman Empire, when painting became a more important art than sculpture, the stress was also on naturalistic, momentary illusionism (Figures 10–11a and 10–11b).

The Romans adopted for their drama most of the practices of the classical and Hellenistic theatre, yet they made many fresh and original contributions. At the time of Plautus and Terence in the second century B.C., the stages were temporary and probably consisted of bleachers arranged around a semicircular orchestra and backed by a five-foot wooden platform which was long and narrow and bounded by a wooden frame stage house at back and ends. The back wall probably had three openings, used in comedy as the entrances to houses. The stage usually became a street in front of the houses. This basic plan remained in force

Figure 10–11a *Head of a Man*, Lateran Museum, Rome, first century A.D. An excellent example of the solid realism in Roman sculpture. Photo courtesy of the Stanford University Art Department Slide Files.

Figure 10–11b *The Aldobrandini Wedding*, Roman fresco in the Vatican Museum, Rome, first century B.C. Photo courtesy of Alinari, Florence.

in the later permanent theatres, but there was a great increase in size and architectural elaboration (Figure 10–12). For example, the theatre at Orange in southern France, with a "scaenae frons" 118 feet high and 338 feet long covered with niches, statues, and columns, is obviously not suited for small comedies but only for the grandeur of the imperial spectacles that were so admired during the period of the Empire.

Costumes and masks in the Roman theatre of Plautus and Terence were based on those used in Greek New Comedy, but other playwrights, who stressed Roman settings and characters, used more native costumes and accessories. Most of the characters in the comedies are types or stock personalities, such as the old man, the young lover, and the parasitical servant, so costumes tended to be standardized, reflecting in color and line the occupation and age of the character. Even wigs were usually conventionalized in color, and masks completed the sense of exaggeration based on type. As in Greek theatre, masks allowed a full range of parts to be played by a limited number of actors (Figure 10–13).

In the plays themselves a number of changes took place during adaptation from the Greek. There was no chorus and no division into acts and scenes. Those divisions that appear today were added at a later time. Music was scattered through the action as in a modern musical rather than being placed in a formal manner. As in Greek New Comedy,

Figure 10–12   A reconstruction of the theatre at Ostia, 30–12 B.C. From D'Espouy, *Fragments d'architecture antique*, Vol. I, 1901.

Figure 10–13 Red figured Calyx-Krater, Italiote, early fourth century B.C. The scene from the *Phylakes* comedy of southern Italy deals with the ribald travesty of mythological subjects and heavily influenced Roman comedy. Photo courtesy of The Metropolitan Museum of Art, New York, Fletcher Fund, 1924.

the themes were everyday domestic affairs rather than political or civic problems; plots were based on mistaken identities, misunderstandings, lost children, lovers' problems, and parental obtuseness. In Plautus, a single relatively complicated plot is introduced by an expository prologue, while in Terence there is frequently a double plot and no prologue. The characters usually varied from about seven to fourteen; the most important figure was the rascally servant or slave, and the action invariably took place in the street in front of characters' houses.

The Menaechmi

STRUCTURE In his plot structure, Plautus subordinates everything to his main purpose of gaining comic effect from mistaken identity, and the story is very contrived in motivation, exits, entrances, and final resolution. In performance the inconsistencies go unnoticed, however, and only in retrospect do they become obvious. The playwright develops his material with great economy, eliminating everything that does not contribute to his principal aim.

CHARACTERIZATION   The characters are two-dimensional types, and this is often suggested by their names: Peniculus (the Broom), who cleans up the house; Erotium (Sensual Beauty), who is the courtesan; Cylindrus (Rolling Pin), who is the cook. All the characters are limited in motivation: the Menaechmi desire sensual gratification, the wife wishes to reform her husband, the father desires to keep peace in the family, and the doctor wants a patient on whom he can practice his quackery. The limitation in character portrayal makes for sharp, clear, uncomplicated roles, and the actors required to perform the roles would need to be highly trained in movement, timing, stage business, and rapid dialogue. The ability to portray a wide range and depth of human emotion is not required.

DIALOGUE   The dialogue in the play is direct and utilitarian. It is used for comic descriptions, to further the narrative action, and to make bawdy or boisterous jokes. It is not subtle and does not grow out of character; it is employed to keep the plot moving and to evoke laughter from the audience by matching an expression, a word, or a brief description to some physical action in the play.

THEME   The idea behind the play is not deep or penetrating, since the play is contrived purely for entertainment. It uses the simple device of twin brothers mistaken over and over again for one another until comic confusion dominates. There is no goal to educate or moralize. When the characters indulge in adultery, stealing, and deception, they merely contribute to the overall tone of good-humored cynicism that seems to lie behind the play.

RHYTHM   The rhythm in the play is fast paced and furious, with few stops for reflection. Only if a rapid-fire rhythm in the dialogue and a fast tempo in the physical action is maintained throughout will the audience be swept along with the boisterousness and general mood of merriment. The music, now lost, originally accompanied over one-half of the dialogue, and a number of songs were interspersed.

SPECTACLE   The scenery and costume requirements for the play are minimal. The original platform with a house for changes and properties at the rear is sufficient to suggest a street backed by a number of houses. The frequent eavesdropping that goes on suggests alcoves or projections in which characters can be concealed. The costumes are based on those from everyday Greek life, although seen through Roman eyes; and there is a strong stress on simplification and conventionalization according to social class, occupation, age, and sex. Although not required by the script, wigs and masks were, of course, part of the original production.

Visual Presentation of The Menaechmi *Today*

After looking briefly at the Roman comedy *The Menaechmi,* one is struck by its close similarity to a certain kind of modern American musical comedy. The use of song, the flute accompaniment to action, the coarse jokes, the flimsy plot, the juxtaposition of sentiment and vulgarity—all of these elements are reminiscent of the musical comedies of the 1920s and 1930s that made use of the best vaudevillians and burlesque entertainers, and reused hackneyed plots that had been serviceable for centuries. In fact, one of the best-remembered musicals of that era is *The Boys from Syracuse,* which is based on *The Menaechmi.*

Given the one-dimensional plot and characters and the similarity to certain early twentieth-century American musicals, the designer of *The Menaechmi,* even if he transposes the play to another period, will be inclined to use flat colors, sharp outlines, exaggerated forms, and lack of textural interest. If it is a Roman street, a modern street, or a street from some other era, the designer will tend to treat it in the exaggerated contours of the cartoon and the comic strip (Figure 10–14). The play has

Figure 10–14   A sketch for a setting of *The Casina* by Plautus, by Donald Oenslager. From *Scenery Then and Now* by Donald Oenslager, Norton, New York, 1936. Courtesy of Donald Oenslager.

even been done as a "Charlie Brown" cartoon, and the designs were very successful.

But what does this mean to the costume designer? First of all, it means that texture is not of major importance in the choice of fabric. In a script which has a strong sense of design and contrivance, it would be a mistake to stress fabric texture; as a result, light reflection and a tactile sense would take precedence over outline and color. In the costumes for *The Menaechmi*, one would not want changing light on texture, in mood, or in atmosphere. To return to our earlier discussion of polar opposites, the category of absolute clarity would be most suitable to this play. Line, form, and color must be simple and direct—not distorted, muted, or disguised by shifts in the effect of light on texture. Even the massed folds and draped lines of Greek and Roman statuary would be out of place in Roman comedy, since the depth and weight of fabric folds are analogous to depth and weight in the structure of the script. Whether one chooses soft or stiff fabrics—and this choice depends on how exaggerated and cartoon-like the production is to be—the fabrics should be almost without texture and cut and fitted with a minimum of folds and draped lines. To take a group of flat but relatively soft textures is to give a more natural look to the human form and to make the characters seem more human; to select a stiff set of fabrics that will tend to distort and exaggerate the human form, if cut and fitted for this purpose, is to make the play far less realistic and to approach more closely the modern cartoon strip.

The lines of the costumes should be simple and sharp in effect, with an emphasis on short broken lines rather than long, unbroken, vertical, diagonal, or horizontal lines. Only in this way will the lines of the costumes reflect the sharp, simple, direct characterizations and the short, broken nature of the rapid-fire dialogue. Also, there is a good deal of rough-and-tumble physical action. Only with costumes that make little or no use of long lines will the full movement potential in the play be achieved. Every costume should be as simple and as easy to work in as possible.

The matter of color has already been suggested by relating the play to the modern musical and the cartoon strip. This loud, hot, and boisterous comedy obviously requires colors that are direct, strong, and primary—the colors that are printed in cartoon books and Sunday supplements or the harsh, strong pigments in much abstract modern art. Subtlety of color is no more called for in this play than is subtlety of characterization.

In ornament, one might choose a few simple, exaggerated, flat forms and use them with little variation throughout the costumes. Again, linear design should take precedence over contour and three-dimensional depth of form. Often such ornamental decoration can be in linear black rather than color to act as an accent and an outline for the exaggerated movements of a character or the distorted outlines of his costume. Such use

Figure 10–15   Costume sketches for *The Menaechmi* by Plautus, by Betsy Leichleiter. Prepared as a class assignment in the Department of Drama, Stanford University. Courtesy of Betsy Leichleiter.

of a heavy black line in ornamentation is very like the black outlines in the cartoon strip, the flat print, or an illustration. Ornamentation, such as three-dimensional jewelry, buckles, and headdresses, should definitely be subordinate to the strong use of linear ornamentation. The best inspiration for this kind of ornamentation as originally used in *The Menaechmi* comes from the vase painting, statuettes, and illustrated manuscripts that show Roman and Greek comedy figures in action. Vase paintings dealing with comic subject matter are particularly helpful in suggesting the strong, linear ornamentation appropriate for this play; statuettes showing figures from Roman comedy are especially helpful in indicating the effectiveness of the short lines in the costumes.

For the accessories, one would have to take a long look at the statuettes still available to us before deciding whether to use masks, wigs, and built-up areas of the human body. The masks would be effective for exaggerating the character of the actor but would hide any effective facial expressions. They would also create a problem when viewed at close hand, since they would make the already stereotyped characters seem even more unreal. To perform *The Menaechmi* in a large theatre would defeat the purpose of having audience and actors in close contact throughout the play for asides and direct statements to the audience. If masks are not used, then one should use a stylized makeup that will make the human faces match some of the distortions and exaggerations in the sets and costumes. Even if masks are not worn, it might be advisable to use wigs occasionally, just to have another major item near the actor's face for strong linear exaggeration in line and form. The same is true of built-up padding on the human figure. If one uses a hunchback, enlarged buttocks, exaggerated feet, and a protruding phallus, one approximates the spirit of the original and makes the comic exaggerations in costume line and form fit the nature of the body wearing the costume.

Finally, there is the key technical question that must be answered by the costume designer: can the twins be made to look exactly alike if no masks are used? If the two people are exactly the same size and have similarly shaped faces, it is usually possible with the use of hats, wigs, and carefully exaggerated makeup to make them look enough alike to fit the demands of the play (Figure 10–15).

In looking at *The Menaechmi,* then, as a problem for the costume designer, one is struck forcibly by the direct connection between the play's structure and characters and their visual equivalent in the line, texture, and color. No matter what the period of the costumes or what the approach used in the direction of the play, the visual equivalents to the plot structure and characterizations are so insistent that the range of variety in visual choices is quite effectively limited.

11

Medieval Plays

Medieval Art and Thought

It has long been fashionable in brief surveys of medieval art and theatre to speak of the Dark Ages as a barbaric backsliding from the naturalism, logic, and organization of Greece and Rome. However, it has also often been written that there were several rises to cultural peaks that did attempt to reestablish classical culture during the thousand years following the fall of Rome, and that the Italian Renaissance was the final full return to the ideals of Greece and Rome. Although there are many similarities, the Italian Renaissance was more than just a return to the ideals of antiquity; the Carolingian and Ottonian revivals of the ninth and tenth centuries and the classical Gothic of the thirteenth century are not classical in method, although they do borrow classical images. As was brilliantly pointed out by Henry Adams in *Mont St. Michel and Chartres,* the thought behind the art of the medieval period is so opposed to the logic and rationalism of classical art that it is illogical even at its most logical— unless the dual world of heaven and earth presented by Aquinas and Dante is completely understood. The Italian Renaissance really was different from both the medieval period and classical antiquity in its nostalgia for the classical past and in its self-conscious desire to affirm the dignity of man in a universe of beauty and logic. And the medieval period, even when it copied directly from antiquity, had a logic that related its art neither to the Renaissance nor to Greece and Rome. Medieval thought always attempted the impossible balance between the world of nature and the world of the spirit, and the subtleties of the scholastic method devised to bring order to this double world could not reduce the

266

degree of contradiction between flesh and spirit. The strain in Dante is severe, and every ledge of Purgatory is a theatre for human beings striving to master their human passions and reconcile them with God's will. Dante clearly presents the two poles: the ideal order of a universe expressing God's unchanging will, and the changing life of each human being who feels the pain of existence. This double vision of reality in the Middle Ages is reflected in the great Gothic cathedrals, in which the aspiring leap to overcome the solidity of the walls and the enclosure of space is opposed by a sense of strain and instability—a sense of danger in those soaring towers and overreaching vaults (Figure 11–1a).

The Gothic period differs from the Romanesque and Carolingian periods in giving man a more central location in art; but even though a cer-

Figure 11–1a   Notre Dame Cathedral, Paris. Example of transitional to high Gothic architecture, 1163–1250. Photo courtesy of the French Government Tourist Office.

tain growing humanism gives much more emphasis to man in nature in this world, it always sees man in relation to the hereafter and the divine. In looking at any aspect of art in the late medieval period, one is aware of the conflict between the personal and the abstract, the logical and the transcendental, the historic and the timeless. Only when full reliance had been placed on man's abilities and powers can we say that the Gothic was superceded by the Renaissance. It arrived when the artist and scientist succeeded in imposing mathematical and aesthetic theories on the loose discoveries of medieval empiricism. It is this empiricism, however, that created the great Gothic cathedrals and their negation of the inert, solid, block-like structures of Romanesque architecture. Gothic architecture rejected the idea of architecture as the enclosure of space. By forming and penetrating it rather than defining and encompassing it, it became a framing device for sculpture and stained glass—an illustrated book of knowledge for the religious community. Illuminated manuscripts and missals could be deciphered only by monks and scholars, but everyone

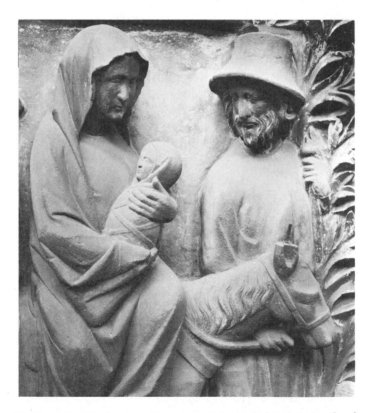

Figure 11–1b *The Flight into Egypt,* a sculptural detail from the facade of Notre Dame Cathedral, Paris, late thirteenth century. The scene shows the combination of realism and idealism in Gothic art. Photo courtesy of Jean Roubier, Paris.

Figure 11–1c *Annunciation to the Shepherds,* two scenes from the Sacramentary of Fulda, Bamberg Library, Germany, second half of the eleventh century. The scene shows the use of properties and framing devices to present the subject matter as scenes from a play. Photo courtesy of the Stanford University Art Department Slide Files.

went to the House of the Lord to worship and learn. One "read" a Gothic cathedral inside and out, in glass or wood, gilded metal or stone, and this Gothic world of flesh and spirit is crowded with intensely human anecdotes, stories, and details presented in a simple linear fashion (Figures 11–1b and 11–1c). In the medallions of a stained glass window, in the statues arranged within a cathedral porch, or in the movement of figures in a manuscript there is a simple, linear progression. Gothic literature also accepts this arrangement of episodes (as in the Mystery plays) in which compartmentalized scenes are presented one after another until the cycle is complete. This one-dimensional story telling is often referred to as processional, because the scenes, dramatic as they may be, do not fit into a unified plot or scheme. The stories lack a dramatic focus, a point of crisis to which all characters and acts converge to form a climax. Gothic art gives us dramatic episodes with very human actors, but it cannot furnish the proper stage and the proper space for an entirely humanist drama.

Medieval Theatre and Drama

Although records show actors and mimes wandering from place to place in the early Middle Ages, the revival of the drama as a part of medieval culture came only with the use of dramatic interludes within the services of the Church. It has never been clear why the Church began to use these dramatic interludes, but the answer seems to be that the Church leaders hoped to make the lessons and the stories more vivid and interesting. Also, since the majority of parishioners could not understand Latin, such dramatizations were added to the already important use of ritual and spectacle to give Church doctrine simplicity, directness, and power.

Figure 11–2 *The Angel Appearing to St. Anne* by Giotto, Scrovegni Chapel, Padua, ca. 1306. An example in painting of the use of theatrical mansions used to stage a scene from the Bible. Photo courtesy of Alinari, Florence.

The two most important dates in the Christian calendar were quite naturally Christmas and Easter, and it was in connection with the services devoted to these holidays that the first short dramatizations developed. By the time the Church moved these dramatized episodes outside to the square in front of the cathedral, the placement of the scenes within the cathedral had become the standard plan that was to remain for most outdoor presentations of religious plays. The altar remained the key point of focus, with little booths or *mansions* set up in the two aisles of the cathedral to mark the place and character of the individual dramatized episodes. These mansions are identical in many ways with the little compartments or framing niches that appear as a framework for the religious scenes and characters that adorn the inside and outside of the cathedral, and they indicate vividly how strong was the influence from art to drama and from drama back to art (Figure 11–2). The area around the individual mansions, which became much more open when the drama moved outdoors, was called the *platea* or "place" and was the neutral playing space within which actors could move from one mansion to another as the action demanded.

In the staging of these plays, there came to be three or four widely used variations besides the open layout in the cathedral square: there was the rectangular platform arrangement on which the various mansions were arranged in an actual linear progression from left to right; there was the pageant wagon method by which each mansion, built on a wagon, moved from corner to corner and square to square throughout the city until all the mobile mansions had stopped and the playlets had been played to the full audience; while still another variation was to use Roman or other primitive amphitheatres as a setting for a circular arrangement of mansions around a central platea. But in all medieval staging there were certain elements that remained basically the same: there was always a series of mansions surrounded by a generalized area; the performances were composed of a series of plays, each more or less complete but tied to the preceding and succeeding play by the position of the story in the Bible or in other Church literature; each cycle of plays made use, in one or more of the plays, of three planes of action, Heaven, Earth, and Hell; and finally, there was a great attempt to make special and miraculous effects as convincingly realistic as possible (Figures 11–3a and 11–3b).

To achieve these special effects a considerable amount of stage machinery was invented, and there was a real determination to make the miraculous events from the Bible as real as possible, so that no doubts about Church doctrine would be raised in the minds of the audience. The major area of concentration in special effects was the Hellmouth, with its fire and smoke and the horrific reality of the devils who emerged from Hell equipped with terrifying masks, tails, claws, cloven hoofs, and exploding fireworks. The costumes and equipment for such devils can be easily seen in the gargoyles of the great cathedrals and in the sculptural programs dealing with the Last Judgment. One can imagine how artists

Figure 11–3a   The stage for the Passion Play produced at Valenciennes, France, in 1547. The various mansions, reading from the left, represent Paradise, Nazareth, the Temple, Jerusalem, a palace, the golden door, the sea, and the mouth of Hell. From a manuscript in the Bibliothèque **Nationale,** Paris. Photo courtesy of the Bibliothèque Nationale.

delighted in depicting these monsters, and producers of the cycle plays took inspiration from the figures they found carved on the exteriors of the churches. In costumes there was a mixture of everyday wear with elaborate overlaid accessories, and when saints and important Biblical personages appeared they usually carried a specific visual symbol which was associated with them throughout the presentation. The costumes of heavenly figures were supposed to inspire awe and reverence, those of Hell

Figure 11–3b   Scene from the Valenciennes Passion Play showing the simultaneous depiction of several scenes involving Christ's curing of the paralytic and the woman with dropsy. Photo courtesy of the Bibliothèque Nationale, Paris.

Figure 11–4   Scene from a production of *Master Pierre Pathelin,* as produced by the Drama Department of Florida State University in 1952. The play was produced on a platform at the end of a hall against simple cut-out mansions. Photo by the author.

were to arouse scorn and terror. Only the common man in such plays appeared as he would in everyday life, a representative of the common man of medieval society caught between the supernatural forces of good and evil.

There were, of course, in the late medieval period, play forms other than the liturgical dramas or Mystery plays. The best known of these are Miracle plays, about the lives of the saints; Morality plays, such as the famous *Everyman;* and secular plays such as *Master Pierre Pathelin.* All were short and included only one or two major incidents, and all are more important for a study of the beginnings of the Renaissance than for an understanding of medieval thought and culture (Figure 11–4).

The Second Shepherd's Play

Probably the single play that is most widely read and seen from the list of English cycle plays is *The Second Shepherd's Play* from the Wakefield Cycle of Mystery dramas. It is the thirteenth play in a long group of thirty-two short playlets dramatizing key Biblical events from the Creation to the Last Judgment.

PLOT AND STRUCTURE   The plot is based on the simple statement in the Book of Luke about the Shepherds who watched over their flocks near Bethlehem when the Angel of the Lord came to announce the birth of the Christ child. The author elaborated and enriched this idea with comic detail, farcical humor, and a strong feeling for contemporary medieval peasant life. This short narrative puts together what may seem to us opposing ideas of supernatural spirituality and earthy, farcical reality. With our religious outlook we cannot envisage placing a scene about the farcical problems of a stolen sheep in the same context with a scene depicting the Nativity, but such a juxtaposition of elements typifies the completely unself-conscious religious thought of the medieval peasant and also vividly illustrates the duality of thought in all medieval art.

CHARACTERIZATION   There are only seven roles in this short play, and all the parts would, almost certainly, have been played by men. In fact, the actor playing Gil may well have doubled in the part of the Virgin Mary, and the Christ child was probably a doll. The shepherds and Mak are simply but effectively characterized as peasants, and the age for all characters is indeterminate except for one shepherd who is a boy. There is little psychological development of character aside from one or two obvious traits for each person. The three shepherds are differentiated merely by the personal problem each indicates at the opening, and all are shown to be basically kind and generous. In fact, it is the generous instinct to give Gil's baby a gift that finally unmasks Mak and his deed. Mak himself is portrayed as a simple but clever thief who is rather cowardly and henpecked. The part must be played by an actor of great skill who can communicate one thing to the audience and another to the shepherds, while making expert use of comic timing. His wife, Gil, who is both clever and shrewish, must be a close second to his action and comic timing. The religious figures of Mary and the Angel of the Lord are seen as typical religious stereotypes.

Physical action throughout is reasonably realistic, although transitional actions such as the shepherds falling asleep and the trip to Mak's house are missing. Thus, many details that are not indicated in the script would have to be supplied by the actors. There are also several demands for song, so the shepherds, Mak, and the Angel must all be capable singers.

DIALOGUE   The dialogue is very simple and has a naive chanted rhythm through its persistent use of obvious rhymed endings. Yet the play contains some beautifully simple, unpretentious phrases that completely illuminate a scene or a character with a minimum of effort. Although probably written by an unlearned author and consequently containing many crudities, the dialogue has an easy and elastic quality that allows it to follow all of the shifts in inflection, pace, and mood.

THEME   The most important theme is, of course, man's basic sinfulness and the need for a Saviour. The play's structure is two-part—a demonstration of sin followed by the possibility of redemption. The shepherds represent the audience personality, Mak represents the sinners who need to be saved, and the Christ child is the symbol of God come to man.

RHYTHM   The rhythm is the same processional, linear unrolling of action that we have discussed as being the basis for most medieval art, while the music that is included in the action highlights this simple, linear rhythm. The musical requirements are quite simple: the first song would undoubtedly be a contemporary popular song, while the Gloria and the shepherds' final song would have been taken from contemporary Church music.

SPECTACLE   The play calls for three scenes—the fields, Mak's house, and the stable at Bethlehem. Whether three mansions would have been required is doubtful; probably the same mansion could have been adapted for Mak's house and the Nativity, while the fields would have been in the open surrounding area. The mansion for the house would need a curtain to hide Gil and Mak when they were not on stage, as well as a door, a cradle, and a bed. If the mansion were placed on a pageant wagon, it is logical to assume that it would pull up to another flat-bedded wagon, or a stationary platform, which could then act as the open area of the fields.

The costume demands are minimal: the shepherds and Mak would wear the tunics or smocks of the medieval peasant, Gil would wear the skirt and blouse of a lower-class woman, and only the Angel and Mary would require some richer ecclesiastical garments as symbols of authority. The Angel would certainly need wings, while Mary would require an upper-class medieval garment embellished with the symbols usually associated with the Mother of God.

Visual Presentation of
The Second Shepherd's Play *Today*

The mood created by any physical arrangement for one of the medieval Mystery plays should approximate the small-scale, naive, realistic method of the medieval artisans, even if strong modern stylization is employed. The craftsmen who did the settings for the medieval Mystery plays were the same men who adorned the cathedrals, chapter houses, and monasteries; over and over again, as one looks at a sculptured Nativity or Last Judgment, one is struck by the theatrical groupings of character and a sense of a recorded moment in a playlet or drama. In a modern production this same sense of vivid, personal, naive decorative reality should be the ideal.

Since the medieval artisans gave full attention to ornamental detail and the individual pieces of stage property, no attempt was made to unify figures and background in a single space-time perspective. The modern designer should stress the discontinuity between the size of the characters and their backgrounds, the decorative unreality of ornamental detail, the continual shift from the real to the unreal. Just as Gothic art places very human actors in realistic "business" in an unrealistic framework, so should a modern production work diligently to capture the very real duality between the worldly and the unworldly that is operative in the Mystery plays.

Obviously, there is an abudance of source material to use as a basis for one's choice of line, texture, and color in the re-creation of a medieval Mystery play, but the danger is in becoming too involved with some specific source (stained glass, manuscript, or sculpture) and allowing the designs for a production to be quaint recreations of some historical art form. One must capture the essence of the medieval usage of line, texture, and color within the duality of effect mentioned above. In medieval times color was used very directly and without complicated gradations and mixtures of hue. One usually thinks of the chalky colors of a Giotto fresco or the bright, clear, undiluted colors of stained glass, manuscript illumination, or heraldry. Line is the all-important item in medieval art, culminating in the fascinating arabesques and decorative linear effects of the international Gothic style of the late fourteenth and fifteenth centuries. Here depth, shadow, and highlight are all subordinate to the fascinating, delicate play of a serpentine line that creates pattern before it creates reality. Texture is secondary to line in medieval art and comes forward only as a surface of the particular media being used: the flat shiny surface of the manuscript, the hard surface of stone, the brilliant transparency of stained glass.

With these abstract elements in mind and the plan to use one or possibly two mansions to represent Mak's cottage and the Nativity scene, what would be the specific design problems involved in a modern presentation of *The Second Shepherd's Play?*

The most important visual idea to be borrowed from medieval art is the processional or linear unrolling of the play so that the various locales are visible at once and characters move from episode to episode without leaving the stage. Usually the physical re-creation of the pageant wagon would be unnecessarily academic, and the more practical arrangement would be to have the mansions (if separate frames are needed for Mak's house and the Nativity) arranged on a rectangular platform stage or grouped in an open "in the round" arrangement.

In producing some of the Mystery plays, one might wish to make use of the double-level arrangement found in so many medieval manuscripts and tympana sculpture; but, for this play, a mansion with a single level is all that is required, and a traverse curtain could be used to indicate the move from outdoors to indoors. One also has to make a decision about the nature of the mansion or mansions to be used. Is it to be a structural pavilion that has no decoration and can be used for any number of scenes, or is it to have a specific interior and exterior design, which would make it imperative to have a different mansion for Mak's house and the Nativity scene? If it has decoration, can it be abstract enough so that the same pavilion can be used for both interior scenes, and what should be the nature of the decoration? Is it relatively rich and architecturally decorative like the frames around a manuscript scene or the pavilion surrounding a cathedral front scene, or is its decoration a suggestion of a shed or hut as in a Giotto fresco? The major choice would be whether to place the play in a decorative architectural framework that might be used for other plays in the cycle or to place it in a basic structural mansion that gives no decorative frame to the action. The designer and director need to make the choice between architectural decoration (which may contrast with the realistic action) or a simple frame for the action.

However, there would seem to be no problem with the few properties and set pieces required. By the very nature of the play and the nature of medieval play production, it would be best to make them all simple and realistic. When one considers the costumes to be designed for *The Second Shepherd's Play,* the requirements are so simple that a mere catalogue of the script's demands would be enough to guide one in choosing from a wardrobe of tunics, tights, and simple gowns. But if the subtle ideals of medieval art are to be projected by the costumes, careful planning and designing must take place.

Figure 11–5 *Shepherds in the Fields,* west portal, Chartres Cathedral, early thirteenth century. An example of the naive simplicity and faith to be found in early Gothic sculpture. Photo courtesy of Jean Roubier, Paris.

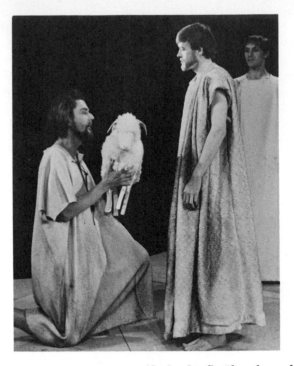

Figure 11–6   A scene from *The Second Shepherd's Play*, from the Wakefield Cycle of Mystery plays, as produced by the Mermaid Theatre, Puddle Dock, London, 1965. Courtesy of the Mermaid Theatre. Photo by Adam Wolfitt.

Since the shepherds and Mak are the key figures in the play, let us consider their costumes first. They would require tunics, tights, soft shoes, and, possibly, a hood for one and a short cloak for another; the youngest shepherd should probably be without cloak or hood. But how should these simple items of clothing look? A famous section of the royal portal from Chartres Cathedral depicts two shepherds with their sheep, and here we can get an excellent idea of the simple costume requirements for this play (Figure 11–5). Note that the most important item that strikes the eye after one absorbs the overall simplicity and naiveté of the scene is the stress on line to achieve decorative effect. The draping of the hood and collar on the shepherd to the left, the folds on the sleeve of his tunic, the wrinkles in the hose of the cloaked shepherd—all make a decorative linear statement. This means that in choosing the fabric for such simple costumes and in cutting them to fit the actor, great pains should be taken to re-create these decorative wrinkles and folds. A very soft and pliable wool would be the most appropriate fabric choice, and linings in the sleeves and under the tights and torso might be necessary so that certain drapings and folds could be sewn permanently in place. The period during which these statues were carved has often been called classical Gothic because of the great formal beauty of the cathedrals and their decoration; it is the simple yet often detailed beauty of the sculpture of this period that gives it a classical note. This balance of naive simplicity and beauty can be admirably adapted to the costumes for the shepherds, and in this way the naive charm of the opening, the farcical humor of the middle scenes, and the religious beauty of the final scene can all be met (Figure 11–6).

12

Renaissance Plays

Art and Culture in the Fifteenth and Sixteenth Centuries

Traditionally, the Renaissance is thought to have begun in Florence at the beginning of the fifteenth century as a reaction against medieval modes of thought. It was an age of burgeoning thought about all aspects of the natural world and an age of rebirth of interest in the art and ideas of antiquity. The historians and philosophers of the nineteenth and early twentieth centuries conceived of the Renaissance as an age that rediscovered man and his world, an age that rose to its highest achievement in Italy at the time of Michelangelo, Raphael, and Leonardo, only to fall gradually into decadence during the following century. A few moments of distinction, like those in Cervantes' Spain and Shakespeare's England, brightened the decline. Today, this is considered to be a romantic and oversimplified view of the Renaissance, and the two centuries from 1400 to 1600 are usually divided into three very separate and distinct artistic periods.

First, the fifteenth century, until approximately 1485 or 1490, is considered to be an age of experimentation—a period of conscious, consistent, objective analysis of the natural world. It was not that naturalism suddenly burst on the scene for the first time, but rather that a new and scientific view of reality triumphed in fifteenth-century Italy. The beautiful curving lines and flat decorative patterns of the international Gothic style gave way to the art of Masaccio, Donatello, and Bruneleschi, who stressed tactile form, mathematical precision, dignity, simplicity, and compactness (Figures 12–1a, 12–1b, and 9–6a). The feeling of this new art was unmetaphysical, unsymbolic, unromantic, and unceremonial, and it stood as a guide for all later fifteenth-century artists to analyze and dissect.

Second, the period known as the high Renaissance, which lasted only about a generation from 1490 to the death of Raphael in 1520, was a period of innovation by several men of genius who were given great scope for their artistic ideas by the Popes in Rome. Several powerful and worldly Popes, including Alexander VI, Julius II, and Leo X, were determined to use the full resources of art to achieve the strongest possible statement of Church authority. The works of Michelangelo, Leonardo, Bramante, and Raphael (in many ways a culmination of the artistic experiments of the fifteenth century) were also something new, based on the absolutism, unity, and power exercised by the towering figures of authority (Figure 12–2).

Third, the years following the death of Raphael are today seen not as a decline in art but as a move toward personal interpretation and even distortion of reality, derived from inner convictions on the part of artists. The optimism of the early Renaissance waned at the beginning of the sixteenth century with the many invasions of Italy, the rise of the Ref-

Figure 12–1a   The Pazzi Chapel, Church of Santa Croce, by Filippo Bruneleschi, Florence, ca. 1430–1433. An early Renaissance example of slender classical arcading used to form the colonnaded loggia facing a public square. Photo courtesy of Alinari, Florence.

ormation, and the final horror of the sack of Rome in 1527. A malaise and disillusionment arose among certain artists, who are today labeled *mannerists*. These artists deliberately distorted and exaggerated many artistic ideals of the Renaissance in order to gain disturbing psychological effects (Figures 12–3a and 12–3b). And, because the ideals of the sixteenth-century Renaissance in Italy spread to the rest of Europe, the art of England, France, Germany, and Spain naturally adopted a mixture of Re-

Figure 12–1b   *The Lame Man Healed by the Shadow of St. Peter* by Masaccio, Brancacci Chapel, Sta. Maria del Carmine, Florence, ca. 1427 (fresco). An early example of solemnity, weight, carefully controlled highlight and shade, and a fully unified perspective layout combined in a monumental work by one of the founders of the Florentine Renaissance. Photo courtesy of Alinari, Florence.

Figure 12–2 *The David* by Michelangelo, The Academy, Florence, 1501–1504 (marble). An example of the heroic scale, monumental grandeur, and unified emotional power of the high Renaissance. Photo courtesy of Alinari, Florence.

Figure 12–3a *The Rape of the Sabines* by Bologna, Loggia dei Lanzi, Florence, 1583 (marble). An example of the self-conscious, artificial, choreographed exercise in spiral movement and forced emotion that characterize much late sixteenth-century mannerist art. Photo courtesy of Alinari, Florence.

naissance precepts and mannerist interpretations. The artists who moved north from Italy after Raphael's death were only nominally of the Renaissance. Although they knew its methods, they were psychologically mannerists, creating and teaching an art that was personal, distorted, ambiguous, and unnatural. During the late years of Henry VIII's reign and most of Elizabeth's reign, this art sifted north to England, and conditioned the artistic and cultural setting in which Shakespeare flourished.

Figure 12–3b *The Last Supper* by Tintoretto, The Church of San Giorgio Maggiore, Venice, 1592–1594. The exaggerated perspective, brilliant night light, and self-consciously choreographed action create a sense of mystery and theatricality in the work of Tintoretto, El Greco, and other late mannerist painters. Photo courtesy of Alinari, Florence.

Theatre and Drama in the Fifteenth and Sixteenth Centuries

ITALIAN COURT THEATRE   With the revival of interest in classical antiquity during the early years of the fifteenth century in Italy, an interest in the plays and theatres of Greece and Rome also developed. This interest is clearly evident even in Shakespeare, in plays such as *Julius Caesar* and *Antony and Cleopatra*.

The books of the Roman architect Vitruvius included much information about the theatre of classical times, but they were first published in 1486 without supporting illustrations. By the beginning of the sixteenth century, with illustrations added, his books were known throughout Europe. This interest in classical staging soon led to a demand for production, and by the late fifteenth century most of the cultured princes and dukes of the small Italian states were using festivals of plays to demonstrate the high development of art and culture at their individual courts (Figure 12–4). In many artistic centers there were academies of intellectuals organized solely to study the arts of antiquity, and they too staged plays to demonstrate their knowledge of the classical past. Both courts and academies used their own members in performance, costumes and scenery were usually done by a local court painter or architect, and the plays were written, adapted, or translated by authors under royal patronage. Actors at court were aristocratic members of the royal household, while in the academies they were chosen from the membership (Figure 12–5).

The staging in these theatres stemmed from two sources—the permanent theatre background described by Vitruvius and the contemporary fascination with perspective in painting. Productions were usually staged in a hall where the stage and auditorium were specifically designed and built for each new production. Although we have many sketches and engravings of such court presentations, the first treatise on the subject did not appear until the architect Serlio devoted a section to theatre in his great work on architecture in 1545. His scenes for both comedy and tragedy are the street scenes of Roman comedy translated into a perspective

Figure 12–4 Perspective scene from *L'Ortensio*, Siena, 1560: from the wood-cut by H. Bols after B. Neroni in the Victoria and Albert Museum, London. An example of perspective scenery in Italy in the middle of the sixteenth century involving a raked stage, canvas wings of diminishing size, and a painted backcloth. Photo courtesy of the Victoria and Albert Museum.

setting; with no thought of a permanent theatre, there is no proscenium frame. No provision for shifting is indicated, since the background is seen as being continuous for each production.

The first permanent theatre to be built for the production of classical plays was the Teatro Olimpico in Vicenza. Designed by the renowned architect Andrea Palladio for the Olympic Academy, it opened in 1585 with a performance of *Oedipus Rex*. Here Vitruvius' plan for a Roman theatre was followed quite closely, and the influence of perspective is very evident in, for example, the alleyways designed to slope up visually behind the doors of the facade. These streets, entirely fixed, could not be shifted, and, in face of the growing demand for shifting scenery and more spectacle, this structure was old-fashioned even at the time it was built (Figure 12–6).

The final form of the Renaissance theatre does not appear until the dawn of the Baroque era, when a permanent framing device (prosce-

Figure 12–5   Designs for costumes in the Florentine "Intermezzi" of 1589: from the original drawing by Bernardo Buonalenti in the Victoria and Albert Museum, London. An example of the fantasy of design and ornament, based on the classical chiton with overfold, that developed in mannerist theatrical designs during the sixteenth century. Photo courtesy of the Victoria and Albert Museum.

Figure 12–6   The stage of the Teatro Olimpico at Vicenza with Palladio's *scenae frons,* 1580, and Scamozzi's added perspective vistas, 1585. An example of the strong interest in the theatre of classical antiquity coupled with the Renaissance preoccupation with perspective. Courtesy of the Norman Philbrick Library. Photo by Keeble and Shuchat.

nium) was built into the Teatro Farnese in Parma in 1618. A combined inheritance, the proscenium uses an enlargement of the central doorway of the Roman theatre in conjunction with the picture-frame idea derived from the perspective school of the Italian Renaissance. By restricting the audience's view with scenery in perspective, the stage machinery for shifting scenes became more effective; with the possibility of full stage illusion, the Baroque age of opera was ushered in.

COMMEDIA DELL'ARTE   Alongside the dramas of court and academy, Italy nurtured the *commedia dell'arte*—groups of itinerant professional

Figure 12–7   A sketch of two figures from the *commedia dell'arte* by Jacques Callot, ca. 1620. Callot's sketches of Italian comedy figures vividly capture the gay, exuberant crudity of early seventeenth-century Italian popular theatre. Photo courtesy of the National Gallery of Art, Washington, D.C., Rosenwald Collection.

actors who toured the countryside playing standard stock characters from an improvised script. The lovers (the straight parts in the action) were handsome, sympathetic, and did not wear masks. The three most famous older characters (who wore masks) were the Pantalone, a miserly Venetian merchant; the Dottore, a long-winded pedant or lawyer who loved long speeches filled with bad Latin; and the Capitano, a boasting soldier who talked of conquests in love and war only to prove the craven coward in the end. To complement these older types there were the comic servants or *zanni*—witty rogues who thought up every conceivable trick and deception to discomfit the older "masks." Usually one or two female servants, with names such as Colombina, Rosetta, Francischina, and Olivetta, attended the young girls in the scenario and furthered the love complications of the plot. They usually received the amorous attentions of the zanni. All of the actors developed set speeches as well as clever bits of business, known as *lazzi*, which were used to spark audience interest whenever the plot or action began to lag (Figure 12–7).

The *commedia dell'arte,* which literally means comedy done by professionals, may well have descended from the farce comedy of ancient Rome, preserved in some limited way through the Middle Ages. It sprang into prominence in the middle of the sixteenth century and spread to all of Europe by the second or third decade of the seventeenth century, appearing as an influence in Shakespeare's comedies as early as the last decade of the sixteenth century. It continued as a powerful influence on literary drama and formal stage presentation up to the opening of the nineteenth century.

POPULAR THEATRE IN SPAIN AND ENGLAND In two European countries where there developed a strong national spirit and a native culture not affected by the limiting rules of neoclassicism, a native drama and a popular theatre grew up that rivaled the Golden Age of Greece. In both England and Spain at the beginning of the sixteenth century, small groups of wandering professional actors, although treated as outcasts from society, were patronized for the exciting if limited theatrical fare they had to offer. Such actors were not recognized legally in the two countries until after the founding of permanent theatres in London and Madrid in the last quarter of the century.

In England the drama that began to emerge was a mixture of influences: school and university plays, which had been performed by amateurs since the beginning of the century; dramas staged by the young lawyers training at the Inns of Court; and the popular playlets derived from the medieval interludes and folk dramas that toured the country. The new plays were frequently a curious mixture of elements from early native drama and the new classical learning. In Spain the dramatic inheritance was similar, although in the plays of one of the most prolific of Spanish playwrights, Lope de Vega, the scope of subject matter—the Bible, saints' lives, mythology, romance, history, and folklore—was far broader than in Shakespeare.

The physical theatre in England in the late sixteenth century was of two types: the outdoor public theatre and the indoor private theatre. Although both were open to the public, the indoor theatres charged higher prices and played to a more select audience. A number of famous public playhouses were built in London between 1576 and 1615, but aside from limited information about The Globe, The Fortune, and The Swan, few concrete facts survive to guide us in building reconstructions of the Elizabethan stage. Usually round, square, or polygonal, the theatres held between 2000 and 3000 persons, who stood in the central yard or pit or sat under roofed balconies surrounding the yard. The stage, a raised platform, projected into the center of the yard. A roof supported by pillars partially covered the stage, which was backed either by a wall with doors, or by an open inner stage flanked by large doors. An upper stage above this inner stage could be used for scenes requiring a second level. Scholars still disagree as to whether the inner and upper stages were permanent features of the theatre, or whether they were constructed only for specific productions. Despite disagreements about specific forms, the basic layout can be deduced from the plays: a large platform reaching out into the pit audience; a door on each side at the rear of the stage; a pavilion or curtained inner stage for "discovering" actors at the opening of a scene; an upper area or stage; windows above the doors on each

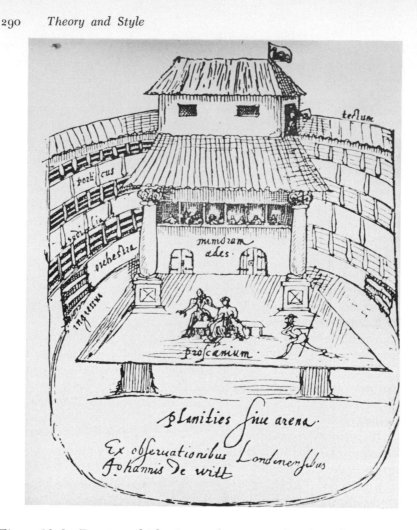

Figure 12–8   Drawing of The Swan Theatre, London, by Johannes de Witt, 1596. The only contemporary drawing of the Elizabethan stage, showing a partially covered platform projecting into the yard, which was surrounded by balconies for spectators and backed by two doors and a stage balcony. From Johannes de Witt's sketch as copied by Arend van Buchell.

side of the stage; and a third level for musicians that could be used for supernatural appearances (Figure 12–8).

The lists of a theatrical businessman, Philip Henslowe, describe the minimal scenery used on the Elizabethan stage; rocks, trees, furniture, Hellmouths, some kind of backcloth representing Rome; no large-scale scenic effects, however, are indicated. Machinery housed below the stage allowed for the appearance of ghosts through trapdoors in the stage floor, while cranes, ropes, and pulleys permitted objects and people to be raised to the upper stage. Resources were also available for producing fire and smoke as well as the sound of cannons, bells, thunder, and other sound effects.

Since performances took place in the daytime, lighting was not required, although torches, candles, and lanterns were used to indicate night scenes. Costumes were of two basic kinds: symbolic and contemporary. Symbolic costumes, used to represent gods, supernatural creatures, animals, exotic foreign characters, and servants in livery, were built specifically for the company wardrobes; all contemporary items (worn by the majority of actors in a production) were usually donations from the households of those noblemen who sponsored the particular troupe (Figure 12–9). The troupes themselves usually included ten to twenty members, some of whom were shareholders and realized a certain percentage of the profits; all other actors and backstage personnel were hired at a fixed fee. The company also had young boys, who served as apprentices, to play all the female roles. As for the audience, it consisted of all levels of society, from the nobility in the balcony or on the sides of the stage to the "groundlings" who stood in the yard.

Public theatres in Madrid were in many ways very similar to those in London. Existing courtyards formed by the walls of houses were often remodeled so that surrounding balconies could be used to seat the nobility, while common people either stood or were seated on benches in the yard. The stage, raised on trestles at one end, did not jut out into the yard as in England, so it was observed only from one side and not from three. However, it did have a curtained inner stage and a balcony that served as an upper stage.

In both England and Spain, strong dramatic and theatrical traditions

Figure 12–9   A sketch from a production of *Titus Andronicus*, 1595. An example of the mixture of contemporary and classical dress on the Elizabethan stage. From the original drawing in the possession of the Marquess of Bath. Courtesy of the Marquess of Bath.

Figure 12–10a   A scene from the final act of *Romeo and Juliet*. An example of the sentimental, romantic approach to Shakespearean production in the late eighteenth and early nineteenth centuries. From the 1785 edition of Bell's *Shakespeare*. Courtesy of the Norman Philbrick Library. Photo by Keeble and Shuchat.

were well established before the arrival from Italy of the neoclassical ideas of writing and staging. In England and Spain, theatrical development was a logical and relatively smooth outgrowth of medieval tradition, and there was never a sharp division between entertainment for the court and that for the common man. In fact, much of the strength of the English and Spanish drama arises from the fact that it was written and performed for all classes.

In both countries, the rigid rules of neoclassicism that had developed in Italy were never fully accepted, and the idiosyncracies of style that did develop in the drama were more natural, less self-conscious, and freer than were those that developed in Italy. Although mannerism in art and literature was an international style by the close of the sixteenth century, it was infinitely varied and complex, and each European country expressed the cultural, political, and religious problems of the century in a very personal and dramatic way.

Shakespeare as a Renaissance Playwright

In the nineteenth century it was assumed that the greatest playwright in the English language and the most popular playwright in the history of the Western world was a product of the Renaissance (Figures 12–10a and 12–10b). This limited view of the Renaissance combined a religious outlook borrowed from medieval philosophy and the best elements of Renaissance humanism. Only in recent years, with the careful study of Renaissance mannerism as the major artistic style of the sixteenth cen-

Figure 12–10b   A drawing of Act I, scene 2 of *Hamlet* as presented at the Lyceum Theatre, London, 1874. An example of the romantic pageantry in Shakespearean production in the nineteenth century. From a scrapbook of Marvin Clarkson. Courtesy of the Norman Philbrick Library. Photo by Keeble and Shuchat.

tury, have critics begun to realize the complexity of Shakespeare's genius. In the nineteenth century his work appeared to be more or less all of one piece, except for certain so-called "inferior" works. Today, when we see the fifteenth century as being primarily an age of scientific analysis of man and nature, we view the turn into the sixteenth century as a period in which art reached a balanced, unified peak known as the high Renaissance. Later sixteenth-century art is then seen not as a decline of Renaissance ideals but as a departure from the unified view of the outer world to the inner world of mannerism. Today we see elements of all of these shifting styles in Shakespeare's plays, just as Michelangelo's works reveal elements ranging from late medieval concepts through artistic ideals of the early and high Renaissance to mannerist ambiguities and proto-Baroque concepts. Shakespeare seems to have been endowed with the genius to absorb and make use of all the cross currents of cultural and artistic life available in the world in which he lived. No scientist or academician, Shakespeare could hardly have written his plays according to rigid theories of unity, proportion, and balance, but he was able to construct his plays psychologically and scenically from dramatic perspectives involving the entire spectrum of methodology from late medieval to Baroque.

In his first chronicle plays, Shakespeare uses a late Gothic or medieval organization, allowing his material to unroll in a processional series of scenes arranged in much the same way as the individual playlets of the great religious cycles. Then, in the early dramas that follow, more form is added, and in comedies such as *Two Gentlemen of Verona* and *Love's Labour's Lost* and the tragedy *Romeo and Juliet* he seems to enter upon an early Renaissance phase. One senses the lightness of touch, the artificial paring of figures, the balanced use of poetic line, and the foreground depth of characterization against a flat plane of two-dimensional background, which has the effect of destroying any "middle ground." These were all effects found in the fifteenth-century Renaissance. Even the values represented in these plays fall into symmetrical patterns of love and hate, rashness and caution, wit and grief, purity and sensuality, day and night, life and death. Although Shakespeare is too free to be described as high Renaissance or classical in his writing, his handling of the subject matter and development of mood in *Julius Caesar* (especially in the forum scene) reminds one of the balanced organization of Raphael's *School of Athens* (Figure 12–11). But Shakespeare lived in a mannerist age, and as the positive outlook of England began to fade along with the health of the aging Queen Elizabeth, Shakespeare came to his most brilliant period of tragic and tragicomic writing in plays such as *Hamlet, King Lear,* and *Measure for Measure.* These works have all the ambiguity, theatricality, and psychological subtlety of mannerism as an art form. Throughout the first decade of the seventeenth century, Shakespeare developed his work along mannerist lines intermingled with elements from the Renaissance past and the future Baroque. The con-

Figure 12–11   *The School of Athens* by Raphael, Stanza della Segnatura, Vatican Palace, Rome, 1508–1513. The balanced organization in this painting is in some ways analogous to the composition of the forum scene in *Julius Caesar*. Photo courtesy of Alinari, Florence.

tinuous mixture of tragic and comic motifs, the contrast between the concrete and the abstract, the play of sensual language against intellectual language, the forced ornamental character of his structure, the emphasis on the contradictory and the unfathomable in life, the compulsions versus the restraints in human psychology—all these are elements linking the bulk of Shakespeare's work with mannerism. Only in the late romances, including *Cymbeline, Winter's Tale*, and *The Tempest*, do we achieve certain visual qualities, a certain calm, symphonic beauty, a progression in clear movement to a final climax that suggests Baroque characteristics within an ornamental, mannerist structure.

Romeo and Juliet

Looking at one of the most famous of Shakespeare's early plays and realizing how much his imagination and creative insight worked on a legendary tale of tragic, star-crossed lovers, we see in *Romeo and Juliet* a play filled with an instinctive understanding of the Renaissance spirit of organization and composition. The action is confined by walls, orchards, squares, and rooms in a manner that reminds one of the geometric composition of Italian fifteenth-century painting.

PLOT AND STRUCTURE   Even at first glance, the mechanics of the plot and its compositional plan seem rather obvious and possibly too clear. The contrasting movements of the plot are arranged like the converging lines in a perspective drawing, and a heightened sense of drama is achieved by forcing the perspective a bit so that there is no middle ground in the play. There are only foreground characters and those who are part of the background. If one recalls his first reading of the play, it is fascinating to note that the visual impression, as well as the organizational principle, reminds one of a scene from Botticelli, a bronze panel from the doors of the Florence Baptistry by Ghiberti, or a crowded scene by Fra Filippo Lippi rather than any of the paintings by Shakespeare's mannerist contemporaries, such as Tintoretto or El Greco.

The Prologue, read by the chorus, sets up the image of the star-crossed lovers. It is an objective framing device that places the story of the family feud clearly before us, suggests the ominous movement of fate, and removes the tale to the level of a legend. It is immediately followed by a clear-cut demonstration of the symmetrically conceived feud which erupts against the backdrop of a square in Verona. The balance of the opposing enmities is given a central focus in the figure of the Prince, who remains above and outside the quarrel. In the final act, all the balanced and symmetrically developed forces converge on a tableau that exemplifies the tragic beauty of the story's ending—the centrally placed bodies of the two young lovers, the flanking members of the two reunited families to right and left, and the benedictory figure of the Prince presiding over his dead kinsmen.

CHARACTERIZATION   The characters in this play are as carefully balanced against one another as are the various scenes and tableaux in the script. Romeo is scaled against Paris and Mercutio; Juliet is placed against Rosaline, the Nurse, and Lady Capulet; Tybalt against Benvolio; Capulet against Montague.

Aside from the two protagonists, the characters may be arranged in two groups. The first and largest includes all the supernumeraries, minor characters such as Peter and the Apothecary, and a few relatively important figures such as Tybalt, the Capulets, Paris, and Benvolio. These are all static, flat characters who are by nature what they are; they present a limited range of values and make the plot operable. Tybalt is choleric and determined to pick quarrels; Benvolio is equally determined to avoid them; Paris is pleasant, bland, with no surprises; the Nurse is garrulous, corruptible, and insensitive, and as long as there is no emergency she is also amusing. They all represent standard types in a representative human community, but their vitality tempts the audience with the possibility that they have more dimension than they actually possess.

The second group consists of three characters who give a doubly strong impression of life because they have qualities of real understanding and perception. The Prince knows from the beginning that keeping peace in Verona is a matter of life and death, and in the end he readily takes his share of responsibility for the tragic deaths in the tomb. Friar Lawrence, also, has from the start a clear perception of the danger and takes steps appropriate to his position to avert disaster. However, unlike the Prince, who moves openly, the Friar works in secret, and his secrecy ultimately betrays both him and the others. Mercutio, the third member of this group, is the character whose action at the moment of the play's crisis is on the threshold of accomplishing what neither the Prince nor his well-intentioned ingenuity had been able to do; but Romeo's sentimental action destroys all. It is Mercutio in his death speech who keeps this key moment in the play from becoming overt melodrama.

Finally, in Romeo and Juliet we have a full development of personality. From the beginning, Juliet is more mature; it is Juliet who leads the conversation in their two great scenes together, and it is she who knows through love what language cannot say, what cannot be expressed in words. She can conjure up the full range of the death images in the potion scene, yet when she wakes to find Romeo lifeless she cannot muster any language to help her deal with such a horror. Romeo's most mature speech is the one he delivers in the tomb, in which he gives dignity, meaning, and finality to the one act that he executes without the help of friends, the Friar, or Juliet. The courtly conventions, borrowed puns, and paradoxes of his earlier scenes are gone, and he achieves a manly directness and power to act in his last scene in the play.

THEME   Just as the characterizations fall into balanced patterns, so do the values that one finds within the play. The theme of love versus hate, courtly love versus romantic love, rashness versus caution, tolerance versus intolerance, or the contrasted ideas of wit and grief, purity and sensuality, day and night—all of these are presented as neatly balanced opposites framed with a Prologue by the Chorus and an Epilogue by the Prince. They set up the play as a tale which exemplifies the relentless mechanics of fate. The major theme of star-crossed lovers is kept before the audience even when the plot seems to hinge on the vagaries of accident; the secondary theme of evil and tragedy that must of necessity arise from a feud between two families is kept as a backdrop or recurring motif throughout the action.

DIALOGUE   The dialogue is noted for its poetic and lyrical values and is tightly organized by the sonnet form—rhyming couplets at the conclusion of a scene. These give symmetrical balance, polish, and a frame to the lyrical beauty of a scene. The language is also admirably adapted to the individual characters and the romantic mood of the play. Shakespeare easily catches the wide range in the social scale from the servingman to the Prince: the Nurse's peasant speech, the country gentry talk of old

Capulet, Mercutio's love for the sensuousness and richness of language, Tybalt's narrow and sharp-tongued insolence, Friar Lawrence's moralizing sententiousness, and even the tiny voice of the complaisant Apothecary. The personalities are simply but fully developed, and they unfold in a natural and direct way through language.

In analogy with the visual arts, it can be said that the language of the play has the lightness of touch, the clarity, the richness and sparkle of fifteenth-century painting. The dialogue in *Romeo and Juliet* is analogous to the color palette of Botticelli or Lippi.

RHYTHM   The rhythm of the play shifts from the light, almost comedic note of the first two acts to a more somber note after the banishment of Romeo. In the changes of mood from street to orchard to ball to upper chamber, we experience shifts from the realistic to the lyrical, from pageantry to simplicity. Only after the banishment, when the scenes follow as night rather than day scenes and tightly enclosed rather than open, do we sense the play rushing to a tragic close. It is this breathless pace of action which is the dominant note in the drama; it is time that runs out in this play, and Shakespeare has used every device to make haste and speed part of the play's rhythm.

SPECTACLE   The various scenes in the play come vividly and clearly to life in the imagination, and each setting offers a clearly marked-off space with characters in the foreground and a measured distance to the background. There seem to be no unlocalized areas; even street scenes seem to be specific. And on the Elizabethan stage much depends on a clear, localized use of the various stage areas: the inner area above for Juliet's bedroom, one of the windows for the balcony scene, the tomb placed in the study below, the doors at either side of the stage for the entrances of the two families. Although the pace of the action cannot allow for a perspective box setting for each major scene, on reading the play one envisions a series of balanced, one-point perspective scenes, and the characters always seem to be foreground accents against the changing backgrounds.

Visual Presentation of Romeo and Juliet *Today*

In staging a production of *Romeo and Juliet* in the contemporary theatre, the director is faced with a major dilemma in choosing the visual background. (Figure 12–12). Stopping after each scene even for backdrop changes is unthinkable because of the pace demanded in the action, and an intermission after the banishment of Romeo seems the only logical break in the forward movement of the play. Thus, the director and his stage designer must devise a method that allows for speed of action coupled with a sense of quite separate stage areas. The Elizabethan stage design provides one solution to this problem by presenting the director with clear-cut areas including the study, the inner area above, the side doors, the forestage, and the windows above the side doors. The end of a scene can take place in one area of the stage, while the following scene may begin in quite another area without stopping the action. For example, Act II, scene 1 (which is set near the orchard and includes Mercutio and Benvolio and a hidden Romeo) is in a space that is clearly "outside" the orchard wall, yet the rhyme scheme that ends the scene is directly tied into the beginning of the following scene "inside" the orchard. Both spaces must be on stage at the same time and yet be clearly differentiated. Following the discovery of Juliet after the potion scene, it is important (for dramatic impact) that the space of her bedroom and her bed within it be visible throughout the action of mourning, and especially during the arrival of the musicians and Count Paris for the wedding. Only if the bed (with the supposed dead body of Juliet) is clearly in evidence when Paris learns of the death, and we can see the flowers and the musicians below contrasted with the mourning in the

Figure 12–12 Act III, scene 1 from *Romeo and Juliet* as produced by the Shakespeare Memorial Theatre, Stratford-upon-Avon, England, 1954, with scenery and costumes by Motley. Photo reproduced by permission of the Governors of the Royal Shakespeare Theatre, Stratford-upon-Avon, England.

bedroom above, can the full dramatic impact of the scene be visually accomplished. Even the short, ironic scene which follows, showing Peter exchanging pleasantries with the musicians, is more effective when it is contrasted with the visual presence of Juliet above, lying on her bed.

The director is usually forced to discard the idea of a set for each scene if he wishes to gain the full visual impact required by the space relationships suggested by developments in the action. This can, however, still be done within the multiple-space relationships suggested in early Renaissance painting: two places, or inside and outside, are often shown together in a single scene. The problem in trying to approach the setting in this manner is, again, one of time for scene changes, and most directors feel that it cannot be spared. A compromise is usually the result in contemporary productions of this play. The mood of early Italian Renaissance painting is often retained in the design forms and decorative elements of the production, while the space arrangements of the setting are analogous to those available on the Elizabethan stage. Some arrangement of steps, doors, windows, and platforms is often designed to give an upper area for the bedroom and the balcony while a raised area is reserved for the Prince, side doors are used for entrances to a street, a large area is available for the ballroom scene, and a small enclosed forward area can be suggested for Friar Lawrence's cell. Within this space arrangement, which does not change during the action, the designer may then work to create the symmetrical forms, simplicity of line and ornament, and the environment that suggests the architecture, painting, and sculpture of the early Italian Renaissance. Even when a period other than the fifteenth century in Italy is used as a setting for the play, the designer, if he is going to work from the structural nature of the script, will feel bound to treat the Renaissance elements in a simple, direct way, with stress on slenderness of proportions, balance and symmetry in structure, lightness and clarity in color, and a delicacy in ornamentation. *Romeo and Juliet* is a play of youth, and the fifteenth century is an age of experiment and youthfulness; it is this quality that must be placed visually before the audience no matter what historical period is chosen for the production. For example, if the play is done in the same period in which it was written, that is, within the artistic styles of the late sixteenth century, the designer must strive to exclude from the designs the twisted complexities, ambiguities, and grotesqueries of mannerist art; he must use simpler architectural and costume lines to suggest a world of strict symmetry, rich simplicity, and youthful exuberance.

When considering the costume design problems in *Romeo and Juliet*, it should already be quite apparent that the most natural period in which to do this play is fifteenth-century Italian Renaissance (Figure 12–13). This period suits both the geographical setting of the story and the mood, characters, and decorative background required by the script. Choosing another period would require a search for artistic effects analogous to

MOTLEY.54

Figure 12–13 Costume design for Mercutio by Motley for a production of *Romeo and Juliet* at the Memorial Theatre, Stratford-upon-Avon, England, 1954. From the Souvenir Program for 1954. Photo reproduced by permission of the Governors of the Royal Shakespeare Theatre, Stratford-upon-Avon, England.

the costume ideals of the Italian Renaissance. For example, an artist who has been requested to design the play for Elizabethan staging must work diligently to lighten the mannerist costume lines, remove the heavy decoration, choose lighter fabrics, avoid exaggerated underpinning and stiffening to make the costumes of 1590 have some of the movement, color, and feeling of the Italian costumes of 1490.

Examining the problem of line in the costumes for this play, the demand seems to be for balance, symmetry, simplicity, and beauty of proportion. Clean-cut, simple lines seem to be necessary in the costumes, including pleated jackets, long skirts, mantles, and robes for ease and

Figure 12–14a   Original sketches for Paris and Tybalt by Lee Simonson for a production of *Romeo and Juliet* as produced by the Stanford Players, Stanford University, 1949. Photo courtesy of Special Collections, Stanford University Libraries.

beauty of movement. Natural body lines, without grotesque exaggeration or distortion, should be stressed, and each costume should have a single central area of focus such as the neckline, collar, chest, or waist. Whatever the period, simple, clear-cut forms in collars, sleeves, hats, dresses, and jackets should be used to suggest the same simple, clear-cut, and balanced lines that are in the script. The heavy romanticism that frequently was poured into the visual presentation of this play in the nineteenth and twentieth centuries is not compatible with the nature of the script. It is the delicate romanticism of Botticelli and other early Renaissance painters that must find its way into the costumes for this play (Figure 9–4a).

Selecting fabrics for a production of *Romeo and Juliet* may take several directions. One is to choose the soft, supple movement and flat surfaces of the woolens seen in fifteenth-century Italian paintings and thus allow the beauty of the folds, accented by a minimum of well-placed ornament, to be the dominant costume effect. Another would be to use the soft, transparent effects of Botticelli's draping with soft sheen fabrics to achieve costumes that are very effective in movement under light.

Another might be to use soft brocades as accents in sleeves, underskirts, and robes, keeping the brocade subordinate to the overall color tonality of the costume. This would give a rich effect and should be carefully controlled if the simplicity and youthful freshness portrayed in the script is to be retained. No matter what the period, the fabrics should not be heavy or stiff, nor their surface texture too complex.

In color the costumes should incorporate the overall blond tonality of the Italian fifteenth-century painters and make little use of the complex light and dark patterns of Shakespeare's contemporaries such as El Greco and Tintoretto. The color should have the freshness, clarity and sparkle of spring or early summer, with darker accents to give sharpness and clarity to the design. Even in the later scenes, when the tone is tragic and the scenes are set at night, the costume colors, although they might be lowered in value, should not be grayed or muddied. Clarity should remain even in the darker colors required by the concluding scenes of the play (Figures 12–14a and 12–14b).

The ornament for a production of *Romeo and Juliet* should be clean-cut, symmetrically placed, and used to carry the eye to the key

Figure 12–14b   Original sketches for Prince Escalus and a man-at-arms by Lee Simonson for a production of *Romeo and Juliet* as produced by the Stanford Players, Stanford University, 1949. Photo courtesy of Special Collections, Stanford University Libraries.

points on the costume. Again the asymmetrical, twisted, complex ornamental patterns of late sixteenth-century mannerism, even though this
is the period in which the play was written, seem completely inap-
propriate to this play's structure and imagery. The costume ornament
should have the kind of clear-cut organization, sparkle, and brilliance
characteristic of the Queen Mab speech, or the paintings of Botticelli,
da Cossa, and Fra Filippo Lippi. The ornament used in the costume designs must not be merely added to the costumes for decoration, but must
be integral to the line of the total costume. The best ornament or trim
for this play includes accents of brocade in sleeves, tiny borders of braid

Figure 12–15   Costume designs for Prince Escalus and attendants by Ann
Roth, for a production of *Romeo and Juliet* as presented at the American
Shakespeare Festival Theatre, Stratford, Conn., 1965. From *Designing and
Making Stage Costumes* by Motley, Watson-Guptill, New York, 1964. Cour-
tesy of Ann Roth.

or gems, small amounts of jewelry, and contrasting linings in sleeves, capes, and robes. Basically, it is the simple structure of the costume itself that creates the major decorative or ornamental effect. (Figure 12–15).

Hamlet

With the opening of the seventeenth century and the writing of his first great "dark tragedy," *Hamlet*, we find that Shakespeare has revised all the dimensions of his dramatic art. England after the Essex rebellion had taken on the trappings of a police state, and, as had happened more than a half-century before in the rest of Europe, a heavy disillusionment and despair took hold of the land and its people. The national pride and patriotic excitement that had accompanied the defeat of the Armada had waned, and in Elizabeth's last few years the country had to look forward to the reign of a foreigner from Scotland. England, which had borrowed only casually from the mannerist styles of the continent since the days of Henry VIII and had used mannerist ideas only in an ornamental way, now had its own optimism shaken and began to accept the disproportions, complexities, and ambiguities of mannerism as a deeply felt expression of the social and psychological disturbances of the time. Hamlet resides in this new world; his mind is tainted, his heart is heavy, he feels there is something rotten in the state, he is obsessed with an almost medieval sense of death. It is for this character, within this tainted world, that Shakespeare devises a whole new technique of dramatic art.

PLOT AND STRUCTURE   It was Aristotle's belief that a well-constructed plot for tragedy should be single in issue; and if any action were to be displaced or removed, the whole structure would be disjointed. The action of *Hamlet* is far from single in issue, and the principal effect of the play is to present the audience with a multiple sense of action that leaves it with a sense of ambiguity and disturbance. Everywhere there seems to be a double statement, a psychological inner world and a concrete outer world; and Hamlet certainly takes this double view of the world, seeing life as a bad dream as well as a horrible reality. Along with other characters in the later Jacobean theatre, Hamlet takes a violently dramatic view of reality. Although his acts seem to be involved with ordinary experience, they are also driven by some obsessive psychology that exists outside the usual ethical-moral world. His insecurity and psychological torment are presented within a framework of scenes shifting from comedy to horror, sanity to madness, brilliant external pageantry to almost impenetrable inner thought. There is also the shift within the same scene from inward emotion to outward action without clear transition, from foreground soliloquy to background pageantry without the usual sense of logic.

Throughout the plot all the characters, in one way or another, share a concern for the welfare of Denmark, but this is the only truth that remains constant. Generally, the truths of this play are unstable and changing, presented either at a high pitch, near hysteria, or so low that they are almost inaudible. All of this is the hallmark of mannerist composition and structure.

CHARACTERIZATION   The characterizations in this play seem ambiguous, operating on two levels as psychological relationships and symbols of the state's decay. The playwriting method used allows abrupt shifts from the deeply psychological to the symbolic and has equally violent shifts of idea and personality within each of these dual levels. One of the major reasons for the sense of instability in this play stems from the character of Hamlet, who is of a mercurial temperament— outgoing yet inward, almost in the same instant. He is a compendium of the contrasts that are evident in all human nature. Even outwardly he must be interpreted both as the typical avenger in a melodrama and as the complex and introspective Prince, powerless to act. Repeatedly, we see the characterization of Hamlet developing from opposing impulses, and the only explicit line of transformation and development that recurs throughout the play is his attitude toward death as it progresses from "To be or not to be" to the Graveyard Scene and finally to "the readiness is all" speech. Throughout the play Hamlet acts as the guide for audience feeling—thinking and mirroring, as the Chorus often did in Greek drama, all the hopes and fears of mankind. In mannerist terms he is like the *Sprecher* or Speaker in paintings by Tintoretto and El Greco—a sharply accented figure in the foreground who faces the spectator while gesturing or glancing toward the background action. Hamlet, through his soliloquies at the edge of the stage, is the intermediate figure leading the audience from the theatrical situation on stage to the nontheatrical world outside, from the world of events to the world of the inner mind.

Each of the other major characters is used to provide contrast to Hamlet and to give a particular view of the state's ill health. All act indirectly; all have a bias, a very partial view of the facts; and all help to define the action. In short, each has a dominant drive placed in opposition or relation to the conflicting motives that drive Hamlet forward through the play.

THEME   The themes of this play are many, but they tend to group about the psychological contrast of father-son and mother-son relationships and the political disease that saps the strength and power of a state. The themes are from many points of view strikingly like those in *Oedipus*, in which the father-son and mother-son relationships are the key to the play, and society must be purged before the plague (or the rottenness in the state) is lifted. Both plays begin with an invocation to the well-being of the state; in both the destiny of the individual and of the society are closely intertwined, and in both the suffering of the royal victim seems to be necessary before purgation and renewal can be achieved. These themes are achieved in *Hamlet* through a series of ritual scenes that are ceremonious invocations of the well-being of society, while in *Oedipus* the whole play is a ritual; and the theme of order in the Rennaissance monarchy is a direct successor to the theme of order in the cosmic framework presided over by the Greek gods.

DIALOGUE   Shakespeare's dramatic poetry in this play is immensely complex. The use of blank verse allows for great flexibility, broken rhythms, and the interjection of prose, while still permitting great formality and elevation of tone when required. The most important element is the imagery developed by the figurative use of language. It provides visual associations, sharp contrasts, and ironic descriptions that portray in a mysterious, ambiguous, yet vivid way the condition of sickness that pervades the state and all who live in it. The pictorial imagination behind the imagery suggests the path of any sickness or infection which strikes, spreads, and finally devours the innocent and the guilty together.

The use of language in the play is firmly designed to create the most sensory impact possible on the audience. For example, the famous description, "What a piece of work is Man," lifts optimistic imagery to great heights, only to be turned inside out by the ironic last line, in which Hamlet indicates his own bitter point of view. Throughout the play, language is used in this same shifting way to build contrasting, changing, complicated images of life.

RHYTHM   The forward pace and rhythm of action in a play such as *Hamlet* is very much complicated by sharp shifts in the mood, texture, and force of the action. The rhythm created by moving from intimate soliloquy to large-scale pageantry, from softly whispered dialogue to shouted verbal climaxes reveals the internal design of the play as seeming to run the gamut of contrasting emotions. The rhythm constantly changes from tension to relaxation, and the audience is never certain what rhythmic pattern will come next.

SPECTACLE   There are three great opportunities for visual splendor and pageantry in the play: the opening court scene, the scene in which the play within the play is presented, and the final duel scene. Each of these ritual ceremonial scenes, representing the social order in the decaying state, allows for full visual splendor. The action of the play takes place in many locales, most of which are in and around the Castle of Elsinore. The play requires the suggestion of many passageways and rooms within the palace, a great hall, a parapet, a graveyard, and even a plain away from the castle. These, in Shakespeare's time, would have been placed in the various areas of the Elizabethan stage. Properties are limited to thrones, tables, chairs, a bed, a grave, and a funeral bier. In contributing to the spectacle, costumes are important in establishing the ritual and ceremony of court life, the mystical quality of the Ghost, the horror of Ophelia's madness, the mourning of Hamlet, and the coldness of the night on the parapet.

Visual Presentation of Hamlet *Today*

The first choice that must be made in presenting *Hamlet* is whether to reproduce the locations found on the Elizabethan stage or to plan a new arrangement. In many ways there is a great advantage in having the upper stage for the parapet, the trap center stage for the grave, the full width from door to door with courtiers above for the large court scenes; but there is also a sense of rigidity and a lack of rhythmic flow when the stage space is not designed specifically for the structural arrangements of the play. If a choice is possible, it would seem better to retain those elements of the Elizabethan stage that really do further the rhythmic flow and structural development of the play, and incorporate them into a plan for stage space which contains the sharp contrasts and tensions of this mannerist composition. The necessity for a forestage is primary. Hamlet, acting like the *Sprecher* in mannerist painting, must come forward and commune directly with the audience and then move upstage to join the pageantry of a larger scene (Figure 12–16).

Another very important consideration is the disposition of the space available for the three great scenes of ritual pageantry. Is the area for the thrones of Claudius and Gertrude to be upstage center, to the right or left downstage, or down close to the forestage? This placement is especially important for viewing the play within the play. The director must decide whether his audience is to read through the backs of the King and Queen to the Players, glance at them on the other side of the stage while watching the play, or observe the Players performing downstage in front of Claudius and Gertrude. To solve the problem of spatial arrangement artistically and effectively is in many ways to set the artistic style and production approach for the entire play. The mannerist qualities in the play's structure will profit most by an asymmetrical, unconventional placement that will give a sense of imbalance and discomfort to the unraveling events of the scene. And then again, the conventional symmetrical plan usually selected for the duel scene would profit from a certain sense of imbalance through placement of the thrones and the grouping of the courtiers. However, an upstage center blocking of Fortinbras would serve to conclude the play on a stable note of balance and order.

Tintoretto's *The Last Supper,* from San Giorgio Maggiore in Venice, with its tilted diagonal composition, sharp shifts in placement and focus, and strong eruptions of light against darkness, is an artistic work that affects the viewer very much like the play *Hamlet* (Figure 12–3b). It

Figure 12–16   Horatio, Osric, and Hamlet, from a production of *Hamlet* as presented by the Stratford Shakespearean Festival, Stratford, Ont., 1957, with scenery and costumes by Desmond Heeley. Courtesy of the Stratford Shakespearean Festival, Stratford, Ont. Photo by Herb Nott & Co., Ltd.

stresses a ritual moment during the Last Supper that in its torchlit, sulphurous, supernatural illumination is analogous to that moment when Claudius rises and rushes from the scene calling for lights. A visual work such as *The Last Supper* cannot be used in any literal way to design this scene in *Hamlet*, but it can serve as an excellent stimulus for the creative imagination and as a visual catalyst for the images and impressions suggested by the play. It can also reinforce the importance of mood, ambiguity, tension, and mystery that are more important in this play than the actual contours of the setting. It is the disposition of space, use of lighting, and establishment of mood through suggested texture and placement of forms, not a specific period style of architectural ornament, that are the keys to a good background for *Hamlet*.

The period chosen for the costumes is relatively unimportant. It is the appropriate choice of texture, line, and color to reinforce the tensions, sharp contrasts, mysteries, and shifting planes of reality that will aid in creating exciting costume designs. For example, a painting such as *The Burial of Count Orgaz* by El Greco, a contemporary of Shakespeare, might become an exciting visual inspiration for *Hamlet* costumes (see Figure 4–9). Although the color in this painting has none of the ease of color transitions found in high Renaissance painting, the sulphurous yellows, heavy golds, acid greens, and unpleasant magenta reds against large background accents of white, gray, and black give an immediate sense of dramatic and theatrical impact. The stiff, crackling satin folds and the heavy brocaded immobility of the robes produce disturbing contrasts. The heavily ornamented armor of the Count completely contrasts with the dead black costumes of the courtiers surrounding him, and the black figure of the boy in the left foreground is in sharp contrast to the rich red and gold robes of the Saints. One can imaginatively identify this boyish foreground figure as Hamlet, while the rich, complicated, and over-large patterns of gold brocade accented with red and white worn by the Church fathers could be used as mantles for Claudius and Gertrude. The Count's armor could be used as inspiration for the Ghost, the black noblemen behind the dead Count as the basis

Figure 12–17   Costume design by the author for Claudius in a production of *Hamlet* as presented by the Stanford Players, Stanford University, 1963. From the collection of the author.

for many of the Danish courtiers required in *Hamlet,* and the cowled Jesuit priests as ominous accents in the court scenes. The magentas, greens, and yellows used as accents in Heaven might be used effectively as accents in the mantles or short gowns of characters such as Rosencrantz and Guildenstern, while the Player King and Queen might be dressed in mantles of black and white to mirror the patterns in the robes of Claudius and Gertrude. This transference of images captures the inner qualities and techniques of mannerist style without depending on a specific period line. Consider, as a second example, the work of a painter completely removed from the period of Shakespeare, Caspar David Friedrich. A German Romantic painter of the early nineteenth century (with many mannerist tendencies), he painted lonely scenes of figures silhouetted in moonlight against gnarled and broken trees, misty harbors and rocks, open windows at sunset, all of which create a sense of pessimism, mystery, and profound melancholy. These works, although lacking the compositional distortions of mannerism, could be used as visual images for a production of *Hamlet* set in the 1820s. By stressing silhouette rather than ornamentation and accessories, using color as melancholic accents against black, exaggerating line, and trying for an ominous sense of decay in certain textural accents, a production of *Hamlet* could be placed in the early nineteenth century. With costumes related strongly to mood as well as to the structure of the play, the result would certainly be both Romantic and mannerist in its effect on the audience (Figure 12–17).

The period chosen as a setting for a production of *Hamlet* is therefore unimportant compared to the choice of the line, texture, and color in the costumes. These must suit the compositional or structural plan of the play and its overall mood of mystery and ambiguity. The play has been successfully produced in every historical period from the early medieval to the present. The measure of success is never the novelty and cleverness of the choice but the sensitivity in choosing fabrics, colors, and ornament, and the integration of these into appropriate costume lines.

The play in its color emphasis suggests a great deal of black, shot through with harsh, peculiar, misty, or offbeat accents of color. Color contrast should often be sharp and even shocking, and the color scheme should at no time be restful, easy, or relaxed. Even when little color is used and stress is placed on value contrasts created by light, these should be strong and the effects dramatic.

For texture, the range of fabrics can be great but should always be chosen for sharply varied effects and a strong tactile response. Subtle gradations in texture from a soft napped surface to one of elegantly refined fur, or from a soft woolen to a heavier one, should be put aside in favor of sharp textural contrasts and abrupt shifts in tactile effect.

If the actual texture of fabric is to be unimportant compared to the line or silhouette of the costume, then these same contrasts should be seen in the exaggeration of line or in the imbalance of silhouette. To use

Figure 12–18   Costume designs for Hamlet, Claudius, Horatio, and Ophelia for a production of *Hamlet* as presented at the Shakespeare Memorial Theatre, Stratford-upon-Avon, England, 1956. From the Souvenir Program for 1956. Photo reproduced by permission of the Governors of the Royal Shakespeare Theatre, Stratford-upon-Avon, England.

the normal fashion line from a particular period is to lose the ominous mystery of the play. This is especially true of the women in the play; if one places Ophelia or Gertrude in the fashionable lines of the late eighteenth century, the early nineteenth century, or the twentieth century, the structure and the mood of the play are completely destroyed by the associations these fashions have for the audience. By abstracting the costume silhouette to its simplest form and then exaggerating those lines that will give a sense of the ambiguities, contrasts, and sharp changes in rhythm, theatrical gowns can be created to reinforce the meaning and mood of the play, rather than illustrate or pictorialize Ophelia or Gertrude within a particular period (Figure 12–18).

Ornament in the costumes should be used as accent, a moment of textural richness in an otherwise flat costume, a point of focus in a complex area of pattern or texture. It should not be used as decoration.

Hamlet is complicated and ambivalent, and there are as many ways to design it effectively as there are designers to design it. But if the costumes are to be effective, they must not be pictorial or decorative—they must reinforce the mood of ambiguity, contrast, shifting rhythms, and ultimate mystery that lie at the heart of this drama.

13

Baroque Plays

Art and Culture in the Seventeenth Century

In an attempt to vanquish Protestants, skeptics, and heretics, the Council of Trent met for an extended period during the sixteenth century and finally closed in 1563. Having given new sanctions to dogma, reaffirmed the essentials of the Catholic Christian faith, and attempted to inspire a new piety in all Christians, the Council (which convened under the full cloud of mannerist doubt) laid the foundations for a renewal of Christian faith and a return to use of the arts in propagating the faith. When the Council had completed its work, it took another half-century for the arts to develop fully the secular richness, sensuous glory, and worldly grandeur that marked the new-found power of the Catholic Church.

While mannerist art and culture had been a universal European phenomenon, the new Baroque embraced so many different tendencies in each individual country that it is very difficult at a glance to give them universality or "oneness" as an artistic style. There was, however, a certain wholeness of outlook and universality of vision in the new view of Man in relation to the Universe that stemmed from the discoveries of Copernicus, Galileo, and Kepler. With the theory that the earth moved about the sun instead of being the center of the universe, the cosmos came to be seen as an infinite continuity of interrelationships that even embraced Man in its unbroken and systematic wholeness. Particularly, the new elliptical patterns of movement established for heavenly bodies had a direct influence on compositional patterns in art, and all of the strivings for exaggerated effect, lighting from within or from beyond, and movement leading outside the frame of a work of art may be viewed as a striving for the infinite. Although it may be an oversimplification, one might say that just as Gothic art seemed to strive for the spiritual, Baroque art strove for the infinite.

The Baroque art of courtly and Catholic circles seems totally different from the middle-class art of Protestant areas. The art of Bernini and Rubens depicts a very different inner and outer world than that expressed by Rembrandt. This art of the high Baroque, besides representing the triumph of the Counterreformation, indicated a renewed sense of absolutism in government. Throughout Catholic Europe, the new art from Rome was used to enhance the grandeur and power of each particular ruler and his court in an attempt to erase the instabilities and insecurities of the Reformation.

An understanding of high Baroque art may be found in the following artistic concepts: (1) an *integration* of the mannerist tensions and energies of the preceding century by interweaving the elements of composition and building to an emotional release of energies; (2) a resolution of tensions and energies in the *richest of materials,* a sense of abundance, a sensuous richness of color, and a clustering of rich and varied forms; (3) *movement and energy,* and in architecture, sculpture, and painting, an excitement of masses in motion; (4) *space*—the illusion of infinity, the stretching of distance, the expansion and contraction of areas controlled by artistically shifting boundaries, all used to give excitement and changing interest to the definition of space; (5) *light* as a theatrical and organizing factor in the creation of artistic works.

This art began in Italy in the opening decade of the seventeenth century in Rubens' paintings and, in the following decade, Bernini's sculpture (see Figures 9–6b and 9–8a). By the middle of the century, the style dominated the Italian scene through the works of Bernini, Cortona, Longhena, and Rainaldi in architecture, Bernini in sculpture, and Cortona, Gaulli, and later Pozzo in large-scale paintings (Figure 13–1).

Even within the courtly Catholic style, there is a major division between the sensualistic, active, monumental tendencies of Bernini and the stricter, more formal "classisistic" style that leads from the Caracci to Poussin to the court art of Louis XIV. This classic Baroque style stresses many of the same elements that were operative in high Baroque, while reinforcing those ideals with rules and regulations: (1) The most important rule was that of *decorum,* the concept that every aspect of a painting is appropriate and correctly used in relation to another aspect of the work, with no hint of overstatement or excess. (2) The art was supposed to encompass composition on a high plane in an *elevated style.* (3) Subject matter was expected to be *mythological* or to depict scenes from *Greek, Roman, and Biblical history.* (4) The treatment of individual aspects of nature and personality were subordinated to the general, the *universal,* and the regular (as opposed to the irregular or abnormal). (5) Finally, all methods of painting were to be based on the *art of the Ancients* as revived in the classic Renaissance work of Raphael.

This art developed under the Caracci family and was continued in

Figure 13–1   *The Triumph of the Name of Jesus* by Giovanni Baptista Gaulli, Church of the Gesu, Rome, 1672–1685 (ceiling fresco). An example of the extreme theatrical illusionism in decorative painting in the last half of the seventeenth century in Italy. Photo courtesy of Alinari, Florence.

the work of their pupils, including Guido Reni and Domenichino; it was then introduced to France by the great classicist, Poussin, who carried this art to its highest point of achievement in the seventeenth century (see Figure 9–8b).

Finally, the Baroque realism of Velasquez, Rembrandt, and Caravaggio was opposed to the grandiose subject matter and large-scale compositions usually associated with both high and classical Baroque. It made effective use of *theatrical lighting* from a single source, it was *closely focused* on its subjects without a great deal of background and accessories, and it stressed *individuality and personality* in its subject matter. It also chose *lower-class subjects* and treated historical or mythological subjects in a genre fashion.

The style developed in Italy under Caravaggio and his many imitators was carried to Holland by certain artists who formed the School of Utrecht, and was very important in the development of Rembrandt's work (Figure 13–2). It also spread to Spain through Spanish painters such as Ribera and was influential in forming the early style of Velasquez. Artists on the trade and travel routes from Italy to the north, such as Georges de la Tour, were also heavily influenced by this realistic style (see Figure 9–12b).

Theatre and Drama in the Seventeenth Century

By 1650 the Italian theatre structure, which would be the dominant stage arrangement throughout the European theatre for the succeeding two hundred years, had fully developed in response to the great demands of

Figure 13–2 *The Night Watch* by Rembrandt, Rijksmuseum, Amsterdam, 1642. An example of a virtuoso performance in movement and theatrical lighting effects. Photo courtesy of the Rijksmuseum, Amsterdam.

the new theatrical form of opera. The auditorium was usually an elong-ated, U-shaped structure lined with boxes in tiers and a gallery at the back for servants and apprentices. Sight lines from the side boxes were, understandably, very poor. The floor area, which was filled with standees who could be removed for grand promenades and spectacular ballets, was considered an area for would-be gentlemen and critics and cost less than the boxes but more than the gallery. The auditorium and the stage were divided by the heavy and usually ornate proscenium arch; the stage raked upward at an angle and was very deep (Figure 13–3). There was usually a considerable amount of space below the stage floor for ma-chinery and trapdoors, and some space above for painted sky borders; on the sides of the stage there was space only for the side wings to move out of sight behind the proscenium arch. Lighting was done with chan-deliers hung in the auditorium and over the front of the stage, from foot-lights set behind reflectors along the edge of the stage, or by lights set against reflectors behind each set of wings (Figure 13–4).

The standard way of shifting from one setting to another (which can still be seen at the eighteenth-century Royal Theatre in Drottning-holm, Sweden) was to have a series of flats covered in canvas and painted with details representing the sides of the setting, set one behind the other, in groups, up each side of the raked stage (Figure 13–5). In each group

Figure 13–3   The Cuvilliés Theatre, Munich, mid-eighteenth century. An ex-ample of the U-shaped Baroque auditorium designed to focus attention on the royal box. Photo courtesy of KaiDib Films International, Glendale, Calif.

Figure 13–4 *Curtain Time* by Charles Coypel, showing the interior of the Petit Royal in Paris about 1700. An example of the tradition of the lowered chandeliers before the beginning of the performance. From an engraving by Joulain and Gosselin as reproduced in *Theater Pictorial* by George Altman, Ralph Freud, William Melnitz, and Kenneth Macgowan, University of California Press, Berkeley, 1953. Photo courtesy of William Melnitz.

there were as many flats as would be needed to indicate all the locations required by the production. The back wall of the setting was formed of two larger flats or shutters which met in the center and, again, as many of these could be set one behind the other as was required. Borders of two-dimensional framed cloths representing clouds or roofs completed the set above. At each change of scene and in full view of the audience, a set of shutters, wings, and a border were drawn away from the stage to reveal the next scene.

The family of scene designers who most fully represent the development of the Baroque style in staging is the Bibiena, who operated throughout Europe from the late seventeenth to the late eighteenth century. Ferdinando Bibiena, founder of the dynasty and a great contributor to seventeenth-century scene design, introduced angled perspective in operatic settings, which gave a double vanishing point rather than the single central point of the usual wing-and-drop plan. He and his sons,

Figure 13–5   A backstage view of the Royal Theatre, Drottningholm, Sweden, 1762. An example of the use of wings, borders, and the slotted floor system in use in the seventeenth- and eighteenth-century Continental theatre. Photo courtesy of the Drottningholm Theatre Museum.

Giuseppe and Antonio, developed to a high point the great descents by machine of deities from the heavens and expanded the ornamental and monumental aspects of stage setting (Figure 13–6).

The costumes for opera and classical tragedy used within these settings were rich, ornamental, formalized garments based originally on the lines of antique dress but abstracted by the seventeenth century into a very carefully structured basic silhouette with rich accessories. A plumed helmet or headdress, breastplate-shaped tunic, flaring skirt to above the knees, and a mantle and short soft boots to below the knee comprised the standard silhouette for men, although long robes were used for certain older or specialized types. The women's costumes usually consisted of a court gown with a hip-length overskirt and labels or tabs to break up the edge of the overskirt, the waist, the collar, and the shoulder. Sleeves were usually full and caught back to the elbow, and the hair or headdress was adorned with plumes. From this basic structure, ingenious designers were able to develop many subtle variations which suggested characters as varied as Turks, Indians, mythological satyrs and nymphs, classical heroes, and Arcadian shepherds. The style was highly developed in England in the work of Inigo Jones and in France by Henri Gissey and Jean Berain, as well as in the Italian opera of the seventeenth century (Figure 13–7). In comedies, such as those written by Molière and the Restoration playwrights in England, the costume style was basically that of contemporary dress with exaggerated effects for comic comment. All costumes designed for the stage had a very structured, classically organized basic silhouette overlaid with rich and decorative ornament. In this sense, stage costume was analogous to the method used in Baroque architecture whereby the basic structure was oriented toward balance and form, while the rich overlaid decoration achieved a dramatic, theatrical effect.

In Italy in the seventeenth century, the favorite dramatic form was no longer tragedy and comedy but *opera*, which had developed from the spectacular *intermezzi* of the sixteenth century. Opera was intended as a new attempt to approach Greek tragedy by stressing the music, dance, and choral dialogue long acknowledged as the essential elements of ancient Greek drama. Opera began to develop about 1597, culminating

Figure 13–6 A design for an opera by Giuseppe Galli da Bibiena, The Metropolitan Museum of Art, 1719. An example of the grandeur and monumentality in painted perspective scenery associated with the work of the Bibiena family. From *Archittetura e Prospettiva,* Augsburg, 1740. Photo courtesy of The Metropolitan Museum of Art, New York, Harris Brisbane Dick Fund, 1931.

Figure 13–7   Design for a theatrical costume by Henri Gissey, from an original drawing in the Victoria and Albert Museum, second half of the seventeenth century. Photo courtesy of the Victoria and Albert Museum, London.

in the experiments in Venice from 1610 to 1640. By 1650, the new form was the rage throughout Italy and was rapidly spreading to all of Europe; and it was through the medium of opera that Italian ideals of spectacle and theatricality were introduced into other European courts and capitals.

In addition to opera and ballet, the third dramatic form that dominated the late seventeenth-century stage (particularly in France) has been labeled *neoclassicism*. It was based on the work of sixteenth-century critics in Italy who had analyzed classical Greek and Roman tragedy and set down many rules for playwriting. The drama was supposed to teach as well as please. It was supposed to have but a single action that developed in one place at one time, and the particulars and specifics of life were to be put aside in favor of the general and the universal. Characters were to be seen as representative types rather than as individuals, and all action was to conform to the appropriate expectations of the current social scene in matters of class, morality, and background. Both Molière and Racine followed this prescribed method in their plays while still adding much that was based on their own personal experience.

Tartuffe

Molière's comedies were greatly influenced by his exposure to *commedia dell'arte* and the classical comedies of Plautus and Terence. Through his efforts French classical comedy was accepted as equal to neoclassical tragedy in depth of insight into the human spirit. One of Molière's most controversial yet representative plays is *Tartuffe* (Figures 13–8a, 13–8b).

Figure 13–8a A costume sketch for Molières' *L'Étourdi,* by L. Wolffram. Courtesy of the Norman Philbrick Library. Photo by Keeble and Shuchat.

Figure 13–8b A costume sketch for Molière's *Les Précieuses Ridicules,* by M. Sand. Courtesy of the Norman Philbrick Library. Photo by Keeble and Shuchat.

PLOT AND STRUCTURE   In this play, carefully organized form is always paramount, and the plot encompasses several distinct developments of action. The major portions of the play are clearly and logically developed, but the final change in the action that results in the arrival of the King's representative is forced and contrived. We may feel pleased that justice triumphed, but in terms of dramatic construction carefully prepared to lead to an inevitable conclusion, the resolution is open to criticism.

The unities are strictly observed in this play, with only one room required for the action and the length of the action confined to a single day. The room requires little furniture, there are no extra characters except Mme Pernelle's maid and the guards, and all of the action is directly related to the main theme of the play. With the possible exception of its ending, *Tartuffe* is directly a part of the neoclassical tradition and can be admired for its purity of form.

CHARACTERIZATION   All of the major characters are carefully developed to fit into the play's plot structure. Cléante is used to present the "common sense" view in the play and thus appears only in Act I, before Tartuffe has arrived, and again at the close of the play to point up the major theme of true piety versus false piety. He is not at all involved in the action of the play and acts only as a commentator.

Tartuffe, by being withheld from the action until the beginning of the third act, has had his character so fully developed by others that he is able to devote himself fully to his two love scenes. From his first speeches, urging Dorine to cover her bosom, to his later attempts to seduce Elmire, Tartuffe is portrayed primarily as a repressed sensualist. Only in the scene in which he is denounced by Damis do we glimpse some of the false humility and unctious self-criticism that have duped Orgon. For the most part, what the audience concludes about his character is dictated by descriptions from the other characters.

The maid Dorine, although appearing in each act, has her major part in the action early in the play as a foil to Orgon's extreme gullibility. Her charming candor is also used to contrast with the naiveté of the lovers and the falseness of Tartuffe. In fact, she provides most of the humor in the early part of the play through her witty and saucy exposé of all the exaggerated, self-conscious, and overly serious behavior surrounding her.

The lovers, Marianne and Valère, have one full scene in Act II that has a certain humorous charm, and thereafter they are of little importance. Marianne and Valère, like most lovers in Molière, are handsome, winning young people who deserve one another and are being kept apart by a biased, strong-willed parent.

Elmire is a worldly but moral woman who acts as the catalyst in exposing Tartuffe's rampant sensuality. Her appearances are unevenly distributed throughout the play, and she becomes crucial to the action only in those scenes in which Tartuffe pursues her. Orgon, on the other hand, is the key to the action, as it is only through men of his foolish good nature that shams such as Tartuffe are able to flourish. Orgon is not really a fool, but more the typical prosperous businessman who is impulsive and stubborn and feels rather guilty about the money he has made. As in the case of many contemporary men of wealth, he wants to ease certain doubts that trouble his conscience by giving impulsively and generously to someone he feels is worthier than he. He totally misjudges Tartuffe because he does not analyze his character. Even when Tartuffe has been exposed, he misinterprets the difference between hypocrisy and piety and declares that henceforth he will turn his back on all pious people. Unlike Cléante, he cannot take a balanced view.

This play is usually viewed as a comedy in which the principal action of the plot lies in the revelation of character. Yet if the play is so dependent on character, it is surprising how little information is given about age and personal appearance. What we must realize is that Molière wrote for a specific group of actors, and that their individual characteristics would have expanded the roles as written in the script. For example, Tartuffe was played by a plump actor named Du Croisy, and because the actor looked healthy and well fed, much could be made of the dialogue about fasting and scourges. We also know that Molière, who was noted for his expressive face and body, played Orgon. Elmire was played by Molière's wife, who was only twenty-nine at the time. Mme Pernelle was played by a man and so would have been extremely comic in her exaggerated denunciations of all pleasure.

In summarizing the development of character in this play, one may say that the humor derives from the psychological relationships between character and situation. The norm of behavior is established by Cléante and Dorine, and all deviations from it are treated in a satirical manner.

THEME   As in all of Molière's plays, the basic theme is the importance of a balanced view of life. To Molière, the philosopher of moderation, true piety reveals itself through actions and not talk. A secondary theme, widely used in Roman comedy and *commedia dell'arte,* is the folly of forced marriage. The playwright insists that such marriages lead only to rebellion and adultery.

DIALOGUE   Although Molière wrote within the accepted Alexandrine form of his day, with brilliance and polish, his dialogue is essentially realistic prose. His verses, twelve feet long with a rhyme at the end, are clever, witty, and satirical, and they fully express peculiarities and idiosyncracies of character, but they are seldom used for poetic purposes. To play Molière in prose translations is to miss the witty comment he makes on the traditional usage of Alexandrines. Only the polished symmetry and neat precision of English rhyming couplets is an approximation of the verse style.

RHYTHM   The urbane, gem-like, classical wit in Molière's plays is transmitted to an audience only when the rhythmic unrolling of the plot progresses with clear-cut precision. There is a sprightly, direct, onward movement from beginning to end, without sharp contrasts, abrupt breaks, or strong shifts of mood. The rhythmic flow is closely tied to the polished delivery of the symmetrically written rhymes of the Alexandrine.

SPECTACLE   The requirements for the visual spectacle are limited in this play, as in most Molière comedies. A place representing a room in Orgon's house, with a table, several chairs, a closet, and a door, is all that is required, although a staircase is frequently included from which Tartuffe may make an impressive first entrance. It can be produced in almost any period, but if it is placed in the time of Molière the costumes need not be complex nor richly ornamented as long as they represent the personality and social standing of each character. The lighting need not be varied at all; in Molière's time chandeliers hung over the acting area, and the effect of such constant static lighting is quite appropriate to the play.

Visual Presentation of Tartuffe *Today*

If one looks at a representative selection of stage settings for this play in recent years, the scenery falls into two general categories: (1) those settings that attempt to stress the structure and symmetrical balance of the play in a rather simple, abstract, decorative manner, and (2) those that attempt a more realistic portrayal of the interior of Orgon's wealthy, upper-class, bourgeois home. Each interpretation presupposes a particular approach to the total production. If it is considered important to stress the background of the characters, particularly Orgon's bourgeois temperament and taste, then the director may make many specific recommendations about scenery and property details that will set the mood (Figure 13–9). If the play is produced primarily to present the wit of the dialogue, the symmetry of the plot, and the universal types represented by the characters, it is often presented within an architectural suggestion of a room with balanced lines and simplified ornamentation acting as a framing device (see Figure 9–15). One approach obviously gives a more varied presentation of ornamentation, texture, and color to represent the wealth and comfort of a bourgeois home, while the other offers a setting which is as spare and simple as the structure of the play and acts only as a frame to the action. In either case, only those items that will clearly reveal the character and personality of the household should be used.

In costume, the difference between the two approaches will not be as striking. If a semirealistic approach is chosen in order to stress the

Figure 13–9   A scene from *Tartuffe* by Molière as produced by the American Conservatory Theatre, 1967. Directed by William Ball. Sets by Stuart Wurzell. Costumes by Jane Greenwood. Courtesy of the American Conservatory Theatre. Photo by Hank Kranzler, Palo Alto, Calif.

personality and status of the various characters, more variety in texture, line, and color will be needed; if one chooses to stress the classical nature of the script, then the designs should be simple, abstract parts of an overall pattern.

When designing a production of Molière, it could be beneficial to turn to a contemporary Dutch painter such as Vermeer for inspiration. In Vermeer's work are found both the classical spirit operative in Molière's play and the domestic bourgeois setting. A study of Vermeer's painting can be helpful even when the play is produced in a period other than the seventeenth century. His subtle and simple use of color, line, and texture is similar to Molière's spare craftsmanship and can give the designer an insight into how to translate the verbal methods of Molière into the visual designs for the play (Figure 13–10).

If one is to produce the play in a domestic bourgeois setting, the choice of color should have a greater range than if one uses a more restricted and abstract approach. In either case, the colors should be clear and cool, not muddied or warm. If a designer is to relate color usage correctly to Molière's compositional method, a restriction should be made on

Figure 13–10 *The Letter* by Jan Vermeer, Rijksmuseum, Amsterdam, ca. 1666. An example of the cool, carefully composed, classic, bourgeois interiors painted by this contemporary of Molière whose compositional method is similar to that of the French playwright. Photo courtesy of the Rijksmuseum, Amsterdam.

the number of colors used in a particular costume. Usually a costume is most appropriate for a play such as this if it is primarily of one basic hue accented or complemented by another color or a neutral. Even in a bourgeois setting, the approach should be one of clarity and simplicity in the use of color. In the more abstract approach to background, the costumes can be still more sharply defined in simplicity of color and accent. The costume can be designed in a single, cool, clear color accented very sharply with ribbons, bows, or braid of contrasting hue. The placement of such accents becomes a test for the eye, since the width, length, and location of each color accent must be exact.

Texture in the domestic setting may be varied, and the use of pattern can be greater than that used in a more abstract concept. However, great variety of textural surface within a single costume should be avoided. If, for example, a single rich brocade is used for a coat, the pattern of the brocade should be subordinate to the shape of the coat and to its overall color tonality. One major texture per costume is best, accented by small amounts of another texture. When a more abstract approach is taken, a clean, crisp, but not too insistent texture is best for the major fabric for each garment, with a strong minor texture used as accents. For example, a crisp, shiny bengaline faille, accented with velvet ribbon in various widths and carefully selected amounts (Figure 13–11), might be used for all the major costumes.

The line of the costume is extremely important when simplicity is used in color and texture. The silhouette of each costume must be exactly right for the character and action in the play. Every precaution in boning, corsetting, padding, and stiffening must be taken to ensure that the silhouette remains as sharp and clear as the dialogue and plot structure. The exact silhouette should be achieved before it is submitted for final approval by the director, and the designer should oversee the construction period to ensure that the costume is exactly as he and the director had envisioned it. In a domestic setting, the variety in line may be greater than in an abstract production. However, it will not be a great

Figure 13–11   Another scene from *Tartuffe* by Molière as produced by the American Conservatory Theatre, 1967. Directed by William Ball. Sets by Stuart Wurzell. Costumes by Jane Greenwood. Courtesy of the American Conservatory Theatre. Photo by Hank Kranzler, Palo Alto, Calif.

factor in the designs, since the texture and color will have as much interest as the line. In an abstract setting, texture and color are often subordinated to line; the silhouette and internal shapes within the costume will attract the most attention. The width of a cuff, the flair of a bow, the fall of a piece of lace, the size of curls on a wig—all become very important when the method of design is spare, simplified, and intellectually planned. If the comments in costume are exactly right and are complemented by polished acting, the performance will be as pleasing visually, despite its simplicity, as the play is verbally. American audiences, weaned on Shakesperean comedy, often fail to understand how Molière's plays are conceived. Many American and British designers, impressed by the richness and variety of the courtly costumes of the late seventeenth century, squander their wit and ingenuity to achieve a rich, lavish spectacle of varied costumes. This buries a Molière play, rather than projecting and reinforcing it. To design Molière in the same way that one designs Restoration comedy is a mistake. The latter has much more variety of character and scene than does Molière, and demands more complex

Figure 13–12   Costume designs by the author for a production of *Tartuffe* as produced by the Stanford Repertory Theatre, Stanford University, 1965. From the collection of the author.

visual effects. A careful study of Molière's comedies and a direct attempt to equate the visual approach to the literary method will produce costumes and settings that (although not lavish in themselves) will reinforce and support the play (Figure 13–12).

Phèdre

The plays of Racine mark the height of French classical tragedy, and Racine is to the French tradition of tragedy what Molière is to comedy. Racine's reputation rests assuredly on *Phèdre*, which was written in 1677 and adapted from the Greek tragedy *Hippolytus*. It is a perfect example of the tragedy of reason based on a single moment of experience and a single angle of vision. In Racine's tragedies there is little external action; the drama results from internal psychological conflict centered on a single character, and this conflict is usually found in terms of passion versus reason or love versus duty.

PLOT AND STRUCTURE   In French classical tragedy, form is more important than any other single factor. Originally, French classicists based their ideas on a misinterpretation of Aristotle; "a serious action of a certain magnitude" was construed as referring directly to an action involving people of rank whose every action had the correct measure of appropriateness, a decorum that worked itself out in good manners and high breeding. The word "action" meant the results of action, the facts, deeds, and chain of events that produce a final psychological result. Action is never physical or actual stage action. The "action" demonstrates the tragic life of the soul as it struggles with the problems of reason versus passion. It is reason that is the only value; it is reason alone that is to be obeyed. In his writing, Racine develops the gnawing power of passion to demonstrate to the audience the importance of a rational mode of action, an importance he politely assumes they will recognize.

The external action is simple, while the inner, psychological action and character relationships are very complex. Each action in the plot is thus magnified by the varied and involved emotional reactions to it on the part of each character. In its action, the play develops with absolute clarity and simplicity; the unity of time is completely observed; the action is entirely within the palace; and the development of the plot is completely focused on the consequences of a single great psychological aberration.

It is also interesting to look at the changes made by Racine in remodeling Euripides' *Hippolytus* for the seventeenth-century French court. Racine attempts, as much as possible, to eliminate reliance on the gods, even treating the death of Hippolytus as a result of the inevitability of fate rather than as the work of the sea god, Poseidon. He also eliminates

Figure 13–13   A wood engraving of Mlle Rachel in *Phèdre* by Racine at the St. James Theatre, London, in 1846. From the Enthoven Collection, Victoria and Albert Museum, London. Courtesy of the Victoria and Albert Museum. Photo by Malcolm Keep.

the chorus, substituting confidences to a close servant or companion for the revelation of inner thoughts. The neoclassical tradition assumed that both long soliloquies and a chorus acting as if of a single mind violated the rules of "natural" or acceptable speech and action.

Finally, it is very evident that the religious, natural, and large world view of Greek dramatic ritual is missing, and a new, limited, and artificial ritual has replaced it in the guise of a strategy regulating all social functions at the court of Louis XIV. There is a lesser sense of life and ritual than in Greek tragedy, but the rational planning and polished structure are superb.

CHARACTERIZATION   The role of Phèdre is to French drama what the role of Hamlet is to English drama. It is one of the most difficult parts for a woman to play, because there is so little external action and so much internal conflict to communicate to an audience. The shifts in mood and subtle changes of emotional climax must be clearly projected. Resignation turning to hope in the opening scene, passion then overwhelming reason, humiliation after Hippolytus' rejection, the horror and terror of Theseus' return, the jealousy of Aricia, the bitter denunciation of Oenone, and her final moment of greatness in death—all these emotional changes must be shown, as well as the smaller feminine emotional shifts within each scene. In every way, it is one of the most outstanding female roles in the history of the theatre. Audiences have always both admired and pitied the Queen and suffer with her in her passion and remorse. At the play's end she has achieved a truly tragic stature (Figure 13–13).

Other characters are confronted with less violent conflicts that are central to their personalities but not to the main line of the tragedy. Theseus, for example, is late in arriving on the scene and acts as a catalyst rather than an initiator of action. He has the natural responses expected of a king, a great warrior, a strong husband, and a stern father, and he shares fully in the tragic emotions of the play's conclusion. Hippolytus is torn by typical Racinian dilemmas: love for Aricia versus a sense of duty to his father, respect for his step-mother and her position versus the strong desire to protect his father's honor. In short, all of the major characters attempt to act rationally, but they are swayed by irrational forces that seem beyond their control. They all act within the ritual strategy or courtly game that is the basic plot of neoclassical drama. All follow the character dictums of the period: they are drawn with dignity, they act with decorum, they are of noble birth, and they live by the rules of personal honor.

THEME   The theme is so intricately bound to plotting and character that it is apparent at every moment of the play. It can be stated in several ways and viewed from a number of angles, but it basically involves the moral and rational idea that tragic results occur when passion is allowed to usurp the position of thought, reason, decorum, and good breeding in society.

DIALOGUE   The language of the play is ordered in the most logical and musical manner, and the dialogue, even when expressing the full power of passion, is outwardly rhetorical and static while expressing the most brilliantly subtle shifts of inner emotion. The tightly controlled Alexandrine verse form can be built step by step to towering climaxes, and then be made to ebb to devastating quietness like the waves of the sea. When such great speeches or "tirades" are brilliantly performed, they can bring an audience to its feet in thunderous applause, and all actors who have essayed *Phèdre* agree that to do justice to the form takes tremendous technique, power, and emotional control.

RHYTHM   The rhythm or underlying musical progression in *Phèdre* is closely connected to the dignified rise and fall of the carefully ordered verse. Since there are no abrupt breaks in the action or sharp and unaccountable shifts in mood or personality, the progression throughout the play is as clear and ordered as the rhythm of the sea. For each climax there is a carefully controlled rise and an equally ordered fall. The ebb and flow establishes the essence of the "tragic rhythm" of the drama.

SPECTACLE   The physical appearance of set and costumes is not indicated in the script at all, and the audience is aware only that the play takes place in the Palace at Troezen. Furnishings should be minimal or nonexistent in a setting of a simple, classic, monumental background. The costumes should reflect the station and the inherent decorum of the noble-spirited character, and the lighting could remain unchanged throughout the play.

Visual Presentation of Phèdre *Today*

What sources to use as a basis for designing the production is the major question to be faced in presenting this play to a modern public. Should the play be designed in authentic Greek styles reflecting the costume and architecture of the fifth century B.C., when the original *Hippolytus* was written, or should the production attempt to suggest the neoclassical theatrical dress of the age of Louis XIV? Since the play differs sharply in mood and story line from the original by Euripides, it may seem more logical to recreate for a modern audience that feeling for the classical past and the art of antiquity familiar to the seventeenth-century audience that first saw this play. However, after a closer look at the visual sources, especially for costume, the designer may despair at achieving anything but laughter from full-bodied wigs, plumed helmets, and over-ornamented breast plates. Another possibility, which has been attempted once or twice in recent years, is to use neither fifth-century sources nor those from the age of Louis XIV, but only the style of the play itself as a basis for costumes and settings, suggesting no specific period. A fourth idea is to use the modern period with as little detail as possible. With careful planning, insight, and ingenuity this great tragedy can be successfully designed in any of these major ways, as long as the essential nature of the play's composition is kept clearly in mind.

In designing the play (as it has most frequently been interpreted in the twentieth century) in modifications of Greek dress of the fifth century B.C., the designer would be wise, before turning to specific architectural or dress sources from the period, to look at the paintings of Racine's contemporary, Poussin. Both men wanted to liberate seventeenth-century art from excess, from superficial or external detail; both base their work on a central idea or moral theme, and both strip their work to a formal, organized disposition of the simplest visual or emotional effects. Racine and Poussin distill earlier Baroque masses and expanding energies into essences of pure emotion or pure feeling rationally conceived and organized. It is not so much the garments in Poussin that will help the designer of *Phèdre*, but the handling of outlines, the use of draping, the application of color, and the balance and proportions so carefully controlled in a group of people placed in front of some temple or palace (see Figure 9–8b). Once the art of Poussin has been studied, the designer may turn to specific Greek sources and abstract those elements of form and line which he knows will be most appropriate for *Phèdre*, without getting involved in the intricacies of Greek ornamental detail. If this approach is taken, the designer will be able to suggest a Greek setting of time and place while developing fully the monumental, cold, heroic, artificial, artistic effects of Poussin, which contain that sense of removal and decorum needed for Racine.

However, there is one problem with this approach. Despite the most careful innovations on the part of the designer, the Greek draperies of Poussin based on fifth-century styles can never completely capture the formality, decorum, and artificiality of the court of Louis XIV. Only in the late seventeenth-century stage costume versions of classical dress do we find this. Therefore, if a designer has fully absorbed the painting of Poussin and is fully aware of how far he can proceed with his seventeenth-century theatrical sources without getting a comic effect or a laughing response, then a carefully modified and subtly abstracted late Baroque approach to production may most closely capture the essence of the play. Full-bottomed wigs could be replaced by formally waved long hair, which gives grandeur and stature without looking ludicrously artificial. The heavy ornamentation of seventeenth-century stage dress should be avoided, complexity in color and fabric should be discarded, and the structure of the costume should be accented in exactly the right places with the appropriate ornamentation. Everything should be calculated to reinforce the formal, polished structure of the play and its characters, and nothing should be added that is merely picturesque, rich, or decorative.

Finally, if the designer and the director choose to produce the play in a more contemporary way for a modern audience, an abstract modern setting or one that attempts to suggest no particular period may be chosen. Certainly modern-dress items such as full dress formal evening wear for men have the formality and classical restraint of Racine, while simple uniforms and classically inspired gowns can be designed to capture the essence of both Poussin and Racine. Even a palace background can be designed in the modern manner to have all of the coolness and simplicity demanded by Racine's dramaturgy.

Looking specifically at the problem of costume and the nature of the visual effects required by *Phèdre*, no matter what the period in which the play is being presented, the texture of the fabrics chosen for the play should not be complicated and varied (Figure 13–14). A single major texture that is not too insistent, yet not monotonous, and that will hold the carefully chosen shape and line desired throughout the action should be chosen for all the major costumes in the play, with other textures used only as accent. Woolens that do not absorb too much light and hold their carefully planned line might be used; or if a richer effect is desired, a bengaline faille, velveteen velour, or wide-wale corduroy might be chosen. These could be trimmed with gold cord, jewels, small quantities of rich brocade, or heavy lace, but only a single major accent or ornamental effect should be used throughout; the various accents should not be mixed.

The colors could be selected from the clear, pure, rich hues of Poussin, and there should be no subtly grayed or changeable color effects. Each costume, as in Poussin, could be primarily of a single color trimmed with neutrals or metallics and another minor color used for accent. For example, if Phèdre is costumed in a deep, rich red gown, it can be trimmed with gold and accented with white. Hippolytus may be costumed in yellow-gold trimmed with metallic gold and accented in white,

Figure 13–14   A scene from *Phèdre* by Racine as produced by the University of Kansas City in 1958 with costumes by the author. All gowns were of heavy wide-wale corduroy, breastplates were of felt, and trim was of heavy gold braid. Photo by the author.

Figure 13–15   Costume designs by the author for a production of *Phèdre* by Racine as produced at the University of Kansas City in 1958. From the collection of the author.

while Theseus might be gowned in purple accented in metallic gold and relieved with a neutral beige.

Most important is the choice and use of the costume line. It must be grand, imposing, formal, graceful, and theatrical, and great amounts of fabric carefully disposed are needed to give this effect. Mantles and long trains can help to achieve this sweeping line, and a variety of hanging sleeves ending in a tassel might be used to accent and reinforce the carefully planned upward-reaching gestures of Phèdre. Even if a modified or abstracted modern-dress approach is adopted, mantles and trains can be used effectively in the costume scheme. And at the beginning and end of each major costume line, the designer should create an accent through ornamentation. In the theatrical dress of the seventeenth century this frequently was a clasp, an edging in gold braid, or a tassel, but even in Greek clothing there is ample possibility for use of Greek decorative pins or fibulae and ornamental borders. In modern dress there are manifold possibilities in brooches, orders, sashes, and military buttons, for example. This ornamentation should never be simply decorative but must act as an accent for the entire costume (Figure 13–15).

14

Eighteenth-Century Plays

Art and Culture in the Eighteenth Century

The development of courtly art and culture, which had proceeded in a rather uninterrupted fashion since the Renaissance, finally came to a standstill in the eighteenth century. It was superseded by bourgeois subjectivism and sentimentality, which are still the foundation of most popular art today. Even before one arrives at the bourgeois world that appears in the paintings of Chardin and Greuze, there is a tendency in the Rococo art of France and all of Europe in the early eighteenth century to neglect the solemn, the ceremonious, and the monumental in favor of the natural, the casual, and the intimate. Even though in certain ways the Rococo style is a continuation and a consummation of the Baroque splendor of the seventeenth century, the grand manner and the pompous taste of that style are completely foreign to the refined, elegant, intimate ideals of the eighteenth century. Only the basic sources and compositional approach remain from the earlier Baroque style.

Rococo art is an anticlimax, a dying fall in the history of art devoted to monarchy and aristocratic aggrandizement. The aristocracy began to accept middle-class patterns of thought, while clothing them in the most elegant aristocratic trappings. There was a slackening of personal discipline, a growing scepticism and even atheism in religion, and more unrestrained personal conduct among the nobility. Since Louis XV in France allowed his succession of mistresses to have more influence in social matters than he himself, the society developed a feminine bias, and the art a most feminine sensibility.

The paintings of Watteau set the tone for the new culture, and the transition from the grand Baroque "machines" of Charles Le Brun to this master of the delicate *fêtes galantes* expressed fully the change in taste.

338

The art, in spite of its delight in the senses and joyful surrender to pleasure, was full of melancholy and nostalgia—an attempt at the age-old Arcadian ideal of merging nature and civilization, beauty and spirituality, seriousness and intelligence (Figure 14–1a). The style that we call Rococo is not illustrative or even very expressive. It is ornamental, and its decorative patterns seem to be without constraint, like the shepherds and shepherdesses in Watteau, who, endowed with a natural liberty, seem to drift effortlessly in a delicate and airy landscape.

In England the transition from seventeenth- to eighteenth-century culture was not as obvious as in France. Even at the opening of the century, English power was held by a commercial aristocracy which had a more realistic grasp on the meaning of mercantile growth and middle-class power than did the aristocrats in France (Figure 14–1b). The transition from the aristocratic Rococo to bourgeois romanticism in England is not affected by the violence to cultural values that occurs in France and Germany.

Figure 14–1a *The Halt During the Chase* (detail) by Watteau, The Wallace Collection, London, ca. 1720. An example of the aristocratic and artificial dream world of this early eighteenth-century French artist who invented the *fête galante*. Photo reproduced by permission of the trustees of The Wallace Collection.

Trifling as it sometimes seems to be, the Rococo is the last coherent style before the final loss of style in the late eighteenth and early nineteenth centuries, and the replacement of a European-wide cultural style with many individual artist's personal interpretations. Only with the birth of *art nouveau* (in many ways related to the Rococo) and the rise of modern art in the early twentieth century is there a return to a coherent cultural style.

The decline of Rococo art and its traditions inherited from the Baroque began gradually during the middle of the eighteenth century as a result of a continuing attack on bourgeois taste that took two different directions. The emotionalism and naturalism represented by the French philosopher and novelist Rousseau, the English novelist Richardson, the English painter Hogarth, and the French middle-class artist Greuze was one trend; the rationalism and classicism represented by the German philosopher and playwright Lessing, the German painter Mengs, the German historian and archeologist Winckelmann, and the French painter David is the other. Both emphasize an ideal of simplicity, earnestness, clarity, and morality over the courtly softness, ostentation, and

Figure 14–1b   "After the Marriage" from the series *Marriage à la Mode* by Hogarth, National Gallery, London, ca. 1745. An example of Hogarth's moral and satirical tone in a painting from a narrative series dealing with the social evils of eighteenth-century English society. Photo courtesy of the Trustees of the National Gallery.

Figure 14–2a *The Father's Curse: The Ungrateful Son* by Greuze, The Louvre, Paris, ca. 1765. An example of the moralistic, sentimental painting admired by Denis Diderot in the latter part of the eighteenth century. Photo courtesy of Le Directeur des Musées de France.

decadence that are expressed in Rococo art. Greuze, in particular, represented the new middle-class taste in his realistic, story-telling paintings, which project a strong bourgeois ethic. They are literary, banal, moralizing, anecdotal paintings that are the prototype for much of the inartistic work that followed in the nineteenth century. The work of Chardin was much more honest, simple, and truly artistic, yet in his day Greuze was more popular, since his weapons proved very effective in the battle against the decaying Rococo (Figure 14–2a).

However, it is the painter David who represents the renewal of the classic and the rational in painting (Figure 14–2b). What must be understood about art and public taste after 1750 is that picturesque romanticism and severe classicism were two sides of the same coin: the associational concept by which all art forms were chosen—not for intrinsic or structural values, but to evoke rich associations which could inspire the viewer to muse about past history or literature. Such art appealed to middle-class sentiment, snobbishness about learning, and love of prestige and position. Architecture after 1750 swings from neoclassical commercial temples in the city to neogothic villas in the country in deference to this

Figure 14–2b   *The Death of Socrates* by David, The Metropolitan Museum of Art, New York, 1787. An example of the coldness and austerity in the "new classicism" of David, which stressed the stoic virtues and civic duty in classical antiquity. Photo courtesy of The Metropolitan Museum of Art.

associational desire; painting turns from the heroic, stoical, republican virtues in works by David to the romantic, picturesque ruins of Hubert Robert (Figure 14–2c). All art after 1750, even the most fully documented archeological classicism, is used for associational values. By the end of the eighteenth century bourgeois sentimentality and associationalism had spread from England to Germany and France, and by the second quarter of the nineteenth century this artistic ideal lead to the tasteless eclecticism that dominated Western European culture in the nineteenth century.

Theatre and Drama in the Eighteenth Century

STAGING METHODS   The staging methods of the eighteenth century were generally a continuation of the theatrical practices of the preceding Baroque period, although theatre size increased greatly toward the end of the century as the size of the middle-class audience expanded. On the Continent, where the forestage was relatively small and the proscenium doors of the English stage did not exist, the action took place on a rather narrow plane to the front of the raked stage, with a one- or two-point perspective arranged behind it. The grand drape within the proscenium was used only at the beginning of the evening to hide the stage until the play began, and at the end of the evening as a conclusion to all theatrical entertainment (Figure 14–3). Changes of scenery and the famous "transformation" scenes (when one set magically changed into another) occurred in full view of the audience through the use of the chariot system (on the Continent) or the wing-and-groove method (England). In the former, all flats moved on and off the stage by turning a single winch in the basement, and little chariots supported the wings and shutters on masts that came up through slits in the stage floor. The best single example we have today of this type of theatre in operation is the Drottningholm Theatre in the small royal palace of the same name just outside Stockholm. Here a group of full settings and all stage machinery were found intact in the early twentieth century, and today one may enjoy complete performances of many eighteenth-century ballets, operas, and plays (Figure 14–4).

SCENERY The eighteenth century saw a growing interest in archeology, historical objectivity, and the art and culture of the past, and by the

Figure 14–2c *The Old Bridge* by Hubert Robert, National Gallery, Washington, D.C., Samuel Kress Collection, ca. 1775. An example of the romantic ruins that became one of the most popular of subjects in the late eighteenth century. Photo courtesy of the National Gallery.

latter part of the century there were movements in both England and France demanding scenery that had far more detail, more sense of reality, more of an illusion of the time of day or a particular weather condition. Thus, stage lighting improved, as did the quality of mood painting in wings and backdrops. New asymmetrical stage plans, the use of transparent drops, and the addition of individual set pieces not painted on the backgrounds were added.

COSTUMES   The costumes of this period were either based on the theatrical garb developed in the seventeenth century (inspired by supposedly antique lines), which were still prevalent in opera and classical tragedies, or on the use of contemporary dress with certain modifications (Figure 14–5). But the eighteenth century, which showed a great interest in more archeological correctness in stage dress than had been the

Figure 14–3   The Opera House in Stuttgart by de la Guépierre. A cutaway sketch of the interior. From the *Encyclopédie* by Denis Diderot, 1751–1772. Photo courtesy of The Henry E. Huntington Library.

Figure 14–4   Stage setting, Royal Theatre, Drottningholm, Sweden, ca. 1765. One of the few extant examples of a stage house completely equipped with stage scenery and machinery of the eighteenth century. Courtesy of the Drottningholm Theatre Museum. Photo by KaiDib Films International, Glendale, Calif.

case in the past, saw a number of innovations and changes in theatrical costume by 1800 (Figure 14–6). In England, Charles Macklin played Macbeth in plaids, David Garrick played Lear and Richard III in approximations of certain Renaissance garments, and Sarah Siddons and John Philip Kemble appeared in classical plays costumed in garments based on Greek and Roman originals (Figure 14–7). In France, a similar development occurred when Voltaire suggested a number of costume reforms at the Comédie Française; the great French actress Claire Hippolyte Clairon and her leading man Henri Louis LeKain were, with Voltaire's help, able to bring many more historically correct costume effects into the plays of the standard repertoire.

The School for Scandal

Although the art and culture of the eighteenth century has very complicated cross currents and continuous shifts from the classical to the protoromantic, the descriptive words that continually reappear in any

Figure 14–5   Costume sketches by Jean Eric Rehn for the Royal Theatre, Drottningholm, Sweden, ca. 1765. An example of the picturesque and exotic romantic effects achieved in stage costume in the late eighteenth century. Courtesy of the Norman Philbrick Library. Photo by Keeble and Shuchat.

assessment of the period and its drama are "sentimental" and "moralizing." And even though the best playwrights of the period, including Beaumarchais, Goldsmith, Sheridan, and Goldoni, worked to reestablish true comedy, the mark of eighteenth-century sentimentality and its accompanying moral tone appears to a greater or lesser degree in the work of every one of these major playwrights. *The School for Scandal* by Sheridan is frequently said to be the greatest comedy of manners in the English language. However, it in no way achieves the wordly wit and amoral tone of Restoration comedy, and although it was written to escape some of the excesses of sentimental comedy, it still has a strong note of sentiment and a very direct moral tone (Figure 14–8).

PLOT AND STRUCTURE   The play begins with a Prologue and ends with an Epilogue, as is the case with most plays written during the Restoration and eighteenth century. The Prologue was used to introduce the script, make public a quarrel between the playwright and the theatre manager, and put the audience in the appropriate mood; the Epilogue was an appeal for audience favor and a summary of the play's overall intent. Neither is essential to an understanding of the play, and both are frequently cut in modern productions.

Although the scandalmongers play only a small part within the action, they are very important in setting the background tone of the play and acting as framework for the action. The group is also used for exposition, since their gossip frequently introduces much of the information from which character conflict arises. In many ways they seem (in modern productions) to be the freshest and most humorous part of the play as we see how their commodity—scandal—is planned, cooked, and served to cause the downfall of reputations all around them. Even the hero, Charles, is all but ruined by them, and only Snake's exposure of the group's intrigues leads to the happy conclusion of the main action. Their conversation has a crisp and witty tone that supplies much of the play's humor, and their viciousness seems too superficial to be a real danger to the leading characters in the play. They are the background to the action, always available to complicate or untangle the plot and to set the correct comic tone for the play's development.

Figure 14–6   The actor Quin as Coriolanus, 1749. The stiff skirt or "tonnelet" and the heroic plumes were the standard dress for classical tragedy at the middle of the eighteenth century. Courtesy of the Victoria and Albert Museum, London.

Sheridan's structural approach is inherited far more from English comic writing (dating back to the Elizabethan period) than from the French comic tradition of Molière. There is a major plot and a minor plot which at first have little connection, with a gradual entwining of the two toward a common resolution. This contrasts sharply with the single plot action that we find in classic French comedy. If one judges a play by its story telling, then real praise is in order for the playwright who carries his audience with ease and a sense of keen expectation from one scene to another despite the two threads of action. This sense of easy casualness wedded to a sure sense of control is even more admirable when one realizes that there are fourteen different scenes in the play, which take place in various portions of four different households.

Although the audience is prepared from the beginning for Joseph to be unmasked, Lady Teazle to come to her senses, Charles to be ex-

Figure 14–7   Mrs. Siddons in the tragedy, *The Grecian Daughter*, ca. 1790. An example of the pseudoclassical costume at the close of the eighteenth century. From a steel engraving. Courtesy of the Norman Philbrick Library.

Figure 14–8   Costume sketches for Sheridan's *The School for Scandal* by Nancy Potts, as produced by the Association of Producing Artists at the Lyceum Theatre, New York, 1967. From *Theatre Crafts Magazine,* July–August 1967. Courtesy of Nancy Potts and Theatre Crafts Magazine.

onerated, and Maria to be happy, they do not know how all of this is to come about; hence, a marvelous dual sense of clearly knowing the purpose of the action while following it with curiosity and suspense is established. This particular skill on the part of the playwright has always been particularly admired in the Screen Scene. All of the preceding conflicts in the action are brought together in this scene, and a marvelous series of comic reversals ensues until Lady Teazle is revealed behind the screen. Then, like the final pieces of a puzzle fitting into place, Lady Teazle has the necessary discussion with Sir Peter, Joseph is exposed, and Charles' basic goodness is revealed.

CHARACTER   Before analyzing the individual characters in the play, one should be fully aware of the clarity of these characterizations and their relationship to one another and to the plot. The playwright clearly sets the natures of Joseph, Charles, Sir Peter, and Lady Teazle before us, and whenever a sense of ambiguity about their thoughts or motives arises they are allowed to make direct asides to the audience. In the case of minor characters whose personalities cannot be fully described, names are given such as Snake, Sir Benjamin Backbite, and Lady Sneerwell. As was the case in the Baroque theatre, the characters are developed with a sense of decorum or good manners and built on social types so that we expect them to act in a certain manner.

Charles is particularly important as a character type that was greatly admired in the late eighteenth century. He is the natural young man who has not been corrupted by society; a man of frankness, openness, sensibility, and filial affection, who represents an ideal of goodness despite his rashness and lack of social grace. Joseph, on the other hand, pretends to have the social graces and maturity admired in a man of class, but he is shown to be a hypocrite, a dissembler, a mere facade of manners, and is finally exposed as unnatural, corrupt, and somewhat ludicrous. Sir Peter at first place appears to be a man who fulfills the ideals of his age and class, and yet he has married someone far too youthful and so is made the recipient of much barbed satire. Maria, Old Rowley, and Sir Oliver seem to fit the norm of their ages and their positions in society, and so they are treated well at the end of the play. Only those who have deviated from the appropriate social patterns of behavior are punished.

The minor characters are differentiated only slightly through age, sex, or the way they speak. For example, Mrs. Candour can be differentiated from Lady Sneerwell only by a certain flightier tone to her chatter and gossip. It is also important to realize that all of the characters, except Old Rowley, Moses, and the servants, are of the leisure class and are not concerned about making a living. Although the author makes a great point of exposing dishonesty and hypocrisy, no doubts are raised about the social system within which the play operates. As with Molière, the social scene itself is fully accepted, and only the deviations from it are ridiculed. Thus, the play has a certain sense of sophistication and urbanity which sets it clearly within the main stream of the comedy of manners tradition. Only the notes of sentimentality that reflect eighteenth-century bourgeois taste (in the characterizations of Charles and Maria) give an emotional tone to the play quite unlike that found in Molière, Restoration comedy, or the modern plays by Oscar Wilde and Somerset Maugham.

THEME   Just as it is interesting to compare Sheridan and Molière in matters of plot and characterization, so is it instructive to look at the similarities and differences in the ideas or themes in their plays. For instance, both *Tartuffe* and *The School for Scandal* deal with the unmasking of hypocrites, but in the Molière play religious hypocrisy is a real threat to individuals and society, while the social hypocrisy of Joseph Surface, or even the scandalmongering of Sir Benjamin, Lady

Sneerwell, and the others is never a serious threat. *The School for Scandal,* clearly reflecting the lighter touch in all eighteenth-century art and literature, is less serious in purpose than *Tartuffe.* The theme of this play is not so much the exposure of Joseph Surface and the members of the "school for scandal" as a defense of the new "natural man" ideal. Like Goldsmith before him, Sheridan is attacking the tearful sentimentality and complacent false morality that had been rampant in English comedy for fifty years. However, despite this clear intention of indicating the difference between true and false sentiment, his "good" characters still succumb to moralizing and sentiment. In fact, in the final analysis, the entire play illustrates the standard lesson of eighteenth-century sentimental comedy—that virtue will be rewarded and evil will be punished.

DIALOGUE   The language of the play serves admirably to give the play its tone of polish and wit. As with Restoration comedy, the characters generally make their points with polished epigrams and witty descriptions, and the idealized conversations that take place make every phrase seem spontaneous yet sparkling and apt. Such witty talk is far removed from the language of everyday living needed for buying, selling, and functioning within a broad spectrum of society. Although it shows the English language at a polished peak of conversational brilliance, it also reflects a certain aspect of society that is artificial, somewhat tarnished, and rather useless. Certainly the polished prose in much of this play demands a precise and exact technique of delivery, and when it is appropriately spoken it makes the play a dazzling stage piece—the superlative box office comedy that has been kept before the public since 1777.

RHYTHM   The movement and rhythm of a play such as *The School for Scandal* are closely tied to the sharp, rapid, witty dialogue and to the polished gestures of the actors rather than to the vagaries and complications of the plot. Although the unraveling of the story line is interesting and helps to sustain a sense of curiosity and suspense, the movement and pace of the play are ultimately keyed to the conversational games from which the climaxes of all major scenes are built. The give and take of dialogue in such scenes creates a rhythm that is light, clear, and fast moving.

SPECTACLE   The play is set in London in 1777 and reflects, especially in costume, the manners and customs of late eighteenth-century society. A famous engraving of the time, which shows the Screen Scene from a performance at Drury Lane in 1788, gives some idea of the original costumes and settings, the nature of the theatre with its apron stage and proscenium doors, and the relationship of the audience to the stage. It is important to note in this engraving that the actors' costumes closely approximate those worn by members of the audience (Figure 14–9).

By the time this play was written, more emphasis was being placed on each of the settings demanded in the action of the play, and although most of the settings are simply designated as a room in someone's house,

Figure 14–9   "The Screen Scene" from *The School for Scandal* as produced at the Drury Lane Theatre, London, 1778. An example of the use of the fore-stage, proscenium doors, stage boxes, clearly defined wings, and contemporary dress in an English production of the late eighteenth century. From an engraving of the period. Courtesy of the Victoria and Albert Museum, London.

the wings and shutters used at the time would probably have been quite detailed in their architectural adornment; also, they would have been changed in full view of the audience. Much of the action undoubtedly took place on the forestage, with entrances and exits through the pro-scenium doors, using the set simply as background. But in scenes such as those involving the auction of the pictures and the concealment be-hind the screens, the action and the properties required are specifically identified, and the setting would have become more directly involved in the action.

Visual Presentation of The School for Scandal *Today*

In presenting *The School for Scandal* for a contemporary audience, the producer and director must decide whether to adopt the visual methods of the original production or one of a number of contemporary visual approaches. Since the scenic methods used in the eighteenth century can be used to capture a certain period charm that is also inherent in the play, it is possible to use wings and shutters to depict the various locations needed and allow the audience to observe the shifts from one scene to the next. This can give an added interest and charm to the production. If such an approach is taken, the wings and shutters obviously should not be painted in a manner that suggests historical re-creation of late eighteenth-century scene painting, but should take a contemporary artistic approach in capturing the decorative feeling of eighteenth-century architectural ornament. This approach will allow the audience to feel that the production is being presented as a contemporary interpretation of the eighteenth-century theatrical scene while still taking full advantage of the charm, style, and removal from reality inherent in observing the scenery shifted by a wing-and-shutter method. With this concept of production, the acting will be removed almost completely from the level of realism to one of artificiality and a mannered style. The costumes will support the decorative and pictorial needs of the play rather than being tied primarily to the psychological demands of characterization.

However, if quaintness is not desired, a production may be designed which contains detailed box settings for each room, with a certain sense of fullness and period correctness; hence, the characters and plot would have more reality for the audience than in a wing-and-shutter setting (Figure 14–10). If designed in this manner, the details of interior decoration must be specific and detailed; the costumes must be tied closely to special idiosyncracies of character and period, while the acting must be more fully based on a three-dimensional psychological interpretation of individual characters.

Finally, there is the completely contemporary approach, in which a number of modern staging methods could be used to project the script visually. A thrust-stage approach, where only the rear wall is set with eighteenth-century architectural decor and the acting takes place on the thrust stage away from the background would be one way. (Eighteenth-century acting took place similarly on the forestage before the proscenium.) Another approach is to use a few architectural or decorative set pieces rather than a full setting to suggest the various rooms in the play; still another is to frame the entire production in a formal, permanent eighteenth-century architectural framework, with only furniture being shifted from scene to scene. In any of these approaches (both of which would be possible in the contemporary theatre), the stress would be on an abstracted essence of the eighteenth-century world in which the play takes place, and in neither of them would the major stress be on absolute character reality in acting and costumes.

For costume design, these varied staging methods include two basic interpretations of the stage dress to be created for this play: (1) the very detailed, psychologically based character approach to costume; (2) a much more limited, abstracted decorative approach to costume, in which the individual designs are less important than the overall effect of mood, style, and suggestion of period in modern terms. This is not to say that if the costumes are designed with great attention to personality and characterization they will lack unity or any sense of period style, but that these latter elements will remain subordinate to characterization. Neither is it easier or better to design the production in terms of decorative comment on the period, the play, and the visual style of the times. It is simply a fact that most costumes for a production of this play will assume one of these basic interpretations. Like all plays which can be interpreted several ways without violating the integrity of the play's structure, characterization, theme, and dialogue, *The School for Scandal,* unless it is produced for pure novelty of effect, will show certain elements remaining constant in the costume design, no matter how the script is presented.

First, the elements of eighteenth-century culture that have been described in this chapter and clearly lie at the heart of this play (includ-

Figure 14–10   A neoclassical interior of the period of Louis XVI, from the California Palace of the Legion of Honor, San Francisco. Gift of Mr. and Mrs. Richard Rheem. An example of straight lines and elegant restraint in late eighteenth-century interiors. Photo courtesy of the California Palace of the Legion of Honor, San Francisco.

ing artificiality versus casualness, false sentiment versus honesty, and morality versus evil) should be as clearly evident in the costumes as in the characters who wear them. The lighthearted treatment of all these themes, as contrasted with the more serious interpretation in *Tartuffe,* should be directly apparent in the stage dress. Since the effect of *The School for Scandal* is completely dependent on a clear interpretation of upper-class English society in the late eighteenth century, the artistic and cultural ideals of the time must be clearly presented—especially in terms of the costumes worn by characters of various ages and social levels.

The fabric textures chosen for the play should, therefore, reflect the social level of the character and the artistic ideals of the society as well as the character's personal taste. The major fabric surfaces will probably be hard, shiny, and brittle, with some accents of softness. This means that taffetas, moiréd silks, satins, and hard wool gabardines will predominate over soft woolens, heavy velvets, and dull cottons. Only in collars, cuffs, and vests will the softer touches of velvet and lace be apparent. This use of texture also reflects the nature of the script, which makes its first impression through its hard, clever, witty dialogue and sophisticated urbanity, and only a secondary impression through its softer underlying accents of sentiment and subtle sermonizing. A major source of ideas could well be the work of the painter Gainsborough, who was a close friend of Sheridan and his wife. Exquisite portraits of them both show that Gainsborough was a painter adept at capturing the image of the social class which Sheridan represented. Both men lived at Bath for some time, and nowhere in England during this period was the social game more carefully and fully played for image and effect than at this lovely spa. In the work of Gainsborough one can find the transparent, soft, sentimental, casual effects in fabric side by side with the hard satins and reflective taffetas of a more brittle, formal, artificial society; one need only look at the portrait of Mrs. Graham next to one of Mrs. Richard Brinsley Sheridan to see the double effect (Figure 14–11). Whether the costumes are to be quite realistic and tied to character or more abstracted and intended for comment on the period, the fabrics chosen will be similar, although they will probably be more subtle when chosen for character reality than when chosen for period comment or decorative effect.

In color, it seems quite obvious (from looking at the works of Gainsborough and the colors admired by society at this period) that heavy, dark, rich colors were not popular. The late eighteenth-century love of lightness, casualness, sentiment, and subtle decorative effects—borrowed from Antiquity—meant the use of a scale of values above medium tonalities, and only occasionally does one find dark, rich colors used in accent. The lightness, the lack of seriousness in the treatment of theme, and the surface brilliance of dialogue in this play would also suggest lightness of color. Only in a minor character or in someone of a

Figure 14–11   *Mrs. Graham* by Gainsborough, National Gallery, Edinburgh, ca. 1785. An example of the delicacy, elegance, and light brushwork of this portrait painter, who is described as the only Rococo artist that England produced in the eighteenth century. Courtesy of the National Gallery of Scotland.

lower social order would a muddied or dark color seem appropriate. Since this play so clearly reflects the social ideals of its day, the colors chosen for the costumes should reflect the taste of the times.

Finally, the line of the costumes should reveal both the soft and sentimental lines found in younger women's costumes of the day and the more artificial, formal lines found in the costumes worn by the powerful leaders of society. Again, comparing the lines in Gainsborough's portrait of Mrs. Graham with those in his portrait of Mrs. Sheridan, one can see the contrasts possible in this same period and possible in this play if one wishes to contrast sharply the costume worn by Maria with that worn by Lady Sneerwell. The humor gained by slightly ridiculous costume effects in garments worn by Lady Teazle and the ladies of the "school for scandal" can be given full rein by even a minimal look into women's styles of the period. Lady Teazle's naive attempts to fit into society versus the crass and heavy impression created by Lady Sneerwell and Mrs. Candour can be beautifully illuminated through just the slightest simplification, exaggeration, and subtle differences in costume line.

Closely related to costume line is the use of ornament, through which much of the comic tone for the production may be suggested. The use of ribbons and bows, braid edging a man's coat, floral accents, and the treatment of buttons and buckles may, through their size and placement, make a distinct character point or strike exactly the correct comic note as a strong focal point in a particular costume (Figure 14–12).

One must always remember how much costumes for a comedy of manners such as *The School for Scandal* depend on a pointed and slightly satirical interpretation of high fashion of the particular period. In this play especially, the designer must strive to obtain the correct balance in the costumes of those who dress in the artificialities of current fashion and those who wear more unpretentious garments.

Figure 14–12   Helen Hayes, Dee Victor, and Rosemary Harris in *The School for Scandal* as produced by the Association of Producing Artists, Lyceum Theatre, New York, 1967. Reproduced by courtesy of the APA Repertory Company. Photo by Robert Alan Gold.

15

Romantic Plays

Art and Culture in the Early Nineteenth Century

Romanticism, as a fully conscious Western European style, was impossible until the late eighteenth century; European society had for several centuries been based on a tightly organized caste system that placed great stress on organization and form. Not since medieval times had aspects of art and culture arisen in any full and meaningful way from subjective emotion alone. Even in the art of the sixteenth century, the subjective qualities of mannerism had been achieved primarily by very conscious manipulation of composition and form. Following the events culminating in the French Revolution, artists began to break from the strictures and inhibitions of the aristocratic and bourgeois world in which they had lived to the lonely, alienated, existential world of personal emotion and subjectivity. In this drive to break with reality, the leaders of romanticism always attempted to escape into a world that was more exciting, more fulfilling, more beautiful (or more terrible) than the world of bourgeois industrialism which was developing at the opening of the nineteenth century. The inexpressible was to be conveyed by any means possible in art and literature, but the great problem of the romantics was a lack of method, a lack of technique for expressing this personal and subjective reaction to life.

The only romanticist who was both a great representative of the style and an enemy of its formlessness and excesses was the painter Eugène Delacroix, who refused to surrender to the irrational and the emotional at the expense of form and composition (Figure 15–1a). Although we know from his *Journal* that he suffered from fits of melancholia, ennui, emptiness, and discontent with his work and so was fully involved in the

358

"sickness of romanticism," he despised being labeled a "romantic" and protested against being called a "master" of the romantic school. It was Rubens, not the "Bohemian" romantics who surrounded him, who was his artistic and human model, and Delacroix was one of the few artistic personalities since the early seventeenth century to combine the highest intellectual culture with the *grand seigneur* mode of life. What Delacroix lacked was a new technique with enough power to match his emotion. In England, Turner's canvases, scrubbed with a "hot" pigment, almost matched the romantic vision, but only van Gogh and the expressionist painters found a technique to match their subjective feeling (Figure 15–1b). The Baroque, early Renaissance, and medieval techniques borrowed by most romantic artists merely indicated the many directions in which artists and even writers searched for a method to project their personal search for meaning in life (Figure 15–2). These borrowings also indicate how much romantic art is based on escape, psychotic fear of the present, and a deep desire to find a haven, answer, or release in a world of the past or of the imagination.

Figure 15–1a   *The Death of Sardanapalus* by Delacroix, The Louvre, Paris, 1827. An example of the exotic subject matter, violent movement, rich color, and loose, thick brushstroke in the developed romantic paintings of Delacroix. Photo courtesy of Le Directeur des Musées de France.

This new, personal, subjective reaction to life and to the whole past history of the world also led to a totally new idea of history. Instead of the idea that history unfolds as a continuous drama of progress toward a fixed and discernible goal, there was a new, very subjective, and quite fearful idea that history and historical destiny are precisely tied to who we are and what we have been, that nothing is mutable in political or governmental institutions. This led to both pessimism and optimism, hope and despair. It was the basis for the whole development of nineteenth- and twentieth-century thought and institutions and is at the very heart of a present-day sense of relativity in art, morality, and science. This concept, astounding and frightening at the time, made students of history more aware of past ages than at any time in the history of Western man, while at the same time it made them feel alienated from the concept of a historical continuum of Western civilization. In this way romanticism is the first awakening of the modern outlook, rooted in the torment of the "individual mind," in the personal, subjective feel-

Figure 15–1b   *The Slave Ship* by Turner, Museum of Fine Arts, Boston, H. L. Pierce Fund, 1840. An example of the tempestuous, "scrubbed-in" brushwork of Turner, by which he hoped to express the cosmic power behind the elements of air, fire, and water. Photo courtesy of the Museum of Fine Arts, Boston.

Figure 15–2 The Houses of Parliament, London, by Barry and Pugin, 1840–1860. An example of England's Gothic and medieval inheritance used as exterior dressing on a series of rectangular architectural forms for associational and emotional values. Photo courtesy of the British Travel Office.

ing of loneliness and homelessness brought on by this new concept of history. Artists and writers now talk about the dignity of the unknown the way they used to talk about the dignity of man or of reason, and the new art is to become a human document in which the tormented personal confession—the baring of the personal wound—is acceptable as a complete subject in art and literature. In romanticism we see the beginnings of a complete alienation of the artist from public and patron, an autonomy that created art for other artists, an individualism that turned in horror from the crass world of bourgeois materialism. The romantic artist or writer considered himself part of a new aristocracy raised above the rest of society, and this removal led to the modern concept of the artist as half-seer, half-Bohemian, removed from the usual moral and cultural values and devoted to art for its own sake.

This concept also led to a second concept, in which introspection and analysis of one's self created the figure of the "second self" among romantic artists and writers. This tendency to consider one's self over and over again as a being unknown, a remote stranger, was an attempt to escape the responsibilities of one's own historical and social situation. In this flight, the unconscious is the worshipped source of dreams, wish fulfillment, mystery, excitement, and grotesquerie, and the artist or writer replaces experiences in the world with self-experience and natural objects with infinite interest in the "second self."

Theatre and Drama in the Early Nineteenth Century

The period between the late eighteenth century and the latter half of the nineteenth century saw a number of changes in the theatre, most of which were developments from earlier trends. The major method of organizing theatrical production was still the resident repertory theatre with its leading actors and supporting players presenting a rotating series of plays during any given theatrical season. The great companies on the continent were the government-supported national theatres such as the Comédie Française and the Vienna Burgtheater, while in England there were key companies such as the Royal Theatre at Drury Lane, which attracted the very best theatrical talent. Only the coming of the railroads in the 1840s led to the beginning, especially in the United States, of what was eventually known as the long tour, which used a production as a vehicle for a star actor or actress attracting an audience by reputation and personality. The rise of the star system and the long-run "hit play" changed the entire nature of theatrical production in the late nineteenth and early twentieth century. It turned theatre into a great money-making investment for theatrical managers and their stables of stars.

As a result of increasing urbanization and industrialization in Western Europe and the United States, the cities became flooded with workers from the lower classes, and the audiences changed from a middle-class majority in the late eighteenth century to a truly mass audience by the middle of the nineteenth century. Thus, the total spectrum of theatrical experience was greatly enlarged, ranging from performances of mere variety entertainment to grand opera and the classics. During the early nineteenth century the theatre was in many ways an entertainment medium for the masses, just as television is today. Productions often included a play, short song and dance acts, a short light comedy, even a short light opera, and they lasted from seven in the evening until after midnight. The size of the theatre also expanded, until major theatres in large cities seated 3000 or more spectators. At first the old box, pit, and gallery arrangement prevailed, but as it became more and more difficult to see and hear from the boxes, comfortable seats were gradually placed in what had formerly been the pit and is now called the orchestra. In the latter part of the nineteenth century, orchestra seats finally replaced box seats in price and desirability (Figure 15–3).

STAGING   The staging methods of the entire nineteenth century were dominated by an ever-increasing drive for historical accuracy in background and costume. The neoclassical ideal that had dominated the major dramatic developments from Shakespeare's day until the late eighteenth century had always stressed universality rather than detailed reality in theatrical presentation—historical accuracy was felt to have little connection with truth in art. When an interest in archeological accuracy began to develop in all the arts in the late eighteenth century, the theatre could not escape. As in literature and art, the importance of the individual in a particular time and place replaced a more generalized and cavalier attitude about past history and far-away places. In the production of plays in the early nineteenth century, actors and managers studied the architecture, sculpture, painting, literature, dress, social customs, and minor arts with as much, if not more, enthusiasm than they studied the play and its characters. Gradually plays were written which demanded many historical settings and scenes of historical pageantry, and even Shakespearean revivals became an excuse for a great museum of historical arts and facts to be paraded before the public. This trend flowered with the famous London production of *King John* by Charles Kemble in 1824 in which all visual details were designed with great accuracy by the antiquarian and costume historian, J. R. Planché (Figure

Figure 15–3   The interior of the Drury Lane Theatre by Pugin and Rowlandson, 1808. From Ackermann's *Microcosm of London*, 1808. An example of the enormous size of an English theatre in the early nineteenth century. Photo courtesy of The Metropolitan Museum of Art, New York, Harris Brisbane Dick Fund, 1917.

15–4). It reached its zenith in the early 1850s with the Shakespearean revivals of Charles Kean, for which teams of art historians and archeologists would spend months of preparation gathering the background material for a production. The program notes were pages long, and the productions were supposed to teach and enlighten more than entertain the spectator (Figure 15–5).

The scenery for these productions consisted primarily of wings and backcloths painted in perspective. A series of perspective wings with sky or foliage borders above framed the back scene and created an illusion of foliage or architecture moving forward to the proscenium arch. Such wings were still often moved in grooves in the stage floor or on chariots whose poles came through a slit in the stage floor; but such symmetry of visual effect was undesirable for an illusion of reality, and, gradually, wings were set at asymmetrical angles by hand or were developed as partial three-dimensional pieces to frame in the backdrop. In fact, every attempt was made to create an illusion of reality, and many of the

Figure 15–4   Costume sketch for King John, second dress, by James Robinson Planché, for a production of *King John,* 1823. Another example of the stress on archeological correctness in the costumes for this British production early in the nineteenth century. Photo courtesy of the Stark Collection, University of Texas Library, Austin.

Figure 15–5   Charles Kean as Richard II in a production of Shakespeare's play at the Princess Theatre, London, 1857, directed and produced by Charles Kean. A further example of the ideal if not the fact of archeological realism in historical stage dress. Photo from Clement Scott's *The Drama of Yesterday and Today,* Vol. I, Macmillan, London, 1899, p. 240.

theatrical effects and visual scenes placed on the stage during these years were workable and exciting. This was due partially to the adoption of gas light for the theatre, which allowed for the dimming and raising of light on the stage; it was the arrival of electricity for stage production, at the end of the century, that put an end finally to painted wing-and-drop scenery. Throughout the early part of the century, the stage was still sloped for perspective effect, and only when, in the 1840s, experiments with three full walls for the creation of a box set were undertaken were there strong demands for a flat platform stage.

COSTUMES   As with staging in general, costume was now based on careful research, and beauty, unity, and theatricality were prized much less than archeological authenticity (Figure 15–6). There was not, however, an overall feeling of authenticity in nineteenth-century production, but rather a sense of much detail without regard for the overall effect.

Figure 15–6 Costume sketch by Alfred Crowquill for the character of Manuel in a production of *Manfred* by Lord Byron, showing the romantic realism in stage costume that was the ideal in the early nineteenth century. Courtesy of the Norman Philbrick Library.

For example, actresses such as Mrs. Charles Kean would wear a very authentic Greek costume over Victorian crinolines and top it with a Victorian hairdo. Few questioned the final result (Figure 15–7). The great gain for theatrical costume during these years was in careful research and planning; the great loss was in theatricality, unity, and beauty. Important theatre artists of the past, including Inigo Jones and Jean Berain, would never have deigned to occupy their time with the theatrical mass media of the nineteenth century.

Faust

Goethe is to German literature what Shakespeare is to English literature, and *Faust* is considered by many critics to be the greatest literary work in the German language. But since it is more literary than theatrical in its vast size, technique, and development, the play must be cut, condensed, and adapted to make it stageworthy. The play is really a summation of Goethe's ideals and growth as a writer throughout his life; in that he began writing Part I in 1780 and Part II was not published until 1831, the entire work literally grew with him. It is in this very personal record of the author's quest for life's meaning that the play most accurately can be called a romantic epic.

PLOT AND STRUCTURE Romanticism, in attempting to create a picture of life on an extended scale, employs a diffuse and loosely connected plot structure that usually depends more on ideas than on form. *Faust*

Figure 15–7 Mrs. Charles Kean as Hermione in a production of *A Winter's Tale* presented at the Princess Theatre, London, 1856. An example of ambiguities in costume effect achieved by an actress who continued to wear Victorian petticoats under a Greek chiton. An engraving from Joseph Jefferson's *Autobiography*, Century, New York, 1890, p. 268.

is very loosely structured, and although it quite obviously is modeled after Shakespeare's large-scale dramas, it has none of the economy of effect or unity of action that one finds in *Macbeth* or *Othello*. In *Faust* one can see the weaknesses as well as the virtues of romanticism. In reaching for tremendous breadth of experience and scene, it often tends to be confusing and formless. While Shakespeare, in his mature work, sets the basic dramatic situation at the beginning of his play, Goethe waits until the fourth scene of *Faust* to establish the dramatic action in the pact between Faust and Mephistopheles. The introductory material in the two prologues takes a great deal of time, the various aspects of Faust's personal search are extended or contracted at the whim of the playwright, and the amount of attention focused on each of the supporting characters is determined by the author's personal preference rather than the demands of the action. This two-part drama is held together only by Faust's quest for fulfillment and salvation. In Part I, the story of Margarete and Faust tends to hold the play together in its sequential cause-and-effect development, and it is for this reason that only Part I is usually produced. It can be played as a full-fledged tragedy despite the interruptions of many psychological and philosophical scenes which break and confuse the plot structure.

Part II continues Faust's search in the realm of ideal beauty, humanistic learning, and the relationship of man to society. The conclusion is one of the great positive world statements of modern times, equating salvation with an individual's work for the collective good. Only through a two-evening presentation can the entire story be staged with the full breadth of its philosophic vision. In many ways, Part I is only a prologue to Part II.

Even when Part I alone is produced, the action is spread over twenty-five scenes, two prologues, and sixteen changes of locale. Time and place shift rapidly, there are many complicated scenic effects required, and costumes and masks for the *Walpurgisnacht* scene are a challenge to any designer.

CHARACTERIZATION   The cast of *Faust* is always very large. It is composed of crowds, choruses, witches, wizards, and spirits, and only a minimal number of characters are developed with any psychological reality. Faust, Mephistopheles, Wagner, Margarete, Martha, Valentine, and Lieschen have some three-dimensionality as characters, but the large number of other characters who populate the stage are mere abstractions designated by a group label rather than by individual names.

One of the key points of characterization in romanticism is the concentration on the emotions and psychology of the leading character or hero, and in the case of *Faust* this is precisely how Goethe has developed his work. The author uses the other characters only to illustrate, give insight to, and illuminate Faust's mind and soul, and it is an all but impossible task for the actor playing Faust to develop fully all aspects of the

Figure 15–8   Henry Irving as Mephistopheles in his production of *Faust* as presented at the Lyceum Theatre, London, 1887. From *Art Journal,* July 1887. Courtesy of the Norman Philbrick Library.

character without repeating the emotions of longing, groping, and reaching upward that mark Faust's dissatisfaction with life. Mephistopheles is less complex, depending primarily on cynicism, smiling duplicity, and cunning to pose a continuous threat to the fulfillment of Faust's search (Figure 15–8). Margarete is in many ways the typically innocent heroine of melodrama brought to a sad end by naive trust and love. Although she must run the gamut of emotions from love through happiness, shame, madness, and despair, she develops primarily as a stock character, without any great subtleties of personality and character. She is individualized through emotion rather than through character. Other roles must be filled by actors who need to develop only the most limited sense of characterization, yet who must be very accomplished in movement, dance, and sometimes song. In fact, the choruses and the extras can make the difference between failure and success in a production of *Faust*.

THEME   The theme is in many ways the most important part of *Faust* as a play. In his view of man as an aspiring, learning, creative spirit, Goethe takes a large-scale, optimistic view of man's innate strength and capability and clearly sees him as being capable of providing for his own salvation. The basic theme is established in the first prologue: although man cannot avoid loneliness, suffering, and grievous mistakes in judgment, he can hope to achieve salvation through striving for a better world. Both parts of *Faust* are a continuing dramatization of this theme. In Part I the audience is shown Faust's dissatisfaction with life. his solemn pact with Mephistopheles, and his search for salvation through enjoyment and sensual pleasure. Part II depicts the conclusion of the search and an acceptance of God's statement at the opening of the play; Faust finally rejects both poetry and beauty in favor of service to mankind as the final goal in life. Although Faust loses his wager with Mephistopheles, he has gained his own soul, and in the end it is Faust who has conquered and Mephistopheles who has been defeated.

The playwright is obviously concerned with the ageless problem of good and evil, and when Goethe indicates that God lives in eternal light and witches and evil spirits reside in eternal darkness, he is dealing with imagery in a typically romantic way. He builds on this image by posing the theory that man lives poised between good and evil—half in the dark but longing for the light. The *Walpurgisnacht* scene, in particular, makes great use of this contrast by stressing the sinister, dark, and evil nature of the scene, while making it clear that man is part of this scene and that it is part of him. The witches and evil creatures of darkness are part of Faust's own nature, representing the animal drives and the selfishness which he must surmount if he is to find salvation. Goethe also conceives of Faust's love for Margarete within this same image of darkness and light. Since his love is carnal, selfish, and narrow, it has been conceived in darkness and so must end in the darkness of Margarete's death and Faust's failure to find the light. In Part II Faust thinks that he has achieved the light with the attainment of Helen, only to find the light as transitory as his goal is selfish. Only in service is the true light reached and darkness banished.

DIALOGUE   The language in this play is developed in an infinitely complex series of heavy, involved, poetic speeches. Although the poetry is often more literary than theatrical, there are many moments when the total effect of its rich imagery and soaring rhythms is very impressive, especially when spoken by experienced German-speaking actors trained in the classical tradition of the Vienna Burgtheater. Long, poetic speeches similar to the arias of an opera are frequently used to build up the philosophical themes of the drama without furthering the action or developing the characters, and key images in the play, like the opposition between light and dark already discussed, are developed to the fullest poetic extent with little consideration for the events of the plot.

RHYTHM   The general pattern of rhythm in this huge and sprawling play consists of great sweeping crescendos and abrupt shifts and contrasts as the poetic dialogue travels from scenes of interior monologue to those of action and pageantry. The use of the spoken word, song, dance, folk festival, supernatural voices, and dramatized visions gives an endless series of stage effects that assault the senses and give great variety to the rhythmic progression of the play. At no point in the drama could one say that the rhythm becomes light-hearted, gay, or easy. Throughout the unfolding of the drama the rhythm, though rich and varied, is always heavy, sonorous, symphonic, and grand.

SPECTACLE   The staging requirements for the two parts of *Faust* are probably as demanding as for any play ever produced on the stage. The drama was originally conceived for the stage of the imagination, and the challenge to choreographer, musicians, costumer, set designer, lighting designer, and stage director is immense. To orchestrate properly color and light, mass movement, disembodied visions, music, voice, and shifts from one locale to another is a truly stupendous task, necessitating the use of every possible theatrical effect. This assault upon the senses and imagination of the audience is a challenge to the total visual and physical resources of the theatre.

Visual Presentation of Faust *Today*

An epic, cosmic drama such as *Faust*, which takes place on the stage of the imagination with little reference to a particular place and time, should not be produced today as a historic re-creation of how the play might have been done if both parts had been supervised by Goethe himself, in a two-evening production at Weimar. The wing-and-drop method, which has become fixed in the public mind with nineteenth-century melodrama, would have all the wrong connotations for an audience. A rich use of theatrical effects appealing to the senses would seem the logical way to bring this drama of the inner mind to life today. A realistic period approach would be much better left to the films.

Given the total forces of the modern stage, what directions might a producer and director take in presenting this epic on the modern stage? There are many possibilities, but, as in any production, structure, theme, and poetic imagery must be kept clearly in mind. *Faust* is a sweeping romantic drama, and this should not be forgotten while approaching a master plan for its production (Figure 15–9).

One direct and quite common approach to the production of *Faust* is to use light and darkness (one of the great images from the play) as the organizing factor in the drama and to reveal only small pieces of setting rising out of a darkness symbolizing a large area or world that cannot be seen. In this way full settings do not have to be built and so can be quickly shifted. Shafts of light are used to suggest the cosmic background for the drama and are theatrically effective in concentrating attention on one figure or a small group; later they can be expanded to illuminate a full stage scene. Some producers and directors would find this approach too related to the past, tied to the design methods of Jones, Craig, and other symbolists in the visual theatre, but it is a relatively uncomplicated and appropriate way in which to approach this mammoth work.

Another more modern approach would be to admit, as so many dramas have since Pirandello's *Six Characters in Search of an Author,* that the stage is a stage and the characters on it merely actors "describ-

Figure 15–9   Faust and Mephistopheles in Faust's study, from The Theatre Guild production of *Faust, Part I,* 1928. An example of the play produced in the romantic period of the play's composition. Courtesy of the Theatre Collection of The New York Public Library at Lincoln Center, Astor, Lenox, and Tilden Foundations. Photo by Vandamm.

ing" or "presenting" the parts they are to play. *Faust,* because of its Prologue in Heaven, obviously lends itself to this kind of interpretation, in which everything that takes place after the Prologue is a kind of cosmic charade or an acting out of a drama of search and salvation. In this approach the stage must remain a stage, a cosmic platform for events, using only stage properties to suggest a fuller reality. Changes of locale can be indicated by changes in projections, properties, and lighting, or by a combination of the three; only the costumes would have to have a certain dimension of visual effect, although they would be "costumes" and not character clothes.

Probably the most popular approach in the current German theatre is a full production with full sets and costumes, all of which make the play more contemporary, using modern concepts in art to determine the use of line, form, texture, and color. Modern nonobjective art usually falls into two camps: (1) the abstract expressionist school, in which the strongest possible emotional effects are achieved through a heavy use of broken lines, thick textures, and rich colors; and (2) the hard-edged, smooth-surfaced, limited color effects of geometric abstraction. These modern productions, then, are almost always inspired by one or the other of these camps. The abstract expressionist approach might be more suitable for the romantic, subjective, emotional, sensuous grandeur of the play, but this approach neglects the intellectual, philosophical, larger-than-life monumentality of the script. However, the hard-edged, geometric approach seems to leave out the emotion and sensuous imagery of the play. In a 1967 production of Part I at the Burgtheater in Vienna, Faust's study contained a desk built of scraps of broken iron, pieces of wood, bits of burlap, and odds and ends of leather and paper against a wall that was a collage of wood framing, broken books, bits of leather, pieces of manuscript, and ends of old cloth painted, sprayed, and aged to the color and surface of an old cave interior. The concept was one of total assault on the senses through the fullest use of a very textured surface, while simultaneously symbolizing the dusty decay in Faust's mind. It was completely modern and fully in keeping with the sensuous and imaginative power of the script, which exists above and beyond real life, yet it lacked stress on the intellectual, philosophical content of the drama. In a 1966 production of Part II at the Schiller Theater in Berlin, an almost opposite approach was taken (Figure 15–10). The intellectual, philosophical aspects of the drama were stressed, with exciting minor accents of mystery and theatricality. The settings were composed of glowing, colorless shapes made of plastic and metal; the music was abstract, cosmic, and mysterious; Helen appeared inside a transparent plastic sphere; and the general impression was one of a cosmic no man's land between Heaven and Earth. Again, the concept was very modern and fully in keeping with the monumental philosophical and intellectual concepts in the play, while playing down its sensuous aspects.

In the presentation of *Faust* one must be conscious of the importance

Figure 15–10   A scene from *Faust II* as produced by the Schiller Theater in West Berlin, 1966. Directed by Ernst Schröder. Scenery by Bernhard Heiliger. Costumes by Alexander Camaro. An example of this metaphysical drama produced in terms of extremely contemporary visual images. Courtesy of the Schiller Theater, West Berlin. Photo by Ilse Buhs.

of visual spectacle. The direction should take full account of stage depth, with intimate scenes in smaller areas downstage contrasting with large scenes in full depth filling the entire stage; long curving arcs and diagonal movement should be used to give epic sweep to the action, while an artistic use of space and variety is important to achieving a larger-than-life, emotional, visual effect. Also, the acting should be broad, sweeping, larger-than-life, with a great variety and range in the use of voice and gesture. Finally, in examining the costumes needed for this drama, one should realize how important a factor they are in adding to the over-all effect of the play. If the play is presented in a symbolist vein, with pieces of setting looming out of darkness to suggest a fuller and larger reality, then the costumes must add to this effect and be designed in rich color and texture in order to take full advantage of the lighting. A pictorial equivalent for these effects can be seen in Delacroix' water color of *Faust in His Study* (Figure 15–11). Small detail and complex trim should not be used, since it will be lost in the angular shafts of light;

pleating, deep folds, tacks, draping, puckering, and puffing of fabric surfaces will be the most effective way to take advantage of the lighting.
Colors should be rich but subordinate to silhouette and texture, and the
full effect of the costumes should come from the sculptured form of the
actor moving in light. If the play is presented on a stage that always remains a platform, then the costumes may be the major accent in the production. In this case they may be designed as simple costume props or
accessories added to the basic clothing of the actor, or they may be full,
lavish romantic costumes that read as rich accents to an otherwise bare
production. In the latter case the costumes should always have the aura

Figure 15–11 *Faust in His Study* by Delacroix, Fogg Art Museum, 1827.
A watercolor sketch done by this famous French romantic painter after reading Goethe's great work. Courtesy of the Fogg Art Museum, Harvard University. Bequest of Grenville L. Winthrop.

of theatrical stage items even when fully and richly designed to project both character and the sweeping, sensuous images of the play. Color, line, and texture could then be closely related to emotional effects, and the costumes would have the major role in carrying the visual impact of the drama. Finally, in a production designed to make full use of the shapes, lines, textures, and color of modern art, the costumes would either have to be abstractions of period dress or garments that created no illusion of period. The major stress would be placed on the texture, line, and color effects chosen from sources in modern sculpture or modern painting. If an abstract expressionist effect is desired, then many layers of texture composed of diverse materials such as shredded rope, plastics, and melted synthetics might be used to achieve the appropriate sensuous mood. If a cooler, machine-tooled effect is desired, then costumes made of smooth surfaces in glazed, metallic, or plastic textures with hard crisp edges might be appropriate.

The textures used in costumes for a drama such as *Faust* are very important in achieving the monumental, emotional, sensuous mood that the

Martha   Valentine

Figure 15–12   Costume sketches for Valentine and Martha by Frank Bevan for the Yale University production of *Faust, Part I*, 1949. Note the simplicity, monumentality, and strength in the mass and line of these costumes for *Faust*. From *Theatre Arts Magazine*, July, 1949. Reproduced by courtesy of Frank Bevan.

production requires, and great thought should be given to gaining the correct strength and mood unity in the choice of these textures. The lines of the costumes, although there are no limitations of period or shape, should be strong, monumental, and grand, with a larger-than-life silhouette in the finished costume (Figure 15–12). The color may be either strong or richly muted and subordinate to texture, but in no instance should it be weak, pastel, or superficial. Even if color is almost missing and the production is designed in neutrals or in a limited range of very dark tonalities, the particular scheme selected should be clear and forceful, not weak and fuzzy.

In a play of this size and scope, visual prescriptions cannot be few, and because this play strains every possibility of the physical theatre, it is ever a challenge for the designer to attempt something new and exciting in order to transmit the power, infinity of experience, and vitality of Faust's quest.

16

Realistic Plays

Art and Culture in the Midnineteenth Century

About the middle of the nineteenth century the idealistic, subjective views of romanticism began to seem meaningless and overblown. Although there had been several revolutions against repressive political regimes, there had been no real reform, and the principles of liberty, equality, and fraternity, in the face of the exploitations of the Industrial Revolution, appeared outworn and passé. In the face of a factory system that drew ever more workers into urban slums, the romantic tendency to see solutions in the inner heart, soul, and imagination of man seemed vague and impractical. Intellectual leaders and artists began to insist that dreams and the imagination be put aside in favor of systematic research into human personality and human society. Observation, clinical analysis, and scientific study of people and institutions were to replace the subjective idealism of romanticism.

A major contribution to this new outlook was the positivist philosophy of Auguste Comte, the father of sociology, whose writings between 1830 and the early 1850s argued for the study of society in a carefully controlled scientific manner. He felt that events in society could be predicted and determined in a clear cause-and-effect relationship by using the scientific method. This concept was further reinforced by the published theories of Charles Darwin, who developed the doctrine that all forms of life had evolved from a common ancestry and that this evolution was based on the concept of the survival of the fittest. These theories, coupled with those of positivism, suddenly made heredity and environment very important to both sociologist and artist and came to be considered the principal explanation of why individuals and societies developed in a particular direction. Behavior became something beyond the control of the individual, and only improvements in heredity and environment could better the human condition.

Thus, knowledge and truth in the realistic movement were limited to scientific observation obtained through the five senses, and intuition, imagination, visions, and all forms of the supernatural were removed from art and literature. Visually, the new ideal was given great support through the invention of photography, and the objective visual reporting that the camera made possible became a tremendous influence on all the arts during the latter half of the nineteenth century. A peephole glance at life, a scene caught by a camera in the corner of a room, on a street corner, at a café, in which people and objects were framed by the edge of the film, became a way of seeing for painters and writers alike. Edgar Degas gives an excellent indication of how such seemingly accidental views of life become the framework for the carefully planned structural effects and craftsmanship to be found in realistic plays (Figure 16–1a).

The very narrowness of the envelope within which a story could be

Figure 16–1a   *Interior: The Rape* by Degas, Collection of H. P. McIlhenny, Philadelphia, 1874. An example of the apparently casual "peephole" view of Parisian life, in which every item of furniture, the placement of the actors, and the use of light is very carefully selected and planned for dramatic effect. Photo courtesy of the H. P. McIlhenny Collection.

Figure 16–1b *The Romans of the Decadence* by Thomas Couture, The Louvre, Paris, 1847. An example of the contrived "academic exercise" in painting that was admired in the salons of the nineteenth century. Note its superficial and artificially contrived subject, which enables the artist to demonstrate his technical ability. Photo courtesy of Le Directeur des Musées de France.

developed led to a great stress on subtlety, form, and intricate character-story relationships. At a time when those opposed to realism were decrying the loss of style in art, the practice of the new method was leading novelists such as Flaubert and playwrights such as Ibsen to a new and deeper sense of style, a harsh and demanding craftsmanship, and a distilled human poetry which eventually lead to symbolism and the abstractions of modern art and literature. Forced to discard the clichés of romanticism, the realist narrowed his work and his vision to go beyond outer action to a study of what Francis Fergusson calls the "movement of the psyche." At its peak, realism triumphs over its limitations of place, character, and language.

The same is true in painting; artists such as Courbet continually rise above the limitations they set for themselves and inspire subjective, sensuous responses rather than coldly scientific ones. In fact, it is the salon art and its "academic machines" of the latter half of the nineteenth century which produce works with a scientific objectivity. *Romans of the Decadence* by Couture (Figure 16–1b), the teacher of Courbet, is more accurate in form, more technical, and more objectively rendered than a work such as Courbet's *The Stone Breakers* (Figure 16–1c); yet the latter

Figure 16–1c *The Stone Breakers* by Courbet, formerly in the State Picture Gallery, Dresden (destroyed during World War II), 1849. An example of the new realism in subject matter and painterly detail led by the artist Courbet. Courtesy of the State Picture Gallery, Dresden.

transcends mere reporting and delves deeply into subjectively experienced personal values. In giving up the broad sweep of vision available to artists since the Renaissance for the narrow confines of the everyday scene, the realists either succeeded with sharply focused concentration and depth or failed with a superficial reproduction of certain small areas of life.

Realism in Theatre and Drama

REALISTIC STAGING   The later part of the nineteenth century saw an ever greater attempt at historical reality in staging, with more pieces of scenery built in three dimensions than in the past, and perspective backdrops painted, masked, and lit to give as much illusion of reality as possible. For plays requiring one or more interiors to set the action, the movement was entirely away from side set pieces and painted drops to the three solid walls of a box set. The plays that represented the "new drama" at midcentury were basically romantic melodramas disguised as realism, and it took the work of Ibsen, Dumas *fils*, Augier, and others to create plays in which the setting and the overall visual environment of the action were an integral part of the drama.

Along with the increasing demand for the integration of background and action came the call for the integration of all other aspects of production, and from this need arose the role of the stage director. George II, Duke of Saxe-Meiningen, is usually credited with developing the completely integrated, large-scale realistic production. He himself designed all the scenery and costumes, worked out blocking, picturization and movement, and organized the extended rehearsal period. Depending on no stars, his entire company was subordinated to the overall stage effect, and in his many tours to the leading cities of Europe the "Theatre Duke" spread the gospel of the realistic, ensemble performance for the stage classics of the day (Figure 16–2).

But it remained for independent noncommercial groups in Paris, Berlin, and Moscow to introduce these staging methods into productions of the new dramas of realism. André Antoine, at the Théâtre Libre (founded in Paris in 1887), stressed absolute naturalness in his stage pictures, with every property and item of set decoration taken from real life. The Freie Bühne in Berlin in 1889, the Independent Theatre in London in 1891, and the Abbey Theatre in Dublin in 1904 all focused on the new realism, but the group with the most lasting influence, especially in the training of the actors, was the Moscow Art Theatre founded in

Figure 16–2   An engraving of the Saxe-Meiningen Company in a performance of Shakespeare's *Julius Caesar*. An example of the dynamic and precise planning of crowd scenes that made the work of this company admired throughout Europe. Photo courtesy of the Victoria and Albert Museum, London.

Figure 16–3   Act I of the original production of Chekov's *The Cherry Orchard* at the Moscow Art Theatre in 1904. An example of the untheatrical, everyday realism practiced by Stanislavsky and his associates in their productions of Chekov's plays. Photo courtesy of the Stanford University Drama Department Theatrical Slide Collection.

1898 by Constantin Stanislavsky and Nemirovitch Dantchenko (Figure 16–3). Stanislavsky eventually developed his theories on actor training into two books: *My Life in Art* and *An Actor Prepares,* and his basic precepts might be summed up as follows: The actor must be superbly trained in the use of body and voice, while also developing psychological techniques that permit emotional recall of personal experiences that can be related to a particular role. The actor must be able to define and outline the core of his role, particularly the key desires that motivate his character throughout a play, but such knowledge cannot be projected to an audience unless the actor can fuse all his onstage work into a single purpose through concentration. His response to other actors, his sense of the rhythmic development of the play, and his ability to work continuously toward refinement and perfection in his art are all tied to the ideal of onstage concentration. Again, as in writing and painting, the new realism led to a concentration of focus and a depth of penetration.

REALISM VERSUS NATURALISM   Of the many contributors to the drama of realism, the two greatest are undoubtedly Ibsen and Chekov—the first making use of the careful plotting of the "well-made play" to project themes of social import, the second developing the play of mood to project the hidden longings and frustrations of human nature. Ibsen stresses structure and craftsmanship in his playwriting, while Chekov is so skillful at concealing the mechanics of his work that the audience has the feeling that it has seen scenes from real life.

Before discussing plays by Ibsen and Chekov in detail, the distinction that is frequently made between realism and naturalism must be considered. The term naturalism is usually said to have originated in the essays of Émile Zola in France, who insisted that the drama go beyond the well-made problem play in which the author selects and arranges events to gain particular dramatic effects. Zola demanded a scientific, objective analysis of life presented on the stage and suggested the "slice-of-life" technique, which restricted the playwright to the recording of case studies. The importance of an absolutely accurate environment in order to show its influence on character was considered to be very important, and actors were urged to live, not play their parts. Although no purely naturalistic drama was ever written, many playwrights reveal aspects of this form, including August Strindberg, Maxim Gorky, Gerhardt Hauptmann, Eugene O'Neill, and Elmer Rice.

Ghosts

Ibsen's *Ghosts,* which depicts the hollowness of a conventional, nineteenth-century marriage, is a typical thesis play that also includes the thrill and tricks of boulevard entertainment. On the one hand, the play pretends to be not art, but life itself; on the other, it is more artfully crafted than any acknowledged "well-made play" by Scribe or Sardou.

. PLOT AND STRUCTURE   Structurally, *Ghosts* can be viewed on two levels: as a rational welding together of a series of events with a clear-cut moral, and as the "soul" or inner story of the outward action. It is actually organized as a series of debates on conventional morality between Pastor Manders and Mrs. Alving, the Pastor and Oswald, and Oswald and Mrs. Alving. There is a mounting, carefully controlled element of suspense maintained throughout, and each act ends with an exciting moment which sets the issues to date and promises intriguing new developments. But behind the surface events of the story there is a vaguely suggested tragic form, containing a deep and brooding view of the human condition.

CHARACTER   Each principal character in the play suffers, searches for answers, and gains new personal insights with each reversal of the action. Mrs. Alving, like Hamlet and Oedipus, is involved in a search for her true human condition, but as in Greek tragedy, we are shown only the end of the search, when the events of the past are illuminated by the present. Like Oedipus, as one veil after another is removed from the past and the present, Mrs. Alving begins to realize what the past and its dead ideas have done to her. The theme of the play—the "ghosts" of the past that have come to haunt the present—follows her to the end of the drama, and she becomes both a symbol and at the same time a very real, warm, and deeply understood human being. Oswald is also both a symbol of dissolution and decline and a very pathetic individual, and Pastor Manders, representing all the clichés about bourgeois morality, is but a pathetic shell of a man. All of the major characters are thus symbols, believable human beings, and stereotypes who might appear in a boulevard melodrama.

THEME   The central idea behind this drama is a strong and vivid attack on the emptiness of a conventional bourgeois marriage and a strong demonstration of the horror that can develop when a marriage such as that between Captain and Mrs. Alving is not terminated. Within the course of the action the playwright attempts to prove that Mrs. Alving should have left the Captain twenty years before and that such a marriage is evil and wrong.

DIALOGUE   Through the fumbling phrases of everyday conversational speech, Ibsen attempts, by the use of symbolic words and phrases such as "ghosts," to suggest a half-uttered, half-hidden poetry of feelings and ideas that can be fully demonstrated not in words but in acting. There is no verbal music, only a hidden poetry masquerading as reporting, a poetry not of words but of the theatre, and the dialogue in a play such as *Ghosts* can only come alive in the theatre in the performances of outstanding players.

RHYTHM   The rhythm of the play also operates on at least two levels: (1) that of everyday life and events within the circumscribed setting of the bourgeois home, and (2) that which develops from the movement of the intrigue toward climaxes at the end of each act—a series of reversals and revelations that lead directly to the final moment of resolution.

SPECTACLE   Ibsen's realistic technique can be fully seen in the visual elements needed for *Ghosts*. A detailed description of the setting is given, and the setting is very important to the play's action, especially the photographically accurate parlor in the foreground contrasted with the large window in the background, which reveals snowy peaks and suggests the exhilarating wilderness beyond the cramped interior. The characters are heavily influenced by the physical conditions around them, and this must be made abundantly clear through an adequate and accurate representation of the environment. The characters really seem to live in the setting, and they in turn help to create the environment. Therefore, the set designer must be as subtle and aware as the playwright of the actions and characters in the drama. The movement and physical action of the play must also be based on observations from life and on the organization of effects evident in the plot structure. Furniture can be used to assist, block, or complicate the action, and it can be arranged visually to give great meaning to the personal relationships in the play. Costumes must also act on one level to provide a sense of real clothing and on another to complement and assist the relationships, mood, and action of the drama.

Visual Presentation of Ghosts *Today*

In a contemporary production of a play such as *Ghosts,* there are not many choices of staging. Any direct approach to stage realism demands a fourth-wall production, in which the audience is shown the three walls of a room with an illusion of reality in all its furnishings and accessories. This means that the designer working with realism must work with more subtlety and care than the designer working in any other style, since all the elements of mood, shape, texture, line, and color must be subordinate to the overall reality of the scene. At no time can the designer of scenery and costumes allow his personal predilections or any abstract artistic ideals to dominate the visual scene; every artistic choice must be dictated by the need to develop the reality of the play's characters and the environment in which they live (Figure 16–4).

The size of the setting for *Ghosts* need not give the illusion of size and monumentality. This is based on the intimate, private nature of the

Figure 16–4 An original sketch for Hedvig in *The Wild Duck* by Henrik Ibsen designed by Laurence Irving, 1953. From the Norman Philbrick Library. Courtesy of Laurence Irving.

Figure 16–5 A scene from *Ghosts* by Henrik Ibsen as produced by the National Theatre of Oslo. The production approach is that of selective realism. Courtesy of the National Theatre, Oslo. Photo by Sturlason, Oslo.

place of the action, Mrs. Alving's parlor, and on the limited, concentrated nature of the play's construction. Since the play has only five characters, it is important to establish a setting in which each character's actions illuminate their interpersonal relationships. The shape, size, texture, and color of the setting must be carefully considered in order to support the environmental mood needed at the inception of the drama. The single most important mood to be established is that of the ghost of Captain Alving, the sense of what the past twenty years of Mrs. Alving's life with this man must have been like. The decorative detail, unlike the effects in pure Belasco naturalism, should avoid cluttering the walls and furnishings so that these primary effects of mood and environment are not blocked or obscured. In a play such as *Ghosts* a selective realism, whereby every item of set decoration is chosen to reveal the past history of a room, is far more important than merely presenting the audience with a replica of a Victorian parlor in Norway in the 1880s (Figure 16–5).

Probably the single most important item for both director and actors in a realistic play such as *Ghosts* is the furniture. It must be chosen to suit the environmental mood of the room and the character of its owners, but more important is its placement to give the strongest visual possibilities to the sharp conflicts and long debates which shape the drama. Tables and chairs must be the right height, have the right shape,

Figure 16–6   David Waller as Manders, Clifford Rose as Engstrand, and Dame Peggy Ashcroft as Mrs. Alving in *Ghosts* as produced by the Royal Shakespeare Company at the Aldwych Theatre, London, 1967, with designs by Jocelyn Herbert. An example of the strong feeling of mood that can be established within the narrow limitations of realism. Reproduced by permission of the Governors of the Royal Shakespeare Theatre, Stratford-upon-Avon, England. Photo by Dominic.

and have the right weight to be used as barriers or support. More than anything else, the furniture can help to evoke the hothouse, prison-like atmosphere that has been the center of Mrs. Alving's life since her marriage to Captain Alving (Figure 16–6).

Many painters of the late nineteenth century have illuminated interpersonal relationships through the placement of the people and furniture, and none has accomplished this more brilliantly than Edgar Degas. For example, there is his painting, *The Bellelli Family,* in which the father is facing upstage and is separated from his family by the edge of the fireplace and the placement of his chair. The mother dominates one daughter by pulling the girl against her, while the other daughter shows a more independent nature, balanced between the mother and the father (Figure 16–7). Another painting by Degas, variously labeled *Interior: The Rape* or *The Seduction* (Figure 16–1a) uses the placement of the two principals within a particular furniture arrangement to achieve a heavy and ominous atmosphere. The woman is seated weeping at her dressing table, the iron bed illuminated by a small table lamp lies in the center of the painting on a diagonal, and the man is lost in shadows leaning on the door at the far right. It is exactly like the climactic scene in a realistic play, and a study of the so-called camera angle and "snap-shot" effects of Degas can be of great help to a set designer and a director of any realistic play. The plays of Ibsen are as carefully devised in the logical plotting of the structure of events as are the lines and forms in a Degas painting.

It is difficult to give any secure guidelines about costume design, since each costume must be designed to fit exactly the reality of the character wearing it. The subtleties of personality and character suggested by each costume must precede any thought of overall design or atmospheric mood. At the same time, it is a mistake in realistic costume design to work so carefully for evocation of individual characters that the overall mood or atmosphere of the setting is lost.

One important distinction to make in designing costumes for a play such as *Ghosts* is that the costumes must not be laden with natural-

Figure 16–7 *The Bellelli Family* by Degas, The Louvre, Paris, 1859. An example of family relationships presented through placement of the members of the family in relation to one another, to the furniture, and to the room. Photo courtesy of Le Directeur des Musées de France and S.P.A.D.E.M. 1969 by French Reproduction Rights, Inc.

istic detail. It is a selective realism that suits Ibsen's method of character and plot development. This means the inclusion of only those items of dress essential to illumination of character and reality, not the inclusion of busy details that suggest authentic period garments. It is important to realize that the clarity of accent and detail in costume should be as sharp as the accent and detail in the plot and development of character.

Concerning the specifics of costume, the above ideas about selective realism can readily be related to the choice of line, texture, and color. The line chosen both for costume silhouette and ornamentation should be simpler and sharper than if the costumes were reproduced exactly from period sources, as the development of story and character is clearer and sharper than in real life. The textures used should be tied first to personality and character and second to the mood of the setting and the mood of the entire play. The thick, heavy, complex, oppressive textures that we associate with Victorian dress or Victorian parlor fabrics is completely right for the characters in this play. Although there is little opportunity to use any variety of these effects in individual costumes, it should be kept in mind as an image during design. It is certainly true that Pastor Manders must be in the black frock coat and clerical collar of his profession, that Regina wears a maid's costume, that Oswald dresses in a dark Victorian suit with a few Bohemian touches, and that Mrs. Alving wears a severe gown suggesting her position as the widow of Captain Alving; but in each case a very subtle difference of effect will occur with each choice of fabric if the oppressive, heavy atmosphere of the Alving's parlor is retained as an image, and if the symbolic images suggested by the "ghosts" of the play's title are also recalled. This last point might be particularly important concerning color. The requirements of the character's positions demand grayed, dark, oppressive color, with only tiny accents to break the monotony, but the exact tonalities selected can best be inspired by the oppressive images created by the Alving parlor and the "ghosts" so frequently mentioned in the play.

The Cherry Orchard

If the range of realism is to be understood, then it is important to contrast Ibsen's *Ghosts* with a play such as *The Cherry Orchard* by Anton Chekov. The difference between the two writers' methods is very illuminating for the designer, especially when their individual approaches to plot and character are used as the basis for the visual design of their plays.

PLOT AND STRUCTURE   By the time Chekov wrote *The Cherry Orchard*, the ambitious machinery of the thesis thriller had begun to fade in favor of presenting the human spirit and human emotions, not in action, but in the pauses in life. This play is often said to have no plot, but by being free of the mechanical plotting of the "well-made play," it becomes a series of apparently casual incidents—a theatrical poem dealing with the pathos and suffering that accompany individual and social change. Chekov believes that those perceptions that precede rational analysis are the most true in life, and he selects those moments in his character's lives between their rational strivings when they are most vulnerable, open, and obvious—when their personal situations are most directly felt and perceived. The action of the play is then built around four ceremonial family moments that make up the four acts of the play: the arrival back from Paris to take up the old way of life; the pause at sunset when all of the characters see themselves and their lives fleetingly for what they really are; the slightly hysterical party when the announcement about the sale of the cherry orchard is finally made; and the final departure.

CHARACTER   In characterization there is a great difference between what we learn about the characters and the dimly perceived personal perceptions presented on stage. Chekov is extremely dependent on the subtle interpretive abilities of his actors, and only in a superbly orchestrated production will the poetic subtleties of characterization crystallize. For example, Lopahkin is a man of action and could have been used as a symbol of Russia's move into the future, but he is shown at moments of reflection when he is forced to examine his own motives in a rather pathetic way. Mme Ranevsky, who has traveled throughout Europe and might have been shown by another playwright with her lover in Paris, is here shown in all her pathetic, impractical, emotional immaturity, at a moment of pause in her frivolous life when she has to face herself and her past. Particularly in Act II, Chekov allows each character to reveal himself within a mood that suggests all rational processes have ceased to allow subconscious longings their full expression.

THEME   Unlike *Ghosts*, this play does not have a theme or thesis in a true sense of that word. In the final analysis, the play appeals to the poetic and emotional sensibilities, and all so-called themes must be read into the play or interpreted into it in production.

DIALOGUE   The dialogue is as difficult to define as the characters. Once again, it is not the dialogue itself but the ability of the actor interpreting it that makes it have life, poetry, beauty, and meaning. The pauses, breaks, half-phrases, whispers, giggles, exclamations, tears, and laughter are as much a part of the dialogue as the words themselves; and only if all are included can one sense the inexpressible poetry underlying modern life as evoked by the playwright. It is because Chekov says so little that he reveals so much; he knows that the poetry of modern realistic drama is to be found in those inarticulate moments when the human creature is shown responding directly to his all too human situation.

RHYTHM   Nothing could indicate more clearly the difference between *Ghosts* and *The Cherry Orchard* than their rhythms. In the first the rhythm is tightly developed through developing conflict to crisis and denouement, while in the latter it is loosely tied to three ceremonial occasions related to the return to the estate, its sale, and the final departure. Although the rhythm is subordinated to the emotional moods of the characters and the subtle poetry of the setting, it is one of the strongest values in the play—like the inexorable flow of an underground stream occasionally observed through an opening in the ground.

SPECTACLE   The play demands three realistic settings, two indoors and one out, and in the original production at the Moscow Art Theatre each was very literally reproduced; but it should already be obvious that photographic fact in Chekov should be put aside in favor of suggestion, and that lighting in particular will be very important in creating mood. Like music, lighting is able to define mood and atmosphere indirectly, and in this sense Chekov visually demands a production that is balanced between strict realism and symbolic-impressionism. By Chekov's day, the symbolist movement in literature and the impressionist movement in art had reached full development, and much of the secondary level of effect in Chekov comes from this artistic "impressionism." The impressionist painters had begun as realists and then felt that they were deepening their realism through underlining nature's or people's moods. Only by understanding what light filtered through cherry blossoms, the sunset hours of the day, a chandelier-illuminated party would mean to an impressionist painter can a designer have an appropriate feeling of the settings for *The Cherry Orchard*.

In the use of furniture, again the contrast between Ibsen and Chekov should be stressed. Ibsen, like Degas, uses furniture to strengthen conflict, control action, and focus movement and climax. Chekov, using a looser playwriting method, uses furniture for purposes of mood, as symbols of the past, reminders of events and feelings long forgotten. Furniture may also act to break up the usual direct patterns of movement in order to match the halting, broken rhythms of the play's development. Nothing could be more symbolic of this effect than the clumsiness of Epihodov, who is made to stumble over chairs.

In costumes, the requirements are not merely those of character, but also of mood and atmosphere. Suggestion is more important than detailed fact, and a strict realism in choice of garments is less important than the overall interplay of costume effects to establish the mood of the four semiceremonial occasions that make up the four acts.

Visual Presentation of The Cherry Orchard *Today*

In his stage directions, Chekov is uncomfortably bound by the realistic conventions of his time, and to fabricate in a very literal manner three settings for this play out of cyclorama, flats, cut-out silhouettes, heavy furniture, complex bits of set decoration, and strong lighting effects would be to create the interesting but unbelievable antique effect that we still amusedly associate with the settings of David Belasco. The best strategy is to pay only lip service to photographic realism and to keep all the elements as simple as possible, so that the imagination of the audience can be stimulated rather than inhibited by the number and complexity of the set decorations. Even more than Ibsen, Chekov adds the extra dimension of symbolism to his setting demands.

The textures used in the setting should appeal to a sense of association and nostalgia for a past that is rapidly drifting away. Curtains and upholstery should have a softness and a vagueness that would be in sharp contrast to the harsh effects in *Ghosts*. The cornices and mouldings, the door panels and the details of set decoration should suggest rather than state; one should have to guess when the house was built and pay little specific attention to its overall period decor. All textural effects should help to establish that poetry behind the realism that we have described in relation to the plot, characters, and dialogue of this play.

The line of setting and the colors used should also evoke the moody and indefinite. It must be a "real" set, not some poetic abstraction, but the suppressed mood and poetry beneath that realism can only come through if the colors are rather faded and indefinite and if the lines are not too harsh and rigid. The outdoor mood of Act II is completely enmeshed with the line of the trees that are used, and the poplars indicated in the script must have all the mournful character and mood of a "dying fall" that will support the nostalgic and sad "passage of time" indicated by this act of the play. The chandelier-lit party mood of Act III can be effective only if the drawing room is a complex mixture of fading grandeur and sad happiness. The softness of tears, which continually erupt in this act, must be in the colors of the upholstery and draperies and in the soft lines of furniture, paneling, and set decorations (Figure 16–8).

Finally, the costumes must be capable of adding to the same effect, and straightforward realism based on turn-of-the-century fashions will be quite wrong. Once again, vagueness and suggestion must be the key, and since we have mentioned Chekov's visual affinity to much of the work of the impressionist painters, a study of costume in the works of Renoir and Monet would do much to prepare the designer to make appropriate choices for *The Cherry Orchard*. Looking at costumes in impressionist paintings, the viewer is struck by the studied indefiniteness with which the artist has suggested rather than stated a suit or a gown. It is admittedly easier to get some of these indefinite effects in women's clothes than in men's, since male clothes in the nineteenth century were so rigidly set regarding cut and line, and so devoid of ornament, that an indefinite line is almost impossible. Subtle effects can be achieved, however, through the use of soft-textured woolens for suits and coats rather than hard-surfaced gabardines, or through color choices that are muted and rather indefinite. Sometimes accessories can be used, such as a shawl or a smoking jacket, to further soften the hard line of late nineteenth-century male attire. In the case of the women's dress the problem is simpler, although here the specific requirements of a hunting costume for Charlotta and a maid's uniform for Dunyasha do limit the design choices. Fabric choices should be in terms of changeable fibers, laces over solids, soft, absorptive textures, surfaces that suggest through light reflectivity and absorption a sense of indefiniteness, changeability, or subtlety. Lace is a particularly useful costume effect, whether in a full-lace dress over a subtle solid-color fabric beneath—an effect that is particularly close to many impressionist paintings—or as an item of trim or an element of accessory decoration. Since lace is one of the chief fashion fabrics of the period, it is also an acceptable choice without contradicting the fashion line of the times. In color, also, subtlety, indefiniteness, and suggestion should be paramount, and heavy, rich, strong colors should be avoided except as accent. Muted colors, pastels, changeable colors, mottled colors, and broken color effects are needed to match the broken

Figure 16–8   Act II of *The Cherry Orchard* as produced by The Stanford Repertory Theatre, Stanford University, 1967, with settings by Richard Hay, costumes by Richard Odle. An example of simplified realism to project mood through changes in lighting. Photo courtesy of Hank Kranzler, Palo Alto, Calif.

Figure 16–9   Costume sketches by the author for Mme Ranevsky and Gaev in Act II of *The Cherry Orchard*. An example of the use of light color tonality to create mood and to reflect changes in the lighting. From the collection of the author.

and shifting effects in the dialogue, rhythm, and characterizations in this play. The strong lines of plot organization and character delineation found in *Ghosts*, which demand equally strong and clear costume effects, are completely missing in *The Cherry Orchard*. The costumes for this play must evoke a mood, suggestion, wispiness, a sense of the passage of time and the disappearance of the past (Figure 16–9).

17

Symbolist Plays

Art and Culture at the Close of the Nineteenth Century

To the poets, realism seemed a betrayal of the role of the artist in society, a debasement of art from the realms of the artistic to a mere reporting of life. The artists who rejected realism as an answer to the challenge of modern industrial society were not late-blooming romantics but modernists who were probing beneath the surfaces of life and art. While the earlier romantics surrendered themselves to feeling in order to become emotionally involved in their art, the artists who followed the theories of Baudelaire had an unremitting care for composition, style, and how to turn the intuitive and the irrational into carefully planned artistic products. Art was seen as a movement, a shape, a rhythm to be imposed on feeling—a quite self-conscious attempt to impose a personal style and form on the raw materials of life. Each artist hoped to assure his own view of experience as the direction of a new, cohesive cultural style that would reunite the artist with the general public. Throughout the nineteenth century, with cultural absolutes all but destroyed, the true artists had been waging war against the false prestige and historic superficialities purveyed by the great academies and salons of art and literature. Finally, in the last decade of the century they promoted a new style, *art nouveau,* which was the first great Europe-wide artistic movement since the Rococo.

In this new movement, which has been given the overall name of *symbolism,* concentration was on form over content and the inner life of the material over the outward fact. It divided itself roughly into three methods: (1) that art which stresses the inner secrets of life through mood and suggestion (impressionistic symbolism); (2) that art which stresses style and manner of presentation over content (neomannerism); (3) that art which depicts inner emotional states of being through violent, harsh, and distorted attacks on the senses (expressionistic symbolism). All of these movements can be grouped under the title of symbolism because all turn their back on reality and the objective facts of life and use symbols to make their artistic points.

Figure 17–1a　*Rouen Cathedral* by Monet, The Metropolitan Museum of Art, Theodore M. Davis Collection, 1894. An example of the dissolution of reality and structural form by mist and light in the later work of Monet. Mood, atmosphere, and a personal vision take precedence over visual facts. Photo courtesy of The Metropolitan Museum of Art, New York, bequest of Theodore M. Davis, 1915.

Impressionistic symbolism is an art of suggestion in which the early symbolist poets and artists such as Redon used vague symbols to suggest deeply buried inner states of feeling. Even impressionism in painting, originally intended to expand optical reality through the creation of momentary effect, gradually drifted in the work of Monet into vague, moody dream-like effects in which the results were often close to the sublimated reveries of the symbolist poets (Figure 17–1a). In sculpture, impressionistic symbolism is exemplified in the shifting, changing surfaces in the work of Rodin (see Figure 9–11a). Like the famous descriptive phrase in *The Journal* of the artist Delacroix, art was to be like "the memory of music" that has passed away. Odillon Redon was the painter who came closest to this ideal in works entitled *Silence, The Thought,* and *The Dream.* He

Figure 17–1b   *Reverie* by Odillon Redon, The Museum of Modern Art, New York, ca. 1900. An example of the ambiguity and mystery in symbolist painting. Redon hoped to "put the logic of the visible at the service of the invisible." Photo courtesy of The Museum of Modern Art.

Figure 17–2   *Fatata Te Miti* by Gauguin, National Gallery of Art, Washington, D.C., Chester Dale Collection, 1892. An example of the strong sense of mood and style through pattern that made Gauguin a leader among the symbolists as well as among the craftsmen of the *art nouveau*. Photo courtesy of the National Gallery.

used the resources of the inner mind and not the world of the senses to develop his images, and his hope was to create an art that had the uncertain, indefinite, mood effect formerly possible only in music (Figure 17–1b). In drama this method was followed by Maurice Maeterlinck, while in music Claude Debussy was the great exponent of the impressionist tradition of the symbolist poets. In his vague, moody, shifting evocations of the moon and sea we have in music what the painters and poets longed for in their art.

But impressionistic symbolism tended to be formless, and it was to this problem that the *neomannerists* addressed themselves. They used many of the same images and symbols, but stressed form, design, and pattern as equal to mood in the content of their work. They developed artificiality and style as an end in itself in much the same way as the sixteenth-century mannerists. For example, in the work of Gauguin, the flat poster, the woodcut, and the Japanese print are as evident in the shaping of the decorative pattern of the composition as is South Seas mythology in shaping the content (Figure 17–2).

In *expressionistic symbolism* it is the quality of assault on the senses

Figure 17–3   *The Scream* by Munch, National Gallery, Oslo, 1893. An example of the swirling brushstrokes and exaggerated shapes that carry the artist's subjective and overpowering image of fear to the level of nightmare. Photo courtesy of the National Gallery, Oslo.

that is important. Its beginnings are apparent in the 1890s in the paintings of Edvard Munch, James Ensor, and Vincent van Gogh and in the plays of August Strindberg, and in each case the art was due to a very subjective development in the personality of a neurotic and tortured individual (Figure 17–3). Patterns and symbols are used in a distorted, explosive, violent, nightmarish manner to depict the outward world through the inward world of the artist. In lashing out and attacking the suffering, horror, and injustice in life, an art results that is often distorted to near abstraction, and eventually this led to abstract expressionism following World War II. But in the painting of the German expressionists and the work of the fauvist Rouault, the artist is specifically tied to a distorted yet recognizable assault on the senses and an attack on the nature of society.

The Revolt Against Realism in the Theatre

The theatrical ideals of the symbolists had their origin as early as the middle of the nineteenth century in the theories of Richard Wagner, who dedicated himself to a fusion of music, dialogue, color, light, shape, and texture to give a unified theatrical mood. In his theatre at Bayreuth he

Figure 17–4   Design for *Electra* by Gordon Craig, ca. 1905. An example of the simple and magnificent forms given mood and beauty through dramatic lighting effects that marked the work of the "new stagecraft" and the arrival of symbolism in theatrical design. From *On the Art of the Theatre* by Edward Gordon Craig, Browne's Bookstore, Chicago, 1911. Original in the University of California Library at Los Angeles. Reproduced by courtesy of Edward Carrick Craig.

used a double proscenium, a curtain of steam, and a darkened auditorium to create a mystic division between audience and stage that would allow spectators to lose themselves in the artistic magic of the production. The symbolists borrowed many of his precepts when they premiered *Pelléas and Mélisande* at the Théâtre l'Oeuvre in 1892 with a transparent curtain in front of the action and a great stress on mood. At about the same time, Adolphe Appia, in an endeavor to bring the ideals of Wagner to real fruition, developed stage lighting as the great unifying factor in production—defining the actor in space against simple, abstract three-dimensional forms and supporting the continually shifting moods in the action and in the music.

A few years later, the young English designer Gordon Craig further developed the same ideals, placing even more emphasis than had Wagner and Appia on the super artist-director who would blend action, words, line, color, and rhythm into a great artistic work in which the script was only a part of a much larger whole (Figure 17–4).

The influence of Appia and Craig was immense and could be seen in most artistically designed productions before World War II. The scenic philosophy of the symbolists might be condensed as follows: a simplification of means and effects; an appropriate relationship of actor to background; suggestion, by which a single candelabrum could symbol-

Figure 17–5   A sketch of Romain Rolland's *Danton* as produced by Max Reinhardt at the Grosses Schauspielhaus, Berlin, 1920. An example of the spectacular, style-conscious productions of this master of artistic eclecticism. From *Theater Pictorial* by George Altman, Ralph Freud, William Melnitz, and Kenneth Macgowan, University of California Press, Berkeley, 1953. Photo courtesy of William Melnitz.

Figure 17–6   A sketch for Act III, scene 4 from Shakespeare's *Macbeth* as designed by Robert Edmond Jones for a production at the Apollo Theatre, New York, produced and directed by Arthur Hopkins, 1921. An example of violent theatrical expressionism used in presenting the psychology of the protagonist. From *The Theatre of Robert Edmond Jones,* edited by Ralph Pendleton, Wesleyan University Press, Middletown, Conn., 1958. Courtesy of Mrs. Honor Leeming Luttgen Collection.

ize the entire culture of the Baroque era; a synthesis of all elements of a production into a complex and rhythmic fusion of sets, costumes, lights, actors, and script.

The theatre artist who best transformed these ideals into exciting theatrical productions was Max Reinhardt, who took Craig's slogan, "Not Realism, but Style," coupled it to the concept of the director as master theatre artist and seer, and created a new meaning throughout Europe for the title *régisseur.* He paraded before the public the theatrical styles of the past and of the East in great eclectic revivals that used visual and aural symbols to unify the production, and although his eclecticism was criticized by the modernists, he did bring design back into the theatre as a major artistic form (Figure 17–5). He became the master showman of the new theatre, and his name became a household word in the United States and in Europe. It was American artist-designers such as Robert Edmond Jones, Lee Simonson, Donald Oenslager, Norman Bel Geddes, and Jo Mielziner who carried the ideals of Appia, Craig, and Reinhardt into that exciting era of American theatre that followed World War I (Figure 17–6).

Pelléas and Mélisande

One of the most fully symbolist dramas written to exemplify the precepts of impressionistic symbolism is Maurice Maeterlinck's *Pelléas and Mélisande*. In many ways the moody tale cries out for music, and the perfect wedding of composer and author took place when Claude Debussy made the play into an opera in 1902 (Figure 17–7).

PLOT STRUCTURE   Based on Dante's tale of Paolo and Francesca, the structural development of this play consists of a series of loosely connected scenes which seem to have little relation to the main story line. The opening scene, in which a group of women are vainly attempting to wash the stains from the castle steps, is typical of the scene-by-scene development. It creates a mood of mystery and hopelessness, but it has nothing to do with the story of Pelléas' love for Mélisande. There are many more such scenes: the scene in which Mélisande's doves leave her forever, the scene in which she loses her ring, symbolizing the loss of her marriage vow, the scene in which Yniold tries to lift a stone that symbolizes the weight of sin fallen on the family. Mood and theme are the im-

Figure 17–7   A scene from *Pelléas and Mélisande* by Maeterlinck and Debussy as produced at the Metropolitan Opera, New York, 1965. An example of a few simple set pieces used as symbols to be picked out by dramatic lighting to achieve the mood and impression required. Courtesy of the Metropolitan Opera. Photo by Sedge Le Blang.

portant elements in the structure of this play, not the development of a story or plot. In fact, the number of scenes between the first meeting of the lovers and their deaths could be expanded or contracted without much effect on the development of the story, although each is intricately bound to the developing mood of the play. The scenes are connected by a thread of symbolic atmosphere rather than by a cause-and-effect chain of events.

Although the playwright used the five-act play form, the act divisions are purely arbitrary and do not mark any clear breaks or high points of suspense in the action. The true unit of division in this play is the scene, and each of the sixteen scenes suggests some aspect of the theme or deepens some mood effect.

CHARACTER The characters are as vague and mysterious as the mood. They are embodiments of vague feelings and desires that yearn for enlightenment, yet are destined to live and die governed by some inexplicable law of fate. About all we are given is their age, their social class, and their names, plus a vague stroke or two to suggest personality. Fate is the great life force that hangs over all the characters. Maeterlinck is not interested in three-dimensional, flesh-and-blood people, but in states of feeling which creep upon his characters mysteriously and lead to mysterious and inexplicable consequences.

THEME Since his theme is that fate rules all, the playwright presents all ideas indirectly in terms of repeated motifs and symbols. For example, water is used over and over again: there is the pool by which Mélisande is first discovered, the fountain in which she looses her ring, the bottomless pits of water under the castle, the water used to wash the blood stains from the steps, and the sea, which is a soul-beckoning place of release. The same repetition occurs with darkness and light. The forests are ever dark, the characters are seated in darkness groping toward light, lamps die out and cannot be relit. There are many more, and it is difficult to assign definite meanings to them, but throughout, love, happiness, and light are in continuous struggle with fate and the forces of darkness, with the fountains and pools of water symbolizing that reflecting element into which the characters peer in vain in an attempt to unlock life's mysteries. Maeterlinck is obsessed with an even more deterministic philosophy than the realists and naturalists and sees all life as a mysterious and impenetrable unknown.

DIALOGUE The language of the play is extremely simple and repetitive, so that words and phrases ring in the inner ear as symbols for feelings that cannot be expressed. In his long essay, *The Treasure of the Humble,* Maeterlinck speaks of this second level of language as the dialogue "for the soul"—those seemingly unnecessary and superfluous words and phrases that speak to man's deepest strivings toward beauty and truth. The playwright expects the audience to search behind the words and pauses for the play's ultimate significance.

RHYTHM   The rhythm of *Pelléas and Mélisande* is predominantly gentle, shifting, and soft and has no harsh, abrupt changes. It allows for a deepening awareness to grow within the audience, and silence amid pauses is as important as the forward movement of the play. The rhythm of this play, like symbolist poetry and symbolist painting, is close to the moods and rhythms of quiet, flowing music.

SPECTACLE   The demands for appropriate visual effects are very insistent in a play such as *Pelléas and Mélisande*, yet it is difficult to establish the visual effects required. In the original production at the Théâtre de l'Oeuvre in Paris, the stage lighting was overhead and kept low in intensity; a gauze curtain was hung at the front of the stage so that the action seemed to take place at a distance and enshrouded in a light mist. The scenery and costumes were designed in pale gray tones to emphasize the poetic removal of the action from real life; the movement and gestures were unreal and trance-like; the characters' bodies and limbs seemed to be moved by some unseen force. A key to the visual presentation of this play is the word "mist," and a key item in the design concept is the use of light.

Visual Presentation of Pelléas and Mélisande *Today*

Since we have only recently emerged from the period in which aspects of symbolist design were apparent in almost all artistically conceived commercial productions, and we are all somewhat involved in the reaction against this style, it might be very difficult today, at a time when epic and absurdist theatre are admired, to expect an audience to take a production of *Pelléas and Mélisande* seriously. In *New Theatres for Old*, Mordecai Gorelik, who opposed symbolist theatre even at the height of its acceptance, quotes a description of a mock performance in which an audience enters a theatre in 2100 A.D. and falls into a dream-like trance suffused with floating images, perfume, pulsating rhythms, seductive music, overpowering emotions, and symbolic moods. And it is true that the symbolist impulse in theatrical production, if carried to its logical conclusion, could easily remove concrete ideas, clear-cut meaning, and fully developed plots completely from the theatre in favor of the trance-like reverie, the nebulous image, and the sensual stupor. Thus, the producer of *Pelléas and Mélisande* must concentrate less on vagueness and diffuseness of effect and more on emphasizing strong mood derived from simple sets and visual images. Curtains between scenes should be removed; there should be a continuous flow of action from scene to scene, accented and focused by the lighting. Although the use of transparent gauze might still be useful in suggesting vagueness in certain settings, to place the entire action behind such a curtain is probably not possible today. The transparent drop was to symbolist theatre what the painted backcloth was to nineteenth-century romanticism.

It is very appropriate to place all aspects of the physical production on the stage at once in a simultaneous setting that demands no shifting of scenery during the course of the play. This necessitates total reliance on the lighting to lead the audience from scene to scene and place to place. In a sense, a production of *Pelléas and Mélisande* has to be orchestrated by light and developed as if it were a musical composition (Figure 17–8). Each shape and form used must be modeled to the outline and textural surface that suggests the exact mood desired. Sharp, bleak rocks, jagged branches against a dying sky, heavy, shadowed castle stones lost in a veil of mist—each specific image must be simple and direct without the clutter of detail frequently found in symbolist productions in the early twentieth century. The pattern of movement within the setting must

Figure 17–8 A sketch for Act IV, scene 3 of *Pelléas and Mélisande* by Maeterlinck and Debussy as designed by Robert Edmond Jones as a project, 1921. A further example of simple forms used in an impressionistic way to achieve mood and mystery. From *The Theatre of Robert Edmond Jones*, edited by Ralph Pendleton, Wesleyan University Press, Middletown, Conn., 1958. Courtesy of the Yale School of Drama Print Collection.

be close to that of ballet and dance—choreographed to achieve a vague, floating, musical effect that is the essence of characterization in this play. Acting and gesture must project the total mood rather than individual characterization. Textures within the setting should be soft, vague, and light absorbing; harshness in textural effects should be avoided. Color, if it is to be used in the setting, should be soft and grayed (never harsh or brilliant) and able to be softened and changed by the play of light. All lines within the setting should be created to give the maximum mood and symbolic effect with a minimum of means (Figure 17–9).

Specifically, in the costumes for *Pelléas and Mélisande* the designer should try not to treat the period in a direct and obvious way. The key word is "suggestion," not period education. In the original production in 1892 the costumes were modeled after those found in the paintings of Hans Memling, but to use a specific source such as this today would distract from the indefinite mood of the entire playscript. The costumes may

Figure 17–9   A scene from *Pelléas and Mélisande* by Maeterlinck as produced by the Belgian National Theatre, 1963. Another example of indefinite mood-producing forms and wispy or light-reflecting costumes used to create an impression through atmosphere. Courtesy of the Belgian National Theatre. Photo by Carl Hensler.

Figure 17–10   A costume sketch by Dale Hennon for Mélisande in *Pelléas and Mélisande* for a classroom project in the Department of Drama, Stanford University. An example of the transparent, wispy, mood-evoking draperies that are intended to suggest rather than create a specific costume. Courtesy of Dale Hennon.

be vaguely medieval with fairytale overtones, but the audience should not be readily able to place them as to period or place. A generalized, vague, unspecified period in the past should be the goal, with concentration on the subtle, abstract effects of color, texture, line, and movement rather than on period detail. Probably the best medieval source from which to abstract the general lines of the costumes would be the flowing, draped lines of the Romanesque or very early Gothic, rather than a choice of fourteenth- or fifteenth-century sources with the consequent stress on pattern, decoration, and rich accessories. Simplicity, as was noted in the discussion of the play's dialogue, is essential to capturing the moodiness, the vagueness, the shifting sense of reality that comprise this play.

The single most important item in designing the costumes is the choice of fabric or texture to achieve the flowing line and vague, transparent effect that will complement the play's tenuous nature. Chiffons, gauzes, and china silks are appropriate fabrics; changeable silks and soft, flowing, lightweight woolens might also be used. Costumes that are being gently waved by an unseen breeze is the important image to keep in mind when choosing the fabrics. Sometimes filmy layers of transparent fabric can be used over shimmering metallics to give an indefinite, ethereal effect, or soft and absorbent pile can be used to shift and change with the subtle play of the lights. The garments should have a suggested, indefinite effect that changes and shifts with the pattern of the movement.

In color, the key must be the pale and the indefinite. This is one reason why changeable fabrics in which the color shifts with each movement are useful. Color itself is less important in this play than value contrasts and the reflection or absorption of light from fabric surfaces.

In line, the key must again be the suggested and the indefinite. The emphasis must be on garments that float and move with the choreographed action of the play. Heavy, strong, clear-cut costume outlines should be abandoned in favor of full-flowing sleeves, floating mantles, trains, and scarves which lend themselves to arabesques of choreographed movement. The accents and points of focus achieved through ornament and accessories should be kept to a minimum. The ornamentation used should glint and shimmer vaguely in the light rather than achieve specific outline and shape; also, ornament should be seductive and suggestive of mystery rather than focusing attention on parts of the costume and specific areas of the actor's body (Figure 17–10).

Because of its lack of concrete effects, impressionistic symbolism, as in *Pelléas and Mélisande*, appeals to a limited audience, and as a style, has produced few important and lasting plays. But as an influence in the theatre and as a way of designing and producing plays of the past, it has had a very great effect, and its heritage is still strong today.

From Morn to Midnight

From Morn to Midnight was written by the German dramatist George Kaiser before World War I, but it was not produced until 1917. It stands as a clear-cut example of expressionism, since it retains the personal subjective vision of symbolism while lashing out in a direct assault on audience sensibilities—depicting a world twisted and distorted by inhuman social forces. *From Morn to Midnight* obviously owes something to the medieval Morality play, since it is written in scenes rather than acts, depicts the end of modern man in seven steps, and uses the Cashier as a contemporary Everyman. The time span from morning to midnight also seems to symbolize man's journey from birth to death, while the Cashier's search, like that of Oedipus, Faust, and Mrs. Alving, seems to be toward personal fulfillment—a quest that ends not in hope but in the debasement of modern man.

PLOT STRUCTURE　As with most expressionist dramas, the seven scenes that compose the structure of the play are held together by the symbolic search of the Cashier, and all attention is focused on the experiences of this central character. Unity comes not from any logical organization of the scenes or from any causally related events, but through the illumination of the play's theme by concentration on the psychological deterioration of the Cashier as a modern Everyman.

The first two scenes are primarily introductory and serve to establish the dehumanizing effects of modern materialism and the mistaken values in modern society. The Cashier, as the common man, is presented as the mechanized slave to the bank and to the system, a robot who pays out money, enters sums in a book, and taps for attention—all with the exactness and precision of a soulless automaton. With the arrival of the Lady from Italy, the Cashier's automatic routine is jarred, and in his desire to possess her he reacts as one would expect in a system in which money is success: he steals a great sum of cash.

Then begins the search of this modern Everyman. He decides that his whole life has been wasted and empty, and with his new-found freedom and his large sum of money he sets out to explore life and all its possibilities. He soon meets Death for the first time; in succeeding scenes he finds no answers in family, politics, money, sensual pleasure, or religion. His final disillusionment comes when the Salvation Army girl who pretended interest in his soul turns him over to the police for a reward. At the end a tangle of wires outlines the form of Death, and as the Cashier runs into the wires with arms spread like Christ on the Cross, there is a great crackling of electricity and an exploding of lamps. The ultimate comment is given by the policeman who says that there seems to be a short circuit in the wiring.

CHARACTER　The characters in this play are given only labels, not names, and their speeches and actions are composed of a series of clichés that make them stereotypes or symbols rather than individual personalities. It is the mechanical robot quality in each character that is important in projecting Kaiser's mechanistic view of modern life. Only the Lady from Italy, who represents an older way of life, and the Cashier, who symbolizes the search for a new way of life, escape to some extent from the overall mechanistic pattern.

The responsibility for carrying the play forward falls almost entirely on the shoulders of the Cashier. After the introductory scenes he is the spokesman for the playwright and the only character who senses that there must be an escape from the machine-like existence of modern society. Although he is a symbol, he does grow in understanding as the play progresses, and his search makes him seem more and more sympathetic as the scenes pass. However, he never becomes a three-dimensional psychological character because he must ever remain a symbol of modern man's escape from the deadening effects of modern life.

THEME   The theme of this play is strongly stated, repeatedly stressed, and single-mindedly pursued though all the scenes of the drama: the mechanistic, materialistic ideals of modern life must be changed, a search must be instituted for a way out of our present social goals, and human beings must once again be human, individualized, and free. Although the ending is quite pessimistic, it does suggest that a new man was about to emerge from the soulless automaton that was the Cashier, and one is left with the suggestion that it might be possible to redeem mankind. Were this to occur, the author suggests that a complete rebirth of society could then begin.

DIALOGUE   The language as it is developed in this play has a very mechanistic quality. It is frequently intended to be hammered out in a quick, staccato pattern like a telegraph message, reflecting the violent, direct impulses of the messages transmitted by modern machines. The dialogue is often deliberately repetitious, loud, fast paced, and harsh in its effect so that the maximum aggressive, subjective effect on the sensibilities of the audience will be achieved.

RHYTHM   The rhythm of an expressionist drama such as *From Morn to Midnight* is very strong, shows violent shifts from moment to moment, and never drops its insistent, mechanical forward drive. It seldom allows a sense of rest and relaxation for the audience. The beat established by the rhythm of the play is one of the most powerful means of suggesting the mechanized and inhuman feelings that the playwright is saying are a part of modern man.

SPECTACLE   The visual setting must be distorted in the same mechanistic way to indicate the unfeeling, mechanical forms the author sees all around him in modern life. Scene 3, in particular, offers one of the most standard visual clues for the design of this and other expressionist plays. A tree becomes a skeleton before the eyes of the Cashier and the audience and then returns to its normal shape, expressing the idea that the author's vision of reality as seen through the eyes of the Cashier is the distorted view of life the audience must experience. The other characters in the play would presumably see everything as normal; it is only the "awakened Cashier" who sees things as they really are. The implication is, of course, that the audience has been deadened to the truth and that only through these visual exaggerations and distortions in setting and costumes can any of the truth about modern life be expressed.

In developing settings and costumes for expressionist plays in the period between World War I and World War II, designers made great use of changing fragments of distorted form rather than complete settings;

Figure 17–11 A scene from *The Adding Machine* by Elmer Rice as produced by the Stanford Players, Stanford University, 1948. An example of scenery distortion to give a subjective expressionistic effect to this graveyard scene. Photo courtesy of the Stanford Collection, Stanford University Libraries.

color was unnatural and exaggerated; walls, windows, and doors often leaned and tilted at unbelievable angles; sizes of things were diminished and enlarged for psychological effect; lighting was bold, unrealistic, and violent; and costumes were exaggerated or turned into uniforms to give subjective mechanized effects (Figure 17–11). The rationale behind such design is symbolism; all items are distorted and exaggerated to gain violent symbolic effects that assault the sensibilities of the audience rather than lulling them into a trance-like mood receptive to subtle inner truths. Both impressionistic symbolism and expressionism work to gain an overall subjective effect through symbols, and the design principles for both are those of symbolism. Where one is attempting to reach subjective truth through inner mood, the other is trying to achieve it through violently exaggerated outer effect.

Visual Presentation of From Morn to Midnight *Today*

In the complicated, unsentimental, nonidealistic world of the contemporary theatre, it might be more difficult to revive *From Morn to Midnight* successfully than other plays with longer histories, because this play seems much too simplistic and naive in its analysis of human ills and in it recommendations for a brighter future. Although the world it describes is basically our world, we have come to see it as a more complicated, many-layered compilation of problems than there are in this play of pre-World War I. Therefore, great stress should be placed on the visual production. The story and its conclusion should take second place to the texture, color, shape, and lighting effects derived from modern art and films. The simple leaning and tilting of exaggerated and distorted forms would not be enough. These effects would connect in their simple naiveté with the Pre-World War I simplicities of emerging cubism and futurism, rather than with the repellant textural effects found in modern junk art, the light effects found in modern op art and psychedelic "light shows," and the forms found in modern welded sculpture. One could choose any one of these modern art forms and a number of others as a point of departure, and each of the seven scenes would then be a variation on a basic, tortured distortion of modern reality.

The basic mechanization that must lie behind any design for this play might follow either the smooth, riveted, machine-tooled surface and lack of color that we observe in industrial machinery or the corroded, broken, decaying forms and surfaces of the junk yard, dump, or waste bin of modern industry. The first approach would lend itself best to the large, mechanized scenes in the bank and at the race track; the second would lend itself best to the scene in which Death first appears in the gnarled tree and finally reappears in the tangled wires of the last scene. However, to mix the two would take away the single, horrific, exaggerated view from which the Cashier sees the modern world, although a progression of effect might take place once the Cashier is awakened to a view of himself in relation to this world.

No matter what image or visual source is used as the basis for the various set pieces and framing devices for stage space in the production, the lighting would, by the nature of the final moments of the play when the lights go out and the skeleton of Death is outlined in a fury of sparks, be a tremendously important emotional device in unifying and projecting the script. All of the methods found in modern "light shows," such as spiraling, swirling, and bursting color, could be used with brilliant effect to support the emotional climate of each scene. This lighting would be more attuned to the sensibilities of a modern audience than the abrupt shafts of light and strong contrasts of light and dark that were characteristic of the original expressionist lighting methods. Color in light is as important to the emotional presentation of the play as the movement and shape of the lighting, and together they can set the mechanistic, staccato rhythm of the play and the mood of the Cashier's mental state (Figure 17–12).

Music would also be important in a modern production, especially if it were the new electronic music that frequently gives a strong feeling of mechanization and an inhuman rhythmic form. Amplification of the music would also be important, to make the sound even more unreal and mechanized. It would also be effective in underlining the rhythmic progression of the drama.

Exaggeration of form in costumes and a sense of uniformity in the dress of certain groups of characters would not be enough visual comment, as it once was, to make the play acceptable to a modern audience. These effects were new and interesting at the time of World War I, but today they are a theatrical cliché. What is needed is an approach in which the quality of the setting, music, and lights has completely pervaded the dress. If the smooth, polished, mechanistic approach is used, then clothes should have metallic, plastic, manufactured surfaces that reflect our knowledge of the space suits of the modern age, even though the cut would still suggest the dresses and suits of current fashion. Trim could run to tubing, small spheres, prisms and cubes, and the movement

Figure 17–12   A scene from *From Morn to Midnight* by George Kaiser as produced at the Gate Theatre, London, 1932. Courtesy of the Enthoven Collection of the Victoria and Albert Museum, London. Photo by Malcolm L. Keep.

within such costumes could be as labored and mechanized as when wearing a space suit. If the decaying, corroded approach to metallic and plastic surfaces is taken, then melted nylon, burned sponge rubber, acid-eaten plastics painted to further the effect of decomposing surfaces would be effective in indicating the decay of our modern mechanized world. The principle behind either of these seemingly opposed approaches is an attack on the sensibilities of the audience through a strong and violent statement in color, line, and texture. The effect of modern life as a destroyer of the human spirit is the key concept for the costume designs. Therefore, all visual effects must be exaggerated, violent, distorted, and horrifying for the audience.

The history of true expressionism may be limited, but the emotional effects engendered by it can be easily updated for modern production. Many plays from the past, not just the standard expressionist examples, can be presented for modern audiences in a neoexpressionist manner that will fit exactly the mood of much current theatre and will effectively make a modern point about a script that might otherwise seem to lack relevance if presented in a straightforward period manner.

18

Relativist Plays

Art and Culture in the Twentieth Century

Through its various modes of expression, including impressionism, expressionism, neomannerism, *art nouveau,* and many other related styles, the symbolist movement in art and theatre finally precipitated a crisis of subjectivism in the early years of the twentieth century. From the paintings of Turner and Delacroix to the paintings of Munch, Ensor, and van Gogh, the nineteenth century had demonstrated an inability or unwillingness to utilize science intelligently in art. Even the impressionist painters who had begun with a scientific interest in light and optics had drifted into subjectivism. The science that did arouse a response among artists was Darwinian biology, but even this appeared to sanction strong subjective impulses and romantic feelings rather than intelligence. During the nineteenth century art and science became alienated, and no major attempts were made to relate the great discoveries in science to the world of art. In the final analysis, the greatest of the artists in all media suffered from lack of a firm intellectual basis for their art. Rodin's sculpture, for example, was energetic, dynamic, theatrical, and highly emotional, but his late work substitutes vagueness for sculptural realization. In fact, he never found a sculptural style, and there is an abiding conflict between his cloudy implications and his inherent love of the flesh. His vagueness is reminiscent of Maeterlinck, his mass of Michelangelo, and what he lacks is an intellectual concept of simultaneous space, in which time and movement are flattened and become another dimension of space. Rodin can render only one profile at a time, and so his surfaces appear to burst and change within a succession of instants rather than in a single space-time perception. Not that anyone would want to change the sculptural work of

Figure 18–1a   *Guernica* by Picasso, The Museum of Modern Art, New York, 1937. An example of the fragmentation and exaggeration of nature reconstituted to form a new reality. Photo courtesy of The Museum of Modern Art.

Rodin, but it should be understood that he does lack a sound intellectual basis for his work. He is a product of the late nineteenth-century drive for energy, force, emotion, and theatricality, and in these drives he is rebelling against the static qualities of Euclidian space without finding a substitute sculptural structure (see Figure 9–11a).

The painter-innovator who wished to give impressionism the solidity and intellectual foundation of classical art was Paul Cézanne. He wished to break down space and time so that one no longer looked at a subject from a particular point of view at a given moment in time, but observed all of its structural facets and its appearance during many moments in time in one long analytical glance.

It is from this concept that most of the great abstract movements of the twentieth century have evolved. Cubism was the first great conscious movement to break away from the idea that three-dimensional space must be seen from a fixed point of view at a particular moment, and most of the later artistic developments of the twentieth century, up until the middle of the 1960s, have been largely a return to the Renaissance coupling of art and science—that the artist must think as well as feel and see (Figure 18–1a).

The cubists, and the other schools of abstract art which followed, literally destroyed objects of the natural world in order to reorganize the world through the mind. Unlike the symbolists and the expressionists, who distorted life for emotional effect, the cubists and other abstractionists took things apart in a semiscientific way to see how they worked, and then they reconstituted them to see both the inner and the outer dynamics simultaneously. From this process a new art was born: the collage, in which real objects and textures were juxtaposed with painted effects to underline points of intersection between levels of reality. A collage is both a painting and an object, a surface and a picture—a kind of diagram or symbol of the many diverse perspectives or realities in which modern man lives and thinks (Figure 18–1b). In a world in which there are no longer any simple absolutes and relations are multiple and complex, modern painting has attempted to show space and time as an extension of the way man lives—an image of the way the artist thinks rather than the way he sees (Figure 18–2).

The same concepts and ideas also underlie much of the prose and poetry of the twentieth century. T. S. Eliot wrote that there are many

Figure 18–1b *Merz Construction* by Kurt Schwitters (painted wood, wire, and paper), Philadelphia Museum of Art, A. E. Gallatin Collection, 1921. An example of the so-called "trash pictures" that attempted to make interesting abstract arrangements of elements taken from a number of levels of reality. Such work was very influential in the area of stage design. Photo courtesy of the Philadelphia Museum of Art.

Figure 18–2 *Internal and External Forms* by Henry Moore, Albright-Knox Gallery, Buffalo, N.Y., 1953–1954. An example of the interpenetration of space and form in order to create a number of changing levels of reality. Photo courtesy of the Albright-Knox Gallery.

simultaneous levels possible in verse writing in an age of relativity, and one can react to a word simultaneously as a word, a word among other words, a sound, a symbol, and a point in a structural development. Probably the most important literary landmark in the new style was the publication of James Joyce's *Ulysses,* in which each phrase is an intersection of meanings on three or four different levels. In Joyce's work, as in the work of Thomas Mann, Franz Kafka, Gertrude Stein, André Gide, and many others, a relationship on many levels at the same time is the structural basis of the work. There is always an ambiguity, an indeterminate quality, a feeling for multiple images, a cinema-inspired "montage" of effect, a shifting backward and forward in time, a compression and expansion of facts and details.

The great new form that developed along with the new perspectives in art and literature was the cinema. The twentieth-century artist or writer, like the film maker, sees reality not in an object or a sequence of causally connected events, but as a graphic conflict among slightly

Figure 18–3   A series of photographs of a nude woman by Muybridge, George Eastman Museum of Photography, Rochester, N.Y., 1885. An example of early experiments that lead to the art of the cinema and the concept of a simultaneous multiple reality. Photo courtesy of George Eastman House.

Figure 18–4   *Autumn Rhythm* by Pollock, The Metropolitan Museum of Art, New York, George A. Hearn Fund, 1950. An example of free-form action painting, in which texture rather than a defined pattern is created. Nature is reduced to the movement of forces in a field. Photo courtesy of The Metropolitan Museum of Art.

different recurring images and points of view. Such merged images are known as a montage, and the montage has become the symbol of the new reality in art and literature. Reality is a series of changing relationships rather than a single story or event. What the box camera was to realism in the nineteenth century, the cinema is to the arts of the twentieth century (Figure 18–3).

The logical result of all this experimentation in abstract relationships was the liberation of art from subject matter in the late 1940s. Although the retreat from the real object began before World War I in the work of Kandinsky, Malevich, Severini, and others, it did not reach its climax until the triumph of abstract expressionism and neoplasticism after World War II. As practiced by Jackson Pollock and his successors, the first tended toward an emotional attack on the canvas that had characterized the painting of the German expressionists. However, now liberated from subject matter, the artist moved toward a physical relationship with his art—drooling, dribbling, and spurting pigment onto the surface of the canvas. The texture of the field became more important than objects in the field, and the sense of the physical action of the painter more important than images, moods, or ideas (Figure 18–4). In the second school of painting, led by Piet Mondrian, the painter dealt only with the simplest coordinates of mathematical organization—the horizontal and the vertical—and the three primary colors plus black and white. The artist aimed at an abstract expression of pure relationships without relation to a real world of objects. It was the field of relationships that was again important (Figure 18–5).

Figure 18–5 *Composition* by Mondrian, Philadelphia Museum of Art, the Louise and Walter Arensburg Collection, 1936. An example of geometric composition in painting. Photo courtesy of the Philadelphia Museum of Art.

In the art of the early 1960s, field relationships were still stressed, but variety and humor had been added to the purity of Mondrian and Pollock. Shapes, figures, and textures came back into the art of relations, not as objects but as important parts in a field of relationships. Whether one looks at the "aliterature" of Robbe-Grillet, or the antiart of pop art and op art, one seldom finds a secure point of view. Until the mid 1960s, the denial of the complexities in our culture was so strong that most artists and writers did not bother to interpret nature but merely recorded certain physical facts and relationships. It was an exhaustive conclusion to the idea of multiple reality, the multifaceted levels of *Ulysses,* the early experimental cinema, and cubism.

Theatre in the Twentieth Century

Although realist and symbolist approaches to staging have certainly not vanished from the scene of contemporary theatrical production, the major developments in the presentation of these two forms had reached their peak by the 1930s. By the beginning of World War II, several other forms of theatrical presentation, related to the concept of relativism in art, began to dominate Western theatre.

CONSTRUCTIVISM   The first major breakthrough in experimentation occurred in Russia after the revolution of 1917. To reach a new audience of workers and to use the theatre as an instrument of instruction and propaganda, a number of experiments were undertaken to present plays that escaped the mood, illusionism, and sense of environment found in realism and symbolism and that stressed physical action and theatrical abstraction. The most influential exponent of this revolution in theatre was Vsevolod Meyerhold.

Meyerhold had three major concepts, all of which he used to establish his theatrical revolution: biomechanics, theatricalism, and constructivism. Like Craig and Reinhardt before him, he believed in the absolute power of the director. He shaped every element of a production to his own ideas, and insisted that all theatre personnel give him and his concepts absolute obedience.

Meyerhold believed, first, that the theatre must always remain a theatre, not a temple for dreams, a place of illusion, or a setting for reality. He wished his audiences to remain completely conscious of the fact that they were in a theatre, and he wished to use the theatre in a self-conscious, artistic way to achieve his theatrical effects. Thus, he removed the front curtain, placed lighting instruments in view of the audience, used a mechanical-gymnastic approach to acting, rewrote his plays so that elements of realism were replaced by obvious theatrical effects, and used abstract structures, which he called "constructions," as settings. "Constructivism" had developed in the field of sculpture in Russia just before World War I, and the idea was developed to its fullest extent by two brothers, Naum Gabo and Antoine Pevsner, whose sculptural work at the close of World War I brought constructivism to the very forefront of modern art. The idea behind constructivist sculpture was that instead of the artist working with intersecting planes and masses, he constructed skeletal structures of metal and plastic in space. The aim in all of these productions and production methods was to comment on social, political, and economic problems and to incite audiences to desirable social action by strong theatrical statements (Figure 18–6).

Meyerhold's second major innovation in theatrical performance was a system of actor training which was the exact opposite of the Stanislavsky system and which he labeled "biomechanics." He was not interested in any kind of psychological realism but wanted an actor trained as an efficient biological machine to carry out the orders of the master director. The actors trained in ballet, acrobatics, and gymnastics were capable of performing on trapezes, slides, open "constructions," and machinery.

Although these methods finally proved too abstract and experimental for the governmental forces in the Soviet Union, they are the first major examples in twentieth-century theatre of intellectual improvisation. This was based on the idea that the stage houses intersecting places of shifting contrasts between life and the theatre, between the reality of the actor and the reality of his role, between the reality of a play and the reality of the presentation of that play. In short, it was the first use of the simultaneous ideas of cubism in the theatre—the first use of the intellectual concept of relativity.

THE VIEUX COLOMBIER   A less radical development in France just before World War I also contributed to the idea that the fourth-wall concept of proscenium realism was passé, that the stage must remain a stage no matter what the play to be produced. In 1913, Jacques Copeau turned from a career as a critic to become a producer and director of the famous Théâtre Vieux Colombier in Paris. This theatre, which Copeau fashioned from a Parisian warehouse, had a permanent architectural setting for all plays on which only the essential properties and set dressings were placed. Stage and auditorium were considered to be an organic whole; there were no footlights, only a low step made the break from the audience to the stage, and the architectural background consisted

Figure 18–6   Stage design for *The Man Who Was Thursday* from the maquette by Alexander Wesnin in the Theater-Museum, Munich, ca. 1930. An example of constructivism, in which the setting becomes a structure for organizing action and space on a platform in front of an audience. Photo courtesy of the Theater-Museum, Munich.

Figure 18–7   A setting for Le Théâtre Vieux Colombier, Paris, ca. 1913. An example of the use of a basic architectural stage as developed by Jacques Copeau, in which the stage remains part of the auditorium and is changed by the minor use of props and set pieces. From *Continental Stagecraft* by Kenneth Macgowan and Robert Edmond Jones, Harcourt Brace Jovanovich, New York, 1922. Courtesy of Harcourt Brace Jovanovich.

of an arch with a stairway at one side leading up over the arch. Lighting came from above and from the sides, and certain sources were openly displayed within the auditorium (Figure 18–7). Once again the concept of a formal stage that remained a stage and a theatre that remained a theatre throughout all productions paved the way for the death of illusionism and an acceptance of the idea that one can be simultaneously aware of himself, the audience, the theatre, the actor, and the play during a theatrical performance.

ELIZABETHAN STAGING REVIVED   As early as the 1890s, a zealous devotee of Elizabethan staging methods named William Poel produced Shakespeare on a re-creation of an Elizabethan stage set up in rented halls in London and vicinity. With his largely amateur Elizabethan Stage Society, Poel dedicated his life to producing Shakespeare's plays and those of his contemporaries in the Elizabethan manner on a stage that was meant to be a close approximation of what was then known about the Globe and Fortune Theatres. His work influenced the great producer-critic Harley Granville-Barker, who also advocated producing Shakespeare on an open stage in which the division between the stage and the audience was minimized. The audience was made aware that it

Figure 18–8   The Players Scene from *Hamlet* as produced by the Oregon Shakespeare Festival, Ashland, Ore., 1961. An example of a modern use of the Elizabethan stage, based on the dimensions of the Fortune Theatre and inspired by the work of William Poel and B. Iden Payne in the early part of the twentieth century. Photo courtesy of the Oregon Shakespeare Festival.

was seeing the reality of the stage at the same time as it was absorbing the reality of a particular play. Poel's Elizabethan staging ideals also heavily influenced the work of B. Iden Payne in his American Shakespearean productions, and a number of U.S. Shakespearean festivals continue to use modifications of Poel's staging concepts (Figure 18–8).

BRECHT AND EPIC THEATRE   Reinhardt, in his monumental productions at the Circus Schumann and later at the Grosses Schauspielhaus and in many outdoor productions, stressed the direct "presentational" approach to theatre, in which the proscenium was banished and direct contact was established between actor and audience. The value of such direct contact remained with Reinhardt from the days when he had worked in the cabaret theatre Schall und Rauch in Berlin. It was this same background in cabaret theatre and this same feeling for intimacy that was to infuse the theatrical experimentation of one of the greatest playwright-producers of the twentieth century, Bertolt Brecht.

Brecht began his work in the theatre at a time when the expressionists were at the peak of their popularity. Film projections, weird lighting effects, sound effects, swirling movement on platforms and stairs—every theatrical device was used to create a total assault on the senses at the expense of critical, analytical thought. At first Brecht worked within this style, but he gradually developed a theory of theatrical production in which the intellect rather than the senses was to be aroused. He wanted his audiences to participate in a theatrical event, but he wanted this to be critical and intellectual participation rather than sentimental and emotional participation. Just as modern art had turned its back on mood, symbols, and inner emotions in order to analyze, critically and intellectually, the nature of art in relation to modern life, so Brecht decided that the same thing must happen in the theatre. He called his work "epic" as opposed to "dramatic," and he felt that this term (which derives from the great poetic narrative legends of the Greeks and the Germans) correctly described his ideal of a narrative rather than a dramatic theatre of emotional conflict. For Brecht both the drama and theatrical production needed to be altered and guided toward a new set of goals, which involved the key words "alienation" and "historification."

Historification to Brecht meant material chosen from other places and other times in order to obtain a sense of removal—a dispassionate look at facts and events in which we are not involved yet which have relevance to the present. Brecht hoped that by making events strange and removed that his plays would escape the easy identification with actions and emotion that occurred in realist theatre. He hoped that his audiences would use their minds rather than their feelings to arrive at critical, intellectual conclusions about the social problems introduced in his plays.

This concept is a part of the larger concept of alienation. Although alienation is a rather inaccurate rendering of the German word *verfremdung,* it is basically a further expansion of the concept of making the stage action strange and unreal through the introduction of song, film, description, and direct address to the audience. In short, Brecht does not want his audience to confuse what it sees onstage with reality, but to view such action as a comment on life, to be watched and judged with critical detachment. Each element of the production should contribute to the "alienation" of the spectator, and there should be an interdependence rather than a synthesis of the arts of theatrical production. Scenery should not create an illusion of reality, but should merely suggest locale. Costumes should comment on character, music should comment on action, lighting should illuminate but not create mood, and the actor should think of his role in the third person. Once again, the mechanics of the theatre should remain visible at all times. The audience should be critically aware of the various levels of reality that are created; it should not be lulled into a hypnotic, atmospheric trance.

Figure 18–9   The stage of The Stratford Festival Theatre, Stratford, Ont., as redesigned by Tanya Moiseiwitsch in association with Brian Jackson, 1962. An example of the thrust or apron stage in a permanent structure, acting as a modern adaptation of the Elizabethan stage with seven acting levels and nine major entrances. It provides close audience-actor relationship, in which no seat is more than sixty-five feet from the stage. Courtesy of the Stratford Shakespearean Festival, Stratford, Ont. Photo by Douglas Spillane.

THE CONTEMPORARY EMPHASIS ON OPEN OR THRUST STAGING   From the time of Copeau and the constructivists to the present, the battle between the realistic or single-angle proscenium theatre and the formal, open staging concept, which attempts a return to the precepts of the Elizabethan and Greek theatre, has been a continuing event. Only in the past two decades have more theatres been built that stress the open, thrust-stage form of production rather than the proscenium. Many new theatre buildings have attempted to achieve both, but at major festival theatres such as the Shakespeare Theatre at Stratford, Ontario, the Guthrie Theatre in Minneapolis, and the Festival Theatre at Chichester, England, the theatre has been constructed with an open, thrust stage. Only a few popular commercial productions are still produced completely behind a proscenium arch from a single fixed point of view. The majority of productions in the Western world are produced with varying degrees of a theatrical presentational approach in which the audience is aware that it is part of the theatrical event, concerned with both the reality of the stage and the reality of the story and characters presented on it (Figure 18–9).

Six Characters in Search of an Author

Although George Bernard Shaw is often thought of as the leading playwright of the early twentieth century, he was unable to escape the drawing-room scene for a direct approach to the stage as a platform for comic action and comic criticism. Thus, it is Luigi Pirandello who returns stage action to the direct gaze of the audience under the glare of open stage lighting; and it is *Six Characters in Search of an Author* that should be studied to see how contemporary drama emerged from late nineteenth-century realism and symbolism (Figure 18–10).

Figure 18–10   A scene from *Six Characters in Search of an Author* by Pirandello as produced by the Stanford Players, Stanford University, 1951. An example of the importance of the stage as a stage and the actor as an actor in this seminal drama dealing with the concept that truth is a matter of one's point of view. Photo courtesy of the Stanford Collection, Stanford University Libraries.

PLOT AND STRUCTURE   As Sypher indicates in *From Rococo to Cubism in Art and Literature,* Pirandello, like the cubist painters who preceded him, set out to show a compound image in the drama, a form of theatre in which the stage is a plane for the intersection of art and life, a place for the "collision between art and actuality."

In this stage action, which cannot really be labeled a "play," a company of actors is rehearsing a drama by Pirandello himself when six "characters" enter and ask for a completion to the drama of their lives. The author who has conceived them has not finished their play, and they beg the actors to perform their play instead of the one they are rehearsing. The action then develops on several levels: the struggle of the "characters" against the technical and commercial views of the actors and director, the struggle among the "characters" about the shape and meaning of the events of their story, the struggle in the audience's mind with the levels of reality they see before them. The effort of the "characters" to represent themselves on the stage is finally blocked when the Boy, in a fit of despair, shoots himself. The professionals interpret this as the artistic climax to the play, only to realize that it has been a genuine suicide, and the fictional characters turn out to be more real than the live members of the acting company.

By refusing the movement and forward thrust of plot, the author is left with the formal artistic problem of writing a drama about writing a drama. It is very much like the technique of collage used by the cubists to project the problems of painting or the building of a painting. In fact, the great connection between this play and the visual arts is the collage. Pirandello pieces together and arranges a number of theatrical clichés, including the director's attitude, the commercial theatre point of view, the professional actor's outlook, the stagehands' contributions, a missing playwright's concept, and a group of partially realized characters in a collage form to interpenetrate, intermingle, point up, and illuminate the many different levels of reality they represent.

CHARACTER   The six "characters" belong to life but at the same time do not belong to it. Pirandello stops the unrolling film of his "characters'" lives and allows one crucial episode or sequence to be played repeatedly, to be disputed and argued by actors, director, and even audience on a public stage. It is a fascinating philosophical-theatrical idea. The concept of the "characters" then calls into question the nature of the personal and group realities of actors and director, and finally, of course, the audience watching the proceedings. The director demands a single, simple illusion of reality and insists that actors are serious artists ready to project this reality, while the Father insists that they are merely playing a game and have never found out who they really are. Thus, all characterization in the play, although it seems psychologically realistic on its own level, comes into question when pitted against another world or level of reality. Each individual on the stage is both a personality and a philosophical symbol of a certain level of reality.

THEME   Every moment of the development and every step in the intellectual discussion is used to point up and exemplify the thesis that reality is a shifting thing and that at times the reality of art and imitation may be greater than the reality of life. As research into the plural aspects of identity, the play takes every opportunity to show the many levels of reality on which events can occur.

DIALOGUE   The dialogue is primarily philosophical and argumentative as the "characters" argue the nature of their reality with the actors, and more specifically as the Father and the director debate the nature of theatrical reality. The dialogue shifts from real-life conversation to rational argument to theatrical cliché without transition or warning, to underline the multiple levels of reality.

RHYTHM   The rhythm of the play, by most standards, does not exist since the movement of the play stops, starts, shifts abruptly, and changes levels without warning, in an attempt to create ambiguity, stimulate thought, and frustrate easy acceptance of a forward flow of the drama. The rhythm is closest to that of the experimental film in which story movement can go backward or forward, dissolve into multiple images, or change with the shifting viewpoint of the camera.

SPECTACLE   The demands for the visual background very consciously take on the aspects of collage as the bits and pieces of costume and scenery involved in the play being rehearsed are placed against the realities of backstage equipment and stage walls, which are the only permanent background for the action. When other bits and pieces of property and scenery are rigged so that the "characters" may act out their story, the result is a theatrical collage. Scenery and costumes are thus geared to the simultaneous presentation of theatrical reality, life reality, and "character" reality in a shifting and changing collage effect.

Visual Presentation of Six Characters in Search of an Author *Today*

Since Pirandello's dramas, in particular *Six Characters in Search of an Author,* are very rich intellectually and very spare visually, the design for a contemporary production cannot utilize complex visual effects. Each visual choice must be carefully selected to project a particular intellectual shift in the argument about reality without appealing to the emotions or the senses at the expense of the intellect. However, there is certainly a need to accent the theatricality of the stage effects that Pirandello does use to make his points about reality in the theatre, and these can be the visual highlights in a basically spare production. The entire ritual of actors arriving for a rehearsal on a bare stage lit only by worklights can be an interesting charade not usually seen by an audience. The arrival of the "characters," with pale faces in an eerie and unearthly light unrelated to the worklights of the stage, and the readying of the "white parlor background with the floral decoration" as an impromptu backing for the "characters'" story can both be used as interesting visual highlights. The appearance of Madame Pace after the scene has been correctly arranged to evoke her image is a consummate visual moment—if the appearance really does seem to be a transmigration from another world. In all these examples, the lighting can obviously be very helpful in focusing and supporting the desired effect. However, it is the property or bit of setting, item of costume, or type of makeup used within or against the frame of another reality that creates the excitement.

In all matters of setting and costume there is more a problem of selection and arrangement than there is one of design. As in a collage or an assemblage, it is more important to find the right item of costume, scenery, or properties, to place it properly, and to use it at the right mo-

Figure 18–11 A scene from *Six Characters in Search of an Author* by Pirandello as produced by the American Conservatory Theatre for the Stanford Summer Festival, 1966. A further example of multiple reality, in which a scene is constructed in front of the audience from backstage properties and set pieces. Courtesy of the American Conservatory Theatre. Photo courtesy of Hank Kranzler, Palo Alto, Calif.

ment than it is to design each item as a piece of a unified visual whole (Figure 18–11).

Therefore, the costumes are better obtained from costume storage, from an actor's personal wardrobe, or from a used clothing store rather than designed and built to give a unified single artistic point of view to the production. The variety of sources suits the variety of reality levels operating in the play, while a single source and a single artistic point of view tend to give a unified visual reality that is not in keeping with the play. Clichés of theatrical costume may be placed next to items borrowed directly from the real world in an "assemblage"—an artistic arrangement based on the accents and focus indicated by the author in presenting his multilevel view of reality.

The Blacks

Jean Gênet, one of the controversial and brilliant playwrights of the absurd who have appeared since World War II, has created one of the most bizarre and confusing pictures of the shifting realities confronting modern man that has yet come to the modern stage. His major image is that of man caught in a maze of mirrors, trapped by the reflections of his distorted image, trying to make contact with those around him, but being rudely stopped by the barriers created by the reflecting glass. To Gênet, man is caught in the hall of mirrors of the human condition, trapped by an endless progression of images that are merely distorted reflections. In his play *The Blacks,* which the author labels a "clownerie" or clown show, Gênet presents an ingenious ritual in which a group of Negroes, playing both black and white roles, reenacts a ritualistic revenge on the white man's world.

PLOT AND STRUCTURE   There is no story line or clearly developed plot in this play, but there is a fascinating pattern of mirror images of reality that are played against one another in a most ingenious manner. The author assumes that his audience is white, and his black cast is divided into those who enact the black man's fantasy about himself and those who enact the black man's fantasy about the white reaction to the Negro world. Thus, the Negro actors stand between an actual white audience and the white-masked, colonial, fantasy audience composed of a haughty Queen, a Judge, a Bishop, a Governor-general, a Missionary, and a Valet (who acts the part of the artist or intellectual). In front of this hierarchy of white power the other group of Negroes enacts its fantasies of resentment. The central part of this is the ritual murder of a white woman enacted in elaborate detail. The white woman is presumed to be in the coffin, center stage, and the victim is first described by Village as a drunken hag found on the docks, but when the murder is actually reenacted the victim becomes an attractive white woman who had invited her black seducer to her room because of his superior physical attractions. An additional irony is added by the fact that the Negro appointed to portray the raped white woman turns out to be a clergyman who believes in peaceful integration and the brotherhood of man. Equipped with a blonde wig, an insipid carnival mask, pink knitting, and gloves, he impersonates the woman being raped and killed. When he gives birth to a number of dolls representing the figures of the "white court," the victim becomes the Mother of the White Race and the ritual murder becomes the ritual massacre of all whites.

After the Negroes have acted out their ritual resentment and guilt, the Queen and her court descend as though to punish the blacks. They are trapped and ignominiously put to death, after which Archibald, the stage manager and master of ceremonies for the evening's events, thanks the Negroes who have been impersonating the whites and concludes the play by stating that the blacks remain what the white man wants them to be. Early in the evening this same master of ceremonies makes it quite clear that the action on stage is a make-believe ritual, actors making the subject matter of the play palatable through the distance created by the many levels of impersonation and ceremony. The participants in the entertainment are meant to have a sense of awe, mystery, and ritual participation rather than be involved in any conceptual or rational communication. Yet by the end of the evening there is another reality, of which the audience becomes aware when Ville St. Nazaire, sent off in the first scene with a gun, returns to report an offstage revolt and the resultant conviction and death of a Negro traitor before an all black court. The whole stage ritual is revealed as a blind, a diversion to distract from the deadly real problems involved in the offstage revolt. And yet because the levels of mirror reality are so complex, the offstage revolt may be still another trick, another theatrical improvisation that leaves only the reality of the black actors and the smokescreen of their various levels of diversion.

CHARACTERS   In a play written on as many shifting levels as this one, there are obviously no characters or characterizations, but merely stereotyped or ritualized images donned by the actors. Yet even the Negro actors on stage stand for more than Negroes or blacks; they create an image of all the outcasts in a society; they stand for the author himself, who, as an outcast and thief from the age of ten, always played the role of being what society wanted him to be. Denied the dignity of men, the outcasts, the blacks, are denied the emotions of our "real" world and so must ever play the role for which they have been cast by society. All characters are used only to create an image or make a comment on the human experience.

THEME   Gênet's play is like an explosion of evil which breaks through the surface of rational discussion and social consciousness to the darkest reaches of the inner mind—to the level of myth, fear, masochistic fantasy, primitive ritual, and human sacrifice. As an essay on race relations it is impossible. It must be taken as an imaginative and metaphorical creation of a world underlying our own, appealing to whatever remains unconditioned and uncivilized in modern man. Gènet's purgative ritual or myth is violently subversive but also contains a sense of release and liberation. Through his direct sense of and involvement in evil and cruelty, Gènet attempts to stop the logical discussions and rational debates of the modern community through an art of crime and sacrifice, but also an art of collective ecstasy and purgation—an art about the helplessness of modern man when he realizes that he is caught in an endless progression of images that are his own reflections.

DIALOGUE   The actors, like the improvisers or "clowns" of the subtitle, are expected to manage language filled with images that continually shift from one level of reality to another. All the possible meanings and connotations of the words black and white are played off against each other, until all of our unconsciously accepted ideals are turned inside out and upside down. There is also a poetry or litany of hatred developed to fit with the ritual murder enacted onstage, and again the dialogue makes full use of the possibilities of ceremony and ritual. Like the play as a whole, the language or dialogue operates on the level of imagination, symbol, metaphor, and subconscious feelings and fantasies.

RHYTHM   Like all plays that are deeply involved with shifting realities that change and interpenetrate during the course of the action, the rhythm is like the visual movement of a kaleidoscope, rising and falling with the blending and pulling apart of the various levels of reality. The rhythm of the masked Negroes must differ from the unmasked ones; the rhythm of statements to the audience and the statements of the Negroes among themselves must differ markedly from the rhythm of the ritualistic sacrifice. Each level, each reflection of the human condition must seek its own rhythm rather than an overall rhythm devised for the entire evening.

SPECTACLE   All that is required for the staging is a large hall or room in which a stage has been set up for the reenactment of a ritual murder. It must be easy for the master of ceremonies to address the audience, even to hand things to persons in the front row or bring a member of the audience onto the stage. There must also be a coffin at the center of the stage and a range of seats, platforms, or ramps behind, on which the Negroes playing whites can range themselves to view the action below. The costumes are selections from theatrical storage that can suggest both the primitive ritual elements and the Negro's view of the power figures of the white establishment. Lighting also must be obvious and theatrical, able to move from the white audience to the Negro ritual forestage to the Negroes as whites ranged to the back of the stage, uniting all locations or isolating them as needed.

Visual Presentation of The Blacks *Today*

In a play that has as many shifting levels of reality and as many reflecting mirrors revealing the human condition as does *The Blacks*, it is very difficult to come to any coherent or logical plan for the visual presentation of the script. In fact, the logic that must be used is the logic of the illogical and the irrational. None of the usual rules or guides to a unified production is possible, and the design must shift and change from moment to moment as the script does.

In essence there is no setting at all, merely a place for actors to present their ceremonial ritual murder. In planning the ramps and platforms for the Negroes playing whites, the designer should let his personal reaction to the structure and the shifting images of the play guide him in obtaining a construction in space that is primitive and sophisticated,

Figure 18–12   A scene from *The Blacks* by Jean Gênet as produced by the Akademie der Kunste, Berlin, 1964, as part of the Berlin Festwochen. An example of the many layers of reality that must be suggested in the play by the settings and costumes. Photo courtesy of Heinz Köster, Berlin.

hand-made and machine-tooled, something that is organic yet constructed in material modules of form. Proportion should have the same ambivalent quality: part stage property, part primitive symbol, and part polished "product." The coffin can be at the same time a box from backstage, a sinister primitive hand-hewn container, and a highly tooled modern mortuary product. The challenge to the designer is in suggesting all such levels simultaneously (Figure 18–12).

In designing the costumes, each character cannot be thought of as a single unit to be designed in a unified way from top to bottom. Differing levels of reality must be combined within the same costume. This is particularly true of those costumes and masks worn by the Negroes playing whites, and the costumes for the Queen, the Bishop, the Governor-general, the Missionary, and the Valet. Obviously, the white stereotype each Negro portrays must be presented in all its overdrawn caricature as seen through the hatred of the Negroes: the exaggerated sexuality and accouterments of the Queen, the massive uniform and hat of the Governor-general, the poetic qualities of the Valet, the mitre and cope of the Bishop, and the false purity of the Missionary. But from under and within these exaggerated outward labels could escape the fearful symbols that we associate with the rituals of darkest Africa: bangles, bracelets, claw-like nails, painted bodies, animal teeth, for example. These would suggest to the actual white audience how they still see the Negro in their subconscious. Still another level of reality that can be suggested in the costumes is the reality of the stage and the Negro actor presenting the various reflecting levels of reality. Underneath the ironic paraphernalia of white colonialism and black primitivism could creep the worn shoes, the dirty trousers, or the old wrist watch of the actor, although such things might be hidden through much of the action and allowed to appear only at certain dramatic moments (Figure 18–13).

The Negroes preparing the ritual murder may also wear ridiculous outfits of fake elegance as they dance the minuet around the coffin covered with flowers, again keeping the audience guessing about who they are and what they represent. When Diouf must be done up in yellow wig, cheap mask, and white gloves holding knitting, the bitter caricature must be vicious and unsettling.

The costume designer must deliberately keep his audience unnerved and guessing about the planes of reality represented visually. He must create his mixtures of reality from items that are laden with symbolic values that will violate and upset the white audience's usual feelings and preconceptions.

Textures must not be chosen to give any overall or generalized impression; they must be chosen for symbolic contrasts of reality. The velvet of the Queen's gown may turn abruptly into grass or reeds, a richly sophisticated crown may suddenly sprout teeth, claws, or feathers, or the Governor-general's rich uniform may stop at the knees and his

Figure 18–13   The General from *The Blacks* by Jean Gênet as produced by The English Stage Company at The Royal Court Theatre, London, 1966. An example of multiple reality in costume created with the help of a mask. Photo courtesy of Sandra Lousada, Whitecross Studio, Ltd., London.

feet turn into those of an ape. It is the designer's talent for putting two incompatible and incongruous textural effects together that will give the play bite and disturb the usually accepted canons of visual taste.

Colors can, in the same way, shift in mid-figure or mid-costume from one level of reality to another without any regard for the usual rules of visual choice. The line of a costume may move in one direction and then turn completely in another direction to get the right symbolic visual contrasts across to an audience. A scepter that changes to a shrunken head at the top, medals and orders that turn to claws and shells, animal horns that grow from a mitre or a helmet—these are the shifts in line from one symbolic level of reality to another that can make the costume designer's work a real contribution to the harrowing effect this play can have on a modern, sophisticated audience (Figure 18–14).

Figure 18–14   Costume sketches of Felicity and Archibald by Jean Schultz Davidson for *The Blacks* by Jean Gênet. Prepared as a class assignment in the Department of Drama, Stanford University, 1956. Note the intermingling of African and Western European reality in costume. Courtesy of Jean Schultz Davidson.

19

The Problem of Style: Summary and Conclusion

The Meaning of Style

It should be evident by now, even with the cursory treatment of style development in the Western world in the preceding chapters, that to study "style" is to study the complex path of man transforming his reaction to life into an artistic creation such as a drama, a novel, a painting, or a sculpture. It is the "style" of these artistic works that both tells us about the spiritual and physical reactions of the artist to the society in which he lived and provides a glimpse of one or more aspects of the cultural scene of that time. In short, to understand the development of cultural history, one must understand the meaning and operation of "style" in the history of all the arts.

During the early history of art, when the formal elements of art seemed to evolve in an inevitable and spontaneous way, artists were not nearly as conscious of the problem of style as they are today. The Renaissance gave Western Europe a mixed bag of stylistic self-consciousness as artists returned to the classical past, and the neoclassicism of the eighteenth century and the eclecticism of the nineteenth century compounded the issue. Only in the twentieth century were many of the confusions and distractions cast aside. As a result of the confusion of the nineteenth century, we adopted the word "style" to describe superficial, whimsical preferences such as are seen in the annual showings of women's fashions; what the concept of "style" should summarize is something deep and

440

significant about a person or society. It should be a word associated with mature personal and cultural decisions rather than frenzied improvisation and constantly shifting fashion.

The artist who is the product of a society that cooperates for its own well-being and advancement will have a socially oriented self-confidence and a feeling of belonging, while the artist who identifies with a group that is condescending or antagonistic to the society in which he lives will view his world egotistically and place great stress on fantasy, caprice, accidental effects, and sensationalism. Order versus accident, logic versus sensation, analysis versus intuition, production versus consumption, humanism versus egotism—all are extreme opposites that cluster about the two poles of human personality, and style is that recording point on the graph of time that marks the wavering line between them. It sums up the meaning, records the dominant attitudes, and presents an overall picture of the historical, economic, and cultural forces that may be operating at any given point.

The Various Style Labels in Relation to Life

If the many style "isms" that have been pinpointed and labeled in the past two centuries could all be arranged in relation to the polar opposites in the life of man (that is, between the logical and the spontaneous, between the sensational and the rational), much of the confusion caused by the many modern style "isms" might be removed. The common labels that usually describe the two poles in art are classical and romantic, but these are very confusing since they also refer to specific period developments, and in the case of the word classical, to any great art work of the past. In the art of the theatre, the words classical and romantic tend to be used far more than any other labels to denote the contrasting poles of human experience. The average student *does* tend to think of these words as both period labels and general labels that describe two major kinds of theatrical products. To say the word "romantic" to a student of theatrical design is to conjure up a production that stresses emotions, richness, sensuous appeal, physical action, and all the design elements that can be coupled with the word sensation. To use the word "classical" is to conjure up a production that stresses order, structure, logic, humanism, simplicity, careful analysis, and beauty of form. It is only when a student has this distinction clearly in mind and can quickly respond to these two poles of artistic development that he can then begin to place labels such as expressionism, impressionism, symbolism, surrealism, naturalism, and mannerism in some kind of relation to these two basic stylistic poles.

Another very important distinction that students of the theatre tend to understand and use is the distinction between representation and presentation—between a theatrical production that will be accepted as a picture of real life or a production that will be accepted as an abstraction from reality. Although all productions are, by their nature, unreal or abstracted to some extent from reality, there is a whole spectrum of theatrical production that attempts to represent some aspect of real life in such a way that the audience will accept what they see as a picture of reality. The point at which the artists of the theatre begin to abstract and organize this reality in an obvious way cannot be defined, but there is a point at which an audience will be aware that what they see on stage is an artistic abstraction. Thus all productions, whether they lean toward the romantic or the classical, toward the sensational or the rational, can be divided at some point into those that an audience will accept as "real" and those that will be viewed as "abstractions from reality." Many a theatre artist thinks that he has conceived his production as a very obvious abstraction from reality, only to have an audience accept it as a "real" picture of life in a particular period, thus proving that the division between representation and abstraction is closely allied to artistic knowledge, cultural sophistication, and historical information.

These two areas, romantic–classical and representational–presentational, cut across one another when one is attempting to place a theatrical production on a diagram of style, and although diagrams that attempt to relate "isms" of style to the "life" from which they come can give us little definitive information, such a diagram can help the student visualize the relationships of one style to another better than can the use of words (Figure 19–1).

A diagram such as this makes it clear that a modern style such as *expressionism* will almost always be accepted as an abstraction from

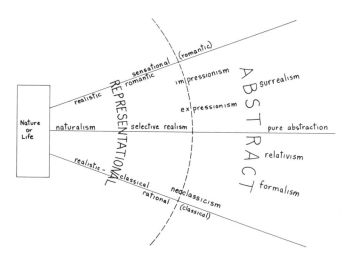

Figure 19–1   A diagram showing an arbitrary placement of styles in relation to reality or life.

reality, will usually tend more toward the emotional and the sensational than the logical and rational, and can be thought of as a direct development from representational realism, since the artist is using the subconscious reality of an individual as the rationale for his art. *Impressionism* will, at times, be acceptable as a representation of reality but is far more likely to move out to the level of abstraction—usually with a strong element of subtle, intuitive romanticism in its composition. *Surrealism* (which is not well represented in the drama) makes use of the reality of dreams and sensations of the inner mind, usually has sensational or romantic overtones, and would almost always be accepted as an abstraction rather than as a representation of reality. *Naturalism* as a stylistic form hugs close to the actual "life" from which it is taken and has few clearly defined characteristics, while *realism* tends to be more logically, rationally, and selectively formed while still attempting to capture the shifting balance between the sensational and the rational in life. Both of these stylistic forms are, of course, representational in intent and never allow an audience to be aware of the organizations and abstractions that are taking place in the production. *Symbolism* may stress either the rational or the sensational aspects of life, and by the nature and strength of the symbols used it can be thought of as either representational or abstract. *Mannerism* is such a loose stylistic term and covers so much artistic ground that it is impossible to tie down easily, but it tends more toward the sensational and the mystical than toward the rational and logical, even when it is most preoccupied with structural effects and rational ideas. It speaks to the spirit rather than the mind, and although it can be representational at times, it is usually viewed as a clear abstraction from reality.

Many more minor stylistic labels can be placed on the diagram if one wishes, but one point is very clear: the great unifying cultural styles (such as the Romanesque, the Gothic, and the Baroque) produce such variety that one cannot tie them down to any single area on a diagram; they take in such wide balances of artistic effect in all directions that one can only discuss this variety, one cannot diagram it.

How the Various Style Labels Affect the Costume Designer

The terms representation and abstraction, when applied to the clothing of the past or present from which the designer is to create his costumes, must mean the difference between costumes that an audience will accept as "real" garments based on the historical fashions of an era and costumes that an audience will accept as "abstractions" created by the designer from historical sources. This difference can apply to plays in any "style," and a majority of plays can be interpreted either abstractly or representationally. In one mode the designer is using his source material as a way to comment on the period in terms of the play and its characters, in the other he is deliberately abstracting his costume effects so that the audience will concentrate on things in the production other than on the cultural background of period. There has been a tendency in the theatre to stress the representational in costume even when settings move toward the abstract, simply because the body of the actor does not lend itself to abstraction as well as do stage sets; but the costume designer should not allow his creative vision to become narrow. If the play and the director's approach allow for an abstract expression of life, he should not be afraid to work in this direction.

The terms romantic and classical, which are the common opposites in theatre terminology, mean to the costume designer the difference between colors, fabrics, and costume lines that possess richness, variety, sensuous appeal, and decorative effect or colors, fabrics, and costume lines that stress balance, overall form, simplicity, logic of structure, and limitation of effect. A stage costume is usually balanced somewhere between the two poles, leaning toward one effect or the other. The costume designer instinctively knows when he must work in one direction or the other, although there has been a tendency in the past century to equate all theatre and things theatrical with the intuitive, the sensational, the romantic outlook on life. This leads the costume designer to "dress up" all productions in essentially romantic costumes. This is obviously a limitation which does not allow the full breadth of our artistic inheritance to be expressed in stage costume.

The Problem of Costume Design in Our Present Culture

One of the great problems of the theatre in the twentieth century is that it has become (or at least it thinks it has become) so well versed in the theatrical styles of the past that its producers are only too ready to display their knowledge and theatrical prowess by presenting each play in its original, distinctive style. Like the great Reinhardt, who attempted to unify all the visual effects in his productions in order to capture the stylistic feeling of the period in which the play was written, many students of costume design become enamored with the idea of presenting each play in a stylistic approach based on the play's original production. Although this is a commendable idea, it leads to an eclecticism that may eventually have only the academic flavor of a museum. The costume designer who prides himself on being able to design equally well in all styles runs the risk of being superficial—of operating as a dilettante instead of as an artist.

On the other hand, the preceding chapters on style have emphasized the importance of understanding the cultural, historical, and artistic background within which a play was written as well as having a clear idea of the play's compositional structure before setting about the design of costumes. Since the costume designer, unlike the painter and the sculptor, is an interpreter of another man's artistic product, the concept of a designer having his own style and forcing it on each production with which he is associated is untenable, if not dishonest. What is needed is a fusion of all that can be learned about a play and its background with the visual sources and design concepts that are prevalent today and will speak to the audiences of our own time. In short, the costume designer must make full use of the latest "breakthroughs" in the visual arts for interpreting the plays of the past, without doing violence to the original stylistic concept of that play. This is a large order, but the costume designer must commit himself to it if he intends to be honest to his playwright as well as to himself as a theatre artist.

The costume designer, like the set designer, the actor, and the director, always works within the limitations set by the script, and only when he is designing for some entertainment or ceremonial occasion that does not include a play script is he free to create like a painter, sculptor, or architect. There are occasions, however, when even painters, sculptors, and architects are required to work under quite strict limitations; we might take example from such limitations to illustrate how the costume designer may solve his artistic problems within the limitations of a script.

Take, for example, the limitations given an architect when he must fit his design into a group of buildings constructed in an earlier era. No self-respecting architect today would create a structure that re-created all the attributes of some historical style, even though this was the *beaux arts* architectural method of the nineteenth century. The architect would study the style of the other buildings very carefully and then, using the abstract attributes of line, texture, and color that he found there, he would design a structure that would harmonize with the older buildings, would contain many of the same ideas of space, form, and surface texture, but would be conceived according to present-day visual usages. At Stanford University, several new and rather interesting structures have recently been built in which the red tile roofs, the sandstone texture, the round arches, and the cloister-like porticos have been retained from the Richardson Romanesque style that was adopted for the earliest buildings of the University (Figure 19–2). In each of these new structures the basic characteristics of the older buildings have been retained while new visual modes have been introduced. The arches are simpler, smoother, and unornamented; the surfaces are smooth plaster or poured concrete rather than cut stone; there is more sense of thrust and balanced

Figure 19–2   The Meyer Undergraduate Library, Stanford University. An example of the tile roofs, columns, and arches found in the Richardson Romanesque architecture of the old campus used in a contemporary architectural design. Photo by the author.

weights than in the piled up block-like forms of the original, and an overall cleanness and lack of ornament replaces the variety of carved stone effects in the earlier buildings. Yet with all the simplifications, expansions, and contractions of form in relation to space, the basic idea of a tile-roofed sandstone-colored structure surrounded by round arches has been maintained in one way or another. The architects, given strong limitations in their design approach, have succeeded in bringing the past and the present together without doing violence to either.

Costume design today should take advantage of the same dual effect. In a Shakespearean production, for example, one may spatter or spray the costumes to bring them closer to the patina of age or the sense of exposure to the elements that one finds prized in much modern art; one may treat raised ornament and jewelry in terms of the melted-metal, free-form look of much modern sculpture and jewelry; fabrics may be treated and dipped and dry-brushed to get a strong statement of surface that has a contemporary look yet is closely derived from historical fabric surfaces; while lines of costumes may be accentuated by outlining contrasts in order to point up the contemporary interest in the structural lines behind an artistic presentation. There are no rules, no way to know how little or how much to change and develop your sources; it depends on sensitivity, intuition, a feeling for the original source as well as for modern artistic ideals, and a great sense of communication with the director of the particular production.

A *Production of* Prometheus Bound

To conclude this discussion of how to bring costume design for the theatre into the mainstream of contemporary art without violating the visual ideals found in an analysis of the script, let us briefly review the thinking and planning that went into a production of Aeschylus' *Prometheus Bound* at the Stanford Repertory Theatre in 1966.

The director wanted a visual production that would stress the sense of primitive ritual and ceremony that he hoped to bring to the play, and since none of the characters are specifically human, the director wished the costumes to suggest natural, organic, universal forces rather than people. A book on precious stones led to a design for the chorus costumes based on a cross section of a piece of malachite. The blues and greens with touches of white suggested the sea as it laps against rock, and this seemed an appropriate image for the chorus, who represent

Figure 19–3   A scene from *Prometheus Bound* by Aeschylus as produced by the Stanford Repertory Theatre, Stanford University, 1966. An example of the use of the traditional Greek mask and costumes interpreted in terms of primitive, ritualistic evocations of natural organic forms. Photo courtesy of Hank Kranzler, Palo Alto, Calif.

Daughters of the Ocean. The shape of the rock also suggested a series of overlapping circular capes, and this gave the conical silhouette eventually used in the chorus costumes, culminating in monumental masks based on primitive votive images from Africa and the South Pacific. The final chorus costume was made of overlapping petals of melted nylon, which gave a broken and coruscated texture of rock and seaweed, and with the use of the mask it suggested the primitive origins of the Greek drama while making an appeal to contemporary visual sensitivities (Figure 19–3).

Io's costume had to suggest not only her intense suffering but also that Zeus had transformed her into a cow, and the finished design made use of a great pink gown suggesting raw membranes covered with pasture grass, hemp garlands, webs at neck and wrists, symbolic horns on the

Figure 19–4 Io from *Prometheus Bound* by Aeschylus as produced by the Stanford Repertory Theatre, Stanford University, 1966. An example of pastoral textures and imagery used to create a ritualistic ceremonial costume. Photo by Hank Kranzler, Palo Alto, Calif.

forehead, and claws instead of hands (Figure 19–4). The costume was fabricated from melted nylon, sisal hemp, shredded rope, and liquid plastic, and although the basic shape of a Greek gown and mask were suggested, the primitive symbolic character of the role was forcefully presented, and the contemporary love of organic surfaces and textures utilizing current synthetics was stressed.

The final costumes for this production were mysterious, primitive, new, exciting, and made a fresh comment using new synthetic textures within the original visual demands of the play. Although most plays will not allow this much abstraction or textural display, many plays which are produced as re-creations of period dress can profit by the right subtle touches of contemporary visual usage.

Contemporary Plays

Finally, a word should be said about the contemporary scene of playwriting and production—the so-called "new theatre" that is in the process of formation, turning its back both on the intellectualism of the absurdists and the emotionalism of the psychological realists.

For half a century, at least, it has been an accepted ideal that the theatre is a unity and all elements should blend under the absolute control of the director. But it has largely been a matter of external unity, and today, when no conventional forms stand firm, the author who cares more about what he is saying than about the external methods of production, must work *with* a director and a cast until what is said is fresh, honest, and direct. A stable and harmonious society need only look to the theatre for reflection and reaffirmation of its harmony, but a shifting, chaotic world must often choose between a playhouse that offers a unified but spurious "yes" and one that offers a provocation so strong that the audience is fragmented into hundreds of vivid and different "nos."

It is obvious and banal to say that sacred, spiritual, or holy art has been destroyed by bourgeois values, but it is also foolish to allow revulsion for bourgeois forms to include reaction against the spiritual and artistic needs common to all men. If the need for true contact with a sacred mystery through the medium of theatre still exists, then all possible vehicles for the projection of this invisible world must be reexamined.

Artists dedicated to this goal are often accused today of wanting to destroy everything admired in the theatre of the past century, particularly the spoken word. There is actually a grain of truth in this assertion, since the word is not the same tool for the dramatist that it once was. Possibly it is because we are living in an age of images that we must go through a period of image saturation before language can reemerge; but dramatists today seem unable to make ideas and images meld through words as they did in the great dramatic eras of the past. The great

Figure 19–5   A scene from the Royal Shakespeare Theatre production of *A Midsummer Night's Dream,* directed by Peter Brook at Stratford-upon-Avon, 1970. An example of Shakespeare designed and directed to make strong, direct, physical communiction with the audience without the interference of illustrative or pictorial material; a production with strong emphasis on physical and even acrobatic presentation of the script. Photo reproduced by permission of the Governors of the Royal Shakespeare Theatre, Stratford-upon-Avon, England. Photo by Joe Cocks.

prophet of this new theatre of images was the French genius Antonin Artaud, who wrote just before World War II. He railed against the sterility of the bourgeois theatre and described from the depths of his imagination and intuition another theatre—a holy theatre whose blazing core was to speak through the forms closest to it; a theatre working like the plague through intoxication, infection, and magic. He saw a theatre in which the play, the event itself, stood in place of the text.

It was the influence of this mad genius, carried forward in the work of the Royal Shakespeare Company under Peter Brook in productions such as *Marat/Sade* and *A Midsummer Night's Dream,* and through workshops devoted to the "theatre of cruelty," that have made such an impact on the contemporary playwriting and theatre scene (Figure 19–5).

In American works such as *Hair, Tom Payne,* and *Futz,* in the efforts that have come out of the workshops of the Polish visionary Jerzy Grotowski, and in much of the experimental work going on in theatre centers such as Prague, Paris, and Rome, this new theatre of image and action has taken a strong hold (Figure 19–6). By making words secondary to movement and gesture, by limiting the alternatives of expression, actors are trained to summon all of their reserves, all of their concentration, all of their will to communicate or express a true dramatic action. The leaders of this movement speak of making the invisible visible through the mere presence of the performer. Masks, makeup, and the traditional properties and accessories of the theatre are rejected in favor of silence, noise, the ritual use of repeated patterns, the climaxes and denouements of group action. To the followers of Artaud, the surprise element and surrealistic incongruity of absurdist drama is as dead as the psychological drama of naturalism. From the phrase "theatre of cruelty," these followers are groping toward a new theatre—more violent, less rational, more extreme, less verbal, more dangerous than the theatre of the immediate past. But the problem that must be faced in the very near future is the age-old one: "What follows the shock?" Once the great excitement and participation

Figure 19–6 Eron Tabor (center) and the Tribe in a scene from the San Francisco production of *Hair,* presented by Michael Butler, Marshall Naify, and the American Conservatory Theatre, 1969. An example of the new theatre of image and action, in which verbal communication is secondary to ritual communication through group action. Photo courtesy of the Press Representative of the American Conservatory Theatre.

in this new order of theatre has worn thin, will inertia set in? This is the major question being asked by leading critics and commentators on the contemporary theatrical scene.

The Happening, developed in artistic circles after World War II, used impulsive, meaningless acts and exercises to awaken the senses and instincts of the participants. Such Happenings screamed at a deadened and desensitized industrial society: "Wake up; live; see and feel." The impulsive, instinctive excitement of the Happening has now become a part of theatrical performance, but the "new theatre" will quickly die unless purpose and meaning are allowed to flow into the receptive instincts, reflexes, and sensitivities opened by the shock and excitement. The theatre today has awakened a great and powerful sleeping hunger in us all, and designers, directors, actors, and playwrights are implicitly challenged to meet the need. Whether new forms containing new depth, perception, and meaning can be developed from the experiments of the "new theatre" remains to be seen, but it is an exciting period of transition and change in which the best insights and instincts of all workers in the theatre may be shared and developed.

III

OUTLINE HISTORY OF WESTERN COSTUME

This outline may be used by students wishing to refresh their memories about the major developments in costume during the history of the Western world. It is in no way meant to take the place of or to be used in place of the standard texts in costume history, but is appended here merely as an aid to the student who needs to keep his period, dates, and costume silhouettes clearly in mind as he reads the body of the text.

Recommended Sources on the History of Western Costume

(These references appear in abbreviated form in the outline history of Western costume. The numbers in parentheses before items by the same author indicate which book by the author is intended in the sources listed for each period.)

American Magazine (1876–). New York.

Barton, Lucy. *Historic Costume for the Stage.* Boston: W. H. Baker, 1935.

Beazley, Sir John D., and Ashmole, Bernard. *Greek Sculpture and Painting to the End of the Hellenistic Period.* Cambridge: Cambridge University Press, 1932.

Benesch, Otto. *The Art of the Renaissance in Northern Europe: Its Relation to the Contemporary Spiritual and Intellectual Movements.* Cambridge, Mass.: Harvard University Press, 1945.

Berenson, Bernard. *Italian Painters of the Renaissance,* 2 vols. London: Phaidon Press, 1957.

Blum, André. *Histoire de Costume: Les Modes aux XIXième Siècle.* Paris: Hachette, 1931.

(1) Boehn, Max von. *Die Mode: Menschen und Moden in achtzehnten Jahrhundert.* . . . Munich: Bruckmann, 1909.

(2) ———. *Die Mode: Menschen und Moden im Mittelalter.* . . . Munich: Bruckmann, 1909.

(3) ———. *Die Mode: Menschen und Moden im neunzehnten Jahrhundert.* . . . Munich: Bruckmann, 1907–1919.

(4) ———. *Die Mode: Menschen und Moden im sechzehnten Jahrhundert.* . . . Munich: Bruckmann, 1923.

(5) ———. *Die Mode: Menschen und Moden im siebzehnten Jahrhundert.* . . . Munich: Bruckmann, 1913.

(6) ———. *Modes and Manners* (trans. by Joan Joshua), 4 vols. London: Harrap, 1932–1935.

Bon Ton, le and *le Moniteur de la Mode* (1853–). Paris and New York.

Boucher, François. *20,000 Years of Fashion.* New York: Harry Abrams, 1967.

Breasted, James Henry. *A History of Egypt,* 2nd ed. rev. New York: Scribner's, 1924.

(1) Brooke, Iris. *English Costume in the Age of Elizabeth.* London: A. & C. Black, 1933.

(2) ———. *English Costume of the Early Middle Ages.* London: A. & C. Black, 1936.

(3) ———. *English Costume of the Eighteenth Century.* London: A. & C. Black, 1931.

(4) ———. *English Costume of the Later Middle Ages.* London: A. & C. Black, 1935.

(5) ———. *English Costume of the Nine-*

456

teenth Century. London: A. & C. Black, 1929.

(6) ———. *English Costume of the Seventeenth Century.* London: A. & C. Black, 1934.

(7) ———. *Medieval Theatre Costume.* New York: Theatre Arts, 1967.

(8) ———. *A History of English Costume.* New York: Theatre Arts, 1968.

(9) ———. *Western European Costume.* Vol. 1, London: Harrap, 1939; Vol. 2, London: Theatre Arts, 1964.

(1) Brown, H. C. *The Golden Nineties.* New York: Valentine, 1928.

(2) ———. *New York in the Elegant Eighties.* New York: Valentine, 1927.

Burckhardt, Jakob C. *The Civilization of the Renaissance in Italy* (trans. by S. G. C. Middlemore), 3rd rev. ed. London: Phaidon, 1950.

Carcopino, J. *Daily Life in Ancient Rome.* New Haven, Conn.: Yale University Press, 1940.

Clinch, George. *English Costume.* London: A. & C. Black, 1923.

Connoisseur, The (1901. In 1927 merged with International Studio). London.

Contini, Mila. *Fashion.* New York: Odyssey Press, 1965.

Court Magazine and Monthly Critic (1832–). London.

(1) Cunnington, C. Willett. *English Women's Clothing in the Nineteenth Century.* London: Faber, 1937.

(2) Cunnington, C. Willett, and Cunnington, Phillis. *Handbook of English Costume in the Eighteenth Century.* London: Faber, 1957.

(3) ———. *Handbook of English Costume in the Seventeenth Century.* London: Faber, 1955.

(4) ———. *Handbook of English Costume in the Sixteenth Century.* London: Faber, 1954.

(5) ———. *Handbook of English Medieval Costume.* Philadelphia: Dufour, 1952.

(6) ———. *A Picture History of English Costume.* London: Longacre, 1960.

Cutts, E. L. *Scenes and Characters of the Middle Ages.* London: Daniel O'Connor, 1872.

Davenport, Millia. *The Book of Costume.* New York: Crown, 1948.

Davis, William S. *Life in Elizabethan Days.* New York: Harper, 1930.

Dewald, Ernest T. *Italian Painting 1200–1600.* New York: Holt, Rinehart and Winston, 1961.

(1) Dimier, Louis. *French Painting in the Sixteenth Century.* New York: Scribner's, 1911.

(2) ———. *Les Peintres Français du XVIIIième Siècle.* Paris: Editions G. van Oest, 1928–1930.

Enlart, Camille. *Manuel d'Archaeologie Française. Tome III, Le Costume.* Paris: Auguste Picard, 1916.

Esquire Magazine (1937–). New York.

(1) Evans, Joan. *Art in Medieval France.* New York: Oxford University Press, 1948.

(2) ———. *Dress in Medieval France.* Oxford: Clarendon Press, 1952.

Evelyn, Sir John. *Diary (1641–1705),* 2 vols. Washington, D.C.: Dunne, 1901.

Faniel, Stephanie (ed.). *French Art of the Eighteenth Century.* New York: Simon & Schuster, 1957.

Fletcher, Sir Bannister. *A History of Architecture on the Comparative Method,* 17th ed. New York: Scribner's, 1965.

Frankfort, Henri. *The Art and Architecture of the Ancient Orient.* Baltimore: Penguin, 1955.

Frankl, Paul. *The Gothic.* Princeton, N.J.: Princeton University Press, 1960.

Freedberg, Sydney J. *Painting of the High Renaissance in Rome and Florence,* 2 vols. Cambridge, Mass.: Harvard University Press, 1961.

Friedlander, Walter F. *Mannerism and Anti-Mannerism in Italian Painting.* New York: Columbia University Press, 1957.

Gallery of Fashion (1794–1802). London.

(1) Gardner, Arthur. *French Sculpture of the Thirteenth Century.* London: Medici Society, 1915.

(2) ———. *Medieval Sculpture in France.* New York: Macmillan, 1931.

Gentleman's Magazine, The (of Fashions, Fancy Costume, and Regimentals of the Army) (May 1828–December 1894). London.

Gernsheim, Helmut. *The History of Photography from the Earliest Use of the Camera Obscura in the Eleventh Century up to 1914.* London: Oxford University Press, 1969.

Ghorsline, Douglas. *What People Wore.* New York: Viking, 1952.

Godey's Lady's Book (1830–1898). Philadelphia.

Good Housekeeping (1885–). New York.

(1) *Harper's New Monthly Magazine* (1850–). New York.

(2) *Harper's Weekly* (1857–1916). New York.

(3) *Harper's Bazaar* (1867–). New York.

Hartley, Dorothy. *Medieval Costume and Life.* New York: Scribner's, 1931.

(1) Hartley, Dorothy, and Elliot, Margaret M. *Life and Work of the People of England (The Eleventh to the Thirteenth Century— A.D. 1000–1300).* New York: Putnam, 1931.

(2) ———. *Life and Work of the People of England (The. Eighteenth Century).* New York: Putnam, 1931.

Heuzey, Léon, and Heuzey, Jacques. *Histoire du Costume dans L'Antiquité Classique l'Orient.* Paris: Les Belles Lettres, 1935.

Holiday Magazine (1946–). Philadelphia.

Hope, Thomas. *Costume of the Ancients.* London: Chatto and Windus, 1875.

(1) Houston, Mary G. *Ancient Greek, Roman and Byzantine Costume.* London: A. & C. Black, 1931.

(2) ———. *Medieval Costume in England and France.* London: A. & C. Black, 1939.

Houston, Mary G., and Hornblower, Florence. *Ancient Egyptian, Assyrian and Persian Costume.* London: A. & C. Black, 1920.

Illustrated London News (1842–). London.

L'Illustration (1843–). Paris.

International Studio (1897–). New York.

Janson, H. W. *History of Art.* New York: Harry N. Abrams, 1964.

Jastrow, Morris. *The Civilization of Babylonia and Assyria.* New York: Lippincott, 1915.

Kelly, Francis M. *Shakespearean Costume for Stage and Screen.* Boston: Baker, 1938.

Kelly, Francis M., and Schwabe, Randolph. *Historic Fashion, A Chronicle of Fashion in Western Europe (1490–1790).* London: Batsford, 1925.

Kimball, Sidney Fiske. *The Creation of the Rococo.* Philadelphia: Philadelphia Museum of Art, 1943.

Kitson, Michael. *The Age of Baroque.* New York: McGraw-Hill, 1966.

Köhler, Carl. *A History of Costume.* New York: Dover, 1963.

Lacroix, Paul. *The Eighteenth Century, Its Institutions, Customs, and Costumes.* New York: Scribner's, 1876.

Ladies' Home Journal (1883–). Philadelphia.

Larkin, Oliver. *Art and Life in America.* New York: Rinehart, 1949.

Larousse Encyclopedia of Byzantine and Medieval Art (ed. by René Huyghe). New York: Prometheus Press, 1958.

(1) Laver, James. *Costume.* London: Hawthorn, 1964.

(2) ———. *Costume Through the Ages.* London: Thames and Hudson, 1963.

(3) ———. *Style in Costume.* New York: Oxford University Press, 1949.

(4) ——— (ed.). *Costumes of the Western World.* New York: Harper & Row, 1951.

(5) ——— (ed.). *Costume in Antiquity.* London: Thames and Hudson, 1964.

Lawrence, Arnold W. *Classical Sculpture.* London: Cape, 1929.

Leloir, Maurice. *Histoire du Costume.* Paris: Henri Ernst, 1933.

Life Magazine (1883–). New York.

Linthicum, M. Channing. *Costume in the Drama of Shakespeare and His Contemporaries.* Oxford: Clarendon Press, 1936.

Mahaffy, Sir John P. *Social Life in Greece from Homer to Menander.* London: Macmillan, 1877.

Mâle, Émile. *Religious Art in France in the Thirteenth Century.* New York: Dutton, 1913.

Marinatos, Spyridon. *Crete and Mycenae.* New York: Harry N. Abrams, 1960.

Martindale, Andrew. *Man and the Renaissance.* New York: McGraw-Hill, 1966.

Men's Wear (1937–1950). New York.

Mode Illustreé, la (1869–1873). London.

Modes Parisiennes, les (1843–1875). Paris.

458

(1) Morey, Charles Rufus. *Christian Art*. New York: Longmans, Green, 1935.

(2) ———. *Medieval Art*. New York: Norton, 1942.

Morse, Harriet K. *Elizabethan Pageantry*. . . . London: Studio, 1934.

(1) Norris, Herbert. *Costume and Fashion*. London: Dent, 1925, Vol. I; 1940, Vol. II. New York: Dutton, 1938, Vol. III.

(2) ———. *Church Vestments*. London: Dent, 1949.

Norris, Herbert, and Curtis, Oswald. *Costume and Fashion*. London: Dent, 1933, Vol. VI.

Novotny, Fritz. *Painting and Sculpture in Europe, 1780–1880*. Pelican History of Art. Baltimore: Penguin, 1960.

Payne, Blanche. *History of Costume*. New York: Harper & Row, 1965.

Pepys, Samuel. *Diary and Correspondence of Samuel Pepys*, 10 vols. New York: Dodd, Mead, 1885.

Perrot, Georges, and Chipiez, C. *A History of Art: Egypt, Judea, Chaldea, Assyria, Persia, Ancient Greece*, 10 vols. Paris: Hachette, 1882–1894. Translated in 1883 and published by Chapman and Hall, London.

Peterson's Magazine (1846–1898). Philadelphia.

Pevsner, Nikolaus. *An Outline of European Architecture*. Baltimore: Penguin, 1963.

Piton, Camille. *Le Costume Civile en France du XIIIième au XIXième Siècle*. Paris, 1913.

Price, Julius M. *Dame Fashion*. New York: Scribner's, 1913.

Quicherat, Jules E. J. *Histoire du Costume en France*. . . . Paris: Hachette, 1877.

Racinet, Albert C. A. *Le Costume historique*, 6 vols. Paris: Firmin-Didot, 1888.

Rice, David Talbot. *The Art of Byzantium*. New York: Harry Abrams, 1959.

Richter, Gisela. *A Handbook of Greek Art*, 2nd rev. ed. London: Phaidon, 1960.

Robertson, Donald A. *A Handbook of Greek and Roman Architecture*. Cambridge: Cambridge University Press, 1954.

Sears Roebuck Catalog, The (1894–). Chicago.

(1) Skira, Albert (ed.). *The Great Centuries of Painting: Roman Painting*. Geneva: Editions Albert Skira, 1953.

(2) ———. *The Great Centuries of Painting: Byzantine Painting*. Geneva: Editions Albert Skira, 1953.

(3) ———. *The Great Centuries of Painting: Early Medieval Painting*. Geneva: Editions Albert Skira, 1957.

(4) ———. *The Great Centuries of Painting: Romanesque Painting*. Geneva: Editions Albert Skira, 1958.

(5) ———. *The Great Centuries of Painting: Gothic Painting*. Geneva: Editions Albert Skira, 1954.

(6) ———. *The Great Centuries of Painting: Italian Painting of the Renaissance*. Geneva: Editions Albert Skira, 1951.

(7) ———. *The Great Centuries of Painting: The Sixteenth Century*. Geneva: Editions Albert Skira, 1954.

(8) ———. *The Great Centuries of Painting: The Seventeenth Century*. Geneva: Editions Albert Skira, 1951.

(9) ———. *The Great Centuries of Painting: The Eighteenth Century*. Geneva: Editions Albert Skira, 1952.

Soehner, Halldor, and Schonberger, Arno. *The Rococo Age*. New York: McGraw-Hill, 1960.

Speltz, Alexander. *The Styles of Ornaments etc.* (trans. and rev. by R. P. Spiers). London: Batsford, 1910.

Strong, Eugene. *Art in Ancient Rome*, 2 vols. New York: Scribner's, 1928.

Studio, The (1893–). London.

Sullivan, Mark. *Our Times, 1900–1914*. Vol. I, *The Turn of the Century;* Vol. II, *America Finding Herself;* Vol. III, *Prewar America;* Vol. IV, *The War Begins*. New York: Scribner's, 1927–1932.

Swarzenski, Hanns. *Monuments of Romanesque Art*. Chicago: University of Chicago Press, 1954.

Tapié, Victor L. *The Age of Grandeur*. New York: Praeger, 1960.

(1) Tilke, Max. *The Costumes of Eastern Europe*. London: Benn, 1926.

(2) ———. *Orientalische Kostüme in Schnitt und Farbe*. Berlin: Wasmuth, 1923.

Tilke, Max, and Bruhn, Wolfgang. *A Pictorial History of Costume*. London: A. Zwemmer, 1955.

(1) Tissot, James. *The Life of Our Savior, Jesus Christ* (trans. with notes and drawings by Mrs. Arthur Bell). New York: Doubleday-McClure, 1899.

(2) ———. *Old Testament Selections*. Paris: M. de Brunoff, 1904.

Vecellio, Cesare. *Habiti antichi et moderni*. Venice, 1598.

Vingt Ans (1947–). Paris.

Vogue (1892–). New York.

Volbach, Wolfgang F., and Hirmer, Max. *Early Christian Art*. New York: Harry Abrams, 1961.

(1) Wilcox, Ruth Turner. *The Mode in Costume*. New York: Scribner's, 1946.

(2) ———. *The Mode in Furs*. New York: Scribner's, 1951.

(3) ———. *Five Centuries of American Costume*. New York: Scribner's, 1963.

(1) Wilson, Lillian May. *The Clothing of the Ancient Romans*. Baltimore: Johns Hopkins University Press, 1938.

(2) ———. *The Roman Toga*. Baltimore: Johns Hopkins University Press, 1924.

Wittkower, Rudolf. *Art and Architecture in Italy, 1600–1750*. Pelican History of Art, Baltimore: Penguin, 1958.

(1) Wölfflin, Heinrich. *Classic Art*, 2nd ed. London: Phaidon, 1953.

(2) ———. *Principles of Art History* (trans. by Mary D. Hottinger). New York: Holt, 1932.

Worth, J. P. *A Century of Fashion*. Boston: Little, Brown, 1928.

OUTLINE HISTORY
OF WESTERN
COSTUME

Egyptian

The earliest civilization of our Western world arose along the Nile River in Egypt and the Tigris and Euphrates Rivers in Mesopotamia several thousand years before Christ; both flourished for roughly 3000 years, but because the material used for temples and pyramids was stone, Egypt left many more remnants of this civilization than did Mesopotamia.

The Egyptian style is characterized by severity, regularity, order, and rhythmical repetition. Flowers and plants such as the lotus and the papyrus were incorporated into the rigid patterns used on columns, capitals, wall decorations, and costume accessories. Costuming, like the other arts, was sophisticated, symbolic, removed from the level of the natural to a formal, frozen, unchanging silhouette that would always suggest the triumph of man's organizing powers over man's natural subordination to nature.

THE OLD KINGDOM. In the first period of Egypt's prosperity, the major masculine garment was a short, plain *loin cloth* of linen wrapped tightly around the hips and secured by a belt with a loop. Loin cloths of the Pharaohs were often woven with gold thread and made a great point of carefully arranged folds at the front of the figure. This stress on many stiffened, lightweight, even transparent folds is a characteristic stressed in most Egyptian costume. The feminine dress was also a single garment: a close-fitting *skirt* covering the body from under the breasts to the ankles and supported by two shoulder straps. As time progressed, the skirt was often overlaid with a girdle with all emphasis drawn to the front of the figure, and the male loin cloth added a stiffly starched and pleated triangle of fabric at the front of the figure.

THE MIDDLE KINGDOM. In the next period of prosperity, men's dress was complicated by the addition of a skirt. The skirt was often semitransparent, over a loin cloth frequently finished with a girdle and again stressing a decorative emphasis at the front of the figure. The head was often covered with a stiffened cloth such as we see on the Sphinx. Women's clothing, though more richly adorned, did not change appreciably during this time.

THE NEW KINGDOM. After a period of disruption caused by foreign raids, a period of great expansion and wealth developed. At this time the seamed tunic or *kalisiris* became a part of Egyptian dress, with men wearing it either over or under a skirt, while women used it as a principal garment coupled with a short cape knotted on the breast; the fabric chosen was so thin and fine in texture that it was almost completely transparent. These tunic dresses, especially at the time of the artistic naturalism of Akhenaten or Amenhotep IV, were often finely pleated and followed the line of the body without the severity of line found in earlier Egyptian dress. The great rectangular robe with a hole in the center for the head was also used at this time. There are many artistic depictions of such well-known symbolic accessories as the sacred *uraeus* or asp, the *scarab* or beetle symbol, the vulture headdress, the combined red and white crown of Upper and Lower Egypt, the winged solar disk, and the famous Queen's Headdress of the Empress Nefertiti. Flowers and jewelry were used extensively in geometric patterns of decoration, the most vivid decorative accessory being the richly colored round collar used by both men and women. Cosmetics were used extensively. Women's eyes were outlined with kohl and shadowed in green, while the body and false wig were bathed in sweet-smelling oils. Men of the nobility frequently used false wigs and beards.

In the long history of Egyptian dress the basic costume ideal underwent very few modifications, because in Egyptian culture respect for tradition was far stronger than the need for change.

EGYPTIAN

DATES
Old Kingdom 2980–2160 B.C.
Middle Kingdom 2160–1580 B.C.
Empire 1580–1090 B.C.
Saite Period 1090–323 B.C.

COMMON TERMS (for others see glossary)
kalisiris
sacred uraeus
mitre of Osiris
vulture headdress
schenti
postiche
pectoral
ankh

RECOMMENDED SOURCES
Houston and Hornblower: Section I
Payne: Chapter I
Köhler: Chapter on Egypt
Boucher: pp. 91–103
Fletcher: Chapter on Egyptian
architecture
Speltz: Chapter I
Barton: pp. 3–18
Davenport: pp. 15–35
Contini: pp. 15–26
Breasted
Tilke: *A Pictorial History of Costume,*
Plates 1–5

Typical Figures

Mesopotamian

The area of the Tigris and Euphrates Valleys and the surrounding areas, which include Persia, Southern Turkey, and Palestine, gave birth to a highly developed series of civilizations at approximately the same time that Egyptian culture developed. However, since the major architectural structures were of brick rather than stone and the transition from one culture to another was quite rapid, we have far fewer artifacts from which to judge each succeeding culture than is the case in Egypt. The most consistent image left to us from these various cultures is that of fierce and war-like conquerors whose major interests were hunting and fighting. Their physical image, draped in fringed woolen shawls over woolen tunics surmounted by heavy beards and headdresses, is far heavier, less sophisticated, and less carefully ordered than the Egyptian figure.

SUMERIAN CIVILIZATION. The few artistic representations of dress from this period show the men in what must be shaggy sheepskin skirts wrapped around the waist. Women wore a simple tunic. Toward the end of this early period the famous fringed shawl was introduced, worn either diagonally over the shoulder and under the other arm or (usually for women) fastened about the neck with a brooch.

ANCIENT BABYLONIAN EMPIRE. The decline toward the end of the third millennium of the Sumerian empire of Ur allowed the city of Babylon to become the center of a new Mesopotamian empire, which further developed the use of thick, richly decorated garments. There was a great emphasis on the use of fringe. The basic garments for both men and women were a fringed shirt or tunic surmounted by the diagonally draped shawl. Headdresses tended toward metal circlets or truncated metal cones, while footwear included an open sandal and a partially closed and laced shoe.

ANCIENT ASSYRIAN EMPIRE. The period of Northern ascendency under the rule of the Assyrians at Nineveh lasted about 600 years, and it is from the reigns of the great kings such as Ashurbanipal and Ashurnasipal that we get the most striking and best-preserved artistic representations of Assyrian dress. The square-cut hair and beard, the long tunic, the heavy, diagonally draped, fringed shawl, the heavy metal ornaments at wrist and waist, and the truncated cone headdress all make it easy to distinguish Assyrian figures. Women wore simply a modification of these garments.

SECOND BABYLONIAN EMPIRE. This brief period of resurgence of the city of Babylon lasted only from 612 B.C. until the invasion of the Persians in 539 B.C. and produced no marked change in dress except for added richness and decoration.

THE PERSIAN EMPIRE. The Persians, who swept into the Tigris–Euphrates Valley from the East in 539 B.C., accepted much of the architecture and artistic decoration of those they conquered, but they did bring with them a longer-sleeved and tighter tunic or coat, sometimes open down the front, and also trousers for covering the legs. The *candys*, a great rectangle reaching from wrist to wrist with a hole for the head and seamed together up the sides, was used as a ceremonial garment. Beards were pointed rather than square; crowns flared out instead of tapering in, and feet were covered with slipper-like shoes. Women still wore the tunic and shawl with the addition of head veils.

HEBREW DRESS. The Hebrews were originally desert people. When they settled in Palestine they kept the enveloping, striped, woolen garments and draperies that protected head and body from the sun. The basic garments were the long-sleeved tunic, a short, wide-sleeved overtunic, and the very wide-sleeved coat or *aba*, a rectangular robe similar to the robe used by the Egyptians and the shawl used by the Assyrians. Women usually wore a sleeveless tunic, often covered with the wide-sleeved aba or a shawl. Priests wore the tabard-like *ephod* with its jeweled purse over their tunics and a dome-shaped mitre on their heads.

MESOPOTAMIAN

DATES
> Sumerian Civilization 4000–2232 B.C.
> Ancient Babylonian Empire 2232–1275 B.C.
> Assyrian Empire 1275–612 B.C.
> Second Babylonian Empire 612–539 B.C.
> Persian Empire 539–331 B.C.

COMMON TERMS (for others see glossary)
> aba
> ephod
> candys
> caftan
> kilt
> kaunakes
> Phrygian bonnet

RECOMMENDED SOURCES
> Houston and Hornblower: Sections II and III
> Tissot (1)
> Tissot (2)
> Heuzey
> Jastrow (background)
> Frankfort (background)
> Köhler: pp. 64–85

kidaris

caftan

Assyrian ca. 1300 B.C.

Typical Figures

Aegean and Archaic Greek

In certain Egyptian tomb paintings we see long-legged ambassadors from Crete wearing costumes that have a freer and more lightly decorative aspect than those worn by the Egyptians. But it was not until Schliemann excavated Tiryns and Mycenae on the Greek mainland and Sir Arthur Evans uncovered the royal palaces of Crete that historians became aware of the brilliant Bronze Age civilization that existed in the Aegean centuries before the rise of Greek civilization. The most astonishing thing about the clothing of the Cretan and Mycenaean civilizations was its tight, fitted, artificial lines and its light, gay, and charming ornamental decorative patterns.

CRETAN DRESS. Since the ideal Cretan male and female were tall and supple, with slender waists and a backward tilt to the upper part of the body, costume was calculated to emphasize these effects. For men, a loin cloth was often the only covering, resting high on the hips and held in place by a belt that held in the waist like a corset.Women's dress, revealed through votive figures and frescoes, was a two-piece costume consisting of a bell-shaped, tiered skirt and a small jacket, the skirt having a pattern of bright colors running in alternating squares and stripes over the tiers. The waist, as in the male costume, was constricted by the use of a tight belt, while the jacket consisted only of a back and sleeves, and material supporting the bust line. The breasts were completely exposed. Both men and women wore their hair over the forehead in loose, twined curls which repeated the characteristic motif of Cretan art—the supple, vigorous line of the spiral.

MYCENAEAN DRESS. The inhabitants of mainland Greece during the late Aegean period were probably a different race from the Cretans, but the women did copy Cretan styles, although the men tended to wear a short, tight-fitting tunic from Asia Minor. This garment eventually became the basis for the looser draped *chiton* of the Greeks. Mycenaean color and ornament was also heavier and less playful in effect than that used in Cretan costume.

ARCHAIC GREEK DRESS. Greek immigrants overwhelmed Cretan–Mycenaean civilization in several waves between 1200 and 1000 B.C. First they captured and burned the Cretan palaces, which were largely unfortified because of the protecting sea, and then they took the fortresses on the Greek mainland in spite of their complex defenses. The two strongest tribes in these invasions were the Dorians and the Ionians, the former finally dominating mainland Greece, the latter settling on the coast of Asia Minor. The beginning of this new civilization, now known as Archaic Greek, began in the eighth century B.C. and continued up to the time of the Persian invasions.

The standard garment for men was the short, close-fitting chiton or tunic or the long, smooth ceremonial chiton with a decorative pattern. Overgarments consisted of a short rectangular cloak or *chlamys* and the rectangular shawl or *himation*. The major feminine garment was the tubular *peplos*, with an overfold at the top held at the shoulders by two pins. Toward the end of the Archaic period, light pleated linen chitons from Ionia began to replace the tight-fitting tubular peplos, and the move toward the beauty of draped lines and soft folds that was to characterize classical Greek costume began.

The ornament used during the Archaic period was rigidly geometric, and the general feeling of the overall costume silhouette was one of tightness and geometric formality.

AEGEAN AND ARCHAIC GREEK

DATES
    Cretan–Mycenaean,
        early 3500–2200 B.C.
        middle 2200–1600 B.C.
        late 1600–1104 B.C.
    Archaic Greek 1104–490 B.C.
COMMON TERMS (for others see glossary)
    Doric chiton
    Ionic chiton
    kolobium
    himation
RECOMMENDED SOURCES
    Fletcher: pp. 69–113
    Richter: Section I
    Heuzey: Part I
    Speltz: pp. 43–57
    Houston (1): Chapter I

Cretan

Typical Figures

Classical and Hellenistic Greek

The beautifully draped garments that we see on Greek and Hellenistic statues developed gradually, just as Greek art developed to a more natural, more relaxed, more idealized sense of beauty. During the transitional period from roughly 500 B.C. to about 460 B.C., we find all manner of experimentation with soft fabrics, draped lines, and pins instead of seams in order to gain more subtlety, beauty, and graceful relaxation in the form and manner of wearing garments.

THE CLASSICAL PERIOD. The basic masculine costume during the fifth century B.C. was the *Ionic chiton,* which was often formed without seams, being a rectangle whose center fold was placed on the left side of the figure while the right side was open. It was then caught at the shoulder with *fibulae* or safety pins, and thus no seams were needed. There were also, however, chitons that had shoulder and side seams and fitted the body more closely. Most masculine chitons were short, the length adjusted by belting, but the long pleated chiton of linen or soft wool was worn by drivers at races, musicians, certain older men, and actors. The male cloak or shawl was still the rectangular *himation,* usually draped over the left shoulder, under the right arm, and back over the left shoulder. The short cloak or *chlamys,* fastened on the right shoulder with a brooch and leaving the right arm free, was also worn over the short chiton.

The women of the classical period usually wore the *Doric peplos* or *chiton,* which was also a rectangle but with an overfold at the top. It was full and fell in graceful folds, in contrast to the close-fitting archaic *peplos;* its material had a woven border but no overall pattern, and it was not sewn together in a tubular shape but was left open on the right side. It could be worn fastened with pins all the way down the arm and loosely draped without a belt, or it could be belted with a cord at several points above the hips to allow for a blousing of fabric at the hips—this was called the *kolpos.* Sometimes women wore the Ionic chiton without overfold, which gave a lighter and more slimly draped silhouette than that achieved by the Doric peplos or chiton. Women also wore the draped himation as an overgarment.

Men's hair was usually cut relatively short during the fifth century. The faces of the young men were clean shaven, the old were bearded. The only headgear was a straw hat, the *petassos;* a *fillet* was used to hold the hair during games and tournaments. Women dressed their hair to the top and back of the head into a knot or cone held variously with pins, nets, bands, or a diadem known as a *stephanie.* Both men and women wore simple laced sandals.

THE FOURTH CENTURY B.C. During this period the distinctions between garments began to disappear, and one type of chiton might be worn over another of a completely different style, especially in the case of women.

HELLENISTIC PERIOD. After the conquests of Alexander the Great, Greece was brought into contact with the East and cotton and silk were imported and woven into a number of fabrics, especially a semitransparent gauzy material called *coan.* Costumes also displayed more orientalized embroidery techniques, with much use of metallic threads, and in general were richer and more ostentatious.

In general, Greek costume of the classical and Hellenistic periods made full use of effects that could be obtained from unseamed garments, emphasizing grace of movement through constantly changing folds, and the beauties of repose through the subtle lines of the draped garments. Greek costume reflects the same simplicity, lucidity, and monumentality that characterizes Greek art and architecture.

CLASSICAL AND HELLENISTIC GREEK

DATES
    Age of Pericles 490–429 B.C.
    Fourth Century 429–338 B.C.
    Hellenistic 338–146 B.C.
COMMON TERMS (for others see glossary)
    kolobus
    chlamys
    fillet
    stephanie
    petassos
    peplos
    kolpos
    fibulae

    bandelette
    cothurnus
    buskins
    Phrygian bonnet
RECOMMENDED SOURCES
    Houston (1): Chapter II
    Heuzey: Part II
    Norris (1): Volume I, Chapter 2
    Perrot and Chipiez: Volumes II–VIII
        (background)
    Mahaffy (background)
    Hope
    Laver (5): pp. 39–103

Typical Figures

Roman

The Etruscans inhabited that part of Italy which is now called Tuscany from about 1000 B.C. until they were finally conquered and merged with Roman civilization about 300 B.C. At the height of their power they influenced a region extending from the Alps in the north of Italy to the Greek colonies in the south.

Rome, founded about 700 B.C. according to tradition, quickly expanded in all directions, asserting its power over the entire Italian peninsula by 300 B.C., conquering Greece by 146 B.C., and controlling the entire Mediterranean Basin by the end of the first century B.C. Octavian proclaimed the Empire in 27 B.C. Rome remained at the height of its power until the rise of Christianity and barbarian invasions weakened the imperial system in the third century A.D. The Emperor Constantine recognized Christianity in 313 A.D. and moved his capital to Byzantium in 323 A.D. Thereafter, there was rapid decline until the final collapse of Rome in 476 A.D. Throughout its rise and fall, Roman culture was strongly influenced by the Greeks, often adding to and improving on Greek ideals and forms for more practical ends.

ETRUSCAN DRESS. The male dress was either a long *chiton* resembling Greek ceremonial garb, or a short chiton like a tunic or doublet. The rectangular cloak could be worn transversely below the right arm and across the left shoulder, wrapped over the lower part of the body, or draped over both arms.

The feminine dress was at first a tight, tunic-like chiton, later a loosely hanging, beltless chiton of transparent spotted material. Footwear for both men and women were either sandals or closed shoes with pointed, turned-up toes.

ROMAN DRESS. The Greek *chiton* reappears in Roman feminine costume as the *tunica*, but over it was worn the *stola* or outer chiton with the rectangular *palla* or cloak draped over all. The head was usually covered with a *flameum* (later called *ricinium*) or veil, and the hair was built up in a halo of curls across the front of the head. Fabrics ranged from very fine woolens to the most precious of silks at

the time of the empire.

The male *tunica* could be sleeved or sleeveless, short or long, the long-sleeved version being known as the *tunica talaris*. The key Roman garment was the half-circle cloak or *toga*. There were many versions: the *toga praetexta* of white wool with a purple border for senators; the cream-white *toga pura* or *virilis* for the ordinary citizen; the dark-colored *toga pulla* for mourning; the bleached white *toga candida* for those running for office; the embroidered *toga picta* for triumphal occasions; and the particolored *toga trabea* for ceremonial occasions. It was folded down its length, then placed on the left shoulder with a fold against the neck. The front material reached the left ankle or toe, while behind the material was passed across the back, under the right arm, across the chest, and once more over the left shoulder. The remaining material fell down the back. The great toga of Imperial Rome evolved from the semicircular to an elliptical shape four to five yards long, about three yards wide, and folded lengthwise before draping. The top layer of this fold was frequently brought up over the head and was called the *sinus,* while the bottom layer or folds on the left side were lifted over the draping across the chest to form a pouch or *umbo.* Late in the imperial period the toga was folded lengthwise several times, was diminished in size, and was no longer draped but fastened rigidly in place with brooches. Also in the late imperial period, it became the practice to wear several sleeved tunics one over the other; the top one, with very wide sleeves, was called the *dalmatica.*

Besides the toga, other cloaks worn by the Romans included the *pallium,* which was worn like the Greek *himation;* the *sagum,* which was a short military cloak; and the *paludamentum,* which was a larger officer's cloak fastened with a brooch at the neck or shoulder. Footwear consisted of sandals *(solea)* or the military boot *(caligulae).* Soldiers wore a breastplate *(lorica)* of solid metal, metal strips, or metal studs on leather over a short tunic; a crested metal helmet protected the head.

ROMAN

DATES
>   The Age of Monarchy 753–500 B.C.
>   The Age of the Republic 500–31 B.C.
>   The Age of Empire 31 B.C.–323 A.D.

COMMON TERMS (for others see glossary)
>   tunica
>   balteus
>   augustus clavus
>   latus clavus
>   toga praetexta
>   toga pura or virilis
>   toga candida
>   toga pulla
>   toga picta
>   toga trabea
>   tunica talaris
>   tunica palmata
>   sinus
>   pallium
>   lacerna
>   sagum
>   paludamentum
>   paenula
>   solea
>   calcaeus
>   crepida
>   lorica
>   caligulae
>   bracchae
>   palla
>   stola
>   flameum
>   dalmatica

RECOMMENDED SOURCES
>   Houston (1): Chapter IV
>   Norris (1): Volume I, Chapter 3
>   Wilson (1)
>   Wilson (2)
>   Heuzey: Part III
>   Skira (1)
>   Strong (background)
>   Carcopino (background)

Typical Figures

Early Christian and Ecclesiastical

The dress worn in the lands designated as the Western Roman Empire in the fourth century A.D. continued to be based closely on the conventions and usage of the late Empire period until the rise of Charlemagne at the beginning of the ninth century A.D. It was during those centuries that the liturgical dress of the Roman Catholic church began to be formed. During the early years the dress of a priest differed from that of a dignified layman only in the cleanliness of his apparel, but by the ninth century A.D. the basic ecclesiastical garments, the *dalmatic,* the *chasuble,* the *stole,* the *pall,* the *cope,* and the *alb* had been separated from lay dress and established as vestments.

ECCLESIASTICAL VESTMENTS. One of the first vestments to appear was the *pall* or *pallium* —originally a folded, draped strip derived from the Roman *toga* and *pallium*—which eventually developed into a circle dropped over the shoulders with a long tab front and back decorated with four crosses. It is part of a bishop's full vestments for the mass. The *stole,* a long narrow silk strip with fringe on the ends and decorated with three crosses, was also an early vestment used by priests, deacons, and bishops during the Mass. It may have derived from the fringed *orarion* waved by the Emperor Aurelian in the third century to applaud the games. The poncho-like rain cape, the *paenula,* used by the common people throughout the Roman period, was transformed into a clerical garment called the *chasuble* by the fourth century, and continued as the basic overgarment for priests and bishops officiating at the Mass.

By the sixth century, the *dalmatic* with its wide sleeves became the official outer tunic for priests and bishops, while the *cope* or half-circular cloak fastened at the front of the neck by a brooch called a *morse* became the standard processional outer garment for priests and bishops by the end of the eighth century. In the ninth century the *alb,* derived from the Roman *tunica alba,* became the standard undertunic, worn over the cassock and under other liturgical vestments by bishops and priests. The embroidered patches at the center front and back of the hem, at the wrists, and sometimes at the breast and back, were known as *apparels* or *orphreys* and were added in the Middle Ages. The *cassock,* which developed into the everyday wear of all clerics, derived from the basic tunic of the Roman common people, while clerical footwear developed from Roman *sandals* and *buskins.* The Roman *mappula* or folded linen napkin, which symbolized service when worn over the arm of a Roman consul, was adapted by the church into the *maniple* or silken band decorated with three crosses that was hung over the left forearm during Mass. The *mitre,* a liturgical and processional headdress worn by the bishops of the church, developed from the cone-shaped caps of the early popes, which in turn may have derived from the cone-like headdresses of Hebrew priests, while the *biretta,* derived from the medieval *beret,* developed into a non-liturgical headgear for the clergy.

Most of these items of dress are still very much a part of Roman Catholic clerical garb, although fabrics, shapes, and colors have changed somewhat over the centuries.

EARLY CHRISTIAN
AND ECCLESIASTICAL

DATES
   Early Christian 323–604 A.D.
COMMON TERMS (for others see glossary)
   cassock
   alb
   surplice
   pallium
   dalmatic
   chasuble
   orphrey

   apparel
   mitre
   cope
   stole
   maniple
RECOMMENDED SOURCES
   Norris (2)
   Davenport: pp. 93–103
   Morey (1) (background)
   Volbach and Hirmer (background)

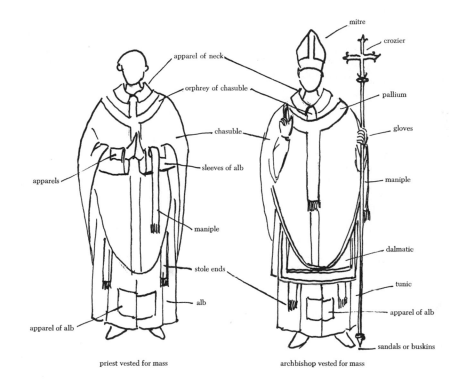

priest vested for mass   archbishop vested for mass

Typical Figures

Byzantine

Byzantium, later called Constantinople and today Istanbul, became the second capital of the Roman Empire in 323 A.D.; after the division of the Empire into two parts, it was the capital of the Eastern section. After Rome fell to the Teutonic armies and Odoacer dethroned the last of the Roman emperors in 476, the Eastern Empire and its Eastern Orthodox version of the Christian faith held out against all invaders until it fell to the Turks in 1453.

Byzantine culture was a combination of the richness and ornamental formality of the Orient, the beauty and proportion of the Greeks, and the practical outlook of the Romans. As in Egypt, hierarchy and tradition played a great part in preserving the character of Byzantine culture for over a millennium.

THE DRESS OF SACRED FIGURES. The basic dress for sacred Biblical figures was a wide-sleeved, wide-bodied, unbelted white dalmatic with purple vertical stripes over each shoulder extending down to the hem and known as a *clavus*. The cloak, which was usually based on the Roman *pallium* and Greek *himation*, was loosely draped over the body in varying ways, sometimes over one shoulder, sometimes over both, or pulled over arms and shoulders like a shawl or mantle. Female sacred figures were dressed in the garments of a Roman matron, always with strong emphasis on the veil. All such figures retained the draped folds and plastic effects of classical antiquity, and preserved such visual concepts deep into the medieval period.

ECCLESIASTICAL DRESS. The basic garments worn by the bishops and priests of the Eastern Church were, as in the West, the *chasuble*, the *dalmatic*, and the *pallium*. At first these ecclesiastical robes retained the folds of Graeco-Roman costume, but in time they became stiff and embroidered, enveloping the body like a box.

SECULAR DRESS. The basic decorative qualities of court dress can best be seen in the famous Ravenna mosaics of the Emperor Justinian and the Empress Theodora. The strong oriental influence is indicated by richly jeweled decoration. The masculine costume usually began with a belted long-sleeved *tunica* with embroidered *segmentae* on the shoulders. This was worn over *hosa* or leg coverings cut to fit close to the body. Sandals had given way to soft shoes or slippers. The outer garment was usually a cloak or mantle derived from the *paludamentum* and fastened with a buckle or brooch on the right shoulder. A large embroidered rectangle known as the *tablion* appeared on the front and back of the mantle. Later, emperors appear to have placed greater stress on the use of the long *dalmatic* worn over a tunic, and decoration became far heavier and richer.

Feminine dress, also based on the long-sleeved *tunica* or sometimes on the Roman *stola*, dropped to jewel-studded slippers and was heavily embroidered and set with jewels. Women also wore the great mantle fastened on the right shoulder, but without the *tablion*. In later Byzantine women's costume, the dalmatic was completely encrusted in jewels, and embroidery was frequently added, tending to make the figure look like a walking mosaic. Wigs set with crowns or a diadem and covered with jewels were used, and jeweled collars reminiscent of the Egyptians were worn.

All of Asia's treasures of gold and silver cloth, pearls and precious stones, and richly woven silks were used for Byzantine court dress, and by about 550 A.D. silk was being manufactured within the Empire. The use of silk material woven with gold thread and adorned with pearls and precious stones made Byzantine dress very different from the dress of Greece and Rome. Light cannot reflect over the folds of a plain, soft fabric, but in the overpowering splendor of the jeweled garments, light was caught and reflected as in the glowing mosaics of Byzantine churches.

BYZANTINE

DATES
  Proto Byzantine 323–565 A.D.
  Early Byzantine 565–726
  Period of Iconoclasm 726–843
  Early Byzantine Renaissance,
    Macedonian Dynasty 843–1067
  High Byzantine Renaissance,
    Comenian Dynasty 1067–1185
  Late Byzantine 1185–1453
COMMON TERMS (for others see glossary)
  tunica
  dalmatic
  segmentae
  tablion

  paenula
  paludamentum
  hosa
  camisa
  colobium
  superhumeral
RECOMMENDED SOURCES
  Houston (1): Chapters IV and V
  Norris (1): Chapter IV
  Skira (2)
  Larousse: Part II
  Rice (background)
  Mosaics, ivory carving, manuscripts,
    sculpture

ca. 1000 A.D.

Typical Figures

Romanesque

About 150 years ago, when a critical historical sense began to develop in Western man, the period of the early Middle Ages was labeled Romanesque since it was thought of as being a culture derived from a Roman heritage, in much the same way that Romance languages derived from Latin. Unfortunately this is a misleading term, since the culture that developed from the fall of Rome to the end of the twelfth century in Western Europe was more Germanic in inspiration than Roman. Although the style flourished only from the time of Charlemagne to the beginning of Gothic style, its heritage reaches back well beyond the times of the Teutonic invasions of Rome. Its major characteristics are heaviness, weight, distortion, and rigidity, with strong accents of the primitive, the geometric, and the supernatural.

BARBARIC DRESS. The major garment worn by the barbarians that was not a part of Graeco-Roman dress was trousers or *bracchae*, which had been worn by mountainous northern tribes since before the Christian era. Roman troops in Gaul had worn short versions of these trousers, and the Byzantine *hosa* were a refinement of the idea. In Germany and France during the period before Charlemagne, they became the symbol of the barbarian. They were usually laced with thongs and covered with leggings. A short, coarsely woven tunic covered the body, and a cloak of animal skins or coarse wool was fastened on the shoulder with a huge metal clasp. Hair was long, the face bearded, and metal helmets set with wings and horns were worn on the head. The women's hair was very long and frequently braided; they wore a long coarse tunic, often woven in stripes or squares, and a mantle was again pinned on the shoulder.

CAROLINGIAN DRESS. At the time that Charlemagne united the petty tribal kingdoms of Western Europe, the standard male dress was a linen undershirt and drawers, a long-sleeved tunic bloused over a girdle that extended to the middle of the thigh, and close-fitting leggings. A half-circular mantle was fastened with a large metal *fibula* on the right shoulder. A metal circlet held the hair, and soft leather shoes completed the dress. The *dalmatic* was in evidence for all ceremonial occasions, and the longer tunic was used by older men. A metal helmet with noseguard was used for battle, and a shirt of mail formed of leather sewn with metal disks or constructed of tiny interlocking metal circles was worn. By the time of Charlemagne, women wore a *chemise* or *camisa* as an undergarment, a long-sleeved undertunic, and a wide-sleeved overtunic or *dalmatic,* with a semicircular or circular mantle fastened on the right shoulder. The hair was often completely covered by the *couverchief* or large kerchief.

ROMANESQUE DRESS. The basic lines of dress changed very little, although refinements in cutting and fitting developed over the three centuries from the rise of the Ottonian emperors to the beginning of the Gothic style. The most stylish male tunic was laced and lifted at the sides of the waist to give a play of draped folds at the front of the figure and was known as the *bliaut*. The feminine version of this garment was floor length, with a slight train, laced to the body at the sides or back, and gave a smooth fit to the hips without special darting or complex cutting. The older, loose tunic of floor length for men and women was now called the *cote,* and the overtunic with wider sleeves was called a *surcote*. A woman's neck and chin were now frequently covered by a kerchief or *gorget,* while the kerchief over the head was called a *wimple.* For men, a distinctive new outer garment developed at this time—the hooded cloak, which also became an important item in the dress of monks. Originally worn by the common man, the hood eventually became a separate item for court dress, with a long tail at the back of the head and a full collar-cape over the shoulders.

ROMANESQUE

DATES
- Barbaric 400–752 A.D.
- Carolingian 752–900 A.D.
- Romanesque 900–1200 A.D.

COMMON TERMS (for others see glossary)
- bliaut
- cote
- corsage
- surcote
- hauberk
- wimple
- couverchief
- mantle
- fibulae

RECOMMENDED SOURCES
- Brooke (2): pp. 10–58
- Brooke (7) (theatre costume)
- Norris (1): Chapters V–VII
- Enlart: Part I
- Evans (2): Part I
- Houston (2): Chapter I
- Cunnington (5): Part I
- Skira (3)
- Skira (4)
- Morey (2): Chapter IV
- Swarzenski (background)
- Sculpture, manuscripts, mosaics, frescoes

ca. 1000 A.D.

Typical Figures

Early Gothic

During the Renaissance, when enthusiasm for things classical had reached a peak, Giorgio Vasari, artist and art historian, called the art and architecture of the preceding period Gothic. He assumed that it had been invented by the so-called Goths, who had destroyed the architectural wonders of antiquity. Although the Gothic style that was invented in France at the close of the twelfth century had nothing to do with the Goths of the great migration, the name has remained and today refers to art from the twelfth to the fifteenth centuries. Entirely opposed to most classical conceptions of style, the Gothic is vertical, strongly linear, stresses open framework rather than solid form, and is highly and complexly decorative. The figures in illuminated manuscripts indicate the active decorative aspects of Gothic dress as opposed to the static and rigid effects of Byzantine dress, as well as the tendency to go beyond the limits of the human body to achieve verticality of form.

MASCULINE DRESS. The long Byzantine tunic, which before had been worn only on special occasions and by royalty, now became the standard dress for men, having been popularized by the Crusaders who had passed through Byzantium on the way back from the Holy Land. Known as the *cote,* it usually had very wide sleeves cut in one with the shoulder and narrowing to the wrist. It was usually covered by a second, sleeveless tunic or *surcote,* which was often left open up the sides to the hips. Sometimes the *surcote* had hanging sleeves and was known as a *gardcorps,* or it had flaring cape sleeves to the elbow and was known as a *garnache.* When it was fur lined, it was frequently known as a *peliçon.* As a military garment, the *surcote* with a coat of arms emblazoned on it was worn over a *hauberk* of chain mail. With the long tunic that stressed the vertical line of the human figure were worn pointed shoes or boots of soft leather. Separate leg coverings or hose worn over underwear were of cloth or leather shaped like long stockings and fastened to a belt around the waist. The hood was also a prominent accessory, with *scalloped* or *dagged* edges around the bottom of the cape-collar giving a strong decorative accent.

At the close of this period in the early decades of the fourteenth century, a close-fitting tunic to the hips, known as a *cotehardie,* came into fashion for younger men. It was usually worn with a decorative caped hood, a jeweled hip girdle, and long pointed shoes, all related to the slim decorative lines of late Gothic art.

FEMININE DRESS. At first, feminine dress was the same as in the Romanesque period, with the use of the undertunic or *cote,* the overtunic or *surcote,* and the *wimple* and *gorget* for covering the head. Sometimes the hair was placed into a pillbox cap or *toque* with chin strap, sometimes coiled over the ears and held by jeweled nets, or loosely confined by a circlet or coronet. Gradually, the lines of the costume became more fitted to the body; the surcote was cut away under the arms and opened up the sides to show more of the figure. At the end of the period the name *cotehardie* was applied to a close-fitting princess-line gown with a low neckline and a full skirt.

PARTICOLORING AND HERALDIC DEVICES. In the early Gothic period, costumes were frequently divided in color down the center to tie the color usage in dress to that found in a family's coat of arms; this particoloring became one of the most characteristic effects of the period. It was also fashionable to have a coat of arms or a crest embroidered on the costume, or at times to have the entire costume constructed as if from a large coat of arms.

EARLY GOTHIC

DATES
    Early Gothic 1200–1350

COMMON TERMS (for others see glossary)
    garnache
    gardcorps
    surcote
    cotehardie
    couvrechef
    wimple
    gorget
    doublet
    jupe
    cyclas
    toque

RECOMMENDED SOURCES
    Norris (1): Volume II, Chapters I–III
    Hartley (1) (background)
    Brooke (2): pp. 58–86
    Brooke (4): pp. 10–24
    Morey (2): Chapter V
    Evans (1): Part II
    Evans (2): Part II
    Houston (2): Chapters II–IV
    Frankl: Part I (background)
    Mâle (background)
    Gardner (1) (background)
    Gardner (2) (background)
    Sculpture, manuscripts,
        frescoes (especially Giotto)

ca. 1250

Typical Figures

Middle Gothic

In the middle Gothic period, the classical semi-draped lines of the early Gothic gave way to extravagant fashions. They moved from the close-fitting contours of the *cotehardie* to the flamboyant lines of the *houppelande,* just as architecture, sculpture, and manuscript illuminations moved from simple, clear-cut vertical lines of structure to highly decorative, graceful, curvilinear lines of design. Throughout Western Europe, the Age of Faith was giving way to an age of worldly power and material prosperity, despite the terrible plagues that stopped artistic and cultural development in the middle of the fourteenth century. The Renaissance that had been in preparation in Italy in the late thirteenth and early fourteenth centuries through the work of Dante, Giotto, Petrarch, and Boccaccio was slowed by many decades, and the final fruition in Florence did not occur until the first two decades of the fifteenth century.

In general, the costume of the last half of the fourteenth century and the early years of the fifteenth century was composed of slim, close-fitting body garments overlaid with flowing draperies, with the edges of all things scalloped, dagged, and foliated until the human figure in movement was all aflutter. Particoloring, emblazonment, and the powdering of garments with family crests increased, giving a far more sophisticated and decorative look to the general costume silhouette.

MASCULINE COSTUME. The hip-length, tight-fitting *cotehardie* remained a basic body garment throughout the period, usually worn with a hip girdle and a hood or *capuchon* with cape-collar and richly cut edges, the hood now having a long tail or *liripipe*. Often the cotehardie had cuffs on the sleeves that flared into hanging *foliations* or hung in long bands called *tippets*. Later in the century, a voluminous overgown with trailing bell sleeves and a high collar made its appearance. This *houppelande,* with all its flamboyant movement of foliated edges and flowing fabric, was worn over the cotehardie. The hood was now frequently worn with the band of the face opening placed around the head, the dagged edges of the collar falling to one side, and the long tail or liripipe wrapped about the head or draped over the shoulder. This fantastic headdress was known as a *chaperone*. Shoes were now exaggeratedly pointed; in the more advanced fashions, the toes were even fastened to the knee by a chain. Hair was worn shoulder length or in an allover bowl cut; mantles were often made the ground for a complete coat of arms; and jewelry and jeweled accessories included bells, hanging baubles, tassels, and chains.

FEMININE COSTUME. Women also continued to wear the cotehardie, but it was soon covered with various overgowns. The first was the famed *cyclas* or *sideless gown,* in which the entire gown was cut away to the hips on each side, leaving only a central panel or *plastron* with fur or embroidered edges over the breast. Sideless gowns, often completely emblazoned with the family coat of arms, continued as official court wear throughout the fifteenth century. At the end of the fourteenth century the houppelande was also added to the female wardrobe, as were the foliated and dagged edges that made for flamboyant effects in sleeves, collars, and gown edgings. The *reticulated headdress,* with its metal cages for holding the hair coiled over the ears, was the most prominent form of hairdressing, while the wimple and gorget arrangement continued to be worn by older women. Larger horned and cone-shaped headdresses known as *hennins* began to develop in the early years of the fifteenth century. With their veils, jeweled decoration, and heavy metallic net accessories, they were to become the major headdress of the late Gothic period. Women shaved their brows and temples and completely concealed their hair under all headdresses. All movement was flowing and graceful, and skirts were often as long in front as the train in back; the lady was expected to lift her skirts and hold them over her abdomen in movement.

MIDDLE GOTHIC

DATES
   Middle Gothic 1350–1425
COMMON TERMS (for others see glossary)
   chaperone
   liripipe
   coif
   capuchon
   jupe
   pourpoint
   jacquette
   courtepy
   houppelande
   foliated
   bagpipe sleeve
   dagged
   castellated
   jupon
   reticulated headdress

   corset
   plastron
   sideless gown
   tippets
   particolored
   caul
RECOMMENDED SOURCES
   Norris (1): Volume II, Chapters IV–VI
   Skira (5)
   Houston (2): Chapters IV and V
   Cunnington (5): Part II
   Evans (1): Part III
   Evans (2): Part III
   Brooke (4): pp. 24–46
   Larousse: Part V
   Sculpture, book illuminations, frescoes,
      panel paintings (especially the
      Lorenzetti brothers)

ca. 1350-1360

Typical Figures

Late Gothic

The late Gothic period was a time of rich and sophisticated effects in art and in costume—a final complex and flamboyant use of all the decorative elements in the Gothic vocabulary. It was also an era divided between two great cultural and artistic centers—Flanders in the north and Florence in the south. The styles and the art that dominated each area were radically different. In the south, all the elements of a revived classicism and a renewed interest in antiquity prevailed, while in the north, the final rich, decorative, flamboyant effects of the late Gothic achieved fulfillment. In the fifteenth century the towns of Ghent and Bruges were two of the greatest centers of European trade and industry. Flemish cloth was famous throughout Western Europe, and the court of Burgundy shared the leadership in fashion with the court in Paris. Simultaneously with the dawn of the Renaissance in Florence and later throughout northern Italy, Gothic costume reached its final phase of richness and splendor in Ghent, Bruges, and Brussels.

MASCULINE DRESS. In Burgundian costume, all the sartorial variations which had gradually appeared during the medieval period were combined into a final magnificent flourish. Shoes were elegantly pointed, and doublets, which had replaced *tunics, cotehardies,* and the sweeping *houppelande,* were tight-fitting, often pleated, and had large padded sleeves that increased the width and height of the shoulders. The long gown was now slim and elegant, again stressing the height of the wearer through padded sleeves and raised shoulders. Sometimes hanging sleeves were used on both doublets and gowns, with an undersleeve coming through a slit in the outer sleeve. Padded, carefully placed pleating in gowns and doublets added to height and elegance, while fur was a preferred trim on collars, sleeves, and hemlines. Hats were divided between the *roundel*—a stuffed, donut-shaped piece of headgear with a wide strip of material still called a *liripipe* draped over the shoulder—and the tall, bag-shaped sugarloaf hats which comple-

mented the pleated lines and padded shoulders of the male figure. Hose, sometimes particolored, covered both legs and were tied with points to the belt of the underdrawers. A voluminous mantle occasionally lined in fur was the chief outer garment, although loose gowns were also worn for this purpose. Armor was now of solid plate in carefully planned overlapping and interlocking pieces and finished with a heraldic tabard.

FEMININE DRESS. The woman's gown now had a slightly lifted waistline, a train that was more voluminous than ever, a deep V-shaped neckline in front partially filled in with the top of the undergarment or *corset,* and a wide belt just above the waist. The wide shawl collar rolled back from the bare neck was usually trimmed in fur, as were the cuffs of the tight sleeves that came down over the hands. The *cotehardie,* covered by a *sideless gown,* usually emblazoned with family or national arms, was still the formal ceremonial dress for women, as was the emblazoned, half-circular mantle. Over the heads of the women rose the steeple-shaped headdress or *hennin* with its floating veil, the most typical headcovering of the period. Variations of it were the *heart-shaped headdress,* the *escoffion*—a padded and embroidered high-rising round headdress set with jewels, the *horned hennin* with its two or three conical points, and the *butterfly hennin* with its wired wing-like veils. In fact, the women's headdresses of the middle of the fifteenth century are some of the most exaggerated and flamboyant headdresses seen in the entire history of female costume. As with men, any loose upper garment might, on occasion, become an outdoor wrap—especially if it were fur lined. Shoes were tiny slippers worn over stockings or hose.

NORTHERN ITALIAN DRESS. During these same years, in styles emanating from Florence, the Italian projected a simpler, natural silhouette with a stress on pleated short and long gowns, natural headdresses, and very limited ornamentation.

LATE GOTHIC

DATES
    Late Gothic 1425–1485
COMMON TERMS (for others see glossary)
    hennin
    escoffion
    journade
    roundel
    poulaines
    crackowe
    pourpoint
    plastron
    liripipe
    sideless gown
    houppelande

RECOMMENDED SOURCES
    Houston (2): Chapters V–VII
    Norris (1): Volume II, Chapters V and VI
    Cutts (background)
    Skira (5)
    Skira (6)
    Brooke (4): pp. 46–86
    Boucher: Chapter VII
    Contini: pp. 74–110
    Book illuminations, paintings (especially
        Van Eyck, Van der Weyden, Masaccio,
        Fra Lippo Lippi, Piero della Francesca),
        sculpture

Typical Figures

Renaissance

While Gothic costume was reaching its final phase at the court of Burgundy, the first stirrings of the Renaissance brought a new concept of dress—or rather a revival of a classical concept—to Italy. The Gothic style had never really been "at home" south of the Alps, and early in the fifteenth century Florence became the center for a revival of interest in the art of antiquity. The new style in clothing that developed by the end of the century was a fresh exploration of certain Roman ideals and artistic effects integrated with garments inherited from the late Gothic style. The new artistic style stressed the horizontal over the vertical, the simple and geometric over the complexly decorative, blond color over the strong color of heraldry, and richly patterned fabrics of silk, velvet and brocade over woolens. The new Renaissance concept of style stressed that perfection lay in the rational and harmonious relationship of all of the separate parts; nothing could be added, subtracted, or changed without impairing the overall effect.

MASCULINE DRESS. The undergarment was usually a sleeveless doublet to which two long stockings or hose could be fastened with points. These hose, of cloth or leather, were sometimes sewn together to form one garment with a *codpiece* that tied in over the front opening, or they remained separate and were pulled loosely up over the underdrawers. The collarless shirt under the doublet was now much in evidence, with sections of outer sleeves laced over it or slashed to show the shirt sleeve beneath. The doublet front was laced loosely across the shirt, which bloused casually at the waist between hose and doublet. Eventually, the doublet was cut low enough to display the shirt at the neck, the edge being finished with embroidery in gold or silk or with a ruffle. Overgowns were loose, rather short, worn casually and often open up the front, the general line being horizontal and somewhat square, with a wide collar falling over the shoulder. Very long gowns were now worn only by the elderly; these too were wide and square, with emphasis placed on a wide collar, large cuffs, and thick pleats. The headgear of the period turned to wide, flat, slightly turned up brims decorated with feathers and jewels, or to small skull caps, truncated cones of heavy felt, large soft fur hats with turned-up brims, and tiny felt pillboxes. Hair was usually shoulder length, either falling loosely or curled under at the bottom. Shoes were like slippers, without the heavy accent on a pointed toe.

FEMININE DRESS. The lacing characteristic of male dress also appeared in women's dress at the breasts, under the arm, and at the shoulder, where the long, often tight, and sometimes slashed sleeves were laced to the armhole of the bodice over the looser sleeves of the chemise. Whereas elderly women still wore long, loose trailing gowns under a cloak, younger women followed the male trend toward shorter gowns, sometimes without a train. The gown was often divided into bodice and skirt and was frequently worn under a sleeveless outer gown slit below the waist on each side or in the front. Sometimes the outer gown was loose and flowing, but more frequently it was fitted smoothly to a slightly raised waistline. The neckline of the undergown was square, in contrast to the pointed Gothic neckline, although the outer gown often showed a V-shaped outline. On the head, elderly women still wore kerchiefs, but younger women preferred to leave the hair uncovered and to knot and twist it into complex hairdos that could be adorned with pearls or nets of gold. Sleeves were the key area for complex lines of trim, with tiny slits in the outer sleeve allowing many interesting effects when the fabric of the chemise was pulled through the slits from underneath. This fashion for slashes was to grow and become more complex and rigid in the early sixteenth century. The loose, casual effect of its original design was to change to restriction, tension, and complexity in both masculine and feminine dress in the later Renaissance.

484

RENAISSANCE

DATES
    1485–1520
      Early Renaissance in France
      Early Tudor in England
      High Renaissance in Italy
COMMON TERMS (for others see glossary)
    bases
    points
    slashing
    simar
    caul
    codpiece
    jerkin
    kirtle
RECOMMENDED SOURCES
    Norris (1): Volume III, Book 1, pp. 1–232
    Vecellio (patterns)

Martindale (background)
Laver (4)
Berenson (background)
Burckhardt (background)
Dewald (background)
Freedberg (background)
Statues and relief sculpture
Brass rubbings
Useful painters: da Vinci, Carpaccio,
    Bellini, Mantegna, Messina, Botticelli,
    Filippino Lippi, Ghirlandaio, Raphael,
    Pinturicchio, del Sarto, Fra Carnavale,
    Signorelli, Gozzoli, Baldovinetti,
    Verrochio, the two Pollaiuoli,
    Perugino, Rosselli, di Credi, di Cosimo,
    Ercole Roberti, Cosimo Tura, Dürer

Typical Figures

Later Renaissance

After the crest of optimism and artistic accomplishment was achieved in Italy during the first two decades of the sixteenth century, foreign invasions, loss of morale, the rise of the Reformation, and the decline of Italian artistic and cultural nationalism brought about a change in art and culture today referred to as the rise of mannerism. Heavily influenced by German and Spanish artistic ideals brought to Italy by the forces of the emperor, the new style was heavier, more complicated, more distorted, and, in general, reflected the new malaise and loss of faith that was to mark the development of all European culture during the sixteenth century. From roughly 1520 to 1560, the German influence in fashion was predominant, while from 1560 into the second decade of the seventeenth century, Spanish styles tended to be the major source of inspiration in dress.

MASCULINE DRESS. The major artistic development of this period took place in puffs and slashing. One colored fabric was placed over another, the top one was slit to show the fabric underneath, and the two fabrics were then puffed out so that all slashes spread to the fullest extent. The major points of usage were on legs and sleeves, although in German military costume they covered the entire costume. The effect of the interpenetration of two planes of fabric was similar to the scroll work on contemporary ornament, in which tongues from one scroll passed through slits in another.

The predominant male silhouette of the period was square, the major garment being a short gown, usually fur lined with hanging sleeves. It was loose, with ample folds; a large collar covered the shoulders, making them appear wide and square. The open front showed the jerkin, which had a gathered or formally pleated knee-length skirt (sometimes called *bases*) and was frequently cut very low to show the doublet. At the beginning of the period the neckline was low, but later the shirt fitted closely around the neck and ended in a ruffle. By the end of the period the doublet also rose to a standing collar. At first the tops of the hose were slashed, later the tops were covered with loose, often slashed breeches fitted with an ornamented *codpiece*. These puffed breeches reached their greatest excess in the extravagant *pluderhose* of the German *Landsknecht* or mercenary soldier. Shoes were broad at the toe with slashes. The headdress was a wide-brimmed flat cap trimmed with ostrich feathers, usually worn at a rakish angle and sometimes over another cap. Hair was relatively short, and beards were popular. Full, heavily ornamented plate armor was still worn by the nobility for war.

FEMALE DRESS. At the beginning of the sixteenth century the now stiffened bodice of the gown had a low-cut square neckline, but it gradually moved upwards and frequently ended in a standing collar finished with a ruffle. The amount and weight of fabric was voluminous and heavy, with a tendency to width. Skirts were pleated to the bodice over a heavy V-shaped front panel of rich ornamentation. Sleeves were fur-lined, bell-shaped appendages open or folded back over a series of slashed puffs that made up the undersleeve, or were alternately puffed down the entire length of the arm. Headdresses included flat caps, wide turbans, or complicated *coifs* or *hood* structures derived from the Flemish and German middle-class headgear of the late fifteenth century. While Italian ladies continued to prefer their hair caught only by a jeweled net or *caul* (or at the most, partially hidden by a slashed turban), northern ladies preferred the *gable kennel* or pedimented headdress or a crescent-shaped variation. In all of these headdresses a heavily stiffened and ornamented frame outlined the face, while a rich fall of fabric or *hood* covered the back of the head. Outer garments consisted of the large circular mantle or a loose, often fur-lined gown.

LATER RENAISSANCE

DATES

> 1520–1560 Period of First-Generation
>   Mannerism in Italy
> Tudor Period in England
> Renaissance in France and Germany

COMMON TERMS (for others see glossary)
> chamarre
> duck-billed shoes
> morion
> basquine
> farthingale
> gable headdress
> barbe
> fall
> cale
> panes

RECOMMENDED SOURCES
> Norris (1): Volume III, Book 1,
> pp. 232–377
> Brooke (1): pp. 10–56
> Laver (4)
> Morse: Part I
> Skira (7)
> Berenson: Volume II
> Boehn (4)
> Dimier (1) (background)
> Friedlander (background)
> Sculpture on tombs, statuary, engravings,
>   painting, miniatures
> Useful painters: Giulio Romano, Titian,
>   Tintoretto, Holbein, Brueghel,
>   Bronzino, Mor, Pontormo, Rosso,
>   Pinturicchio, Jean and François Clouet,
>   Vasari, Giorgione, Michelangelo,
>   del Piombo, Bordone, Primiticcio,
>   Parmigianino, Baroccio

Typical Figures

Elizabethan

Shortly after the middle of the sixteenth century, Spain achieved European dominance in matters of taste and fashion, and the nature of mannerist art and culture began to be more formal, more elegant, and more reserved but still stressed tension, distortion, and exaggeration. Art, as well as fashion, turned its back on nature in favor of the "mannered," the charmingly contrived, or the deliberately grotesque. In the paintings of El Greco and Tintoretto, in the sculpture of Bologna, and in the architectural inventions of Zuccaro, broken rhythms, elongated forms, tense lines, and rich, often grotesque ornamentation characterize this late sixteenth-century style. In fashion, the complex Spanish tailoring which elongated the figure, exaggerated the shoulders and hips, extended the waist, and held the whole body in a tense, elegant, and overly formal envelope was the admiration of all Europe.

In the Spanish style the body was stiff and motionless—a mannequin on which was mounted a richly ornamented case, following its shape on the inside, but showing exaggerated contours on the outside. The wearer was encased in an armor of ornament, adorned like an idol with gold, pearls, and precious stones, while the fabrics used were often black or dark-colored silks and velvets, like the soft lining of a jewel case.

MASCULINE DRESS. The Spanish fashion replaced the wide-brimmed hat with a high-crowned, sometimes bag-shaped hat with a narrow brim, and the short gown now became a circular short cloak with a collar. The short puffed upper hose breeches, ornamented with slashings or strips of fabric called *panes*, were called *trunk hose, melon hose,* or *pumpkin hose* and were stuffed with horsehair bombast or straw to hold their distended shape. The *codpiece,* rarely noted after 1575, all but disappeared by the early seventeenth century. At the same time, stuffed shoulder wings were sewn around the armhole, and a peplum or *picadils* were added to the *doublet,* which was very long waisted, sharply pointed in the front, and frequently padded into a *peascod* belly.

The legs were usually enclosed in tight hose of soft cloth, although knitted silk stockings became more and more prevalent as the century wore on; they were pulled up and gartered over tight breeches called *canions* worn under the trunk hose. These were sometimes referred to as *upper stocks,* in contrast to *nether stocks* or knitted hose. Wider breeches to the knee were known as *Venetians.* Shoes became narrower, covered more of the foot, and had a firmer sole than in the past. With the introduction of the starched circular *ruff* (supporting the head like a platter), the high standing doublet collar became the central point of focus in the costume. The *jerkin* was still used as an outer garment over the doublet, usually sleeveless or with sleeves tied in with *points* under a *shoulder wing.*

FEMININE DRESS. Women's costume followed men's in the use of padding, exaggeration of the width of the hips, and the emphasis on the horizontal line of the shoulders. Two new garments made their appearance under the gown: the corset of stiff material with steel stiffeners in the lining to flatten the bust completely, and the *farthingale* or *vertugale,* which was a cone-shaped cage first of felt and later of hoops to hold out the distended lines of the skirt. The skirt usually had a triangular opening in front to show the rich underskirt. As in male fashions, the waist was elongated and pointed in front and known as a *stomacher,* the hips were frequently distended, with a sausage roll or stuffed *bolster* under the petticoat, and the shoulders frequently were finished in *crescents* or *wings.* Sleeves were padded into great tapering "demi-canons," slashed, tucked, embroidered, and stitched with precious stones, while necklines were either low cut, filled in with a soft *partlet,* or finished in a great platter-shaped ruff. Hair was done in a heart-shaped roll away from the face, frequently framed by a heart-shaped cap or covered with jewels, while female versions of male headgear were reserved for riding or outdoor occasions.

ELIZABETHAN

Dates
1560–1590
  England: Early Elizabethan
  France: Late Valois
  Italy: Late Mannerism
  Spain: High Renaissance or Golden Age

Common terms (for others see glossary)

canions	upper stocks and
Venetians	nether stocks
ruff	underproper or
peascod	supportasse
codpiece	picadil
jerkin	aiglettes
doublet	bombast
pumpkin hose	panes
round hose	mandilion
trunk hose	falling band
galligaskins	vertugale
bell farthingale	bolster
wheel farthingale	partlet
slops	stomacher

Recommended sources
Norris (1): Volume III, Book 2
Morse: Part II
Kelly (theatre costume)
Linthicum (theatre costume)
Laver (4)
Dimier (1) (background)
Boehn (4)
Dewald (background)
Benesch (background)
Sculpture, miniatures, paintings,
  engravings
Useful painters: El Greco, Veronese,
  Tintoretto, Brueghel, late Bronzino,
  Moroni, late Titian, late Mor,
  François Clouet, Eworth, Federigo
  Zuccaro, Gheeraerts, Sanchez Coello,
  Pourbus

Typical Figures

Late Elizabethan and Jacobean

As the sixteenth century came to an end and Europe moved into the early years of the seventeenth century, the rigid and grotesque effects of mannerism reached a kind of peak and then gradually began to relax as if in preparation for the rise of the new art and culture of the Baroque era. The tensions of European politics and the divisions of the Reformation began to give way to the new optimism of the Counterreformation, and the art and culture of the last decade of the sixteenth century and the first two decades of the seventeenth century may be seen as a time of change and transition. Although it is a period that produces many of the most fantastic artistic whimsies of the mannerist mind, it is also the period which gave rise to a new classicism in art found in the work of the Caracci family in Italy as well as a new realism in the art of the Italian painter Caravaggio.

MASCULINE COSTUME. During this transitional period men's clothing lost its elongated vertical look and once again became broader, stressed horizontal lines, and lacked some of the more complicated exaggerations of the preceding period. The headgear was now heavier, with a stiffened sloping crown and a wider brim, while the neck, though still frequently encased in fanciful variations of the circular ruff, was more apt to be surrounded by a stiffened flat collar or *whisk* (*golilla* in Spain), which was beautifully trimmed in lace and still framed the face like a platter. *Shoulder wings* were still popular, but the heavy padded sleeves gave way either to tight-fitting sleeves or to loosely paned outer sleeves showing a shirt or undersleeve beneath. The wrists, like the neck, were finished in stiff, lace-edged cuffs rather than ruffles or miniature ruffs. The doublet was now neither as long waisted nor as pointed in front and was seldom padded underneath, while the breeches were now either loose and knee length or flat and square at the bottom, of thigh length and tapered to the waist over tight-fitting *canions*. Rosettes or cross gartering were frequently seen at the knee, silk hose was now the standard wear for the lower leg, and shoes were heavier, had heels, and were usually adorned with shoe roses. Longer circular cloaks were worn outdoors; the jerkin, often of leather to protect the doublet, was still in use. Military garb gradually dropped full plate armor in favor of metal helmets and breastplates over quilted leather jerkins and high leather boots.

FEMININE DRESS. The major shift in silhouette from the previous period, as with men, was toward a broader line with great stress on the horizontal width in the hips and shoulders. The *wheel farthingale* or *vertugale* took precedence over the older bell-shaped line, although the latter was still favored in Spain, and the waist, though not as low as before, was given emphasis by a large, cartwheel *ruff*. Sleeves were not as heavily padded as in the past and frequently consisted of a series of puffs and tiny slashes down the entire length of the arm. The wrist was now usually finished in a stiff, lace-edged cuff, and the low-cut neckline was now backed with a great, stiffened, fan-shaped collar profusely trimmed in delicate lace. Only in Spain and parts of Italy did the elongated Spanish line ending in a high neckline and wide ruff maintain its fashionable popularity. The hair was still drawn up and away from the face in a vaguely heart-shaped line and was set with precious stones, a jeweled cap, or a tiara. Only for riding and traveling were hats used, and these were close approximations of those worn by the men.

LATE ELIZABETHAN AND JACOBEAN

DATES
  1590–1620
    Italy: Late Mannerism
    France: Early Bourbon
    Germany: Late Renaissance
    England: Late Elizabethan and
      Jacobean
    Spain: Decline of the Golden Age
COMMON TERMS (for others see glossary)
    whisk
    golilla
    canions
    Venetians
    baldric
    kirtle
    pantofles
    shoe roses
    shoulder wings or crescents
    bombast
    cross gartering
    cartwheel vertugale or farthingale
    chopines
RECOMMENDED SOURCES
    Norris (1): Volume III, Book 2,
      Chapter IV
    Laver (4)
    Hartley and Elliot (2) (background)
    Leloir: Section on sixteenth century
    Clinch: Section on sixteenth century
    Morse: Part III
    Davis (background)
    Sculpture, painting, engravings
    Useful painters: early Rubens, El Greco,
      Caravaggio, the Caracci, Gheeraerts,
      prints of Visscher, Pourbus, Brueghel
      the younger.

Typical Figures

Early Baroque or Cavalier

The Counterreformation reached its full stride in Italy during the second quarter of the seventeeth century, and the church gave its full support to art as one of the great weapons to be used in glorifying God. Art, following many of the precepts of Michelangelo, threw off the tensions, ambiguities, and distortions of the past in favor of vigorous movement, sensuous richness, and theatrical effects. The name Baroque, meaning extravagantly ornamental, was eventually given to this expansive new artistic ideal. In architecture, straight lines gave way to curved, oval, and elliptical forms, and focus was placed on great central portals or domes. In painting, figures were shown in violent motion or in strong contrasts of artificial light, while in sculpture, figures expanded out into space in dramatic, momentary movement. Ornament became massive and voluminous, with lines that curled and twisted like the cartilage of the ear. In fashion, as in art, a dashing flamboyance superceded the stiffness and tension of mannerism. Although the richest art and fashion effects were to be found in Italy, France, and Southern Germany, more sober but none the less theatrical effects were achieved in Holland, Flanders, Northern Germany, and England. Spain in many ways remained outside the major lines of development, creating an artistic style that retained many mannerist effects.

MASCULINE COSTUME. The overall line of the male costume by 1630 was relaxed, easy, dramatic, and quite simple in comparison with the complexities that had preceded. The doublet was now unstiffened, with a slightly raised waist and skirts that were either cut in one with the top or casually set on as loose overlapping tabs. The waistline was frequently decorated with metal-tagged ribbons or *points* made into bows, which had originally been drawn through eyelets in the waist to hold up the breeches, but were now merely decorative. Breeches lost their padding and, after being baggy and loose, became long and tapering, had buttons or bows on the sides, and finished in loose garter bows at the bottom. Sometimes breeches were loose at the bottom, finishing in points or bows, and this style grew in importance after the middle of the century. High, soft leather boots were frequently worn indoors as well as outdoors over silk boot hose that fell in a lace cuff over the top of the boot. If shoes were worn, they had a raised heel and rosettes. The smooth white collar, trimmed or made entirely of lace, replaced the pleated ruff and now fell softly over the shoulders. Sleeves were full, usually with one or more slashes the length of the arm in order to show the rich shirt beneath. Such slashes were frequently set with a full line of buttons and holes down the length of the sleeve, and cuffs were of rich lace. Circular, calf-length cloaks were worn over one shoulder and fell diagonally down across the back. Hats were soft and wide-brimmed, of felt or beaver, decorated with ostrich plumes and worn at a jaunty angle. Military wear continued the use of the metal *cuirass* over a leather jerkin and a helmet.

FEMININE DRESS. During this period both the corset and the *farthingale* disappeared, the waistline rose and no longer dipped in front, and several skirts, the top one usually draped up over the one beneath, gave a healthy, homey, slightly pregnant look. The dress was usually low cut, and a rich lace collar either framed or covered the bosom. The sleeves, which ended in wide, turned-up lace cuffs, were large, elegant, sometimes slashed, and often gathered in at the elbow with silk ribbons finished in bows. A similar silk ribbon sash with a bow emphasized the wasitline above the tabs of the peplum. The hair was worn shoulder length, often with a fringe of bangs on the forehead and two long ringlets falling forward over the ears. Masculine hats were reserved for riding, while the hooded cloak was used for travel.

EARLY BAROQUE OR CAVALIER

DATES

1620–1660
    England: Cavalier
    France: Louis XIII
    Italy: Early Baroque
    Germany: Thirty Years' War
    Spain: Reign of Philip IV

COMMON TERMS (for others see glossary)

    casaque
    sacque
    canons
    la modeste
    la friponne
    la secret
    pinners

RECOMMENDED SOURCES

    Laver (4)
    Brooke (6): pp. 10–58
    Kitson (background)
    Skira (8)
    Boehn (5)
    Wittkower (background)
    Tapié (background)
    Wölfflin (background)
    Sculpture, paintings, engravings,
        drawings
    Useful painters: Rubens, Hals, Callot,
        Van Dyck, Brose, Hollar, Inigo Jones,
        Vouet, Champaigne, Terborch,
        Rembrandt, Ostade, Brouwer,
        Jordaens, Velásquez

Typical Figures

Restoration or Middle Baroque

After the middle of the seventeenth century, the Baroque style became more sumptuous and dignified. The favorite ornament was the acanthus of classical antiquity combined in decorative designs with large fruits and flowers or with trophies composed of cannons, weapons, Roman armor, antique helmets, and flowing ostrich plumes. In Italy, undulating walls and higher domes distinguished church architecture, sculpture made use of even more violent motion in draperies and action, and paintings became more operatic, expansive, and sumptuously grand, especially on palace and church ceilings. A new Baroque classicism began to develop in France under the leadership of Louis XIV and his artistic dictator, Le Brun, based on the work of the great French artist Poussin. A dramatic realism still flourished in Holland and Flanders. For the first time since the middle Gothic period, France took the lead in art and fashion, and after Louis XIV became king in his own right in 1661, every aspect of French culture was organized under the central government. All European fashion emanated from the palace at Versailles after the Sun King and his court moved there in 1664. In England after the restoration of Charles II, French styles in art and fashion were predominant, since the majority of the court had spent the years of the Commonwealth in France.

MASCULINE DRESS. During the years which coincided with Louis XIV's youth to middle age, the elegant, soldierly costume of the Cardinal Richelieu period disintegrated into a costume of overlapping layers of fabric covered with ribbons and bows. The doublet became a mere bolero jacket worn open with sleeves only to the elbow, so that the wide shirt sleeves, edged with lace and tied with ribbons in several places, were visible. Boot hose disappeared, but their lace tops survived as wide lace ruffles below the knee, while breeches, decorated at the top with bunches of ribbon loops or *galants*, hung low on the hips and revealed the shirt at the waist. Open and very wide, so that they resembled a short skirt, they sometimes were an actual skirt worn over full, bloused knee breeches. Called *rhinegrave breeches* in Paris, after the Rhinegrave of Salm who introduced them there, and *petticoat breeches* in England, they were worn from 1655 to 1680. Shoes were now high heeled, square toed, very prominent, and finished with stiff bows over the tongues, while stockings were of pale colored silk. Necks were dressed with a lace-edged, box-pleated collar under the chin known as a *rabat,* or a lace fall or *cravat.* Hair was worn shoulder length, often with curls caught into ribbons, and by 1665–1670 this long hair was replaced by wigs. Hats were usually tapered and had tall crowns, and the stiff wide brims were trimmed with ostrich, though lower crowns were more in evidence after 1670. Also by 1670, the short bolero jacket had given way to the long jacket or coat known as a *casaque* which eventually became the fitted *justaucorps* or formal coat. This garment was the key to military wear along with high boots, breastplate, baldric, and sash.

FEMININE DRESS. In the early years of Louis XIV's reign, women's dresses were low cut in a boat-shaped neckline and were worn either with a collar or with a lace edging falling from the top of the bodice. Sleeves were three-quarter length and full, often of lace or material contrasting with the dress, and puffed many times with ribbon bows. The bodice, with its vertical row of bows *à la echelon,* was pointed in front, had a natural waistline in back; the corset underneath kept the figure smooth and trim from bustline to waist. The open *manteau* or overskirt was frequently looped up slightly at one or two points with ribbon bows to show the *jupe* or underskirt, or it opened naturally in a triangle. The necklace at the throat was frequently replaced by a small brooch on a chain known as a *lavallière,* named after the mistress of Louis XIV. Hair was done in full hanging curls over the ears. Hats and coats were reserved for riding, while the hooded mantle was still used for travel.

RESTORATION OR MIDDLE BAROQUE

DATES
    1660–1685
        England: Restoration
        France: Louis XIV
        Italy: Middle Baroque
COMMON TERMS (for others see glossary)
        petticoat breeches
        rhinegrave breeches
        rabat
        cassock
        lavallière
        echelon
        manteau
        galants
        cravat
        boot hose
        canon
        peruque

RECOMMENDED SOURCES
    Pepys (background)
    Evelyn (background)
    Brooke (6): pp. 58–82
    Cunnington (3)
    Leloir: Section on seventeenth century
    Skira (8)
    Tapié (background)
    Wittkower (background)
    Paintings, engravings, drawings, and
        some sculpture
    Useful painters and illustrators: Lely,
        Kneller, Mignard, Champaigne,
        de Hooch, Terborch, Vermeer,
        Van Tilborgh, Jan Steen, Van Oost,
        Le Nain, Largillière, Careño, Murillo,
        Hollar, Bérain, late Rembrandt,
        Le Brun, Van der Helst, Dolci,
        late Jordaens

Typical Figures

Late Baroque

The whirling movement and flamboyance of the Baroque style began to become quieter and more dignified as Louis XIV and his regime grew older and more conservative. France still remained the center of art and fashion, but the rigid autocracy of the king's personal dictatorship in all matters of culture eventually brought a heavy-handed formality to all the arts and fashion. French painters such as Le Brun, Mignard, and Rigaud set a style that was a heavy, ponderous echo of the flamboyant, dramatic work of Rubens; sculptors such as Coysevox and Girardon echoed the excitement of Bernini only vaguely in their formal, dignified statues; and architects such as J. H. Mansard stressed formality and weight over curves and movement in structures built in Paris and at Versailles. All of the petty courts of Germany, the imperial court in Vienna, and the conservative court of William and Mary and Queen Anne in England followed suit. Only in the very last years of the Sun King's reign did the early work of Watteau and other younger artists foreshadow the lightness and gaiety of the Rococo.

MASCULINE DRESS. The *casaque* had, by 1685, become the heavy, tightly fitted coat with flaring skirts and slits to the waist up sides and back known as the *justaucorps*. Its sleeves now reached to the lower forearm, ending in large, turned-back cuffs, while the shirt now showed only as a large lace ruffle below the cuff. Underneath the coat the *rhinegrave breeches* were gradually replaced with tight knee breeches, with hose drawn up over the knee and gartered on top of these *culottes*. The short doublet was now lengthened to form a knee-length waistcoat with large flap pockets, while the cravat at the neck was formed of a soft silk scarf wrapped about the neck with the lace ends falling in a *jabot* under the chin. The *cravat* was often used with a stiff bow at the neck when a formal effect was desired. However, after the Battle of Steinkirk, when the French troops did not have time to tie their cravats and so stuck the ends through a buttonhole in the coat, fashionable men wore the cravat as a *steinkirk*

in this casual manner. Wigs or *peruques* were now large, elaborate, full-bottomed affairs with cascades of heavy curls over the front and back of the shoulders and with two horns of curls above the forehead. The face was clean shaven, and the hats worn over the wigs were huge, broad-brimmed affairs trimmed in ostrich and, after 1695, usually turned up in three places to create a *tricorne*. Shoes were still heavy, high heeled, and square toed, often finished in buckles rather than bows over the tongue. For the nobility, shoe heels were always red. Accessories included muffs, walking sticks, dress swords, baldrics, snuff boxes, and lorgnettes, while ornamentation ran to heavy braiding and embroidery, with the occasional use of bunches of bows on the right shoulder. Uniforms made even greater use of heavy braiding on the coat.

FEMININE DRESS. Women's fashions also aspired to height and dignity. The headdress known as the *fontange*, made of silk ribbons, starched lace fans, and a cap covering the back of the head, rose, as did the peaks of the man's full-bottomed wig, to a high, vertical effect like the pipes of an organ. Two little curls were arranged artfully on the forehead in front of this headdress, while two ringlets were brought forward over the shoulder from under the lace frills of the cloth cap. The dress consisted of a bodice or *taille* sewn to an open-fronted skirt or *manteau* with a train, which was looped up at the back and along the front edges so that the underskirt or *jupe* could be fully seen. The richly draped *manteau*, like the voluminous hangings adorning the beds of the time, was a magnificent garment of heavy satin or velvet heavily embroidered, while the *jupe* was either richly patterned and bordered at the bottom with heavy trim called *pretintailles* or plain and covered with horizontal flounces or *falbalas*. Sleeves reached only to the elbows, where the lace frills of the chemise appeared, while an ornamental apron was popular for the waist. The corset was rigid, tight, and pointed, the decolletage square, and the front of the bodice either laced over an embroidered stomacher or finished with a vertical line of bows.

LATE BAROQUE

DATES
  1685–1715
    England: Late Restoration or Queen Anne
    France: Baroque or Late Louis XIV
    Italy: Late Baroque
    Germany: Period of the Great Elector
COMMON TERMS (for others see glossary)
    cravat
    steinkirk
    fontange
    commode
    peruque
    spatterdashes
    falbalas
    mante
    manteau
    habit à la français
    Ramillies wig
    pretintailles

    culottes
    justaucorps
RECOMMENDED SOURCES
    Quicherat: Section on late seventeenth
      century
    Boehn (1)
    Cunnington (2): Part I
    Lacroix (background)
    Piton: Part VI
    Boucher: pp. 291–318
    Contini: pp. 165–191
    Faniel (background)
    Racinet: Section on eighteenth century
    Sculpture, paintings, engravings,
      illustrations
    Useful painters and illustrators: Kneller,
      Largillière, Rigaud, early Watteau,
      early Nattier, Van Loo, A. S. Belle,
      de Troy

Typical Figures

Rococo

On the death of Louis XIV in 1715, the Duke of Orléans became regent during the minority of Louis XV; these transitional years between the Baroque and Rococo are referred to as the Regency. From 1730 to 1774—the high period of the Rococo style—the elegant, feminine tastes of Louis XV dominated art and fashion. Aristocratic society now stressed the virtues of individuality, relaxation, delicacy, naturalness, and intimacy as opposed to the heavy formality of the previous reign. Painters such as Watteau, Boucher, and Fragonard formulated the pastoral, the *fête galante*, with its shimmering aristocrats amorously disporting themselves amid the delicacy of forest glades. Sculptors such as Clodion and Pigalle created creamy, rounded figures in pink stone, and architects scaled down the size of their structures and lavished their knowledge on the delicate, gay, playful, and extravagant interiors which they designed for their aristocratic patrons. Rococo decoration made great use of asymmetrical shell ornament, S- and C-shaped forms, and motifs such as bat wings and palm branches; straight lines and right angles were systematically avoided. The enthusiasm for the Far East was reflected in ornamental effects from the Orient known as "chinoiserie." This style, as well as the major attributes of the Rococo, were avidly copied throughout Europe.

MASCULINE DRESS. In the early Regency period, the man's coat and waistcoat were narrow at the shoulders and longer than in the past and the coat was left open; the wig was powdered white and not as full as in the past, and the general silhouette was of a conical or funnel shape expanding toward the knees. After 1730 the silhouette changed to a dome shape as the skirts of the slightly shorter coat as well as those of the knee-length vest were stiffened with canvas and horsehair. Sleeves were full length, ending in large cuffs over the shirt frill, while knee breeches were still tight and fastened over the stockings or rolled and gartered over the breeches above the knee. Shoes were less heavy than in the past, had a lower heel, and invariably finished with a buckle over a much shorter tongue. Fashion required that the head appear small despite the wig, and the hair, now powdered white, was drawn back into a bag and tied with a silk bow or *crapaud*. From this, another ribbon, the *solitaire*, frequently came around the neck and tied over the *cravat*, which was now a ruffle attached to the shirt. The neck itself was wrapped in a *stock* of plain linen. Hats, though somewhat smaller than in the past, were still three cornered and often trimmed in ostrich or embroidered in gold. Suits were heavily embroidered with gold, silver, or silk thread. Pale color harmonies were subtle and exquisite, and silk fabrics were preferred. Uniforms stressed braiding and began to be of a set color for entire regiments or armies.

FEMININE DRESS. During the early Regency period, the *contouche* or loose-fitting housecoat became the most prevalent style, laced loosely over an underdress in front with flowing box pleats in back. These were referred to as *robes volantes* (flying gowns) or *robes batantes* (ringing gowns) because of their bell shape when worn over the wicker-basket *panier* or hoop that appeared about 1719. After 1735 these hoop *paniers* gave way to the lateral-spreading collapsible baskets which often stretched gowns after mid-century to as much as four yards at the hem. The gown or *robe à la française* had a square neckline, the bodice was tightly fitted over a corset, sleeves were narrow and reached to the elbows, where lace flounces still appeared, while the spreading lines of the open skirt showed a richly decorated underskirt or *jupe*. The fanciful, asymmetrical festoons of wall decorations were repeated on the tightly stretched silk of the dress in the form of gathered lace, gathered silk ribbon, or garlands of artificial flowers. The gown was edged with ruching, and large bows on the sleeves matched the ladder-like bows *à la échelle* on the breast. The coiffure was set close to the head and powdered white, and cosmetics were heavily applied.

ROCOCO

DATES
1715–1774
England: Early Georgian
France: Rococo or Louis XV
Italy: Rococo

COMMON TERMS (for others see glossary)
polonnaise
jabot
solitaire
tricorne
paniers
robe à la française
parapluie
perspective
mante
modestie
robe volante
Watteau sacque
cadogan

RECOMMENDED SOURCES
Brooke (3): pp. 10–56
Lacroix (background)
Faniel (background)
Soehner and Schonberger (background)
Cunnington (2)
Skira (9)
Boehn (1)
Kimball (background)
Sculpture, paintings, illustrations
Useful painters and illustrators: Watteau, Boucher, Fragonard, Chardin, Lancret, Nattier, Perroneau, Quentin la Tour, Drouais, Coypel, Van Loo, Hogarth, Gainsborough, Reynolds, Zoffany, Longhi, Tiepolo, Guardi, Pater, Moreau le Jeune, Cochin Chadowiazchi

Typical Figures

Neoclassical

Halfway through the eighteenth century the ruins of Herculaneum and Pompeii were rediscovered, and Europe developed a passion for classical antiquity. In his first history of the fine arts, published in 1775, the German archeologist Winckelmann emphasized the classical qualities of "noble simplicity and tranquil grandeur." The style of Louis XVI, or the neoclassical style, was an amalgam of late Rococo elements mixed with the simpler "English style" based on the new classicism. It was not an authentic Greek or Roman revival, but a "dream of the antique"—a charming, delicate, refined use of antique ornament and, after the excesses of the Rococo, a return to horizontal and vertical lines. In painting, the passion for the picturesque in the work of Fragonard and Robert changed to an admiration for the stark, cold, stoical compositions of David; in sculpture, the direct simplicity of Houdon was now admired; and in architecture, a severe structure such as the Panthéon in Paris was the ideal. This period saw Rococo costume ideals reach their final form and then merge into the new modes which crossed the Channel from England.

MASCULINE DRESS. Men's dress in the 1770s consisted of the *justaucorps*—with large cuffs, pocket flaps, and a cutaway line to the coat skirts in front—or the more closely fitting frock coat. With this was worn a waistcoat that now reached only to the top of the thighs, tight-fitting knee breeches or *culottes* which fitted over white silk stockings, and black shoes with buckles and low red heels. The material used was usually silk in delicate shades, and the edges as well as the front of the coat were richly embroidered in gold, silver, or silk thread. The hat was still three cornered, but smaller. The wig, which was dusted with white or gray powder, was dressed into elegant side curls brushed steeply up from the forehead in front and caught either into a bag or by a ribbon bow in back. At home, the wig was replaced by a soft turban or hat and the coat by a silk dressing gown. Only after 1780 did the man's costume *à la anglaise,* in which shoes and silk stockings were often discarded for close-fitting riding breeches and boots, become fashionable. The *tricorne* was replaced with a low- to medium-crowned, flat-brimmed traveling hat, a smaller jockey hat, or a *bicorne*. Wool was now preferred to silk for men's coats, standing turnover collars were added, coat skirts were either cut back even more sharply or stepped back at the waist, and cuffs either disappeared or were merely marked by a bit of horizontal trim on the sleeve. Waistcoats were short and frequently double breasted, uniforms were usually double breasted and garded with braid and buttons.

FEMININE DRESS. In feminine fashion the large *panier* with the full *robe à la française* was used only in formal wear, and for all other occasions the knee-length hoop was used. With this the underskirt or *jupe* was usually ankle length, and the gown or *robe* was often caught up *à la polonaise* in three large loops over the skirt. Shoes were of silk with high heels, and when ladies went walking they always carried parasols or long walking sticks. In the early 1770s, coiffures were enormous—built up over frames and pads, held with pins and pomade, and often culminating in flowers, fruit, or a frigate in full sail. But new ideas were arriving from across the Channel by 1780, and for a time England became the leader in European fashion. Corsets were still worn, but hoops disappeared and the dress fell softly around the body—held in position by a wide sash. Instead of an elaborate coiffure, the hair was arranged in loose curls down the back, and the shoulders were covered by a small scarf or *fichu*. Long, close-fitting sleeves covered the arms to the wrist, while large, broad-brimmed straw hats made a charming frame for the face. A masculine touch was added by the use of the double-breasted *redingote*, similar to a man's riding coat, with skirts to the floor, and the *lévite* gown—tight and double breasted to the waist, with a trailing skirt over a bustle pad at the rear.

NEOCLASSICAL

DATES
  1774–1790
    France: Louis XVI or Neoclassical
    England: Late Eighteenth Century or
      Late Georgian
    Italy: Neoclassical
    U.S.: Colonial
COMMON TERMS (for others see glossary)
    lévite gown
    Gainsborough hat
    redingote gown
    pelisse
    calash
    dormeuse bonnet
    mob cap
    hedgehog hairdo
    circassienne gown
    cadogan hairdo
    caraco gown

fichu
bicorne
RECOMMENDED SOURCES
    Brooke (3): pp. 56–85
    Skira (9)
    Dimier (2): (background)
    Lacroix (background)
    Boehn (1)
    Faniel (background)
    Novotny (background)
    Gallery of Fashion
    Sculpture, cameos, medallions,
      engravings, illustrations
    Useful painters and illustrators: Reynolds,
      Gainsborough, Romney, late Fragonard,
      David, Greuze, Vigée le Brun, early
      Goya, Guardi, Canaletto, Boilly,
      prints of Moreau le Jeune, Copley,
      Stuart, Trumbell, Charles Wilson Peale

Typical Figures

Directoire and Empire

With the coming of the French Revolution, the Republican virtues of classical antiquity triumphed in society. The artist David became the leading painter of the new Republic. During the early years of the Napoleonic Empire, David was dictator of the arts for the Emperor. The Romans, in particular, provided the models for literature, art, and oratory; in every way, Napoleon hoped to create a modern equivalent of the Roman empire. The Church of the Madeleine and the Arc de Triomphe are architectural examples, the busts and statuary of Canova are the sculptural models, and the efforts of David and his pupils Gerard, Girodet, and Prud'hon were the painting ideals of the period. But this was also an age of a growing romanticism, and after the Egyptian campaign many oriental and Near Eastern elements, along with historical touches from the medieval, Renaissance, and Baroque, mingled with the classical.

MASCULINE DRESS. England remained the source of masculine tailoring during this period despite some exciting aberrations in dress brought on by the Revolution and Empire in France. The garb of the revolutionaries usually consisted of the red *Phrygian cap*, worn by galley slaves; a sleeveless, loose-fitting jacket called the *carmagnole*, worn by peasants; and the long, wide trousers worn by sailors and referred to as *sans-culottes*. During the Directoire the most radical fashion figures were referred to as *incroyables*, and they were judged by the elegance of their extravagant disarray. They carried heavy, knotted sticks, sported unruly hair to the shoulders, and hid their jaws in enormous neck cloths. They wore tight, striped trousers, riding boots, square-cut waistcoats with high waistlines, and coats with huge lapels and high, turned-down collars. With this ludicrous outfit was worn a *beaver* or cocked hat. As the Directoire merged into the Empire, men's costume saw the development of the long trousers of today, some very snug, others somewhat looser in fit. Leather and knitted breeches, fitted and ending in knee-high boots, were also popular. Knee breeches and stockings were now worn only with court dress. The fashion in England during the period of the Regency, which coincided with the Empire in France, was set by Beau Brummel, who prided himself on spotless linen—a two-pointed collar now rose above the carefully wrapped *stock*. Frills still decorated the shirt front and sleeve cuffs, waistcoats were usually double breasted and often showed below the buttoned coat front, and coats had a high, rolled collar, slightly gathered sleeves at the armseye, and *clawhammer* tails. Hair imitated the wind-blown Roman look, and headgear was based on variations of the top hat. Caped overcoats were worn for travel. Uniforms were heavily braided, and heads were covered with tall *shakos*.

FEMININE DRESS. At first, during the height of the Revolution, the only changes in female dress came in the casual disarray of the hair, fichu, and muslin gowns, plus the addition of cockades and sashes of the blue, white, and red of the Republic. Toward the end of the Revolution the "antique garb" of the "new classicism" appeared. The waistline moved up to just below the breast, all corseting disappeared, and the dress, cut very simply in white muslin or batiste or some other quiet color, was held by a ribbon under the breast. Flat slippers replaced high-heeled shoes, the large brim of the straw hat was turned down around the face to form a bonnet, and the hair was done in a loose series of corkscrew curls clustering down to the shoulders. During the Directoire those wearing exaggerations of this costume were referred to as *merveilleuse*. By 1800 the upper part of this chemise dress became a small, separate bodice with a square neckline, a tunic was frequently worn over the dress like a Greek *peplos*, and the hair was arranged to imitate a Greek coiffure. After Napoleon was crowned in 1804, heavier fabrics such as silk and satin were reintroduced, small puffed sleeves came in, and for court wear a heavy, separate train or *courrobe* of dark colored velvet was fastened and trailed from the waist. The short *Spencer jacket* and the longer *redingote* were worn outdoors, shawls or stoles were still popular, and the poke bonnet fitted close to the face was fashionable. Toward the close of the Empire, long sleeves returned and heavy trim adorned the bottom of the skirt.

DIRECTOIRE AND EMPIRE

DATES
  1790–1815
    England: Regency
    France: Directoire and Empire
    Germany: Biedermeier
    Italy: Empire
    U.S.: Federal
COMMON TERMS (for others see glossary)
    merveilleuse
    incroyables
    sans-culottes
    muscadine
    redingote
    clawhammer tails
    chemise à l'anglaise
    escarpins
    cherusses
    Spencer jacket

Garrick greatcoat
coal-scuttle bonnet
RECOMMENDED SOURCES
    Price (background)
    Blum (background)
    Norris and Oswald: Part I
    Brooke (5): pp. 8–24
    Laver (2): pp. 70–81
    Cunnington (1): Part I
    Novotny (background)
    Paintings, sculpture, engravings,
      illustrations, fashion plates
    Useful painters: David, Ingres, Gros,
      Prud'hon, Gerard, Gericault, Le Brun,
      Raeburn, Opie, Lawrence, Isabey,
      Goya, Hoppner, drawings by Vernet
      and Debucourt, Stuart, Copley,
      Trumbell, Earle

clawhammer tails

spencer

Typical Figures

Romantic

The nineteenth century was an age of revival. As much more became known about the styles of the past than ever before, architects, sculptors, and painters drew unceasingly on the riches catalogued by art historians and archeologists. The major reaction to the classicism of the Empire was in the direction of Baroque movement, Gothic mystery, and Rococo elegance and charm—the latter being especially influential in the arts of costume. In painting, the Baroque borrowings of Delacroix and Géricault tended to take precedence; in architecture, the Gothic style of the English Houses of Parliament were given great emphasis; while in sculpture, the dramatic effects of Rude and Barye reflected admiration for the work of Bernini. This was a new age of capitalism and the machine, and with the expanding middle class, which had little taste and much money, factory imitations superceded the quality craftsmanship of individual workmen.

MASCULINE DRESS. Although the long trousers, coat, and waistcoat had by now become permanent features of men's dress, the masculine silhouette echoed the women's silhouette in its wasp waist and fullness in chest and hips. The trousers fastened under the instep and were padded at the hips, the coat and overcoat were fitted very closely with leg-of-mutton sleeves joined to the coat below the shoulder, and the cap or shawl collar gave the shoulders a rounded appearance. Coats were fitted either with tails or the flaring skirts of the frock coat, and a corset or *Basque belt* was often used to pinch in the waist under the pidgeon-breasted waistcoat. Short jackets were used only for sport. Height was given by the tall, flaring top hat that was worn for all formal occasions except court dress, when the cocked *bicorne* was carried. Men wore full side whiskers and clustering curls around the ears, and toward the close of the period beards and mustaches began to make their appearance. The crisp points of the shirt collar were still held in place by a wide *stock* that usually tied in a bow in the front, and rich ruffles still showed at the chest above the waistcoat. The mantle and the caped overcoat were standard wear for travel, knee breeches and slippers were used only for court presentation, and pointed boots were now worn under the trousers except for riding or sporting occasions. In uniforms, the braided frock coat superceded tails, and long trousers often replaced high boots.

FEMININE DRESS. Under the Empire, dresses had already become shorter at the hem and were closed around the neck, but now the girdle moved down from below the bust to the slimmest point of the waist, the corset returned, and skirts flared out in many folds over full petticoats. Appliqué trimming, ruching, and many ruffles came back in force. The poke bonnet was still in use, but now it flared out into a huge brim decorated with plumes and ribbons framing a hairdo that had great sausage curls at the temples and a complexly curled top knot at the back. Flat shoes, fastened with cross lacings up the legs, continued to be worn, and shawls of all sizes continued to be carried or worn. As the width of this costume expanded at shoulders and hips, the collar of the low-cut bodice increased in size and formed a kind of roof over the greatly distended leg-of-mutton sleeves, which were attached to the bodice well below the shoulder line. From about 1835 on, the upholsterer, rather than the cabinet maker, dictated in matters of interior decoration, and just as the basic shape of furniture was lost under padded fabric, tassels, and fringe, so women's fashions ceased to have the lightness of the ballet line, and the female figure was gradually covered in heavy fabric and decoration. The skirt lengthened to the floor and was further extended with petticoats. The leg-of-mutton sleeve disappeared in favor of snug-fitting sleeves, exaggerated hairdos were modified to ringlets over the ears and a smooth part across the forehead, and bonnets closed in about the face. The hourglass silhouette gave way to the tea cozy look, and heavier fabrics and trim replaced light ruffles and flowers.

ROMANTIC

DATES
  1815–1848
    England: Period of William IV and the
      Young Victoria
    France: Romantic or Restoration and the
      July Monarchy
    Italy: Restoration
    Spain: Restoration
    Germany and Austria: Biedermeier
    U.S.: Early Republic

COMMON TERMS (for others see glossary)
  stock
  crinoline
  robe d'intérieur
  bertha
  beret
  pèlerine
  canezou
  pelisse
  mantellette

RECOMMENDED SOURCES
  Laver (2): pp. 81–92
  Norris and Oswald: Part I
  Brooke (5): pp. 24–48
  Gentleman's Magazine
  Modes Parisiennes, les
  Novotny (background)
  Gernsheim (background)
  Boehn (3)
  Paintings, sculpture, illustrations,
    engravings, drawings, fashion plates
  Useful painters: Delacroix, Sully, Samuel
    Morse, Cruikshank, Ingres, Lawrence,
    Raeburn, Bouguereau, Meissonier,
    Horace Vernet, Daumier, Gavarni,
    Friedrich

stock or cravat

bertha

crinoline underneath

ca. 1830

Typical Figures

Late Nineteenth Century: Crinoline

The revolts and pressures against the status quo which had erupted throughout the romantic period reached their culmination in 1848. Revolutions arose in all the capitals of Europe and, if not in the mass middle-class taste of the European bourgeoisie, many changes began to take place in intellectual and artistic circles. A new interest in social problems, urban living, and the increasing misery caused by industrialization led to the development of realism in art and literature. In France, Dumas *fils*, Augier, Flaubert, the Brothers Goncourt, and others pioneered in the new field, as did Ibsen in Norway and Dickens in England. In painting, Courbet and Millet pioneered new subjects and new ways of viewing based on the world around them. However, taste at the court of the Emperor Napoleon III was still imitative of past styles, particularly the Rococo.

MASCULINE DRESS. At the beginning of this period the romantic silhouette still retained a tight-fitting, slim-waisted line, but without the previous exaggeration in shoulder and hips. The top hat was still obligatory, but in 1848 the beaver was supplanted by the silk hat. The hair was still full, although not as tightly curled around the ears, and beards were now becoming more and more prevalent. The most fashionable was the pointed "imperial," worn with side whiskers and a mustache. By 1860 a man's daily outfit tended to be uniform in color, and was now known as "a suit of clothes." Trousers, though narrow, were no longer tight fitting and fastened under the shoe, frock coats and tail coats were no longer as snug at the waist, and standing collars and cravats were replaced by starched collars and ties. Special suits of clothes for different occasions also began to be used at this time: the frock coat and top hat for formal afternoon wear, the bowler and short sack suit—usually with waistcoat, pants, and matching coat—for business wear, and short hunting or fishing jackets with leggings and straw hats for country wear. The full black outfit of tails with a white vest was established at this time as the standard for formal evening wear. Overcoats now superceded the cloak for outdoors, and uniforms stressed long trousers, braided frock coats, and visored caps or *shakos*.

FEMININE DRESS. About mid-century the weight of the many petticoats that had achieved the tea cozy silhouette brought about the reintroduction (for the third time in the history of dress) of a frame to hold out the skirts. This *crinoline* was made of bamboo, whalebone, or metal hoops suspended from tapes and increasing in width toward the bottom, and with it came the possibility of extra width in the skirt—a fact which was exploited to the full. The hair was now either parted in the middle, waved over the forehead and caught in a bun or bunch of curls over the ears, or drawn in soft waves from center part to the back of the head and held in a *chignon* or soft roll. The former style was preferred by Queen Victoria, the latter by the Empress Eugénie, who was Spanish by birth, married Napoleon III in 1853, was considered by many the most beautiful woman in Europe, and who, with the help of her couturier, the House of Worth, was the leader of European fashion until 1869. Under the influence of the Empress Eugénie, the poke bonnet was replaced by the small straw hat with a ribbon at the back and the *capote,* a tiny bonnet at the back of the head. In the new style, based in many ways on the Rococo, the lower part of the skirt could be divided into horizontal layers of ruching or garlands of flowers. It might consist of several layers of different lengths, or there could be a major use of overlapping flounces at the hem. The effect of the flouncing on the skirt was repeated in the *bertha* around the shoulders and spread also to the sleeve, which became funnel shaped—the famous *pagoda* sleeve—with undersleeves of white tulle. For evening wear, short cap sleeves and low decolletage were the fashion, while daytime wear required long sleeves and a high neck, except in certain summer frocks. Fabrics ranged from silk taffetas, damasks, brocades, and velvets to light muslins, gauze, and crepe-de-chine, which made women look like floating clouds. Stockings were now colored; cloth boots were used by day, slippers at night. At the close of the period the crinoline changed to an oval shape with emphasis at the back.

LATE NINETEENTH CENTURY: CRINOLINE

DATES
  1845–1868
    England: Victorian
    France: Age of Realism in Painting
      Period of Second Republic and Empire
    Italy: Age of Revolution and
      Independence
    Germany: German Confederation
    U.S.: Antebellum and Civil War
COMMON TERMS (for others see glossary)
    frock coat
    tails
    morning coat
    sack suit
    bowler
    burnous
    raglan coat
    paletot
    cage américaine
    shirtwaist
    Dundreary
    imperial
    muttonchops
    pagoda sleeve

    zouave jacket
    princess gown
    pork-pie hat
    Empress Eugénie hat
    Prince Albert coat
    Inverness cape
RECOMMENDED SOURCES
    Godey's Ladies Book
    Modes Parisiennes, les
    l'Illustration
    Illustrated London News
    Court Magazine
    Cunnington (1)
    Boehn (3)
    Norris and Oswald: Part II
    Brooke (5): pp. 48–64
    Laver (2): pp. 92–100
    Larkin (background)
    Paintings, illustrations, photographs
    Useful painters and illustrators: Manet,
      Delacroix, Ingres, Millet, Courbet,
      Daumier, Guys, Gavarni, Phiz,
      Winterhalter, Lami

muttonchops

frock coat

pagoda sleeve

princess gown over hoop
or cage américaine

ca. 1860

Typical Figures

Late Nineteenth Century: Bustle

During the last decades of the nineteenth century, the imitation of styles became a confusion of styles, each applied to a different purpose. Studies and dining rooms were Renaissance, smoking rooms oriental, girls' rooms Rococo. Coziness was everything, and heavy door hangings, thick upholstery, elephantine furniture, and accessories which ran to wax flowers, lacquered bulrushes, and peacock feathers created a crowded chaos of confused ornamentation. It is no wonder that true art moved outdoors into the light and air as the impressionists, using the new art of optics and a sensitive eye, made people see things "as if for the first time." Even a sculptor such as Rodin gave an "impressionistic" immediacy to his work through the surging, flickering line of tactile surfaces, while other artists experimented with pattern and form at the expense of subject matter.

MASCULINE DRESS. Dress, like interior decoration, followed the mass taste of the times, and men's costume became very conservative in line and color and very organized as to what should be worn when. Formal dress in the morning now consisted of stiff-bosomed shirt, wing collar, bow tie, light gray vest, cutaway morning coat, gray striped trousers, pearl gray gloves, and a top hat—all items still a part of daytime formal wear. Afternoon formal wear consisted of starched shirt, standing collar, *four-in-hand* or *ascot* tie, a rich but sober waistcoat, a dark double-breasted frock coat with matching or lighter trousers. Informal evening wear saw the introduction of the black *tuxedo* or satin-lapeled dinner jacket of fingertip length, while formal evening wear still consisted of white tie and waistcoat with black tails and trousers. For business wear, the bowler hat and the sack suit, the latter frequently in checks and narrow stripes, was the standard. For sports there was a variety of belted *Norfolk jackets* and knee-length knickerbockers worn with billed caps, fore-and-aft caps, and straws. These sporting suits were usually worn with collar and tie, and with buttoned leggings over long woolen stockings. The *Inverness cape* and the *Chesterfield overcoat* were used against rain and cold, faces still sported beards, side whiskers, and full mustaches, hair was moderately full, and shoes were buttoned to the ankle and frequently worn with spats. Uniforms showed innovations in headgear but remained much the same in silhouette.

FEMININE DRESS. The material in dresses was now cut into complex small pieces before being sewn to fit the female figure, in order to demonstrate the masterful art of dressmaking. Folds were draped across pleats, drapings draped over drapings, and velvets were used with dull silks and glossy satins. Everything seemed to strive toward a complex juxtaposition of lines, fabrics, and colors. With the transition from the crinoline to the bustle, the fullness in the 1870s moved firmly to the back. This bustle was either a small pad of horsehair or a small metal cage with the overskirt draped up over it. All draping was as imaginatively contrived as in the portières and curtains of the day. The upper part of the figure was firmly encased in a corset that pushed up the bust and pushed out the abdomen, necks were high, and sleeves were full length during the day, décolleté and short for evening. Long white or pastel gloves were worn with evening wear to cover bare arms. By the late 1870s, the bustle began to disappear as the draped outer skirt wrapped more tightly about the lower part of the body. In this *fish-tailed* style, which reached its peak in 1880, the hips, waist, and bust emerged with a magnificent flourish owing much to corsetry and padding; a long row of buttons down the front emphasized the central line of the figure. In the early 1880s, the bustle returned, now worn higher on the waist and giving the female silhouette the look of a centaur. A skirt with a bustle was worn with tailored jackets, skating outfits, and topcoats, all of which were cut to accommodate this exaggerated line at the rear of the figure. Hair was built up toward the back of the head with tight curls falling down the back; small hats with flowers, ribbons, and feathers perched atop this hairdo were kept on by a ribbon or a hatpin. Shoes were ankle high, buttoned affairs except for evening, when the heeled slipper was worn.

LATE NINETEENTH CENTURY: BUSTLE

DATES
  1868–1890
    England: Victorian
    France: Third Republic and
      Age of Impressionism
    Italy: Age of Nationalism
    Germany: German Empire
    Spain: Carlist Wars
    U.S.: The Gilded Age
COMMON TERMS (for others see glossary)
    Norfolk jacket
    tuxedo
    spats
    wing collar
    monocle
    knickerbockers
    windsor tie
    fore-and-aft cap
    Chesterfield overcoat
    ascot
    fedora
    homburg
    frou-frou
    four-in-hand tie
RECOMMENDED SOURCES
    Brooke (5): pp. 64–80
    Godey's Lady's Book
    Harper's (1)
    Harper's (2)
    Harper's (3)
    Peterson's Magazine
    Sullivan (background)
    Brown (2): (background)
    Norris and Oswald: Part III
    Laver (2): pp. 101–111
    Boehn (3)
    La Mode Illustreé
    Paintings, illustrations, photographs
    Useful painters and illustrators: Manet,
      Monet, Degas, Lautrec, Renoir,
      Thomas Nast, Homer, Whistler,
      Sargent, Eakins, du Maurier

homburg

spats

ca. 1875

Typical Figures

The Birth of Modernism or *Art Nouveau*

With the last decade of the nineteenth century, the first modern mass style began to make itself felt in design and decoration. Artists such as Monet and Whistler, who throughout the last half of the nineteenth century had stressed design, pattern, and form over subject, saw their ideals vindicated in a Europe-wide style variously labeled *art nouveau* or *Jugendstil.* As it spread, eclecticism went out of fashion and the pattern and lines of decoration and ornament, which were based primarily on "organic" growth lines, influenced architecture, painting, sculpture, and interior decoration. As designs were stripped to their basic forms, and beauty began to be equated with function and use, costume was affected and by 1913 the female figure, draped in kimono-like lines, was involved in a tremendous fashion revolution.

MASCULINE DRESS. Male fashions changed only slightly during this period, with casual clothing for outings and the sack suits for everyday wear becoming more prevalent. The fashionable ideal was the subtly tailored, square-shouldered, smooth-waisted elegance of the dandy or "dude." Hair was now most frequently parted in the middle, cleanshaven faces began to return, and many varieties of soft *homburgs, fedoras,* and billed caps began to replace the rigid "topper" and bowler. Very high, stiff collars were still the rule, whether they were winged, turnover, or standing, and the *ascot* and *four-in-hand* ties were rivaled in popularity by the bow tie. Shirts were stiff bosomed for all formal occasions and buttoned up the back, while with all informal outfits the soft, often striped shirt with separate collar was worn. There was still the formal *morning coat,* the square-skirted *frock coat, tails,* the *tuxedo,* and the *sack coat,* with informal *blazers,* knitted *cardigans, Norfolk jackets,* and pullover sweaters for sporting. There was great variety in both double- and single-breasted waistcoats, either matching or contrasting with the coat and trousers, sometimes in rich patterns. Trousers were slim and often pressed into a crease, sometimes turned up into a cuff, while knee-length *knickers* worn with woolen stockings were also still seen in sports wear. Ankle-length button shoes were worn in winter, low *oxfords* in summer, and *spats* were fashionable. Heavy or light overcoats, sometimes in plaid, with a shoulder cape, at other times with fur lining and trim, were worn. Field uniforms moved to khaki brown jackets, riding pants, and leggings.

FEMININE DRESS. By 1890 the bustle disappeared, leaving behind a certain amount of residual drapery in the skirt, but this did not remain, and by the mid 1890s the skirt became a smooth, many-gored, flaring skirt with extra fullness at the back, large *leg-of-mutton sleeves,* and a tiny waist to give an hourglass figure. The dresses were still high necked and long sleeved for day wear, décolleté with short capped sleeves for evening. A feminine version of the male suit appeared in the 1890s which consisted of a tailored jacket and ankle-length skirt worn with a shirt blouse and tie. This blouse, smothered in every conceivable kind of trimming—lace, buttons, frills, and flounces, influenced dress styles toward having a great fullness of material in front. This, coupled with the introduction in the late 1890s of a new corset that pushed the bust forward and the hips backward, produced the famous sway-backed S-curved figure of the opening years of the new century. Hair, which had been drawn up fairly close to the head in the style of Mme de Pompadour, became fuller and surrounded the temples, ears, and forehead with a massive halo of hair. Flowered and be-ribboned hats, which had small brims in the 1890s, expanded into great, broad-brimmed creations saturated with plumes. By 1908 the silhouette was taller and slimmer, the bust had become higher and more prominent, and the hips were held in tightly by the corset; two or three years later the real revolution in female fashion took place. At first there was a brief revival of pseudo-Empire styles, then the corset was completely thrown aside, and the one-piece, *kimono-like costume* began to predominate, with much tight draping about the legs to gain a diamond-shaped silhouette and the famed *hobble skirt* effect. Large floral and oriental patterns derived from *art nouveau* decoration became fashionable, hats became smaller, and hair became simpler, softer, and shorter.

THE BIRTH OF MODERNISM
OR *ART NOUVEAU*

DATES
  1890–1914
    England: Late Victorian and
      Edwardian Age of Imperialism
    France: Third Republic
    Germany: German Empire
    U.S.: Gay Nineties and
      Age of Immigration
COMMON TERMS (for others see glossary)
  boater
  Gibson Girl blouse
  leg-of-mutton sleeves
  bloomers
  chatelaine bag
  windsor tie
  street sweepers
  Panama hat
  string tie
  kimono dress
  beehive hat
  lampshade dress

peg-top skirt
hobble skirt
RECOMMENDED SOURCES
  Vogue
  Life Magazine
  American Magazine
  Ladies' Home Journal
  Sears Roebuck Catalog
  Wilcox (2)
  Worth (background)
  Good Housekeeping
  Sullivan (background)
  Brown (1): (background)
  Gernsheim (background)
  Paintings, sculpture, photographs,
    engravings, drawings
  Useful painters and illustrators: Sargent,
    Gibson, Henri, Eakins, Lautrec, Maillol,
    Bonnard, Boldini, Bottini, Picasso,
    Beardsley, Klimt, Munch, Matisse,
    Van der Velde

ca. 1902

Typical Figures

Age of Relativity

Between the beginning of World War I and the beginning of World War II, the revolution in art and culture that had begun in the last decade of the nineteenth century finally became an integral part of life in the Western World. The new concept of relativity influenced thinking in art, morals, science, literature, and world outlook. Particularly in the arts, with the invention of the motion picture and the establishment of cubism, reality was seen changing from moment to moment, varying widely when seen from different points of view, and capable of being presented as a simultaneous view from many angles. This led to the simultaneous inner and outer levels of reality in the work of James Joyce, to the many visual angles and points of view of Picasso, and to the interpenetration of space and object in the work of Moore, Gabo, and Giacometti. A second major concept was that of functionalism, wherein beauty lay not in ornament and decoration but in the practical function for which a house, a gown, a chair, or an automobile was designed.

MASCULINE DRESS. Masculine dress changed only very slowly and subtly during this period, becoming more functional and less formal. The frock coat finally disappeared altogether, leaving only morning coats and tails as leftovers from the nineteenth century in formal wear. Collars, except for the formal winged collar, became moderately soft turnovers; the soft felt *slouch hat* or *fedora* finally came to dominate the *derby, bowler,* and *top hat*—the latter remaining only for formal wear. High laced and buttoned shoes gave way to the low *oxford.* In the 1920s the male silhouette tended to have rather a slim and boyish look, with the exception of the *Oxford bags* or knee-length *plus fours* for golfing and sports. In the 1930s the silhouette became very broad shouldered and the trousers quite wide and pleated, while hat brims increased in width. Bright-colored sport shirts made their appearance, double-breasted coats were very popular, white tuxedo jackets for summer wear were introduced, and there was great emphasis on swimming trunks, beach wear, and walking shorts. In outer garments the unique item of the 1920s was the raccoon coat, of the 1930s, the trench coat. Throughout the whole period the sack suit was dominant, while in uniforms the khaki brown color became standard and lapel jackets replaced high-collared tunics.

FEMININE DRESS. 1914 is the watershed date in women's fashions, when functionalism finally began to triumph over the complexities of line and superfluous decoration. After the first introduction of the draped kimono lines, dresses and coats fell loosely about the body and showed a marked tendency to become shorter, to reveal that a woman, like a man, had two legs to walk on. After the War, straight lines began to become the ideal, and by 1923 women's costume had developed into a short, absolutely straight dress hanging from the shoulders, usually sleeveless, with the waist around the hips. The curves of the body were ignored, the female form was presented as a sort of tube without hips or breasts. The low waist marked the tops of the legs, and more and more of the leg, clad in light silk stockings, was exposed until the dress reached minimum length in 1928. At the same time, the *Eton crop* and bobbed hair appeared along with the *cloche hat*—the result was a youthful figure of indeterminate sex. The dress of this period was a clear expression of a sober, practical functionalism in design. About 1930, evening gowns grew longer, first at the back and then all the way around. The material was cut on the bias to stretch and shape itself over the bust, hips, and thighs; thus, feminine curves reappeared, while décolleté tended to shift to the rear with backless gowns. In day wear the waist was once again normal, but, as with men, shoulders were broadened and long straight lines in dress and coatskirts predominated until skirts began rising to knee length at the end of the decade. Hats were either felts with a tiny brim, pillboxes, or turbans, and hair was generally parted in the middle and waved or rolled up and to the back. Great experimentation took place in wide slacks or trousers, play suits, tennis dresses, bathing suits, sandals, and shirtwaist frocks.

AGE OF RELATIVITY

DATES
    1914–1940 World War I to World War II
COMMON TERMS (for others see glossary)
    Oxford bags
    plus fours
    polo coat
    blazer
    raccoon coat
    cummerbund
    trench coat
    dolman wrap
    cardigan
    shingled and bobbed hairdos
    arctics or galoshes
    jodhpurs
    monkey fur coat
    bandeau
    halter dress
    culottes
RECOMMENDED SOURCES
    Harper's (1)
    Harper's (2)
    Harper's (3)
    Vogue
    Life Magazine
    Illustrated London News
    International Studio
    Connoisseur
    Studio
    Esquire
    Men's Wear
    Sears Roebuck Catalog
    Ladies' Home Journal
    Good Housekeeping
    Wilcox (1)
    Wilcox (2)
    Contini: pp. 283–306
    Paintings, illustrations, photographs,
        drawings, fashion plates
    Useful illustrators and painters: Grosz,
        Chagall, Benton, Kirchner, Kokoschka,
        Marsh, Schmidt-Rotluff, Sloan, Shahn,
        Wood, M. Parrish, Van Dongen, Dufy

ca. 1920

Typical Figures

Contemporary

Culture has changed radically in the years since World War II. Through increasing methods of communication, the threat of destruction by a "super" bomb, and expanding speed and efficiency of travel, the world has grown smaller. The two greatest technical influences have been transmissions to all parts of the world via communications satellites, and the lurking fear in every country in the world of atomic and hydrogen bombs. Together, these have caused a continuing growth in uniformity of culture from place to place throughout the world, plus a growing anxiety neurosis felt in every aspect of contemporary culture. Acceptance of the *avant garde* in painting, sculpture, architecture, theatre, and the arts of fashion is widespread; there is a greater breakdown of boundaries among all the arts; and there is more violence, neurosis, and hysteria in all aspects of culture than at any time in the history of Western man.

MASCULINE DRESS. The basic form of male dress established at the time of Napoleon has varied in sympathy with the times but has not changed substantially in 150 years. Various new items have been added to it, it has been considerably modified for sport, new fabrics have been introduced, but the basic construction is so practical that it has remained the same. Formal dress such as tails and morning coats are disappearing, and dinner coats in black, white, checks, or velvets, often without vests, are more and more acceptable for all formal occasions. The major changes in cut have been toward slimmer lines, smaller lapels, less padding, and a closer fit. Hats have also narrowed to much smaller brims, sandals have begun to return for men as well as women, and colors and patterns (at least in sportswear) have finally brightened for men so that they now sometimes equal women in the brilliant effect created. Wash-and-wear fabrics, creaseless and stainless materials, and longer wearing synthetics of all kinds have made men's clothes ever more efficient and practical, while in sportswear the variety of fabrics, shapes, and numbers of garments has greatly increased.

FEMININE DRESS. During World War II military wear influenced fashion, and many forms of the male and female uniforms of the time made their way into civil dress, but it was not until 1947 that a great change came to the short-skirted, tubular, square-shouldered look that had been in vogue since 1939. The "new look," established by the House of Christian Dior in Paris, stressed narrow shoulders, smooth bust, normal waist, and a long skirt with a wide hem. This dress silhouette was not really new at all, but merely a return to past styles, and in the years that followed, it was modified, especially in the length and width of the skirt. In the early 1950s, not too many years after the "new look" appeared, the House of Balenciaga was first in the field with a chemise or sack dress, and by 1956 Dior produced his H-line and A-line dresses. Since then the general silhouette of women's clothes has more resembled the modes of the mid-1920s, except when skirts are abandoned altogether in favor of trousers. In recent years the mini skirt length has surpassed the skirt lengths of the mid-1920s for shortness. In the case of young men and young women today, the clothes are often indistinguishable and equally informal. Space-age plastics and protective jumpsuit forms have also influenced fashion, as well as the love for the exotic, the oriental, and the primitive that has so infused the dress and accessories of youth. These clothes of the young, besides being a symbol of rebellion against society, also represent the new romanticism of the present age.

In general, since World War II, one can say that fashion, like art, has become more geometric, often taking its inspiration directly from a painting by Mondrian, an op or pop art design, or the psychedelic patterns based on a revival of *art nouveau*.

CONTEMPORARY

DATES

   1940–   Cold War Period

COMMON TERMS (for others see glossary)

   "The new look"

   A line

   sack dress

   Teddy boy outfits

   mod clothing

   duffle coat

   Eisenhower jacket

   pilot coats

   car coats

   mini skirts

   shifts

   blue jeans

   hippies

   op and pop art

RECOMMENDED SOURCES

   Harper's (1)

   Harper's (2)

   Harper's (3)

   Vogue

   Life Magazine

   Ladies' Home Journal

   Illustrated London News

   Esquire

   Connoisseur

   Holiday

   Studio

   Vingt Ans

   Contini: pp. 306–317

   Boucher: pp. 415–421

   Wilcox (1)

   Wilcox (2)

   Newspaper photographs, magazine illustrations, drawings, fashion plates, catalogs

   Useful illustrators and painters: Kokoschka, Chagall, Picasso, Bérard, Koudine

1950s

Typical Figures

Glossary of Terms
Relating to the History of Costume

EGYPTIAN
(ca. 2980–325 B.C.)

Ankh: A decorative piece symbolizing life, in the shape of a cross and appearing on the crown or carried in the hand.

As: Prince's Lock, which hung down one side of the head.

Crook and Flail: Symbols of the Pharaoh were a crook, originally the boomerang, a flail with three lashes, and a tall animal-headed staff.

Henna: Hand and nail dye, from a shrub or tree whose leaves gave a red-orange dye.

Horus Lock: A braid of false hair worn behind the right ear by fashionable women.

Kalisiris: A tightly molded body-fitting sheath or tunic which stopped underneath the bosom when worn by women.

Kilt: Pleated wraparound skirt worn by men.

King's Apron: A colored triangular apron worn by the Pharaoh; usually carefully decorated.

Klaft: A kerchief which wrapped around the front of the head and fastened at the back of the neck, usually horizontally striped. Later, it was cut away so that it fit over the shoulder, and was decorated heavily with beads and trim.

Kohl: A black cosmetic substance used in Egyptian makeup for eyes and eyebrows.

Menyet: A necklace composed of a hank of green beads, balanced by a gold plaque of equal weight at the other end, which could be carried and waved during religious ceremonies.

Mitre of Osiris: The crown of the North, or Upper Egypt. Also called *Atef.*

Pectoral: A trapezoidal-shaped piece of metal jewelry worn about the neck by nobility.

Postiche: False beard, made of leather, felt, or metal. Reserved for royalty.

Pschent: The red crown of Lower Egypt, worn on the white crown when the two kingdoms of Egypt united.

Sacred Uraeus (Asp): Crowns were often decorated with the uraeus, a rearing viper, the symbol of royalty.

Schenti: A loin cloth; a rectangular piece tied in front in a knot and made of linen.

Stibium: A mixture used for staining eyelids and eyebrows.

Vulture Headdress: A headdress reserved for royalty, symbolic of Maati, Goddess of Truth.

Was and Tsam: Two staffs or scepters, carried by dignitaries to signify support of heaven. Was—straight; Tsam—wavy.

MESOPOTAMIAN
(3400–539 B.C.)

Aba: A robe resembling Egyptian or Persian garments, still worn in Palestine today. Folded rectangle, left unseamed at the sides and held in place by cords under each arm. A garment of virtually the same shape, seamed at the sides and open up the front, was put on like a coat.

Breastplate of Judgment: A 9-inch rectangle, doubled over to form a 4½-inch pocket, ornamented with four rows of jewels, three in a row, which stood for the twelve tribes of Israel.

Caftan: A close-sleeved, long-skirted tunic, trimmed with fringe or tassels on the edges.

Candys (Kandis): A long, flowing cloth gown, looped up to a belt at the sides; with or without voluminous sleeves, widening from shoulder to cuff as the garment itself widened from shoulder to hem.

Catogan: Male or female hair, arranged in a ball at the nape of the neck, sometimes decorated with pins and bands. The hair was often looped or braided.

Ephod: A kind of scapular (two rectangles about 30 inches by 10 inches, fastened together by shoulder straps about 10 inches long), worn on top of the robe. Attached to it was a girdle like that of the Levites, wrapped around the waist and tied in front.

Kaunakes: A long, shaggy skirt, probably closed in front. It was made of hanks of wool fastened in horizontal lines like coarse fringe on cloth, or perhaps twisted locks of wool still fastened to the hide. Sometimes it covered the left shoulder.

Kidaris: Ribbed tiara or embroidered hat, worn by a king.

Kilt: A short wraparound skirt, made of strings or grass; worn by fishermen for protection.

Kulah: High, cylindrical felt hat.

Kyrbasia: A hat similar to the Phrygian bonnet, under the Persian Empire. It also included Median caps with a soft, high crown which fell forward; usually there were flaps at the neck and at either side which could be fastened under the chin.

Petassos: A brimmed sun hat or traveling hat.

Phrygian Bonnet: A segmented conical casque or hat worn by heavily armed Parthian and Sarmathian cavalry.

Phylacteries: Narrow bands of parchment with sacred passages written on them, bound about the foreheads and wrists of devout men.

Tiara: A king's headdress—a truncated conical shape of white felt with a spiked top; purple infulae, two narrow tabs hanging almost to the waist in back.

Tyrian Purple: Purple dye, made from a sea creature, the murex; very rare and very expensive, originally manufactured in the Phoenician city of Tyre. Color most probably a blue-red, a rich plum, or garnet.

AEGEAN AND ARCHAIC GREEK
(3500–490 B.C.)

Catogan: See *Mesopotamian*

Doric Peplos: A garment worn by all Greek women after the sixth century B.C. It was of wool dyed indigo, madder, or saffron, frequently patterned, especially at the turn of the fifth century; used also as a blanket. Its upper edge was folded over to hang down on the breast; it was folded around the body, caught together on each shoulder by pins, leaving the arms uncovered, and though open down the right side, was held in place by the girdle, over which it bloused. In Corinth and Attica it was sewn together down the side below the waistline. With time, the garment grew wider and the overfold deepened so that it was included in the girdling or hung over and concealed the girdle. When not girded, the overfold could be raised over the head in back as a shawl.

Himation: A rectangle of wool with weighted corners, slung over the left shoulder, leaving the right arm free; or worn by married women with the corner over the head like a shawl. Dorian men wore it as their only garment (as did the Athenians in their return to an earlier simplicity, in the third to the second century B.C.). A man wearing the himation alone was always adequately dressed. It served also as a blanket. The colors were gamut (natural wool colors), white, natural, brown, and black, or dyed scarlet, crimson, and purple; woven patterns, selvages, and embroidery were also used.

Ionic Chiton: Of Phoenician origin. It was worn first by men, later by women. It was made of thin woolens, probably crepe-like, similar to materials still woven in Greece; also of linen, or the gauzy materials from Cos in Asia Minor, patterned in murex (Tyrian) purple. It was cut with ample width from two pieces, then sewn together, frequently pleated, and was long, sometimes trailing. It was often sewn or caught together all the way down the arm, into the equivalent of sleeves, and sewn up the right side. It was worn in a number of ways by both men and women. The chiton was often worn with a short wrap, the chlamydon.

Kolobium: A one-piece shirt-like garment worn by men. It opened on the side for the arm rather than along the upper edge as in the chiton. Often it was woven in one piece, with openings cut for arms or head.

Petassos: Wide-brimmed felt hat.

CLASSICAL AND HELLENISTIC GREEK (490–146 B.C.)

Aegis: Animal skin worn with a slit for the head, with the head of the animal, usually a goat, on the breast.

Ampyz: A diadem, female headdress.

Apodesme: Bands of leather used as a brassiere.

Boss: Point on shields and knees (armor).

Buskins: Common men had feet or legs bound or swathed in skin or cloth, called buskins.

Carabitina: A sandal with a large toe, worn by peasants.

Causia: A Thessalonian traveling hat for men or women, worn also by actors to indicate an arduous journey.

Ceryphalos: Bandage-shaped fillet which fitted snugly about the head.

Chlamydon: Short wrap, pleated over a band, which ran from the right shoulder under the left arm. Mainly for women.

Chlamys: A smaller woolen rectangle than the himation, of Macedonian or Italian origin; sometimes bordered, pinned at right shoulder or front; worn with a short chiton or alone, by younger, more active men.

Chloene: Like the chlamys, of coarse wool, worn hooked on one shoulder, running below the other breast; often folded over before fastening; originated in Macedonia or Thessaly.

Cothurnus: Boots to midleg, with platform soles, worn by tragic actors.

Diplax: The female equivalent of the chloene.

Exomia: An intermediate form of sleeveless chiton, caught on one shoulder, worn by athletes and workmen; often of sheepskin or leather.

Fillet: Piece of fabric bound around the head, as a sweatband.

Kolobus: Another form of chiton, which came into use around the beginning of the fourth century B.C. In shape it was two pieces of fabric, cut square and sewn together on the shoulders, leaving an opening in the middle for the head, and sewn down the sides with sufficient space left at the top for the arms to pass through. When the kolobus was girded at the waist, it had very much the same appearance as the chiton, the difference being that the arms emerged at the top edge of the chiton and at the side edge of the kolobus.

Kolpos: The bloused part of the chiton, made by pulling up the chiton over the girdle to make it the proper length from the ground.

Nimbus: A linen headband embroidered with gold.

Peplos: The overfold of the Doric peplos or Doric chiton. Also called *Apotygma*.

Petassos: Wide-brimmed traveling hat, worn also by peasants and shepherds.

Pharos: Linen equivalent of the himation, worn only by noblemen on special occasions.

Phrygian Bonnet: See *Mesopotamian*. Shows Scythian, Persian influence.

Pilos: Cape worn by workmen, shepherds, sailors.

Saccus: A completely enveloping form of hair binding.

Soccus: Comic actor's boot.

Sphendone: A felt, leather, or metal sling, holding up the hair.

Stephanie: A tiara-like crown worn as a headdress by women.

Strophion: A type of corset made of linen, wool, or soft skin, consisting of shoulder straps and three supporting bands, one for the bust, one for the waist, and one for the hips.

Tellex: Hair binding for athletes; refers to segmented windings around the hair, which was clubbed at the neck. Also called *Cricket*.

Tribon: A small oblong cloak of Balkan origin, worn by Spartan males over the age of twelve as the only garment.

ROMAN
(146 B.C.–A.D. 323)

Bracchae (Braeis): Northern English breeches, tied with strings, worn by Roman provincial soldiers.

Bulla: Medallion put around a male child's neck to ward off evil until he became an adult.

Calcaeus: Strapped, cut-out, and laced sandals, varying in height from ankle to well up the calf. Senators wore black, patricians and magistrates wore purple.

Caligula: Heavy, often hobnailed, military boots, rising well up on the leg.

Chlamys: Semicircular cape, hung over the left arm and fastened by a fibula or clasp at the right shoulder. It continued for many centuries as the outer garment for the upper classes of Western Europe.

Clavii: Purple bands on the tunica indicating the wearer's rank. With time, the clavus lost distinction, and by the first century it was worn by everyone. The clavii then became more elaborately decorative in character, broke into spots of decoration and amalgamated with borders at the hem of the garment. *Augustus Clavus:* For equestrian knights; narrow bands running up over each shoulder and down to the hem on tunic or ungirded dalmatic. *Latus Clavus:* Single wide clavus worn by senators down the center of the tunica.

Colobium: The Greek kolobus. It was like the tunica although sleeveless. When more than one tunica was worn, the undertunics were called the tunica interior or subucula.

Crepida: Half-shoes, soles to which a piece of leather or fabric was attached to enclose the heel and sides of the foot. Fastened across the instep by straps or bands laced through eyelet holes set in the sides.

Cuculla: An overdress without sleeves, practically an oblong piece of cloth with a hole in the middle for the head. Used by all classes as a protection from weather and when traveling. Later prescribed for monks of the Benedictine order. (About 1500, given the name of scapular as an ecclesiastical garment.)

Dalmatica: An outer garment, originally male. Introduced ca. 190 A.D. from Dalmatia. Prominent in Rome by the third century A.D., it was cut like a tunic, but wider, with wide sleeves to the forearm. It went on over the head, was worn without a girdle, and was characteristically decorated by the clavus.

Flameum: Veil of the Roman matron.

Lacerna: Cloak similar to the chlamys, but light and short, worn by everyone in the last century of the Republic. Even senators wore it, in place of the toga, although this was frowned upon.

Lorica: A cuirass of brass or bronze, molded to the shape of the body with perfect fit and following the line of the abdomen. Frequently enriched with reliefs and ornaments in metal work.

Mappa: Used at table for wiping the mouth and hands, after washing, before and after a meal, in a basin brought by a slave.

Orarium: Large napkin, carried by servants and slaves over the left shoulder and used for cleaning vessels of all sorts.

Paenula: A hooded, bell-shaped, weatherproof garment of leather or wool. It was already in use by the Etruscans in the fourth century B.C. It was worn by everyone, civil and military, particularly by centurions.

Pallium (Palla, f.): Roman outdoor garment which could also be used as a bed covering. It was originally Greek, and in Rome it was draped like a Greek himation, held by a fibula, not hooked as in Greece. It was a rectangle as wide as from the wearer's shoulder to the floor, about three times as long, and was worn by men, women, children, civil servants, and military. Women wore the palla outdoors, often draped over the head but always in conjunction with a veil or cap. The pallium was the characteristic garment of the scholar and philosopher (as the sole garment, it was the conventional mantle of Christ).

Paludamentum: A purely military mantle, used as the official military mantle of the general in command, or the Emperor while in the field. Used particularly in the earlier years, before the first century A.D. In cut, it resembled the chlamys or lacerna, with two corners truncated to form an elongated, primitive semicircle.

Saggum: Gallic in origin. Became the military wrap of the Roman army, used also as a blanket. Generals, also, wore it in red and purple. "Putting on the saggum" was the equivalent of declaring war. Square in shape, of thick, heavy, tightly woven wool.

Soccus, Cothurnus: Other terms for caligula.

Solea: Strapped slippers, like sandals.

Stola: Woman's garment. Worn over the tunica intima (which was of similar cut, might or might not have sleeves, and which served as a house dress). The stola had sleeves like the men's tunica, or was pinned along the shoulder line and down the arms. It was girded once under the breast and often girded again at the hips.

Sublagaculum: Small garment or piece of cloth, worn bound around the hips as a loincloth. This was worn under the toga, or frequently without any other covering. It was a fashion copied from the Greeks, who themelvses derived it from the Egyptians and Assyrians.

Sudarium: Small piece of fine linen, often embroidered with silk or gold and equivalent to the modern handkerchief.

Toga: General: Outer garment, which was the badge of the Roman citizen, rich or poor. Originally, the rectangular Greek pallium made into an ellipse, the draping of which was infinitely complicated. Of wool, it was characteristically white.

    Toga Candida: Worn plain by candidates for public office.

    Toga Picta: Purple embroidered official robe of the Emperor, worn over the tunica palmata and, in the second century A.D., became part of the official garb of Roman consuls. Essentially a ceremonial dress, it constituted the correct costume of the court during the whole of the Empire period, until the center of government was transferred to Constantinople, where it was superseded by the paludamentum. From the toga picta all imperial and regal robes have descended.

    Toga Praetexta: Had a purple hem; worn by senators, certain officials, and priests.

    Toga Pulla: Black, worn as a mourning robe, or for sacrifices; of darker colored wools, worn draped over the head.

    Toga Pura: Natural-colored wool, not a bleached white; worn by the Roman citizen.

    Toga Trabea: Worn by the equestrian knights, small toga striped in scarlet; basically white for soldiers.

    Toga Umbo or Contabulatum: The ordinary toga, with a red or purple band, draped so that a pocket or pouch was formed. Came into fashion among high dignitaries toward the end of the second century A.D.

    Toga Virilis: An all-white toga, worn by young males, fourteen to sixteen years of age.

Tunica: Wide, shirt-like undergarment, the indoor dress of the Roman; worn outdoors without the toga only by working people. It was not, like the toga, distinctly Roman. Originally sleeveless and woolen, usually white, it acquired sleeves and was later made of linen and cotton as well. The tunic was girded with meticulous care to the exact length considered correct for the rank and sex of the wearer.

    Tunica Interior or Subucula: Another name for the colobium.

    Tunica Palmata: Part of the official garb of emperors. With the toga picta, it constituted part of the ornamenta triumphalia. Decorated richly and elaborately with gold embroideries of conventional foliage. It was also usual to have the tunica embroidered all over with the same design as that used on the toga picta, in circular, square, and lozenge-shaped motifs, with a border at the neck, wrists, and bottom.

    Tunica Talaris: Fell to the feet and had long, loose sleeves; it was the marriage dress for men, but was looked down upon by the citizens of Rome and did not compete with the short tunic until the fourth century A.D.

EARLY CHRISTIAN AND ECCLESIASTICAL
(323–604 A.D.)

Alb: A liturgical vestment of the Catholic church; derived from the tunica alba, which passed out of Roman civil use in the sixth century. Of white linen, narrow sleeved, slit for the head to pass through, and girded to clear the ground. Worn over the cassock and under other liturgical garments.

Amice: The first liturgical vestment to be assumed by the priest vesting himself for Mass. Developed out of the Roman neckcloth, it is a strip of linen laid hood-like over the head, dropped to the shoulders, and tied in position around the upper body wtih tapes sewed to two corners, forming a collar.

Cassock: Originally derived from the daily wear of the dignified and elderly, it was retained by the Catholic church after the change in lay fashions in the seventh and eighth centuries. It is now the ordinary dress of the Roman Catholic and, to a more limited extent, the Church of England clergy, on which vestments, eucharistic and processional, and monastic habit are superimposed. Its color is black, purple, red, black with red pipings, or white, all of which indicate rank: priest, bishop, cardinal or pope. Monk's cassocks are the color of the order.

Chasuble: Outermost and one of the most important liturgical garments of the Catholic church. Its shape has varied by period and country, but it is essentially a cape of silk or metallic cloth (never linen or cotton), with a hole for the head, shortened at the sides to the shoulder to leave the arms uncovered, and falling down the front and back. Derived from the Roman paenula or casula, it was originally a barbaric garment to ward off bad weather.

Cope: A liturgical vestment of the Catholic church and a choir vestment of some Anglican churches; it is a semicircular cape embroidered or brocaded and fastened across the chest by a wide ornamental band. This is sewn to one edge and hooked or pinned by a jeweled morse to the other. It has a vestigial hood or embroidered flap hanging down the back. It usually substitutes for the chasuble in all ceremonies outside the Mass.

Dalmatic: A knee-length, wide-sleeved gown slit up the sides, it derives from the Roman dalmatica and is decorated with two vertical stripes over the shoulder to the hem—taken from the augusta clavii of Roman dress. The dalmatic of a bishop is fringed on both sides and sleeves, and that of a deacon is fringed on the left side and left sleeve only. Since the fourth century, the dalmatic has been a vestment worn as a festal garment during Mass, benedictions, and processions. It can be worn under the chasuble, never under the cope.

Maniple: A narrow strip of silk three feet long, decorated with three crosses hung or fastened over the left forearm. It is one of four distinctly Roman contributions to liturgical costume, originally a linen handkerchief or cloth derived from the folded consular mappula. It is part of liturgical vestments of all orders above subdeacon.

Mitre: A liturgical headdress of the Catholic church specifically worn by bishops but occasionally worn by abbots and other church dignitaries. It is a high hat composed of two identical stiffened pieces which fold flat against one another when not spread horn-like by the head; from the back hang two narrow fringed strips. It seems to have developed out of the cone-shaped caps of the early popes, which in turn may relate back to the mitres of the Hebrews.

Pallium: A vestment worn by Catholic archbishops, it is a woven band of white lamb's wool "three fingers broad," worn over the chasuble. Derived from the Roman pallium, it was originally a longer strip draped over both shoulders and pinned to the left one; now it is a strip decorated with four crosses, made into a circle, which is dropped on the shoulders and pinned front and back.

Pastoral Staff: A five-foot staff that is the insignia for cardinals, bishops, and abbots of the Catholic church. Heads were originally of four kinds: shepherd's crook, the knobbed crook, the bent crook, and the cross or crozier top. Today, either the crozier or the pastoral shepherd's crook is seen.

Stole: A liturgical vestment of the Catholic church for Mass, never for processional use. It is a long strip of material, usually silk, now decorated by three crosses at the ends and middle, and frayed at the hem. It is worn over the shoulder in different ways and is characteristic of deacon, priest, or bishop. It probably descended from the *orarion,* adopted by the Emperor Aurelian in the third century to be waved in applause at games.

Surplice: Originally, as the Latin name indicates, it was worn over fur-lined garments. Made of white linen like the alb, it was initially long, then became much shorter after the thirteenth century. It is usually trimmed in lace or embroidery.

Tunicle: A garment peculiar to deacons at Mass; bishops wear it under the dalmatic, but always under the chasuble, never under the cope. It is basically a plainer, narrower-sleeved dalmatic without clavii and usually fringed.

BYZANTINE
(323–1453 A.D.)

Bracco or Braies: Semiclose-fitting leg covering sometimes worn over hose; used with or without cross gartering.

Camisa or Chemise: An undergarment with long sleeves that showed beneath the sleeves of the outer garment for women.

Colobium: A garment similar to the Greek kolobus; made of linen or wool and sewn on the sides and at the shoulder if not woven all in one piece.

Dalmatica: One of the most important garments of the Byzantine Empire, it had the same general wide-sleeved shape as in Roman days but with far more embroidery and decoration.

Hosa: A close-fitting covering for the leg.

Lorum: A long, narrow scarf originating from the pallium and worn with Byzantine court costume from the eighth to the twelfth centuries.

Orb: A celestial sphere usually topped with a cross, carried by the emperor and empress.

Paludamentum: The Roman general's cloak now became the half-circular imperial mantle of rich material, often of purple silk embroidered in gold or gold and jewels.

Pedule: Short hose usually turned down at the knee.

Sarcenet: A fine, thin silk cloth originating in the orient and named from the Saracen.

Segmentae: Embroidered circular decorations worn on the sleeve of a tunica or dalmatica.

Sudarium: A handkerchief, often embroidered with silver or gold.

Superhumeral: A jeweled collar, usually worn by the empress or ladies of the court.

Tablion: The very elaborate oblong decoration embroidered in red and gold on the back and front of the imperial mantle. For other high officials and courtiers it varied in color.

ROMANESQUE
(400–1200 A.D.)

Amusse: A hood with a small cape worn by monks and the nobility.

Barbe or Barbette: A piece of linen, often pleated, worn under the chin, especially by a widow or a person in mourning.

Bliaut: A garment worn by men and women, it originated about 1130 in the East and was brought to Europe with the end of the First Crusade. As worn by the upper classes at the end of the twelfth century, it consisted of a snug-fitting torso, often wide embroidered sleeves, a low skirt pulled into elegant pleats across the hips, and snug lacing up the back or under each arm. It is one of the first garments to depend on fit as well as cut.

Cagoule: A semicircular cape of cloth or fur, with a hood; usually worn by peasants.

Cainsil or Chainsil: A very fine, lightweight or heavyweight cloth of simple weave.

Capuchon: A hood usually attached to a cape,

often with a long tail later known as a liripipe.

Caul: Close-fitting gold hairnet worn by ladies of the aristocracy.

Chape: Similar to mantle, sometimes slit at sides with cap-like or long, loose sleeve.

Chaplet: A headband of gold or silver filigree, set with jewels, flowers, or leaves.

Chausses: Leg coverings of cloth, shaped and sewn to fit.

Chemise: A long feminine undergarment with tight sleeves and a skirt frequently showing from beneath the underdress.

Coif: A close-fitting cap of silk, linen, or cotton, tied under the chin. A circlet or band of jewels might be worn over the coif by royalty.

Corsage: A tight-fitting, sleeveless jacket resembling a corset, worn over the bliaut.

Corse: A tight-fitting, sleeveless jacket of leather or metal disks laced up the front and worn under a male tunic or bliaut.

Cote, Cotte, or Cotta: A long tunic with the sleeve cut in one piece with the garment. The length varied from the calf to the instep.

Crispine or Crispinette: A headdress of gold net and pearls.

Diaper: Silk, linen, or cotton cloth of one color woven in a sprinkled ornamental pattern.

Fibula: The heavy metal or jewel-encrusted brooch used to fasten the mantle at the shoulder.

Girdle: A type of waistband or belt that encircles the hips.

Gorget: A wimple or couverchief worn under the chin and tucked under the neckline of the gown.

Gown: A "gunn" (from the Anglo-Saxon) was a tunic for women somewhat like the Roman and Byzantine stola.

Guimpe: A chemise worn with a low-cut dress.

Gypsire: A pouch or bag worn at the hip from which alms were given.

Head Rail: A colorful rectangular veil draped over the head and shoulder from left to right, passed around the neck and tied under the chin.

Jube or Jupe: An undergarment or shirt, some-times fur lined; worn by both men and women.

Kirtle: Anglo-Saxon for tunic.

Liripipe: The long, pointed tail on a hood.

Rheno: A mantle without a hood.

Sherte: A straight, knee-length garment with slits at front, back, and sides, resembling a modern shirt.

Smock: Innermost garment of fine linen worn by women.

Surcot or Surcoat: A loose, lightweight garment originally worn by the Crusader over his armor as a protection against the sun. It soon became an overtunic worn over the cotte, sometimes unseamed, sometimes sleeveless, sometimes with wide-open sleeves like a dalmatic. It could be belted or unbelted, and the length varied from the knee to the ankle.

Wimple or Couverchief: A fine silk or linen covering for the head, usually brought under the chin and pinned to the gown and to the head; frequently worn with a separate gorget under the chin.

EARLY GOTHIC
(1200–1350)

Aglet, Aiglet, Point, or Poynt: A metal tag or point used to fasten pieces of plate armor, or various parts of other garments such as sleeves and paltock.

Bateau Neckline: A boat-shaped neckline.

Button: A solid, dome-shaped top, with an eye at the base, used as trimming at the beginning of the Middle Ages; used as a fastening with buttonholes from the middle of the thirteenth century on.

Castellated, Dagged, or Foliated: Deep-cut scallops at the hem or other edges of a garment shaped in triangles, half-circles, squares, or leaf-like foliations.

Cointise or Quintise: Cut-out decoration of the cyclas; also applied to a garment so decorated.

Coronet: An ornamental circlet worn about the head.

Cotehardie: A shaped garment, tight-fitting around the shoulder, waist, and hips. When worn by a woman it had a circular skirt; when worn by a man it usually ended at the hips or slightly below, often with dagged or scalloped edges. It could be hooked or laced up either the front or the back.

Cyclas: An overgarment cut from a single piece of cloth, with a hole in the center for the head, sometimes lined with fur or silk.

Emblem or Badge: The distinguishing symbol worn by the Crusader which developed into the system of heraldry.

Ganache or Garnache: A surcoat or robe with short, caped sleeves worn for extra warmth.

Gardcorps: A surcoat or robe with hanging sleeves slit to allow the arms to pass through.

Gueules: A small, fur-lined shoulder cape with the lower corners of the cape turned back in front; it was usually attached to the peliçon.

Herlot or Lachet: A string used to tie the hose to the paltock or the sleeve in the armhole of the paltock.

Paltock: A short jacket to which undersleeves and hose were attached, later called pourpoint.

Particolored or Pied: A two-colored garment, often with one side embroidered.

Passemente: Gold, silver, and colored braid.

Pel;çon: Any fur-lined garment of robe length.

Plastron: A type of garment which later became the stomacher. It was most frequently of fur and was worn as a decorative front to a female costume.

Tippet: A band sewn around the elbow of the sleeve with the end hanging as a streamer.

Toque: A pillbox-shaped headdress worn by women in the thirteenth century attached either to a barbe or barbette, or worn with a caul or crispinette.

MIDDLE GOTHIC
(1350–1425)

Bellows or Bagpipe Sleeve: A gathered sleeve with a cuff and a long vertical slit through which the hand could pass.

Castellated: Square or rectangular dagges or cuts into the hem or edge of a garment; named after the wall tops of castles.

Chaperone: A caped hood with long liripipe, worn with the face opening around the head and the tail or liripipe wound about the head and then draped under the chin.

Corset: A fitted garment worn over the chemise with skirt attached and usually laced up the front.

Courtepy or Jacquette: A very short overgarment or cotehardie, often particolored or embroidered with gems. It usually had a high collar.

Cracow or Poulaine: A long-tipped hose and shoe introduced during the reign of Richard II and named after the city of Cracow in Poland; later the length of the toe became so long that it had to be tied to the knee.

Doublet or Doblet: A short jacket or variety of pourpoint, sleeved or sleeveless, worn under a close-fitting pourpoint. When used as an outer garment it was padded and had a short skirt.

Galoche: A wooden platform with an ornamental strap fastening the base beneath the heel and ball of the foot; elevated to varying heights.

Hennin or Cornet: A truncated cone or steeple headdress with veil completely covering the female hairdo.

Houppelande: A loose and comfortable gown of great size introduced during the reign of Charles VI in France which became very fashionable during the reign of Richard II in England. One style worn by men had long, flowing, bell-shaped sleeves, a long, fitted waist, and a floor-length skirt slit to the knees; another style, known as the "bastard houppelande," was only knee to calf length. A high standing collar was usually part of this flamboyant costume. The woman's version of this robe had a soft, open collar, a short waist, a full skirt, and long, flowing sleeves.

Journade: A short, circular garment which at first had large, full sleeves and later had long, slit sleeves. It was often worn for riding.

Jupe: A form of shirt or undertunic, sometimes fur lined; worn by both men and women.

Jupon: An overgarment having armorial blazonry, worn over armor in the fourteenth century; the term sometimes was also used to refer to a petticoat.

Mahoitres: The name given to the shoulder padding of a gown or jacket.

Patten: Iron support worn under a shoe.

Plastron: A stomacher-shaped appendage, usually of fur or embroidered fabric, worn at the front of the sideless gown as both support and decoration.

Pomander: A ball or hollow ornament, often made of filigree, containing a sponge of perfume suspended from a necklace or a girdle.

Pourpoint: A short jacket with tight sleeves buttoned from elbow to wrist, worn under the cotehardie and formerly known as a paltock.

Reticulation: Decorative metal cages which confined the hair at the side of a woman's head.

Roundel or Roundlet: A headdress made of a doughnut-shaped roll of material with a scarf or liripipe hanging down one side and draped over the shoulder.

Sideless Gown: A woman's overgown cut away at the sides from under the arms to the hips to show the cotehardie or kirtle underneath; it was usually worn with a plastron at the front of the figure.

Tussoire: A chain and clasp which hung from the girdle and held up one side of a long skirt.

LATE GOTHIC
(1425–1485)

Bag Cap: A cloth or velvet brimless cap with fur band and ornament which resembled a turban.

Butterfly Headdress: Made of semitransparent linen, it was draped and wired to resemble a butterfly and was worn over a tall hennin.

Cracow or Poulaine: See *Middle Gothic.*

Escarelle: A pouch or purse attached to the waist on a hip belt, into which a knife was frequently inserted.

Escoffion: A tall, richly brocaded headdress, sometimes shaped like two horns, sometimes like a narrow, tall turban; it usually had a veil of fine lawn about a yard wide.

Hennin: See *Middle Gothic.*

Journade: See *Middle Gothic.*

Kirtle: A dress which evolved from the cotehardie after 1450. It was close fitting at the shoulder, waist, and hip and had a very full skirt. The neckline, edged in fur, velvet, or brocade, was very low in front, on the shoulders, and in the back.

Liripipe: Still retained from the chaperone as a tail of material coming from the doughnut shape of the roundel, draping under the chin and over one shoulder.

Pourpoint: The name usually given to the short jacket with a pleated skirt during this period. Sleeves were either full at the top and tapering to the wrists, open and hanging behind a tight undersleeve, or slashed to allow the arm to come through.

Roundel: The doughnut-shaped, turban-like headdress worn by most men of fashion until the latter part of the fifteenth century.

Sideless Gown: This gown, cut away under the arms to the hips, was usually covered with armorial bearings and remained the ceremonial dress for women during this period.

RENAISSANCE
(1485–1520)

Barret: A flat Spanish cap of gorgeous material which was slashed, puffed, and embroidered.

Bases: Sixteenth-century cartridge-pleated skirts for men, worn separate from the doublet. To be noted in many portraits of Henry VIII.

Breeches or Hosen: Leg coverings, either cut from fabric or knitted, all in one piece.

Calotte: A cape or coat, usually of expensive material, over which the barret was worn.

Caul: Developed from the crespinette. A meshwork covering for the hair, sometimes edged with jewels in a border.

Clog, Chopine, or Patten: A wooden-soled platform attached to the shoe, worn as a protection from mud and to gain height.

Codpiece: A pouch-like appendage made from the same fabric as the jerkin or upper stocks and fastened by ties or buckles as a decorative covering for the opening in the front of breeches.

Jerkin: A short velvet or leather jacket, usually sleeveless.

Kirtle: A dress which evolved from the cotehardie about 1480. It was close fitting at shoulder, waist, and hips and had a full skirt.

Little Hennin: A headdress shaped like a truncated cone.

Mancheron: A false, hanging sleeve.

Pantoffle: A mule or slipper with a cork sole, worn as a protection for the shoe.

Points: Metal-tipped ribbons or lacings sewn in corresponding pairs to sleeves and armseyes or to doublet and hose.

Simarre: A robe for men, derived from chimer or chimere, an ecclesiastical garment very much like it in shape. The neck part is shaped somewhat on a double-breasted line with no collar in back, but with wide revers turned back from the front edge of the robe. The robe is worn either ungirded or confined at the waist by a narrow silk scarf, knotted with one loop and two ends.

Slashing (Puffs and Slashes): Vertical, horizontal, or diagonal slits in the fabric of the garment through which appeared a fabric different from that of the garment which was slashed. Often the shirt was the garment which puffed through.

Solleret: A shoe with a rounded toe.

LATER RENAISSANCE (1520–1560)

Barbe: Pleated neck and shoulder covering with a hood (or béguine) worn by widows until the time of Catherine de Medici, when it was replaced by a wired-out hood, dipping low over the forehead or carried out into a beak. For the white mourning of a young queen (i.e., Mary of Scotland), a veiled hood over a wired cap and a pleated barbe under the chin was worn.

Basquine: A fitted restraining underbodice of heavy material used in the late fifteenth century. Origin of the term Basque.

Bombast: Stuffing of wool, flax, or hair.

Busk: A rigid piece of wood set in the fake front or stomacher, which gave a straight line effect.

Cale: Bag of black velvet to conceal the hair; for the gable headdress or for the French hood.

Chain or Order: A heavy chain worn by a man as decoration across the chest and neckline which often denoted an order or organization to which the man belonged.

Chamarre: Large, square piece of fabric, slit up the front vertically and into a T-shape to leave a neck opening; a collar was attached to the top of the T-shaped slit and the sides folded back into revers. Worn as a coat and principally a French style.

Cordelière: A long chain, usually of gold, which hung from the girdle.

Duck-Billed Shoes (Also called *Splay-Footed*): Very wide, square-toed, slipper-like shoes, usually decorated with jewels, puffs, and slashes.

Fall: Like the cale, for the gable headdress, of black silk or velvet.

Farthingale: Hoops of graduated size inserted in a petticoat. Of several types. See also *Elizabethan.*

Fraise: A small ruff which edged the standing collar. It is said that Henry II adopted the neckline to hide a scar.

Gable Headdress (Also *Kennel* or *Pedimental*): Resembled in outline the pediment of a Greek temple. Its essentials were a piece which went over the front part of the head and covered the ears and a veil or bag cap covering the rest of the head; the forehead was covered with rolls or folds of cloth. With the formal styles of this headdress, no hair was visible. There were, however, linen coifs shaped in the same outline which left the parted hair visible on the forehead. The front roll was of diagonally striped material or velvet. The kennel consisted of a stiff plane covered with rich material, pieces of which extended down the sides and might be pinned back on themselves. The cap at the back, joining the kennel, was like a bag with a square bottom. One side was turned back and pinned to the other at the back of the head. The bag was generally of black velvet.

Lower Stocks or Bas de Chausses: Silk or cloth stockings showing beneath upper stocks or trunk hose.

Mary Stuart Cap: A heart-shaped cap worn by the Scottish queen.

Medici Collar: The lace-edged ruff which opened into a standing fan-shaped frill, high in the back with low decolletage. Accompanied by cuffs to match.

Morion: Brimmed helmet; English, Spanish.

Panes: Loose, vertical bands used on sleeves, doublets, and trunk hose.

Shakefold: A stiffened pad on a wire frame, an early form of farthingale. The name was given to this part of the garment because it swayed back and forth as the wearer moved.

Stomacher: False front or ornamental covering on front of bodice.

Trunk Hose, Melon Hose, or Haut-de-chausses: Upper hose or full trunks that extended from upper thighs to waist.

ELIZABETHAN—JACOBEAN (1560–1620)

Aglet, Aiglet, Point, or Poynt: A metal tag or point used to fasten armor or various parts of other garments including sleeves and hose to a paltock or underdoublet.

Baldrick: Some kind of band, ribbon, or leather, usually to hold a sword; goes through several centuries. Here, a shoulder sash of satin, the fashion for both men and women; white was reserved only for the King.

Basquine: A boned bodice resembling a corset.

Bombast: Padding for shaped breeches, composed of flock, rags, or any other serviceable material. Also used to stuff the peascod belly.

Busk: A rigid piece of wood set in a fake front or stomacher to give a straight line effect.

Canions: (Upper stocks.) Virtually tight knee breeches. The lower edges were covered by the nether stocks or stockings, usually rolled above the knee and secured by garters.

Cartwheel Vertugale or Farthingale: The circular wheel support worn under the full, drum-shaped hoop skirt, also with underskirt.

Chopines: High clogs, worn by Spanish women, serving both to increase their stature and to protect them from the surfaces of dusty roads. These were usually made of cork covered with leather or velvet. They came to Europe from the Middle East by way of Venice.

Codpiece: The stuffed and slashed appendage at the front opening of male hose.

Cross Gartering: Criss-crossed bands, ribbons, or cords tied below the knee.

Falling Band: Wide, flat collar, known as the Louis XIII collar, of sheer white fabric, with or without lace edge. Bands diminished in size from about 1640.

Fers: Metal buttons used by a woman of rank, worn as decoration on costume.

Galligaskins: Loose knee trousers that remained wide and open at the knee.

Gauntlets: Elbow-length gloves of velvet or satin, silk- or gold-fringed, with backs embroidered or sewn with jewels; for courtier wear.

Golilla: The starched, dish-like neckband introduced by Philip IV of Spain. It remained in favor for some fifteen years after his pragmatic of 1623 against the large ruff (gran gola). It was worn usually in conjunction with plain turned-back wristbands.

Jerkin: An outergarment, often of leather, which had a shoulder puff or wing, sometimes hanging sleeves or tied-in sleeves; it was worn over the doublet.

Kirtle: Fundamental woman's garment of the period, often composed of the two separate parts which go to make up its form— the bodice and the skirt. For most of this period these two elements of the kirtle had emphatically contrasting forms, the bodice tapering to a sharp point at or below the waistline, while the skirt was in the shape of an upright cone, bell, or drum. The skirt derived its form from the shape of the farthingale.

Neck whisk: A standing, fan-shaped, wired collar.

Pantoffles: Shoes or pumps of crimson, red, or violet velvet; cut in the shape of a lobster tail.

Peascod Belly: A padded doublet with a front shaped like a peascod.

Picadil: The tabbed finish on the edge of a garment; also a collar support or underprop at tabs.

Shoe Roses: Large ribbon ties in the form of rosettes for men's shoes; worn at the buckle, with heeled shoes, during the reign of James I.

Shoulder Wings or Crescents: Decorative pieces extending outward at the shoulder of the doublet.

Slops: Unpadded trunk hose, termed Spanish slops. Very full breeches, bagging at the knees, were termed full slops. Small, very short trunk hose were called pansid slops.

Under Proper or Rebato: A frame to hold up ornate, starched lace collars.

Venetians: Full, loose breeches without codpieces, fastening below the knee.

EARLY BAROQUE OR CAVALIER (1620–1660)

Bucket-Top Boot: Wide-topped boot, sometimes turned in a large cuff.

Cadanette: Lovelock, a long curl or strand over one shoulder, tied with a ribbon or a string with a rosette.

Canons: A lace flounce attached just below the knee to the same stocking which was drawn up over the breeches.

Casaque: A loose greatcoat, with big sleeves, usually three-quarter in length, with turned-back cuffs.

Galant: Ties or loops of ribbons used on sleeve, bodice, or skirt.

Lovelock: Plait or curl of hair near left ear and tied with a ribbon; worn by both men and women.

La Modeste, la Friponne, la Secret: The modish woman of the period wore a chemise, a corset, then several petticoats over the vertugale, or hoop. The hoop had grown smaller but continued to be worn until 1630. Over that was the gown, consisting of skirt and bodice or stomacher, with sleeves of light-colored satin or other fabric. Over that, a robe or sort of redingote of darker or contrasting colored material opened the full length in front. The robe usually had slashed sleeves showing the undersleeves. This robe was generally worn until 1645. The outer robe was called la modeste, and when there were two skirts the outer one was called la friponne (hussy, in English), the under one la secret.

Pantoffle: Type of soft slipper.

Pinners: In women's dresses, aprons of exquisite workmanship, matching lingerie accessories, such as sheer lingerie cuffs and collar.

Points: See *Elizabethan, Aglet.*

RESTORATION OR MIDDLE BAROQUE (1660–1685)

Boot Hose: Ornamental topped stocking worn under boots, the decorated edge of which fell over the top of the boot.

Canons or Cannons: Bunches of ribbon loops affixed at the knee from 1660–1670.

Cassock: Between 1650 and 1660 or 1670, the doublet of Charles I's reign was sometimes lengthened almost to the knee. Like its predecessor, it could be worn either belted or beltless, but following the new trend it had a lower waistline; its skirts flared slightly. Except for length, it was essentially like the modern clerical cassock.

Cravat: Any type of neck dressing other than a collar. Of various types through several periods. Here, the rabat, or lace falling band with round corners, became broad and long, and the jabot, or frill on the shirt front, frequently appeared with it. By the end of the 1670s the ends of the cravat became full lace tabs, tied under the chin with a "cravat string," which was of ribbon or lace.

Culotte: Breeches tied below the knee and trimmed in braid.

Echelon: Bowknots of graduated size on the stomacher. The bodice often laced in back, but when fastened in front it had jeweled clasps, buttons, or many bowknots with which to fasten it.

Falbala: Ruffle of lace on sleeve falling three-quarter or elbow length.

Galants or Favors: Bunches of ribbon loops of variegated colors. Extravagant ornamentation in passementerie of gold or silver; laces and ribbons became the standard decoration for women's dress.

Hurluburlu: Short curls worn over the entire head; introduced by Mme de Maintenon, 1670.

Justaucorps: A long, fitted coat with full skirt, buttoned down the front, with sleeves usually turned back in large cuffs; replaced cassock about 1675–1680.

Lavallière: A necklace with a pendant, worn by Louise de la Vallière, first mistress of Louis XIV; the style became known as the lavallière.

Manteau: The formal female gown of the period of Louis XIV. The overskirt was looped back and held by ribbon bows. The looped-up folds were often bunched in back over an underskirt of taffeta, the looped-up outer skirt of brocaded silk ended in a train, the length of which was determined by the lady's social position. The train was carried over the left arm, except in the presence of royalty, when it trailed on the floor.

Montero: A round fur cap with a turned-up brim.

Palatine: A small shoulder cape introduced in 1671 by the Princess Palatine to avoid exposing her shoulders.

Peruque: (Periwig—a misconstruction of the French word *peruque.*) The peruque, or wig, gained favor during the period of Louis XIV, at a time when hair was worn shoulder length in flowing curls. Then the head was regularly shaved and the wig took the place of the man's own hair. At first, it was made to look like natural hair, but eventually an artificial effect was cultivated. Masses of ringlets fell over the shoulders and down the back. By 1660, wig making in France reached such a stage of perfection that the French peruque was in demand all over Europe.

Petticoat Breeches (Rhinegrave Breeches): Full breeches, ending in deep ruffles or canons.

There were two styles of petticoat breeches; one which resembled a kilt, the other like a divided skirt. By about 1660 the breeches were so wide that it is not always easy to distinguish between rhinegrave breeches and a short skirt. In certain cases, although they still fell under the heading of breeches, the legs of these garments attained a width of six feet.

Rabat: A type of cravat, with a vertically pleated or gathered fall.

Taure: A hairdress resembling a bull's head, introduced in 1673.

LATE BAROQUE
(1685–1715)

À la Maintenon: A coiffure with hair parted in the center, trimmed in graduated lengths, curled and fluffed; designed by Mme Martin, hairdresser to Mme de Maintenon.

Apron: A length of cloth hemmed and usually ornamented, gathered into a waistband having long, ornamental strings; worn at the front of a full court gown.

Cravat: More variations during this period of the wrapped neckcloth or cravat which first appeared during the reign of Louis XIV.

Falbalas: Heavy ruffles, the name of which, when anglicized, became the "furbelows." The ruffles, gathered up the center, were used as decoration on women's garments.

Fontange: In 1680, the Duchesse de Fontanges, having her hat blown off at a royal hunting party, tied her curls in place with her garter, arranging a bow with ends in front. From that incident grew tier upon tier of up-standing wired and pleated ruffles of lawn, lace, and ribbons fastened to a cap. The hair dressed in that fashion was called "coiffure à la fontange," and the cap with its narrow rising front was known as "le bonnet à la fontange." The cap often had two floating lappets of ribbon or lace in back, and over the whole arrangement was often worn the black silk hood or kerchief. In 1691 the headdress was reduced to two tiers of pleats and became known as the commode.

Habit à la français: Adhering to the three fundamentals of coat, vest, and breeches, set in the reign of Louis XIV, it was perfected in design during the Regency, then became the formal attire of the gentlemen of Europe and lasted a century. The coat retained its name, "habit à la français," and its cut to the end of the eighteenth century. It was slashed up the center back to the waist, originally necessary for riding. The sleeves, usually split part way up in the back, were straight with wide cuffs. The skirt of the coat, reaching to the knees, was reinforced with linen, buckram, or whalebone and cut to flare when buttoned at the waist.

Mante: The wrap of the period for women. A short scarf-like cape, edged with ruffles or lace. This wrap and the manteau were probably made of silk imported from Italy and called Mantua silk. Mantes or broad scarfs of gold or silver tissue were worn only by women of high rank at court.

Manteau: A loose, beltless, coat-like robe worn at home for a negligée. It was not unlike the kimono version of modern times and was a dark color or black.

Palatine: A small cape introduced by the Princess Palatine ca. 1671.

Passecaille: The ribbon on which a muff was hung.

Pèlerine: A short shoulder cape, usually with long ends hanging down in front.

Periwig: See *Peruque.*

Peruque: Continuation and variation of the false wig which was introduced during the previous period.

Pretintailles: Cut-out motifs of lace or gold embroidery, appliquéd or gummed to the bottoms of skirts, making elaborate ornamentation.

Ramillies Wig: Of English origin, named in honor of the Battle of Ramillies, won by the Duke of Marlborough. The wig had one or two hanging braids tied top and bottom with black ribbon. Later, the end of the braid was often looped under and tied.

Roquelaure: A large, full overcoat with cape, named after the Duc de Roquelaure.

Spatter Dashes: High leather leggings which

came in ca. 1700. The joining of legging and shoe was covered by spur leathers.

Steinkirk: A scarf of lace or lawn loosely tied, with the ends casually twisted into the vest or shirt front or drawn through a buttonhole or ring. Black silk steinkirks were also worn. These were introduced in the 1690s and were named after the Battle of Steinkirk, where the hurriedly garbed French, unable to take time to tie their cravats, twisted the ends through buttonholes in their coats.

ROCOCO
(1715–1774)

Bag Wig or Crapaud: A wig with a bag in the back which held loose ends of the hair, tied at the nape of the neck with a bow.

Bagnolette: Hood wired away from the face.

Banyan: Men's eighteenth-century dressing gown, same cut as the coat.

Cadogan: In the catogan or cadogan wig, the back hair was looped under and tied with a concealed string or solitaire. The name of the wig is attributed to the first Earl of Cadogan.

Calash: Eighteenth-century hat, attached to capes, to cover women's high wigs, folds back like a baby-buggy cover.

Festoons: Decorative elements on women's gowns; pieces of sheer fabric or flowers.

Frills: Decorative ornamentation—fabric gathered on one side, in contrast to furbelows, which are fabric strips gathered down the center.

Furbelows: See *Late Baroque, Falbalas.* Decorative ornamentation for gowns.

Jabot: The military tied the ends of the large, flat collar in front with a band, and from the loose ends the jabot was later developed as a falling lace ruffle, which filled in the opening of the shirt.

Leghorn: Large, straw picture hat.

Mantle: The long winter mante. Fully lined throughout and buttoned down the length of the front.

Modestie: When the neck in front was low on a woman's dress, often the stomacher was ornamented with graduated ribbon loops or lacings of narrow ribbon, finished with gauze or lace, known as the modestie. In English, the "modesty bit."

Monterro: Skull cap, often fur trimmed, worn with banyan.

Paniers: These baskets to hold out the skirt returned in 1717 to France, by way of England, where they had already been in fashion for six or seven years under the name of hoop skirt. They did not really take hold in France until 1730. The hoops were of reed or whalebone, held together with basket-like ribbons, thus the French name, panier, meaning basket. The framework was covered with taffeta or brocade. The hoop was first funnel shaped, but from the 1730s to 1740s it grew very broad at the sides and flat in front and back.

Parapluie: Rain umbrella, made with a folding frame.

Perspective: Women carried the lorgnette, men the single glass, or perspective.

Polonaise: An overgown for women, with fitted back and front and a draped skirt. It lasted from 1776 to 1787, and its special feature consisted of three paniers, one back and two side sections, which rounded away in front. The paniers of the polonaise were drawn up on cords and could also be let down to form a flying gown. The cords were run through slots and were finished with tassels and rosettes. Later the paniers were sewn in position, with the cords merely serving as ornament.

Quizzing Glass: Looking glass on a stick.

Robe à la française: In the 1730s the Watteau gown became the "robe à la française," and by 1770 this loose gown was the formal dress for court functions, six box pleats stitched flat to the back, and ending in a train. Under the upper part of the gown, attached to the bodice, was a fitted lining which was laced in back.

Robe Volante or Flying Gown: A variation of the gown with the Watteau pleat. The soft pleats flowed from shoulder to hem, both back and front. Usually ankle length, worn over a wide hoop which created an undulating movement while walking.

Solitaire: A concealing string of black taffeta, satin, or velvet, which tied the back hair of the cadogan wig. The solitaire, which no doubt is the origin of the black tie, was the black ribbon tied to the wig in a bow at the back, with the ends brought around under the white cravat and tied in a bow in front. Sometimes the solitaire was held in front by a diamond pin or a barrette.

Tricorne: The standard three-cornered hat worn by gentlemen of the period.

Watteau Sacque: The gown named after Watteau was the principal style of the Regency. The original Watteau gown was a loose sack or dress, worn over a tight bodice and very full underskirt. The loose folds falling from the shoulders in back became part of the skirt. The front of the gown varied in design, either hanging loose or fitted at the waist, worn closed or open, and, if open, revealing a bodice and underskirt. The elbow-length sleeves had vertical pleats and soft, wide cuffs. But from the 1740s on, the pagoda-shaped sleeve took hold, tight from shoulder to elbow, where it spread into flaring ruffles headed by ribbon bows. See also *Modestie.*

Neoclassical
(1774–1790)

Bicorne: A type of man's hat having a front and back flap, with the highest point or corner in center front caused by a pinching of the front flap, thereby resembling a tricorne. Developed from a variation of the Swiss military hat.

Cadogan Hairdo: Wig having ends of hair turned under; named in honor of the first Earl of Cadogan.

Calash: A cage, covering huge hairdos and therefore very large. It had reed or whalebone hoops which could be raised or lowered by a ribbon like the hood of a carriage. See also *Rococo.*

Caraco Gown: A gown with long basque, finished with a peplum ruff, and often a train called a Figaro which was attached under the peplum.

Circassienne Gown: A variation of the polonaise. It too had three paniers run on cords, but very short and of even length. The gown had double sleeves; the outer bodice had short cap sleeves worn over the longer sleeves of the under bodice.

Cockade: A rosette or similar ornament worn on the side of the hat.

Dormeuse Bonnet or Sleeping Bonnet: So named because it was also worn at night. It hugged the head tightly, covering the cheeks, and was threaded with a ribbon, tied into a bow on top of the head. For daytime wear it was worn higher on the head, revealing the ears and back of the head.

Fichu: A piece of lightweight, almost transparent fabric, worn like a shoulder scarf with the different styles of gowns. It was bunched above the small, tight waist, giving a pouter pigeon look to the figure.

Gainsborough Hat: A type of wide-brimmed hat, decorated with ribbons or ostrich plumes, that appeared in Gainsborough's paintings.

Hedgehog Hairdo: A woman's hairdo that appeared in 1778. It resembled a short male hairdo, cut fairly short in front, frizzed to the ends, and brushed up high off the face with long loose curls or the catogan in back.

Le Gilet: A copy of the English sleeveless waistcoat, with a laced back of lining material, which fitted the figure.

Lévite Gown: A type of redingote with train. Its creation was inspired by the Englishman's redingote, or riding coat, of the same period. There was also a definite *redingote gown*, which had a double-breasted jacket, with wide lapels. This costume was considered very mannish.

Liars, Menteurs, or Trompeurs: Wires which supported the fichu.

Macaroni: Member of a London club who dressed in extreme fashions. His costume consisted of a bobtailed coat and wig a foot high topped by a small tricorne hat.

Mob-cap: Large cap with soft, full crown and wide brim which almost hid the face; usually trimmed with ribbon bands and loops; known in England and therefore not restricted to use during the French Revolution.

Pelisse: A fur-trimmed wrap, cape-like, with armholes and broad collar. For women.

Pouf: A huge headdress with ornaments which were attached to a framework of gauze.

Redingote: A man's double-breasted long coat with turned-down collar and two or three shoulder capes; of English origin.

DIRECTOIRE AND EMPIRE (1790–1815)

À la Titus or à la Victime: Type of coiffure resembling a condemned person's locks before execution; worn with a red shawl and red necklace.

Barouche Coat: Tight-fitting, three-quarter-length coat with full sleeves, fastened down the front with gold barrel-shaped snaps and confined at the waist with an elastic girdle and buckle.

Cabriolet: Huge hat with elaborate silk trimming.

Canezou: A bodice with a high neckline and long sleeve.

Chemise à l'anglaise: A soft, full lingerie gown with crushed satin sash; it was worn both summer and winter, and it originated in England.

Cherusses: Long sleeves, divided into several cuffs by narrow bands or ribbons.

Circassian Wrapper: A dress similar to a night chemise, with very low-laced bodice and sleeves of lace and muslin in alternate stripes.

Clawhammer Tails: Any male coat with stepped-back front at the waist and very long tails at the rear.

Coal-Scuttle Bonnet: A bonnet with a huge, shovel-like lip in front, worn during the Directoire period.

Curricle Cloak: A half or three-quarter-length shaped cloak with sloping sides, edged with fur or lace, ca. 1801–1816.

Escarpins: Pumps of soft leather with pointed toes, worn with silk stockings, either plain white or striped on white.

Garrick Greatcoat or Capote: Overcoat of the period, with several capes over the long-skirted redingote.

Incroyables: A group of young dandies who went to extremes in their dress, right after the French Revolution. Their coats, which sloped away in front from the waist when buttoned, had a high, turned-down collar, very wide lapels, and were usually worn open. Sometimes the coat had bulky pleats across the back, giving the ugly effect of a hump. The "incroyables" strove for a careless, wrinkled appearance. With this coat was worn a waistcoat of contrasting colored satin and a very full, sheer white cambric cravat. The cravat or neckcloth was loosely wound around the neck several times, often over padded cushions so that it rose up over the chin with ends tied in front.

Merveilleuses: The feminine counterpart of the "incroyables." The neck of the short, tight bodice was very low, the fabric diaphanous. A sheer lingerie muffler resembling the masculine neckcloth was often added and worn in the same fashion. The woman either went bareheaded or wore an extreme style of hat, frequently a bonnet with a very large brim, rising high off the forehead—an exaggerated version of the English jockey hat.

Muscadine: A pastille scented with musk. The name was applied to effeminate men who overdressed and used quantities of this scent. The muscadine carried a short or long stick weighted with lead.

Pantalettes: A separate leg covering of lace and ruffles that extended below the hem of the dress.

Redingote: The long cloth or velvet coat which became a fashion for women ca. 1812. It was high waisted, was at first knee length and later reached to 9 to 10 inches above the hem of the dress. By the end of the decade, the coat was full length and edged with wide bands of fur.

Reticule: A small drawstring purse used in lieu of pockets.

Robespierre Collar: High, turned-down collar worn with frilly jabot and stock tied in a bow in front. Worn by the French statesman ca. 1790.

Roguelo Dress: A morning dress with a loose back and bias front.

Rotonde: Short cape of the same material as the dress.

Sans-culottes: Those who wore trousers were called sans-culottes (without breeches), distinguishing them from the aristocracy, who wore breeches; eventually the term came to signify the patriot.

Spencer: A very short-waisted jacket, worn by women with the Empire dress. Named after Lord Spencer.

Wellington Mantle: Garment which resembled a Spanish cloak of merino lined with sarcenet.

Yeoman Hat: A triangular hat turned up in front and ornamented at the top with button and tasseled cord.

ROMANTIC
(1815–1848)

Angoulême Bonnet: Bonnet with a high crown and tied at the side.

Beret Sleeve: Until 1813, the sleeves of evening gowns, while short, were full and stiffened and called beret or pancake sleeves.

Bertha: Wide collar on women's gowns of the period, which accentuated the dropped-shoulder look.

Bishop Sleeve: A wide, long sleeve gathered at the cuff.

Byron Collar: An unstarched collar left open at the throat and held together by a silk scarf carelessly tied.

Canezou: Refers to Canezou Spencer. A short, separate, transparent jacket with sleeves, its two scarf-like ends held in place by the dress belt. Usually of sheer muslin with embroidery, it was worn over the bodice. The false canezou was a deep ruffle or bretelle, falling over the short puffed sleeves.

Crinoline: Made its appearance in the early 1840s and was, at first, a band or braid of horsehair—crin is the French word for horsehair. The crinoline was a petticoat, corded and lined with horsehair and finished with a braid of straw at the hem.

534

Donna Maria: A full sleeve puffed to below the elbow and then tight to the wrist.

Frock Coat: A double-breasted coat having long skirts of equal length in front and back.

Frog Fastening: Ornamental fastening with cord loops and suspended buttons.

Hessian Boot: A rather tight-fitting high boot.

Mameluke: A sleeve that was full nearly to the wrist.

Mantelette: Shaped scarf. Covered the back almost like a jacket and descended to the knees in front, narrow and sloping from the shoulders down.

Montespan: A sleeve with the upper part full, a band at the elbow, and a ruffle extending over the forearm.

Pantalettes: Underdrawers that were often false, just ruffles held at the knees with tapes.

Pèlerine: A short, separate cape deriving its name from the shoulder cape of the medieval pilgrim; often of fur.

Pelisse: A fur-lined or fur-trimmed cloth coat, used in France, although the English applied the name to any long outer coat.

Robe d'interieur: At home for "negligée," men wore lounging clothes or smoking suits with a velvet cap. The robe d'interieur was of brilliantly figured silk or velvet.

Sautoir: A silk cravat worn to support ruff.

Stocks: During the 1840s the wide stock was still a fashionable neck covering. As before, it was often neatly shaped to the neck, whaleboned at the sides, and secured by a strap and buckled in back. Often the stock was plain across the front. At other times, it had a piece brought around the back and fastened in a knot or bow.

LATE NINETEENTH CENTURY: CRINOLINE (1848–1868)

Antimacassar: An ornamental washable covering used to protect chair backs from the oil used on men's hair.

Basque: The outer part of a dress sewed onto a boned bodice.

Bavolet: A flounce sewn on the back of a bonnet.

Bertha: A cape-like collar of cloth or lace.

Bloomers: Loose oriental trousers gathered at the knee; popularized by Amelia Bloomer in 1851.

Bolero: A small jacket with rounded corners in front.

Bournouse or Burnous: A fringed, knee-length, Arabian-style mantle with hood worn in the 1850s.

Bowler or Derby Hat: A stiff felt hat with a low round crown and narrow brim; the bowler, which is the British term for derby, has a slightly wider brim and roll at the sides.

Braces: Suspender straps extending from the waist belt in the front over the shoulder to support trousers.

Cage Américaine: Another term for the whalebone, metal crinoline, or hoop skirt.

Canezou: At first a sleeveless outdoor garment developed from the Spencer jacket; later it referred to a neckpiece on a dress.

Capote: Elaborate mid-Victorian bonnet with ribbon bows tied at the side or front.

Chignon: A heavy twist or knot of real or false hair worn high or low at the back of the head.

Chimney Pot or Stovepipe Hat: A tall, cylindrical hat with very little brim; worn by men.

Crinoline: A stiff or unpliable material used to stiffen a costume; the name is also given to the spring steel hoops set into a petticoat or onto cloth strips to hold the petticoats and skirts away from the body in a bell shape.

Dundrearys, Dundreary Whiskers, or Piccadilly Weepers: Long side whiskers worn by Lord Dundreary in *Our American Cousin* by Tom Taylor, 1858.

Empire Jupon: A petticoat with gores and two or three steel frames at the bottom.

Empress Eugénie Hat: A flat-crowned straw with a rolled brim and ribbons falling down the back, used by the Empress Eugénie for riding and traveling.

Figaro Jacket: A close-fitting short jacket with epaulets on the shoulder, cut away at the side in a bolero style.

Frock Coat or Prince Albert: A double-breasted

coat with a long skirt of equal length in front and back; the skirts had less flair than in the romantic period.

Garibaldi Jacket: A shirt of bright scarlet merino wool, decorated on the front with black braid and buttons and named after the popular Italian hero.

Imperial: A small, tufted beard on the chin, usually worn with a waxed mustache; named after the style worn by the Emperor Napoleon III.

Inverness Cape: A full, sleeveless cape which fitted closely around the neck; from Inverness in Scotland.

Morning Coat: The swallowtail or curved, cutback, skirted coat worn by gentlemen for formal morning wear.

Muttonchops: Heavy sideburns at the side of the face.

Pagoda Sleeve: A sleeve shaped like a funnel, tight above and gradually widening at the bottom, often finishing in several ruffles over a soft lawn undersleeve.

Paisley Shawl: A copy of an Indian shawl made in Paisley, Scotland.

Paletot: A cape-like outdoor garment hanging in stiff pleats from shoulder to flounce of dress, with a flap over the armhole and a number of short shoulder capes.

Peignoir: A dress with a boneless bodice and bishop sleeves.

Pork-Pie Hat: A low, flat hat worn with a dish-shaped fold in the crown.

Princess Gown: A full-length gown cut in one from shoulder to waist with a number of gores and full enough in the skirt to go over a hoop. Usually it buttoned up the front.

Raglan Coat: A coat with sleeves cut to fit into the shoulders all the way to the neckline of the garment. Named after Lord Raglan.

Russian Jacket: A sleeveless short coat.

Russian Vest: A loose blouse resembling the Garibaldi jacket.

Sack Suit: A loose-fitting combination of vest, coat, and trousers of the same material, with the coat ending at the finger tips and having high, short lapels. It was used in commerce and in sports wear.

Shirtwaist: A masculine style of bodice that looked like a male shirt with high collar and cuffs.

Victoria Mantle: A knee-length mantle with collar and wide, hanging sleeves. Usually a deep-colored border was used as a decoration for this garment.

Waistcoat: The forerunner of the present-day vest.

Waterproof Coat: An outdoor garment with or without a cape, worn as a protection from the rain.

Zouave Jacket: A short, loose jacket for women which revealed the Algerian influence on certain French uniforms. Usually the chemisette showed at the neck and below the three-quarter sleeve.

LATE NINETEENTH CENTURY: BUSTLE (1868–1890)

Ascot Tie: A scarf with horizontal ends, tied in a knot and then crossed diagonally; the whole usually held in place with a jeweled stick pin.

Balayeuse, Dust Ruffle, or Street Sweeper: A ruffle on the inner side of the hem of a skirt to protect it from the ground.

Blazer: A lightweight sport jacket.

Bustle: Whalebone or steel strips placed in the top back of the petticoat or in a separate panier puff in order to hold out the elaborate draping at the back of the overskirt.

Camargo: A jacket with a built-in panier.

Camisole: The light cloth cover worn over the corset.

Cardigan: A collarless sweater with a front opening.

Chesterfield Overcoat: A fitted dress overcoat with hidden buttons and a velvet collar, worn in the late nineteenth century.

Dolman: A three-quarter-length, out-of-doors wrap made of brocade, silk, or woolen fabric with sleeves cut in one with the body of the wrap.

Eton Jacket: A short jacket with side lapels first worn by the students at Eton in England.

Fedora: A velour hat with a fairly high, tapering crown that was usually creased in the middle.

Fore-and-Aft Cap: A cap having a visor front and back, worn with an Inverness cape.

Four-in-Hand: A type of necktie tied in a slip knot.

Frou-Frou Dress: A dress with a low corsage and a light pink underskirt covered with many small flounces.

Homburg: A carefully blocked, stiff felt hat with a medium tapering crown creased in the middle and a brim that was rolled up on the sides and finished in grosgrain ribbon.

Hussar Jacket: A jacket with braiding and frog fastenings; it was worn with a waistcoat and heavily influenced by military uniforms of the English in Egypt.

Jersey Sweater: A slipover sweater, fairly close fitting, copied from a fisherman's sweater.

Knickerbockers: Full, knee-length breeches gathered in at the knee; named after Father Knickerbocker, who came to New Amsterdam in 1674.

Langtry Bonnet: A small, close-fitting bonnet.

Monocle: A single glass with a ribbon, fitted into the eye socket to help the wearer both to improve the vision of one eye and to appear aristocratic.

Norfolk Jacket: A jacket with box pleats or straps of the same material passing over the belt and extending from shoulder to hem in front and back; usually worn for sport occasions.

Pompadour: A style of hairdress formed by drawing the hair straight up and back from the forehead.

Reefer: A double-breasted, close-fitting jacket.

Russian Bonnet: A type of bonnet with a large bow tied under the chin, a steel embroidered crown, and a lace brim.

Spats: Short coverings for the ankles and instep, usually made of felt and buttoned on the outside.

Swallowtailed Coat: Formerly a riding coat with skirts buttoned back, it now had the skirts cut back at the waist. Also called tails.

Tam-o'-Shanter: A round, flat cap with a tight-fitting headband.

Toque: A small, close-fitting female hat without a brim.

Tucker: The fabric used to cover the neck above the very low bodice.

Tuxedo: An informal dinner jacket introduced from England, although the name is of American origin.

Ulster: A fitted, double-breasted coat having several capes; at first made of frieze, a coarse woolen cloth with shaggy mat on one side made in Ulster, Ireland.

Windsor Tie: A large, flowing tie.

Wing Collar: A high, stiff collar with turned-back corners.

THE BIRTH OF MODERNISM OR
Art Nouveau
(1890–1914)

Aigrette: A feather or plume from the egret, a kind of heron.

Balkan Blouse: A low-bloused bodice with a belt girding the hips.

Bateau Neck: A wide, fairly low female neckline.

Beehive Hat: A large hat shaped like a beehive that came down well over the head and was fashionable from 1910 to 1914.

Bloomers: Loose underdrawers usually gathered at the knee.

Boa: A long or short cylindrical neck scarf of fur or feathers.

Boater: A stiff-brimmed, flat-crowned straw hat worn by young men with summer sporting outfits.

Brassière: A band worn around the bust, usually as a support.

Bulldog Toe: The high, rounded, and blunt toe of a shoe.

Bungalow Apron: A simple, straight-line dress.

Bust Improver: A device used to make the bust appear larger.

Buster Brown Collar: A wide, starched collar worn with a windsor tie and identified with the character, Buster Brown, in the comic strip of the period.

Châtelaine Bag: A pouch bag of pin-seal attached to a belt.

Diadem: A form of tiara or small jeweled crown for evening.

Dog Collar: A close-fitting necklace that hugs the throat; also known as a *choker*.

Duster: A coat of panama, pongee, alpaca, or

natural linen used for driving and motoring.

Fascinator: A lacy woolen square or triangular head covering.

Friendship Bracelet: Consisted of similar links given by various friends and later put together to form a bracelet.

Gainsborough Hat: A velvet, beaver, or straw hat having a low crown and a broad brim, trimmed with feathers.

Gibson Girl Blouse: A blouse with a single pleat which extended over each shoulder front and back, hiding the armseye of the shirtwaist.

Gigot Sleeve: A full sleeve with more fullness at the elbow than at the shoulder or wrist.

Godet Pleats: Fluting held in place by a fine steel in the hem; used on the back and sides of a skirt.

Harem Skirt: A divided skirt.

Hobble Skirt: A very narrow skirt that inhibited walking.

Kimono Dress: A loose gown with sleeve and body cut in one piece; popular about 1912, when there was a great interest in Japanese art and culture.

Knickers: Full breeches gathered or pleated into kneebands and buckled at the knee; based on the knickerbockers of the preceding period.

La Pliant: An invention of 1896 consisting of pieces of steel enclosed in cotton or silk ribbon tapes, which held out the stiff and heavy skirt in the back and was much lighter than the use of numerous petticoats. It was possible to transfer the steels to different skirts.

Lampshade Dress: A two-tiered skirt with the top tier flared out in the shape of a lampshade. This style became popular just before World War I.

Leggings: Fitted coverings for the legs, usually fastened with a strap under the shoe and extending above the knee or to the waist.

Leg-of-Mutton Sleeves: A sleeve that is extremely wide at the top and tapers to the wrist.

Mackintosh: A waterproof coat bearing the name of the originator of rubberized cloth garments.

Marabou: Trimming made from the feathers of a certain species of stork; also a kind of raw silk or fabric made from it.

Marcel Wave: A type of artificial waving of the hair devised by Marcel of France in 1907.

Merry Widow Hat: An extremely large hat named from the musical comedy of the same name.

Mesh Bag: A bag made of interwoven metal links.

Morning Glory or Serpentine Skirt: A skirt which fitted snugly at the hip and flared bell-like at the hem.

Mother Hubbard: A loose-fitting housedress worn for comfort when doing housework.

Mushroom-Style Hat: A large female hat suggesting the shape of a mushroom; worn between 1908 and 1913.

Napoleon Costume: A woman's dress of 1905 having a straight standing collar with deep turnover, wide revers, and braid trimming.

Opera Hat: A tall silk hat that folded flat.

Pajama: Loose trousers and jacket, usually of silk, that were beginning to be worn for sleeping and lounging.

Panama Hat: A handwoven hat of fine straw from Ecuador and Colombia.

Peek-a-Boo Waist: A very thin blouse.

Peg-Top Skirt: A skirt with fullness of drapery around the hip and very narrow at the hem.

Peg-Top Trousers: Trousers that are wide and pleated at the top and very narrow at the ankles. The name peg-top originally applied to a boy's cone-shaped spinning top.

Peter Pan Collar: A small, soft, turnover collar, named from the costume worn by Maude Adams in the stage production of *Peter Pan.*

Pettibockers: Related to bloomers, these were ankle-length, silk jersey pantaloons worn by women.

Prince Rupert: A velvet or plush jacket worn open at the front and resembling a Louis XV coat.

Rainy Daisy Skirt: The nickname given to the skirts of women who belonged to the Rainy Day Club; a walking skirt, 2 to 3 inches off the ground in rainy weather.

Rat: Padding worn to make the hair extend outward from the head.

Rough Rider Shirt: A khaki shirt similar to that worn by Theodore Roosevelt and his cavalry in Cuba in 1898.

Slit Skirt: A narrow slit upward from the hem in the side, back, or front of a skirt to facilitate walking.

Street Sweepers: Ruffles worn under the hem of a skirt to protect it from dust and dirt.

Sun-Ray Skirt: A skirt with accordion pleating.

Switch: A separate tress of real or artificial hair bound at one end.

Umbrella Skirt: A full, bell-shaped skirt.

Wrapper: The name given to an unshapely housedress, about 1905.

Yoke Skirt: A skirt which had a shaped piece in front and two side pieces which extended around the hips and joined in the back. The lower part of the skirt was attached to this yoke.

THE AGE OF RELATIVITY
(1914–1940)

Algerian Purse: A purse made of Algerian leather, usually tooled and embossed in colors or gold.

Apron Tunic: A tunic having an overskirt, cut away in the back and forming an apron in front.

Arctics or Galoshes: A rubberized overshoe worn as a protection against rain and snow.

Babushka: A scarf worn around the head and tied under the chin. Babushka is the Russian word for grandmother.

Balkan Blouse: A blouse with full, loose sleeves gathered into a wide band around the waist; came into fashion after the Balkan Wars.

Balmacaan: A type of loose-fitting, flaring overcoat with raglan sleeves.

Bandeau: A band worn around the head to hold the hair tightly to the head.

Bed Jacket: A short jacket worn while resting in bed.

Blazer: A bright colored sport jacket, originally vertically striped.

Boutonnière: A real flower or an artificial nosegay worn in the buttonhole of the left lapel.

Box Coat: A loose, short, finger-tip-length coat of a boxy cut.

Bush Jacket: A belted, hip-length jacket with tailored collar and two sets of pockets, worn by a hunter in the African jungle.

Camisole Neckline: An evening dress with a neckline resembling that of a camisole-top slip, which was straight above the bustline with a strap over each shoulder.

Cardigan: A knitted sweater-jacket that opens up the front.

Chemise Dress: A one-piece dress slipped over the head. It had short sleeves, a long waist, and a narrow belt, and became the basic style for all dresses in the 1920s. It was also called the tube or pillowslip dress.

Cloche: A close-fitting, bell-shaped hat.

Compact: A small ornamental box containing powder and rouge.

Cowl Neckline: The loose neckline of a dress falling in graceful curves across the chest; the draping of the fabric resembled the soft folds of a monk's cowl.

Crew Cut: Hair cut very short and combed upward to create a brush on the top of the head.

Crew-Neck Sweater: A sweater with a flat, close, round neckline.

Culottes: A trouser-like garment that has the fullness to make it look like a full skirt when the wearer is not in movement.

Cummerbund: A wide band of cloth wound tightly around the waist to imitate the same item worn by Spanish and Latin American gentlemen; usually worn with a tuxedo.

Dolman Wrap: A coat with sleeves cut in one with the body and the whole tapering toward the ankles.

Ferris Waist: The trade name given to a fitted waist which had buttons on tabs to hold the supporters. It was worn mainly by young girls.

Foulard: A thin, soft material of silk, or silk and cotton.

Halter Dress: A strap or band around the neck to hold the bodice of a backless dress.

Handkerchief Tunic: Tunic made from a square of material, the center of which was cut out for a waistline, the corners falling in graceful folds at the side of the skirt.

Harlequin Hat: A hat with wide, turned-up brim and oblique at the sides.

Helmet: A close-fitting cap worn toward the back of the head with sides extending over the ears.

Hollywood Top Slip: A fitted slip with a single or double-V top.

Hoover Apron: A wraparound, coverall apron with sleeves. It originated in World War I when Herbert Hoover was Food Administrator.

Irene Castle Bob: A haircut, loosely waved and combed back from the forehead. It was introduced by the dancer Irene Castle.

Jodhpurs: Breeches used for riding; designed with fullness above the knee, close-fitting below, cuff at ankle, and often with a strap under the instep.

Kiki Skirt: An extremely tight, knee-length skirt which appeared after it was worn in the play *Kiki* by Lenore Ulric.

Lindbergh Jacket: A heavy, warm, woolen or leather jacket with large pockets and elastic, fitted waist and wrist bands. It was worn by Charles Lindbergh on his 1927 flight over the Atlantic.

Middy Blouse: A young girl's straight blouse with a braid-trimmed sailor collar, bearing the nickname of the English midshipman; the three stripes on the collar represent the three great naval victories of Lord Nelson.

Monastic Silhouette: A dress resembling a monk's robe, hanging loosely from the shoulder, with fullness held in place by a belt at the hips.

Monkey Fur Coat: A woman's outer coat actually made of monkey fur or imitation monkey fur.

Off-the-Face Hat: Also called halo hat, it was worn to the back of the head with the brim framing the face.

Oxford Bags or Plus Fours: These loose knee trousers were an exaggeration of the earlier knickers and were usually reserved for golf.

Parka: A long-skirted woolen garment having an attached hood and often fur lined. The garment was used for winter sports and was originally the outer garment of animal skins worn by Eskimos.

Patch Pocket: A pocket sewn on the outside of a garment and made of the same material.

Peter Pan Hat: Small hat with a feather at the side, similar to that worn by Maude Adams in the play of the same name.

Pinch Back Coat: A coat with inverted pleats at the back which were stitched into the belt.

Planter's Punch: A firm straw hat, shaped like a fedora, which originated in Jamaica about 1923; it had a creased crown and a wide, pleated ornamental band.

Pocket Cascade: A pocket formed in the folded and draped section at the side of the skirt.

Polo Coat: A light-colored, soft-surfaced top coat for informal wear and sports.

Polo Shirt: A sport shirt, usually knitted, with an open collar and short sleeves.

Profile Hat: A hat worn on one side of the head, forming a background for the profile of the wearer.

Raccoon Coat: A very bulky outer coat or overcoat of raccoon fur, worn for display as well as for warmth at sporting events, particularly at football games.

Saddle Shoe: A two-toned oxford with an ornamental strip of leather across the instep.

Sash Blouse: A blouse with wide pieces, crossing in front like a surplice with attached ends forming a sash or girdle, which was tied or fastened in the back.

Sequin Calotte: A small hat decorated with sequins.

Shawl Collar: An attached collar having a rounded, unbroken outline, often extending to the waistline.

Shingle Bob: A mode of cutting the hair very close to the head in the back to show the natural contour of the head.

Shirtwaist Dress: A one-piece belted and tailored dress having a tucked shirtwaist.

Shorts: Short cotton pants worn under trousers

or short cotton pants worn at the beach or for various sports.

Skimmer Sailor: A flat-crowned sailor hat with a heavy, wide, and straight brim.

Slacks: Loose trousers worn for informal wear.

Swagger Coat: A coat having a very loose skirt, or flare from shoulder to hem.

Swing Skirt: A circular skirt with gores that gave a swinging motion when the wearer was walking. The skirt was also popular in the 1930s when swing music was popular.

Tab Collar Shirt: A collar with a long point on each side extending down the front.

Teddies: A straight garment, combining a shapeless brassiere and a straight skirt with a wide strap separating the garment into two separate parts or legs.

Trench Coat: A tan-colored top coat with a belt, a double yoke at the shoulder that was loose at the bottom, and epaulet straps at the shoulder; it was designed to resemble a military coat and was used as a protection in bad weather.

Turtle-Neck Sweater: A slip-on, knit sweater with a high turned-over collar.

Tyrolean Hat: A hat with a feather, usually of soft, fuzzy felt similar to those worn in the highlands of Bavaria and Austria.

Windbreaker: A lined leather or closely woven cloth jacket with a zipper that was used as a protection against the weather when a sport shirt and slacks were worn, in place of a longer or heavier coat.

CONTEMPORARY
(1940-1965)

A *line:* A triangular or **A**-shaped dress, either belted or unbelted and usually sleeveless.

American Blade: A coat with a broad shoulder and with fullness at upper arm and back to prevent strain.

Ballerina Skirt: A very full, usually ankle-length, gored or flared skirt, sometimes made of three or four tiers of ruffles, resembling the type worn by a Spanish dancer.

Ballet Slipper: A flat, low slipper laced around the ankle and worn for casual or evening wear.

Beach Coat: A short, loose coat of terrycloth, plain cotton, or synthetic fiber used for beach wear.

Blücher: A shoe with a long vamp and a strap across the instep, derived from the style of boot worn by General Blücher during the Battle of Waterloo.

Blue Jeans: Trousers made of denim, a heavy, twilled cotton cloth; formerly worn by cowboys and workmen, they have become the standard day-to-day wear of young people and students in many parts of the United States and Europe.

Boy Coat: A short jacket with collars and cuffs that resembles the jackets worn by small boys.

Butcher Linen: A strong, heavy cloth originally made of long-fiber flax and used for the aprons worn by butchers; when it is white it is used for dresses and suitings; today it is usually of rayon or rayon and cotton.

Cabin Boy Breeches: Short, tight-fitting knee pants laced at the knee.

Cache-chignon: A velvet bow used to catch loose ends of hair.

Car Coat: A fingertip-length coat with patch pockets and a turned-up collar used for traveling in an open sports car.

Cinch Belt: A tight, wide elastic belt.

Cobbler's Apron: A sleeveless, hip-length, belted apron with huge pockets across the front, worn for dress or for utility.

Cocktail Dress: A party dress appropriate for wear in the late afternoon; often longer than a daytime dress.

Convertible Jumper: A sleeveless dress worn with a sweater for sportswear, with a dressy blouse for daytime, and without a blouse for evening.

Cowichan or Siwash Sweater: A sweater with a striking Indian pattern in black on white or grey background, made by the Siwash Indians of Vancouver Island, B.C.

Directory Suit: A suit with high midriff and very short cutaway jacket; in general, a suit that follows the silhouette of the French Directoire.

Dirndl: A very full, gathered skirt resembling the skirt of Tyrolean peasants.

Duffel Coat: A warm woolen coat of fingertip length with hood attached, having frogs of wood and rope.

Eisenhower Jacket: A waist-length military tunic in khaki worn by General Eisenhower in World War II and adapted for civilian use after the War.

Flyaway Collar: A collar with points that flare to the side in the manner of a winged collar.

Flyaway Jacket: A very short jacket with a very full back.

Four-Way Dress: A dress that can be worn for various occasions.

Gaucho Pants: Calf-length pants, wrapped across the front, with trouser leg tapered below the knee; resembling pants worn by the cowboy of Argentina.

Halter Top: A blouse with bare back, with the neckline continued around the back of the neck.

Harem-Hem Skirt: A soft hem, draped to give a bloomer effect.

Hippies: A cult of young people of the 1960s devoted to a primitive look through the use of old or worn clothes and accessories; they are usually associated with long hair, beards, bare feet, and the use of drugs.

Huarache: A sandal woven of leather or raffia strips; used by the Mexican Indians.

Levis: A tight-fitting denim trouser with a U-shaped crotch, worn by boys and younger men; originally part of a western cowboy outfit, the trousers were and still are manufactured by Levi Strauss of San Francisco.

Lumber Jacket: Short, heavy, plaid woolen jacket, belted and with patch pockets.

Mandarin Jacket: A loose-fitting jacket resembling a Chinese tunic coat.

Martingale Belt: A half-belt in back of a jacket or coat. The word has been long applied to a leather strap extending from the bit or reins in a horse's bridle to the girdle.

Mini Skirt: A very short skirt that ends well above the knees.

Mixed-Match Separates: A jacket and skirt of unlike but harmonizing fabrics worn interchangeably with other garments.

Moat Collar: A narrow standing collar worn around a high, broad neckline.

Mod Clothing: A contraction of "modern" clothing used to apply to the exaggerated, smartly cut clothes for young people that have come out of Carnaby Street, London, since 1960.

Monk Shoe: A low shoe, plain across the instep and fastened with a buckle.

New Bold Look: An organized program of manufacturers and retailers to assist men in coordinating an ensemble and to create a demand for new male styles.

New Look: Styles for women introduced in 1947.

Op and Pop Art: Op art is the name given to designs based on optical illusions, while pop art is based on either a photographic or cartoon approach to the artifacts and advertising of our materialistic culture; both are used in patterns for clothing.

Pedal Pushers: Close-fitting pants extending below the knee, made in various colors, frequently of blue denim, and with or without a cuff.

Poncho: A large square or rectangular piece of material, often in gay colors, with a hole cut out of the middle for the head; worn by Mexican peasants and popular in the United States as a gay outer garment.

Poodle Cloth: A woolen material with a surface of thickly woven loops, popular in 1952.

Poodle Haircut: A woman's hairdress in which the hair is cut uniformly over the entire head to about 1½ inches and loosely curled.

Puggree: Wide, soft band arranged in a fold around a hat.

Reefer: A single- or double-breasted tailored coat.

Sack Dress: A straight dress with no shape, cut from shoulder to hem like a bag or sack.

Sarong: A short, wraparound skirt of colorful fabric, usually with Polynesian designs.

Sheath Dress: A tight-fitting dress.

Shift: Another straight dress without shape, worn without a belt at the waist, which rides on shoulders and hips.

Shrug Jacket: A very short jacket or sweater with sleeves cut in one with the body.

Sleeveless Blazer: A short, sleeveless jacket with pockets, knitted or made of fabric.

Sleeveless Look: A dress or a blouse without sleeves or decorations at the armhole.

Sling Neckline: A pointed neckline that extends diagonally and joins the side opening of a dress.

Sloppy Joe: A costume including a man's shirt, usually several sizes too large and worn on the outside over blue jeans carelessly rolled up at the knee; also the name given to a loose, baggy sweater, worn several sizes too large.

Snap Brim: A soft felt hat with a medium crown and medium brim, pulled down in front in a jaunty fashion.

Square-Dance Dress: A dress with a full blouse, sleeveless or with puff sleeves, and a full skirt.

Stocking Bodice: A knitted woolen tube, to be pulled over the head and fastened with a drawstring or shirred-on elastic, worn with shorts, skirts, or dinner dresses.

Sun Dress or Sunback Dress: A cotton dress with the back cut out.

Teddy Boy: Exaggerated outfits worn after the War in England by those young boys who were trying to attract attention by their outlandish dress and gang behavior.

Toreador Pants: Short, tight-fitting pants buttoned at the knee, resembling those worn by the Spanish toreador.

Tremont Hat: A man's hat with a tapered crown and center crease and a fairly narrow brim worn up or down; sometimes it has a pinched crown and a snap brim.

Trumpet Coat Dress or Trumpet Skirt: Garments that are fairly tight over the hips with pleating or fullness from just above the knee.

TV Lounging Jacket: A loose-fitting jacket.

TV Sets: Lounging separates.

Wedgie: A shoe having a very thick sole and a wedge-shaped heel.

Weskit: A waist-length, tight-fitting, sleeveless jacket.

Bibliography

This bibliography lists some of the more useful works to be consulted in costume, theatre, and art in connection with the study of this text. The bibliography is divided into categories which correspond to the divisions in the text.

GENERAL

Altman, George, et al. *Theater Pictorial, A History of World Theater as Recorded in Drawings, Paintings, Engravings, and Photographs.* Berkeley: University of California Press, 1953.

Baker, Blanche. *Dramatic Bibliography.* New York: Wilson, 1933.

Beaumont, Cyril. *Ballet Design: Past and Present.* New York: The Studio, 1946.

Brockett, Oscar. *The Theatre: An Introduction,* 2nd ed. New York: Holt, Rinehart and Winston, 1969.

Burris-Meyer, Harold, and Cole, Edward. *Scenery for the Theatre: The Organization, Processes, Material, and Techniques Used to Set the Stage.* Boston: Little, Brown, 1938.

Cheney, Sheldon. *The Theatre: Three Thousand Years of Drama, Acting and Stagecraft.* New York: Longmans, Green, 1929.

———. *Stage Decoration.* New York: Day, 1928.

Cleaver, James. *Theatre Through the Ages.* London: Harrap, 1946.

Freedley, George, and Reeves, John. *A History of the Theatre.* New York: Crown, 1941.

Fuller, Edmund. *A Pageant of the Theatre.* New York: Crowell, 1941.

Gascoigne, Bamber. *World Theatre: An Illustrated History.* Boston: Little, Brown, 1968.

Gassner, John, and Allen, Ralph. *Theatre and Drama in the Making.* Boston: Houghton Mifflin, 1964.

Hartnoll, Phyllis. *The Oxford Companion to the Theatre,* 3rd ed. London: Oxford University Press, 1967.

———. *The Concise History of the Theatre.* New York: Abrams, 1968.

Macgowan, Kenneth, and Melnitz, William. *The Living Stage.* Englewood Cliffs, N.J.: Prentice-Hall, 1955.

Nagler, Alois. *Sources of Theatrical History.* New York: Theatre Annual, 1952.

Nicoll, Allardyce. *The Development of the Theatre,* 5th ed. London: Harrap, 1966.

Odell, G. C. D. *Annals of the New York Stage,* 15 vols. New York: Columbia University Press, 1927–1949.

Oenslager, Donald. *Scenery Then and Now.* New York: Norton, 1936.

Roberts, Vera Mowry. *On Stage: A History of the Theatre.* New York: Harper & Row, 1962.

Sachs, Curt. *World History of the Dance* (trans. by Bessie Schoenberg). New York: Norton, 1937.

Simonson, Lee. *The Stage Is Set.* New York: Harcourt, Brace, 1932.

Sobel, Bernard. *The Theatre Handbook and Digest of Plays.* New York: Crown, 1948.

Whiting, Frank M. *An Introduction to the Theatre.* New York: Harper & Row, 1954.

CHAPTER 1

Adams, J. Donald. *Naked We Came.* New York: Holt, Rinehart & Winston, 1967.

Albright, H. D., Halstead, W. P., and Mitchell, Lee. *Principles of Theatre Art.* Boston: Houghton Mifflin, 1955.

Broby-Johansen, R. *Body and Clothes* (trans. by Erik I. Friis and Karen Rush). New York: Reinhold, 1968.

Burris-Meyer, Elizabeth. *This Is Fashion.* New York: Harper, 1943.

Burris-Meyer, Harold, and Cole, Edward C. See *General.*

Flügel, John Carl. *The Psychology of Clothes.* London: Hogarth, 1950.

Jones, Robert Edmond. *The Dramatic Imagination.* New York: Theatre Arts, 1941.

Komisarjevsky, Theodore. *The Costume of the Theatre.* London: Bles, 1931.

Laver, James. *Costume in the Theatre.* New York: Hill & Wang Dramabook, 1965.

———. *Drama, Its Costume and Decor.* London: Studio Publications, 1951.

———. *Taste and Fashion.* London: Harrap, 1945.

Parker, W. Oren, and Smith, Harvey. *Scene Design and Stage Lighting.* New York: Holt, Rinehart & Winston, 1963.

Selden, Samuel, and Sellman, Hunton. *Stage Scenery and Lighting.* New York: Appleton-Century-Crofts, 1959.

Smith, Milton. *Play Production for Little Theaters, Schools and Colleges.* New York: Appleton-Century-Crofts, 1948.

Young, Stark. *The Theatre.* New York: Doubleday, 1927.

———. *Theatre Practice.* New York: Scribner's, 1926.

CHAPTER 2

Arnheim, Rudolph. *Art and Visual Perception.* Berkeley: University of California Press, 1954.

Clark, Kenneth. *The Nude: A Study in Ideal Form.* New York: Pantheon, 1956.

Doten, Hazel R., and Boulard, Constance. *Fashion Drawing: How to Do It.* New York: Harper, 1939.

Emerson, Sybil. *Design: A Creative Approach.* Scranton, Pa.: International Textbook, 1962.

Gombrich, E. H. *Art and Illusion: A Study in the Psychology of Pictorial Representation.* New York: Pantheon, 1965.

Gordon, Conni. *You Can Paint.* New York: Conni Gordon, 1965.

———. *You Can Draw.* New York: Conni Gordon, 1963.

———. *You Can Watercolor.* New York: Conni Gordon, 1962.

Gutierrez, Jose, and Roukes, Nicholas. *Painting with Acrylics.* New York: Watson-Gupthill, 1962.

Hale, Robert Beverly. *Drawing Lessons from the Great Masters.* New York: Watson-Gupthill, 1964.

Hill, Adrian. *The Beginning Book of Watercolor Painting.* New York: Emerson, 1964.

Mayer, Ralph. *The Painter's Craft; An Introduction to Artists' Methods and Materials* (rev. ed.). Princeton, N.J.: Van Nostrand, 1966.

———. *The Artist's Handbook of Materials and Techniques,* rev. ed. New York: Viking, 1957.

Motley. *Designing and Making Stage Costumes.* London: Studio Vista, 1965.

Pope, Arthur. *The Language of Drawing and Painting.* Cambridge, Mass.: Harvard University Press, 1949.

Ruth, Jan de. *Painting the Nude.* New York: Watson-Gupthill, 1960.

Schmid, Frederic. *The Practice of Painting.* London: Faber & Faber, 1948.

Sotto, Marilyn. *The Art of Costume Design.* Laguna Beach, Calif.: Walter Foster, n.d.

Taylor, Joshua C. *Learning to Look.* Chicago: University of Chicago Press, n.d.

Yochim, Louise Dunn. *Perceptual Growth in Creativity.* Scranton, Pa.: International Textbook, 1962.

Zinkeisen, Doris, *Designing for the Stage.* London: The Studio, 1945.

Chapter 3

Anderson, Donald M. *Elements of Design.* New York: Holt, Rinehart & Winston, 1961.

Burris-Meyer, Harold, and Cole, Edward. See *Chapter 1.*

Fry, Roger. *Vision and Design.* London: Chatto & Windus, 1920.

Kepes, Gyorgy. *Language of Vision.* Chicago: Theobald, 1951.

Lenssen, Heidi. *Art and Anatomy.* New York: Augustin, 1944.

Lowry, Bates. *The Visual Experience: An Introduction to Art.* Englewood Cliffs, N.J.: Prentice-Hall, 1961.

Motley. See *Chapter 2.*

Oxenford, Lyn. *Playing Period Plays.* London: Miller, 1958.

Panofsky, Erwin. *Meaning in the Visual Arts.* Garden City, N.Y.: Anchor, 1955.

Parker, W. Oren, and Smith, Harvey. See *Chapter 1.*

Philippi, Herbert. *Stagecraft and Scene Design.* Boston: Houghton Mifflin, 1953.

Sheringham, George, and Laver, James. *Design in the Theatre.* London: The Studio, 1927.

Teague, Walter Dorwin. *Design This Day; The Technique of Order in This Machine Age* (rev. ed.). New York: Harcourt, Brace, 1949.

Watkins, Charles Law. *The Language of Design.* Washington, D.C.: Philips Memorial Gallery, 1946.

Weismann, Donald L. *The Visual Arts as Human Experience.* Englewood Cliffs, N.J.: Prentice-Hall, 1970.

Chapter 4

Burris-Meyer, Elizabeth. *Color and Design in the Decorative Arts.* Englewood Cliffs, N.J.: Prentice-Hall, 1935.

Burris-Meyer, Harold, and Cole, Edward. See *Chapter 1.*

Ellenger, Richard G. *Color Structure and Design.* Scranton, Pa.: International Textbook, 1961.

Evans, Ralph M. *An Introduction to Color.* New York: Wiley, 1948.

Graves, Maitland. *The Art of Color and Design,* 2nd ed. New York: McGraw-Hill, 1951.

Green, Joyce Conyngham. *Planning the Stage Wardrobe.* London: Nelson, 1941.

Itten, Johannes. *The Art of Color: The Subjective Experience and Objective Rationale of Color* (trans. by Ernst von Haagen). New York: Reinhold, 1961.

Jacobson, Egbert. *The Science of Color.* Chicago: American Photographers Association, 1937.

Luckiesh, Matthew. *Light and Shade and Their Applications.* New York: Van Nostrand, 1916.

———. *Color and Its Applications.* New York: Van Nostrand, 1915.

Motley. See *Chapter 2.*

Parker, W. Oren, and Smith, Harvey. See *Chapter 1.*

Pope, Arthur. See *Chapter 2.*

Chapter 5

Denny, G. G. *Fabrics and How to Know Them.* Philadelphia: Lippincott, 1947.

du Pont de Nemours. *A Brief History of Dyes.* Wilmington, Del.: E. I. du Pont de Nemours, n.d.

Fernald, Mary, and Shenton, Eileen. *Costume Design and Making.* London: Black, 1958.

Green, Joyce Conyngham. See *Chapter 4.*

Healy, Daty. *Dress the Show: A Basic Costume Book.* Evanston, Ill.: Row, Peterson, 1948.

Hess, Katharine. *Textile Fibers and Their Use.* Philadelphia: Lippincott, 1941.

Jacobsen, E. A., and McCullough, H. E. *Fundamentals of Textiles: A Workbook.* New York: Wiley, 1941.

Köhler, Carl. *A History of Costume.* New York: Dover, 1963.

Mathews, J. M. *Textile Fibers.* New York: Wiley, 1947.

Prisk, Berneice. *Stage Costume Handbook.* New York: Harper & Row, 1966.

Wingate, Isabel. *Textile Fabrics and Their Selection,* 5th ed. Englewood Cliffs, N.J.: Prentice-Hall, 1964.

Woolman, M. S., and McGowan, E. B. *Textiles.* New York: Macmillan, 1934.

Chapter 6

Arnold, Janet. *Patterns of Fashion: Englishwomen's Dresses and Their Construction*

(2 vols.: 1660–1860, 1860–1940). Washington, D.C.: Hobby House Press, 1965.

Barton, Lucy, and Edson, Doris. *Period Patterns*. Boston: Baker, 1942.

Bernstein, Aline. *Masterpieces of Eighteenth and Nineteenth Century Women's Costumes*. New York: Crown, 1959.

Bradford, Nancy. *Costume in Detail*. Boston: Plays, Inc., 1970.

Brooke, Iris. *Medieval Theatre Costume*. New York: Theatre Arts, 1967.

Evans, Mary. *How to Make Historic American Costumes*. New York: A. S. Barnes, 1942.

Fernald, Mary, and Shenton, Eileen. See *Chapter 5*.

Gassner, John. *Producing the Play* (Including *The Scene Technician's Handbook* by Philip Barber). New York: Holt, Rinehart, 1953.

Healy, Daty. See *Chapter 5*.

Hill, Margaret Hamilton, and Bucknell, Peter A. *The Evolution of Fashion: Pattern and Cut from 1066–1930*. New York: Van Nostrand Reinhold, 1968.

Houston, Mary G. *Technical History of Costume* (2nd ed.). London: A. & C. Black, 1954.

Köhler, Carl. See *Chapter 5*.

Norris, Herbert. *Costume and Fashion*. London: Dent, 1941.

Payne, Blanche. *History of Costume*. New York: Harper & Row, 1965.

Prisk, Berneice. See *Chapter 5*.

Prisk, Berneice, and Byers, Jack. *The Theatre Student, Costuming*. New York: Richard Rosen Press, 1970.

Singer Sewing Machine Company. *Métado Singer de Corte y Costuma*. New York: Singer Sewing Machine Company, 1955.

Tilke, Max. *Costume Patterns and Designs*. New York: Praeger, 1957.

Walkup, Fairfax Proudfit. *Dressing the Part*. New York: Appleton-Century-Crofts, 1950.

Waugh, Norah. *The Cut of Men's Clothes 1600–1900*. New York: Theatre Arts, 1964.

———. *The Cut of Women's Clothes 1600–1930*. New York: Theatre Arts, 1968.

CHAPTER 7

Barton, Lucy. *Historic Costume for the Stage*. Boston: Baker, 1935.

Crider, James. *Costuming with Basics and Separates*. New Haven, Conn.: Whitlock, 1954.

Fernald, Mary, and Shenton, Eileen. See *Chapter 5*.

Green, Joyce Conyngham. See *Chapter 5*.

Healy, Daty. See *Chapter 5*.

Jackson, Sheila. *Simple Stage Costumes and How to Make Them*. London: Studio Vista, 1968.

Lippincott, Gertrude (ed.). *Dance Production: Music, Costumes, Staging, Decor, Lighting, Photography, Makeup, Planning and Rehearsing*. Washington, D.C.: American Association for Health, Physical Education and Recreation, 1957.

Paterek, Josephine. *Costuming for the Theatre*. New York: Crown, 1959.

Prisk, Berneice. See *Chapter 5*.

Young, Agnes Brooks. *Stage Costuming*. New York: Macmillan, 1927.

CHAPTER 8

Barton, Lucy. See *Chapter 7*.

Corson, Richard. *Stage Makeup*, 4th ed. New York: Appleton-Century-Crofts, 1967.

Healy, Daty. See *Chapter 5*.

Heffner, Hubert; Selden, Samuel, and Sellman, H. D. *Modern Theatre Practice*, 4th ed. New York: Appleton-Century-Crofts, 1959.

Macgowan, Kenneth, and Rosse, H. *Masks and Demons*. New York: Harcourt, Brace & World, 1923.

Motley. See *Chapter 2*.

Nicoll, Allardyce. See *General*.

Prisk, Berneice. See *Chapter 5*.

Winter, Garry. *Crafts and Hobbies*. New York: Arco, 1965.

Zarchy, Harry. *Creative Hobbies*. New York: Knopf, 1953.

CHAPTER 9

Aristotle. *Aristotle's Theory of Poetry and the Fine Arts*, 4th ed. (critical text and trans. by S. H. Butcher). New York: Dover, 1951.

Bowman, Walter P., and Ball, Robert H. *Theatre Language, A Dictionary of Terms in English of the Drama and the Stage from Medieval to Modern Times.* New York: Theatre Arts, 1961.

Brooks, Cleanth, and Heilman, R. B. *Understanding Drama.* New York: Holt, Rinehart, 1948.

Cole, Toby, and Chinoy, Helen K. (eds.). *Directing the Play: A Sourcebook of Stagecraft.* Indianapolis, Ind.: Bobbs-Merrill, 1953.

Edman, Erwin. *Arts and the Man.* New York: Norton, 1939.

Fergusson, Francis. *The Idea of a Theatre: A Study of Ten Plays.* Princeton, N.J.: Princeton University Press, 1949.

Fry, Roger. *Vision and Design.* New York: Brentano's, 1924.

Hauser, Arnold. *The Social History of Art,* 4 vols. New York: Vintage, 1959.

Heffner, Hubert. *The Nature of Drama.* Boston: Houghton Mifflin, 1959.

Holt, Elizabeth. *A Documentary History of Art,* 2 vols. Garden City, N.Y.: Doubleday, 1957.

Langer, Susanne K. *Problems of Art: Ten Philosophical Lectures.* New York: Scribner's, 1957.

Laver, James. *Style in Costume.* New York: Oxford University Press, 1949.

Levy, Mervyn. *Pocket Dictionary of Art Terms.* Greenwich, Conn.: New York Graphic Society, 1961.

Nicoll, Allardyce. *The Theory of Drama,* rev. ed. London: Harrap, 1931.

Read, Herbert. *Art and Society.* London: Faber & Faber, 1945.

Rothschild, Lincoln. *Style in Art: The Dynamics of Art as Cultural Expression.* New York: Yoseloff, 1960.

St. Denis, Michel. *Theatre: The Rediscovery of Style.* New York: Theatre Arts, 1960.

Wölfflin, Heinrich. *Principles of Art History: The Problem of the Development of Style in Later Art.* New York: Dover, 1950.

———. *The Sense of Form in Art: A Comparative Psychological Study.* New York: Chelsea, 1958.

CHAPTER 10

Allen, James T. *Stage Antiquities of the Greeks and Romans and Their Influence.* New York: Longmans, Green, 1927.

Arnott, Peter D. *An Introduction to the Greek Theatre.* London: Macmillan, 1959.

Bieber, Margarete. *The History of the Greek and Roman Theater.* Princeton, N.J.: Princeton University Press, 1939.

Brooke, Iris. *Costume in Greek Classic Drama.* New York: Theatre Arts, 1965.

Gaster, Theodor. *Thespis: Ritual, Myth, and Drama in the Ancient Near East.* New York: Abelard-Schuman, 1950.

Hamilton, Edith. *The Greek Way.* New York: Norton, 1952.

———. *The Roman Way.* New York: Norton, 1932.

Harsh, Philip W. *A Handbook of Classical Drama.* Stanford, Calif.: Stanford University Press, 1944.

Havemeyer, Loomis. *The Drama of Savage Peoples.* New Haven, Conn.: Yale University Press, 1916.

Hunningher, Benjamin. *The Origin of the Theatre: An Essay.* New York: Hill & Wang, 1961.

Jaeger, Werner. *Paideia: The Ideals of Greek Culture,* 3 vols. (trans. by Gilbert Highet). New York: Oxford University Press, 1939–1944.

Webster, T. B. L. *Greek Theatre Production.* London: Methuen, 1956.

CHAPTER 11

Brooke, Iris. See *Chapter 6.*

Chambers, E. K. *The Medieval Stage,* 2 vols. Oxford: Clarendon Press, 1903.

Kernodle, George. *From Art to Theatre.* Chicago: University of Chicago Press, 1944.

Nicoll, Allardyce. *Masks, Mimes and Miracles.* New York: Harcourt, Brace, 1931.

Southern, Richard. *The Medieval Theatre in the Round: A Study of the Staging of The Castle of Perseverance and Related Matters.* London: Faber & Faber, 1958.

Wickham, Glynne. *Early English Stages 1300–1660,* 2 vols. New York: Columbia University Press, 1959–1962.

Williams, Arnold. *The Drama of Medieval England.* East Lansing: Michigan State University Press, 1961.

Young, Karl. *The Drama of the Medieval Church,* 2 vols. Oxford: Clarendon Press, 1933.

CHAPTER 12

Beckerman, Bernard. *Shakespeare at the Globe 1599–1609.* New York: Macmillan, 1962.

Bentley, Gerald E. *The Jacobean and Caroline Stage,* 5 vols. Oxford: Clarendon Press, 1941–1956.

Burckhardt, Jakob C. *The Civilization of the Renaissance in Italy,* 3rd ed. Vienna: Phaidon, 1937.

Campbell, Lily Bess. *Scenes and Machines on the English Stage During the Renaissance.* Cambridge: Cambridge University Press, 1923.

Hewitt, Barnard (ed.). *The Renaissance Stage: Documents of Serlio, Sabbattini, and Furttenbach.* Coral Gables, Fla.: University of Miami Press, 1958.

Hodges, C. W. *The Globe Restored.* London: Benn, 1953.

Hotson, John Leslie. *Shakespeare's Wooden O.* New York: Macmillan, 1960.

Joseph, Bertram. *Elizabethan Acting.* London: Oxford University Press, 1951.

Kennard, Joseph S. *The Italian Theatre,* 2 vols. New York: Rudge, 1932.

Kernodle, George. See *Chapter 11.*

Nagler, A. M. *Shakespeare's Stage.* New Haven, Conn.: Yale University Press, 1958.

Nicoll, Allardyce. See *Chapter 11.*

———. *Stuart Masques and the Renaissance Stage.* London: Harrap, 1937.

Shoemaker, William H. *The Multiple Stage in Spain During the Fifteenth and Sixteenth Centuries.* Princeton, N.J.: Princeton University Press, 1935.

Symonds, John A. *The Renaissance in Italy,* 7 vols. London: Murray, 1909–1937.

Sypher, Wylie. *Four Stages of Renaissance Style: Transformation in Art and Literature.* Garden City, N.Y.: Doubleday-Anchor, 1955.

Wölfflin, Heinrich. *Classic Art: An Introduction to the Italian Renaissance.* New York: Phaidon, 1952.

CHAPTER 13

Beijer, Agne. *Court Theatres of Drottningholm and Gripsholm* (trans. by G. L. Frölich). Malmo, Sweden: Kroon, 1933.

Campbell, Lily Bess. "A History of Costuming of the English Stage Between 1660 and 1823," *University of Wisconsin Studies in Language and Literature, 1918,* pp. 187–223.

Hathaway, Baxter. *The Age of Criticism; The Late Renaissance in Italy.* Ithaca, N.Y.: Cornell University Press, 1962.

Hotson, John Leslie. *The Commonwealth and Restoration Stage.* Cambridge, Mass.: Harvard University Press, 1928.

Lough, John. *Paris Theatre Audiences in the Seventeenth and Eighteenth Centuries.* London: Oxford University Press, 1957.

Mayor, A. H. *The Bibiena Family.* New York: Bittner, 1945.

Summers, Montague. *The Restoration Theatre.* London: Macmillan, 1934.

Sypher, Wylie. See *Chapter 12.*

Thaler, Alwin. *Shakespeare to Sheridan.* Cambridge, Mass.: Harvard University Press, 1922.

Turnell, Martin. *The Classical Moment; Studies of Corneille, Molière, and Racine.* New York: New Directions, 1946.

Wiley, W. L. *The Early Public Theatre in France.* Cambridge, Mass.: Harvard University Press, 1960.

Wittkower, Rudolf. *Art and Architecture in Italy 1600–1750.* Baltimore: Pelican, 1958.

Wölfflin, Heinrich. *Principles of Art History.* See *Chapter 9.*

Wright, C. H. C. *French Classicism.* Cambridge, Mass.: Harvard University Press, 1920.

CHAPTER 14

Beijer, Agne. See *Chapter 13.*

Boas, Frederick. *An Introduction to Eighteenth Century Drama 1700–1780.* Oxford: Clarendon Press, 1953.

Burnim, Kalman. *David Garrick, Director.*

Pittsburgh: Pittsburgh University Press, 1961.

Campbell, Lily Bess. See *Chapter 13.*

Hawkins, Frederick. *The French Stage in the Eighteenth Century,* 2 vols. London: Chapman & Hall, 1888.

Kimball, Sidney Fiske. *The Creation of the Rococo.* Philadelphia: Philadelphia Museum of Art, 1943.

Odell, George C. D. *Shakespeare from Betterton to Irving,* 2 vols. New York: Scribner's, 1920.

Scholz, János. *Baroque and Romantic Stage Design.* New York: Dutton, 1962.

Sypher, Wylie. *Rococo to Cubism in Art and Literature.* New York: Vintage, 1963.

Thaler, Alwin. See *Chapter 13.*

Theatrical Designs from the Baroque Through Neo-Classicism, 3 vols. New York: Dutton, 1962.

CHAPTER 15

Abrams, M. H. *The Mirror and the Lamp: Romantic Theory and the Critical Tradition.* New York: Oxford University Press, 1953.

Clement, N. H. *Romanticism in France.* New York: Modern Language Association of America, 1939.

Delacroix, Eugène. *The Journal of Eugène Delacroix* (trans. and ed. by Walter Pach). New York: Crown, 1948.

George, A. J. *The Development of French Romanticism: The Impact of the Industrial Revolution on Literature.* Syracuse, N.Y.: Syracuse University Press, 1955.

Lucas, F. L. *The Decline and Fall of the Romantic Ideal.* Cambridge: Cambridge University Press, 1936.

Novotny, Fritz. *Painting and Sculpture in Europe 1780–1880.* Baltimore: Penguin, 1960.

Odell, George C. D. See *Chapter 14.*
———. See *General.*

Rowell, George. *The Victorian Theatre.* Oxford: Clarendon Press, 1956.

Scholz, János. See *Chapter 14.*

Vardac, Nicholas. *Stage to Screen: Theatrical Method from Garrick to Griffith.* Cam-

bridge, Mass.: Harvard University Press, 1949.

Walzel, Oskar F. *German Romanticism* (trans. by Alma E. Lussky). New York: Putnam's, 1932.

Watson, Ernest B. *Sheridan to Robertson: A Study of the Nineteenth-Century London Stage.* Cambridge, Mass.: Harvard University Press, 1926.

Willoughby, Leonard A. *The Romantic Movement in Germany.* London: Oxford University Press, 1930.

CHAPTER 16

Gassner, John. *Form and Idea in Modern Theatre.* New York: Holt, Rinehart & Winston, 1956.

Gorelik, Mordecai. *New Theatres for Old.* New York: Dutton, 1962.

Hunter, Sam. *Modern French Painting 1855–1956.* New York: Dell, 1956.

Macqueen-Pope, W. *Nights of Gladness.* London: Hutchinson, 1956.

Melcher, Edith. *Stage Realism in France from Diderot to Antoine.* Bryn Mawr, Pa.: Bryn Mawr College Press, 1928.

Nicoll, Allardyce. "History of Late Nineteenth Century Drama," *A History of English Drama, 1660–1900,* Vol. V. Cambridge: Cambridge University Press, 1930.

Rowell, George. See *Chapter 15*

Sloane, Joseph C. *French Painting Between the Past and Present: Artists, Critics and Traditions from 1840 to 1870.* Princeton, N.J.: Princeton University Press, 1951.

Stone, Edward. *What Was Naturalism? Materials for an Answer.* New York: Appleton-Century-Crofts, 1959.

Sypher, Wylie. See *Chapter 14.*

Vardac, Nicholas. See *Chapter 15*

Waxman, S. M. *Antoine and the Théâtre-Libre.* Cambridge, Mass.: Harvard University Press, 1926.

CHAPTER 17

Appia, Adolphe. *The Work of Living Art: A Theory of the Theatre.* Coral Gables, Fla.: University of Miami Press, 1960.

Bergson, Henri. *The Creative Mind* (trans. by

Mabelle L. Andison). New York: Philosophical Library, 1946.

Cole, Toby (ed.). *Playwrights on Playwriting: The Meaning and Making of Modern Drama from Ibsen to Ionesco.* New York: Hill & Wang, 1960.

Craig, Edward Gordon. *On the Art of the Theatre.* New York: Theatre Arts, 1957.

Fuerst, Walter, and Hume, Samuel. *Twentieth Century Stage Decoration,* 2 vols. New York: Knopf, 1929.

Gorelik, Mordecai. See *Chapter 16.*

Jones, Robert Edmond. See *Chapter 1.*

Lehmann, Andrew G. *The Symbolist Aesthetic in France, 1885–1895.* Oxford: Blackwell, 1950.

Macgowan, Kenneth, and Jones, Robert E. *Continental Stagecraft.* New York: Harcourt, Brace & World, 1922.

Moussinac, Leon. *The New Movement in the Theatre. A Survey of Recent Developments in Europe and America.* London: Batsford, 1931.

Simonson, Lee. *The Art of Scene Design.* New York: Harper & Row, 1950.

———. See *General.*

Stein, Jack M. *Richard Wagner and the Synthesis of the Arts.* Detroit: Wayne State University Press, 1960.

Sypher, Wylie. See *Chapter 14*

Vardac, Nicholas. See *Chapter 15.*

CHAPTER 18

Artaud, Antonin. *The Theater and Its Double* (trans. by Mary C. Richards). New York: Grove, 1958.

Barr, Alfred H. Jr. (ed.). *Masters of Modern Art.* New York: Museum of Modern Art, 1954.

Brustein, Robert, *The Theatre of Revolt.* New York: Atlantic-Little, Brown, 1964.

Clurman, Harold. *The Fervent Years: The Story of the Group Theatre and the Thirties.* New York: Hill & Wang, 1957.

Cole, Toby (ed.). See *Chapter 17.*

Esslin, Martin. *The Theatre of the Absurd.* Garden City, N.Y.: Doubleday-Anchor, 1969.

Fuerst, Walter, and Hume, Samuel. See *Chapter 17.*

Goldwater, Robert. *Primitivism in Modern Painting.* New York: Harper, 1938.

Haftmann, Werner. *Painting in the Twentieth Century,* 2 vols. (trans. by Ralph Manheim). New York: Praeger, 1965.

Hainaux, René (ed.). *Stage Design Throughout the World Since 1935.* New York: Theatre Arts, 1956.

———. *Stage Design Throughout the World Since 1950.* New York: Theatre Arts, 1964.

Ritchie, Andrew C. *Sculpture of the Twentieth Century.* New York: Museum of Modern Art, 1952.

Soby, James Thrall. *Modern Art and the New Past.* Norman, Okla.: University of Oklahoma Press, 1957.

Southern, Richard. *The Open Stage.* New York: Theatre Arts, 1959.

Sypher, Wylie. See *Chapter 14.*

CHAPTER 19: CONCLUSION

Langer, Susanne. See *Chapter 9.*

Richman, Robert (ed.). *The Arts at Mid-Century.* New York: Horizon, 1954.

Rothschild, Lincoln. See *Chapter 9.*

St. Denis, Michel. See *Chapter 9.*

Sources of Theatrical Supplies

Atlanta Costume, 2409 Piedmont Rd. N.E., Atlanta, Ga.

Brooks-Van Horn, 117 W. 17th St., New York, N.Y.

Costume Associates, 381 Canal Pl., Bronx, N.Y.

Dallas Costume Shoppe, 3400 Perry Ave. at 3rd, Dallas, Texas.

Eaves Costume Company, 151 W. 46th St., New York, N.Y.

Hooker Howe Costume Company, Haverhill, Mass.

Krause Costume Company, 2445 Superior Ave., Cleveland, Ohio.

New York Costume Company, 10 W. Hubbard St., Chicago, Ill.

Northwestern Costume House, 3203 North Highway 100, Minneapolis, Minn.

Salt Lake Costume Company, 1701 S. 11th E., Salt Lake City, Utah.

Stagecraft Studios, 1854 Alcatraz Ave., Berkeley, Calif.

Variety Costumes, 353 W. 48th St., New York, N.Y.

Waas and Sons Company, 922 Walnut St., Philadelphia, Pa.

Western Costume Company 5335 Melrose Ave., Hollywood, Calif.

Index